HARD
LESSONS

For sale by the Superintendent of Documents, U.S. Government Printing Office
Internet: bookstore.gpo.gov   Phone: toll free (866) 512-1800;   DC area (202) 512-1800
Fax: (202) 512-2104 Mail: Stop IDCC, Washington, DC 20402-0001

ISBN 978-0-16-080817-3

HARD
LESSONS

THE IRAQ RECONSTRUCTION EXPERIENCE

Hard Lessons: The Iraq Reconstruction Experience

Contents

PREFACE

Hard Lessons: The Iraq Reconstruction Experience appears virtually upon the five-year anniversary of my appointment as Inspector General in Iraq. Shortly after that appointment, I met with Secretary of Defense Donald Rumsfeld, to whom I reported, to discuss the mission. His first words were: "Why did you take this job? It is an impossible task." I began to understand why he offered so startling a "welcome" during the following week, when I made my first trip to Iraq to begin setting up oversight of the Coalition Provisional Authority (CPA), then in charge of Iraq's reconstruction. My office in the Republican Palace, which housed the CPA—and would later house the U.S. Embassy—was adjacent to the CPA Comptroller's. What I saw was troubling: large amounts of cash moving quickly out the door. Later that same day, walking the halls of the palace, I overheard someone say: "We can't do that anymore. There is a new inspector general here."

These red flags were the first signs of how challenging executing oversight in Iraq would be. But it has not been impossible, chiefly because of the professional, productive, and courageous conduct of the many auditors, inspectors, and investigators who have worked diligently to fulfill the mission of the Office of the Special Inspector General for Iraq Reconstruction (SIGIR).

SIGIR's oversight jurisdiction covers about $50 billion in U.S. funds appropriated by the Congress for Iraq—the largest relief and reconstruction effort for one country in U.S. history. This sea of taxpayer dollars flowed to a wide spectrum of initiatives, ranging from training Iraq's army and police to building large electrical, oil, and water projects; from supporting democracy-building efforts to strengthening budget execution by provincial councils; and from funding rule-of-law reforms to ensuring that the Iraqi government sustains what the U.S. program provided. Some of these initiatives succeeded, but, as this report documents, many did not.

Hard Lessons reviews the Iraq reconstruction experience from mid-2002 through the fall of 2008. Like SIGIR's previous lessons learned reports, this study is not an audit. Rather, it arises from our congressional mandate to provide "advice and recommendations on policies to promote economy, efficiency, and effectiveness" in programs created for Iraq's relief and reconstruction.

The report presents a chronological history of the reconstruction program, threading together a number of themes including:

- the enormous challenges that security problems posed for rebuilding efforts

- the dramatic and frequently reactive course-changes in reconstruction strategy

- the turbulence engendered by continual personnel turn-over at every level

- the waste caused by inadequate contracting and program management practices

- the poor integration of interagency efforts caused by weak unity of command and inconsistent unity of effort.

The text of this report—through vignette, interview, and factual detail—explicates these themes by, in turn, laying out the blinkered and disjointed prewar planning for postwar Iraq; the CPA's large and ultimately too ambitious expansion of the reconstruction program; the security-driven reprogrammings required by the exploding insurgency; the strongly resourced response of the surge; and the rise of Iraq's role in its own reconstruction.

Hard Lessons answers some important questions about the U.S. relief and reconstruction program in Iraq:

- *Did the program meet the goals it set for itself?* Generally no on the infrastructure front, but generally yes regarding the development of Iraq's security forces. Electricity and oil outputs remain below goals set by the CPA more than five years ago, and the number of successful project completions in the key water and health sectors fell far short of hopes. But after several false starts and greatly increased U.S. investment, Iraq's security forces have achieved substantial operational capabilities, despite remaining doubts about overall unit readiness and potential performance levels.

- *Was the program grossly burdened by waste and fraud?* Regarding waste, yes; regarding fraud, no. The overuse of cost-plus contracts, high contractor overhead expenses, excessive contractor award fees, and unacceptable program and project delays all contributed to a significant waste of taxpayer dollars. Although SIGIR and other law enforcement agencies have uncovered egregious examples of fraud, the size of the total criminal wrongdoing known to date amounts to a relatively small percentage of the overall reconstruction investment, and the number of individuals involved was relatively low. The vast majority of those who served the U.S. reconstruction program—soldier, civilian, and contractor— did so honorably.

- *Why did reconstruction efforts so often fail to meet their mark?* Security. That single explanation has been offered up thousands of times since the 2003 invasion as the prevailing reason for shortfalls, large and small, in the U.S. program. But this explanation leads to a further question. Why was an extensive rebuilding plan carried out in a gravely unstable security environment? This question underscores an overarching hard lesson from Iraq: beware of pursuing large-scale reconstruction programs while significant conflict continues. But beyond the security issue stands another compelling and unavoidable truth: the U.S. government had neither the established structure nor the necessary resources to carry out the reconstruction mission it took on in mid-2003. As Under Secretary of Defense for Policy Douglas Feith said, "Every time the United States has had a substantial stabilization and reconstruction project, pretty much from World War II forward, we've [had to] improvise."

The research for *Hard Lessons* comprised interviews with hundreds of individuals and the review of thousands of documents. SIGIR reached out to virtually every major player in the Iraq reconstruction experience and almost all agreed to be interviewed or provide useful responses. Among others, Secretaries Powell, Rumsfeld, Gates, and Rice; USAID Administrator Natsios and Deputy Administrator Kunder; Deputy Secretaries Wolfowitz, England, Armitage and Negroponte; Under Secretary Feith; Ambassadors Bremer, Khalilzad, Crocker, Jeffrey, Satterfield, Speckhard, Taylor, and Saloom; and Generals Garner, Abizaid, McKiernan, Strock, Eaton, Sanchez, Casey, Petraeus, Odierno, Chiarelli, Dempsey, and McCoy were all interviewed by SIGIR or gave helpful information or advice. We also interviewed Iraqi leaders, including former Prime Ministers Allawi and Ja'afari, Deputy Prime Ministers Chalabi and Salih, Ambassador Sumaida'ie, Judge Radhi, and Minister Baban.

Equally important to the study, SIGIR staff interviewed hundreds of military members, government officials, and civilian contractors who carried out the "brick and mortar" work of Iraq's relief and reconstruction. The report also draws on the body of SIGIR audits, inspections, and investigations, as well as reports from other investigative bodies.

Finally, a somber note. Although this oversight mission has not been "impossible," it has been dangerous. During 2007, five SIGIR staff members were injured by indirect fire in Iraq. And on March 24, 2008, SIGIR auditor Paul Converse died from wounds he received during the Easter Day rocket barrage of the Green Zone. This report is dedicated to him and to all who gave their lives in Iraq in service to our country.

Stuart W. Bowen, Jr.
Inspector General
February 2, 2009

Key U.S. Figures in Iraq Reconstruction

General John Abizaid – Commander, United States Central Command (July 2003-March 2007)

Elliot Abrams – Special Assistant to the President and National Security Council Senior Director for Near East Affairs (December 2002-February 2005); Deputy National Security Advisor for Global Democracy Strategy (February 2005-January 2009)

Hilda "Bambi" Arellano – USAID Iraq Mission Director (August 2006-August 2007)

Richard Armitage – Deputy Secretary of State (March 2001-February 2005)

Joshua Bolten – Director, Office of Management and Budget (June 2003-April 2006); White House Chief of Staff (April 2006-January 2009)

Major General Thomas P. Bostick – Commanding General, U.S. Army Corps of Engineers-Gulf Region Division (June 2004-June 2005)

Ambassador L. Paul Bremer III – Administrator, Coalition Provisional Authority (May 2003-June 2004); Presidential Envoy to Iraq (May 2003-June 2004)

President George W. Bush – President of the United States

General George Casey – Director, Joint Staff (October 2001-January 2003); Commander, Multi-National Force-Iraq (June 2004-February 2007); Chief of Staff, U.S. Army (April 2007-present)

Ambassador Wendy Chamberlin – Assistant Administrator for the Bureau for Asia and the Near East, USAID (December 2002-December 2003)

Vice President Richard B. Cheney – Vice President of the United States

Lieutenant General Peter Chiarelli – Commanding General, 1st Cavalry Division (2003-2005); Commander, Multi-National Corps-Iraq (January 2006-December 2006)

Robin Cleveland – Associate Director for National Security Programs, Office of Management and Budget (March 2001-June 2005)

Ambassador Ryan Crocker – United States Ambassador to Iraq (March 2007-present)

Christopher Crowley – USAID Iraq Mission Director (September 2007-present)

Lieutenant General Martin E. Dempsey – Commanding General, 1st Armored Division (June 2003-July 2005); Commander, Multi-National Security Transition Command-Iraq (August 2005-June 2007); Deputy Commander, United States Central Command (August 2007-March 2008); Acting Commander, United States Central Command (March 2008-October 2008)

Major General Paul Eaton – Commander, Coalition Military Assistance Training Team and the Office of Security Cooperation (June 2003-June 2004)

Gordon England – Deputy Secretary of Defense (January 2006-January 2009)

Douglas Feith – Under Secretary of Defense for Policy (July 2001-August 2005)

Henrietta Fore – Administrator, United States Agency for International Development (November 2007-January 2009)

General Tommy Franks – Commander, United States Central Command (July 2000-July 2003)

Lieutenant General (Ret.) Jay Garner – Director, Office of Reconstruction and Humanitarian Assistance (January 2003-May 2003)

Robert Gates – Secretary of Defense (December 2006-present)

Brigadier General Steven Hawkins – Commander, Joint Task Force Four (December 2002-March 2003); Commanding General, Task Force Fajr (April 2003-June 2003); Commanding General, Task Force Restore Iraqi Electricity (September 2003-June 2004)

Charles Hess – Director, Project and Contracting Office (August 2004-April 2005)

Ambassador James Jeffrey – Deputy Chief of Mission (June 2004-March 2005); Senior Advisor to the Secretary of State on Iraq (August 2005-August 2006); Principal Deputy Assistant Secretary, Near Eastern Affairs (August 2006-July 2007); Deputy National Security Advisor (August 2007-January 2009)

Ambassador Zalmay Khalilzad – United States Ambassador to Iraq (June 2005-March 2007)

James Kunder – USAID Deputy Assistant Administrator for Asia and the Near East (July 2002-July 2004); USAID Assistant Administrator for Asia and the Near East (July 2004-January 2009); USAID Acting Deputy Administrator (July 2006-January 2009)

Dawn Liberi – USAID Iraq Mission Director (April 2005-July 2006)

Lewis Lucke – USAID Iraq Mission Director (March 2003-February 2004)

Major General William H. McCoy – Commanding General, U.S. Army Corps of Engineers-Gulf Region Division (June 2005-October 2006)

Lieutenant General David McKiernan – Commander, Combined Forces Land Component Command (September 2002-May 2003)

Peter McPherson – Chief of Economic Policy, Coalition Provisional Authority (April 2003-September 2003)

Frank Miller – Chairman, Executive Steering Group of the National Security Council (August 2002-March 2003); Senior Director for Defense Policy and Arms Control, National Security Council (January 2001-March 2005)

Christopher Milligan – Iraq Deputy Director, USAID (March 2003-2005)

Rear Admiral (Ret.) David Nash – Director, Program Management Office (July 2003-May 2004); Director, Project and Contracting Office/Iraq Reconstruction Management Office (June 2004-August 2004)

Andrew Natsios – Administrator, United States Agency for International Development (May 2001-January 2006)

Ambassador John Negroponte – United States Ambassador to Iraq (June 2004-March 2005); Deputy Secretary of State (February 2007-January 2009)

General Raymond T. Odierno – Commanding General, 4th Infantry Division (October 2001-June 2004); Commander, Multi-National Corps-Iraq (December 2006-February 2008); Commander, Multi-National Force-Iraq (September 2008-present)

Rear Admiral (Ret.) David Oliver – Director, Office of Management and Budget, Coalition Provisional Authority (June 2003-November 2003)

General David Petraeus – Commanding General, 101st Airborne Division (March 2003-June 2004); Commander, Multi-National Security Transition Command-Iraq (June 2004-September 2005); Commander, Multi-National Force-Iraq (February 2007-September 2008); Commander, United States Central Command (October 2008-present)

General (Ret.) Colin Powell – Secretary of State (January 2001-January 2005)

Dr. Condoleezza Rice – National Security Advisor (January 2001-January 2005); Secretary of State (January 2005-January 2009)

Donald Rumsfeld – Secretary of Defense (January 2001-December 2006)

Ambassador Joseph Saloom – Director, Iraq Reconstruction Management Office (May 2006-May 2007)

Lieutenant General Ricardo Sanchez – Commander, Combined Joint Task Force-7 (June 2003-June 2004)

Ambassador David Satterfield – Deputy Chief of Mission in Iraq (May 2005-July 2006); Senior Advisor to the Secretary of State on Iraq (August 2006-present)

Major General Darryl A. Scott – Commander, Joint Contracting Command-Iraq (January 2006-January 2008)

Brigadier General Stephen Seay – Commander, Joint Contracting Command-Iraq/Head of Contracting Authority (October 2004-2005)

Ambassador Daniel Speckhard – Director, Iraq Reconstruction Management Office (June 2005-August 2006); Deputy Chief of Mission (August 2006-November 2007)

James "Spike" Stephenson – USAID Iraq Mission Director (February 2004-March 2005)

Lieutenant General Carl Strock – Deputy Director of Operations, Coalition Provisional Authority (June 2003-September 2003); Commanding General and Chief of Engineers, U.S. Army Corps of Engineers (2004-2007)

Ambassador William B. Taylor – Director, Iraq Reconstruction Management Office (July 2004-May 2005)

Brigadier General Michael Walsh – Commanding General, U.S. Army Corps of Engineers-Gulf Region Division (October 2006-October 2007)

Thomas Warrick – Director, Future of Iraq Project (April 2002-March 2003)

Ross Wherry – USAID Senior Reconstruction Advisor for the Bureau for Asia and the Near East (October 2002-August 2004); and USAID Director, Office of Iraq Affairs (2004-March 2006)

Dr. Paul Wolfowitz – Deputy Secretary of Defense (March 2001-May 2005)

Acronyms

AIRP	Accelerated Iraq Reconstruction Program
BSA	Board of Supreme Audit
CAP	Community Action Program
CCCI	Central Criminal Court of Iraq
CENTCOM	United States Central Command
CERP	Commander's Emergency Response Program
CFLCC	Coalition Forces Land Component Command
CJTF	Combined Joint Task Force
CMATT	Coalition Military Assistance Training Team
CPA	Coalition Provisional Authority
CPA-IG	Coalition Provisional Authority Inspector General
CPATT	Coalition Police Assistance Training Team
CPI	Commission on Public Integrity
CSIS	Center for Strategic and International Studies
CSP	Community Stabilization Program
DART	Disaster Assistance Relief Team
DCAA	Defense Contract Audit Agency
DCMA	Defense Contract Management Agency
DFI	Development Fund for Iraq
DoD	Department of Defense
DoJ	Department of Justice
DoS	Department of State
ePRT	Embedded Provincial Reconstruction Teams
ESF	Economic Support Fund
FAR	Federal Acquisition Regulation
FEST	Forward Engineering Support Teams
FOB	Forward Operating Base
FPS	Facilities Protection Service
GAO	Government Accountability Office
GRD	Gulf Region Division
GST	Governorate Support Team
IAF	Iraqi Armed Forces
IAMB	International Advisory and Monitoring Board
ICDC	Iraqi Civil Defense Corps
ICITAP	International Criminal Investigative Training Assistance Program
IDIQ	Indefinite Delivery, Indefinite Quantity [contract]

IED	Improvised Explosive Device
IG	Inspector General
IGC	Iraqi Governing Council
IIF	Iraqi Intervention Force
IIG	Iraqi Interim Government
IJ	Investigative Judges
IMF	International Monetary Fund
ING	Iraqi National Guard
IPS	Iraqi Police Service
IRDC	Iraqi Reconstruction Development Council
IRMO	Iraq Reconstruction Management Office
IRRF	Iraq Relief and Reconstruction Fund
ISF	Iraqi Security Forces
ISFF	Iraq Security Forces Fund
ITAO	Iraq Transition Assistance Office
JCC-I	Joint Contracting Command – Iraq
JMD	Joint Manning Document
JSAT	Joint Strategic Assessment Team
JSPA	Joint Strategic Planning and Assessment
JTF	Joint Task Force
LGP	Local Governance Program
LOGCAP	Logistics Civil Augmentation Program
MAAWS	Money as a Weapons System
MBPD	Million Barrels Per Day
MNC-I	Multi-National Corps – Iraq
MNF-I	Multi-National Force – Iraq
MNSTC-I	Multi-National Security Transition Command – Iraq
MoD	Ministry of Defense
MoI	Ministry of Interior
MW	Megawatt
NGO	Nongovernmental Organization
NRRRF	Natural Resources Risk Remediation Fund
NSC	National Security Council
NSPD	National Security Presidential Directive
OIF	Operation Iraqi Freedom
OMB	Office of Management and Budget
OPLAN	Operations Plan

ORHA	Office of Reconstruction and Humanitarian Affairs
OTI	Office of Transition Initiatives
PCO	Project and Contracting Office
PHC	Primary Healthcare Center
P.L.	Public Law
PMO	Program Management Office
PRB	Program Review Board
PRDC	Provincial Reconstruction Development Council
PRT	Provincial Reconstruction Team
QRF	Quick Response Fund
REO	Regional Embassy Office
RFP	Request for Proposal
RIE	Restore Iraqi Electricity
RIO	Restore Iraqi Oil
RSCMA	Reconstruction and Stabilization Civilian Management Act of 2008
S/CRS	Department of State-Office of the Coordinator for Reconstruction and Stabilization
SAMP	Single Acquisition Management Plan
SIGIR	Special Inspector General for Iraq Reconstruction
SOE	State-owned Enterprise
SOMO	State Oil Marketing Organization
SOW	Statement of Work
SPMO	Sector Program Management Office
TAL	Transitional Administrative Law
TNA	Transitional National Assembly
TRA	Transition Readiness Assessment
UN	United Nations
UNSCR	United Nations Security Council Resolution
USAAA	United States Army Audit Agency
USACE	United States Army Corps of Engineers
USAID	United States Agency for International Development
USIP	United States Institute of Peace
WMD	Weapons of Mass Destruction

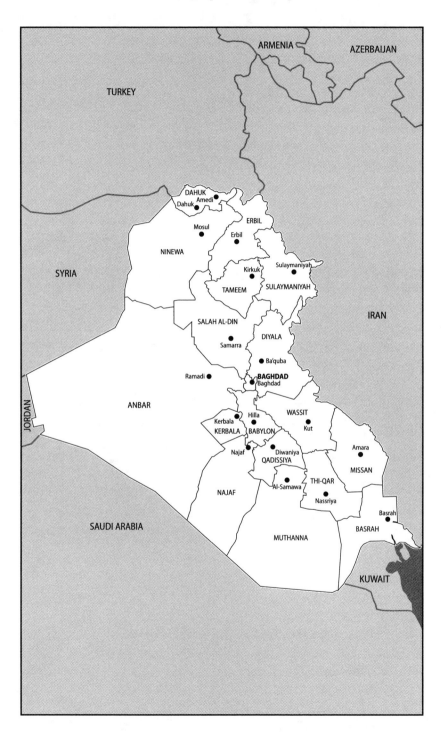

PART I
PLANNING FOR POSTWAR IRAQ
SEPTEMBER 2001 TO MAY 2003

CHAPTER 1
PLANNING BEGINS

*I have no idea what CENTCOM was planning, and I
have absolutely no idea what the Joint Chiefs of Staff were
planning. I do know that the political guidance they were
getting from Rumsfeld, the NSC, and the White House
was, 'You got about three months to get [the postwar Iraqi
government] up and running.'**

General Colin Powell
Secretary of State (2001-2005)

The origins of U.S. reconstruction policy in Iraq are rooted in a series of debates that occurred during the fall of 2001, when President Bush ordered the
Pentagon to revise its plans for deposing Iraqi dictator Saddam Hussein.[1] From
the outset, Secretary of Defense Donald Rumsfeld believed that, after Saddam's
fall, power should rapidly transfer to an interim Iraqi authority. Reflecting this
belief, Pentagon officials conceived of U.S. forces as liberators who would leave
Iraq within months of toppling the regime. In this scenario, the United States
would not need to administer the functions of Iraq's government after major
combat operations ceased.[2]

A different view of regime change developed at the State Department. Some
senior officials in Foggy Bottom believed that Iraq, with its history of sectarian
violence, could not be easily reshaped. They concluded that invading Iraq and
replacing its totalitarian regime would require a U.S. commitment of enormous
scope, carried out over a period of years, engaging everything from Iraq's judiciary
to its electrical grid. Secretary of State Colin Powell pointedly told the President
that "when you hit [Iraq], it's like a crystal glass. It's going to shatter. There will be
no government. There will be civil disorder. You'll have 25 million Iraqis standing
around looking at each other."[3]

The tense interplay between these competing visions fundamentally shaped
the process of prewar planning for postwar Iraq in the fifteen months that pre-
ceded the March 2003 invasion. As planning moved forward, experts inside and
outside government—including some at the Department of Defense—warned
that failing to prepare for a more extensive engagement after regime change exposed the United States to extraordinary risks. Although the NSC agreed that

---

* SIGIR interview with General (Ret.) Colin Powell, former Secretary of State, February 4, 2008.

Iraq should be liberated from Saddam's tyranny, the disagreements about the postwar plan remained unresolved right up to the invasion. They arose from differing assessments of prewar conditions in Iraq and what the consequences of deposing Saddam would be.

A Brief History of Modern Iraq

Shortly after World War I, Winston Churchill, then head of Britain's War Office, told the commander of British forces in Iraq: "The fate of the province depends entirely upon whether a reasonable scheme for maintaining order can be devised at a cost which is not ruinous."[4] Creating a "reasonable scheme," however, proved exceedingly difficult.

The British shaped and laid claim to modern Iraq through the 1916 Sykes-Picot agreement, negotiated by the United Kingdom, France, and Russia in anticipation of the fall of the Ottoman Empire at the end of World War I. By 1920, Iraqis living under British military occupation had compiled a list of grievances against their foreign rulers. Shi'a clerics in the south demanded an independent Islamic government. The Kurds in the north wanted autonomy. Tribesmen throughout the country opposed the British-imposed tax system and forced labor. Eventually, senior Sunni and Shi'a clerics joined together to issue a *fatwa* calling for rebellion. An insurgency started in Baghdad and quickly spread across the country, forcing the British to move up their timetable for granting Iraq full sovereignty.[5]

In their efforts to build an independent state, British officials faced the challenge of melding three distinct social structures (tribal, clerical, urban), three ethno-religious groups (Sunni Kurds, Sunni Arabs, Shi'a Arabs), and three territorial regions (north, central, south).[6] The solution they ultimately settled on, undertaken with the advice of British Arabists Gertrude Bell and T.E. Lawrence, was to install a king, Emir Faisal, to lead the new country. The 1921 investiture of Faisal—a Sunni—entrenched a pattern of volatile sectarian politics that would burden Iraq for decades.[7]

The exercise of power by the minority Sunnis over the majority Shi'a produced instability: 58 separate governments ruled Iraq in the 37 years between 1921 and the 1958 revolution that overthrew the monarchy.[8] In 1963, the Sunni-controlled Ba'ath party took power in a coup.[9] By the mid-1970s, a middle class had emerged in Iraq that was a model for its neighbors. High oil prices briefly pushed the country's per capita gross domestic product past that of Spain's. A secular state with an excellent education system and a thriving economy, Iraq seemed poised to break with its turbulent past. But this relative renaissance was not to last.

In 1979, a law school dropout named Saddam Hussein seized power. He would rule Iraq for the next 24 years at ruinous cost. In 1980, Saddam launched his country on a disastrous eight-year war with Iran that left a half million Iraqis dead. The war ended the country's brief period of prosperity, decimated a generation of young men, and roiled tensions between the regime's Sunni Arab elite and their Shi'a and Kurdish coun-trymen. In 1990, Saddam invaded Kuwait and the United States quickly responded, leading to the 1991 Gulf War.[10] Saddam was badly defeated by a broad coalition of forces, and his regime became an international pariah. By the year 2000, the impact of multiple wars, severe international sanctions, and repressive rule had left Iraq a broken country.

Iraq Under Saddam

In 2003, Iraq's population of around 27 million people lived in an area about the size of California. The land between the Tigris and Euphrates Rivers, known as the cradle of civilization, had given birth to remarkable innovations in writing, farm-ing, law, medicine, and governance. But Iraq suffered under a brutal tyrant whose destructive policies had led to the imposition of harsh United Nations (UN) sanctions. The deterioration of the country's physical infrastructure stemmed, to varying degrees, from these sanctions, Saddam's neglect, the Iran-Iraq War, and the 1991 Gulf War.

During the Gulf War, Iraq inflicted significant damage on Kuwait. Under the supervision of then-Secretary of Defense Richard Cheney, Kuwaiti and U.S. of-ficials planned the reconstruction of Kuwait in advance of its liberation. Kuwait's quick recovery largely resulted from work carried out by the U.S. Army Corps of Engineers (USACE) and private contractors, including Bechtel, and Brown and Root, both of which would later play major roles in Iraq's reconstruction.[11]

Although Saddam restored some essential services after the Gulf War, the larger recovery of Iraq proved more daunting. United Nations-imposed sanc-tions and an international trade embargo, aimed at preventing the regime from acquiring ballistic missiles and weapons of mass destruction, limited the country's capacity to recover.[12] Iraq's non-oil economy was especially hard hit. By the mid-1990s, unemployment and under-employment exceeded 50 percent.[13] Iraq's gross domestic product, which peaked in 1990 at $74.9 billion, remained below $20 billion throughout most of the decade.[14]

Under Saddam, Iraq had plunged from a gradually advancing middle-income country to a poor and underdeveloped one. In its shift "from relative affluence to massive poverty," 60 percent of Iraq's population was left heavily dependent on the government-provided food ration for their livelihood.[15] By the mid-1990s, these rations, delivered through the country's public distribution system, provided only 1,100 calories per person per day, causing widespread malnutrition.[16]

Faced with rising social and economic instability, Saddam acceded in 1995 to a UN proposal, on the table since 1991, to allow the use of proceeds from controlled oil and gas sales to purchase food and medicine.[17] Under the new "Oil-for-Food Program," the UN managed monthly distributions of 450,000 tons of flour, clarified butter, peas, lentils, beans, sugar, tea, salt, and soap through a network of 44,000 privately owned corner stores. At one level, the program worked, effectively doubling the population's per capita caloric intake.[18] But beneath the sanctions and authorized oil sales, an illicit economy flourished. Institutionalized corruption infected both the government and the supporting UN programs, spawning powerful criminal elements within Iraq.[19]

The reversal in U.S.-Iraqi relations during Saddam's rule—with Saddam first an ally and then an enemy—increased Iraqi suspicion that the West had designs on its territory and oil wealth. These suspicions—together with the effects of internal political violence, Saddam's ceaseless propaganda, a corrupt public sector, regular shortages of food, medicine, and everyday goods, and frequent U.S. bombing of air-defense installations in the no-fly zones—led to a siege mentality among many Iraqis.

The peculiar mix of charity and harsh sanctions that defined the international community's relations with Iraq in the years following the Gulf War presented a paradox. Saddam's brutal secrecy and intrigue shrouded the inner workings of the Iraqi state, while the UN's distribution scheme for goods and services provided the international organization with extensive connections in the country.[20] Thus, in 2003, the UN sanctions committee had a list of every good it had permitted Iraq to import for about a decade, down to fuses in power plants.[21] Although the UN's records were not organized as a needs assessment of the infrastructure, a diligent review of them could have revealed how much cement a particular Iraqi factory produced or what spare parts an Iraqi electricity plant had ordered.

Initial Planning

On September 29, 2001, Secretary Rumsfeld ordered a review of existing Iraq war plans.[22] Shortly thereafter, General Tommy Franks, Commanding General of the U.S. Central Command (CENTCOM)—the combatant command with responsibility for the Middle East and Central Asia—removed a small group of key planners from the Afghanistan campaign and directed them to revise plans to attack Iraq.[23] At the outset, Secretary Rumsfeld did not advise the planners to prepare for a lengthy occupying military administration after Saddam's regime fell.[24] He presumed that others in the government, probably the Department of State, would handle the governance aspects of "Phase IV," military parlance for operations after the end of major combat.[25]

The concept of operations Rumsfeld and Franks devised in four videoconferences between Thanksgiving and late December 2001 focused chiefly on the combat phase. The war plan Secretary Rumsfeld briefed to President Bush on December 28, 2001, anticipated a rapid postwar handoff to a provisional Iraqi government and a minimal continuing military footprint.[26]

In early 2002, the State Department's Bureau of Near Eastern Affairs launched the "Future of Iraq Project" to assess postwar requirements. Six days after the President named Iraq as part of the "Axis of Evil" in his January 29, 2002 State of the Union address, project director Thomas Warrick submitted an outline of subjects to Ambassador Ryan Crocker, then serving as Deputy Assistant Secretary of State for Near Eastern Affairs. The outline anticipated seventeen working groups, composed primarily of Iraqi exiles, that would evaluate post-invasion needs in areas ranging from rule of law and public finance to oil, energy, and anticorruption.[27] The project would serve both as a means to expand postwar planning and as a vehicle to consolidate competing Iraqi exile groups, who were involved with the project from its earliest days.

White House coordination of nascent planning for Iraq began in the spring of 2002 during twice-weekly meetings of the National Security Council's Deputies Committee, which comprises the second-in-command officials—or their representatives—from the Departments of State and Defense, the CIA, and the military's Joint Staff.[28] Ideas about how to handle the postwar phase took shape during these meetings. The Deputies Committee focused on three concepts: a liberation model in which Iraqis would quickly take charge through a provisional government; a military administration led by CENTCOM; or a civilian transitional authority, perhaps run under UN auspices. Irrespective of which concept or combination of concepts would apply, policymakers addressed three linked issues: how to secure public order, what relief and reconstruction operations would be necessary, and how to promote U.S. interests in Iraq's longer-term economic and political stability.[29]

"One of our main themes was liberation rather than occupation," Under Secretary of Defense for Policy Douglas Feith said. "There was this constant debate between those of us who said we've got to push the Iraqis forward," Feith recounted, and others who judged that the Iraqis would be ready to govern themselves only after several years.[30] Reflecting the views of Secretary Rumsfeld, Feith advocated a rapid transition to Iraqi control. Drawing lessons from past nation-building efforts, he and Rumsfeld believed that minimizing the military's presence would force local populations to rely more rapidly upon their own leaders to resolve problems. They were convinced that by limiting the military's postwar role in Iraq, the United States could avoid the "culture of dependency" that had taken root in other post-conflict interventions.[31]

The U.S campaign in Afghanistan appeared to support the rapid-transfer approach.[32] After a small U.S. force achieved military victory, political authority passed to Hamid Karzai, an Afghan exile leader selected by a *loya jirga*—a grand assembly of Afghan tribal leaders—and subsequently appointed president of Afghanistan at an international conference in Bonn. Per capita reconstruction expenditure in Afghanistan had remained modest. Officials viewed this seemingly successful postwar transition as a vindication of the Administration's break with conventional wisdom about nation building, buttressing arguments of Defense officials that Afghanistan should serve as the model for Iraq.[33]

The State Department argued against applying the Afghanistan model to Iraq. State experts believed that Iraqi exile leaders were unlikely to garner the same level of support from their countrymen as Karzai had enjoyed from Afghans. Moreover, State's analyses suggested that Iraq would need a longer transitional period because of the need to reconcile Iraq's competing ethnic and sectarian groups. The State Department advocated a U.S.-led "Transitional Civil Authority" that would govern postwar Iraq during a "multi-year transitional period to build democratic institutions."[34] This approach ultimately was embodied by the Coalition Provisional Authority, which ruled postwar Iraq from May 2003 to June 2004 ostensibly under the Defense Department's aegis.

Interagency Planning Accelerates

By mid-2002, an invasion of Iraq remained in the realm of speculation for all but a handful of senior officials in Washington. The machinery of interagency planning in the National Security Council largely sat idle, leaving open the fissure between planning for war and planning for war's aftermath. The differences among the three underlying policies for a postwar framework—rapid transfer to

Iraqi control, military administration, or civilian transitional authority—had yet to be seriously addressed, much less resolved. Nor had officials reached consensus on the public order and reconstruction requirements for each scenario.[35]

In August 2002, the President and his advisors enlarged the Iraq planning effort to include civilian agencies that ostensibly would administer the postwar phase. *Iraq: Goals, Objectives, Strategy*, a national security document signed by President Bush on August 29, 2002, articulated an evolving strategy that would employ "all instruments of national power" to free Iraq from Saddam. The document stated that the United States would "work with the Iraqi opposition to demonstrate that we are liberating, not invading Iraq, and give the opposition a role in building a pluralistic and democratic Iraq, including the preparation of a new constitution." As for rebuilding, the U.S. strategy would:

> ... demonstrate that the United States is prepared to play a sustained role in the reconstruction of post-Saddam Iraq with contribution from and participation of the international community, that rapidly starts the country's reconstruction, that preserves but reforms the current Iraqi bureaucracy and reforms Iraqi military and security institutions.[36]

Secretaries Powell and Rumsfeld and Vice President Cheney met with Iraqi exile leaders to show support and to express the seriousness of U.S. intentions.[37]

To help execute the ambitious mission envisioned by the August 29 document, the Joint Staff instructed CENTCOM that it should begin planning to administer Iraq for an interim period after the invasion. This order appeared to counter the earlier Rumsfeld presumption that the Defense Department would not bear principal responsibility for managing the country after the combat phase concluded. Despite the Joint Staff order, "there wasn't a whole lot of intellectual energy being focused on Phase IV," one of CENTCOM's key planners said.[38] While most of CENTCOM's staff focused on Phases I, II, and III, Major Thomas Fisher and Major Ray Eiriz, two mid-level officers who had served in Bosnia and Kosovo, took charge of Phase IV.[39]

To jump-start postwar planning efforts across the government, National Security Advisor Condoleezza Rice established a National Security Council (NSC) Executive Steering Group on Iraq in August 2002 and asked Frank Miller, an NSC senior director, to chair it. The Joint Staff had already formed a political-military team to link detailed operational planning at CENTCOM with interagency planners in Washington. An energy infrastructure working group, a diplomatic working group, a global communications office, and a humanitarian working group eventually joined the planning effort.[40]

Under Secretary Feith also enlarged the Pentagon office responsible for Iraq policy planning. Until then, only four people in Defense's Near East and South Asia Office had worked full-time on Iraq.[41] Feith brought together a staff of about a dozen under a new "Office of Special Plans" to engage in large-scale planning for war. Later, officials working on the management of postwar Iraq would discover that this office had produced relevant analyses and concept papers that were not shared during interagency consultations or with those who eventually played a leading role in postwar Iraq—emblematic of the extensive compartmentalization of prewar planning for postwar Iraq.[42]

NSC's Humanitarian Working Group

Assessing how the war might disrupt the provision of food, water, and shelter fell to an interagency Humanitarian Working Group led by Elliot Abrams, an NSC senior director, and Robin Cleveland, associate director of the White House Office of Management and Budget (OMB).[43] The working group, which began weekly meetings in Cleveland's office in September 2002, included officials from the CIA, United States Agency for International Development (USAID), the Joint Staff, and the Departments of Defense, State, Treasury, Justice, and Commerce.[44]

One nightmare scenario loomed above all others—the possibility that Saddam would use chemical or biological weapons against an invading force or his own people. In the wake of such a disaster, hundreds of thousands or even millions of Iraqis might flee. Very large refugee flows were thought by Pentagon analysts to be the most likely challenge the United States would face in the aftermath of an invasion.[45] Accordingly, Cleveland and Abrams focused their working group on how the U.S. government would respond to large-scale humanitarian contingencies.

They also considered the role of the UN. Several officials initially resisted continuing the Oil-for-Food Program—which partially financed Iraq's public distribution system, through which 25 million Iraqis received a monthly food staple—on grounds that it ceded too much control to the UN. But USAID and State officials argued that the program would help prevent starvation if food became scarce. A related question was how to administer oil revenues accruing under the Oil-for-Food Program. Several working group members again argued against continuing UN control, with State and USAID officials again urging that the international body was best suited to serve as custodian of Iraq's oil wealth. Several rounds of adjudication through the Deputies Committee left the UN in control of the Oil-for-Food program and its revenues.[46]

Under the leadership of Elliot Abrams, the Humanitarian Working Group quietly coordinated with the international aid community to develop a "no-strike" list of civilian infrastructure, such as hospitals and power plants. To separate the regime's military command and control facilities from known civilian sites, the UN and NGOs familiar with Iraq nominated locations that the military would then cross-walk through an intelligence-community database.[47]

Although the working group had been chartered to evaluate only humanitarian contingencies, its participants soon realized that Iraq's infrastructure and ministries would play essential roles in postwar operations.[48] Ambassador Wendy Chamberlin and Ross Wherry of USAID thus began a reconstruction assessment that considered what it would take to get the infrastructure and ministries up and running after the invasion.[49] This raised a fundamental strategic question: how extensive should postwar reconstruction be? Reconstruction geared to repair war damage would differ greatly from attempting to reverse the deleterious effects of the Iran-Iraq war, sanctions, and Saddam's own destructive policies.[50]

The lack of information about Iraq's infrastructure and government institutions made it difficult to determine what was necessary to restore essential services. "We never had anything more than a PowerPoint briefing," a Defense official later commented. "We might have had some financial estimate papers, but it was a lot of back-of-the-envelope, 'what will it take to fix the Ministry of fill-in-the-blank.' It was all guesstimates made on top of suppositions."[51] The few detailed reports reviewed by the working group suggested that sanctions had significantly limited Iraq's recovery from the first Gulf War. For example, a UN assessment of the electrical sector concluded that a lack of spare parts left the system remarkably fragile. In light of Iraq's substantial oil wealth, however, the scope of expected infrastructure repairs seemed manageable. The group assumed that long-term repairs could be undertaken and funded by the Iraqis.[52]

With military, political, and democratization plans developed out of sight of the Humanitarian Working Group, its members could consider only in general terms how reconstruction might help legitimize a new Iraqi state. The group asked for but never received a briefing on how public-order requirements would be met. It was also not permitted to examine the potential role of reconstruction in civil administration. Department of Justice proposals to employ police trainers were dismissed as falling outside the group's mandate.[53] The Defense Department asserted that it had plans for postwar security well in hand.[54] As one working group member said, it appeared that "a lot of things were decided but never discussed."[55]

In the absence of direction from above, the working group's co-chairs, Abrams and Cleveland, developed a set of core judgments about postwar Iraq. "It was taken as an assumption," one participant said, "that the war would be brief, war damage would be minimal, and oil revenues would finance almost all of reconstruction."[56] They also assumed that the political people would somehow "pull a Karzai out of the hat," and that the Iraqis would take care of the rest.[57]

Towards the end of 2002, with time running out and war a few months away, working group officials were putting in eighteen-hour days to make sure their parts of the plan came together. General Franks at CENTCOM did not seriously question the approach developed under Abrams's and Cleveland's leadership. Briefed twice by the working group's members on their findings, General Franks reacted favorably. "On both occasions, he said this was good," an official recalled. Franks said that the reconstruction and humanitarian planning "basically jibes with what we're thinking."[58]

Structuring Postwar Administration

On October 15, 2002, Under Secretary Feith briefed the National Security Council on a proposed structure for CENTCOM's military administration of postwar Iraq. The structure consisted of a military headquarters, known as Combined Joint Task Force-Iraq (CJTF-I), headed by a three-star general, and a civil administration, headed by a civilian "Iraq coordinator." Both would fall under CENTCOM's command.

The briefing recommended that the Secretary of Defense be placed in charge of the entire effort, reflecting Rumsfeld's view that political, economic, and security activities in postwar Iraq should not be managed by separate institutions.[59] This proposed structure touched off a vigorous debate among interagency planners. Lieutenant General George Casey, who would command military forces in Iraq from 2004 to 2006, later said, "We lost, in my view, two months while we fought over who was going to be in charge."[60]

CENTCOM divided Phase IV into three overlapping stages—Alpha, Bravo, and Charlie.[61] During Alpha, the military would have the lead; during Bravo, a U.S. civilian authority would move to the forefront; during Charlie, the Iraqis would take charge. "None of this was exclusive," CENTCOM's chief of war plans explained. "It was who dominated and who had the lead during those phases."[62] The "A-B-C" approach was a way for the military to conceptualize what and when certain tasks would have to be performed, given that planners did not yet know whether U.S. policy ultimately would call for a rapid handoff to Iraqi leaders or to a civilian transitional authority of longer duration. The phases were set; their duration was not.

On October 18, 2002, Secretary Rumsfeld asked Feith to stand up the postwar planning office that would prepare for the civil administration of Iraq. But Rumsfeld canceled that order just a few days later. Feith later learned from Deputy National Security Advisor Steven Hadley that the reversal came from a

Presidential decision that the U.S. government should not engage in highly visible postwar preparations while in the middle of international efforts to defuse the threat posed by Iraq without war.[63]

These decisions reflected a strategic resistance to bringing postwar planning into the open. All the interagency Iraq planning groups worked in secret. Few knew the others existed. Officials justified the extreme secrecy on the grounds that ongoing diplomatic negotiations would be undercut if Saddam knew that postwar planning was well underway. "There was a reluctance to pull that all together," Feith explained, "because, while you're saying that you want to resolve this dispute through non-military means, there's a sense that you're contradicting yourself if you're not only planning for the war but planning for the postwar."[64] While postwar planning efforts progressed under strict secrecy, the build-up of troops and materiel around Iraq's borders continued—a necessary threat to make diplomatic negotiations credible in the eyes of Saddam.

The structure of postwar administration and the mechanics of political transition remained undecided through the fall. A revised version of the strategy paper, *Iraq: Goals, Objectives, Strategy*, issued in late October 2002, reflected the lack of a clear decision on these matters. Rather than articulating a detailed timetable for transition to Iraqi control, the memorandum spoke only of an interim administration that would provide for "external and internal security," "humanitarian assistance," and "the country's political, economic, and security reconstruction."[65]

Early Warnings
As planning for the invasion moved forward, the Departments of Defense and State produced assessments of what could go wrong. In October 2002, Secretary Rumsfeld, Chairman of the Joint Chiefs of Staff General Richard Myers, Vice Chairman General Peter Pace, Deputy Secretary Wolfowitz, and Under Secretary Feith developed a "Parade of Horribles" memo that presented 29 possible catastrophes the invasion of Iraq might engender. In retrospect, the memo proved remarkably prescient. Number thirteen was not finding weapons of mass destruction. Other fears included sectarian and ethnic strife among Sunnis, Shi'a, and Kurds; the failure to capture Saddam Hussein; Iraq fracturing into two or three pieces; U.S. postwar involvement lasting ten years, rather than two to four; the cost of the postwar effort being too high; and a turnabout in world opinion.[66] Rumsfeld shared the memo at an NSC meeting with the President, the Vice President, the Secretary of State, the National Security Advisor, and the CIA Director.[67]

In mid-December, Secretary Powell received a twelve-page warning—co-authored by Ryan Crocker, eventual Ambassador to Iraq—titled "The Perfect

Storm." This memo accurately warned that the struggle for dominance after the fall of Saddam would inspire violent clashes among Iraq's sects, tribes, and ethnic factions, possibly leading to the country's fragmentation.[68] Deputy Secretary of State Richard Armitage believed that this memo was shared with the NSC, although members of Frank Miller's Executive Steering Committee were not privy to it or to Rumsfeld's "Parade of Horribles" memo.[69]

Caveats about what lay ahead could also be found in the history of nation building.[70] Of the sixteen countries in which the United States attempted to implant institutions of democratic government over the past century, only four—West Germany, Japan, Panama, and Grenada—remained democratic a decade after U.S. forces ended their active involvement in governance. In three countries—Cuba, Haiti, and Nicaragua—intervention led to worse misrule and greater economic decline.[71] Some political scientists and historians noted that Iraq's social and political attributes could make the country inherently resistant to political reform by outsiders, and that any effort there would be unlike the U.S. occupation of Germany and Japan.[72] Both Germany and Japan were highly developed societies with homogeneous populations and established bureaucracies. Operational planning for their occupation began within months of the bombing of Pearl Harbor, and thousands of native speakers were trained.[73]

The potential difficulty in remaking Iraq's political system was underscored in January 2003 by a then-classified National Intelligence Council assessment, *Principal Challenges in Post-Saddam Iraq*, which predicted that establishing a democratic system in Iraq "would be a long, difficult, and turbulent process."[74] CIA Director George Tenet and his deputy, John McLaughlin, did not highlight the findings of the assessment to interagency planners or ask that it be briefed to the NSC's Executive Steering Group on Iraq or to the NSC's Deputies Committee.[75]

Several other studies outlined how the expected difficulties of regime change would affect the military and civil missions in Iraq.[76] The most comprehensive was by Conrad Crane and Andrew Terrill of the Army War College Strategic Studies Institute. In coordination with the Army Deputy Chief of Staff for Operations, Crane's interdisciplinary team began work on their study in October 2002. Two dozen officials from the Joint Staff, Joint Forces Command, and the Departments of Defense and State vetted its interim findings in mid-December. Published February 1, 2003, the report identified 135 tasks that military and civilian agencies would need to perform across 21 categories of activity.[77]

The Congress also examined postwar scenarios. On August 1, 2002, the Senate Foreign Relations Committee held a hearing at which members heard warnings from scholars about potential challenges an invasion of Iraq could bring. It would be the only congressional examination of postwar scenarios before the

Congress authorized the President to "use the Armed Forces of the United States as he determines to be necessary and appropriate" to defend the United States against the threat from Iraq and to enforce UN resolutions regarding Iraq.[78] Although six committees and two subcommittees held more than a dozen hearings subsequent to the vote in Congress to approve the use of force, most of the hearings focusing on post-Saddam Iraq did not occur until just before hostilities began in March 2003.[79]

The Future of Iraq Project

By late 2002, participants in the State Department's Future of Iraq Project began formulating their own vision of postwar administration. Working independently of other planning teams, fourteen of the project's seventeen working groups met between July 2002 and April 2003, bringing some 200 Iraqi exiles together with government and international experts.[80] The project identified a range of issues that an invading army inevitably would confront, from the possibility of political violence to the decrepit electricity, oil, and water infrastructures. The richly developed reports constitute the single most rigorous assessment conducted by the U.S. government before the war. Although the findings of each working group did not amount to an operational plan, their reports contained facts and analysis that could—and in some cases did—inform operational planning.

Several factors—particularly timing—kept most project findings from influencing interagency deliberations. Of the fourteen working groups that did meet, many carried their deliberations into 2003—too late to influence prewar planning.[81] Moreover, the completed reports proved of varying utility. The Transitional Justice Working Group, for example, offered a detailed analysis of Iraq's political-military establishment. The specific suggestions it contained came close to constituting an action plan on the legal front. Others, such as the Public Health and Humanitarian Needs Working Group, offered only a generalized set of recommendations drawn from previous international crises.

The NSC's Executive Steering Group invited the project's director, Thomas Warrick, to brief the group shortly before the invasion, but the project's unwieldy reports—which in toto ran more than 1,000 pages—could not be easily reduced to a set of slides that policymakers could absorb.[82] Warrick's briefing did not raise a single issue for decision and was not viewed as useful at the time. To planners preparing for war and a short postwar operation, the Future of Iraq Project did not look like a coherent operational plan.[83] Only when Warrick produced an edited volume of findings after the war began could the project be seen as a comprehensive guide to issues the United States could face—and, by then, was already facing.[84]

Perhaps most critically, the project's reports did not capture the attention of the State Department's senior decision-makers. Secretary of State Colin Powell and his Deputy Secretary Richard Armitage did not use them to bolster their cautionary views or to push for more detailed planning on worst-case scenarios. Without a high-level patron, the project's reports lacked the visibility and clout to reach key decision-makers in time.[85] "I never felt that the Future of Iraq Project was embraced or connected to the actual planning effort for regime change," Ambassador Ryan Crocker said, "and the farther we went into the calendar, the more noticeable that became."[86]

Fragmented Planning
The divergence Crocker noticed was the consequence of a planning process that had been fragmented from its beginning. For nearly a year, the NSC exercised loose coordination over separate efforts by State and Defense and did not seek the participation of post-conflict experts at USAID. The marked separation between civilian and military preparations, which had existed since late 2001, was followed by further fragmentation within the interagency planning process, which had begun in earnest in August 2002. Even as officials thought they were moving toward an integrated master plan, the building blocks of that plan were being developed in a piecemeal fashion that rendered risks and needs less visible.

The reasons for the fragmentation were in part bureaucratic, but, in an important sense, they were also the product of higher-level strategic judgments. Calls for better-integrated planning and greater capacity to address worst-case scenarios were subordinated to the views of Defense Department officials who were committed to a rapid transfer of power. The liberation approach they and others backed became the operative strategy, with the White House elevating it to official U.S. policy by late fall 2002.[87]

As the fall turned to winter, NSC officials moved to integrate this vision of regime change into operational plans being prepared by the government's civilian agencies. USAID was among the first to be mobilized.

ESSENTIAL SERVICES OVERVIEW: PREWAR LEVELS IN IRAQ

Metric[88]	Pre-invasion
Electricity Production	
Megawatts	4,075
Oil Production	
Million Barrels per Day	2.58
Iraqi Security Forces	
Soldiers and Police	1,300,000[89]
Telecommunications	
Landline Subscribers	833,000
Mobile Subscribers	80,000

Iraq's electricity sector suffered from years of inadequate maintenance and poor management under Saddam.[90] According to the International Monetary Fund (IMF), Iraq's monthly electricity production, from March 2002 to March 2003, averaged 4,075 megawatts per day.[91] The distribution of power under Saddam heavily favored Baghdad, which received between 16 and 24 hours of power per day, while the average Iraqi household outside the capital received power for just 4 to 8 hours per day.[92]

The U.S. Department of Energy estimated that Iraq's oil production fell to 2.0 million barrels per day (MBPD) in 2002, but increased to 2.58 MBPD just before the war.[93] Although oil production itself is not an essential service, oil feeds the refineries that produce petroleum products for domestic consumption, is critical to electricity generation, and provides Iraq with much of the revenue that supports other services.

Chapter 2
The Agencies Engage

We needed to be thinking at a much different order of magnitude
of what is required to reconstruct a failed state, in the context of a
U.S. military invasion.

James Kunder
USAID Deputy Assistant Administrator for
Asia and the Near East (2002-2004)*

In 2002, the United States Agency for International Development administered nearly $7.5 billion in foreign aid programs.[1] Its 2,000 employees and 5,000 contractors worked in more than 100 developing countries across the world.[2] Many in government nonetheless viewed USAID as a minor player running small projects in faraway places. Despite its relative lack of capacity, USAID was fast becoming an essential player in the late 2002 planning for postwar Iraq. The National Security Council assumed that USAID's disaster response teams could help contain humanitarian crises that might follow the invasion, and that its development know-how could help repair Iraq's infrastructure and support the country's transition to democracy. Some Pentagon planners—particularly those unfamiliar with USAID's missions in Bosnia, Kosovo, and Afghanistan—imagined that the agency had vast powers to rush in civilians behind the troops and establish conditions that could lead to the soldiers' deployment home.

USAID officials first learned of their expected role in Iraq well after war planning had begun. Notably, USAID Administrator Andrew Natsios was not formally consulted in the early planning phases.[3] Ross Wherry, who ultimately directed much of the agency's reconstruction preparations, began to learn about Iraq planning in mid-2002 through a series of chance encounters, cryptic notes, and indirect suggestions that the agency should develop contingency scenarios.[4] The agency did not become formally involved until August 2002, when USAID Assistant Administrator Wendy Chamberlin was asked to serve on the NSC's Humanitarian Working Group.

White House officials would ask several USAID officials to join the planning efforts over the next month.[5] The agency's Asia and Near East Bureau soon took charge of reconstruction planning, while the Bureau for Democracy, Conflict and Humanitarian Assistance prepared for humanitarian relief operations.[6] In early October 2002, Administrator Natsios formed USAID's Iraq Task Force, chairing

---

* SIGIR interview with James Kunder, USAID Acting Deputy Administrator, February 15, 2008.

its weekly meetings thereafter to coordinate the agency's efforts. Several hundred USAID employees eventually would work full time on Iraq plans.[7]

When it came to mobilizing resources for possible humanitarian disasters in Iraq, USAID officials proceeded with full Administration support.[8] Mobilizing reconstruction resources, however, was a different matter. The NSC conceived of reconstruction primarily in terms of brick-and-mortar work, but USAID viewed such rebuilding as only part of a long-term social and political transformation necessary to achieving a fully democratic Iraq.[9] This divergence reflected larger disagreements among the President's advisors over what the postwar mission in Iraq demanded, making for a difficult and tense planning process.[10] In every aspect of the effort—in both the humanitarian and reconstruction areas—complex contracting regulations and time pressures pushed USAID's capacities to the limit, exposing structural weaknesses in the U.S. government's capacity to mobilize for contingency relief and reconstruction operations.[11]

USAID's *Vision for Post-Conflict Iraq*, first drafted in October 2002, stated the Administration's emerging policy that "reconstruction will aim to bring Iraqi facilities back to a modestly improved pre-conflict level." It also included this pointed—and, in retrospect, markedly accurate—assessment: "complete reconstruction to the economic and institutional capacity of 1980 (conditions prior to the Iran-Iraq war) will require years of public investment."[12]

Planning to Prevent a Humanitarian Disaster

The fear that Saddam would severely damage his own country in response to a U.S. invasion drove much of USAID's humanitarian planning. "What happens if Saddam blows up the dikes, the dams, floods the country?" Natsios asked.[13] Refugees also were a paramount concern. In response, USAID mobilized its cadre of U.S.-based and international NGOs that carry out the agency's humanitarian missions. The agency's disaster relief expert, Jonathan Dworken, chaired regular meetings in the USAID crisis room to plan their deployment.

USAID's Office for Foreign Disaster Assistance built the largest Disaster Assistance Response Team in the agency's history.[14] USAID's Office of Transition Initiatives (OTI), which works to stabilize countries making the transition from violence to peace, also mobilized much of its staff to work on Iraq planning.[15] Programs to prevent or minimize acts of reprisal and to maximize high-visibility projects that would symbolize U.S. goodwill were geared toward best-case, worst-case, and middle-range scenarios.[16]

Food was also a top priority.[17] The World Food Program, the food-aid branch of the UN, was deemed best suited to manage the logistics; it had the capacity to rush in 600,000 metric tons of food to feed 25 million people each month.[18] In the early fall of 2002, the Director of USAID's Office of Food for Peace alerted World Food Program officials in Rome that hostilities in Iraq might be imminent. Robin Cleveland, co-chair of the NSC's humanitarian working group, then authorized up to $200 million for the World Food Program to survey roads, identify warehouses, and preposition trucks, supplies, and staff.[19] It was the first U.S. down payment on postwar Iraq.

Success in Iraq would depend significantly upon synchronizing civilian relief efforts with military combat operations. In early November 2002, a contingent from the NSC's Humanitarian Working Group spent two days at CENTCOM headquarters in Tampa, Florida.[20] The Humanitarian Planning Team, as this contingent came to be known, worked to improve coordination between planners at CENTCOM and USAID.[21] In Tampa, the planning team and its military counterparts walked through what each agency and the military would do in the event of mass civilian casualties, refugee flows, and disruptions in the water and food supply.

Institutional differences made this joint planning difficult.[22] In the view of some USAID officials, CENTCOM planners had a circumscribed view of postwar operations. Military planning naturally emphasized the combat phase. "They were very focused on operations orders: take this hill by this date, take this crossroads," Wherry said. USAID planners realized that meeting humanitarian needs would fall almost entirely on their shoulders."[23]

Planning for Reconstruction
The evolving postwar plan called for a shift to reconstruction efforts once humanitarian needs were met. The scope of reconstruction would depend upon the amount of damage.[24] The Humanitarian Working Group developed reconstruction plans for various sectors and assigned an agency to lead each one. USAID would bear responsibility for most sectors, including health, water and sanitation, electricity, education, transportation, telecommunications, and agriculture/rural development. It also would complement governance efforts by the Department of State. Officials at Treasury would handle plans for financial recovery and economic development. Oil was assigned to the Pentagon.[25]

Wendy Chamberlin, Ross Wherry, and Christopher Milligan managed USAID's reconstruction planning.[26] The agency's institutional culture embraced a concept of development that went beyond merely rebuilding what war destroyed. Physical rehabilitation of damaged infrastructure would be one step in a larger democratic transition. Neighborhoods would need to elect their own governing councils to restore civil order. Teachers and civil servants would have to stay on the job. Employment programs, micro-lending, and other economic stimuli would be offered alongside programs that fostered reconciliation. This conflict transformation framework had informed international peacekeeping missions in Somalia, Haiti, Bosnia, and Kosovo.[27] USAID officials proposed that it should also be adopted in Iraq.

White House officials were skeptical. This was exactly the kind of nation building-ing the Administration had wanted to avoid. Robin Cleveland, co-chair of the NSC's Humanitarian Working Group, articulated a more limited view of U.S. objectives, insisting that only war damage would be repaired; the new Iraqi state would do most of the rebuilding, paying for it with Iraqi oil revenues. USAID planners, however, warned that achieving a stable and economically prosperous Iraq would require significant U.S. investment.[28]

The postwar policy for Iraq envisioned a democratic state that would threaten neither its regional neighbors nor U.S. interests. "Security, humanitarian assistance, and reconstruction aid," National Security Advisor Condoleezza Rice stated, would be deployed "in support of this vision."[29] How much reconstruction aid would be enough to achieve these goals was a matter of dispute between White House and USAID officials.

The U.S. postwar strategy had a two-phased approach. USAID would attend first to providing food, water, public health, and emergency electricity. Once Iraq stabilized, it would expand its focus to improving basic infrastructure, including electricity, roads, irrigation systems, hospitals, markets, and schools. The overarching goal of infrastructure repair was to return service delivery to pre-conflict levels.

Alongside physical reconstruction, USAID planned to promote economic renewal by bolstering Iraq's private sector, improving its banking system, and modernizing its agricultural economy. One of the primary goals was to establish a regulatory regime favorable to private enterprise that would, in time, make Iraq competitive in the world market. USAID put forth its plans, recognizing that fostering democratic governance in Iraq based upon the rule of law would be an enormous challenge.

The Department of State had the lead on developing a specific governance strategy, with USAID participating by preparing assistance programs that would help reform Iraq's local governance. USAID expected State to provide guidance, but in the absence of a detailed framework from the Department, the agency developed its own plan in which authority over funding many civic services would devolve to local governments, which had no previous experience in managing the delivery of essential services or administering the rule of law.[30] This proposed radical restructuring of Iraqi governance institutions was meant to promote a clean break from Saddam's highly centralized control.

USAID's approach to reconstruction embraced the Administration's transformational ambitions for Iraq, but also revealed the gulf between those ambitions and the limited resources that White House officials were willing, at the time, to commit. These differences came into stark relief when USAID's *Vision for Post-Conflict Iraq* contrasted the goals for each sector with the status of Iraq's dilapidated infrastructure. In the electricity sector, for instance, restoring service to prewar levels depended on finding enough portable generators and securing adequate supplies of fuel, substantial logistical challenges in a country with minimal refining capacity.[31]

A similar gap between goals and resources existed in the agricultural sector, Iraq's largest industry after oil. Fostering "commercial processes and a market-based food economy" would require repairing irrigation systems on more than two million acres of land, engaging in extensive technology-transfer programs, and immediately providing assistance for upcoming rice and barley harvests.[32] To meet the education sector's goal of reopening schools for the new term, the United States would need to repair 3,000 schools and provide supplies and instructional kits to 12,500 more.[33]

Conflicted Planning

Planners framed reconstruction policy for postwar Iraq by setting benchmarks in each sector at one month, three months, six months, and twelve months. These benchmarks developed through a sustained back-and-forth debate between White House officials and those at USAID and other agencies. For example, OMB's Robin Cleveland argued that the number of schools rehabilitated would be a good indicator for progress in the education sector. But the idea of counting buildings was anathema to USAID, whose subject-matter experts insisted that the percentage of children in school would be a more accurate measure of progress toward primary-education goals. The number of schools became the benchmark.

Cleveland's demands often pushed planners beyond what they believed they could reasonably deliver. Missing from the intelligence, according to USAID's Wherry, were assessments of the economy, governance, agriculture, and other "soft" aspects of Iraq's condition. "If it couldn't be got by a satellite, we just didn't have it," he said.[34] At one point, Chris Milligan was directed to establish indicators for the transportation sector. "I had a turn-around time of four hours to determine how many miles of roads would be re-opened or repaired," he said. To meet the deadline, he went to the USAID reference library, researched the available data on Iraq's road networks, and provided his "best estimate" based upon limited information.[35] The estimate went directly into USAID's *Vision for Post-Conflict Iraq.* "A targeted 50 percent, or about 2,200 kilometers, of economically important roads and bridges open to high speed traffic," was the sector goal.[36]

USAID Reconstruction Sector-Goals Timeline

	Immediate Post Conflict	60 Days	6 Months	12 Months	18 Months
Water and Sanitation	Rubber water bladders and purification equipment for up to one million displaced persons. Generators will be provided to power water systems pumps as required.	Repairs will begin on up to 10 urban water systems, assuming secure access to them.	Dependable minimum water supply will have been re-established in 15 cities.	Water systems will begin to be returned to local control. Revenue generation will be an issue at that point.	Dependable minimum water supply will have been re-established in all cities greater than 25,000 persons. Primary sewage treatment will have been restored in ten urban centers.
Public Health	Delivery of medicines and consumable surgical supplies to treat injured civilians and operate medical facilities.	Basic health services will be available to a targeted 25% of the population, and maternal/child health up to 50% of the populations, in secure areas.	Basic health services will be available to a targeted 50% of the population, and maternal/child health up to 100% of the populations, in secure areas	The reformed Ministry of Health will begin operating the health care system. Referral hospitals will be functioning in 21 urban locations.	Basic Health services available to the entire population. Advanced surgical services available.
Transportation	Damage assessments will be reviewed to prioritize reconstruction efforts. Repairs to Umm Qasr and Basra International proceed.	Port of Umm Qasr and Basra International Airport reopened for humanitarian traffic. Flour mills connected to seaport.	A targeted 50%, or about 2,200 kilometers, of economically important roads and bridges are open to high-speed traffic. Ports of entry for highways are appropriately controlled.	Reconstruction of roads, rail and barge landings completed to minimal level.	The Ministry of Public Works will be restructured, and furthered transportation assistance will make a transition to being the responsibility of the Ministry and local governments.
Electricity	Install emergency generators at hospitals, pumping stations, other priority sites.	A targeted 550 diesel-driven emergency generators will be installed. Rapid assessments conducted as security permits, and a power restoration plan prepared.	15% of the high voltage (132Kv and 33Kv) distribution net repaired, including rehabilitation of a targeted 50 substations and 5 generation plants in key urban areas. 40% of the previously served population has electricity.	Generation of 6,750 MW achieved.	An additional 60 substations and another 5 generation plants operational. Total electric supply a targeted 75% of pre-1991 level, with electricity reaching most, if not all, of the urban population.
Local Development	Prevent destruction of land records, ration lists, public documents.	Identify key local leaders and councils; connect them to opportunities for relief and reconstruction assistance, using small grants for immediate assistance as appropriate. Radio stations operating in secure areas.	Reconstruction offices established in all 18 provinces to coordinate projects and facilitate service provision. Interim local assemblies have clear roles and responsibilities.	Local governments counterbalance recentralization tendencies; interim democratic institutions demonstrate representative and transparent local governance.	Local administrations have responsibility for revenue generation for local services.
Economic Governance	Technical assistance teams will begin work outside Iraq to prepare for the needs of the Finance Ministry and the banks.	Technical teams ready to move into Iraq to assist a vetted Iraqi financial leadership team. Small business lending facility prepared to open.	Central Bank and MOF operating. Central Bank and SOMO cooperate on oil sales and food imports. Permissive environment for private banks. If a new currency is needed, ready for issuance. Programs promote competitiveness and global trade	MOF handles all government payrolls. Legal framework is hospitable to private business.	Privatization of state-owned businesses is occurring. Widespread access to private commercial banks.

Source: USAID, *Vision for Post-Conflict Iraq*, February 19, 2003.

Although some USAID officials had taken part in interventions in Bosnia, Kosovo, and Haiti, the agency had not had a role in large-scale contingency relief and reconstruction operations since the Civil Operations and Revolutionary Development Support (CORDS) program in Vietnam.[37] USAID's office computers were not even outfitted to email the classified plans agency officials were developing. Each time its planners completed a new draft, they had to hand-carry copies to the White House.[38]

Navigating between agency views and White House demands proved difficult. Realizing that he could not bridge some of the divides, USAID's Milligan decided to "jump through hoops" to get as many resources as possible to mobilize contractors and agency personnel in advance of the invasion. "Just tell me what I need to do to secure the money so we can be reasonably prepared," Milligan remembers thinking.[39] Although members of the Humanitarian Working Group had disagreements along the way, at no point did they take these issues to the level of Frank Miller's Executive Steering Group on Iraq or to Stephen Hadley's Deputies Committee.[40]

By December 2002, USAID had arrived at a picture of what the agency thought it would take to reconstruct Iraq within the policy guidelines set by the NSC. Officials consolidated humanitarian and reconstruction plans in a huge spreadsheet that became known as the "horse blanket."[41] The horse blanket showed the order in which USAID would mobilize its workforce and the many contractors it employed. It was a checklist of what would need to happen inside the agency to get ready for postwar Iraq.

In a briefing to the NSC Deputies Committee on December 10, 2002—with war just over three months away— Robin Cleveland and Elliot Abrams presented the Humanitarian Working Group's final recommendations. Most of the briefing slides detailed humanitarian preparations; a few dealt with reconstruction and the complex Iraqi political situation that would emerge after the invasion.[42] The presentation listed the assumptions on which the group had based its plans. A secure environment was first.[43] The briefing also made clear that the working group had planned for only a modest intervention. After the meeting, USAID was "instructed to go full bore with detailed planning," including drawing up the contracts to carry it out.[44]

USAID Mobilizes Contractors

Like most U.S. civilian agencies, USAID had little in-house surge capacity. Almost all of its mission in Iraq would be executed by NGOs and the small circle of companies that traditionally bid on the agency's contracts. By early 2003, six in ten of the personnel running USAID's overseas missions were contractors, the result of a 37 percent cutback in government staff in the decade following the Cold War.[45] "We lost a third of the Foreign Service and a third of the civil service in the mid-90s," Administrator Natsios said, "and we never got them back."[46]

Mobilizing USAID's contractors was complicated. By law, U.S. agencies must follow the Federal Acquisition Regulation (FAR), an encyclopedic compendium of rules governing federal contracting.[47] The FAR values procedural fairness and transparency over expediency.[48] Its mandatory reviews and restrictions would later rankle officials in Baghdad, who thought its provisions were not well-suited for contingency contracting in a war-zone. A number of FAR exemptions allowed for flexibility in unusual circumstances.[49] One of the most important was the "notwithstanding authority" clause, which permitted USAID's Office of Foreign Disaster Assistance to award grants to relief organizations outside normal FAR processes, if international disaster relief demands required it.[50]

USAID had existing contracts for frequently used services, which enabled it to set up some postwar contingency programs for Iraq rapidly. These "indefinite delivery, indefinite quantity" (IDIQ) contracts were held by firms that maintained ready-response capabilities. As planners identified needs, agency officials would issue "task orders" under an IDIQ contract, which the contractor would then carry out. Pre-authorization letters also enabled USAID to mobilize contractors and emergency-relief organizations before specific task orders were written or grants awarded.[51] In extraordinary situations, agency officials could waive the FAR's "full and open competition" requirement.

On January 16, 2003, with war looming, USAID Administrator Andrew Natsios did just that, waiving the FAR's full and open competition requirement for all war-related contracts. USAID's late entry into planning, Natsios argued, made it impossible to use the normal bidding processes.[52] The agency's Inspector General later certified that USAID properly justified the waivers for each contract it let with less than full and open competition.[53]

A number of USAID's contractors received urgent phone calls during this period. The day after Christmas 2002, Bruce Spake, Vice President at Development Alternatives, Inc. (DAI), heard from USAID official Rob Jenkins: "Bruce, we're interested in talking to you about some possible work in a place in the Middle East. You read the newspapers, don't you?" Jenkins asked Spake to write a concept paper for working in a destabilized country in the Middle East "without using that country's name." Spake turned in a paper the next day, and DAI was awarded a contract shortly thereafter. In February 2003, the company dispatched an advance team to begin operations in Kuwait, weeks before senior U.S. civilian leadership arrived in the region.[54]

USAID also awarded a total of $41 million in international disaster assistance to a broad array of NGOs, including Mercy Corps, Save the Children, and the International Rescue Committee.[55] By the end of February, the agency had provided $17.3 million for prepositioning relief commodities in theater.[56]

Contracting was more complicated on the reconstruction side, in part because USAID's development ethos had long since moved away from viewing large infrastructure projects as catalysts for economic growth. Although the agency activated several of its standing IDIQ contracts, it still needed new contracts for the large-scale construction tasks looming ahead.[57] Crafting their language was a crucial step in the mobilization process. To ensure that reconstruction policy formulated by the NSC translated into the right assets on the ground, contracting officers from USAID's management bureau had begun working with experts across the agency in the late fall of 2002 to write the necessary "statements of work," which are basic—but critical—descriptions of a project and what is required to implement it. Many of the statements of work mirrored the goals outlined in USAID's *Vision for Post-Conflict Iraq* and the indicators developed by the NSC's Humanitarian Working Group.[58]

Eleven teams finalized the statements of work in early December and wrote requests for proposals during the last two weeks of the year.[59] "The instruction was … get in, get it [done], get out," Ross Wherry recalls. But because USAID's experts believed rebuilding would take longer, its contracting officers added options to extend each contract.[60]

From February through May 2003, USAID awarded eight major contracts worth $1.3 billion, the largest short-term burst of contracting in the agency's history.[61] This was just the beginning. The agency would soon let many more contracts, and it would dramatically increase the value of those already awarded.[62] The contracting surge put the agency in a cash crunch. Officials drew $110 million from existing accounts on an emergency basis, "mortgaging the fourth quarter of AID's budget in order to do what we had to do in January, February, and March," Wherry said.[63] The Iraq Relief and Reconstruction Fund (IRRF 1), which the Congress created in April 2003, ended up funding most of these contracts.[64]

USAID's Initial Reconstruction Contract Awards

Date Awarded	Contractor & Sector	Original Contract Amount ($ Millions)	Original Contract Ceiling or Current Obligation ($ Millions)	Contract Length	Contract Type & Procurement Method
02/07/03	International Resources Group (IRG): Personnel Services Contract	$7.000	$27.10	3 month, with 2 option years	CPFF: Sole Source
03/17/03	AFCAP: Logistics	$26.00	$91.50	2 years	CPAF: Inter-agency agreement
03/21/03	SkyLink Air: Airport Administration	$10.200	$27.20	18 months, with 2 option years	CPFF: Less than full and open
03/07/03	SSA Marine: Iraq Seaport Assessment	$4.800	$14.32	1 year with no option year	CPFF: Less than full and open
04/11/03	Research Triangle Institute: Local Government I	$168.000	$241.91	I year, with 2 option years	CPFF: Less than full and open
04/11/03	Creative Associates, Inc. (CAI): Education I	$62.628	56.50	1 year, 2 option years	CPFF: Less than full and open
04/17/03	Bechtel National: Infrastructure	$680.000	$1,029.83	18 months	CPFF: Less than full and open
04/30/03	Abt Associates: Health Systems	$43.800	$23.03	1 year	CPFF: Less than full and open
06/01/03	Army Corps of Engineers: Architecture and Engineering Services	$3.00	$38.09	1 year, 2 option years	Interagency agreement
06/25/03	Management Systems International: Monitoring and Evaluation	$5.038	$15.12	1 base year and 2 option years	Task Order: RFP to all holders of IQC
07/24/03	Bearing Point: Economic Recovery I	$79.583	$79.58	1 year with 2 option years	CPFF: Less than full and open
10/15/03	Development Alternatives, Inc.: Agricultural Development	$36.900	$106.70	1 year with two option years	CPFF: Full and Open

Source: SIGIR, "Iraq Reconstruction: Lessons Learned in Contracting and Procurement," July 2006, 32.

By far the most substantial IRRF 1 contract during this period—and the largest single contract ever let by USAID—went to Bechtel International on April 17, 2003: $680 million for major infrastructure reconstruction. The expedited bidding process shortened the procurement time normally required for so large a contract from seven months to three.[65] Of the seven contractors invited to compete, only two submitted bids.[66]

The Bechtel contract's statement of work reflected the planners' beliefs that rebuilding Iraq's infrastructure would help achieve U.S. foreign policy goals. "The

U.S. government envisions a postwar reconstruction effort," the statement read, "as a highly visual symbol of good faith toward building trust for economic, social and cultural benefits as well as for political stability in the region."[67] Five months later, USAID would increase the Bechtel contract's value to $1.03 billion.[68]

Defense's Oil Sector Plan

As USAID planned for its sectors, the Department of Defense prepared for the oil sector, while Treasury focused on financial and economic recovery plans. Senior officials believed that a rapid post-invasion restoration of Iraq's oil sector was central to achieving U.S. strategic goals. The prospect that oil revenues could finance Iraq's reconstruction led the Administration to assert in March 2003 that total costs to the American taxpayer would be limited.[69] With 115 billion barrels of known reserves and potentially 100 billion more lying in wait—the world's third-largest reserves—Iraq, in theory, could rely exclusively on oil to provide not only electricity, gasoline, and cooking fuel, but also most of the revenue it needed for reconstruction.[70] But Iraq's dilapidated oil infrastructure stood in the way.

During the 1991 Gulf War, the U.S. bombing campaign severely damaged the country's refineries and oil distribution networks.[71] The lack of proper maintenance during the sanctions era further degraded the oil sector to the point that Saddam was unable to make use of a 1998 UN authorization that allowed oil sales to double.[72] Despite the import of more than a billion dollars in spare parts and equipment under the Oil-for-Food program, Iraq's production capacity only marginally improved during the latter half of the 1990s.

On September 20, 2002, Under Secretary Feith established the Energy Infrastructure Planning Group inside the Department of Defense, placing it under the leadership of Michael Mobbs.[73] Representatives from the Departments of State, Energy, and Defense, and the Central Intelligence Agency eventually joined.[74] Formal meetings began in November, with draft plans due by mid-December.[75]

The task of determining how to revitalize Iraq's oil sector far exceeded the U.S. government's in-house expertise. The need to turn to a specialized private sector company led to the first significant—and the most controversial—contract in Iraq reconstruction. Although a number of firms could repair oil infrastructure, the decision to classify the oil cell's planning restricted the universe of supporting contractors to those with security clearances.[76] Mobbs thought that the Houston-based firm of Kellogg Brown and Root (KBR), the prime contractor for the U.S. Army's massive Logistics Civil Augmentation Program (LOGCAP), was a logical choice.[77] LOGCAP is the Army's standing IDIQ contract for the worldwide support of military operations, chiefly providing troops in the field with food, fuel, and billeting.

Just as USAID had outsourced much of its work in the years after the Cold War, the military also had turned to the private sector to perform work once done by its own personnel. Under the LOGCAP contract, which KBR held for all but a few years since the program's inception in 1985, contractors provide services ranging from building bases to cooking food and doing laundry. LOGCAP grew out of the post-Vietnam downsizing of the armed services, reflecting the government-wide growth of outsourcing, which would dramatically affect the war and reconstruction efforts in Iraq.[78] In World War II, one contractor was deployed for every seven soldiers.[79] During the 2003 invasion, that number had increased to one for every 2.4.[80] By 2006, contractors outnumbered soldiers in Iraq.[81]

KBR's responsibilities under LOGCAP meant that it was already working in support of the Defense Department's Iraq war plans. Mobbs wanted to capitalize on this existing relationship. Hiring KBR, though, could create the appearance of a conflict of interest, because Vice President Cheney was the former CEO of KBR's parent company Halliburton.[82] Under Secretary Feith raised this issue at a Deputies Committee meeting and even alerted the Vice President's office. According to Mobbs, White House officials said the mission took priority over whatever political fallout might occur from granting a sole-source contract to KBR.[83]

A second possible conflict arose. The General Counsel of the Army Materiel Command ruled that asking KBR to assist the oil cell was outside the scope of activities permitted under the LOGCAP contract. The legal opinion acknowledged that a contract for the logistical support of military operations was not an appropriate vehicle for funding plans to repair a foreign country's oil infrastructure. The matter was forwarded up the chain, first to the Army General Counsel, and then to the Department of Defense General Counsel, who settled the matter on November 8, 2002.[84] So long as the job did not extend to actual repair work, the opinion stated, the contract could go forward under LOGCAP.[85] A task order for $1.9 million was issued to KBR the same day.[86]

The link between planning and executing oil sector repairs, however, could not be easily severed. On March 8, 2003, just three months after KBR had received its planning contract and one week before the invasion of Iraq, the U.S. Army Corps of Engineers (USACE) awarded KBR a $7 billion sole-source contract for repair work on Iraq's oil sector.[87] As the contracting documents reveal, part of the basis for this award was the previous task order issued to KBR.[88] This would be the single largest reconstruction contract in Iraq and the largest known sole-source contract in U.S. history.

A subsequent review by the Government Accountability Office (GAO) found that the original November task order was beyond the scope of the LOGCAP contract and that the Army Field Support Command should have prepared a written justification to authorize the work without competition.[89] But Defense officials later justified their use of LOGCAP by citing overriding national security interests in getting planning started. "We certainly did not have time to run a competition to see who was going to support us," Mobbs said.[90]

USACE mobilized to help with the oil sector work. General Robert Crear, commander of the Corps' Southwest Division, established Task Force Restore Iraq Oil (RIO) as part of the plan to rush engineers into theater. Task Force RIO's projected strength was 129 personnel, 90 of whom would be civilians.[91] By February 2003, a Task Force RIO advance team had deployed to Kuwait.

As Task Force RIO and the Energy Infrastructure Working Group proceeded, Frank Miller and NSC staffer Pamela Quanrud developed a longer-term plan for moving control of Iraq's oil infrastructure back to Iraqis. Avoiding the perception that the United States would annex Iraq's oil wealth for its own purposes was a crucial goal. Miller and Quanrud devised a way to manage downstream and upstream production while also assembling a governing board of Iraqis. Decisions about Iraq's oil wealth were not to be seen as made by the United States alone. Their plan was approved by the President—who came to call Quanrud "the petroleum lady"—in January 2003, when war with Iraq was two months away.[92]

Treasury's Financial Reconstruction Plan

The NSC gave the Treasury Department a unique mission for postwar Iraq— preserving and restoring the country's financial system—that Treasury ultimately executed with success in the chaotic months after Saddam's fall. Treasury officials recognized that the financial recovery of Iraq depended upon the simultaneous accomplishment of two interdependent feats: maintaining confidence in the country's currency and restoring operations at Iraq's financial institutions, including its central and commercial banks and the Ministry of Finance. Without a functioning financial system and a stable currency, commerce in Iraq—and thus much of ordinary life—would grind to a halt.

Addressing these and other economic challenges fell to Treasury Under Secretary John Taylor, who, beginning in September 2002, led the agency's Iraq planning efforts, along with Van Jorstad, George Mullinax, and David Nummy.[93] Taylor established the Treasury's Task Force on Iraq Financial Reconstruction, setting up offices in the Treasury Department's Market Room. Taylor and his team soon found that reliable information about Iraq's economy was almost nonexistent.

The International Monetary Fund had not done a technical analysis of Iraq's economy for twenty years, and Iraqi data-collection entities had atrophied under Saddam. Almost no bank in Iraq transferred money electronically, and the regime had co-opted the once-functional Central Bank to "lend" money to Saddam's cronies. There was also the issue of dealing with Iraq's dual system of currency—the "Swiss" dinar used in the Kurdish region in northern Iraq and the "Saddam" dinar used everywhere else.[94]

Taylor worked with Iraqi participants drawn from the Future of Iraq Project and experts across the government to draft contingency plans to prevent a monetary collapse and stabilize Iraqi assets.[95] The plan focused on securing key financial institutions after Saddam's regime fell and then using seized Iraqi assets to pay the government's employees and pensioners until a permanent system could be established. In support of this planning, the President issued an executive order on March 20, 2003—the day the war began—authorizing the freezing of Iraqi funds held in U.S. banks. The United States ultimately vested about $1.9 billion of these assets in the Treasury Department for—among other things—paying Iraqi salaries.[96]

NSC's Asymmetry

A striking asymmetry resulted from the NSC-led planning process: the U.S. government planned for the worst-case humanitarian scenario while it simultaneously planned for the best-case reconstruction one. Humanitarian planning for postwar Iraq advanced smoothly because the humanitarian disaster contingencies involved were straightforward, and the President had backed the effort from the beginning. Consequently, humanitarian planners could mobilize any part of the government and were free to reach out to international institutions to obtain help in formulating what became a robust multilateral approach. By contrast, irreconcilable views of how extensive the U.S. financial and administrative role in Iraq might become impeded reconstruction planning. Repairing war damage ultimately became the policy goal, but little connection was made between how the rebuilding would—or even could—bring about a democratic transition.[97]

The reality was that most policymakers considered reconstruction a relatively minor issue. They saw USAID's contract with Bechtel as a "standby" measure—for emergency use only.[98] USAID officials—who, in 2002, had privately predicted a $90 billion rebuilding scenario over three to five years—could not have gotten "traction" for a large reconstruction plan with the officials to whom they reported in the interagency planning group.[99]

The responsibility for reconstruction, along with all the other bureaucratic and administrative duties playing out in the fragmented planning process, would soon fall under the Department of Defense, which, at Secretary Rumsfeld's request, would be given full responsibility for administering postwar Iraq.

CHAPTER 3
THE DEPARTMENT OF DEFENSE TAKES CHARGE

*It has long been a concern of mine that the U.S. Government
lacks a standing capability in the area of reconstruction and
that there is no long-established team of civilians, let alone an
experienced joint civilian-military team, to handle the challenges
of major post-conflict tasks.* *

Donald Rumsfeld
Secretary of Defense (2001-2006)

In the wake of the October 2002 decision to delay establishing a civilian office in
the Department of Defense to coordinate interagency planning for postwar Iraq,
the existing planning groups pressed on independently.[1] USAID created a detailed plan for humanitarian relief and reconstruction operations. A Department
of Defense team prepared to restore Iraq's oil infrastructure, and a team at the
Department of the Treasury planned to restore Iraq's financial infrastructure.
An interagency humanitarian planning team, with representatives from agencies
across the government, worked at CENTCOM headquarters. But the absence of
a single coordinating office meant there was no management locus around which
postwar planning could coalesce. "What was lacking," Under Secretary Douglas
Feith would later say, "[was] the integration."[2]

The postwar structure briefed to the National Security Council in mid-October—a three-star military headquarters and a parallel civilian administration—still
existed only as a diagram on a briefing slide. The Administration lacked a consensus policy on key matters, such as the formation of an interim Iraqi authority and
a timeframe for transferring power to it. "Liberation" had become the dominant
assumption, but whether liberation could be easily achieved and stability secured
was viewed differently by defense, diplomatic, and development officials. All the
while, troops and materiel flowed to the Gulf.

At CENTCOM headquarters in Tampa, Florida, the small building that
housed Iraq war planners was a beehive of activity. Every week seemed to bring
a new major event requiring action. First was the President's speech to the UN
in September 2002, then the war resolution before the Congress in October.
Next came the issue of obtaining basing rights in the region. Periodically, yet
another Rumsfeld-directed revision of the war plan would arrive, triggering

---

* Donald Rumsfeld, former Secretary of Defense, letter to SIGIR, April 4, 2008.

• 32 •

commanders' conferences, new iterations of deployment schedules, and a blizzard of briefing slides.[3]

Through all of this activity, Phase IV got short shrift—but not without notice. Since late August 2002, the Joint Staff had worried that Phases I through III had swamped CENTCOM and that planning for Phase IV had fallen behind.[4] The Joint Staff recognized that CENTCOM had devoted insufficient resources to integrate government-wide postwar planning within Phase IV and to coordinate it with phases I through III.[5] Majors Thomas Fisher and Ray Eiriz, the CENTCOM planners working on Phase IV, had other responsibilities that pulled them from their postwar planning work.[6]

On December 11, 2002, the Phase IV planners, spurred by the Joint Staff, started catching up. Major Fisher quickly initiated an intense postwar planning session with a 40-person interagency team. Three days later, he briefed the Joint Staff on the draft Phase IV plan. It predicted rough going ahead. "We were assuming that there would be no government that moves in, so we were anticipating chaos," Major Fisher said. "We did make the assumption that at some point there would be an international mandate, either of the Coalition or of the United Nations."[7] After Fisher's briefing, the Director of the Joint Staff, Lieutenant General George Casey, realized that CENTCOM needed to augment the Phase IV effort, so he created a joint task force—designating it JTF-4—to supply 58 more personnel to help with postwar planning.[8]

Defense Leads Postwar Planning

On December 18, 2002, the President used the phrase "war is inevitable" at an NSC meeting.[9] The remark prompted Secretary Rumsfeld to launch the long-awaited civil-administration office that would help manage postwar Iraq. Soon thereafter, the President resolved the question of its chain of command.

At Secretary Rumsfeld's request, and with Secretary of State Colin Powell's concurrence, the President placed the Defense Department in charge of all postwar activity.[10] "State does not have the personnel, the capacity, or the size to deal with an immediate postwar situation in a foreign country that's eight thousand miles away from here," Secretary Powell explained.[11] Lodging oversight of both military and civilian functions in the Defense Department, Rumsfeld had argued, would ensure a seamless transition from combat to reconstruction. A unified chain of command, running from the Secretary down through CENTCOM, would prevent the split between the military and civil reconstruction seen in Bosnia and Kosovo.[12]

The President formalized the decision on January 20, 2003, by issuing National Security Presidential Directive 24 (NSPD 24), consolidating responsibility for managing postwar Iraq in a new organization, the Office of Reconstruction and Humanitarian Affairs (ORHA), housed within the Defense Department.[13] With a stroke of his pen, the President superseded the existing system for interagency postwar planning inside the NSC. This dramatic shift shocked some Iraq planners. "Within a 24-hour period all of a sudden Robin and Elliot go away," USAID Administrator Natsios said, referring to the Humanitarian Working Group led by Robin Cleveland and Elliot Abrams.[14] "We were just stunned," the agency's acting Deputy Administrator James Kunder said. "It was our first insight into the fact that there were big processes going on that we were oblivious to."[15]

As Defense officials consolidated control, the period of adjustment that followed was turbulent. Some compared the implementation of NSPD 24 to a hostile takeover. "You don't need to worry about the nuts and bolts of basic reconstruction," NSC Senior Director Frank Miller remembers two Defense officials saying. "It's now an [Office of the Secretary of Defense] operation." "Thereafter," Miller said, "it was 'you guys stay out, we don't need your help.'"[16]

NSPD 24's new arrangements directly affected CENTCOM's Phase IV planning. "There were two phases to the plan we had developed," Major Eiriz said. First, the Humanitarian Planning Team would ensure that the rest of the government be "in synch" with CENTCOM's plans for humanitarian contingencies. "Then there was going to be the reconstruction planning team," to address the restoration of Iraq's civil institutions and infrastructure. But after NSPD 24 was issued, CENTCOM stood down the Humanitarian Planning Team and assigned the reconstruction mission to JTF-4.[17]

Strategy and Force Levels

The standing war plan for Iraq, developed by General Franks's predecessors at CENTCOM, called for a half million troops—a number Secretary Rumsfeld and his aides thought much too high in light of advances in war-fighting technology and service integration.[18] Relying on a large force would bring more troops into theater than needed, Rumsfeld argued, and would also constrain the President's ability to respond quickly to any other provocations.[19] "We got told that it was old think, too big, wasn't innovative, and to readdress the planning using a different set of assumptions," said Colonel Mike Fitzgerald, CENTCOM's chief of war plans.[20]

Secretary Rumsfeld pushed General Franks to develop a more flexible plan, one that would rely on fewer troops. "It was clear to the planners, over time," Fitzgerald said, "that some of the assumptions we had made were not going to be accepted very well unless they went the way the Office of the Secretary of Defense was thinking."[21] The revised war plan significantly reduced aggregate force levels. General Franks ultimately recommended to the President that he send only 160,000 combat soldiers, two-thirds less than the number initially suggested by CENTCOM planners.[22]

The President questioned whether this lower troop level would affect security after the invasion. "In the area of law-and-order, the President and Rice asked Tommy Franks if it was covered," Frank Miller recalled. "He said it was—'every village will have a mayor, a lieutenant, captains, a structure.' He was asked again if he was sure—he emphatically answered, '*It's covered.*'"[23]

The Coalition ground forces commander, Lieutenant General David McKiernan, "really felt strongly about the inadequacy of the force," said Colonel Mike Fitzgerald.[24] The idea of fewer troops similarly unsettled CENTCOM Phase IV planners, as Major Fisher explained:

> The thing we kept going back to was we've only got so many people. Do you want them on the streets protecting people? Do you want them on the borders keeping WMD from getting away and keeping terrorists from getting in? Do you want them on the oil pipelines to keep the oil flow flowing? Do you want them handing out food to people that need food? Do you want them securing bank vaults and things of that nature? Do you want them conducting [medical programs] to build good will? I would sit there and talk to these people from [the office of the Secretary of Defense] and they'd say, 'You know, we need to improve security on the borders.' And I'd say, 'Do you know when you stretch the border of Iraq out, it's longer than our border with Mexico? How many divisions would you have to put in Arizona, New Mexico, California, Texas to secure our border?'[25]

Building ORHA

On Thursday, January 9, 2003, Jay Garner, a retired Army Lieutenant General and president of the defense contractor SY Technology, was lunching at a restaurant in New York when Under Secretary Douglas Feith called his cell phone. Garner had successfully led Operation Provide Comfort, a humanitarian mission in Northern Iraq, after the 1991 Gulf War. "We just got out of the Secretary's office," Feith said, "The Secretary would like for you to consider coming in and helping us put together a postwar organization."[26]

Garner and Rumsfeld had served together on a federal advisory panel, and the Secretary thought it would be easier for a former military man—especially one who knew Iraq—to work with CENTCOM.[27] Garner met with Feith and Rumsfeld the following week. When he agreed to lead ORHA, Lieutenant General Garner could not have known he was "embarking on mission impossible," as one national security aide described his job.[28] Just 56 days after ORHA moved into its empty Pentagon offices, the United States would be at war.[29]

Created by NSPD 24, ORHA started with no staff, was barely integrated into the military command structure, and—from day one—encountered hostility from the very parties whose activities it was asked to coordinate. Three military commands, two civilian agencies, and the circle of White House officials expecting to oversee postwar administration learned of Garner's appointment after the fact.[30] "Rumsfeld pulled the rug out from under them," Garner recalls. "They never forgave us for that."[31]

The success of ORHA was premised on the idea that Garner would "operationalize" plans that had already been well developed through the interagency process. But when Lieutenant General Garner arrived at the Pentagon, no master civilian plan was there to greet him. "They hadn't lined up anybody to brief us … we really had to find out what they were doing by word of mouth." Garner later learned about the Office of Special Plans—Feith's Pentagon unit dedicated to postwar planning—but its products, Garner said, were "never given to us, we never saw it, didn't know about it." Garner learned of the office's existence just before the invasion, when one of his aides happened across it by chance.[32]

The logistical and staffing challenges inherent in starting ORHA from scratch were overwhelming. "We didn't have a desk, we didn't have an office, we didn't have a telephone, we didn't have anything," Garner recalls. Arabic linguists, regional specialists, and military planners were nowhere in evidence. Garner himself started work on a volunteer basis when the Pentagon was unable to process his hiring as a temporary employee.[33]

Lieutenant General Garner moved quickly to build a team. He brought in retired Lieutenant General Ron Adams as his deputy and hired retired Lieutenant General Jerry Bates and Colonel Paul Hughes as senior advisors. Colonel Thomas Baltazar was assigned by Feith's office, and Chris Milligan came over from USAID. USACE sent Major General Carl Strock to be ORHA's seventh member. National Security Advisor Condoleezza Rice meanwhile urged government agencies to provide more personnel to support the fledgling organization.[34]

Garner organized ORHA into three pillars: humanitarian assistance, civil administration, and reconstruction.[35] When Chris Milligan moved into the Pentagon the week of January 20, 2003, he helped Garner and Bates flesh out the pillar structure.[36] The reconstruction and civil administration pillars would oversee Iraq's 22 ministries. To get the ministries back on their feet, an American "senior advisor" assigned to each would serve as the liaison between ORHA and the new Iraqi government.

Garner wanted a U.S. government agency in charge of each pillar. "Adams and I sat down," he remembers, "and we put State Department over humanitarian affairs, and we put State Department over civil administration, and we put USAID over reconstruction."[37] It was a division that reflected each agency's expertise, as well as existing interagency plans. But Rumsfeld objected to Garner's decision, demanding that a Defense official control all three pillars. "I had a running gun battle with the Defense Department on who were the leaders of each of these pillars," Garner recalled.[38]

Secretary Rumsfeld eventually relented, claiming only the civil administration pillar as Defense's own, but he still questioned the appropriateness of several officials selected by State and USAID. "The White House," Rumsfeld later wrote, "believed [the selections] would not be a good fit within ORHA."[39] Garner named Ambassador George Ward to lead the humanitarian pillar, with Dick Owen, a USAID official, as his deputy. USAID official Lew Lucke took charge of the reconstruction pillar, with Christopher Milligan in the deputy slot.[40]

Finding a lead for civil administration proved difficult.[41] Feith eventually nominated Michael Mobbs, who had overseen the department's oil-planning cell.[42] The State Department immediately protested the appointment of a lawyer rather than a professional diplomat to such a key position. Under Secretary of State Marc Grossman told Garner that Mobbs was unqualified for the job. Garner brokered a compromise in which Ambassador Barbara Bodine, an experienced Arabist who had previously served in Baghdad, would join ORHA to support civil administration and provide experience that Mobbs lacked.[43]

Unable to assemble a large civilian support staff quickly, Garner filled much of the rest of his staff with military personnel. When he asked the Joint Chiefs for 90 military personnel, Lieutenant General Casey, Director of the Joint Staff, initially refused. "No, too many people," Casey said, telling Garner that ORHA would not be operating 24 hours a day. "If you think we're not going to have a 24/7 operation over there," Garner thundered, "where the hell have you been in your career?"[44] Only after Garner scheduled a meeting with Secretary Rumsfeld to protest the refusal did Casey relent.[45]

The staff Garner cobbled together was an ad hoc team—a portent of things to come in post-invasion Iraq. Many of the leadership positions were filled by officials pulled from retirement or outside government. Senior State Department officials were conspicuously absent. "There was not a lot of participation or enthusiasm for the mission even at senior levels at the State Department," George Ward said. "It was 'if you don't want us, we're not going to play the game.'"[46]

Struggling for Resources and Control

As ORHA organized itself at the Pentagon, JTF-4, the Joint Staff's Phase IV task force, was doing the same thing at CENTCOM headquarters in Tampa. In mid-December, Casey had tapped Brigadier General Steven Hawkins, his subordinate from operations in Bosnia, to command JTF-4. Hawkins arrived at CENTCOM the same day Garner was asked by Secretary Rumsfeld to lead ORHA.[47] Phase IV planning was transferred from the CENTCOM planning cell to JTF-4 during the third week of January 2003, about two months before the invasion would begin.[48]

The division of duties between ORHA and JTF-4 was ambiguous. Hawkins saw JTF-4 as more than just an organization to assume control of CENTCOM Phase IV planning. Casey, who launched JTF-4 before ORHA's formation, had intended it to become the command center for postwar operations in Iraq, led by a three-star general.[49] In this formulation, JTF-4—not ORHA—would have the postwar operational lead after the fall of Saddam's regime. Dozens of area specialists and the best military planners would help it work directly with USAID, the Department of State, USACE, and the Coalition Forces Land Component Command (CFLCC).[50] ORHA's creation fundamentally altered this vision, but the new arrangement was anything but clear.

CENTCOM's leadership was not happy with either ORHA or JTF-4. Although Rumsfeld envisioned ORHA as a "module that fit within the CENTCOM structure," military commanders viewed it as an unwanted interloper. "I was getting phone calls from Jay Garner, even after he deployed," Feith said. "CENTCOM was referring to ORHA as 'they' and ORHA would refer to CENTCOM as 'they.'"[51]

JTF-4 received the same arms-length treatment from CENTCOM. "I couldn't even get office supplies back [at CENTCOM headquarters in] Tampa," Brigadier General Hawkins remembered. "I went to the craft trade show at the Officers' Club and took office supplies off of every display table," he said. "That's how I put the first pads of paper on the desk to put the task force together."[52]

The cold receptions Garner and Hawkins received reflected the frustration within CENTCOM over the ever-shifting management of Phase IV. "What we had asked for was a Corps Commander and staff that was already developed," Colonel Fitzgerald said in reference to the three-star command the Joint Staff envisioned for postwar Iraq. "What we got [with JTF-4] was General Hawkins—a one-star general—and 50 great Americans trying to do great work, but with no guidance, no headquarters to accept them, no resources available. They were just orphan children."[53]

Others at CENTCOM viewed ORHA and JTF-4 as the long-promised "interagency cavalry" riding to the post-invasion rescue. ORHA and JTF-4 personnel, however, had an opposite view, seeing CENTCOM as subject to their direction on postwar matters and obligated to furnish the military resources they needed to manage postwar Iraq. Each side tried to have its way. CENTCOM Commander General Tommy Franks cited an operational order that placed ORHA under his control. In response, Garner asserted his independence by invoking his reporting relationship to the Secretary of Defense and the Presidential charter for ORHA. "It was a continual battle on who worked for whom," Fitzgerald said.[54]

In a period of three weeks, the Pentagon's military and civilian leadership had launched what became competing postwar organizations. This failure in organizational unity hobbled the efforts of both ORHA and JTF-4 to mobilize for the mission. The resulting "confusion-of-command" dynamic foreshadowed problems that would afflict the Iraq reconstruction program in various ways over the next six years.[55]

Two Chains of Command

ORHA's Garner tried to broker a solution to the crossed lines of postwar authority. He asked that ORHA and JTF-4 be merged, with Hawkins becoming commander of "ORHA's operational arm." When this was rejected, Garner advocated placing General John Abizaid, CENTCOM's Deputy Commanding General, in charge of the Iraq theater, with McKiernan and Garner as co-equal subordinates.[56] McKiernan would oversee security and troop movements, and Garner would handle civil administration, reconstruction, and humanitarian relief.[57] It seemed logical to have a "military guy" in charge, Garner reasoned. "I didn't own any helicopters, and I didn't own any fuel, and I didn't own any trucks," he said.[58]

The Department of Defense weighed this option, but, on the eve of war, Rumsfeld backed away from it as well. Garner made one last phone call to Rumsfeld from Kuwait. "He finally got so mad at me, he said, 'We're not discussing this anymore,' and hung up."[59] General Franks also opposed a major postwar military command and told his planners he did not see a headquarters commanded by a four-star general—which the military would eventually create in June 2004—as necessary.[60]

Ironically, this chain-of-command confusion was exactly what Secretary Rumsfeld had hoped to avert by placing postwar administration under the control of the Department of Defense. Yet, by establishing ORHA in parallel to JTF-4, and then not having the CENTCOM commander effectively arbitrate between them, Rumsfeld created the very situation he had sought to prevent. "I pointed out to the President and to Dr. Rice," Secretary Powell said, "that they authorized and set up two chains of command." "They said 'no we didn't,'" but then "checked and realized that's what they had done."[61]

ORHA Prepares

While Lieutenant General Garner navigated through the colliding chains of command, his staff focused on preparing for postwar Iraq. The humanitarian pillar took charge of the food program and the disaster relief that the NSC's Humanitarian Working Group had planned. Food, water, medicine, and shelter were being positioned in Kuwait and Jordan.[62] The reconstruction pillar began using the new USAID contracts, especially the International Resources Group (IRG) contract for technical experts.[63]

Tom Wheelock, IRG's chief of party, arrived at the Pentagon in February 2003 to augment ORHA's reconstruction staff, which now numbered more than 30. He reviewed the reconstruction targets previously established by the NSC, and immediately noted that they went well beyond what could be accomplished with the level of funding provided. The $680 million Bechtel reconstruction contract, according to Wheelock, would be "a drop in the bucket."[64]

The arrival of more USACE personnel into ORHA reignited debates about what reconstruction should accomplish. USACE saw physical rebuilding as reconstruction's primary goal. "When [USACE] said reconstruction," Major General Strock said, "[those at USAID] were not thinking of bricks and mortar and concrete. They were thinking of governance and human rights and those kinds of softer aspects of reconstruction, which are very important," Strock said. "But at the end of the day, the laws of physics apply, and if you're going to get water to people you need to understand Bernoulli's equation."[65]

The civil administration pillar was the least developed.[66] Finding reliable information about Iraq was a challenge. CIA briefings on public services and ministry functions were of limited use. "Nobody could tell how many ministries currently existed in the Iraqi government," an ORHA official said. Garner kept asking, "Where is my list of ministries?"[67]

Iraq's Postwar Politics

Ordinarily, a political-military plan would have clearly articulated a detailed strategy for engaging with the leaders of Iraqi factions in postwar Iraq. But because Defense officials intended to transfer control rapidly to an interim Iraqi authority, ORHA was told it would not need such a plan.[68] "The expectations derived from policy set in Washington were that the establishment and devolution of authority to an Iraqi entity would proceed quickly," an ORHA planner wrote, obviating the need for a governance strategy.[69]

Garner wanted a second opinion on how to approach the politics of Iraq. In late February, one of his staff placed a call to Len Hawley, a former NSC staffer with expertise in political-military planning. After evaluating ORHA's staffing structure, Hawley advised Garner that—at a minimum—he needed a political deputy and a political intelligence section.[70] Trying to govern Iraq with the civil-administration staff he had, Hawley said, would be akin to "running Fairfax County [a major suburban area in northern Virginia] with eight people." Failure to move immediately to control the struggle for power would permit powerful criminal constituencies to develop. "In this kind of work," Hawley said, "the clock ticks. Nothing can wait."[71]

ORHA's Resource Problem

Iraq's postwar politics was only one of many worries. At the end of February, just three weeks before the invasion, Garner was still trying to hire enough staff. The President authorized agencies to "detail" personnel temporarily to ORHA, but they were not compelled to do so—and few did.[72] ORHA secured some personnel through defense contractors, but these personnel were prohibited by law from formulating policy or managing government resources.[73] To help solve its personnel shortfalls, Garner exploited a temporary-appointment category within U.S. law that is normally used to staff boards and commissions.[74] These "3161 appointments" enabled ORHA and later the CPA to bypass the cumbersome hiring procedures required by civil service regulations.[75]

ORHA also needed administrative, logistics, and other operational support. Colonel Robert Costello, detailed by the Department of Defense to serve as ORHA's logistics chief, joined the team on January 27, 2003. With Garner's approval, Costello immediately began using the LOGCAP contract to meet ORHA's support needs. Costello developed a statement of work that envisioned an ORHA contingent in Baghdad of 200, with 50 more in three regional offices.[76] Although the military staff ORHA needed was forthcoming, Garner ultimately had to rely on a commercial contract to supply the organization's communications support because his request for dedicated military communications assistance was denied. This denial proved to be a consequential decision. Rather than being seamlessly integrated into the secure communications systems used by war planners at CENTCOM as well as McKiernan's theater ground command, ORHA had to rely on commercial services, such as Internet connections and personal email accounts. Unable to send or receive classified information, ORHA's staff, at a critical juncture, would effectively be cut off from both war planners in Kuwait and officials in Washington.

Securing resources for postwar relief and reconstruction was yet another battle. In several meetings with National Security Advisor Condoleezza Rice, Garner presented anticipated requirements for reconstruction funding.[77] At each successive meeting, he brought Rice an ever-expanding list of requests, but few were granted.[78] "I needed $28 million up front for judicial reform, indigenous media, food, refugees, internally displaced persons, and energy," Garner recalls. "Never did get any of those."[79]

Garner also approached Rumsfeld for reconstruction funding, but the Secretary was similarly unpersuaded by Garner's long list. Garner laid out four rebuilding scenarios for Rumsfeld, from "do what absolutely needs to be done and no more" to "redo the whole country of Iraq."

"What do you think that'll cost?" Rumsfeld asked.

"I think it's going to cost billions of dollars," Garner said.

"My friend," Rumsfeld replied, "if you think we're going to spend a billion dollars of our money over there, you are sadly mistaken."[80]

In the five years following that remark, the United States appropriated nearly $50 billion for Iraq's relief and reconstruction.

The "Rock Drill"

One month before combat operations began, representatives from all military and civilian agencies involved in postwar administration met together for the first time. The occasion was a "Rock Drill," an interagency rehearsal convened by Garner. In a packed conference room at the National Defense University, ORHA's staff joined officials from the NSC, the Vice President's office, the Joint Staff, the Office of the Secretary of Defense, USAID, and the Departments of Treasury, Commerce, and State. Admiral James Robb, head of policy and planning at CENTCOM, flew in. From Kuwait, Lieutenant General McKiernan dispatched Major General Albert Whitley, his British deputy, whom he had put in charge of Phase IV planning. JTF-4's Brigadier General Hawkins was also there.[81]

Not everyone made it to the Rock Drill, and some of those who came had orders not to participate fully. Senior State Department officials were conspicuously absent.[82] Officers from CENTCOM, CFLCC (CENTCOM's ground combat arm), and JTF-4's Hawkins arrived with instructions that limited the extent of their cooperation with ORHA. These "red lines," an ORHA planner wrote, "related both to the supporting/supported commander issue and to the feelings of inadequate force structure to address post-conflict planning requirements."[83] Most worrying, General Abizaid—who Garner assumed would be named the overall commander in Iraq—was absent.[84]

During the two-day conference, key ORHA officials briefed six aspects of their evolving strategy: planning assumptions; requirements; high-impact actions; measures of effectiveness at 30, 90, 180, 270, and 360 days; policy decisions required; and "showstoppers." Security was the number-one showstopper.

Official meeting notes state that "current force packages are inadequate for the first step of securing all the major urban areas, let alone for providing an interim police function."[85]

Ambassador George Ward, head of ORHA's humanitarian pillar, asked, "How am I going to protect humanitarian convoys, humanitarian staging areas, humanitarian distribution points?" A flag officer who had flown in from CENTCOM said, "Hire war lords." "Wait a minute," Ward thought, "folks don't understand this. There are warlords in Afghanistan, not in Iraq. There were no warlords to rent." "At that point," Ward said, "I thought this was going to fail because no one is paying serious attention to civilian security."[86]

Dick Mayer, a former police officer and deputy director of the Department of Justice's International Criminal Investigative Training Assistance Program, proposed that 5,000 international police advisors be rushed into Iraq to bolster rule-of-law efforts after the military victory. But no plans were made for such a deployment. "What happens to law and order in the meantime?" the meeting notes say. "We risk letting much of the country descend into civil unrest and chaos whose magnitude may defeat our national strategy of a stable new Iraq."[87]

The lack of adequate reconstruction budgets was the second showstopper. "It seems likely that we will begin military action before we know whether sufficient Phase IV funds will be available," the notes read. Everyone was desperate for skilled interpreters. Participants were told to expect "economic-related violence." "We should expect to see the economically disadvantaged residents of Saddam City [the Shi'a slum in Baghdad, renamed Sadr City after Saddam's fall] do a bit of Robin Hooding ... in short, civil unrest will be the rule, not the exception." The absence of a governance plan also concerned Rock Drill participants. "What sort of future Government of Iraq do we have in mind," the summary notes read, "and how do we plan to get there?"[88]

The Rock Drill exposed problems created by the disjointed postwar preparations. "It became clear," said one participant, "that not everything was going to be as well organized by the civilians as it was by the military. In part the civilians either weren't fully on board, or didn't take [planning and preparation] seriously, or didn't throw their best people at [the subjects]—but the civilians weren't prepared."[89]

Lieutenant General Garner noticed a man seated near the front who asked tough, insightful questions. It was Thomas Warrick. When Garner pulled him aside during a break, he learned that Warrick had led a year-long State Department study on postwar Iraq.[90] Dumbfounded that no one had told him about the Future of Iraq Project, Garner asked Warrick to join ORHA on the spot.

Briefing the President

On March 10, 2003, just over a week before the bombing started, Garner briefed President Bush in the White House Situation Room on ORHA's postwar plan. Rice, Rumsfeld, Powell, CIA director George Tenet, and General Franks sat around the table. Vice President Cheney joined by video link.

Garner's briefing slides outlined ORHA's pillars, the gaps the Rock Drill revealed, and what remained to be done. He told the President that a tremendous amount of work was still necessary to make the interagency postwar plans operational. Garner outlined his major concerns, including some of the "showstoppers" identified at the Rock Drill. He focused on the need to fund Iraq's public servants, police, and army; to rush in international stability forces after Saddam's fall; and to employ the Iraqi army for reconstruction.[91]

The President authorized Garner's proposal to use the Iraqi army on reconstruction projects. Envisioning something like the Depression-era Civilian Conservation Corps, Garner hoped to help demobilize the army and use it to populate a large labor force for reconstruction efforts. The plan, first developed by USACE's Major General Strock, anticipated marching the disarmed soldiers into camps, forming 200-man construction units, and putting them immediately to work.[92] Everyone in the situation room agreed that this was an excellent idea.

The President was receptive to Garner's briefing, asked a few questions, and thanked him for his service. The meeting was over in less than an hour.[93] On the same day, Frank Miller presented the President with an overview of postwar political strategy, specifically addressing de-Ba'athification and recommending that it be undertaken lightly, so as to preserve Iraqi administrative capacity. The President approved Miller's recommendation for a "light" de-Ba'athification policy.

Two days later, Under Secretary Feith, echoing Garner, briefed the President that the Iraqi Army would not be demobilized.[94] Feith also presented a plan to transfer governance authority shortly after Saddam's fall to a new entity called the "Iraqi Interim Authority." The President previously had decided against forming a provisional Iraqi government in advance of the invasion, a decision conveyed to the Iraqi opposition by Zalmay Khalilzad, the President's Ambassador to Free Iraqis, in late February 2003 at the Salah al-Din political conference in Kurdish Iraq. Feith proposed brokering a formal power-sharing agreement between the new Iraqi Interim Authority and the U.S.-led Coalition shortly after Saddam was deposed. The leadership committee formed at the Salah al-Din conference, comprising Iraqi exiles and Kurdish leaders, would serve as the core group for the new authority, which would work in partnership with the Coalition's transitional authority.[95] This concept would allow Iraqis to exercise some political control from the outset, with the Coalition controlling the pace at which power was transferred. The President endorsed Feith's proposal. Because it was premised on the notion that Iraqi governmental institutions would emerge from the war reasonably intact, the plan's actual implementation would depend on the course of the war.

The Eve of Departure

Garner's last week before deploying was a tough one. Shortly before his briefing to the President, Secretary Rumsfeld asked him to remove two key members of his staff—Thomas Warrick, head of the Future of Iraq Project, and Meghan O'Sullivan, a young State Department employee who worked in the agency's Office of Policy Planning.[96] Rumsfeld eventually permitted O'Sullivan to return, but Warrick was gone for good. A separate "hold" by the Department of Defense was placed on Garner's request for seven ambassadorial-level appointments from the State Department, three of whom were Middle East experts. In exasperation, Secretary Powell told Secretary Rumsfeld, "Don, we're trying to help."[97]

The final surprise came on March 14, 2003, two nights before deployment. Late in the evening an aide called to say that Rumsfeld wanted to see Garner at eight the next morning.[98] Rumsfeld told Garner that he was not comfortable with the people selected as ORHA ministerial advisors, and that he would rather make the appointments himself.[99]

"I'm going to give you a new set of ministry officials," Rumsfeld said.[100] Garner was incredulous.

"It's too late. I'm leaving tomorrow. In a month from now we'll be doing this."

"No," Rumsfeld shot back. "I want [Defense] to run all these."

Garner asked, "Is [Defense] going to run Agriculture? [Defense] is going to run Health?"

Rumsfeld requested that Garner send a list of advisors essential to keep. "I never told anybody about this," Garner said, figuring that "if they show up, we'll give them the job."[101]

Garner's frustration led him to reflect on lessons learned just before he deployed. "The Administration started way too late," Garner said. "We've only really been in business six weeks, and we only began to get people three weeks ago." Garner nevertheless was hopeful that ORHA would overcome its late start. "We'll get there," he said. "It will look like hell, but we'll all come together on the objective."[102]

Chapter 4
Staging in Kuwait

The funding was too little, it was too late, and it was too damn hard to get. *

Lieutenant General Jay Garner
Director of ORHA (2003)

In the six weeks since Jay Garner started work as coordinator of postwar relief and reconstruction, 167 military and civilian personnel had joined ORHA. On the morning of March 16, 2003, they gathered in a parking lot at the Pentagon to begin their journey to Baghdad. Secretary Rumsfeld stepped outside the building to wish the men and women of ORHA well. They then took buses to Andrews Air Force Base, where they boarded a chartered plane bound for Kuwait.[1] In less than a week, the invasion would begin.

Jay Garner had barely arrived in Kuwait before a second round of sparring broke out over senior advisors. Now the Office of the Secretary of Defense was calling to say that the candidates Rumsfeld was in the process of selecting had been superseded by new White House selections. The 23 senior advisors on board the flight—Garner's original picks—would arrive in Kuwait unaware there had been two attempts to strip some of them of their positions. As he had done with Rumsfeld's candidates, Garner decided he would ignore the White House appointees until they arrived—if they ever did.[2]

The start-up of ORHA had turned into a tug of war between cabinet secretaries. Ten of thirteen USAID contracts had yet to be signed. ORHA had no directive authority over military resources. Only about a dozen passengers on the flight knew any Arabic.[3] So much of Garner's time had been spent arguing over who was to deploy that he was still developing basic plans for managing postwar Iraq.

Camp Villa

General Franks placed ORHA under the operational control of the Coalition Forces Land Component Command (CFLCC), Lieutenant General McKiernan's ground command in Kuwait. Garner wanted to co-locate with McKiernan's headquarters at Camp Doha, one of several U.S. military bases outside Kuwait City, but the advance party he dispatched found there was no room left at the base.[4] ORHA would have to find its own place to stay.

---

* ORHA/CPA Historian interview with Lieutenant General (Ret.) Jay Garner, former Director of ORHA, April 22, 2004.

Garner turned to the LOGCAP contractor KBR, which quickly arranged quarters for ORHA at the Kuwaiti Hilton Resort. Locating the Coalition's postwar headquarters at a four-star hotel seemed extravagant at first, but few alternatives existed, and the Hilton's perimeter walls gave a measure of security. McKiernan's soldiers, who slept in tents and portable trailers, dubbed it "Camp Villa."[5]

ORHA's staff members from USAID did not remain at the Hilton long, moving instead to the Radisson, some 30 miles away, where the NGOs they worked with were staying. Garner's logistics chief argued with USAID's mission director, Lew Lucke, urging that it was important for all of ORHA's staff to stay together, but Lucke saw advantages to the Radisson. Garner sided with Lucke, deciding that it was acceptable for USAID to co-locate with its implementing partners.[6]

This left ORHA, JTF-4, and CENTCOM's postwar planners scattered among five places: on three sides of Kuwait City, at CENTCOM rear in Tampa, and CENTCOM forward in Qatar. Sophisticated military networks are set up to allow "real-time" communication of classified material, but without a supporting military communications unit, ORHA was unable to tap into these networks. Passing classified plans through the hotel's Internet network would have been a criminal offense. Nor could the plans be discussed on unsecure phones. When Rumsfeld could not reach Garner on a protected line his first night in Kuwait, two aides brought a secure satellite phone on the next flight.[7] The rest of the staff bought phone cards at the poolside gift store and did what they could with their personal email accounts.

Garner soon found he could not buy much, either. The Army contracting command serving as ORHA's purchasing department refused to "warrant" the officers sent to Kuwait with letters authorizing them to sign contracts on the government's behalf.[8] Without this crucial authority, ORHA could not purchase the resources it needed. The Defense Contract Management Agency stepped into the breach, but by the time Lieutenant Colonel Steve Elliot arrived in late March 2003 with a minimal staff, a long list was waiting.[9] The $146 million ORHA had in its account, hardly enough for staff and supplies, was supposed to pay for interpreters, translators, start-up funds for a new Iraqi media, seed money for demobilizing the Iraqi military, and Iraqi expatriates to serve as subject-matter experts.[10]

Coordination in Chaos

ORHA had barely unpacked its bags in Kuwait before war was unleashed in Iraq. Operation Iraqi Freedom began on March 20, 2003 (Iraq time).[11] Shortly thereafter, Garner's deputy, Ron Adams, flew to Qatar to meet with General Abizaid, only to discover a large parallel universe of planners and plans at the CENTCOM forward command. "I felt frustrated, betrayed," Adams said, "that we were having access to this kind of material and this kind of energy so late in the game." "Why," Adams wondered, "weren't they co-located with us in February?"[12]

McKiernan's staff at Camp Doha had its hands full. To the great displeasure of its commander, Brigadier General Hawkins, JTF-4 had been subsumed at Doha into the staff of Major General Albert Whitley, the British two-star general whom McKiernan had deputized to lead Phase IV planning for CFLCC.[13] By the end of March, little of JTF-4 remained intact. Whitley and McKiernan supported Garner, at least rhetorically, but in the end they did not meet ORHA's needs—not the least of which was the implementation of a unified Phase IV effort. CENTCOM treated ORHA's requests as low priority, setting many of its incoming communications in a pile that remained untouched until April 19.[14]

Garner was one of the few go-betweens among the four postwar-planning factions—ORHA, JTF-4, CFLCC, and CENTCOM. He demanded that everyone meet.[15] On March 27 and 28, representatives from each staff convened at the Hilton, but no unified mission plan emerged, as Garner had hoped. With the war underway, all that could be done was de-conflict the separate plans in places where the execution of one would interfere with another. By the time two ORHA staffers managed to produce a unified plan, it was largely overcome by events.[16]

As Garner made last-ditch efforts to coordinate plans on the ground in Kuwait, the fight over personnel continued. Determined to keep as many of his senior advisors as possible, Garner contacted Secretary Rumsfeld by commercial email from the Hilton. "Sir, on Saturday you questioned the Agency leads for 12 of the 23 Iraq Ministries … We might not agree with State's nominees, but they did step up to the plate a month ago and began nominating people," Garner wrote. An enclosed chart outlined who among his senior advisors should stay and whom he could permit to go. "Of greater concern," Garner noted, were vacancies in ministries for which the Defense Department assumed responsibility. Five of them still had no assigned senior advisor.[17]

Two days later, a briefing slide from the Office of the Secretary of Defense arrived. It listed a star-studded mix of former cabinet members, senators, and governors, both Republican and Democrat, as ministerial advisor candidates. Harvard President Larry Summers was listed for Finance; the former head of General Electric, Jack Welch, for Electricity; Bill Bennett for Education; and Senator Rick Santorum (R-PA) for Trade.[18] Few had ever worked in developing countries. None spoke Arabic.

Secretary Powell reacted immediately. "We have identified qualified people to fill all eight positions that Garner assigned us. All have regional, functional management experience, several of them speak Arabic," Powell wrote Rumsfeld.

"We have frozen these assignments until you and I deal with this at an early opportunity."[19] Powell's intervention helped. Garner kept his State Department senior advisors.

USAID Efforts

As the invasion got underway, USAID accelerated its humanitarian assistance preparations. Dozens of NGOs and hundreds of workers were in position. Tens of thousands of hygiene kits, plastic sheeting, and blankets were at the ready.[20] The UN World Food Program mounted the largest relief operation in its history, filling warehouses in Kuwait, Jordan, and Turkey with food, water, and medicine.[21]

To coordinate its army of relief workers, USAID set up a Humanitarian Operations Center in Kuwait. This meeting place for USAID and its NGO partners was about ten miles away from the Radisson in a compound donated by the Kuwaiti government.[22] Maps, communications equipment, and computers were spread among the buildings. After USAID entered Iraq, it established similar Humanitarian Operations Centers across the country. Together with their military equivalent—Civil-Military Operation Centers—the humanitarian centers coordinated delivery of aid in each of Iraq's regions.[23]

Behind the army of soldiers and the army of relief workers came a third organized force—the army of contractors. They were the last to arrive. Because the order to begin the long and complicated contracting process was not issued until December 2002, most reconstruction contracts were not awarded until late April 2003. The compressed timetable meant that, at war's start, many companies had yet to receive word on their bids.[24]

The gap was the inevitable result of a contracting cycle begun only ten weeks before war started—a consequence of excluding USAID from the planning process for an entire year. As soon as USAID and ORHA made the awards, contractors began mobilizing. But this usually entailed an extended process of activating staff and recruiting the "muddy boots" operators who know how to get things done.[25] Notably, USAID did not award its major infrastructure contract to Bechtel until April 17—over a week after Baghdad fell—and the company did not deploy personnel into Iraq in any strength until May. Contractors working for the USAID's Office of Transition Initiatives arrived sooner. The office used its IDIQ contract (SWIFT I) to mobilize its contractors immediately, including Development Alternatives, Incorporated, which had established a Kuwait office more than two weeks before ORHA arrived.[26]

Governance Questions Answered

How military units would administer Iraqi territory under their control remained an open question as late as mid-March 2003. With no political-military plan formulated in Washington, CENTCOM moved ahead with its own ad hoc plan, deciding to establish Governorate Support Teams (GSTs) primarily from civil affairs units, whose reservist soldiers frequently brought applicable civilian skills. The GSTs would follow closely behind the invasion force, taking charge of towns once they fell under Coalition control. They would serve as the point of contact with town mayors and municipal governments across Iraq, helping to bring order by standing up town councils in places where none existed. The eventual transition to civilian control under ORHA and then to an interim Iraqi authority would open the door for the military's exit.[27] CENTCOM officers had presented a rough version of the GST strategy at Garner's March 27-28 meeting at the Kuwait Hilton.[28]

CENTCOM's GST plan was compatible with USAID's Local Governance Program (LGP), which assumed that a national political process, overseen by the Department of State, would quickly shift the deposed regime's centralized authority to local democratic entities. USAID proposed a "transfer" of central-government civil servants to the local level, paring back national ministries to their essential functions.[29] Teams of experts funded by USAID's LGP would arrive shortly after the invasion to help newly elected town councils improve education, health, water, markets, and roads. By devolving control directly to local officials and empowering them to spend U.S. reconstruction money, planners hoped to quickly break Iraq from the pattern of centralized authoritarianism that had gripped the country for decades.[30]

Implementing these loosely coordinated local governance plans yielded a number of unanticipated consequences. Saddam's regime had been like a giant octopus with tentacles reaching down into every village in Iraq through a system of ministry "directors general." Through these directors general, ministries controlled the disbursal of resources in each Iraqi province. Coalition plans superseded the director general system, shifting authority to town councils created by GSTs or USAID's LGP teams.[31] This radical and rapid restructuring of local government would shape debates about Iraqi federalism for years to come.

Governance plans at the national level were equally loose. Garner planned on using the "big tent" method to bring Iraqi leaders together to form a national interim government.[32] This approach had worked reasonably well with the *loya jirga* process in Afghanistan, which had quickly named Hamid Karzai the leader of postwar Afghanistan. Garner hoped to use his good relations with the Kurds to help move quickly to the appointment of an Iraqi interim authority, as approved by the President on March 10, 2003.

ORHA Expands

In early April 2003, as ORHA continued postwar planning at the Hilton, its staffing needs kept growing. The Office of the Secretary of Defense estimated that the staff of ORHA might reach 1,268, plus a 600-person military police battalion provided for security.[33] Even this estimate—many time higher than originally expected—would prove too small.

After ORHA arrived in Baghdad on April 21, its staff quickly increased, eventually peaking at 2,500—about eight times its original estimate of 350.[34] Back at the Pentagon, the comptroller's office was asked why there was such a huge rise in ORHA's staffing. Dov Zakheim, the Defense Department Comptroller, responded: "ORHA projected staffing levels and budget requirements will vary greatly as they get a better grip on the requirements of their mission."[35]

ORHA's rapid expansion unsettled its contracting staff. Lieutenant Colonel Elliot, ORHA's contracting officer from the Defense Contract Management Agency, had only three officers on staff with warrants to write contracts.[36] As needs mounted rapidly and the details of contracts were often left unspecified, Elliot found he was forced to make policy decisions. "I'm making the decision as to what's prudent. And that shouldn't be my job. That should be the customer's job," Elliot said. From his perspective, "There [was] no planning"—it was all reaction.[37]

Views From Washington

As ORHA struggled to carry out its mission, several Administration officials gave hopeful briefings. During an interview on April 23, USAID Administrator Natsios predicted that the cost of reconstruction to American taxpayers would be minimal. "The American part of this will be $1.7 billion. The rest of the rebuilding of Iraq will be done by other countries ... and Iraqi oil revenues."[38] But National Security Advisor Condoleezza Rice offered a more cautious assessment in an April 4 press briefing. "Our goals are clear," she said. "We will help Iraqis build an Iraq that is whole, free and at peace with itself and with its neighbors; an Iraq that is disarmed of all WMD; that no longer supports or harbors terror; that respects the rights of Iraqi people and the rule of law; and that is on the path to democracy."[39]

The National Security Advisor was circumspect about the details of Administration plans. "Specific means of achieving these goals are being worked out now. Many can only be developed once Saddam's regime is gone. To a large extent, the means to these goals will depend on things outside our current control." She further noted that the Administration did not know what conditions it would find inside Iraq. "We do not know, for instance, what damage Saddam Hussein's regime may inflict on the Iraqi people in the regime's last gasps. We do not know what we'll find on the ground once the regime is gone—for instance, the condition of Iraqi natural resources or its infrastructure."

Rice pointedly observed that a long-term occupation was far from the minds of the President's advisors. "ORHA is not a provisional government for Iraq, civilian or military. The goal is to transition responsibilities to the Iraqi people as soon as possible," she said.[40] Within weeks, this approach would be superseded when the Coalition Provisional Authority was installed to occupy and rule Iraq.

Saddam's regime fell the week after Rice's briefing. Soon looting and chaos began to engulf Baghdad and many provincial capitals. As ORHA's senior advisors watched their ministries burn on CNN, a fatalistic mood took hold at the Hilton. Garner had been so hopeful that things would all come together, but now he had grave doubts. ORHA was about to face a far greater challenge than harnessing the interagency system. They were about to cross the berm into Iraq.

CHAPTER 5
ORHA IN BAGHDAD

*At the end of this there is [a] real simple truth. If you don't plan
and organize and rehearse together, you end up with ad hoc
solutions during execution. [Iraq] is a classic case of not having
done it all together.*[*]

Lieutenant General David McKiernan
Commander of Coalition Forces
Land Component Command (2002-2003)

As the Coalition prepared for war, so did Saddam Hussein. In the fall of 2002,
he declared a general amnesty, freeing thousands of violent criminals.[1] As U.S.
troops massed along the Iraqi border in the spring of 2003, Saddam deployed
Iraqi military units both to defend against the invasion and to prevent a coup
in the rebellious Shi'a south. Ministers made contingency plans, just as they
had in 1991, to weather the conflict and repair damage once hostilities ceased.[2]
Saddam sent a memorandum instructing state agencies to sabotage infrastructure, shoot dissident Shi'a clerics, and burn the regime's records if U.S. troops
entered Baghdad.[3]

As the country braced for impending attack, Saddam's workers moved furniture out of his main palace and removed the palace doors to minimize damage
caused by the concussion of bombing.[4] Bank managers personally safe-guarded
the financial data of customers at 170 branches across Iraq.[5] The director of computer services at the Ministry of Trade secured in his home the list of every Iraqi
household eligible for food rations.[6] After the official Oil-for-Food ration list
vanished amid looting, this copy was later used as a basis for registering voters in
Iraq's first democratic election.[7]

The Iraqi people also prepared.[8] Shopkeepers boarded up their stores, women
stockpiled food and water, and men headed to gun shops.[9] Tens of thousands of
families fled Baghdad and its suburbs for safety in the countryside.

The reckoning began on March 17, 2003. In an Oval Office address,
President George W. Bush gave Saddam Hussein and his two sons, Uday and
Qusay, an ultimatum to leave the country within 48 hours. But they did not
leave. Bombing started on March 20 (Iraqi time), and U.S. ground units rolled
into Iraq the next day.

---

[*] SIGIR interview with Lieutenant General David McKiernan, former Commander of Coalition Forces
Land Component Command, December 5, 2006.

Invasion

The experience of the invasion force differed by region. In the north, a small number of U.S. Special Forces troops linked with Kurdish Peshmerga, the armed force
of Iraq's autonomous northern region, which opposed Saddam. Together they
pushed south against Iraqi Army units dug into defensive positions. In Baghdad,
Iraqis had such confidence in the accuracy of American "smart weapons" that
many watched the bombing from their rooftops, but the precision targeting had
serious second-order effects. Telephone service ceased. Explosions broke pipes
all over the city, causing sewage to contaminate what water still flowed out of
the tap. Then, on April 4, power surges shorted out most of Baghdad's electrical
infrastructure. Much of the city went dark.[10]

Because Turkey and Saudi Arabia had denied U.S. troops passage, the main
invasion force came through Kuwait. Special operations units captured oil fields
and dams almost immediately, and oil engineers from Halliburton extinguished
the few oil-well fires that were set. Thousands of troops with the Third Infantry
Division and First Marine Expeditionary Force then pushed north. Rather than
advancing methodically to capture and hold territory, the war plan called for a
daring sprint to the capital.[11] The idea was to put the regime down before it could
deploy chemical weapons. Lieutenant General McKiernan's troops sped by most
population centers, avoiding combat in favor of pushing to Baghdad.

The fast-moving U.S. invasion force meant that troops engaged Saddam's
forces only briefly in many towns. Some cities were occupied quickly, but in the
west and north, U.S. troops did not arrive until weeks after Baghdad fell. Many
Iraqis were left listening to conflicting accounts of the invasion's outcome on
regime and foreign radio broadcasts, never seeing troops from either side.[12] The
uniformed Iraqi military largely abandoned their posts after little or no fight, but
sustained resistance materialized in many southern towns. Sandal-clad fighters in
civilian garb, both foreign and Iraqi, used rocket-propelled grenades and pick-up
trucks to organize ambushes that frequently turned deadly for the attackers as
they encountered first-hand the lethal power of the invading force.[13]

"The enemy we're fighting is different from the one we'd war-gamed against,"
said Lieutenant General William S. Wallace, commander of V Corps, one of the
main ground units.[14] To General John Abizaid, the only Arabic-speaking senior
commander in theater, the signs were ominous. Garner remembers Abizaid telling him the first week in April: "I've been listening to everything they're saying
on the radio. I've been reading Al Jazeera, and I'm looking at what's happening.
I'm telling you. We're going to have a guerrilla war on our hands."[15]

Initial Assessments

Sixty-two people from USAID's Disaster Assistance Response Team (DART)—
the largest ever fielded—followed quickly upon the heels of the invading force.[16]
On March 27, DART members crossed into Iraq to assess the humanitarian
situation in the port town of Umm Qasr, a major supply node in Iraq where 60
percent of Iraq's Oil-For-Food imports were offloaded. British commandos had
seized the port after sustained fighting. Elements from the U.S. Army's 354th Civil
Affairs Brigades began repair work after British troops took control.[17]

USAID's DART team found the port in poor but working condition. Team
members identified two back-up generators that, with minor repairs, could power
the entire facility. Three grain vacuums were operational, and the port's 24 silos
were available for storage once swept for explosives. A day later, the *Sir Galahad*,
a British relief ship carrying more than 230 metric tons of food, medicine, and
blankets, was able to dock.[18]

All seemed to be going reasonably well. There were no major signs of humanitarian crisis, and no chemical weapons had been used. But worrisome news
soon arrived from USACE, which had embedded Forward Engineering Support
Teams (FESTs) in U.S. combat brigades.[19] Traveling in Humvees equipped with
a satellite link to their headquarters, these highly mobile military and civilian
engineer teams quickly assessed the state of the power plants and other civil infrastructure they came across during their advance into Iraq.[20] The dilapidated
infrastructure reported everywhere by FEST personnel confirmed USACE's
prewar assessment that a major reconstruction effort—on the order of $35 billion
for a "middle-range" damage scenario—would be necessary.[21]

To augment the information from the FEST reports, Garner asked USAID's
DART team to shift its role and begin conducting infrastructure assessments.
At first they refused.[22] The team members were reluctant to take on activities
that fell outside the mandate of a normal DART mission, which is to assess humanitarian conditions—such as food supply availability and likelihood of disease
outbreak. Their leadership, at USAID's Office of Foreign Disaster Assistance in
Washington, was also averse to allowing the unarmed teams to operate in an
environment where residual fighting continued.[23] By the first week of April, the
DART team's failure to carry out Garner's request threatened to unravel the fragile cooperation between the military and civilian communities inside ORHA.[24]

Garner was seething. "They refused to come in," he said, "because it wasn't
permissive. You know, I have this civilian organization in this not-permissive
environment in Suburbans, which are not hardened. Yet you [the DART com-
mander] have $350,000 hard Mercedes. You have body armor, which these

people [ORHA personnel] don't have, and your people refuse to come in here, and they're staying in very expensive hotels."[25]

Ambiguity about lines of authority aggravated the situation. Did a USAID asset, the DART team, report to its agency headquarters in Washington or was the team now under operational control of ORHA, an office of the Department of Defense? Instead of appealing to the NSC for arbitration, Secretaries Donald Rumsfeld and Colin Powell had a "war of memos" trying to settle the issue.[26] Relations between the Departments of State and Defense had become increasingly tense in the late winter and early spring of 2003.[27] Only when Garner phoned Powell and threatened to oust the DART teams did they agree to comply with Garner's direction.[28]

ORHA Enters Iraq

ORHA personnel first crossed into hostile territory on April 1 at the port of Umm Qasr, where the situation had deteriorated rapidly since the DART team's first forays four days before. Coalition soldiers, who cautioned that they did not have enough troops to stop the looting, reported, on April 2, 2003, that more than 200 residents had carried off every useful piece of equipment at the port. Looters took desks and chairs, electrical generators, conveyor belts, and even a forklift. "Anything not nailed down" was gone, the DART team reported on its second visit.[29] Work to rehabilitate the port was set back by weeks. The looting itself—the first major episode reported in Iraq—presaged a period of extraordinary difficulty that the Coalition would face in the weeks ahead.

ORHA used Umm Qasr as a testing ground to calibrate its approach to the post-invasion environment. "We thought of Umm Qasr as a laboratory where we could see what worked and what didn't," an ORHA official explained. "It gave us a chance to get some real work done as opposed to just theorizing and writing position papers."[30]

Restoring Umm Qasr presented three significant challenges. First was simply performing the brute physical work of reconstruction. The port was badly in need of dredging. Sunken obstacles and unexploded ordnance posed a danger to approaching ships.[31] The second was luring Iraqis back to work. Port workers who encountered Coalition soldiers were understandably skittish.[32] The third was coordinating civil and military authorities, which proved extremely difficult, a precursor to similar problems that would burden the U.S. relief and reconstruction endeavor in Iraq for years to come.[33]

On April 11, 2003, Lieutenant General Garner crossed into Iraq at Umm Qasr. He visited the port, delivered a speech before a newly formed town council, inspected a school, and was briefed by his staff.[34] He and his team then began making plans to move to Baghdad, which had fallen four days before.

Baghdad Falls

British troops took control of Basrah on April 6. Baghdad began to capitulate the next day, after armored columns made "thunder runs" into the city center. As U.S. troops took over Saddam's presidential palace on the Tigris River's west bank, jubilant Iraqis, with the help of U.S. Marines, toppled the statue of Saddam Hussein in Firdos Square. Looting on a wide scale began that day, first on the fringe of the fighting and then later in plain view of American military patrols.[35] In response, protective Iraqi militias sprang up in neighborhoods across the city, putting men with AK-47s atop makeshift barricades. Gunfire could be heard throughout the night as robberies and revenge killings took place.[36]

Deteriorating conditions on the ground began to supersede Coalition plans. The rush to the capital meant that fewer than two divisions—about 25,000 soldiers—occupied the capital, a city of about six million, amounting to an approximate ratio of one U.S. soldier to every 250 residents. "That's not enough to control a city of six million people," Lieutenant General David McKiernan said.[37] With U.S. troops scattered across Baghdad, looting seemed almost impossible to prevent. Patrols had no appetite or mandate to stop it, and McKiernan had orders to continue pushing troops north to carry out the search for weapons of mass destruction that were assumed to be in central Iraq. One option was to impose martial law and shoot looters on sight, but McKiernan could not bring himself to issue the order. "This is not just the Saddam Feyadeen that are in there looting the stores, it's the population," McKiernan explained. "It's children and women. What are you going to do? What's a soldier on the street going to do? Fire warning shots around them? The answer is, and I'll accept full responsibility, I said 'we are not going to shoot to kill. We're not going to do that.'"[38]

Laith Kubba, a prominent Iraqi exile who helped found the Iraqi National Congress, later observed that the lack of an effective media organization from day one hamstrung the Coalition, which might have been able to calm the public had it communicated a clear message. "Iraqis are used to military coups. When they take place, they tune in to their radios," Kubba said. "They wait for an announcement, number one, to tell them, 'All important personnel working in electricity and water, report back to work, and you'll be given access. Everybody else is under curfew from so-and-so hours.' Instead there was a day, two days and three days of no authority."[39]

The interactions between occupier and occupied were aggravated by the way troops were assigned to patrol zones. "We had divided the city up into target areas that didn't have any relevance to political boundaries," Lieutenant General Strock said. Some brigade commanders were spread across four neighborhoods. To Strock, the arrangement was far from ideal. "I remember saying, you know, it would be really nice if we could align up our security zones with our political boundaries and then you would have much more synergy."[40]

The frequent movement of units from one zone to the next undermined the incipient personal relationships developing between commanding officers and community leaders. Yet another complication arose when civilians entered the mix. The military used a specialized system of grid coordinates to plot patrol zones, but civilians in ORHA, and the NGOs with whom they worked, normally used longitude and latitude to mark locations.[41] The Coalition was literally not working off the same maps, adding unnecessarily to the confusion on the ground.

ORHA Arrives in Baghdad

Garner was eager to get to Baghdad, but the military leadership had a different view of when ORHA should deploy. "Tommy Franks didn't want us to be there for 60 to 90 days," Garner recalled.[42] The CENTCOM Phase IV plan called for the military to secure Iraq for six to eight weeks before beginning the transition to civil administration. It was all part of the three stages of Phase IV. But Garner believed conditions were right for ORHA to start its operations, even if the timing was in advance of what military planners had expected.[43]

On April 17, Garner flew to meet Franks in Qatar. "I got in a big argument, pretty tense argument," Garner said. "Look, Jay," Franks told him, "there's still fighting going on in Baghdad. The last thing I need is a bunch of damn civilians running around there and me having to worry about taking care of them. Dave McKiernan doesn't have the force to do that." "I realize that," Garner replied, "but what's happening is vacuums are being created and they're being filled up with what you and I don't want them filled up with, and the only way to prevent that is to get us in there."[44]

"He was exasperated with me," Garner remembered. "He finally just, kind of, shook his head and shrugged his shoulders." The next day, Franks called to say that ORHA could go in. "We don't have the force in there to give you the proper amount of security," Franks said. "God bless you and good luck."[45]

Garner immediately dispatched a small advance party. He followed two days later, on April 21, flying with his senior staff aboard a C-130 to Baghdad International Airport and traveling from there to the Republican Palace, one of Saddam's grand edifices on the banks of the Tigris, which would house ORHA for its brief tenure.[46] Most of the rest of ORHA's staff drove up from the south in several convoys over the next week.

During ORHA's first days in Baghdad, achieving effective communications was again a debilitating problem. Some ORHA officials had Thuraya commercial satellite phones, but they were unable to receive calls inside the palace without an outside antenna. No phone system was yet established, so the staff had to walk from office to office to communicate.[47] With the Baghdad telephone exchange down, it was impossible to reach Iraqis. Commercial communications equipment acquired by ORHA had also failed to operate, leaving the Baghdad team out of touch with its regional offices in Erbil, Hilla, and Basrah.[48] After an urgent call from Garner, Lieutenant General McKiernan dispatched a communications unit to the Republican Palace to connect ORHA to SIPRNET, the military's classified network. Even with this support system, bottlenecks still impeded communications.[49]

Looting and its Consequences

Two weeks had passed since Saddam's regime had fallen. Outside the gates of the Republican Palace where ORHA was trying to set up shop, anarchy reigned. "We found the city in utter chaos," said Richard Miller, one of six police advisors sent by the Justice Department. In some places, "corpses littered the streets, AK-47 fire was near constant, and looters operated with impunity."[50] Many government buildings had been destroyed.

"A lot of the ministries turned out to be blasted cinders," noted Ambassador Tim Carney, senior advisor for the Ministry of Industry and Minerals.[51] "They not only took everything out of there, but they stripped the electrical wires out of the wall, and they stripped most of the plumbing out, and then they set the buildings on fire," Garner said.[52] Fires burned so hot that concrete in many buildings exploded.[53] ORHA advisor Christopher Spear waded into ransacked rooms filled three feet deep with paper debris. Clean-up crews hauled away six tons of scattered documents from the Ministry of Health alone. "We would say they took everything but the kitchen sink, [but] they took that, too," Spear said.[54]

The looting quickly changed into organized theft by gangs of Iraqi criminals and insurgents trying to destabilize the country. In a military compound under nominal guard by U.S. soldiers, one of these gangs smashed through a rear wall and used a crane to remove valuable precision milling equipment used to manufacture Scud missiles. "They knew exactly what they were going for," Spear said.[55]

Millions of dollars in cash stored in Rafidain and Rasheed bank branches and at the Central Bank were looted or destroyed, as were the contents of safety deposit boxes.[56] "Organized crime found its golden opportunity," the Iraqi politician Samir Sumaida'ie said.[57] Some government officials joined in the melee. In Mosul, a prison guard sold all the prison beds for scrap.[58] In time, ORHA's senior advisors would learn that the theft of Iraq's assets had, in truth, started years before, when corrupt government officials began regularly selling ministry property "to pad their own pockets."[59]

The looting went on for several weeks. "In a lot of cases," Garner said, "after we began to try to reoccupy buildings, they still got set on fire. The Health Ministry got set on fire two or three times after we occupied it, because there just wasn't enough force to provide security on everything."[60] The Oil Ministry was the only ministry to escape major damage. It was protected by Coalition troops as soon as they entered Baghdad, minimizing but not preventing looting. The ministry was reopened on May 2, in advance of others.[61] To ORHA senior advisors, it stood as a symbol of what might have been.

The oil infrastructure seemed to have emerged from the invasion largely intact. Fewer than ten oil well fires were set. But post-invasion looting in the oil sector went on for ten weeks, from March 20, 2003, through the end of May.[62] Of the oil sector damage the Coalition had to repair, only one-third resulted from the war. The remaining two-thirds of the damage—amounting to $943 million—was caused by looting.[63]

The contours of post-Saddam political life could be seen taking shape in the patterns of destruction. Eleven of Baghdad's thirty-three hospitals were protected by a Shi'ite militia. These hospitals survived completely intact but others left unprotected were stripped clean.[64] Shi'ite militias also took control of the city of Amarah, preventing looting before it could get started.[65] In isolated cases, loyal staff at public institutions held looters at bay. Thirty engineers secured the Basrah refinery by using heavy equipment to block the gates.[66]

The looting had three major effects. The first was its high cost. Estimates vary, but looting clearly caused billions of dollars in damage, greatly adding to the total cost of relief and reconstruction.[67] The second—the looting of conventional munitions depots—had severe long-term consequences for U.S. forces in Iraq. The war plan assumed that some elements of Iraq's security forces would be used to "provide internal security," including guard duty at the hundreds of arms caches across the country.[68] This assumption did not hold. Thousands of tons of munitions were looted in the weeks after Baghdad fell, and some of it doubtlessly was later used to build improvised explosive devices that would be employed against U.S. personnel.[69]

The third effect—the lost opportunity to restore government services quickly—also had long-term consequences. With public institutions and critical infrastructure reduced, in some cases, to smoldering rubble, ORHA's senior advisors would have to rebuild ministries, not just restart them. The unexpected extent of the destruction dealt a critical setback to Administration plans for a rapid transfer of power and would eventually force a significant course change.

Troop Strength

On April 21, the day Lieutenant General Garner arrived in Baghdad, Secretary Rumsfeld—following the advice of CENTCOM Commander General Franks—canceled the deployment of 50,000 additional combat troops scheduled to arrive in the region and ordered the withdrawal of the Third Infantry Division as soon as the First Armored Division arrived.[70] Rumsfeld's decision shocked some commanders on the ground, including CFLCC Commander Lieutenant General McKiernan, who were counting on the additional manpower to provide a secure environment for post-conflict stabilization. The reversal also dumbfounded McKiernan's CFLCC staff, that had just sat through two video conferences with senior Pentagon officials who had affirmed the decision to continue deploying forces.[71] Garner called Rumsfeld and said, "You've got to stop this. You can't pull troops out. In fact, we probably need more right now."[72]

Paying for Reconstruction

The widespread looting and the damage it wrought meant that the reconstruction funds the Congress had just appropriated would be inadequate to quickly restore Iraq's essential services to prewar levels. On April 16, 2003, President Bush had signed Public Law 108-11 creating the Iraq Relief and Reconstruction Fund.[73] The $2.475 billion congressional appropriation funded the program of humanitarian relief and reconstruction planned by the NSC, which had assumed that an extensive reconstruction would not be needed because Iraq's infrastructure would remain largely intact after the war and that Iraqi oil revenues would fund most reconstruction. On the same day, General Franks issued his "Freedom Message," declaring the Coalition's intention to "exercise powers of government temporarily, and as necessary." Franks's message also identified an entity, called the Coalition Provisional Authority (CPA), that would be responsible for the governance of Iraq.[74]

USAID was the largest recipient of IRRF 1 money, receiving just over 70 percent of the appropriation. A separate provision of the bill established an $800 million Natural Resources Risk Remediation Fund (NRRRF) to support emergency fire fighting, repair damage to oil facilities and related infrastructure, and preserve oil distribution capability. NRRRF funds were used to help pay part of the costs of Task Force Restore Iraqi Oil (RIO), administered by USACE.[75]

New Iraqi Politics

Chaos on the ground threw the plan for a rapid political transfer to an interim Iraqi authority into confusion. On April 15, Garner and Presidential Envoy Zalmay Khalilzad assembled more than a hundred key Iraqi leaders in the southern city of Nassriya.[76] To encourage leaders within Iraq to step forward, the United States excluded the heads of exile opposition groups, who had formed the Leadership Committee from the Salah al-Din conference. Although the Nassriya meeting was boycotted by several clerics and the Supreme Council for the Islamic Revolution in Iraq, a larger follow-on gathering was planned for Baghdad later in April.[77]

On April 22, Garner flew to meet with Kurdish leaders he knew from the humanitarian operation he led in 1991. He undertook this trip and other meetings with Iraqi politicians to further the process of forming an interim Iraqi authority, in accord with the President's approved plan. "He was really pushing them both pretty hard," Lieutenant General Strock said of Garner's interaction with Ahmed Chalabi and Jalal Talabani. "He was playing hardball with them, saying, 'Look, you guys got to stand up and come together and set aside your differences,'" Strock said.[78]

Secretary of State Colin Powell then dispatched Khalilzad and Ambassador Ryan Crocker to southern Iraq for talks on political transition, but there were intense disagreements over how to proceed.[79] Garner was trying to carry through the standing plan for a rapid transfer.[80] But in Washington, officials were concerned that conditions were not right for creating the interim authority. The next step would come on April 28, when more than 250 Iraqi leaders would convene a second political conference in Baghdad.

ORHA's Goals

On April 24, 2003, Garner briefed CFLCC Commander Lieutenant General McKiernan on eleven goals he wanted ORHA to help accomplish. McKiernan and Garner both assigned a member of their senior staff to the leadership of each task. The goals were:

1. Security

2. Salaries Paid Nationwide

3. Return Police to Work and Train Them

4. Return Ministries to a Functional Level

5. Restore Basic Services to Baghdad

6. Prevent a Fuel Crisis

7. Purchase Crops

8. Solve Food Distribution Challenges

9. Install Town Councils Nationwide.

10. Deploy and Integrate Government Support Teams With Local Government

11. Prevent Cholera and Dysentery[81]

The goals Garner had set for himself were enormous, as were the obstacles to accomplishing them. For example, adequate and reliable power was unavailable. "It is a Catch-22," senior oil advisor Gary Vogler explained.[82] Without fuel oil, electric plants cannot produce electricity, yet without a steady supply of electricity, crude cannot be refined into fuel oil.

In Basrah, Coalition personnel trying to restart essential services faced a similar conundrum. "The circle was amazing," JTF-4's Lieutenant Colonel Joseph Morgan said. "Just in that one area, just looking at how we could turn on power, so we could turn on water, so we could turn on electricity."[83]

Many of Garner's other goals fell under the purview of the civil administration pillar, where plans were less developed and leadership weakest.[84] The part of the mission that Rumsfeld told Garner would be least essential was now crucial, and ORHA was not well staffed to carry it out.

ORHA's Early Departure

In the last week of April 2003, Baghdad was descending into further disorder. ORHA's limited resources were consumed with finding ministerial staff members who had fled, reconstituting records, and locating workspace for almost the entire central government. Garner could not arrange enough military security escorts for his staff to move unfettered around the city. As for the rest of the country, ORHA had not established formal mechanisms for coordination with the military units occupying towns and villages across Iraq, much less with Iraqi leadership at the provincial level. Coordination was in short supply everywhere: between ORHA and Washington, ORHA and the military, and ORHA and the Iraqis.[85] Suddenly Iraq seemed very large, and ORHA's staff seemed very small.

In this chaotic atmosphere, more than 200 Iraqi leaders arrived in Baghdad for the "big tent" meeting on April 28, 2003. Garner presided, with Ambassadors Khalilzad and Crocker in support. The political conference was attended by all the key Iraqi players, including representatives from the major Shi'a political party, the Supreme Council for the Islamic Revolution in Iraq. Under Garner's guidance, the Iraqis at the conference resolved to create an interim government at their next meeting in four weeks. After the meeting, Garner announced this decision through the Iraqi and U.S. media. It appeared to some in Washington that the concept of an interim Iraqi authority might still be realized.[86] But out of view, a significant change in strategy was developing.

On May 6, just fifteen days after Jay Garner had arrived in Baghdad, President Bush announced that L. Paul Bremer III, a former ambassador and career Foreign Service Officer, as his new Presidential Envoy to Iraq. Bremer also would lead the Coalition Provisional Authority, the civil authority that General Franks announced in his April 16 freedom message.[87]

Ambassador Bremer had first been approached at the beginning of April by senior officials in the Defense Department and the Office of the Vice President.[88] Although Garner had been told when first appointed to lead ORHA that he would eventually be followed by a person with a diplomatic or political background, he did not learn of Bremer's selection until Rumsfeld phoned him with the news on the evening of April 21, Garner's first night in Baghdad. "I never saw CPA coming," Garner said.[89] He did not immediately tell his staff of the impending change.

Bremer's arrival would reflect a sea change in U.S. policy. ORHA was designed as a short-term holding mechanism, to be followed by a rapid shift to an interim Iraqi authority, mirroring the swift transition that occurred in Afghanistan. But the deteriorating situation in Iraq apparently had caused the White House to change plans. Zalmay Khalilzad, the President's envoy to the Free Iraqis, recalled: "The idea that I was working on initially, with support from everyone in Washington, was to form an interim authority that we could work with. A decision was made not to pursue that option until later, and therefore the Coalition Provisional Authority was established."[90]

During the summer of 2003, the U.S. role in Iraq, under Bremer's leadership, rapidly and massively expanded, far eclipsing the minimalist liberation vision that had set planning for war in motion a year and a half earlier, and superseding the quick transfer to an interim Iraqi authority that the President had approved at the March 10, 2003 NSC meeting.

ESSENTIAL SERVICES OVERVIEW: THE EFFECTS OF INVASION

Metric[91]	Pre-invasion	Post-invasion
Electricity Production		
Megawatts	4,075	711
Oil Production		
Million Barrels per Day	2.58	0.30
Iraqi Security Forces		
Soldiers and Police	1,300,000	7,000-9,000[92]
Telecommunications		
Landline Subscribers	833,000	0
Mobile Subscribers	80,000	0
Human Toll		
U.S Troop Fatalities	-	139
Civilian Contractors[93]	-	1
U.S. Civilians	-	~9
Iraqi Civilians	-	7,413
Financial Cost ($ billions)		
U.S Funding	-	$3.45
Iraqi Funding	-	$0.00
International Funding	-	$0.00
Total Funding	-	$3.45

Production of electricity came to a near-complete halt during the 2003 invasion. By mid-April 2003, the grid was generating an average of just 711 megawatts of electricity per day.[94] Postwar looting and sabotage had destroyed nearly 1,000 electrical towers, and the loss of numerous electrical control systems caused frequent blackouts in Baghdad.[95]

Without electricity, oil production also came to a standstill. Many oil facilities were safely shut down, but some oil stocks were destroyed by fire. Although production restarted fairly quickly, it averaged only 300,000 barrels per day—about one-eighth of prewar levels—in May 2003.[96]

Already in a state of severe disrepair, Iraq's essential services declined precipitously after the March 20 invasion due to war damage, looting, and sabotage. ORHA had neither the time nor the resources to fix these problems. Thus, the CPA took them on, shouldering the responsibility for restoring broken essential services and distributing them more fairly among all Iraqis.

PART II
THE COALITION PROVISIONAL
AUTHORITY LEADS RECONSTRUCTION
MAY 2003 TO JUNE 2004

CHAPTER 6
CHARTING A NEW COURSE

> *But the President's instructions to me... when I had lunch with him alone on May 6th, were that we're going to take our time to get it right... The President had effectively, though perhaps not formally, changed his position on the question of a short or long occupation, having before the war been in favor of a short occupation. By the time I came in, that was gone.* *

> **Ambassador L. Paul Bremer III**
> CPA Administrator (2003-2004)

Ambassador L. Paul Bremer III landed in Baghdad on May 12, 2003, less than two weeks after President Bush appointed him Presidential Envoy to Iraq and designated him to lead the Coalition Provisional Authority (CPA). Just under a month had passed since the first members of ORHA had settled into Saddam's Republican Palace. But ORHA's days were numbered. Bremer's arrival and Garner's quick departure marked the beginning of a significant shift in U.S. reconstruction policy.

The new envoy, then 62 years old, enjoyed a solid reputation as a diligent, intelligent public servant. He had enjoyed a long career at the State Department, followed by distinguished private- and public-sector stints.[1] But the choice of Bremer raised some eyebrows. Neither his Foreign Service background nor his private-sector work included experience in post-conflict peacekeeping, contingency operations, or reconstruction. He had never participated in a joint civilian-military operation, had little experience in international development, had never served in the Middle East, and did not speak Arabic.[2]

Ambassador Bremer was first contacted about leading the CPA in early April 2003, when the Vice President's chief of staff, Lewis "Scooter" Libby, called to ask whether he would consider serving in Iraq.[3] Meetings at the Pentagon soon followed, and, by the end of April, he was preparing to deploy to Iraq. All of this occurred just as Jay Garner was settling into Baghdad with his ORHA staff.[4] Secretary Powell recalled that Rumsfeld telephoned him about this time to say that the White House wanted to remove Garner because he did not seem to be the right man for the job. When Rumsfeld asked Powell if he knew Bremer, Powell said yes and that he "didn't have any reason to object."[5] Rumsfeld later said that the Administration always intended that Garner's position within CENTCOM

---

* SIGIR interview with Ambassador L. Paul Bremer III, former CPA Administrator, March 18, 2008.

would be eliminated, and that a senior diplomat outside the military chain of command would be appointed to head the CPA.[6]

On May 6, the President appointed Bremer as envoy to Iraq, directing him to "oversee Coalition reconstruction efforts and the process by which the Iraqi people build the institutions and governing structures that will guide their future."[7] In a May 13, 2003 memo, Secretary Rumsfeld informed Bremer that he, as Administrator of the CPA, would be "responsible for the temporary governance of Iraq." Rumsfeld directed Bremer to "oversee, direct and coordinate all executive, legislative, and judicial functions necessary to carry out this responsibility, including humanitarian relief and reconstruction and assisting in the formation of an Iraqi interim authority."[8]

Ambassador Bremer took charge of a country in political and economic chaos, with no government, no electricity, and no functioning security forces. Not a single drop of oil flowed to export spigots. He now faced the daunting task of restoring virtually every aspect of Iraqi life, from reopening ministries to paying government salaries, from restarting essential services to providing healthcare, and from collecting garbage to cleaning sewage from the streets.

The CPA quickly subsumed ORHA, retaining many of its members. Ambassador Bremer reported to the President through the Secretary of Defense. But, as a Presidential envoy, Bremer also reported directly to the President. "I was neither Rumsfeld's man nor Powell's man. I was the President's man," said Bremer.[9] These parallel chains of command would create problems for the Iraq program. CENTCOM was tasked by Rumsfeld to "directly support the Coalition Provisional Authority by deterring hostilities; maintaining Iraq's territorial integrity and security; searching for, securing and destroying weapons of mass destruction; and assisting in carrying out U.S. policy generally."[10] Despite this order, unity of effort in Iraq proved elusive during the CPA's early days because Ambassador Bremer and General Franks reported to the Secretary of Defense through separate channels.

The Occupation Begins
Within days of arriving in Baghdad, Ambassador Bremer issued three important directives. The first established the CPA as an occupying authority. The second banned certain Ba'ath Party members from public service. The third dissolved Iraq's military and other security forces.

CPA Regulation Number 1: Liberation to Occupation
On May 16, 2003, Ambassador Bremer signed and issued CPA Regulation Number 1, establishing the CPA's mission, authority, and responsibilities.[11] The regulation provided that the CPA "shall exercise powers of government

temporarily in order to provide for the effective administration of Iraq" for an undefined transitional period. The CPA would work:

> ... to restore conditions of security and stability, to create con-
> ditions in which the Iraqi people can freely determine their
> own political future, including by advancing efforts to restore
> and establish national and local institutions for representative
> governance and facilitating economic recovery and sustain-
> able reconstruction and development.[12]

This order also vested Ambassador Bremer with "all executive, legislative and judicial authority necessary to achieve [CPA's] objectives." Iraqi law would continue in effect unless it was "suspended or replaced by the CPA."[13]

The new regulation signaled a developing shift in U.S. policy. The postwar strategy for Iraq—approved by the President on March 10, 2003—assumed that the country's governing institutions would survive the invasion and remain sufficiently intact to continue to administer the offices of government and provide the Iraqi people with essential services. The President's policy anticipated establishing an interim Iraqi authority with which the CPA would work to develop a political process for the eventual permanent transfer of sovereignty to a new, democratically elected government. The March 10 NSC Situation Room briefing to the President, however, did not define how the members of the new interim Iraqi authority would be chosen and what its authority would be during the postwar period.[14] On April 28, 2003, the Office of the Secretary of Defense produced a briefing book on the development of the Iraqi Interim Authority, stating that the Department and "the U.S. government interagency process have yet to decide upon a final structure for the IIA, and have not announced an approach or timetable for implementing the concept."[15]

When Bremer arrived in Iraq on May 12, the United States did not have a well-developed plan in place for transferring political power to an interim Iraqi authority, despite operative orders anticipating a fairly imminent withdrawal of most U.S. forces. The unexpected complete collapse of Iraq's governing institutions, widespread and debilitating looting, and disagreements among U.S. government officials about the composition of the interim authority prevented the Coalition from promptly effecting the hoped-for quick transition. The absence of clarity on the way forward amid Iraq's evolving post-invasion conditions was underscored in Under Secretary of Defense Douglas Feith's May 15, 2003 congressional testimony, given the day before the CPA issued Regulation Number 1. He said: "We are pursuing [our] goals with a two-part determination: a commitment to stay and a commitment to leave."[16]

Ambassador Bremer said that, by the time he was appointed, senior Washington officials had agreed that the political transition would take much longer than initially anticipated at the March 10 briefing. On May 6, President Bush told Bremer "to take the time necessary" to set Iraq on the path to democracy. Two days after Bremer's meeting with the President, Secretary Rumsfeld presented a paper at his morning staff meeting stating that the transition from despotism to a democracy will not happen fast or easily. It concluded that it could not be rushed.[17]

The rapid policy change in Washington was slow to filter to Iraq, where both civilian and military leadership assumed that the March 10 strategy still controlled. When Ambassador Bremer arrived, ORHA's Jay Garner and Zalmay Khalilzad, the President's envoy to Iraqi exile groups, were actively engaging with Iraqi leaders, primarily from the exile community, to quickly form an interim authority. Bremer's issuance of Regulation Number 1 effectively ended this initiative.

On May 22, Bremer proposed a new political plan under which the Iraqis would form a governing council, produce a new constitution, and then hold elections for a permanent government. On that same day, he submitted his first report to the President through Secretary Rumsfeld, stating that he had "re-launched the political dialogue with Iraqi leaders" and that "full sovereignty under an Iraqi government can come after democratic elections, which themselves must be based on a constitution agreed by all the people." The President wrote back, "You have my full support and confidence. You also have the backing of our Administration that knows our work will take time."[18]

Meanwhile, CENTCOM was still following its original strategy. General Franks had issued orders in April—pursuant to prewar plans—to move much of the initial invasion force out of Iraq by the end of July. He anticipated a U.S. military presence in Iraq of "fewer than 30,000 troops by the first of August."[19] By May 1, 2003, CENTCOM had dismantled its forward command-and-control center in Qatar. Two weeks later, the Defense Department announced that Lieutenant General David McKiernan's command (CFLCC) would soon leave Iraq and that his large headquarters would be replaced by a much smaller Combined Joint Task Force 7 (CJTF-7), led by Lieutenant General Ricardo Sanchez.[20] During this period, Lieutenant General Sanchez repeatedly expressed concern to General John Abizaid about the ongoing troop withdrawals, while Ambassador Bremer also warned Washington that security was deteriorating.[21]

General Abizaid assumed command of CENTCOM on July 8. Three days later he issued orders halting the U.S. troop withdrawal. Forces withdrawn during that early summer included U.S. Army Engineer units that could have supported the incipient reconstruction mission. The loss of these units hampered the Coalition's capacity to carry out quick-impact rebuilding projects during the CPA's first weeks.[22]

CPA Regulation Number1, which made the CPA the occupying authority of Iraq and Bremer—in effect—a proconsul, "completely flabbergasted" many Iraqis, according to senior exile leader Ali Allawi, who would serve as the Minister of Trade, Defense, and Finance in successive Iraqi governments. Allawi was shocked that, "within the space of a few days, the entire process that was to lead to a provisional Iraqi government had been abruptly stopped, and then upended."[23] The change raised suspicions among Iraq's indigenous tribal, political, and religious leadership, who chafed at the idea of an occupation by foreigners, after suffering under Saddam's dictatorship for decades.

On May 22, 2003, the UN Security Council approved Resolution 1483, recognizing the CPA as the temporary governing authority in Iraq, directing it to work to "promote the welfare of the Iraqi people," and advising it to "comply fully" with all obligations under international law.[24]

CPA Order Number 1: De-Ba'athification

On the same day that he signed CPA Regulation Number 1, Ambassador Bremer issued CPA Order Number 1, a de-Ba'athification directive that stripped certain former members of Saddam's Ba'ath Party of political influence in Iraq. In his April 16 Freedom Message, General Franks already had done away with the Ba'ath Party, which had about two million members in 2003.[25]

Conceived in Washington and promulgated with little Iraqi involvement, the de-Ba'athification order eliminated all Ba'ath Party structures and banned "Senior Party Members"—those in the top four ranks of the party—from serving in Iraq's public sector.[26] The order also provided for the immediate dismissal of anyone in the top three layers of management in any government institution (including ministries, state-owned enterprises, universities, and hospitals) if he or she had been a "full member" of the Ba'ath Party.[27] Because the vast majority of senior officials in Saddam Hussein's regime were Ba'ath Party members, the order effectively fired most senior leaders in Iraq's government, severely depleting the bureaucracy of key personnel. The order also allowed for exceptions and waivers.

Before the war began, interagency planners debated the delicate trade-off between the need to eliminate the Ba'ath Party and the need to retain an effective administrative bureaucracy in postwar Iraq. A consensus developed favoring a policy to remove the Ba'ath Party's most-senior ranks; but the meaning of "most-senior ranks" was left undefined.[28] The intelligence community estimated that implementing the order down to the Party's fourth level would affect "only about one percent of all party members or approximately 20,000 people, overwhelmingly Sunni Arabs."[29] Many in the Shi'a and Kurdish communities believed that a strong de-Ba'athification policy was crucial to prevent a Ba'athist return to power.

Some senior U.S. officials opposed the de-Ba'athification order. They argued that it would strip Iraq's governance institutions of key senior management and thus jeopardize the Coalition's primary goal of stabilizing the country. For example, ORHA's Jay Garner and the CIA station chief in Baghdad urged Ambassador Bremer to modify the order, believing the policy needlessly would create enemies for the Coalition and undercut national reconciliation.[30] Bremer refused, saying he had his instructions from Washington.[31]

Most Iraqis agreed that some de-Ba'athification was necessary, but many believed that the CPA order had gone too far. For example, Nazar Janabi, the Director General for Defense Policy and Requirements in Iraq's Ministry of Defense from 2004 to 2006, thought that only the top three levels of the Ba'ath Party should have been subject to the order. It would have had a far "less disenfranchising impact" if it had been restricted to just those levels, he said.[32]

The de-Ba'athification order arguably reached beyond what President Bush had approved on March 10, 2003, when the NSC's Frank Miller had briefed him on the policy. The President had then determined that "we ought to remove what we understood to be the top layer" of the Ba'ath Party (although no further definition was given to what the top layer comprised). Whether "the top layer" reached down to the fourth rung is subject to dispute. Miller believed that "the Ba'athist regime ought to [have been] dealt with in truth and reconciliation panels. Membership in the Ba'ath Party ought not to [have been] an immediate disqualification for office."[33]

Whatever its reach should have been, the consequences of the de-Ba'athification order quickly became clear: it reduced the ranks of Iraq's capable bureaucrats and thus limited the capacity of Iraqi ministries to contribute to reconstruction. "The impact of this de-Ba'athification order was devastating," said Lieutenant General Sanchez, Commander of Coalition forces in Iraq at the time. "Essentially, it eliminated the entire government and civic capacity of the nation. Organizations involving justice, defense, interior, communications, schools, universities, and hospitals were all either completely shut down or severely crippled, because anybody with any experience was now out of a job."[34]

Some of Iraq's Sunnis equated the order with a "de-Sunnification" of the government. Samir Sumaida'ie, a Sunni who became a member of the Iraqi Governing Council (IGC) and then served as Iraq's Minister of Interior, criticized the order for focusing on removing people rather than getting rid of an outmoded ideology. "The whole thing was applied in a very negative way," he said. "It was far too wide-ranging, and as a result, created a backlash. There were a lot of people who were just ordinary people who [joined the party simply because they] wanted to survive."[35]

On May 25, 2003, Bremer signed CPA Order Number 5, creating an Iraqi De-Ba'athification Council to "investigate and gather information" on "the extent, nature, location and current status of all Iraqi Ba'ath Party property and assets" as well as "the identity and whereabouts of Iraqi Ba'ath Party officials and members involved in human rights violations and exploitation of the Iraqi people." The council, composed entirely of Iraqis, was tasked to help the CPA Administrator identify and classify former Ba'ath Party members, eliminate Ba'ath Party structures, and reclaim Ba'ath Party assets. Importantly, it also advised Bremer about who should be exempted from de-Ba'athification.[36]

The CPA gave the council responsibility for de-Ba'athification, but "did not provide enough authority, resources, or oversight for them to manage the process."[37] It eventually turned the de-Ba'athification process over to the Iraqi Governing Council.[38] In November 2003, the Supreme National De-Ba'athification Commission replaced the Iraqi De-Ba'athification Council; Ahmed Chalabi, the Shi'a expatriate politician, served as its first chairman.[39]

CPA Order Number 2: Disbanding the Military
One week after issuing the de-Ba'athification order, Ambassador Bremer handed down another momentous order that also had unanticipated and significant consequences. CPA Order Number 2, titled "Dissolution of Entities," abolished seven institutions: the Ministry of Defense, the Ministry of Information, the Ministry of State for Military Affairs, the Iraqi Intelligence Service, the National Security Bureau, the Directorate of National Security, and the Special Security Organization.

The order put every member of Iraq's army, air force, navy, and air defense force, as well as the Republican Guard, the Special Republican Guard, the Directorate of Military Intelligence, and the Emergency Forces—some 500,000 men—immediately out of work, many without any compensation. Although the roughly 300,000 conscripts could receive a small termination payment, no soldier with the rank of colonel or above was eligible for either a termination payment or a pension.[40]

This CPA order surprised some policymakers in Washington. The NSC had not vetted the decision, and NSC Iraq coordinator Frank Miller said that the President had expected the army to continue after regime change because the Coalition could not "afford to put 300,000 men with guns in their hands on the street."[41] Secretary Powell first learned of the order at a May 22, 2003 NSC meeting at which Bremer, via secure video-teleconference from Iraq, announced his intent to issue the order the following day.[42]

"When the Army was disbanded," Secretary Powell recalled, "I called Dr. Rice and said, 'What happened?' Nobody seemed to know about this and [her] answer was, 'We have to back Jerry [Bremer].' There was no meeting on it; there was no, 'Gee, is this a good idea?' You couldn't even tell who had decided it ... I saw Peter Pace, the Vice Chairman, a little later and I said, 'Peter, did you guys know about this?' He said, 'Hell, no!'"[43]

The order was drafted by the CPA's senior advisor for national security, Walt Slocombe, in consultation with the Office of the Secretary of Defense and circulated to senior military leaders, including the Chairman of the Joint Chiefs of Staff.[44] Under Secretary Feith later acknowledged that it was an error in judgment for the Pentagon not to have discussed disbanding the army with senior-level officials of other agencies before formally approving the issuance of the order. But he maintains that it was the right decision substantively because the Iraqi army was top-heavy with generals, otherwise badly organized, corrupt, and had been an instrument of oppression in Iraq.[45] Slocombe later said that the order merely reflected facts on the ground because Iraq's forces had essentially disbanded in the wake of the invasion. Moreover, the Kurdish and Shi'a leaders objected to any reconstituted version of Saddam's army.[46]

Key U.S. generals in Iraq expressed concerns about the order before it was issued.[47] CENTCOM's Phase IV plan, approved by the President, anticipated using the Iraqi army to help stabilize the country and assist with reconstruction. To this end, the military had dropped leaflets across Iraq before the invasion urging soldiers not to fight and promising no reprisals against those who laid down their arms. Some U.S. ground commanders argued that the army had not "dissolved," but that Iraq's soldiers had gone home, awaiting direction. In each region across the country, U.S. brigade commanders had contacted Iraqi military leaders and, through them, had begun to reconstitute army units.[48]

To replace the disbanded forces, Bremer and Slocombe proposed creating a small volunteer Iraqi army.[49] The plan called for the Coalition to train about 40,000 Iraqi soldiers, divided into three light infantry divisions, over the next two and a half years. The first division would be ready for deployment in the fall of 2004, the second division in the fall of 2005, and the third in early 2006.[50] The plan would allow the "New Iraqi Army" to draw on carefully vetted officers from Saddam's old force, but it had to exclude the top ranks of the Ba'ath Party and anyone from the inner circle of the old security forces.[51]

Leading Iraqis disagreed with the CPA's decision to disband the army. Ali Allawi said Iraqi attitudes toward the army were far more complicated than Americans understood. The police (which were not disbanded) and other internal security forces were "detested," but the armed forces "generated considerable sympathy and respect throughout Iraq." According to Allawi, the public at large saw the army "as an integral part of the identity of the state of Iraq," and it was difficult, "even for the Shi'a, to accept a wholesale dissolution of the armed forces and to leave the country bereft of an army."[52]

Laith Kubba—one of the founding members of the Iraqi National Congress, an advisor to the Future of Iraq Project, and later a spokesman for the Iraqi government—said, "the measure to dissolve the Iraqi army was not a smart one." Kubba believed that Ambassador Bremer needed the old army to help Iraq make the transition to democratic governance. "Now if that means you need to utilize some of the people who were in the bureaucracy, in the army, in the regime, and if they're vital and crucial to make that transition, then you take them on board." He added, "Alienating large numbers of people … was not a smart move."[53]

Within days of the announcement of the "Dissolution of Entities," crowds of former soldiers gathered outside the CPA's palace gates in Baghdad and around U.S. military compounds across the country, demanding the restoration of their salaries and pensions. In Mosul, where Major General David Petraeus was commanding the 101st Airborne Division, disbanded military members demonstrated for several days in front of the city hall. Iraqi policemen shot and killed one of the protestors and wounded three others, sparking a riot. Over the next two days, eighteen of Petraeus's soldiers were wounded, and two Humvees were burned. Riots in Baghdad and elsewhere claimed American and Iraqi lives. Ten days later, Bremer modified the policy, announcing that the CPA would pay salaries and pensions to members of the disbanded army.[54]

Major General Petraeus later said that the order to disband the army sparked an anti-Coalition sentiment that fueled the nascent insurgency in Iraq, igniting nationalist impulses against "the occupiers." Petraeus believed that the order created "tens of thousands, if not hundreds of thousands, of additional enemies of the Coalition."[55]

CPA's Shortfalls

> *Jerry [Bremer]—God bless him—he was never given a set of coordinated instructions from the Administration. He went in pretty much on his own.**
>
> General Colin Powell
> Secretary of State (2001-2005)

When Ambassador Bremer arrived in Iraq, he ostensibly had at his disposal both U.S. appropriated funds and Iraqi money that he could use to fund government operations and reconstruction programs. In April 2003, the Congress had approved $2.4 billion for the newly created Iraq Relief and Reconstruction Fund, which would become the primary U.S. funding account for Iraq's reconstruction.

The Office of Management and Budget apportioned the first appropriation to the Iraq Relief and Reconstruction Fund (IRRF 1) among five implementing agencies, with USAID receiving more than 70 percent.[1] USAID already had marked these IRRF 1 funds for use before the CPA's creation, and thus Ambassador Bremer had limited influence over how this money was spent.[2] The CPA's advisors, however, sought to shape specific job orders under the various IRRF 1 contracts USAID managed. Disagreements over these job orders marked the beginning of a disputatious relationship between the CPA and USAID.

Unlike IRRF 1, Ambassador Bremer had virtually complete control over Iraqi money, which came from three sources: vested funds in U.S. bank accounts frozen by an executive order shortly before the March 2003 invasion; seized funds that Coalition forces had recovered in Iraq; and oil and gas revenues controlled by the UN under the Oil-for-Food program. The CPA would expend about $20 billion of these Iraqi funds by the end of its fourteen-month tenure.[3]

U.S. Funding

In the April 2003 IRRF 1 legislation, the Congress directed that the funds be used to pay for "humanitarian assistance" and "rehabilitation and reconstruction in Iraq." The Congress identified twelve humanitarian and reconstruction sectors for fund use, with the OMB apportioning the money among the agencies shown on the following chart.[4]

---

* SIGIR interview with General (Ret.) Colin Powell, former Secretary of State, February 4, 2008.

Breakdown of Iraq Relief and Reconstruction Fund Apportionments by Agency ($ Millions)

Source	Agency	Apportioned
IRRF	USAID	$1,820.3
	Department of Defense	$518.3
	Department of State	$125.4
	Department of the Treasury	$6.0
	U.S. Trade and Development Agency	$5.0
	Total	**$2,475.0**

Source: Data as of September 30, 2004; CPA-IG, *Quarterly Report to the United States Congress*; October 2004, 55.

USAID had initiated contracting for Iraq's reconstruction in early 2003 and, by early May, it had awarded twelve contracts, obligating about $1.5 billion in IRRF 1 dollars. The agency divided the contracts between "hard" projects to restore infrastructure and "soft" programs to support health, education, agriculture, and economic reform initiatives. Bechtel received the largest single contract, $680 million, for infrastructure projects in Iraq.[5]

After the March 2003 invasion, USAID quickly began to establish a presence in Iraq, and, by mid-summer, the agency had 30 offices open in 15 of the country's 18 provinces, staffed by more than 400 people. Reflecting USAID's transformation over the previous fifteen years into an agency heavily reliant on contractors, only about a dozen of the deployed personnel were full-time agency employees.[6]

Iraqi Funds

In May 2003, the U.S. government, the Coalition, and the United Nations took several important steps to give the CPA access to Iraqi funds for reconstruction programs and to fund government operations. An executive order issued on the eve of the invasion permitted Ambassador Bremer to use $1.7 billion in vested Iraqi assets, which had been drawn from various banks and deposited into the U.S. Federal Reserve Bank of New York.[7] During the invasion, U.S. forces seized about $900 million from various locations across Iraq, finding much of it in Saddam's palaces. Bremer generally used the vested funds to pay Iraqi government salaries and the seized funds to support reconstruction projects. The U.S. military carried out many of the first reconstruction projects using seized funds, which marked the beginning of a critical program that Bremer would soon formalize in a CPA order as the Commander's Emergency Response Program (CERP). Vested and seized Iraqi funds alone, however, could not cover the mounting costs of administering and rebuilding Iraq. For that, the CPA depended on the Development Fund for Iraq (DFI).

The DFI

On May 22, 2003, the UN Security Council passed Resolution 1483 (UNSCR 1483), creating the DFI as the new repository for Iraq's oil and gas revenues.[8] The resolution required the deposit of 95 percent of these funds into the DFI account at the Federal Reserve Bank of New York, from which the CPA could draw to pay for "the economic reconstruction and repair of Iraq's infrastructure, for the continued disarmament of Iraq, for the costs of Iraqi civilian administration, and for other purposes benefiting the people of Iraq." The remaining five percent was deposited in the UN Compensation Fund for victims of Saddam Hussein's 1990 invasion of Kuwait.[9]

UNSCR 1483 also created the International Advisory and Monitoring Board (IAMB) to provide oversight of the DFI and to ensure that the CPA used Iraqi revenues for the benefit of the Iraqi people. The IAMB's membership included representatives from the UN, the World Bank, the International Monetary Fund, and the Arab Fund for Social and Economic Development. Notwithstanding the importance of the IAMB's mission, the UN failed to appoint its members until October 24, 2003, and the board did not have its first meeting until December 5, 2003, more than six months after the CPA started using the DFI.[10]

At the end of May 2003, the UN transferred a billion dollars into the DFI account "to provide for immediate reconstruction needs," and the CPA immediately began using it to pay Iraqi governmental salaries and pensions and to finance initial reconstruction projects.[11] Ambassador Bremer created a Requirement Review Board (RRB) to manage the DFI, and the RRB quickly started approving projects, ranging from a $600 water pump to a $4 million radio system for the railroads.[12] "For lack of a better [term]," noted Ambassador James Warlick, the CPA's point person on the Oil-for-Food program, the DFI became CPA's "bank account" for Iraq.[13]

On June 15, 2003, the CPA issued two regulations governing the DFI.[14] One gave Ambassador Bremer complete control of the DFI funds, providing that he alone could direct their disbursement.[15] The other replaced the RRB with the Program Review Board (PRB), directing it to use the DFI in a transparent manner to meet Iraq's humanitarian needs, support the economic reconstruction, fund projects to repair Iraq's infrastructure, continue disarmament programs, and pay for the costs of the country's civilian administration.[16]

Program Review Board

Bremer named his new director of economic policy, Peter McPherson, as chairman of the PRB.[17] Under McPherson's guidance, the PRB reviewed numerous reconstruction project proposals, making recommendations to the Administrator on which the CPA should pursue.[18] Ambassador Bremer instructed McPherson to "promote the CPA's objective of actively involving Iraqis in the financial planning process, and transferring to the Iraqi interim administration the responsibility for budgeting Iraq's financial resources"—but only one Iraqi representative was on the board.[19] The PRB was also supposed to develop a comprehensive funding plan for the "relief and reconstruction of Iraq," but it never produced such a plan.[20]

Because the CPA was legally deemed an "international organization," Iraqi funds under its control were not subject to U.S. contracting regulations. The CPA thus developed its own contracting regulations, embodied in CPA Memorandum Number 4, which detailed the rules for using the DFI. Among other things, Memo 4 established conditions for the award of DFI-funded contracts and defined the documents required for each contract file. Notably, it put the CPA's Head of Contracting Activity (HCA) in charge of executing all CPA contracts.[21]

The HCA also was directed to manage Iraqi ministry contracting unless the CPA's Administrator had exempted a ministry after certifying that it had established capable contracting systems "adequate to ensure the transparent use and management of Iraqi funds."[22] By the end of the CPA's tenure, Bremer had certified just two ministries. Nevertheless, Iraqi ministries regularly engaged in independent contracting, in breach of Memo 4, throughout the CPA's duration. U.S. and international auditors later raised serious concerns about the CPA's weak oversight of the DFI and its failure to enforce its own contracting procedures.[23]

Commander's Emergency Response Program

On June 16, 2003, Ambassador Bremer authorized the use of DFI funds for CERP, an important new program that enabled U.S. military combat units to use Iraqi funds for small-scale reconstruction projects to meet Iraqi needs. Three days later, Lieutenant General Ricardo Sanchez, Commander of CJTF-7, issued Fragmentary Order 89, outlining the regulations governing CERP and defining eligible projects as those for "the building, repair, reconstitution, and reestablishment of the social and material infrastructure in Iraq."[24] CERP grew into a key U.S.-funded reconstruction program in Iraq, ultimately receiving more than $3.5 billion in U.S. appropriations by the end of 2008.[25]

Shortly after creating the program, the CPA expanded CERP's limits on project spending and strengthened its regulations, requiring commanders to appoint trained purchasing agents to document their use of CERP funds. General officers in charge of regional commands could receive $500,000 in CERP money for projects; brigade commanders could receive $200,000. The PRB approved additional tranches upon depletion of these allotments.[26]

The CERP made it possible for U.S. commanders to improve life in Iraqi communities by quickly repairing roads and bridges, rebuilding schools, improving health care, and removing trash.[27] The program would later play a critical role in U.S. counterinsurgency efforts in Iraq.

Staffing Problems

Soon after arriving in Baghdad, Ambassador Bremer replaced ORHA's pillars, organizing the CPA into political, economic, administrative, budgeting, and planning sections, which roughly resembled the traditional embassy structure with which Bremer was familiar. The CPA absorbed 600 ORHA staff members but was still far short of what it needed to manage its burgeoning relief and reconstruction program.[28]

On May 21, 2003, Deputy Secretary of Defense Wolfowitz moved to address the CPA's shortfalls by directing the Department of the Army to meet its administrative, logistical, and contracting needs.[29] The Army promptly opened a contracting office at CPA headquarters in the Republican Palace in Baghdad, appointing an Army colonel to lead the new office. When he arrived at the end of June 2003, he found that there were just three contracting officers on staff to manage all of the CPA's work.[30] He desperately needed more qualified personnel to help produce statements of work—the key element in defining a contract's scope—and more lawyers to review contracting documents. Throughout the CPA's tenure, the contracting office was grievously understaffed.[31]

These personnel problems were symptomatic of those afflicting the entire CPA. With no formal recruiting process in place, the CPA resorted to a "pull system" in which senior advisors determined their staffing needs on an ad hoc basis and then sent the requests to the CPA's human resources office in Baghdad. The Baghdad office would then send the request to the CPA's Pentagon office.[32] This procedure was too slow, so CPA officials in Iraq began recruiting staff directly from federal agencies and presenting them to human resources for immediate processing.[33] The CPA also suffered from a very high personnel turnover rate. Part of the cause was that, in the summer of 2003, the U.S. still expected a short stay in Iraq, and so most people signed up for three-month tours.[34]

Because of the CPA's myriad personnel problems, the White House sent Katja Bullock, special assistant to the President for presidential personnel, to assist in developing a Joint Manning Document (JMD). Bullock promptly produced a JMD that included personnel needs from federal agencies, contractors, and Coalition partners. Submitted to the Joint Staff by July 2003, the JMD called for a CPA staff of around 1,200 people, which would double its size.[35] The Joint Staff quickly filled the military slots, but ignored the civilian ones because it had no mechanism in place for forwarding staffing requests to the civilian agencies.[36] Colonel Dennis DeGraff, CPA's personnel director, said that "the civilian [personnel] piece ... just sat on somebody's desk in [the Office of the Secretary of Defense]."[37]

At the end of 2003, Secretary Rumsfeld deployed a team to Iraq to assess the CPA's personnel situation. Its report concluded that the CPA was "a pick-up organization [seeking] to design and execute the most demanding transformation in recent U.S. history."[38] A CPA Inspector General audit of the organization's personnel management system also found problems, noting that "CPA staffing needs changed constantly in terms of the number of required personnel," and that the CPA could not keep an accurate count of its personnel.[39]

Throughout its tenure, the CPA operated with about one-third fewer people than it needed and turnover was constant.[40] Retired Lieutenant General Jeffrey Oster, who served as the CPA's deputy administrator and chief operating officer during 2004, observed: "If you couldn't get somebody for 90 days, you'd take somebody for 60 days." When the CPA dissolved on June 28, 2004, only seven people had served for the CPA's entire fourteen-month duration.[41]

The 3161 Provision

During mid-summer 2003, it became apparent that the CPA was going to be in Iraq longer than the few months the Pentagon's leadership had hoped. Meeting personnel needs to support the occupation thus quickly moved up on the list of priorities. U.S. civilian agencies were failing to provide enough personnel, so the Pentagon established a new recruiting team within its White House Liaison Office to find and employ staff. Like ORHA, the new team used a special federal law designed for temporary organizations—Section 3161 in Title 5 of the United States Code—to fill CPA positions quickly. The 3161 provision permitted federal hiring free of the usual position classifications and competition requirements.[42]

Although the Pentagon's recruiting team had an efficient and effective hiring tool, it still needed a pool of candidates with the right skills and experience to support a contingency relief and reconstruction operation. Because a ready pool did not exist, many of the personnel that the team recruited were poorly qualified for the jobs to which they were assigned.[43] Furthermore, using the Pentagon's White House Liaison Office as the locus for senior official recruitment exposed the effort to charges of politicization.

By the spring of 2004, more than twenty percent of the CPA's staff had been hired under the 3161 provision. Coalition partners contributed another thirteen percent, and around five percent were contractors. Only 149 of the CPA's 1,196 staff were detailed from the civilian agencies. Most of these came from the State

Department, USAID, and the U.S. Treasury. The Defense Department drew on its military assets to provide the rest.[44] The civilian agencies in the federal bureaucracy failed to muster more staff for Iraq because they had neither the financial nor personnel resources to support a contingency operation.[45] Also, the worsening security situation in Iraq proved a deterrent.

Matching Skills to Jobs
The CPA's Office of Management and Budget staff exemplified the CPA's personnel problems. When Retired Rear Admiral David Oliver, the first Director of CPA's OMB, started in June 2003, he requested 31 people to meet his enormous mission. When he left five months later, in November 2003, only four of his positions were filled.[46] Rodney Bent, who worked for OMB in Washington, replaced Oliver, finding severe shortages in staff numbers and skills. Bent discovered that none of his employees had ever worked on a budget before being deployed to Iraq. "I had a relatively young staff that was completely inexperienced and had no particular training either in the Middle East or on budget matters," said Bent. "I would think, if we're ever in this kind of situation again, that we'd want to draw on some of the professional staff that does exist" in Washington.[47]

The Iraq Reconstruction and Development Council
Deputy Secretary Wolfowitz and Under Secretary Feith created the Iraq Reconstruction and Development Council (IRDC) to bolster cultural awareness and Iraqi outreach. First ORHA and then the CPA used the IRDC's 150 members as technical advisors to Iraq's ministries and provincial offices. These Iraqi exiles—most of whom were American citizens—had an ambiguous status that set them apart from their CPA colleagues (as well as from Iraqi nationals).[48] Some CPA officials had concerns that some IRDC members brought potentially troublesome political baggage with them, including ties to factions controlled by exile politicians.[49]

A few IRDC members achieved success. For example, Dr. Sinan al-Shabibi later became the governor of the Central Bank of Iraq.[50] But the IRDC program was far from an overall success. It suffered from severe attrition. In the waning days of the CPA, only 27 IRDC members still remained on CPA's roster.[51]

A post-mortem of the IRDC effort found that it was poorly planned and inadequately managed.[52] The difficult IRDC experience underscores the need for a preplanned, well-prepared cadre of experts who understand the culture, history, and economic foundations of a country undergoing a major relief and reconstruction operation.[53]

Although the United States was generally unprepared to take on a large-scale occupation and rebuilding mission in Iraq in 2003, one agency notably stepped up and performed its mission admirably. The U.S. Department of the Treasury, having dispatched a well-staffed and well-qualified team, worked first with ORHA and then CPA in 2003 to help prevent the collapse of Iraq's economy.

CHAPTER 8
TREASURY'S TRIAGE

The banking system [in Iraq] was in shambles. Electronic transfer of funds, widely made to people in developed countries, was virtually non-existent, making Iraq's payment system the equivalent of a Model-T Ford.*

John B. Taylor
Under Secretary of the Treasury for International Affairs (2001-2005)

When the first group of U.S. Treasury experts arrived in Baghdad in April 2003, they found Iraq's financial system in ruins. Looters had ransacked the Rafidain and Rasheed banking chains and pillaged safe-deposit boxes. Just two of the 170 Rafidain branches, the largest bank chain in the country, were open.[1] The vault of the Central Bank of Iraq contained only $350 million in gold and waterlogged bank notes.[2] Nearly a billion dollars in foreign currency had been withdrawn from the bank before the war. In early May, Iraq's ministries were bankrupt, unable to pay salaries and pensions, and the country's currency was dangerously unstable.

The U.S. Treasury team worked through the spring and summer of 2003 to battle these devastating problems, shoring up Iraq's banking system, resuming civil servants' payments, stabilizing the currency, and securing a moratorium on repayment of Iraq's international debts. Negotiations that began later in the year would significantly reduce this debt. These efforts, among the most successful and most important during the early CPA period, prevented the country's financial collapse. But the larger goal of transforming Iraq's statist economy into one powered by free-market principles would prove much more difficult.

Paying Iraqi Salaries

In May 2003, the CPA began paying Iraqi governmental salaries and pensions, using vested and DFI funds. To end the inequities of Saddam's payment system, Ambassador Bremer approved a four-tier monthly pay scale that permitted civil servants, based on their grade, to receive $50, $100, $150, or $250 per month.[3] Treasury officials in Baghdad worked with the Iraqi Ministry of Finance to develop a roster of eligible civil servants and pensioners. Ministry officials, who had secured their payroll records when the war started, turned them over to the CPA, and Bremer's senior advisors used them to develop employee registers for each

---

* John B. Taylor, *Global Financial Warriors: The Untold Story of International Finance in the Post-9/11 World* (New York: W.W. Norton, 2007), 200.

ministry.[4] The senior advisors then requested budgets to pay salaries based on the new payroll grades. Some professions received instant pay raises. Teachers, for example, received $50 per month under the new system, a tenfold increase.[5]

The CPA initially used the $1.7 billion in vested Iraqi funds to pay salaries.[6] The cash was packaged at the Federal Reserve Bank in New York, put on pallets, and flown to Baghdad for distribution. These money flights would occur continually over the next year, transporting more than $12 billion—or 237.3 tons of cash—from the United States to Baghdad to fund Iraqi budgets and reconstruction projects.[7]

Ged Smith, the director of Treasury's Office of Technical Assistance, remembered calling the New York Federal Reserve Bank to order the first shipment of $20 million in small bills: "The guy just laughed and asked, 'How many planes do you have?'"[8] When the money arrived, CPA's senior advisors loaded bricks of cash—nicknamed "footballs"—into trucks and Chevy Suburbans, delivering them personally to their respective ministries to pay salaries and other costs. Senior Iraqi officials distributed the money to ministry employees.[9] Although the payment process lacked the controls necessary for proper accountability, it met the urgent need to provide salaries, inject money into the economy, and prevent a political crisis.

Treasury advisors to Iraq's Ministry of Finance and the Central Bank moved quickly to establish a more controlled payroll system. By late June 2003, procedures were in place to pay government salaries through the Rafidain Bank, whose branches were quickly reopening. Forty-six branches were operating by August in Baghdad, with another 85 branches across the country.[10]

More than 90 percent of the salary payments during the CPA's tenure—all paid with either vested or DFI funds flown from the United States—went from the CPA Comptroller to the Central Bank and then out to recipients through the Rafidain Bank chain.[11] John Taylor, the Under Secretary of the Treasury, testifying before the Senate Foreign Relations Committee during the first week of June 2003, reported that more than 1.5 million workers and pensioners had already started receiving regular payments. He described the payments as an "initial financial life-line to the Iraqi people."[12]

Although the CPA's payments and new pay-scale provided a "life-line" for many Iraqis, they nearly caused a revolt among oil workers. "In the one-product economy that Saddam's disastrous economic policies had developed for Iraq," said Admiral Dave Oliver, Director of CPA's Office of Management and Budget, "the oil workers were accustomed to being specially pampered and not reluctant to express their displeasure." The CPA promised to come up with a new pay-scale by September, which "kept the oil and electrical ministries working without significant protest."[13] CPA Order Number 30 created thirteen civil-service classifications, each divided into ten steps on a career ladder that mirrored that of the U.S. civil service.[14]

Flying Billions to Baghdad

The CPA relied on the DFI to fund the operations of Iraq's ministries and to pay for reconstruction projects. Held in a Federal Reserve Bank account in New York, DFI cash was flown to Baghdad in very large sums whenever the CPA requested. These shipments—the largest airborne transfer of currency in history—proved an enormous logistical challenge. A typical pallet of DFI cash had 640 bundles, with a thousand bills in each bundle. Each loaded pallet weighed about 1,500 pounds. The pallets were flown into Baghdad's airport at night and were then driven to the Central Bank of Iraq for deposit.[15]

The first emergency air-lift of money to Iraq was for $20 million, but the shipments rapidly grew in size. In December 2003, the CPA requested a $1.5 billion shipment, at the time the largest single payout of U.S. currency in Federal Reserve Bank history.[16] But that record was soon broken when, in June 2004, more than $4 billion was flown to Iraq, just before the CPA's transfer of sovereignty to the Iraqi Interim Government.

The Currency Exchange

Before the war, U. S. Treasury officials were concerned about the two different currencies in circulation in Iraq. In northern Iraq, the Kurds used the old Iraqi currency, known as the "Swiss" dinar, so named because the currency's original plates were made in Switzerland. In the south, Iraqis used the "Saddam" dinar, which bore Saddam Hussein's picture. The fact that the Saddam dinar was emblazoned with the dictator's portrait was just one of its problems. It was also easy to counterfeit, had only two denominations in circulation, and had plunged in value since the 1991 Gulf War. [17]

Treasury officials knew that a stable and unified currency system would be essential to Iraq's long-term economic health, so they developed a currency exchange program as part of the agency's prewar strategy.[18] In July 2003, Bremer announced the currency exchange plan, noting that the CPA would print and distribute new Iraqi banknotes and make them available to the Iraqi public in mid-October.[19] The Central Bank of Iraq, with Treasury's support, would manage the exchange and the "New Iraqi Dinar" would replace both the Swiss and the Saddam dinars.[20]

"Currently everyone in Iraq carries a reminder of Saddam in their pockets— on the banknotes they're using," Bremer said. "Shortly after October 15, the first batch of Saddam notes will go into the incinerator. At close of business January 15, 2004, Saddam notes will no longer be legal tender."[21] Between October 2003 and January 2004, the CPA carried out the exchange with armed convoys delivering the new Iraqi dinars to 243 banks across Iraq. Insurgents attacked fifteen of the convoys, wounding eleven people.[22] But the attacks did not stop the conversion. Iraqis exchanged their old dinars for new ones at banks across the country, with the old notes shipped to Baghdad for burning.[23]

President Bush hailed the exchange program as an important achievement: "A stable currency, a new currency, a currency without the picture of the dictator or tyrant, or the torturer, however you want to define him, is important for the future."[24] The new dinar was stable enough by the end of 2006 to begin appreciating against the dollar.[25]

Relieving Iraq's Debt

Estimates of Iraq's external debt in 2003 ran as high as $130 billion.[26] Fearing that interest payments on the debt alone could consume most of the country's income, Treasury made it a priority to persuade Iraq's international creditors to forgive or restructure Iraq's mammoth debt.[27] It secured an initial agreement with the G-8—comprising the world's top eight industrialized democracies—to give Iraq eighteen months before seeking interest payments on any Iraqi debt. Treasury then embarked on an intense negotiation process which eventually secured extraordinary debt relief for Iraq.[28]

In December 2003, President Bush appointed former Secretary of State and Secretary of the Treasury James Baker as his special envoy for Iraq's debt to lead the negotiations. Baker heavily engaged with the Paris Club, a debt forum comprising the world's nineteen richest countries, eventually securing a commitment from Club members to write down Iraq's foreign debt.[29]

At their economic summit in June 2004, the G-8 endorsed an IMF finding that Iraq's debt should be reduced by 90 to 95 percent. Iraq's new Minister of Finance Abdul al-Mahdi then asked the Paris Club creditors to reduce Iraq's debt by 95 percent and to reschedule payments of the remaining debt over a 23-year period. The United States, Canada, and Britain supported the request. Baker's negotiations over the next five months produced a hugely beneficial outcome: 80 percent of Iraq's $38.9 billion debt to Paris Club creditors was forgiven.[30] More significant debt forgiveness would follow over the next few years, which helped the country's foundering economy to stabilize and begin to grow. The extraordinary elimination of much of Iraq's debt since 2003 amounts to one of the most generous acts of collective international debt-forgiveness in modern times.

CPA's Economic Reform Agenda

In May 2003, Peter McPherson, the CPA's Director of Economic Policy, oversaw the CPA effort to pay Iraqi government salaries, restart the banking system, and manage the currency exchange program, he began to implement reforms to open Iraq's economy to the free market.[31] Some in the CPA contended that these reforms should be implemented gradually; others urged letting Iraqis resolve their own issues regarding the country's economic structure after the CPA left.[32] The IMF warned that in transition economies like Iraq, "implementation of these reforms has typically been difficult and time consuming, reflecting the need to build political support for reforms to ensure that they are durable, and that adequate institutional capacity exists to ensure effective implementation."[33] But McPherson pointed to the IMF's report on economic reform efforts in Eastern Europe, which concluded that the earlier reforms are made, the faster economic growth will occur.[34] McPherson and his economic team moved briskly ahead, focusing much of the CPA's reformist effort on Iraq's state-owned enterprises and the country's banking system.

State-owned Enterprises

After the March 2003 invasion, most of Iraq's SOEs shut down because of looting. Three wars and a decade of international sanctions had left them "seriously de-capitalized, asset-starved, obsolescent, inefficient, saddled with high production costs, over-staffed, and—as a result of looting—in a state of physical degradation."[35] But Iraq's 192 SOEs were the "sole providers of essential public utilities and the leading providers of a large number of public goods and services as well as of consumer and industrial products." They accounted for 90 percent of the country's industrial capacity. Eleven different ministries oversaw various SOEs, which employed an estimated 500,000 people, or roughly one-eighth of the country's workforce.[36]

The CPA considered three separate but related issues regarding the SOEs. First, how much budget support should it provide to these state businesses? Second, should the SOEs be able to draw upon their deposits held by state banks? And third, should the debt between the SOEs be cancelled?[37]

Regarding budgetary support, McPherson and the ministry advisors differed on the degree to which the CPA should assist the largely inefficient and outdated state-run businesses. The CPA did continue to pay all SOE salaries and, in the early days, gave some financial support to a number of SOEs in the electricity, oil, water, and health sectors. But McPherson, who saw the SOEs as vestiges of Saddam's statist economy, did not want to risk wasting additional money on businesses about which the CPA had little knowledge. He demanded proof that support for the SOEs would stimulate the economy and, in time, create viable companies.[38] Some of CPA's senior advisors, however, pushed to have more money allocated immediately to the SOEs, which they saw as vital to Iraq's economy.[39]

As to SOE bank accounts, McPherson made the controversial decision in July, when the two largest government banks began opening branches, to freeze all SOE deposit accounts at these banks. The move prevented individual SOEs from drawing on their accounts to purchase supplies, make needed capital improvements, or pay debts. McPherson was concerned about the viability of the state banks, which had recorded deposits amounting to about $2 billion but had only about $1 billion on hand.[40] He feared that any attempt by the SOEs to withdraw their money could spark a run on the banks.[41]

At the same time that the CPA froze the SOE bank accounts, it also cancelled all of their debts. McPherson contended that the "maze of obligations between government entities" was so complicated and that so many records had been destroyed by looting, that it would take more than a year to sort them out and "even then you would not have an accurate record."[42] He concluded, with Bremer's concurrence, that "we should clean the slate and move on."[43] McPherson said that many of the SOEs could not survive without huge subsidies, and that he wanted to fund only "those that could make practical use of CPA money."[44]

Some members of the Treasury's economic team and senior advisors to the ministries objected to these decisions. They contended that debt cancellation could weaken the Iraqi government's long-term credit standing. Moreover, they argued that freezing the bank deposits and cancelling all the debt among the SOEs hurt the most viable companies—those with money in their accounts—and risked leaving Iraq without a manufacturing base and with a huge unemployment problem.[45] There were also legal concerns about the CPA's authority under international law to effectively shut down much of Iraq's manufacturing base.[46]

Timothy Carney—the CPA's senior advisor to the Ministry of Industries and Minerals, which supervised a number of SOEs—urged that Iraqis should have a say in this significant economic decision. In a June 15, 2007 memo to McPherson, Carney warned that the proposed SOE policy "risks [undermining the] assets of the Iraqi people" and "was drawn up without adequate Iraqi participation."[47]

The CPA changed course at the end of July, and started to provide additional operating budgets for those SOEs, such as the cement and fertilizer companies, that could produce goods and services needed to support reconstruction. By the end of August, about one-third of the SOEs had reopened.[48] Dr. Sami al-Araji, an American-trained mechanical engineer who had been working for the Ministry of Industry and Minerals, criticized the policy on SOEs, because he believed they "would have been able to support the [reconstruction] work in the electrical, oil, health, water and sewerage, and transport sectors."[49]

Banking Reforms

During Saddam's rule, banks functioned as "vehicles for storing and moving cash around the country and—in some cases—outside the country." They were not commercially viable institutions that promoted economic growth.[50] The CPA economic team and USAID agreed that Iraq's banking sector needed modernizing, but disagreed on how to do it.[51]

The CPA promulgated three orders to reform the Iraqi banking system. The first, issued on July 7, 2003, suspended the country's old banking laws, which had allowed only the Ministry of Finance to authorize loans to government ministries, and gave the Central Bank of Iraq the "authority to determine and implement monetary and credit policy without the approval of the Ministry of Finance."[52] The second order, issued on July 14, 2003, created the Trade Bank of Iraq to manage DFI funds and to help Iraqi businesses finance the imports of goods. Noting that Iraq lacked "financial institutions capable of facilitating imports and exports of goods and services to and from Iraq," the CPA authorized the Trade Bank's capitalization at $100 million.[53] The Trade Bank, one the CPA's more important achievements, would issue letters of credit worth more than $16 billion over the next five years.[54] The third banking order, issued on September 19, 2003, established rules for bank licensing, capitalization, and management.[55]

These orders collectively effected two major economic changes simultaneously. They modernized the banking system—making it more structured and stable—and changed the credit system, giving more Iraqis greater access to capital. Under Saddam, Iraqi banks required hard collateral, such as houses, jewelry, gold, or property, to secure a loan. The CPA wanted the banks to make credit more available, hoping that increased access to financing would spur economic growth.[56]

The CPA's banking reforms, however, did not have a significant effect on credit practices because the bank branches continued to require 100 percent collateral for loans. They could not quickly break their Saddam-era habits, even though the Finance Ministry had provided a written guarantee of 50 percent against possible losses made on small business loans.[57]

The Limits of Economic Change

A number of factors constrained the CPA's ability to make sweeping economic reforms in post-invasion Iraq.[58] Disagreement within the Coalition's ranks over the scope of economic reform measures, together with Iraqi opposition, stalled ambitious attempts to create a more open economy in Iraq and sidetracked SOE reform. There was never any serious discussion about the privatization of electricity, and the oil industry was considered off limits from the beginning.

The deteriorating security situation and the November 15, 2003 decision to accelerate the return of sovereignty to Iraq made it all but impossible for the CPA to tackle other significant economic issues, like the state subsidies for food, electricity, and fuel.[59] By the beginning of 2004, the CPA had set aside its free-market reform agenda, focusing instead on planning the political transition and implementing a wave of new reconstruction projects. According to Ali Allawi, who served as Minister of Trade during 2003, "there was not one [Iraqi] voice raised in support of the CPA's economic plans."[60]

BREMER'S GRAND VISION

> *We seem to have transitioned from a cautious beginning*
> *to requesting funding for everything without a plan or a*
> *thorough justification. And not only have the cost estimates*
> *been unrealistic, the entire postwar experience appears to have*
> *taken us by surprise. We were told that we would be welcomed*
> *with open arms by the Iraqi people and that Iraqi government*
> *institutions would be restored after a short hiatus. The vision of*
> *postwar reconstruction presented to Congress at that time was for*
> *many of us either hopelessly naive or grossly incompetent.* *
>
> **Representative Nita Lowey (D-NY)**
> Chair, House Appropriations Subcommittee on State and Foreign Operations

During mid-2003, several U.S. agencies and international organizations travelled to Iraq to conduct assessments on the country's reconstruction needs. The resulting surveys projected rebuilding costs ranging up to $60 billion, far higher than prewar estimates. In the wake of these assessments, Dave Oliver, Director of CPA's Office of Management and Budget, observed: "Our invasion seemed to have occurred just as the condition of the entire infrastructure teetered on the edge of the cliff of disaster."[1]

The assessments also caused Ambassador Bremer to push the CPA to develop a new and much more ambitious reconstruction plan. His new vision embraced a rebuilding program many times larger than any previously proposed, which would require enormous increases in U.S. funding for Iraq's relief and reconstruction.

2003 Assessments of Iraq

Four organizations conducted major reviews of Iraq's infrastructure and economy during the CPA's first three months: Bechtel, USACE, the UN, and the Center for Strategic and International Studies. Their reporting helped shape the next phase of the U.S. relief and reconstruction effort.

---

* Representative Nita Lowey, Statement before the House Appropriations Subcommittee on Foreign Operations, Export Financing and Related Programs Hold Hearing on FY2004 Supplemental: Iraq Reconstruction Funds, September 24, 2003.

The USAID/Bechtel Infrastructure Assessment

Bechtel's first job under its $680 million contract with USAID was to assess Iraq's infrastructure in six areas: surface transportation, aviation, buildings, water, electricity, and the Umm Qasr Port in southern Iraq. During late April and May 2003, Bechtel teams surveyed dozens of sites across the country. What they found disturbed them. Iraq's infrastructure had collapsed. They estimated rehabilitation costs at about $16 billion.[2]

Bechtel's assessment identified five challenges then confronting the U.S. reconstruction program: (1) worsening security, (2) poor interagency coordination, (3) limited access to information, (4) confusing contracting regulations (5) the prevalence of unexploded ordnance. The report predicted that Iraq's deteriorating security situation would cause reconstruction costs to skyrocket.

The ultimate success of the reconstruction program, Bechtel further noted, demanded improved coordination among the U.S. government agencies involved.[3] Bechtel urged the CPA to adopt a new systemic approach to rehabilitating Iraq's infrastructure because: "Power, water, airports, rail, and the port are all integrated systems, and each has to be understood as critical components of an overall infrastructure network to arrive at the most economic and effective implementation plan."[4]

The USACE Oil Sector Assessment

In May 2003, USACE, working with Task Force Restore Iraqi Oil, KBR, and the Iraqi Ministry of Oil, surveyed Iraq's oil infrastructure. USACE's report approximated oil sector damage at $457 million from the war and $943 million from postwar looting, estimating reconstruction funding requirements at $1.7 billion. But USACE advised that this figure could vary by as much as 40 percent.[5]

USACE's assessment underscored the need to sequence and integrate oil facility repair with infrastructure work in other sectors. The electrical power grid depended on fuel from the oil sector, and oil production facilities required a steady supply of electricity. Power plants and oil facilities needed water to cool generators. The assessment found that "[a] failure of one component in the system [created] a related problem elsewhere in the system."[6]

Systemic interdependence demanded a high degree of coordination between the Iraqi ministries of oil and electricity—coordination that would be missing for most of the next five years. USACE emphasized the importance of obtaining Iraqi input at every step of the rebuilding process, highlighting the need to build capacity so that Iraqis could properly operate and maintain the new parts of their infrastructure. Like Bechtel, USACE flagged the growing security problem as a major obstacle to further progress.[7]

The UN Assessment

A joint assessment team from the UN and the World Bank spent the summer of 2003 in Iraq evaluating the country's development needs, in part to prepare for a donors' conference scheduled for October 2003 in Madrid. The team's report documented the severe consequences of Saddam's neglect of and under-investment in Iraq's infrastructure, economy, and social institutions.[8]

The UN calculated that rebuilding Iraq would cost at least $56 billion over three years, with $36 billion needed for health, education, agriculture, private-sector development, government capacity building, and the rule of law. The assessment addressed neither oil nor security, opting instead to include CPA's $20 billion estimates for these sectors.[9] Like Bechtel and USACE, the UN report warned that, unless the Coalition restored security across Iraq, the economic and political transformation of the country could not proceed:

> Security concerns are paramount to the Iraqi population, influencing their ability to move freely, engage in work and education, and participate in the burgeoning political process. Without security, progress in rebuilding the critical infrastructure, health and education systems, and access to electricity and clean water that have been degraded and destroyed by years of corruption, conflict, neglect, and sanctions may be too slow to provide a noticeable improvement in the quality of life and reassure the Iraqi people of the benefits of a transition to an open and democratic society.[10]

The UN also emphasized the need to strengthen government institutions and to restore "core human services." It identified factors that could impede Iraq's recovery. High on the list was the requirement to restore the almost nonexistent executive and administrative capacities of Iraq's public institutions, most acutely revealed in the absence of an effective financial management system.[11]

The CSIS Assessment

In June 2003, at the request of Secretary Rumsfeld, John Hamre, president of the Center for Strategic and International Studies (CSIS), led a delegation of post-conflict reconstruction experts to Iraq to determine the country's rebuilding needs. Hamre and his team visited nine of the country's eighteen provinces and met with the CPA's senior leadership. The CSIS report concluded that the United States faced an "enormous task" in Iraq, would have "to stay the course" for several years, and would need to provide significant initial funding for reconstruction programs.[12]

CSIS also pointedly warned that the CPA had to address immediately the deteriorating security situation in Iraq. Hamre recommended engaging more Iraqis at every level of the reconstruction effort, expanding programs that could provide Iraqis with employment opportunities, and decentralizing political power to the provinces. The CSIS report advised that "[the] CPA must be given rapid and flexible funding," adding that "business as usual" was "not an option for operations in Iraq, nor can it be for the funding."[13]

A New Strategic Vision
Concurrent with the outside assessments, the CPA's Office of Strategic Planning drafted CPA's *Vision for Iraq*, which supplanted ORHA's *Unified Mission Plan*.[14] Dayton Maxwell, a former USAID official who had served with JTF-4 during prewar planning, was the senior civilian in CPA's policy planning office, and Lieutenant Colonel Robert Polk was the senior military officer.[15] They both had helped craft ORHA's *Unified Mission Plan* before the war.[16]

The *Vision for Iraq* defined the CPA's mission as working to achieve "the conditions for a free, sovereign, democratically elected representative government." The document outlined, in general terms, five "core foundations" that CPA would lay to support Iraq through its democratic transformation: security, essential services and civil society, economy, governance, and strategic communications.

The highest priority, according to the *Vision*, was "to create a secure and safe environment, without which the CPA recognized there could be little progress on other goals." The CPA would work to restore security across the country by recruiting and training Iraqi police and military forces. Other goals included promoting a rapid transition to a market economy and establishing an effective rule-of-law system. The document called for new programs to develop democracy, to create equitable criminal justice processes, to implement a new and fair penal code, and to construct new courthouses and prisons. The success of the *Vision* depended upon a "coherent and coordinated information campaign" that would explain the scope and nature of U.S. programs to all Iraqis.[17]

In mid-July, Ambassador Bremer sent the *Vision for Iraq* to the Pentagon. "I am confident," he wrote, "that this will put us on course for success."[18] By July 18, 2003, senior Pentagon officials had approved it.[19]

In the meantime, Ambassador Bremer had tasked Maxwell and Polk to expand the *Vision for Iraq* by identifying specific tasks aimed at implementing the five core foundations, and they quickly completed a new detailed framework, entitled *Achieving the Vision to Restore Full Sovereignty to the Iraqi People*. In late July, Bremer took the framework to Washington for briefings with the Congress, senior Administration officials, and the press. The 30-page document was the

CPA's first attempt to develop, in some detail, the litany of actions required to achieve the core foundational goals of the *Vision for Iraq*.[20]

The CPA's *Achieving the Vision* suffered from some serious flaws. First, Iraqis were not sufficiently consulted on it. The Iraqi Governing Council, which was appointed on July 13, was never given a chance to provide advice on it. Maxwell and Polk expressed concern at the time that the CPA was handing the Iraqis a fait accompli—a plan they were "just going to have to eat."[21] The CPA also had established overly ambitious infrastructure outcomes before ascertaining baseline conditions and before determining costs. Moreover, the outcomes had unrealistic completion dates, some by October 2003, just three months later.

The ambitious goals contained in *Achieving the Vision* included deploying 30,000 trained Iraqi police, re-establishing the Iraqi Border Guard, reopening all courthouses, building eleven new prisons and detention centers, reforming the ministries, improving electricity generation capacity to 4,000 megawatts, restoring basic health care services to prewar levels, rehabilitating 1,000 schools, and reopening the airports and railroads.[22] Even under the best of conditions, achieving these outcomes on a short timetable was virtually impossible.

Developing Iraq's Budget

In early July 2003, the CPA published a budget to fund ministry needs for the rest of calendar year 2003. CPA's senior advisors, then serving as the de facto ministers for each ministry, compiled what data they could find and developed a budget totaling $6.10 billion. The CPA predicted oil revenues for the rest of 2003 to be $3.46 billion and expected $432.7 million from taxes and the state-owned enterprises, leaving a deficit of $2.2 billion. Bremer planned to cover the difference with vested and seized Iraqi funds, the DFI, and new U.S. appropriations.

The new Iraqi budget provided only $609.5 million for reconstruction and capital improvements.[23] This could not begin to meet Iraq's many reconstruction needs. The CPA's economic team knew that without a major infusion of additional funds, it would not be possible to realize any of the objectives listed in *Achieving the Vision*.

On adoption of the 2003 budget, Ambassador Bremer ordered his senior advisors to develop, with their Iraqi counterparts, a 2004 budget. This effort produced more than $35 billion in ministerial requests, but Iraq's projected 2004 revenues amounted to less than $13 billion, leaving a projected deficit of $23 billion.[24]

"No matter how we pared the list," said Oliver, "we needed [over] $20 billion more than we had available."[25] Faced with a huge shortfall, Ambassador Bremer decided to ask the Congress for a dramatic increase in funding to support Iraq's relief and reconstruction. He would also look to the international community for significant contributions.

In July and August 2003, Oliver and the CPA's economic team developed a new supplemental funding request for Iraq reconstruction that would go to the Congress in September. They also shaped the U.S. proposal for the International Donors Conference planned in October.[26]

Asking Congress for Money

In late July 2003, Dave Oliver directed the CPA's senior advisors involved with infrastructure to contribute to a new reconstruction plan, which would provide the basis for the new supplemental request. Oliver charged Dave Nash, a retired rear admiral recently arrived in Baghdad as the deputy senior advisor to the Ministry of Transportation and Communications, to coordinate the plan's development.[27]

Just a few months earlier, Nash had been working as a construction manager in Birmingham, Alabama, for Parsons Brinckerhoff (a large U.S. contractor that would later receive sizable Iraq reconstruction contracts). He had made his career as a Navy engineer, rising to command the Naval Facilities Engineering Command and serving as Chief of Civil Engineers. Like many of the CPA's early recruits, he was in Iraq on a 90-day contract. With a wealth of experience in large public-works projects, Admiral Nash arrived at the Republican Palace just as CPA's leadership needed someone with significant construction expertise to develop an expansive strategy to rebuild Iraq's infrastructure.[28]

After briefly considering asking the Congress for $5 billion, Nash and his planners developed a much larger request. Working with CPA's senior advisors, Nash pulled together a long list of infrastructure projects that would cost about $27 billion. After whittling it down to $20.3 billion, Bremer approved the proposal in early August and sent it to Washington.

On August 15, 2003, Joshua Bolten, Director of the White House OMB, wrote Secretary Rumsfeld, objecting to the size of the CPA's request. The White House had already told the Congress that it would not ask for additional funding for Iraq and Afghanistan in 2003. Bolten said the CPA would have to provide a detailed justification before the Administration would consider going back to the Congress to argue for more money for Iraq reconstruction.[29]

The CPA had hired Tom Korologos as a senior counselor. Korologos, a veteran lobbyist, addressed Bolten's concerns in a memo to Bremer on August 17, 2003. "To delay getting our funds will be a political disaster for the President," he wrote. "His election will hang for a large part on show of progress in Iraq and without the funding this year, progress will grind to a halt." Korologos added that he did not believe that the Congress would turn down the supplemental request because "the faster the Iraq CPA succeeds, the quicker 'our 150,000 boys over there' will start coming home."[30]

By the end of August, the CPA had answered Bolten's demand for more data, producing a "Program/Integration Management Plan for Recovery, Reconstruction and Redevelopment of Iraq." The plan's stated objective was to "assist in restoring the stability of Iraq and the Iraqi economy by means of infrastructure and development." It emphasized that U.S. funds were essential to meet Iraq's critical infrastructure needs because oil production and revenues were stagnant.[31] "These needs are immediate and urgent," the plan asserted, adding that the CPA would "begin execution of these funds before the end of 2003."[32]

The CPA's answer satisfied Bolten. On September 6, 2003, OMB submitted a $20.3 billion supplemental request to the Congress. President Bush announced the next day that he had asked the Congress for a total of $87 billion to support Iraq and Afghanistan, including the $20.3 billion for Iraq's reconstruction, noting:

> This budget request will support our commitment to helping the Iraqi and Afghan people rebuild their own nations, after decades of oppression and mismanagement. We will provide funds to help them improve security. And we will help them to restore basic services, such as electricity and water, and to build new schools, roads, and medical clinics. This effort is essential to the stability of those nations, and, therefore, to our own security.[33]

USAID's Complaints

USAID officials were perturbed by both the process and the substance of the CPA's supplemental request, having been shut out from its development. They believed Bremer had acted "in a non-transparent way" and expressed grave concerns about the plan's failure to include sufficient money for capacity building, democracy programs, agriculture efforts, and economic development.[34] USAID Administrator Andrew Natsios sharply disagreed with the CPA's premise that a large-scale infrastructure program would quickly create jobs and help solve Iraq's most pressing problems. "Development is not building things," he said. "It's not engineering. It's institution building."[35]

USAID was particularly concerned about underinvestment in the agricultural sector, which, at the time of the 2003 invasion, was the country's second-largest employer. Natsios was shocked to find that the supplemental had zero for agricultural programs, which he said are essential "to stimulate the economy and keep all the young men in the rural areas," rather than have them stream into the cities where they could be recruited as insurgents.[36]

In August 2003, before the submission of the supplemental, USAID's Baghdad office sent a memo to Oliver outlining its objections and encouraging him to revise the request so that it addressed Iraq's long-term needs for capacity building and sustainability. Oliver responded that the Congress would not fund "soft" projects and that the request would not be changed.[37]

The dispute between the CPA and USAID intensified when USAID discovered that the CPA, a Defense Department organization, would manage all of the IRRF 2 funds. Lewis Lucke, USAID's Mission Director in Iraq, complained to Oliver:

> To exclude us—especially considering the success we have achieved and are achieving to date in our programs, and the fact that we are a professional development organization that is by nature operational overseas—seems short-sighted and territorial in the extreme to the detriment of the overall U.S. mission in Iraq.[38]

USAID then developed its own $5 billion supplemental funding request, emphasizing public health and education, the economy, government accountability, and technical support. It called for $3.25 billion to restore essential electricity, transportation, irrigation, and water infrastructure.[39] The proposal gained no traction, either within the Administration or on Capitol Hill. Relations between USAID and CPA officials continued to deteriorate during and after the submission of the 2003 supplemental request. These breakdowns, both personal and bureaucratic, would continue to affect the reconstruction program for years to come.[40]

Congressional Debates on the Supplemental

During the last two weeks of September 2003, the Congress held seven hearings on the supplemental, during which members from both parties demanded to know why Iraq was not shouldering more of the reconstruction program's financial burden. Some argued that the United States should provide support through loans, while others saw CPA's request as an extravagant "wish list."[41]

"When I look at some of these justifications and when I look at some of the postwar planning in general, two thoughts strike me," said Representative David Obey (D-WI), the ranking member of the House Committee on Appropriations. "It looks like it was put together by the president of an Optimists Club, rather than someone with an understanding of the world; and secondly, it looks like the execution plans have been put together more like an MBA term paper than a document that reflects a realistic understanding of the society that we're wishing to operate in."[42]

Senate and House committee members peppered the CPA with written "questions for the record" about contracting, management, and oversight. Some legislators were struck by the fact that the CPA request contained more than $15 billion for construction, but provided virtually no information about the contracting process. Others raised concerns that the CPA had failed to prioritize the sectors or projects within sectors and had not provided timetables for program completion.[43] One member observed that a construction program of the size and scope proposed by the CPA would take five to seven years to complete in the United States.

The CPA brushed off all objections: "Our estimates differ. While some of the most complex projects may take several years to complete, we anticipate that the majority of construction can be completed much sooner."[44]

The Congress also raised concerns that the huge appropriation would serve as a disincentive to international donors. The CPA countered that Iraq would need between $50 billion and $75 billion for reconstruction—well above the supplemental request—and that it planned on presenting a "rich package of projects that should appeal to the donors" at the Madrid conference in October.[45]

The Madrid International Donors Conference

Creating that "rich package" fell to CPA's Council for International Coordination. CPA Regulation Number 5 created the council on June 18, 2003, "to be the CPA's focal point and coordination body for international assistance in the relief, recovery and development of Iraq."[46] Bremer tasked the council, chaired by Marek Belka—an economics professor who had served as Poland's deputy prime minister and minister of finance—to coordinate assistance from governments as well as international and nongovernmental organizations, make recommendations to the PRB on international assistance efforts in Iraq, coordinate with the IMF and the World Bank, and—most important—prepare for the October 2003 Madrid Donors Conference.[47]

As he organized for Madrid, Belka faced two significant challenges. First, he had to put together a plausible list of projects that interested donors might support. Second, he had to overcome the lack of interest on the part of certain countries, such as Germany, France, and Russia, that had opposed the Iraq invasion and thus might be disinclined to support Iraq's economic recovery.

Planning for Madrid suffered a devastating blow when, on August 19, 2003, a truck bomb destroyed the UN headquarters in Baghdad, killing the Secretary-General's Special Representative, Sergio Vieira de Mello, and 21 others.[48] This tragedy caused the UN to pull out of Iraq, and cast a pall over Belka's efforts.[49] The attack eventually led many countries to conclude that security was so bad in Iraq that contributing funds could have little positive effect in the near term.

On October 16, 2003, the UN issued Security Council Resolution 1511, which aimed to assuage international concerns about America's expanding role and lengthening stay in Iraq. The new resolution stressed the temporary nature of the Coalition's occupation and encouraged the United States to transfer sovereignty to the Iraqis as soon as practicable. Issued shortly before the Madrid Donors Conference, UNSCR 1511 was crafted in part to calm the concerns of donor nations about U.S. plans for Iraq and thereby persuade them to contribute to Iraq's reconstruction.[50] But it did not have this effect.

On October 23 and 24, 2003, a total of 76 countries, 20 international organizations—including the IMF and the World Bank—and 13 nongovernmental organizations participated in the Madrid Donors Conference. The United States pledged $18.4 billion (the amount of the pending supplemental), and the other countries combined pledged a total of $13.5 billion in grants and loans. Fewer than half of the attendees announced contributions. Germany, France, and Russia pledged nothing. Japan offered the most, contributing more than a third of the total non-U.S. amount pledged—$1.5 billion in grants for 2004 and $3.4 billion in loans.[51]

To help manage international donations, the UN created the International Reconstruction Fund Facility, which the UN Development Group and the World Bank would oversee. All qualified companies from any country could bid on contracts for projects paid for by the fund.[52]

Congress Passes IRRF 2

The Congress debated the CPA's supplemental request during October 2003, and, on November 6, it passed the "Emergency Supplemental Appropriations Act for Defense and for the Reconstruction of Iraq and Afghanistan for Fiscal Year 2004," allocating $18.4 billion to the Iraq Relief and Reconstruction Fund (IRRF 2). The Congress made the money available for two years, meaning that it had to be fully contracted by September 30, 2006. Notably, the Congress required the CPA to provide an accounting for all revenues—domestic and foreign, including Iraqi—used for Iraq's reconstruction.[53] The Act also created a new oversight office—the Inspector General for the Coalition Provisional Authority—which became SIGIR in October 2004.

Although the Congress approved the CPA's funding request almost intact, the legislators imposed greater controls and more oversight for IRRF 2, dividing the money among ten sectors and giving the CPA limited authority to make adjustments. The Congress provided that the CPA could shift up to ten percent from one sector to another, but no sector could be increased by more than twenty percent without congressional approval.

Iraq Relief and Reconstruction 2 Sector Allocations ($ Billions)	
Sector	Allocation
Electricity	$5.56
Water Resources and Sanitation	$4.33
Security and Law Enforcement	$3.24
Oil Infrastructure	$1.89
Justice, Public Safety Infrastructure, and Civil Society	$1.32
Health Care	$0.79
Transportation and Telecommunications	$0.50
Roads, Bridges, and Construction	$0.37
Education, Refugees, Human Rights, and Governance	$0.28
Private Sector Development	$0.15
Total	$18.44

Source: P.L. 108-106, Emergency Supplemental Appropriations Act for Defense and for the Reconstruction of Iraq and Afghanistan for Fiscal Year 2004, November 6, 2003. Numbers may not add up due to rounding.

The IRRF 2 legislation stipulated that, in addition to the CPA, only five agencies could use the funds to implement reconstruction programs—the Department of Defense, the Department of State, the Department of the Treasury, the Department of Health and Human Services, and USAID. The Congress encouraged each to "provide significant financial resources, technical assistance, and capacity building to counterpart organizations led by Iraqis."[54]

Section 2207 of the legislation required the OMB, in consultation with the CPA's Administrator, to submit quarterly reports to the Congress on the status of IRRF 2 projects. The first *Section 2207 Report* was due on January 5, 2004, and it had to contain a complete list of proposed projects.[55] The CPA now had less than two months to compile the list of projects, develop a spend plan, and build an office to manage what quickly had become the largest foreign reconstruction program for a single country in U.S. history.

CHAPTER 10
CONTRACTING BILLIONS FOR RECONSTRUCTION

They [CPA] sat down in a four-day period and came up with a
list of projects of what they wanted to do. And they were all high-
*end capital expenditures: build the big this, build the big that.**

Lieutenant General Peter Chiarelli
Commander, Multi-National Corps-Iraq (2006)

In early November 2003, the Congress appropriated $18.4 billion to the Iraq
Relief and Reconstruction Fund (IRRF 2). The CPA had established the Program
Management Office (PMO) to oversee the burgeoning reconstruction program,
and Bremer had appointed Dave Nash, the man who had helped develop the
new reconstruction plan, as the PMO's first director. Nash quickly shaped a new
management structure for the CPA's reconstruction efforts and began developing
a program of projects. In the IRRF 2 legislation, the Congress required the CPA
to produce a "spend plan"—a comprehensive list of projects, including estimated
costs and timelines for completion by early January 2004.

The $18.4 billion IRRF 2 program would included $12.6 billion for construction projects and another $4 billion for procurement, including everything from
personal protective gear, weapons, and vehicles for Iraq's security forces to construction materials for the oil, water, and electricity sectors. The remaining $1.8
billion was for capacity development, governance, and economic reform programs.[1] Almost all of the IRRF 2 was designated as Defense Department money,
meaning that the Pentagon was ultimately responsible for the use of this reconstruction money.

Creating the Program Management Office
The CPA created the PMO because USACE and USAID—the two U.S. agencies
with established systems for managing large construction and international assistance programs—reported that they did not have the resources in Iraq to manage
an $18.4 billion rebuilding effort. USAID said it did not have the staff or organi-
zational capacity to manage more than a $5 billion program. USACE was just
starting to establish its new office in Iraq—the Gulf Region Division (GRD)—to
manage infrastructure projects, and it would not open until January 2004.[2]

---

* SIGIR interview with Lieutenant General Peter Chiarelli, former Commander of MNC-I, February
19, 2008.

Ambassador Bremer had to move rapidly on his mammoth new reconstruction plan to demonstrate the U.S. commitment to restoring Iraq's essential services and promoting the country's economic development. The question was how to do so. With USACE and USAID out of the picture, Admiral Nash persuaded Bremer that, by consolidating management of the entire program under the PMO and staffing it largely with contractors, the CPA could launch the IRRF 2 program by the end of 2003. To meet this timeline, Nash proposed outsourcing most of the management to private contractors.

Steve Browning, who headed the CPA's Office of Iraqi Infrastructure, warned Ambassador Bremer that it would be impossible to begin so large a program that quickly because contracting regulations demanded a rigorous bidding process. "You can't get contracts in place by that time," Browning told Bremer. But Nash had assured Bremer that, given the importance of the mission, the CPA could get special dispensation from the Defense Department to accelerate contracting processes.[3] Although the Defense Department did expedite the process, it was not able to award contracts as quickly as Nash predicted.

Dov Zakheim, the Under Secretary of Defense (Comptroller) and chief financial officer for the Department of Defense, initially opposed the creation of the PMO, which he saw as a form of "empire building."[4] He thought it a duplication of existing USAID and USACE expertise. But Nash met with Zakheim at the Pentagon in mid-September and "convinced him that no entity in Iraq or Washington was going to take on this work with existing resources and using current procedures."[5]

At the beginning of September 2003, the PMO had a staff of one—Admiral Nash—and no money. On September 9, Zakheim—despite his reservations about the office—allocated $10 million to it for "personnel, logistics and contractor support for approximately six months."[6] A week later, the Department of the Army authorized USACE to spend another $9 million to support the PMO.[7] USACE then provided Nash with fifteen people from two private firms, Stanley Consultants and Michael Baker Corporation.[8]

Outsourcing Oversight

Nash created a four-tiered organization to oversee the Iraq reconstruction effort: the PMO, the PMO Support Office, six Sector Program Management Offices (SPMOs), and twelve design-build contractors.[9] Although the organizational structure included government supervision of contractors (as required by the FAR), Nash's plan ultimately outsourced to private contractors much of the program-management and oversight responsibilities, thus diluting the government's authority.

Iraq Relief and Reconstruction Design-build Program Management Structure

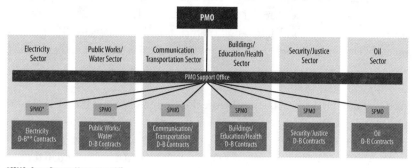

*SPMO: Sector Program Management Office
**D-B: Design-build

Source: SIGIR, *Iraq Reconstruction: Lessons in Contracting and Procurement*, July 2006, 54.

Staffed by a small group of government employees at the top, the PMO nominally oversaw the entire operation. Immediately under it (on the organizational chart) was a private management company that worked with USACE in the PMO Support Office to supervise the six SPMOs, which were run by private contractors who supplemented a handful of government employees. Each of the six SPMOs supervised two design-build construction contractors that carried out projects in a specific reconstruction sector.[10]

Major General Ronald Johnson, the USACE Director of Military Programs, was Nash's deputy director, and he supervised the overall reconstruction operation. USACE engineers provided much of the quality assurance for IRRF 2 contract execution. In January 2004, Major General Johnson became Commanding General of USACE's Gulf Region Division and continued to supply most of the manpower for reconstruction quality-assurance programs.[11]

To staff the management offices, Nash proposed hiring 100 government personnel to perform the inherently governmental management and oversight functions required by government regulations.[12] But the PMO was never able to hire more than half the government staff it needed. Thus, it relied heavily—perhaps excessively—on the contractors in the SPMOs to oversee reconstruction. This unprecedented outsourcing of traditionally governmental responsibilities raised concerns on Capitol Hill.[13]

The six primary infrastructure sectors under the PMO's aegis were: electricity; public works and water; security and justice; communications and transportation; oil; and buildings, education, and health. The SPMOs wrote construction requirements and worked with the design-build firms to develop projects. USACE oversaw construction after project designs were completed and work had commenced.[14]

The twelve "design-build" construction contractors were awarded indefinite delivery, indefinite quantity (IDIQ) cost-plus contracts for design, engineering, and physical work in the sectors. To prevent conflicts of interest, contractors could not win management and design-build contracts in the same sector. The government also reserved the right to restrict any company to a total of four contracts.[15]

Start-up Problems
At the end of October 2003, just before the Congress passed the IRRF 2 supplemental, the PMO had insufficient funds and too few personnel to operate effectively. Although Pentagon Comptroller Zakheim had authorized $10 million for the PMO, it took two months for the money to wend its way through the bureaucracy. The PMO did not receive this operating capital until mid-November 2003. According to Zakheim, OMB acted slowly in allocating the money. "The problem was that the OMB insisted on approval," Zakheim said, "and OMB became kind of a black hole, from which funds would emerge on what appeared to be a whimsical basis."[16] The OMB demanded detailed descriptions from the CPA on how it planned to spend IRRF 2 dollars before it would release them.[17] It released no IRRF 2 funds until after the CPA submitted its spend plan in early January 2004.

When the Congress passed the IRRF 2 supplemental in early November 2003, the PMO consisted of Admiral Nash, two government employees detailed from USACE, and thirteen USACE contractors. Of the 100 government employees Nash requested, only 8 had arrived by January 2004.[18]

Staff shortages were not the only problem; the skills the new PMO employees brought to the job were frequently not the right ones. A year after the PMO was created and just before the Program Contracting Office subsumed it in the summer of 2004, a frustrated Admiral Nash would have just half the number of people he needed—roughly one government employee for every $400 million the PMO was overseeing, or about ten times more than the average State Department contracting officer managed.[19]

The Contracting Plan
In early September 2003, Admiral Nash notified Tina Ballard, Deputy Assistant Secretary of the Army for Policy and Procurement, that the CPA would need a major acquisition plan to award the IRRF 2 contracts. Ballard quickly assembled a joint Department of Defense team, which included contracting personnel from USACE and the Navy, to develop a Single Acquisition Management Plan (SAMP) for IRRF 2.[20]

The SAMP established procedures for the award of twelve large IRRF 2 design-build contracts and six reconstruction management contracts. It created selection boards and developed guidelines to prevent conflicts of interest. To maximize flexibility, the SAMP provided that all contracts would be IDIQ contracts. These contracts allow for the provision of an indefinite quantity of supplies or services during a fixed period of time; they are used when the government cannot determine in advance the precise construction requirements.[21]

The SAMP team issued requests for bids in mid-December 2003.[22] Only companies from the United States, Iraq, and force-contributing nations could bid.[23] All proposals—except for those in the oil sector, which USACE had solicited during summer 2003—had to be submitted by February 5, 2004. The government received 53 bids on the contracts but made no awards until late March.[24]

Several factors caused the IRRF 2 contract-award process to be slower than Ambassador Bremer wanted. Because of concerns raised by the Congress about prewar sole-source contracting and IRRF 1's many limited-competition awards, the SAMP source-selection boards scrupulously complied with the requirements of the Federal Acquisition Regulation. But complying with the FAR's complex procedural requirements meant that more time was needed to review the bids.[25]

The Program of Projects

The PMO built its project list based on the ten sectors defined by the IRRF 2 legislation. Nash and his fifteen USACE contractors, in consultation with the CPA's senior advisors, developed the first master project list. The senior advisors had already developed reconstruction proposals with their ministers, as part of the 2004 budget process, and they incorporated many of these into the IRRF 2 project list. The PMO tracked the projects by using Project Identification Forms (PIFs), which described the justification, scope, and estimated cost of each proposed project and gave it a priority.[26] The information from 5,000 PIFs was entered into a "monster Excel spreadsheet," from which the PMO derived its final project list.[27]

The quality of the project list was uneven. Some ministries, such as Water Resources, had complete designs sitting on the shelf that had been "waiting for Saddam to go away so they could build these projects."[28] But others had nothing. Moreover, some ministries disagreed with the CPA's decisions. For example, the Ministry of Health favored building large hospitals, but the CPA wanted to focus on small primary-care clinics. Although Iraqis were accustomed to providing and receiving medical services through a hospital system, the senior advisor to the Ministry of Health believed that a network of clinics focusing on preventive and primary health care would most effectively and efficiently help Iraq meet nationwide health care needs.[29]

To estimate the costs for each project, the PMO took the base cost of each project and added fixed charges for security, transportation, procurement, program management, and award fees. The PMO estimated that security costs would add seven percent, a figure provided by Bechtel. Bechtel developed this figure, assuming that the environment would be, in military parlance, "semi-permissive."[30] But by late 2003, Iraq's security environment had drastically deteriorated.[31]

On December 1, the PMO presented a list of 1,706 prioritized projects to Ambassador Bremer and representatives of USAID, the military, and CPA's senior advisors. This was the first time that most of the participants, including USAID, had seen a comprehensive project list.[32] The group had nine days to review the plan and comment on it before Bremer sent it to Washington. "It was like a grocery list," said Nash, "You could go down so far, draw a line, and that's how much money you had, and then we took the rest of the projects and we said, 'We'll give those to the Iraqis.'" Projects that fell below the funding cut-off for each sector were assigned to Iraq's Ministry of Development, Planning, and Cooperation.[33] The ministry was expected to find other donors to fund them.[34]

In mid-December 2003, after receiving the CPA's program of projects, the OMB convened an interagency meeting to discuss it, inviting USAID Administrator Andrew Natsios to attend. Other participants included National Security Advisor Condoleezza Rice; her deputy, Stephen Hadley; Robin Cleveland, associate director of the OMB; the Pentagon Comptroller, Dov Zakheim; and Deputy Secretary of Defense Wolfowitz. According to Natsios, Cleveland—who had been skeptical about the CPA's planned use of the IRRF 2 allocations—wanted him in the room because she knew he would make a strong argument against certain aspects of the proposed plan.[35]

Cleveland was right. Natsios told the group: "If this thing gets approved, you'll have no money for elections, no money for rebuilding local governance, no money for building the university system, no money for the health system." Calling the plan "a recipe for disaster," he recommended reserving some of the money for non-construction projects and contingencies.[36] Natsios strenuously objected to the CPA's big infrastructure approach, arguing that it flouted the lessons learned from decades of international development experience. Wolfowitz and Hadley responded to Natsios's concerns by directing that $4 billion in IRRF 2 funds be held in reserve, preventing the PMO from immediately allocating or obligating that money.[37]

Two weeks later, Natsios received an angry call from Ambassador Bremer, accusing him of destroying the IRRF 2 plan. Natsios countered that CPA had put together an unrealistic and excessively optimistic construction timeline. Bremer believed that, under his original plan, the CPA could have begun construction by March. But Natsios, who had managed Boston's "Big Dig," one of the largest and most problem-ridden construction projects in American history, viewed the CPA's timetable as "utterly ridiculous."[38]

On January 5, 2004, the OMB delivered the CPA's project plan in the first *Section 2207 Report*, to the Congress. The submission included the first of what would become many requests for re-allocations of IRRF 2 funds. In this initial re-alignment, the OMB shifted funds within the security sector to allocate additional funds for democracy-building efforts, a step driven in part by the November 15, 2003 decision to transfer sovereignty to Iraq by June 30, 2004.[39] Other readjustments included taking $150 million from the budget for the New Iraqi Army to augment the border enforcement program and moving $25 million from the witness protection program to support democracy projects.[40] The OMB observed that maintaining "flexibility in the allocation of resources among projects and for new projects" was critical, given the evolving security and political situations in Iraq.[41]

Managing Project Information

The Congress authorized $50 million as part of the IRRF 2 supplemental to help the CPA meet its reporting and monitoring obligations. The OMB apportioned the money to the Department of Defense for the CPA's operating expenses, but the PMO did not get any of this money until May 2004, a month before the CPA expired.[42]

The PMO's leadership decided against adopting any existing project information management systems, because none offered "the full complement of integrated capabilities" they believed they needed.[43] The PMO developed a hybrid system, combining an asset-management program with off-the-shelf software, but the hybrid system did not work well.[44] The PMO needed an integrated program management system from the start in order to stay on top of the program, track contracts, prevent overspending, and measure progress. But it would be many months before it had a usable system.

"You lose track of a program, a big program like this with 3,000 projects, you never get it back," observed Nash.[45] The delay in creating an integrated information system that could track projects had long-term consequences, hampering program and project management for years to come.

The "Bridging" Contracts

When it became clear in late 2003 that the Defense Department would take longer than hoped to award the IRRF 2 design-build contracts, USAID and PMO took innovative steps to implement projects by other contractual means.

The Bechtel Contract

In October 2003, USAID solicited proposals for Phase II of its infrastructure program to bridge the period between the end of IRRF 1-funded operations and the time that IRRF 2 design–build contractors could mobilize to Iraq. USAID had awarded its original contract to Bechtel without full and open competition. This time three firms, including Bechtel, submitted bids.

On January 4, 2004, USAID awarded Bechtel another large Iraq reconstruction contract, this one for $1.82 billion. Upon award, Bechtel quickly bolstered its Iraq staff, anticipating an array of new projects from the PMO. But the PMO made little use of this contract, issuing just four task orders to Bechtel—for a total of $180 million of work—between January and March 2004.[46]

The reason for PMO's minimal use of the Bechtel bridge contract may have stemmed from the increasingly fractious relationship between USAID and the CPA. USAID officials believed that, after Natsios's successful fight to put a hold on $4 billion in IRRF 2 money, Admiral Nash reacted by limiting the number of task orders issued to Bechtel.[47] Nash denies this was the case.[48] He said his problems with USAID boiled down to a simple power struggle. Describing it as a great "harangue," Nash said the "argument was over who is in charge" and "how things will be run." He insisted that the CPA needed one central organization, in this case the PMO, to manage the program, but that USAID "did not understand—or agree with—this concept."[49]

The simmering enmity between the CPA and USAID weakened reconstruction progress at this critical juncture. With no new work forthcoming during the winter of 2004, USAID's Mission Director James "Spike" Stephenson confronted Nash in March about the lack of task orders and "reminded him of the Bechtel contract's purpose." Nash demurred, saying that he wanted all the work to move ahead in unison. Stephenson took his complaints to Bremer but nothing changed.[50]

At the end of March 2004, Stephenson met with Tom Gibb, Nash's deputy for programs, and they worked out a truce that resulted in a trickle of task orders. The Bechtel contract, however, would not be fully utilized until after the CPA dissolved in June 2004. During this period of relative inactivity, USAID still had to pay Bechtel's entire overhead costs, ultimately reducing the amount available for reconstruction projects.[51]

The Air Force Center for Environmental Excellence

The CPA's reconstruction priorities in December 2003 included renovating Iraqi military facilities for the New Iraqi Army by June 2004. Realizing that the design-build contracts would be awarded later than hoped, Nash looked for existing contracts that he could use for construction projects.

The Air Force Center for Environmental Excellence (AFCEE) in San Antonio, Texas, had an existing IDIQ contract—called the Worldwide Environmental Restoration and Construction Contract—for a wide range of construction services at U.S. military bases around the world. In January 2004, the U.S. Air Force Chief of Staff approved the CPA's request to use the AFCEE contract to accomplish construction projects in Iraq.[52]

The IRRF 2 supplemental had allotted $745 million for the construction of New Iraqi Army facilities. By the end of May 2004, the PCO had awarded AFCEE fifteen task orders valued at $481.2 million. Three of these, totaling $42.3 million, went to non-military projects, such as the reconstruction of schools, government buildings, and pumping stations. These appeared to be beyond the scope of the CPA's original request. A CPA Inspector General (CPA-IG) audit of the contracts subsequently found that "AFCEE's role in awarding task orders on behalf of the CPA was not clearly defined, and the continued use of AFCEE's contract vehicle provided less than necessary transparency to the public."[53]

IRRF 2 Contract Awards

In March 2004, the Defense Department announced the award of the major IRRF 2 design-build construction and program management contracts for Iraq's reconstruction. Over $5 billion in new contracts had been approved in less than 90 days. A typical contracting process involving awards of this size could take over a year.[54]

AECOM Technology Corporation won the umbrella services management contract, valued at $50 million, to support PMO's program management. The following two tables show the program management contracts and design-build construction contracts that were awarded:

IRRF 2 PMO Program Management Contracts		
Sector	Contractor(s)	Maximum Value ($ Millions)
Electricity	Iraq Power Alliance Joint Venture (Parsons Energy and Chemical Group, Parsons Brinckerhoff – USA/UK)	$55
Water and Public Works	CH2M Hill and Parsons Water Infrastructure (USA)	$55
Communications and Transportation	Berger/URS Joint Venture (Louis Berger Group & URS Group – USA)	$15
Building, Education and Health	Berger/URS Joint Venture (Louis Berger Group & URS Group – USA)	$15
Security and Justice	Berger/URS Joint Venture (Louis Berger Group & URS Group – USA)	$30
Oil	Foster Wheeler (UK)	$30

Source: SIGIR, "Iraq Reconstruction: Lessons Learned in Contracting and Procurement," July 2006, 59-60.

Sector	Contractor(s)	Maximum Value ($ millions)
IRRF 2 Design-Build Construction Contracts		
Electricity, Generation	Fluor-Amec Joint Venture (USA/UK)	$500
Electricity, Transmission and Distribution (North)	Washington Group International (USA)	$500
Electricity, Transmission and Distribution (South)	Perini Corp. (USA)	$500
Public Works (North)	Fluor-Amec Joint Venture (USA/UK)	$600
Public Works (South)	Fluor-Amec Joint Venture (USA/UK)	$500
Water Resources	Washington Group International & Black and Veatch (USA)	$600
Communications	Lucent Technologies (USA)	$75
Transportation	Contrack/AICI/OIC/Archirodon Joint Venture (USA/Egypt/Netherlands/Panama/UAE)	$325
Building, Education, and Health	Parsons Delaware (USA)	$500
Security and Justice	Parsons Delaware (USA)	$900

Source: SIGIR, "Iraq Reconstruction: Lessons Learned in Contracting and Procurement," July 2006, 59-60.

USACE already had awarded two design-build contracts for the oil sector in January. The one for northern Iraq went to Parsons Iraq Joint Venture ($800 million); the one for the oil-rich southern region went to Kellogg, Brown and Root ($1.2 billion).[55]

Nash demanded that the IRRF 2 contractors move quickly, giving them 30 days to deploy to Iraq and directing that each be prepared to execute $500 million dollars in work. This proved an expensive demand. The contractors did quickly mobilize significant numbers of personnel and equipment, putting large construction forces on the ground in very short order. But most contractors did not receive task orders for reconstruction work until months later because of the PMO's slow management practices, the worsening security situation, and the widespread uncertainties that accompanied the CPA's administrative transition, as well as the program review by Ambassador John Negroponte after he took over from Bremer.

By the time the CPA closed its doors at the end of June 2004, the PMO had spent only $366 million of the $18.4 billion IRRF 2 appropriation.[56] Bremer was never able to realize his grand reconstruction vision.

CHAPTER 11
RESTORING IRAQ'S CAPACITY TO GOVERN

The CPA came and they were obsessed [with] decentralized government... I kept telling them, before you devolve power, you have to have power to devolve. We don't have power to devolve.*

Samir Sumaida'ie
Iraqi Governing Council Member (2003-2004)

The CPA, the military, and USAID adopted different approaches to restoring Iraq's national, regional, and local governments. The CPA initially concentrated on finding suitable candidates for the new Iraqi Governing Council and on restarting the national ministries. Ambassador Bremer issued a series of orders to improve governance by reforming Saddam-era institutions and creating new organizations to combat corruption. At the same time, the U.S. military and USAID launched an array of projects to establish regional and local councils across Iraq and to encourage community participation in governance.

Local Governance Needs

In Saddam Hussein's Iraq, Baghdad firmly controlled all aspects of governance. The Ba'ath Party appointed provincial governors—known as "mini-Saddams"—and Saddam's directors general extended ministry control into the provinces, exerting authority over local budgets, administering essential services, and managing state-owned enterprises. The provincial councils possessed nominal power, while local councils protected Saddam's interests at the district and neighborhood level.[1]

The 2003 invasion shattered this repressive system, with most senior Ba'ath Party officials fleeing as local bureaucracies dissolved.[2] Remnants of provincial councils and a handful of directors general continued minimal operations, but virtually all connections between Baghdad and local governments collapsed.[3] Ambassador Bremer arrived in Iraq to find governance in disarray. Several initiatives—some led by the U.S. military, some by USAID—were underway, all seeking to fill the post-Saddam governance vacuum.

---

* SIGIR interview with Samir Sumaida'ie, Iraqi Ambassador to the United States and former Iraqi Governing Council Member, March 11, 2008.

The Military Builds Local Governments

Coalition military commanders entered Iraq with, among other duties, a general mission to establish regional and local councils with whom they could work to develop governance in their areas of operation. They did not, however, have any specific guidance on how to establish new councils. Consequently, each commander devised a political process as he saw fit.

In early May 2003, Major General David Petraeus—then commanding the 101st Airborne Division in northern Iraq—assembled a new city council in Mosul, the capital of Ninewa province, establishing qualifications for council members and deciding how the local populace would select them. Over a 10-day period, Petraeus and his team organized a city-wide convention where some 270 delegates, representing all of Mosul's religious and ethnic groups, elected a new 24-member city council and a mayor.[4] "We had to hammer all this out, and obviously all of it was very torturous and bloody battles, and nobody thought they had enough representation," said Petraeus. "I think it was the ten toughest days of my life because everybody wanted something more than what they had. Everybody had a grievance."[5]

Lieutenant General James Conway, Commander of the 1st Marine Expeditionary Force, which controlled Najaf in central Iraq, took a different approach. He scheduled province-wide elections so that Iraqis could directly choose a new provincial council. Conway, who would later become the Commandant of the Marine Corps, set the elections for July 4, 2003. By mid-June, the Marines had registered political parties and were printing ballots. When Scott Carpenter, CPA's Director of Governance, found out about Conway's plan, he told him that Iraq had neither a constitution nor an electoral law upon which to base such an election.[6] Ambassador Bremer also said he was concerned that Shi'a Islamist parties "would clamor for them across the south since they were most likely to win in those early days."[7] At the last moment, the CPA persuaded Conway to cancel the elections.[8]

As the U.S. military established provincial and local Iraqi councils, they expected civilian agencies to rush in with resources to support the new councils. USAID had awarded three contracts to support local governance, to develop community-based organizations, and to provide local grants for reconstruction projects. The largest governance contract—valued at $168 million—went to the Research Triangle Institute (RTI) for the creation of transparent and accountable local and provincial governments, the provision of training to strengthen civil society, and the restoration of basic services.[9]

USAID's Local Governance Program
On April 22, 2003—eleven days after receiving its contract—RTI sent an advance team to Kuwait, expecting to have about a month to organize before entering Iraq. But USAID ordered RTI to move out immediately.[10] The first group of RTI contractors promptly crossed the border and headed for Basrah, while the second set out for Baghdad to help create the capital's new city council.[11]

Within days of getting the "go order," the first RTI team—driving Chevy Suburbans loaded with tents, fuel, food, satellite phones, and office supplies—pulled into Basrah, the largest city in southern Iraq. What they found was a disaster: public offices stripped of all furnishings, widespread looting, and no basic services.[12] The British forces controlling the city asked RTI to engage with the city's provincial council, and so Aaron Williams, RTI's team leader, consulted with the local Shi'a leaders on the councils "to determine what their priorities and needs were."[13]

The team sought out Iraqi technocrats to identify projects the city urgently needed for essential services.[14] By mid-May RTI had hired about two dozen Iraqis and was working with the local council to implement emergency water and electricity projects. The Basra office was the first of what would become 22 offices that RTI opened across Iraq during the spring and summer of 2003.[15]

Money for the provinces usually came from the Central Bank in Baghdad, but with the collapse of governing institutions, not a single dinar from the bank could make its way to the provinces. In the absence of funding from the capital, the U.S. military supported local councils by providing money through the fledgling CERP program. USAID also provided grants to assist councils with small infrastructure projects.[16]

Clarifying roles, responsibilities, and working relationships among the military, the CPA, and USAID and its contractors proved a major challenge. The military perceived USAID and its contractors as "relief in place" and "expected to rapidly hand over [to them] public services restoration, infrastructure reconstruction planning and coordination, and managing relationships with newly formed local councils throughout Iraq." But neither USAID nor its contractors had sufficient resources to sustain this mission.[17]

The Community Action Program
In April 2003, USAID began a Community Action Program (CAP) in Iraq, awarding contracts worth $120 million to five contractors.[18] Unlike other USAID-funded activities in Iraq, the CAP required local groups to contribute to projects. Implementation depended upon local facilitators and contractors, and "community action groups" composed of Iraqis elected by their neighbors.

The CAP used small amounts of reconstruction funding as a catalyst for local capacity-building initiatives. During the CPA's tenure, CAP contractors started more than 1,700 projects, costing about $61.7 million, ranging from sewage-system repair to rehabilitating schools and health clinics. A USAID Inspector General audit found that CAP generally achieved its intended goals, including citizen participation, local government cooperation, and local employment generation.[19]

The National Ministries

To help restart the looted and broken national ministries, USAID contractor Development Alternatives Incorporated (DAI) created a package called "Ministry in a Box." Each kit cost $122,000 and provided furniture and supplies for 100 civil servants. USAID employed dozens of small Iraqi companies across Baghdad to manufacture and assemble all the elements that went into each package. The ministries soon demanded more of them, and DAI had delivered 132 "Ministries in a Box" by the fall of 2003.[20]

The CPA depended chiefly on its senior advisors for hands-on capacity development. Among other things, the senior advisors assisted new Iraqi ministers in implementing the de-Ba'athification order, appointing and developing new ministry leadership, devising new budgets, identifying reconstruction projects, and securing sufficient CPA funding for ministry operations. But these efforts fell far short of meeting ministry capacity-development needs.

The CPA used the DFI to fund ministry budgets, which included paying for salaries, operating expenses, and capital projects. By April 2004, the CPA had authorized the expenditure of about $20 billion in DFI funds for Iraq's national budget. When the CPA transferred sovereignty to Iraq at the end of June 2004, the ministries had received $8.8 billion dollars to pay for administrative operations. But this money was poorly controlled, as a SIGIR audit would later find.[21]

The Iraqi Governing Council

Soon after his arrival in Baghdad, Ambassador Bremer directed his governance team to create a new Iraqi Governing Council as the first step in a process to transfer political power back to Iraqi control. The IGC would be the initial post-invasion Iraqi authority, although it would serve only in an advisory capacity. The IGC's creation also would satisfy UNSCR 1483's requirement that CPA form an Iraqi transitional administration (to work in partnership with the CPA) until the Iraqi people elected a new government.[22]

To find candidates for the IGC, the CPA's governance team canvassed the country, meeting with economic, religious, and tribal leaders.[23] Under the CPA's plan, the IGC would appoint a committee to draft a new constitution for Iraq. This would pave the way for national elections and a democratically elected government.

At the end of June 2003, while the CPA was still evaluating potential IGC members, Iraq's most respected Shi'a religious leader—the Grand Ayatollah Ali Husaini al-Sistani—issued a *fatwa* declaring that a council chosen by occupying authorities could not be charged with drafting the constitution. Grand Ayatollah Sistani said there was no guarantee that such a committee would write a constitution reflecting the true interests of the Iraqi people and expressing the nation's Islamic identity. Sistani demanded immediate elections for a new national assembly to draft a new constitution and present it to the people for a vote.[24] Bremer rejected Sistani's demand, pressing forward with his plans to form the IGC and have that body name a constitutional drafting committee.

The CPA named 25 Iraqi leaders of different religious and ethnic backgrounds to the IGC in mid-July. By early September 2003, the IGC had appointed new ministers to run the country's 25 ministries. The ministers reflected the religious and ethnic balance of the council. Although the diversity was commendable for its pluralist aims, it was also controversial because it laid the foundations for sectarian strongholds that would later develop in some ministries.[25] With the appointment of new ministers, the role of the CPA's senior advisors changed. They had been serving as the de facto ministers of Iraq, but they now took on an advisory capacity, serving the new Iraqi ministers. The senior advisors still greatly influenced ministry policy, but this shift signaled that the slow process of transferring governance authority back to Iraqi control had begun.

On September 8, 2003, Ambassador Bremer published a transitional roadmap for Iraq in a *Washington Post* opinion piece.[26] The article—a framework for an extended occupation by the CPA—set off alarm bells in Washington. Secretary Rumsfeld said it was the first time he realized that "Bremer was not ready to hand over responsibilities for governance of Iraq to Iraqi leadership" as quickly as originally envisioned and was instead "taking a route somewhat different than what we had believed would be the approach."[27] Bremer said that the op-ed contained nothing new, and that the Pentagon had approved the transition plan. He added that he spoke regularly with Rumsfeld and had sent the opinion piece to the Pentagon three days before it was published.[28]

Washington reacted quickly to the perception that the CPA was planning a long occupation. The White House formed an Iraq Stabilization Group under National Security Advisor Rice's aegis, and a push began to return full sovereignty to Iraqis more quickly than Bremer perhaps had anticipated.[29] Secretary Rumsfeld also convened strategic review meetings with Ambassador Bremer and General Abizaid to discuss the ramifications of Bremer's proposed transition plan.

Accelerating Sovereignty's Return

In late September 2003, Iraqi leaders, representatives of the international community, and senior officials in Washington began to pressure the CPA to announce a new timeline for returning sovereignty to Iraqis. Pentagon officials, in particular, pushed for a shortened timeline. Rumsfeld expressed "enthusiasm for the concept of granting sovereignty as soon as possible to the Council or some other group of Iraqis." Bremer replied that Iraqis should quickly be given more responsibility, but urged that it be done "in a manner that [has] a fair chance of success."[30]

On October 6, Bremer learned that President Bush had put National Security Advisor Condoleezza Rice in charge of the newly created White House Iraq Stabilization Group to coordinate Iraq policy and speed up reconstruction efforts.[31] Secretary Rice said the new organization was to support the Pentagon, not supplant it, but the move reflected growing tensions among agencies in Washington, between agencies and the White House, and between Washington and Baghdad.[32] Rice asked Ambassador Robert Blackwill, who had become deputy national security adviser for strategic policy in August 2003, to manage the new group. According to Blackwill, there was an "estrangement, [a] very serious estrangement, between the Pentagon and the State Department. The interagency process was essentially not working."[33]

Deputy Secretary of State Richard Armitage recalled an exchange illustrating the estrangement of which Blackwill spoke:

> One day, in the fall of 2003 ... we were coming out of the [White House situation] room and Dr. Rice turned to Rumsfeld and I was between the two of them—but she kind of leaned over ... and said, 'Don, would you call Jerry [Bremer] and have him do X, Y, or Z?' And [Rumsfeld] said, 'No, he doesn't work for me.' [Rice] said, 'Yes, he does. Who does he work for?' And [Rumsfeld] said, 'He works for the NSC.' And this is because Rumsfeld found out that Jerry was at least communicating with—if not taking instructions from—the National Security Advisor.[34]

Blackwill travelled to Iraq in September 2003 and quickly concluded that the United States would not be able to sustain its position there on Bremer's timetable because "the occupation would become more and more intolerable to the Iraqis."[35] In close collaboration with Dr. Rice and senior officials at the Defense and State Departments, Blackwill helped implement a major course correction for the occupation. This change was driven in part by the fact that some at the Pentagon and at the NSC believed that Bremer had been making momentous decisions about the future of Iraq that had not been "debated seriously at the principals level."[36]

On October 16, 2003, the international community joined in by formally pushing for a speedier return to full Iraqi sovereignty. UN Security Council Resolution 1511 stated that "the day when Iraqis govern themselves must come quickly," and asked the Iraqi Governing Council, in conjunction with the CPA, to provide the Security Council with "a timetable and a program for the drafting of a new constitution for Iraq and for the holding of democratic elections under that constitution." It further called on the CPA to "return governing responsibilities and authorities to the people of Iraq as soon as practicable."[37]

One month later, on November 15, 2003—barely a week after the U.S. Congress passed the $18.4 billion IRRF 2 reconstruction package—the CPA announced an agreement to pass sovereignty to an interim Iraqi government by the end of June 2004, just seven months later.[38]

The agreement required a series of predicate events. By the end of February 2004, the IGC had to approve the Transitional Administrative Law (TAL), which would define the laws for the interim government. Three months later, local caucuses in each of Iraq's eighteen provinces would elect delegates to an Iraqi Transitional National Assembly, which would then elect leaders of the new government. On June 30, 2004, the CPA and the IGC would dissolve, and the Iraqi Interim Government would take power. Provincial elections would occur on January 30, 2005, the constitution would be written and approved by referendum on October 15, 2005, and national elections would be held on December 31, 2005. The agreement further stipulated that "Coalition forces will continue to work side-by-side with new Iraqi police and security institutions to ensure a peaceful transition to a sovereign, democratic and secure Iraq."[39]

This was an extraordinary timetable: provincial and national elections—and a constitutional referendum—all to be held in a violence-stricken Iraq within thirteen months.

Supporting Provincial and Local Governments
The CPA divided Iraq into four administrative regions—north, central, south central, and south. It also appointed coordinators and established offices in each provincial capital.[40] Because of its gradual expansion into the provinces, most of the CPA's coordinators arrived after the military and USAID contractors had established relationships with their Iraqi counterparts.[41] The ensuing confusion over roles and responsibilities made for a mix of government employees, contractors, and troops whose plans and programs often worked at cross-purposes.

Mark Etherington, the CPA's coordinator in Wasit province, said he had assumed that USAID would help form councils and establish their rules of procedure. Instead, the USAID team in his area "consisted of specialists in subjects such as women's rights, agriculture, and water supply" who "knew nothing about Councils or any of the fields that were pressing priorities for us at the time." Etherington noted that USAID's private contractors made his job more difficult. As he put it, "one was left with a raft of largely unaccountable companies with their own sets of rules and security procedures, arriving at intervals, whose roles had never been properly defined or harmonized with CPA's political objectives."[42]

A SIGIR audit of USAID's local governance program noted a lack of clear policy guidance, and criticized both USAID and its contractor for failing to define the program's goals. USAID's contractor was supposed to submit quarterly work plans, but failed to do so, producing instead an implementation plan in August 2003 that simply listed the core activities planned for the year.[43]

In December 2003, Ambassador Bremer convened a "Commanders and Leaders" conference in Baghdad to address the implications of the November 15 sovereignty transfer agreement. At the conference, Bremer announced that the CPA would triple spending over the next three months to create jobs and foster stability, which would help facilitate the transfer of power.[44]

The CPA created two new DFI-funded programs—the Rapid Regional Response Program (known as R3P) and the Accelerated Iraqi Reconstruction Program (AIRP)—to funnel money into provincial reconstruction projects. The CPA's provincial offices received $120 million in R3P funds to support projects to improve essential services, create jobs, and stimulate the economy.[45] In addition, the CPA approved $277 million for the AIRP to fund high-impact, high-visibility projects in ten strategic cities: Baghdad, Ba'quba, Falluja, Mosul, Ramadi, Samarra, Tikrit, Najaf, Diwaniya, and Kerbala.[46] AIRP projects aimed to improve access to potable water, sanitation, health, education, and transportation.[47]

In April 2004, after ten months of governing Iraq, Ambassador Bremer promulgated CPA Order Number 71, strengthening the powers of local and provincial governments. The order specifically spelled out the powers of local officials, from mayors to police chiefs, and provided that the provincial councils were to be "funded from national budget allocations that are separate from the budgets of the ministries and other national institutions," and were to "perform their responsibilities independently from the control or supervision of any ministry." The provincial councils could even "approve or veto" the appointment of directors general and "local ministerial officials for positions designated as 'senior positions,'" a dramatic departure from Saddam-era practices.[48]

The order's radical decentralization of power was not well received by many Iraqi political parties, who differed about how much control should remain in Baghdad. Thus, the CPA—which had two months left in power—made little attempt to implement the order.

The Iraqi budgets for 2004 did not allocate any money directly to local and provincial governments.[49] Consequently, with no budget and no real authority over any other financial resources, the provincial councils were unable to do much for their constituent populations. By the time the CPA dissolved in June 2004, the Iraqi public had little faith in the appointed provincial councils, seeing them as creations of the occupation authorities.[50]

As the Coalition struggled to assemble local, provincial, and national governments, it also tried, with too few resources, to rebuild Iraq's police and army.

CHAPTER 12
RECONSTRUCTING IRAQI SECURITY FORCES

> *[The U.S.] Army was absolutely focused in May [2003]*
> *on wrapping up the fight… They had just finished combat*
> *operations, and then we went through this terrific problem of*
> *social mayhem, looting, the lawlessness that occurred, so the*
> *Army was absolutely focused on its mission of bringing order to*
> *the country… There was zero thought on what the Army could*
> *do to develop security forces—zero.* *

Major General Paul Eaton
Commander of CMATT and OSC (2003-2004)

The CPA planned to create a new security force—the New Iraqi Army—accountable to Iraq's civil authorities and capable of maintaining national security. But the CPA's efforts in this regard foundered because of poor planning, insufficient resources, and the failure to effectively counter the growing insurgency. However, mounting violence and the November 15, 2003 decision to return sovereignty to the Iraqis forced acceleration of plans to rebuild and deploy Iraq's security forces.

Although a spirit of liberation briefly prevailed in Baghdad after it fell, post-invasion Iraq quickly descended into a maelstrom of looting and violence as Iraqi military and police personnel fell from view and the paramilitary and intelligence services dissolved.[1] CPA Order Number 2 exacerbated matters by essentially "firing" the entire Iraqi military, with—at least initially—no compensation. Amid the ensuing chaos, the CPA sought to rebuild Iraq's security forces, aiming to inculcate Western concepts of accountability and rule of law. Critical resource shortages, a dearth of qualified trainers, and the violent environment finally forced major U.S. policy changes on the security front as the CPA era ended.

The Iraqi Police Service
Contingency operations—particularly in post-conflict situations—usually occur in environments characterized by broad insecurity and unpredictable violence, with indigenous security forces too weak or too corrupt to maintain order.[2] A prewar assessment by the U.S. Department of Justice's International Criminal Investigative Training Assistance Program (ICITAP) recommended that 5,000

---

* ORHA/CPA Historian interview with Major General Paul Eaton, former Commander of CMATT and OSC, December 27, 2004.

international police advisors be deployed to Iraq to reform the country's police system.[3] But NSC planners believed that postwar security in Iraq would not be a significant problem and that the Iraqis would be able to maintain public order, concluding that ICITAP's proposal for police training was unnecessary.

"With the police, we recommended that we leave the administration of justice and law and order in Iraq in Iraqi hands, because we didn't understand the culture, we didn't understand the language, we didn't have a corps of people we could rush there," recalled Frank Miller, who headed the NSC's Iraq group. "We didn't want Americans enforcing the Iraqi law. We did not envision occupation."[4]

Unlike the Ministry of Defense, Iraq's Ministry of Interior with its large Iraqi police force was not dissolved by CPA Order Number 2. The MoI was expected to take on the civil security mission, as part of a quick handover of internal security responsibilities to Iraqi police.[5] "We had bad intelligence," Miller later conceded. "We believed that the Iraqi police were a corrupt, but generally efficient police force. It turns out they were both corrupt and not a particularly efficient police force."[6]

Soon after the invasion, an assessment team comprising personnel from ICITAP and the State Department's Bureau of International Narcotics and Law Enforcement Affairs (INL) travelled to Iraq to assess the Iraqi Police Service (IPS), judiciary, and prison system. By the time this team of 25 experts arrived in May 2003, looters had destroyed most of the Ministry of Interior, as well as many police stations across the country, leaving the police force infrastructure in tatters. Gerald Burke, a member of the six-person team assigned to assess the police, said their conclusions could be summed up in one sentence: "The police need everything."[7]

The assessment team submitted its report to the CPA at the end of May 2003. Its conclusions were troubling: the Iraqi police were incapable of restoring public order and, unless quickly reformed, they could "not constitute a suitable, viable, and sustainable police service that can engender public trust and confidence."[8] The assessment recommended the immediate deployment of 2,500 international police officers to restore order and the recruitment of 360 professional police trainers and 6,600 international police advisors to reform the Iraqi police.[9] But the NSC again rejected these recommendations, viewing them as too ambitious and too expensive. Ultimately, Ambassador Bremer requested IRRF 2 funding for 1,500 police advisors—of whom 1,000 would be American.[10]

Training Iraq's Police

Bernard Kerik became the first senior advisor to the Ministry of Interior in May 2003. The controversial former New York City police commissioner faced dual challenges: quickly reconstituting Iraq's police forces so they could restore public order and reforming an institutional culture in which respect for human rights and community policing was unknown.

The rapidly worsening security environment increased the tension between the need to provide short-term security and the goal of long-term institutional reform. Moreover, criminal looting had gutted law enforcement's public infrastructure. To address these myriad problems, Kerik put six members of the ICITAP/INL assessment team in charge of rebuilding police stations and training academies, retraining the police forces, and improving ministerial capacity.[11]

Although Kerik, according to his own estimates, reopened 35 police stations in Baghdad and recalled 40,000 police officers in three months, some contend he spent too much time conducting tactical operations—leading teams of recalled Iraqi police on nighttime raids in Baghdad—and not enough time on developing a workable strategy to train, equip, and employ Iraqi police across the country.[12] Lieutenant General Sanchez considered Kerik's efforts "a waste of time and effort." He thought they were too Baghdad-centric and neglected critical equipment needs.[13]

Lieutenant General Scott Wallace, Commander of the Army's V Corps, tasked the 18th Military Police Brigade with organizing and mentoring the residual police force. Joint U.S.-Iraqi patrols were policing the streets of Baghdad by May 9, 2003.[14] But when Ambassador Bremer arrived on May 12, only 4,000 poorly trained, pistol-wielding police were on duty in Baghdad, a city of more than 7 million people.[15] Determined to bolster these numbers, Bremer issued a directive in June 2003 that police who failed to return to work by July 3 would be fired; about 38,000 former police returned by the deadline. Their ranks were further strengthened by an additional 30,000 new officers recruited across the country by Lieutenant General Sanchez's Combined Joint Task Force 7 (CJTF-7) staff.[16]

Finding a facility large enough to train tens of thousands of Iraqi police was an important priority. According to John Meiklejohn—the CPA advisor in charge of police academies and curriculum—the Ministry of Interior's infrastructure had been "totally ransacked." USACE began reconstructing police academies by the end of May, and instruction started as classrooms were finished. With the help of U.S. Military Police instructors, the first four classes of 25 to 30 students began on June 28, 2003.[17]

The CPA needed to expand Iraq's police training capacity quickly. Security conditions were deteriorating rapidly, so the CPA looked abroad, first contemplating using an air base in Hungary. Meiklejohn scrapped the idea in late September 2003, when the Jordanians agreed to train 1,500 Iraqi police per month.[18] He flew to Amman in October to manage the rapid construction of and logistics for the new International Police Training Center in Muwwaqqar, Jordan.[19] In late November 2003, the first class of 456 Iraqi cadets began an eight-week training course in makeshift facilities while construction continued on permanent facilities.[20]

The CPA's police training program was constrained by funding and staffing shortfalls. Its various initiatives depended almost entirely on Iraqi funds because no U.S. money was appropriated for this purpose. The 2003 Iraqi national budget initially provided just $2.4 million for police operations. Although 2004 Iraqi funding increased to $122.4 million, chiefly to pay police salaries, the capital budget for police infrastructure remained low.[21]

During the fall of 2003, crime continued to rise in Iraq, forcing CJTF-7 to increase the training rate of Iraqi police. Ambassador Bremer feared that it was doing little more than rearming elements of Saddam's abusive and ineffective police force, so he had INL design a three-week Transition and Integration Program that CJTF-7 could use.[22] Despite marginal improvements brought about by the new curriculum, military trainers still had little understanding of Iraq's police methods or existing Iraqi criminal justice procedures.[23]

Border Enforcement and Facility Protection

The CPA established the Department of Border Enforcement (DBE) on August 24, 2003, but allocated scant resources for training.[24] New recruits had little experience, and previous immigration officials were excluded from employment because of their connection to Saddam's secret police.

After the 2003 invasion, Iraq's borders were porous, subject to easy infiltration by foreign fighters. U.S. soldiers tried to fill gaps, but they had no interpreters, could not read Arabic passports, and were unfamiliar with reviewing customs papers. The soldiers were soon overwhelmed by masses of people trying to enter Iraq; border traffic "backed up literally for miles."[25] By June 2004, only 255 members of the Iraqi DBE had received training from the Coalition.[26] Iraq's porous borders remained an egregious security problem for several years after the 2003 invasion.

The Facilities Protection Service (FPS) was the last major security force to stand up under the Ministry of Interior. It provided site security for ministry facilities and provincial government buildings.[27] By 2004, the FPS ranged from 80,000 to 100,000 personnel, but its members received just three days of training and light equipment, putting it at "the lower end of the spectrum of capabilities."[28] Most notably, some ministers used the FPS to mask militia and sectarian elements within their ministries.[29]

New Iraqi Army

On May 23, 2003, CPA Order Number 2—the order dissolving Saddam's military structures—announced the formation of the New Iraqi Army.[30] Whatever the negative consequences of Order 2, it provided a clean break from the old force and a new slate for the systematic rebuilding of Iraq's army. It failed to address, however, what resources the CPA should use to accomplish this enormous mission.

CPA Order Number 22, issued in August 2003, expanded upon Order 2, establishing the New Iraqi Army as the basis of "militarily effective, professional, and non-political armed forces for the military defense of the nation."[31] The order provided that the army would be civilian-controlled, a tenth of its previous size, nationally recruited on a volunteer basis, and focused strictly on external defense. The CPA believed that the New Iraqi Army—unlike the police force—need not be fielded immediately. Plans called for training three divisions of light motorized infantry battalions over two years. Including headquarters units, the total end strength for the New Iraqi Army would amount to a modest 40,000.[32]

Responsibility for training the Iraqi army fell to Major General Paul Eaton, who arrived in Iraq on June 13, 2003, to take command of the Coalition Military Assistance Training Team (CMATT). Major General Eaton soon realized that the army training mission was "not a high priority" for the CPA or the U.S. military. The only real policy direction came from a 24-page PowerPoint presentation from CENTCOM. It did not contain "execution level" plans for manning, training, equipping, or employing the 40,000-man force, all of which had to be accomplished with a budget of just $173 million drawn from the DFI. According to Eaton, "there was zero participation on the part of the Army Staff. Zero participation on the part of [the U.S. Army Training and Doctrine Command]. Zero participation on anybody's part except for an ad hoc team on personal request from me." With no strategic plan, limited resources, and only five staff members, CMATT "set out to man, train, and equip the Iraqi Armed Forces essentially in a vacuum."[33]

Major General Eaton set August 1, 2003, as the training start date for the Iraqi army, leaving just six weeks to prepare. In the middle of June, he selected Kirkush, northeast of Baghdad, as the site of the first training base, because its isolation provided a measure of security. CMATT contracted with an Iraqi firm to refurbish the barracks and to provide power, water, and sewerage. Two weeks later, another Iraqi firm was contracted to provide water, food, and fuel for the trainees.[34] Using Iraqi contractors helped leverage CMATT's meager resources and established a civilian contracting model that would form the basis of support for Iraq's Ministry of Defense.[35]

A U.S. contractor was placed in charge of recruiting enlisted men, and CMATT selected the officers. On July 15, 2003, CMATT asked U.S. Army division commanders in Iraq to provide 45 former Iraqi lieutenant colonels to populate the new officer corps, hoping these former officers would bring needed experience, but not be so senior that they could not be retrained along Western lines. But when these new officers refused to serve without being reinstated to their Saddam-era rank and pay, CMATT dismissed them and lowered the recruitment requirement to major. Seventy-five percent of the new force—including almost all of the NCOs and officers—had prior military experience.[36]

Security worsened over the summer of 2003 and, during a brief August 2003 visit to Iraq, Secretary Rumsfeld decided to cut the Iraqi army's two-year training time in half.[37] CMATT desperately needed help to meet this new timeline and found some during a visit by Major General Eaton to Jordan to purchase equipment. During his trip to Amman, Eaton asked Jordan's chief of military training to consider whether he could support the training of 2,000 new Iraqi Army officers. In late August, word came that King Abdullah of Jordan had agreed to provide help.[38] Buoyed by this support, CMATT developed a new training model. In the first eight-week segment, the Jordanian military would retrain former Iraqi officers at a base outside Amman, while Coalition partners trained non-commissioned officers (NCOs) at a reconstructed military academy in Taji, Iraq. In the second stage, CMATT would form battalions of Iraqi officers and enlisted soldiers, and the new battalions would train in Iraq as whole units for a three-month period.[39]

Many Iraqi officers resented training in Jordan, but only by using Jordanian and U.S. military units to train officers and NCOs did CMATT have any hope of achieving the training results needed before the new September 2004 deadline. By November 15, 2003, CMATT's plan to stand up the New Iraqi Army was underway, and the CPA had promised more funding through IRRF 2.[40]

Iraqi Civil Defense Corps
As the insurgency grew during the latter half of 2003, CJTF-7's overstretched forces were unable to maintain public order. CENTCOM commander General Abizaid and CJTF-7 commander Lieutenant General Sanchez thus began to develop a new Iraqi security force component that could help fight the insurgency.[41] This force—the Iraqi Civil Defense Corps (ICDC)—would assist with constabulary duties, employ former members of the Iraqi military, and give Iraqis a sense of ownership of security in their communities.[42]

CJTF-7 began training the first six ICDC battalions in July 2003. CPA Order Number 28 officially established it as an institution that was "distinct from the Iraqi police force and the New Iraqi Army" on September 3, 2003.[43] Because the ICDC was not part of the original CPA security sector plan, it posed significant coordination problems from its inception. Its chain of command went from Lieutenant General Sanchez to General Abizaid to Secretary Rumsfeld. There was little coordination with the Iraqi police or army and no accountability to any Iraqi ministry or the CPA.

Some in CMATT feared the ICDC could become a parallel security structure, competing with the police in local affairs and diluting the Iraqi Army's authority at the national level.[44] But Coalition commanders valued the ICDC as a way to enable Iraqis to provide security for their own country, while supplementing CJTF-7's overstretched forces. By April 2004, the ICDC had grown from the six battalions initially authorized to 45 battalions across the country, amounting to 36,000 personnel.[45]

Growing Insecurity

During the summer of 2003, insurgent attacks on Iraq's infrastructure had supplanted looting as the chief reconstruction security problem. Repeated sabotage of pipelines and power lines impeded economic recovery and limited the success of early attempts to restore essential services. The deterioration of the security situation delayed reconstruction projects, interrupted supply delivery, and disrupted daily life across Iraq. All this "fed into Iraqi feelings of resentment and despair, which fueled insurgency and crime, thereby worsening the security climate."[46] The violence prevented many CPA officials from leaving the Green Zone, limiting their contact with—and thus their understanding of—Iraqis.[47]

In October and November 2003, the growing insecurity highlighted the need to hasten security force training and improve its resourcing. Security funding finally received a much-needed boost with the passage of IRRF 2 on November 6, 2003. The sector received $3.29 billion, including $1.22 billion for the police forces, $2 billion for the Iraqi army, and $76 million for the Iraqi Civil Defense Corps.[48]

Reforming MoD and MoI

The impending June 2004 deadline for the transfer of sovereignty forced CPA officials to rethink security sector development. In mid-November 2003, the CPA's Office of Policy Planning warned Ambassador Bremer that Iraq required "legitimate and accountable systems of security to prevent violent conflict." These included not only the security forces, but also intelligence services and judicial and penal institutions. The CPA's Office of Policy Planning further advised that the CPA's narrow focus on Iraq's short-term security problems had limited the efforts to address longer-term reforms.

The CPA needed to pursue "a more integrated approach to security sector reform that will meet Iraq's future needs and enable the coalition to transfer responsibility for security to Iraqis."[49] It also needed to address the absence of a legal framework for the use of force by Iraq's military, the disparity between force requirements and security budgets, the need to ensure that the new Iraqi security forces would operate under civilian control, and the need to insulate the security forces from sectarian influences.[50] The failure to address this last crucial issue would have lethal consequences in 2004 and 2005, as the Iraqi Ministry of Interior became infiltrated by sectarian militias.

Another gap was the need for a new Iraqi Ministry of Defense (MoD). The plan was to create the new MoD in April 2005, but the new date to transfer sovereignty shortened the timeline by a year.[51] The CPA quickly focused on finding senior leadership for MoD.[52] It strove for ethnic balance in the new MoD leadership and sought to ensure that military promotions would be based on merit, not sectarian affiliation. Experience requirements for high-level jobs meant that former military officers (mostly Sunnis) filled a third of the new civilian positions and virtually all of the top military positions.[53] The CPA provided the new leadership with three weeks of training in Washington at the National Defense University and the U.S. Institute of Peace. The training established "a foundation of understanding of civilian control of the military, some basics in defense-sector management and issues, and (not unimportantly) a look at a successful, functional democratic country."[54]

Iraqis themselves had little influence on the new ministry's design. Major General Eaton believed that 30 years of oppression under Saddam had left them unable or unwilling to challenge the ideas posed by CPA advisors and CJTF-7 officials.[55] There was still concern about Iraqi Governing Council involvement in selecting the new Minister of Defense. The CPA feared that political allegiances of IGC members would exert a negative influence.[56] Thus, the choice of the new minister of defense was not discussed with the Iraqis to avoid allegations of politicization.[57]

Reforming the Ministry of Interior was more difficult than restarting the MoD. The Iraqi police force had not been a viable institution during Saddam's reign, so there was no cadre of competent mid-level management from which to draw new leadership. Procurement problems also impeded progress.[58] The State Department's Bureau of International Narcotics and Law Enforcement Affairs had failed to promptly contract with DynCorp for housing, food, security, facilities, and other support for the International Police Liaison Officers (IPLOs). The IPLOs were supposed to train and advise Iraqi police.[59] Because of the contracting delay, only a few dozen came to Iraq during the first six months of the occupation, far short of the 5,000 originally recommended and the 1,500 that Bremer approved.[60]

Security Challenges

A few early successes suggest that a counterinsurgency strategy might have proved effective during the CPA's tenure in Iraq. Shortly after occupying Mosul, Major General David Petraeus and the 101st Airborne Division, worked directly with local community leaders in the city to implement critical reconstruction projects that helped reduce violence.[61] Most units in Iraq, though, had little counterinsurgency training or experience, and the Coalition's campaign strategy was "wrapped around killing and capturing the insurgents," not promoting political participation, economic opportunity, and public buy-in.[62] Replicating the 101st Airborne's methods across the country might have helped tamp down the insurgency, but it would have required more troops and a coordinated counterinsurgency strategy. This was eventually used in 2007, during the surge, and ultimately quelled most violence in Iraq.

On October 14, 2003, the White House reported to the Congress that 70,000 Iraqis were engaged in security operations, and another 13,000 were in training.[63] Secretary of State Colin Powell claimed that the Department of Defense "kept inventing numbers of Iraqi Security Forces—the number would jump 20,000 a week! 'We now have 80,000, we now have 100,000, we now have 120,000.'"[64] But Secretary Rumsfeld later said that changes in how the Defense Department tracked Iraqi troop readiness accounted for the changes over time in the numbers reported.[65]

Some CPA and CJTF-7 leaders felt that the perceived inflation of Iraqi troop numbers hurt the Coalition's effort. According to Ambassador Bremer, "it was increasingly clear that the Pentagon's apparent preoccupation with the spring [2004] troop rotation was creating unhealthy pressures to wish a competent Iraqi security force into being faster than possible."[66] Lieutenant General Sanchez echoed the point, noting that, "at various times, the Department of Defense inflated the numbers of effective Iraqi forces," while ignoring the fact that "the enduring challenge was building capable and effective Iraqi forces rather than simply adding numbers."[67]

Given the CPA's persistent personnel shortages, General Abizaid strongly advocated that the U.S. military take over the security force training responsibilities "because [CPA's] people didn't have the capacity" to do it well. He also pushed for a bigger Iraqi army and said it was necessary to "really put the muscle of DoD" behind the training effort.[68] Unsurprisingly, this idea created controversy. Many civilian police advisors feared that giving the police training mission to the military would sacrifice the Iraqi police force's "long-term institutional and personnel development for expediency and would have negative consequences, saddling Iraq with security forces that could possibly endanger the country's future."[69] Major

General Eaton also had reservations; consolidating training for all Iraqi security forces under a single military command threatened to divert resources from the Iraqi army and thus undermine long-term capacity building there as well.[70]

The Eikenberry Report

In November 2003, Secretary Rumsfeld ordered an assessment by Major General Karl Eikenberry to determine what reforms were necessary to produce enough capable Iraqi forces to take over security responsibilities. Released in February 2004, the Eikenberry report described CPA training efforts as under-resourced and disorganized, noting in particular that the development of Iraq's police force was so far behind that transferring security responsibilities would not be possible for many months. Eikenberry's report concluded that the U.S. military should manage the training of Iraq's army and police.[71]

Rumsfeld accepted Eikenberry's recommendations and authorized CJTF-7 to form the Office of Security Cooperation (OSC). Major General Eaton assumed command on March 9, 2004. Both CMATT and the newly established police training command—the Coalition Police Assistance Training Team (CPATT)—fell under OSC's purview.[72] "At this point, the distinction between an Iraqi military force and an Iraqi civilian rule-of-law police service became almost interchangeable with the use of the term 'Iraqi Security Forces,'" said Gerald Burke, a member of the CPA's first police training team. "It was at this time that input or control of the police training by civilian police experts was significantly reduced."[73]

With the reorganization of training for the Iraqi Security Forces underway, the Department of Defense advanced an ambitious plan to cede security responsibilities to the Iraqis. In March 2004, Lieutenant General Sanchez announced that, as the Iraqi security forces proved capable and credible enough to maintain local security, Coalition forces would redeploy to bases outside major cities. From there, they would coordinate with the Iraqis and provide quick-reaction forces, but the ISF would have daily policing and patrolling duties.[74] As the security situation improved, the size of Coalition forces would decrease from 130,000 to 115,000, and the number of U.S. forward operating bases within the city would drop to eight in May 2004 from its June 2003 high of 60.[75]

Iraqi Force Failures

The first test of this new security sector strategy was a disaster. In April 2004, Sunni insurgents attacked Coalition forces in Falluja, Baghdad, Ramadi, Samarra, and Tikrit, while the Mahdi Army occupied Najaf in the south and Sadr City in Baghdad. Many elements of the newly deployed Iraqi Security Forces proved unwilling or unable to fight. Some abandoned their posts and

aided the insurgency.[76] Others mutinied when they came under fire.[77] Iraqi
police units collapsed in Falluja, Najaf, Kerbala, and Kut, and the number of
Iraqi police dropped by nearly 3,000 in one week in April 2004. The Iraq Civil
Defense Corps fared worst of all. From April 2 to April 16, up to 12,000 ICDC
members deserted; the rates reached up to 30 percent in northeastern Iraq, 49
percent in Baghdad, 30 percent in the south-central region, and 82 percent in
western Iraq.[78] The Defense Department's plan to transfer security responsibilities rapidly to the Iraqis had failed.

Recovery and Reorientation

The April uprisings pitted Iraq's police, military, and civil defense corps against
well-armed insurgents and militias across Iraq. Of the 200,000 Iraqi security
force personnel rushed into service, "no more than 5,000" were "fully trained
and equipped."[79] Few were ready for counterinsurgency operations; only the Iraqi
Army was trained to fight organized enemies (although a mere eight percent of
its force was considered ready before the uprising).[80]

The Defense Department now focused the various Iraqi military and police
forces on a single threat—the insurgency within Iraq. This was a departure not
only for the Iraqi army, whose mandate under CPA Order Number 22 had specifically prohibited its participation in domestic affairs, but also for the police, who
had to add counterinsurgency to their criminal justice responsibilities.[81] But the
disastrous results of the April 2004 uprisings forced the Defense Department to
modify how the Iraqi security forces were being trained. Major General Eaton's
Office of Security Cooperation began to refocus the mission on the development
of more heavily equipped, specially trained counterinsurgency forces.

The Coalition Police Assistance Training Team brought a military approach
to equipping the Iraqi police. CPATT analyzed Iraqi police needs for materiel,
infrastructure, weapons, and other pacing items.[82] Because of the contracting
challenges in Iraq, the requested equipment did not reach the police until after
the transfer of sovereignty. According to Lieutenant General Sanchez, it took 30
to 45 days to document requirements and issue contracts and another 45 to 60
days before deliveries began.[83]

CPATT also improved field training programs for Iraqi police, implementing
specialized programs in four key areas that had been neglected: counterterrorism,
intelligence, organized crime, and corruption. These were implemented at the
Jordan and Baghdad police academies, as well as several smaller regional training
academies.[84] Meanwhile, the Ministry of Defense reoriented its forces toward domestic security missions. Shortly after the April uprisings, an Iraqi general visited
various Iraqi army units, recruiting volunteers for a division that could operate

anywhere inside the country.[85] Named the Iraqi Intervention Force, the unit was heavily armed and trained specifically for counterinsurgency.[86]

Iraqi officials also wanted a larger regular military, demanding an increase at a May 2004 conference between Department of Defense officials and the Iraqi leadership. General Abizaid recalled that Prime Minister Allawi "actually pounded on the table about as hard as I've ever seen a human being pound on the table and said the army was too small, and that he had to have more."[87]

A Hard Lesson Learned

The CPA's July 2003 *Vision for Iraq* declared that "our first priority is to create a secure and safe environment, without which there can be little progress on other goals."[88] This foundational goal proved exceedingly difficult to achieve. During the CPA's tenure, Coalition forces could not provide the secure environment necessary for the Iraqi police and military to develop into competent and accountable security forces. By the time of the June 2004 transition, just half of Iraq's army and two-thirds of its police forces had received any training at all, and the quality of that training varied widely.[89]

A transition team assessment report delivered to the Secretary of Defense on June 23, 2004—five days before Iraq assumed full sovereignty—showed that just six percent of Iraqi Police Service members had completed a police academy program. The report concluded that if this number did not at least triple by the end of the year, the newly sovereign Iraq would be at "high risk."[90] The Iraqi security forces were also poorly equipped. Despite the new IRRF 2 appropriations for security, contracting delays caused serious shortages in weapons, vehicles, body armor, and communications equipment.[91]

The disastrous performance of the Iraqi Security Forces in the April 2004 uprisings revealed that the Department of Defense had prematurely pushed security responsibilities onto Iraqi shoulders. The Iraqi's confidence in the country's security forces—and in their sponsors, CJTF-7 and the CPA—plummeted as violence soared in 2004.[92] The human toll was also severe; thousands of civilians were killed amid the growing violence.[93] Pressed by time and under-resourced, the CPA and CJTF-7 could not adequately prepare the Iraqi Security Forces to fight the growing insurgency. Prematurely substituting Iraqi forces for Coalition forces had proved a mistake. As the performance of the 101st Airborne Division in Mosul suggested, the Coalition needed a new counterinsurgency strategy.

CHAPTER 13
RESTARTING OIL PRODUCTION

> *There's a lot of money to pay for this that doesn't have to be U.S.*
> *taxpayer money... the oil revenues of that country could bring*
> *between $50 and $100 billion over the course of the next two*
> *or three years... We're dealing with a country that can really*
> *finance its own reconstruction, and relatively soon.**
>
> **Dr. Paul Wolfowitz**
> Deputy Secretary of Defense (2001-2005)

Iraq has the third-largest oil reserves in the world.[1] Given this immense oil wealth, Iraq should have been able to pay for its own reconstruction from the start. But three debilitating wars, institutionalized governmental corruption, and crippling international sanctions all contributed to a breakdown of the country's oil sector.

Oil output peaked at 3.5 million barrels per day in July 1990, eight months before the first Gulf War. Because of damage inflicted during that war, production plummeted to less than 500,000 barrels per day, gradually increasing over the next decade to reach an average of 2.5 million barrels per day by early 2003.[2]

Iraq's proven natural gas reserves—112 trillion cubic feet—are the tenth-largest in the world. Natural gas production also declined after the first Gulf War, as processing facilities deteriorated for lack of spare parts and maintenance. In 2003, Iraq was "flaring"—igniting, and burning off—about 60 percent of the natural gas released in the production of crude oil, because it lacked the capacity to capture it for domestic consumption or export.[3]

Iraq's Oil Infrastructure
Iraq's oil industry is an intricate web of what is known in oil-business parlance as "upstream," "midstream," and "downstream" operations. Upstream consists of oil fields, oil wells, and gas-oil separation plants; midstream facilities include refineries, gas-processing and stabilization plants; and downstream operations comprise distribution networks, terminals, and service stations.[4]

Most of Iraq's oil and gas reserves lie in the southeastern and northwestern parts of the country. In 2003, about 70 percent of the oil produced in Iraq came from the north and south Rumaila fields near the southern city of Basrah and

---

* Dr. Paul Wolfowitz, Deputy Secretary of Defense, Statement before the House Appropriations Subcommittee on Defense, March 27, 2003.

the Kirkuk fields in the western part of Kurdistan.[5] About two-thirds of its oil wells were in the Rumaila fields, and about one-third were in the north, in and around Kirkuk.[6]

Oil from the Rumaila fields has two notable attributes. First, it is "light," meaning it has relatively low viscosity and yields a high percentage of desirable products when refined. Second, it is "sweet," meaning that it has only a small amount of hydrogen sulfide and carbon dioxide, both of which corrode production facilities. "Some of the best crude in the world comes out [of southern Iraq]," said Brigadier General Robert Crear, who commanded Task Force RIO. "When it comes out of the ground, it goes through the gas-oil separating unit, and it goes straight to a ship for export," without further treatment.[7]

At the time of the 2003 invasion, the country had two functioning export pipelines. The Ceyhan line carried oil from Kirkuk to the Turkish port of Ceyhan on the Mediterranean, and a pipeline from the Rumaila fields in the south carried oil to off-shore platforms near Basra.[8]

Iraq also had three main refinery complexes—in Baiji, Basra, and Doura—that collectively possessed the capacity to process about 570,000 barrels of crude oil per day. The Doura refinery, with a capacity of 110,000 barrels per day, supplied most of the fuel for nearby Baghdad. The two refineries at Baiji, in north-central Iraq, had a refining capacity of 310,000 barrels per day, and the Basrah facility near the Umm Qasr port could process 150,000 barrels per day.[9]

Despite this significant nominal capacity, Iraq's refineries did not have the technology to process a broad range of refined products. Their obsolete systems left 45 percent of every barrel of crude oil behind as "heavy fuel oil," a thick, sticky residue of limited commercial value. Iraq and other countries in the Middle East use heavy fuel oil to run large thermal power plants. Before the 2003 invasion, Iraq did not produce enough gasoline and cooking gas to meet domestic demand; thus, it traded its excess heavy fuel oil in exchange for refined products. For every three truckloads of heavy fuel oil exported to Jordan and Turkey, Iraq imported one truckload of gasoline.[10]

Task Force Restore Iraqi Oil

Determined to avert the environmental disasters experienced during the first Gulf War—when Saddam started 700 oil-well fires—USACE's Task Force RIO, KBR, and the military developed extensive plans to prevent or put out such fires.[11] One of the first task orders issued under KBR's $7 billion contract with the Army Field Support Command was for a contingency plan to repair and restore Iraq's damaged or destroyed oil structures. A separate contract for $37.5 million was awarded to KBR for the purpose of prepositioning fire-fighting equipment.[12]

USACE prepared to fight up to 1,500 well fires, but most of the RIO team thought Saddam Hussein loyalists would not have time to sabotage more than thirty percent of the approximately 1,000 wells in the south. The team feared losing most of the 500 wells in the north because Turkey denied the Coalition access to Iraq, lengthening the time it would take for U.S. forces to secure the northern Iraqi oil fields at Kirkuk.[13]

During and immediately after the March 2003 invasion, no serious sabotage of the northern or southern oil fields occurred, with only nine fires recorded.[14] Gary Vogler, a former Exxon-Mobil executive who served as a member of the Energy Infrastructure Planning Group in the run-up to the war and later as an oil advisor to ORHA and the CPA, attributed the small number of fires to USACE's "fantastic planning" and to the fact that Coalition forces prevailed so quickly.[15] USACE found and disarmed explosive devices at several wells and many gas-oil separation plants in the south.[16]

If the good news was that Iraq's oil fields suffered little damage during the invasion, the bad news was that Task Force RIO had not expected the widespread damage that post-invasion looting and the developing insurgency would cause. In the south, where U.S. troops bypassed the oil infrastructure on the way to Baghdad, vandals and thieves stripped facilities of anything of value. Oil advisors had identified key installations that needed to be protected, but "[the military] said they didn't have enough people to do that," recalled one advisor.[17] Task Force RIO had more firefighters than it needed but not enough oil people with operational experience to restore the damaged infrastructure.[18]

Reopening the Ministry of Oil
On their first visit to the Ministry of Oil at the end of April 2003, Gary Vogler and Clark Turner, an oil advisor from the Pentagon team, found the offices damaged and most of the files missing. This shocked them because CENTCOM had planned to protect the oil ministry buildings. Apparently, during the brief time between the entry of Coalition forces into Baghdad and the arrival of troops at the oil ministry, significant looting had occurred.[19]

Vogler and Turner's first job was to find an interim minister to oversee restarting ministry operations.[20] On May 3, Vogler, a senior advisor to the ministry, called a meeting of the entire ministry staff to announce that Thamir al-Ghadban, its director of planning before the war, would serve as interim oil minister.[21] Turner recalled that Ghadban then made a short speech that encapsulated Iraqi ambivalence toward the Coalition. He said that, "Whatever you call this unfortunate incident, we don't like to be occupied." He urged the Americans to concentrate on providing security. If the Americans could do that, Ghadban said, Iraqis could handle the reconstruction of the oil sector.[22]

Turner and Vogler then began searching for more employees who could help Ghadban stabilize the ministry. "Our philosophy was we weren't going to change anything," said Turner. "We wanted to keep as many of the Ba'athists there as possible to help out and then later do the de-Ba'athification."[23] Ghadban said that, although the de-Ba'athification order affected some high-ranking technical people, its most deleterious impact was to severely politicize the ministry, which had longer-term harmful effects on the ministry's operations.[24]

In 2003, the Ministry of Oil had about 15,000 employees.[25] They oversaw 22 state-owned enterprises, which engaged in everything from drilling and producing oil and gas to processing and exporting it. Dozens of other SOEs supported the ministry, providing a variety of goods and services.[26] These companies had operated under memoranda of understanding with the UN Oil-for-Food program, as well as agreements among themselves. The ministry's director general in charge of national manufacturing bore responsibility for coordinating the activities of the SOEs. He hoped to get some of them to work on oil sector reconstruction, but most of the factories had been looted and were struggling to survive.[27]

The Task Force RIO engineers made progress. The Rumaila fields in the south were soon producing modest amounts of oil, while the Kirkuk fields in the north were producing more than 30,000 barrels per day. By late April, Doura, Baghdad's main refinery, was processing 40,000 barrels per day—still less than half the refinery's capacity.[28]

Fuel Shortages

In late spring 2003, the CPA faced a serious fuel crisis. Iraq could not meet domestic demand for kerosene, diesel, liquefied petroleum gas, and gasoline. Looting had shut down some refineries, the invasion had disrupted the distribution system, and huge subsidies continued to encourage smuggling. With the refineries operating at low levels—or out of commission altogether—the Ministry of Oil tried to meet growing demand by drawing on supplies from its reserve inventory.[29]

By mid-May, Iraq was almost out of gasoline. Liquefied petroleum gas, sold in twelve-kilogram bottles and used primarily for cooking, had all but disappeared from the markets. The ministry set up a rationing system that reduced the number of truckloads of gasoline delivered to each gas station by almost 70 percent, trying to ensure that all stations would get some gasoline. Many received none at all.[30]

As the lines at gas stations grew longer, the Coalition turned to Task Force RIO and the KBR contract to solve the immediate problem, and they began to fund the massive import of refined products. Defense Department officials did not know how much fuel would be required or how long it would be necessary to import it, but had anticipated that they would need to provide a 10- to 30-day supply.[31]

During the summer and fall of 2003, Iraq's refineries repeatedly shut down because of power shortages, insurgent attacks, or the lack of storage space for the heavy fuel oil that was a byproduct of their refining process. Thus, Task Force RIO's requests for refined fuels rapidly rose during the hot summer in 2003. From July 16 to August 3, USACE continuously raised the amount of fuel that it was requesting under the KBR contract. By the fall, USACE had "increased the funding on Task Order 5 from $24 million to $871 million, a value more than 36 times greater than the initial allocation." Five of the ten task orders ultimately issued to KBR under its $7 billion contract would be for importing fuel.[32]

Rebuilding Begins

In July 2003, the Corps of Engineers, the Ministry of Oil, the CPA, and KBR developed a strategy to get Iraq's oil infrastructure back to prewar production capacity. The resulting "Iraq Oil Infrastructure Restoration Plan" identified 220 projects, divided between "procurement only" activities (to obtain materials) and "engineer-procure-construct" contracts (for design and construction). Procurement-only activities used most of the funding.[33]

The Ministry of Oil drew on its own technical experts, as well as those of KBR and Task Force RIO to survey the upstream facilities—the fields and wells that had sustained most of the serious damage from looting and war—and to develop rehabilitation plans for them. But the ministry used its own engineering and construction firm, the State Company for Oil Projects, for most oil sector construction. KBR focused on purchasing and importing spare parts, new vehicles, and safety gear, as well as heavy equipment.[34]

Infrastructure Security

Iraq exported no oil from March to June 2003. The UN, which managed the country's oil exports under the Oil-for-Food program, had halted exports when the invasion began.[35] UN Security Council Resolution 1483, passed at the end of May 2003, required all income from oil sales to be deposited into the newly created DFI, paving the way for the resumption of exports in June.[36] Northern exports started almost immediately; on June 22, 7.5 million barrels stored in tanks at the Turkish port of Ceyhan were sold.[37]

Meanwhile, Task Force RIO worked to bring the southern oil fields, badly damaged by looting, back on line. In mid-June, Iraq's State Oil Marketing Organization (SOMO) began issuing "spot" tenders—or sales orders—for both southern and northern oil. It was not until the end of July, however, that SOMO signed its first contracts to export 20 million barrels of Basra crude per month.[38]

In June 2003, Vogler estimated that Iraq might be able to produce three million barrels of oil per day within a year.[39] Production climbed steadily during June and July, reaching 1.3 million barrels per day at the end of August 2003.[40] By the end of October, the country was pumping just over two million barrels per day and exporting more than half of it. In the first five months of post-invasion operations, Iraq had earned about $2.6 billion in oil export revenues, depositing them in the DFI for use by the CPA.[41]

Significant insurgent attacks on the oil sector began in June 2003. Seven bombs shut down three pipelines: the Ceyhan line, the north-south pipeline, and a natural gas line. Between June and November 2003, insurgents launched thirteen major attacks on pipelines and oil facilities, severely limiting growth in production and exports.[42] The CPA's senior advisor to the oil ministry said the pattern of attacks indicated an organized insurgent campaign to sabotage Iraq's oil infrastructure.[43]

Building an Iraq Oil Protection Force

Protecting the oil infrastructure soon became an important priority. In mid-July 2003, Vogler requested $50 million from the CPA on behalf of the Ministry of Oil for a security contract to protect the pipelines and facilities. He estimated that the Coalition was losing at least $20 million per day from sabotage and continued looting. Advisors to the oil ministry searched for companies that could provide protection and found six already working in Iraq.[44]

On August 6, 2003, the CPA awarded a $39.5 million, one-year fixed-price contract to Erinys Iraq, a subsidiary of a private British security company, to train a 6,500-person Iraqi guard force to protect 140 oil sites across Iraq.[45] By the end of the year, the CPA had modified the contract eleven times and more than doubled the number of guards it wanted Erinys to train to counter the increasing violence. Erinys ultimately was paid $104 million to provide training and site protection over two years.[46]

A month after awarding the Erinys contract, the CPA established Task Force Shield to oversee the training and operation of the Iraq Oil Protection Force. Task Force Shield reported to CJTF-7 until May 2004, when it began reporting to the Multi-National Force-Iraq, CJTF-7's replacement.[47]

SIGIR's audit of the Task Force Shield programs uncovered numerous problems: too short or ever-changing timelines, confusing lines of reporting authority, competing notions of what the contract required, and ambiguity as to which government entity actually oversaw the contract. The pressure to respond to rapidly escalating attacks accounted for some of these problems, but auditors could not verify the many specific line-item costs, could not determine the total number of guards trained by the contractor, and could not account for most of the equipment procured.[48]

According to Erinys, which recruited most of its staff from the British military, the CPA's directive to get "boots on the ground" meant that the company immediately had to assess needs, draw up plans, and implement a program in a "whirlwind of concurrent activity driven by intense Coalition pressure to deploy guards."[49] The security situation deteriorated faster than Erinys or anyone else could train guards to address it. The oil infrastructure sustained nine serious attacks in November 2003.[50]

Already spread thin, the lightly armed pipeline patrols "found themselves frequently overmatched by insurgents operating in strength and armed with rocket-propelled grenades."[51] James Wilshire, the Erinys manager for the central region, and his Iraqi translator, Majid Husein Jasim, were killed in an ambush on November 11, 2003, while traveling between Baghdad and the Doura refinery. Jasim was the first of 23 Iraqis killed while serving with the oil protection force from August 2003 to December 2004.[52]

Oil at the End of the CPA

Few oil fires occurred during the March 2003 invasion, but subsequent pipeline sabotage and looting of oil facilities caused severe damage to the oil sector, ultimately preventing the CPA from reaching its oil production or export goals. During the CPA's tenure, insurgents launched more than 70 attacks on pipelines, wells, refineries, storage tanks, and individuals working for the Ministry of Oil.[53] Much of the CPA's efforts and Ministry of Oil resources went into repairing pipelines and other oil facilities.

All the oil pipelines suffered at least some damage during this period, but none more than the one connecting the Kirkuk oil fields in the north to the Turkish port of Ceyhan. This important pipeline, the only one for northern exports, was repeatedly shut down by insurgent attacks.[54] Thus, during most of the CPA's existence, Iraq did not export any oil from the Kirkuk fields by pipeline. By the end of June 2004, Iraq was producing more than 2 million barrels of oil per day, almost all of it in the south, still well short of the prewar 2.58 million barrels per day.[55]

The CPA channeled most of the resources it devoted to the oil sector into repairing pipelines, importing refined fuels, boosting production to increase export revenues, and protecting oil sites. It paid less attention to upgrading Iraq's refining capacity because the refineries, although obsolete and decrepit, had not suffered as much from the war and looting. The refineries were crucial, but had so many mechanical failures in 2003 that they were down a third of the time.[56]

With Iraq's refineries unable to meet domestic demand for refined petroleum products, the CPA continued to import diesel and gasoline into oil-rich Iraq. Because many of Iraq's power plants also depended on these refined fuels, the shortage forestalled progress on another major CPA objective: restoring electricity.

Chapter 14
Rebuilding the Electricity Sector

We were measuring the wrong things. [Average daily megawatt production] was a metric that you could easily define and would demonstrate some progress, but we weren't really focused on the right things in putting the electrical grids back on line. *

Lieutenant General Carl Strock
USACE Commander, Chief of Engineers (2004-2007)

Brigadier General Steven Hawkins received a late-night phone call on April 11, 2003, in Doha, Kuwait. The U.S. Army had completed its "thunder runs"—armored thrusts into the heart of Baghdad—and now occupied a city where the power grid had crashed, taking down all the other infrastructure systems with it, including water and sewerage. Lieutenant General McKiernan wanted the lights back on in Baghdad immediately.[1]

Tapped by Lieutenant General George Casey in January to lead Joint Task Force-4, Brigadier General Hawkins had spent the previous four months planning to manage the transition to a new Iraqi government.[2] Now he was on his way into Iraq, suddenly responsible for what would become one of the Coalition's most intractable challenges—Iraq's broken electricity sector.

Twenty-four hours later, Hawkins and his 28-member team boarded a C-130 bound for Baghdad. Tasked to restore power, water, sewerage, and hospital services to the city, they called themselves Task Force Fajr, the Arabic word for "dawn" or "new light."[3]

Task Force Fajr

Task Force Fajr landed in Baghdad at 2:30 a.m. on April 13, 2003. Iraqi electrical engineers who knew the capital's power system met them for a pre-dawn conference in downtown Baghdad. The Iraqis and the Americans recognized the mission's urgency. "All of us knew that potable water, sewer systems, and hospitals would not function without power."[4] They also realized it was just a matter of time before the loss of power would cause a humanitarian crisis.

Devising a solution was difficult because the Iraqi engineers did not have complete drawings showing Baghdad's transmission and distribution networks.[5] Someone said that the Karkh water treatment plant just north of Baghdad had an

---

* SIGIR interview with Lieutenant General (Ret.) Carl Strock, former USACE Commander, Chief of Engineers, May 13, 2008.

operational ten-megawatt generator. Hawkins and his engineers hit on an idea and immediately set to work to get power to Baghdad by routing the Karkh plant's power through an intermediate substation and onto Baghdad's grid. Lights soon began to flicker on across the city, and the grid was gradually patched back together, averting disaster.[6]

After getting Baghdad's lights on, Brigadier General Hawkins and his team then engaged in a form of triage to determine where to distribute the limited available power. Hospitals had first priority, followed by water-treatment facilities and sewerage systems; domestic consumption came next, followed by businesses and factories. Within two weeks, the capital's critical facilities had the power they needed to operate.[7] By the end of April, Iraq's power plants were generating 1,275 megawatts, up 50 percent since the invasion, but still only about a quarter of prewar levels.[8]

While Task Force Fajr pieced together Baghdad's power grid, the Coalition began reconstituting Iraq's Commission of Electricity. The commission, which would later become the Ministry of Electricity, was responsible for the generation, transmission, and distribution of power throughout the country. It had about 38,000 personnel on its payroll before the March 2003 invasion. As with most other ministries, the Commission of Electricity staff had dispersed in the wake of the invasion.

In May, the CPA asked a respected Iraqi electrical engineer, Dr. Kareem Waheed al-Aboudi, to head the commission. He had a doctorate in electrical engineering and previously served as the director general of the commission's technical office.[9] In one of the first acts of U.S. capacity building in Iraq, Hawkins embedded engineers from Task Force Fajr in the commission to help Dr. Kareem and his Iraqi engineers get it operating again.

Task Force Fajr disbanded on June 15, 2003, but many of its members continued working for the CPA on Iraq's electricity problems, some helping to rehabilitate power generation and distribution across the country, which was critical to the CPA's overall mission of establishing a stable and democratic Iraq.[10]

Challenges in the Electricity Sector

An array of problems hobbled CPA's effort to restore Iraq's electrical system. Wars, sanctions, and decades of mismanagement had left the entire network dilapidated.[11] Moreover, the country did not have enough trained personnel to upgrade and maintain the electrical systems. Iraq did not produce enough refined fuels to sustain operations at all of its power plants and the country's pipeline system was inadequately developed to ensure effective delivery of the right fuel to the right power generation facilities.[12] Finally, the insurgency frequently targeted the electricity infrastructure, causing blackouts and impeding progress.

Electricity Infrastructure

In 2003, Iraq's power sector was a network of electrical generation plants, transmission systems, and distribution networks that fed power to hospitals, industries, government buildings, and neighborhoods. Electrical substations, which adjust voltage levels for distribution, connected power plants to transmission systems and distribution networks. Seven large thermal power plants produced more than 54 percent of the country's electricity, two hydroelectric facilities generated another 24 percent, and nine gas-turbine power plants provided 21 percent.[13]

Before the invasion, Iraq had the "nameplate capacity" to produce over 9,000 megawatts of power.[14] But achieving that level of output required all facilities to be operational and running optimally, which was not possible because of chronic maintenance problems and fuel shortages.[15] The first Gulf War severely damaged Iraq's power plants, transmission lines, and electrical substations, reducing average daily power output in 1991 to 2,325 megawatts.[16] Revenue from the Oil-for-Food program helped fund repair work that had increased generation to a daily average of about 4,000 megawatts by the end of 2002.[17] Although the March 2003 invasion deliberately avoided targeting Iraq's power system, looting, poor maintenance, and a lack of spare parts, made it impossible to restore electricity quickly. By the early summer of 2003, Iraq's power plants were generating about 3,500 megawatts, a five-fold increase from immediate post-invasion levels but still at least 500 megawatts below prewar levels.[18]

Iraq's main generating facilities were in serious disrepair because "most plants [had] been operated in a manner that has degraded the output of the plant and eliminated most environmental controls."[19] To make matters worse, because Iraq had not adhered to uniform standards in equipment acquisition, its power plants were a hodgepodge of "parts and repairs ... from many different suppliers using many different codes and standards (and sometimes none at all)."[20]

The transmission systems and distribution networks were even more fragile. "The system was more like a string of old-fashioned Christmas lights than a modern national power grid," said Lieutenant General Strock. "When one key facility went out, the entire system failed."[21] Delicate and deteriorated, Iraq's electricity sector was essentially held together by "Band-Aids and rubber bands."[22]

Security Problems

Soon after Baghdad fell, gangs of looters stripped substations and control centers of copper, computers, and communications equipment. Bechtel found thirteen destroyed transmission towers, all stripped clean of their copper.[23] Although USACE estimated that "fewer than 50 high-voltage electricity transmission towers were toppled or significantly damaged as result of the war," by mid-June vandals and scavengers had destroyed more than 700 towers and taken the copper from thousands of miles of high-voltage wires.[24]

"It was like Pac Man," said USAID's Tom Wheelock, former chief of party for the agency's personnel contractor International Resources Group. "They just started at one end of the transmission line and worked their way up, taking down the towers, taking away the valuable metals, smelting it down, selling it into Iran and Kuwait."[25] At one point the looters had cut all four electric transmission lines connected to Basrah's oil refinery, exacerbating an already severe fuel shortage and causing riots in the city.[26]

In addition to the looting problem, the fledgling insurgency began sabotaging key electricity infrastructure nodes and attacking repair crews. The insurgents "routinely targeted joint U.S.-Iraqi electricity meetings," as well as Iraqis who were associated with the Coalition electricity restoration effort. In early June 2003, insurgents shot to death a senior Iraqi distribution engineer in front of her children as she left her Baghdad home. By the end of June, "attacks on Iraqi electrical engineers and facilities in and around Baghdad" occurred daily.[27]

Many senior Iraqis working for the Commission of Electricity disappeared after the invasion. De-Ba'athification further eroded the commission's staff, and insurgent attacks made some afraid to go to work. Lieutenant General Strock recalled that "many of the local Iraqis with expertise necessary to restore and operate critical infrastructure were either unavailable or fearful of working with the Coalition."[28]

The Electrical Power Security Service (EPSS), which had existed under Saddam Hussein, was supposed to protect power plants and substations. The CPA tried to continue this weak force but found that it lacked trained staff, had limited equipment, and was staffed by personnel with little interest in protecting the power grid.[29] Task Force Shield was charged with training and equipping 6,000 Iraqi EPSS guards for the new Ministry of Electricity. But, as with the Oil Protection Force, Task Force Shield failed to meet its mission.

A SIGIR audit found that only 334 EPSS guards were trained, despite the fact that the contract required 300 per month for two years. Additionally, the EPSS Training Academy at Taji was not built according to the contract's requirements, and $4.7 million in equipment there could not be accounted for. SIGIR's review of the EPSS program concluded that it "barely got underway and only trained a limited amount of guards."[30]

Fuel Problems

In 2003, most Iraqi power plants burned diesel, natural gas, or heavy fuel oil to generate electricity. Iraq's seven thermal power plants, which generated more than half the electricity for the entire country, could run on heavy fuel oil, a thick, low-value byproduct of Iraq's antiquated refining process and the only fuel that the country had in surplus.[31] Iraq's refineries produced more heavy fuel oil than its thermal plants could use, so Iraq exported the excess, mostly to Jordan and Turkey, in exchange for gasoline, diesel, and other refined products. The war disrupted this quasi-barter system. The storage tanks for heavy fuel oil quickly reached capacity, forcing the refineries to shut down and halting production of other refined fuels needed by other power plants.[32]

Iraqis filled the power gap by buying small generators to provide power to their homes, as well as to small businesses, water plants, and hospitals. But these generators did not contribute to the national grid, were relatively expensive on a per-capita basis to operate, and exacerbated fuel shortages. Nevertheless, Iraqi entrepreneurs imported and sold tens of thousands of the portable systems to households all over Iraq. The boom in home generation increased demand for refined fuels such as diesel and liquefied petroleum gas, stoking black market activity.[33]

The CPA's plan to expand power generation focused on importing gas turbine generators—which are relatively easy to transport and install—rather than building new thermal units.[34] This was the quickest way to add generation capacity to the grid. But Iraq did not produce enough refined fuel to power these generators, and its distribution system was inadequate to deliver the fuel it did produce. Moreover, Iraq did not have enough trained personnel to maintain and operate the more delicate gas turbine engines, which require frequent maintenance. The decision to install gas turbines, based in part on the assumption that the Iraqi oil industry could rapidly rehabilitate its natural gas industry, foundered when plans to develop the national gas delivery system fell by the wayside.[35]

Developing a Plan

The first CPA senior advisor on electricity, Peter Gibson, had worked with hydroelectric plants in the Pacific Northwest, but nobody on his small staff of four was an expert in the field.[36] Gibson instituted weekly strategy sessions in the Green Zone that brought together USACE, USAID, Bechtel, and the head of the Commission of Electricity—and his key managers—to develop a work plan for the electricity sector. By the end of June 2003, when Dick Dumford arrived as USAID's electricity specialist, the strategy sessions had yet to produce such a plan.[37] "We started looking around at what needed to be done," said Dumford, "and came up with a list as long as your arm."[38]

The CPA used DFI funds to pay for electricity projects but also had access to U.S. appropriations through USAID's contract with Bechtel. In July 2003, the CPA's Program Review Board approved $77 million from the DFI for the capital expenditures portion of the 2003 Iraqi budget for the Commission of Electricity.[39] The CPA looked to Bechtel, which had received funding from USAID for work in the electricity sector, to advise the commission on how best to spend this money.[40]

Bechtel's Assessment

On April 17, 2003, USAID contracted with Bechtel to assess Iraq's power facilities and systems and to execute critical repairs that would permit and promote "rapid and significant improvements in the quality and reliability of electricity services."[41] After spending the month of May assessing Iraq's electricity system, Bechtel estimated repair costs would amount to about ten times the value of its $680 million contract with USAID.[42] Bechtel warned that the "reconstruction of Iraq's power sector is a long-term effort," and that one of the biggest challenges to come would be conveying to the Iraqi population the reality that "there will be a delay in providing reliable, 24-hour-a-day power."[43]

The Bechtel assessment recommended focusing on rehabilitating power plants, replacing destroyed substations, and installing new generator units. It further advised that the CPA establish a capacity-building program to get Iraqis on the road toward "standardization of operation and maintenance practices," highlighting the need to strengthen coordination between the ministers of electricity and oil.[44]

The Push for 4,400 Megawatts

In mid-summer 2003, Ambassador Bremer surprised many in Iraq and Washington when he announced that the Coalition would have Iraq's average daily electricity supply back up to prewar levels by early October.[45] He expanded the CPA's operations office, asking its director, Peter Andrew Bearpark, to manage the "infrastructure" ministries involved in providing essential services.[46] Bearpark became the Director of Operations and Infrastructure, with then-Major General Strock as his deputy. At the end of July, Bearpark appointed Stephen Browning, a senior civilian from USACE who had served as a senior advisor to several ministries, to take charge of infrastructure.[47]

Browning found that the Coalition's electricity team had no plan for how the CPA and the Ministry of Electricity would restore electricity to prewar levels by October.[48] He immediately created an Electricity Action Team, comprising personnel from USAID, USACE, and the Iraqi Commission of Electricity.

On August 18 and 19, Browning convened a conference with every one of Iraq's power plant managers to shape the plan to reach the 4,400-megawatt target. Capacity for over 9,000 megawatts existed, but only about 3,000 were being generated. The question was how to put some of the idle capacity to work.[49] Browning asked each Iraqi power plant manager to present proposals for improving output.[50]

Browning's team concluded that the only way to reach Bremer's 4,400-megawatt goal was to target quick repairs that would have the greatest impact on generation. The staff put together a list of equipment needs for each plant and then scoured warehouses across Iraq for parts.[51] They found caches of equipment and spare parts, purchased under the UN Oil-for-Food program, which plant managers had been hoarding.[52]

Throughout September, Browning and his team worked diligently with the ministry's engineers to complete targeted repairs. USACE engineers concentrated on downed transmission lines and broken substations; Bechtel provided technical assistance for generation plant repairs; and BearingPoint helped with sector studies and system forecasts. The CPA's senior advisors met with the Ministries of Electricity and Oil once each week to address the recurrent fuel problems. Browning's effort did not include any major construction, but instead focused on minor repairs and technical assistance. The work was feverish, eighteen hours per day. "We pulled out all the stops, and it looked hopeless at times, but we made it," said one team member. On October 6, Iraq produced 4,518 megawatts, exceeding the CPA's target by 118 megawatts.[53]

The effort, though successful, took a toll on the grid's infrastructure. Browning had warned Ambassador Bremer that pushing the system to reach 4,400 megawatts could cause breakdowns that would make sector-wide rehabilitation more difficult. He believed that the focus should have been on building a sustainable power generation system.[54]

The decision to set an output metric like 4,400 megawatts as the goal had both short- and long-term negative effects on management. In the short term, the decision caused senior officials at the Pentagon and the White House to fixate on the metric rather than moving forward on multifaceted improvements of the system. In the long term, the focus created a perennial desire to judge electricity sector performance on one metric—whether current output exceeded prewar levels.

Even before the CPA reached the 4,400 target, Ambassador Bremer set a lofty new goal. In a broadcast to the Iraqi people on August 29, 2003, he said, "About one year from now, for the first time in history, every Iraqi in every city, town, and village will have as much electricity as he or she can use; and he will have it 24 hours a day, every single day."[55] At the time, the CPA estimated the current unsatisfied demand at 6,000 megawatts, but that number would rise as Iraqis anticipated greater amounts of power being available in the foreseeable future.[56]

Task Force Restore Iraqi Electricity

During a visit to Baghdad in July 2003 when the CPA was developing its plans to increase the country's power supply, Lieutenant General Robert B. Flowers, the USACE commanding general, told Bremer that he could bolster electricity reconstruction by deploying a new task force, similar to Task Force RIO. Ambassador Bremer immediately jumped at the idea. In August 2003, CENTCOM authorized USACE to develop and deploy a team, called Task Force Restore Iraqi Electricity (RIE), to provide rapid reconstruction assistance to the electricity sector.[57]

USACE recruited Brigadier General Hawkins, formerly Commander of Task Force Fajr, to return to Baghdad to head Task Force RIE. He and his team—which included 84 USACE civilians and 90 soldiers, many with specialized skills in the electricity field—arrived at the end of September 2003. Task Force RIE also included mechanical, civil, and electrical engineers.[58] Their job was to help CPA reach its 6,000-megawatt goal by the summer of 2004.

Task Force RIE designed a plan for 26 projects to repair and upgrade existing power generation, transmission, and command and control facilities to "restore reliable electricity to national and regional power grids." To manage the work, Task Force RIE established bases in Baghdad and in the northern, central, and southern regions of the country.[59]

USACE used three IDIQ contracts it already had in place with Perini Corporation, Washington Group, and Fluor International to implement the first Task Force RIE projects. These three companies eventually won the three IRRF 2 electricity sector contracts, no doubt in part because of their work with Task Force RIE. USACE tasked each company to start projects to repair the electrical infrastructure in a different region: Perini Corporation in the south, Fluor International in the center, and Washington Group in the north.[60] By October 2003, the contractors had begun many projects, covering everything from refurbishing power plants to restoring transmission towers.[61]

Electricity at the End of the CPA

The Congress allocated $5.56 billion—or nearly 30 percent of IRRF 2—to the electricity sector when it passed the supplemental legislation on November 6, 2003.[62] One week after the supplemental was enacted, Robyn McGuckin, the CPA's deputy advisor to the Ministry of Electricity, called a meeting of CPA's electricity team to review the list of proposed electricity projects covered by IRRF 2. The projects were divided among the categories of new generation, rehabilitation, controls and communications, transmission, and distribution. McGuckin needed to have a prioritized list of projects ready for the first *Section 2207 Report* to the Congress. Her list eventually included 110 generation, transmission, and distribution projects.[63]

In the late spring of 2004, insurgents stepped up attacks on the electricity infrastructure. They targeted contractors working to restore generation plants, substations, and transmission lines, forcing some companies to suspend operations. Washington Group International locked down its power plant construction site in Mosul for three days following an assault that included ambushes, and small-arms and mortar fire.[64] Subcontractors like General Electric and Siemens pulled staff from project sites after attacks in April. Insurgents also targeted Iraqis working on reconstruction projects.[65] Ambushes of convoys carrying reconstruction supplies and materials caused added delays.

The wave of violence drove costs higher, pushing all electricity projects over budget and forcing the prime contractors to spend more on security. Perini's security costs would total $63.4 million, about 18 percent of the $356.5 million it spent; Washington Group's security bill amounted to $44.5 million, 14.3 percent of the $310 million it spent.[66]

Despite the exploding security situation, work in the electricity sector continued. By June 2004, Task Force RIE had launched 66 projects and USACE said it was on target to increase generation by 1,295 megawatts, even though work on seven generation plants was well behind schedule. When the CPA closed its doors on June 28, 2004, Iraq's average daily generation capacity stood at 4,200 megawatts, well short of its 6,000-megawatt goal.[67]

CHAPTER 15
IRAQ RECONSTRUCTION IN TRANSITION

*Sovereignty involves more than a date and a ceremony. It
requires Iraqis to assume responsibility for their own future.**

President George W. Bush

From January to June 2004, the CPA concentrated on preparing to pass sovereignty to the Iraqis and on developing a process for the formation of a new democratic government in Iraq. In collaboration with the UN, the CPA assisted the Iraqi Governing Council in developing the Transitional Administrative Law (TAL), which provided dates for provincial and parliamentary elections and for a referendum on a new constitution. The TAL would serve as the legal foundation upon which the new Iraqi Interim Government would operate.

The CPA also prepared to pass oversight of the U.S. reconstruction program to a new U.S. Embassy, the first in Iraq since 1991. By the end of June 2004, the Department of Defense formally handed over management of the reconstruction program to the Department of State, and a new set of ad hoc organizations assumed control of a faltering reconstruction mission.

The Transitional Administrative Law

The November 15, 2003 transition agreement anticipated the transfer of sovereignty to an interim Iraqi government by the end of June 2004.[1] But certain Iraqi leaders—including the Grand Ayatollah Sistani—disagreed with Bremer about how the new interim government should be chosen. Bremer proposed holding caucuses in each of the provinces; Sistani insisted on national elections.[2]

In early 2004, the United States and the Iraqi Governing Council turned to the UN for help. It appointed Special Envoy Lakhdar Brahimi, a former Algerian foreign minister who had recently served as the Special Representative of the UN Secretary General in Afghanistan.[3] When Brahimi and his UN team arrived in Iraq, they quickly concluded that it was logistically impossible to hold national elections before the June 30 transfer of sovereignty. He proposed deferring the elections until after the transfer. The Iraqis accepted the recommendations, and the CPA turned to the work of developing the TAL.[4]

---

* President George W. Bush, "'We Will Finish the Work of the Fallen," Remarks by the President, April 14, 2004.

Through the TAL, the CPA sought to enshrine the core principles of Western federalism in Iraqi law; but the Iraqis quickly voiced their disagreement. The Sunnis wanted a united Iraq, so they could continue to play an important role, while Shi'a clerics, led by Sistani, were adamant that the law be clearly informed by Islam.[5] Finally, on March 8, 2004, the CPA and the Iraqi Governing Council approved the TAL, a consensus document full of compromises.[6]

The TAL served effectively as Iraq's interim constitution, with 62 articles that, among other things, guaranteed fundamental rights for all Iraqis, outlined the Iraqi Interim Government's authority, and defined a timeline for electing a permanent democratic government in Iraq. It provided that all Iraqi laws—including the regulations, orders, and directives promulgated by the CPA and in place before the June 30, 2004 transfer of sovereignty—would remain in force unless amended or rescinded by the Iraqi Interim Government or its successors. It made Islam the official faith of Iraq, stating that it was "to be considered a source of legislation."[7] In an important concession to the Kurds, the law recognized the Kurdistan Regional Government, giving it control over its police forces and internal security.[8]

The TAL provided for an eighteen-month transition period, requiring three national elections in less than a year. The Iraqi Interim Government would commence operations no later than June 30, 2004, and would hold the first election—for provincial councils and the National Assembly—by January 31, 2005. The National Assembly would draft a constitution by August 15, 2005, with the Iraqi people voting on it no later than October 15, 2005. National elections would occur by December 15, 2005, for the Council of Representatives, which would be seated by the end of the year.[9]

The task of forming the Iraqi Interim Government was given to Brahimi, who worked closely with U.S. officials and Iraq's major political leaders in developing the new government. At the end of May, the Iraqi Governing Council chose one of its members, Ayad Allawi—a secular Shi'a who had lived in exile during the Saddam years—as interim prime minister. On June 1, 2004, Brahimi and Allawi announced the formation of the new Iraqi Interim Government, including the president, the deputy prime minister, two vice presidents, twenty-six ministers, and five ministers of state.[10]

The Use and Misuse of the Development Fund for Iraq

About $20 billion dollars, predominantly from oil sales, were deposited into the Development Fund for Iraq from May 2003 to the transfer of sovereignty to the IIG in June 2004. The DFI roughly equaled the total of both IRRF appropriations ($20.9 billion) approved by the Congress. The CPA used most of the DFI to fund Iraq's national budget, which chiefly supported ministry operations. A smaller portion of the DFI—$7 billion—went to CPA-approved relief and reconstruction efforts.[11]

SIGIR audits found that the CPA failed to exert adequate control of the DFI used to support the Iraqi national ministries or reconstruction projects.[12] An audit of DFI disbursements to Iraqi ministries made through the national budget process concluded that the CPA failed to enforce adequate management, financial, and contractual controls over approximately $8.8 billion of DFI money. SIGIR found that there was "no assurance that the funds were used for the purposes mandated by [UN] Resolution 1483." Ambassador Bremer and the CPA disagreed with SIGIR, arguing that the auditors had failed to account for the very difficult security environment the CPA operated in and ignored the steps taken to improve recognized management weaknesses. Although it acknowledged the extraordinary danger confronting the CPA, SIGIR nevertheless found that the "CPA management of Iraq's national budget process and oversight of Iraqi funds was burdened by severe inefficiencies and poor management."[13] Moreover, SIGIR concluded that the chaotic circumstances required more stringent oversight—not less, as the CPA suggested.

The CPA appeared to be averse to oversight of the DFI. Dov Zakheim, the Pentagon comptroller, said that Bremer "resisted the creation of the IAMB for a very long [time]" because "he didn't want to be audited by a bunch of international auditors." Zakheim added, "You can have rules, but if you resist the auditing and you resist the implementation of the rules ... what kind of rules are they?"[14]

The CPA did not appoint an accounting firm to audit its use of the DFI until March 2004.[15] Work started on this audit only after the CPA signed the contract with KPMG on April 5, 2004—nearly a year after the DFI had been established and less than three months before the CPA would expire.

DFI Spending Frenzy

In late April 2004, as the handover of sovereignty to the Iraqi Interim Government neared, Ambassador Bremer ordered his staff to step up the expenditure of DFI funds while the CPA still had control of them and could use them to support reconstruction projects.[16] Spike Stephenson, the USAID Mission Director in Iraq, described this process as "a frenzied initiation of activities."[17]

On May 15, the Program Review Board approved the very general expenditures of some $2 billion for major projects: Iraqi security forces ($500 million), improvements in the electricity sector ($315 million), oil infrastructure reconstruction ($460 million), and supporting the Iraqi Property Claims Commission ($180 million).[18] Some PRB members disputed the proposed expenditures. Neil Hawkins, an Australian foreign aid official, said that five voting members thought the proposals, initially presented as one package on May 12, were "inadequately documented." He added, "You have one paragraph, half a page, for $70 million ... You had to say, 'That's not good enough.'" The documentation was improved before the final vote three days later, when most, but not all the components were approved.[19] Bremer was furious at the resistance.[20]

During the final six weeks before the handover, more than $5 billion was either transferred to Iraq's ministries or committed to CPA-administered reconstruction projects—amounting to over one-third of all the DFI funds that the CPA disbursed during its entire fourteen-month existence. In the week before the transition, CPA officials ordered urgent disbursements of more than $4 billion from the Federal Reserve, including one shipment of $2.4 billion—the largest in the bank's history.[21]

Operation Plan Sovereign Iraq

In concert with the transfer of sovereignty to the IIG, White House officials wanted to normalize relations with Iraq's new government by establishing a U.S. embassy in Baghdad, moving responsibility for managing the U.S.-Iraqi relationship to the State Department.

On March 19, 2004, an interagency Transition Planning Team arrived in Baghdad to develop what became known as "Operation Plan (OPLAN) Sovereign Iraq." The OPLAN was the first attempt since the 2003 invasion to develop an interagency strategy for the coordination of efforts to stabilize and rebuild Iraq. To develop the OPLAN, joint assessment teams looked at security, staffing, financial management, acquisitions and contracting, and communications.

Not surprisingly, the Transition Planning Team identified security as the foremost problem in Iraq but offered no proposals for reducing the violence.[22] During the CPA's existence, the U.S. military's mission did not include providing security for either U.S. civilian government agencies or private firms contracted for reconstruction projects. Thus, the CPA and the private firms working to rebuild Iraq had to hire private security companies to protect them.

By May 2004, the State Department, USAID, USACE, and the CPA had all contracted with private security firms.[23] The transition team identified twelve different private security contractors providing "various levels of force protection" and recognized that these private contractors would continue to play an important role supporting the U.S. program Iraq.[24]

The OPLAN perpetuated the bifurcated military command and civilian management structures. The military would continue to report to CENTCOM, while the civilians working on reconstruction would report to the new ambassador. Although the OPLAN urged cooperation and coordination, it did not mandate it, stating only that the Commanding General of the Multi-National Force-Iraq should serve as the principal military advisor to the ambassador.[25]

On May 11, President Bush issued National Security Presidential Directive 36, legally formalizing key aspects of the OPLAN.[26] The State Department, through the Chief of Mission to Iraq, would be in charge of all U.S. activities in Iraq except for military operations and the development of Iraq's security forces, which would be the Defense Department's responsibility. The new directive also established new ad hoc organizations to manage the reconstruction program: the Iraq Reconstruction Management Office (IRMO) and the Project and Contracting Office (PCO).

IRMO and PCO inherited the mission of CPA's PMO. IRMO, under the jurisdiction of the State Department, absorbed most of the CPA's former senior advisors (now known as senior consultants), who would continue to provide technical and operational reconstruction assistance to the Iraqi ministries.[27] IRMO eventually concentrated its efforts on building the capacity of the ministries to function independently.

The PCO, a temporary organization within the Defense Department, provided acquisition and project management support for the execution of IRRF construction and non-construction projects. The U.S. Army was responsible for funding, staffing, and operating the new office. Under the transition plan, the PCO would be "responsive" to the U.S ambassador to Iraq "concerning the requirements and priorities for projects to support reconstruction programs that are unrelated to the Iraqi Security Forces" and to the Multi-National Force-Iraq commanding general "with respect to requirements and priorities concerning training and equipping the Iraqi military and police forces."[28]

The PCO took over management of approximately $12.4 billion of the $18.4 billion of IRRF 2.[29] It also took over the financial management systems used to prepare the quarterly *Section 2207 Report* to the Congress. Although the organization was run by USACE, it fell under chief of mission authority, reporting to the embassy's deputy chief of mission, as did IRMO.[30] These crossed lines of reporting created operational conflicts as the IRRF 2 process unfolded.

CENTCOM consolidated Coalition military forces under the new Multi-National Force-Iraq (MNF-I), with Multi-National Corps-Iraq (MNC-I) controlling operations. At the end of June, it also established the Multi-National Security Transition Command-Iraq (MNSTC-I) to organize, train, and equip Iraq's security forces.

Leaving the Provinces

The CPA had opened offices in seventeen of Iraq's eighteen provinces. The OPLAN eliminated all but four: Kirkuk, in Tameem province; Mosul, in Ninewa province; Basrah, in Basrah province; and Hilla, in Babil province. Although driven by security concerns and budget constraints, the decision also reflected an attempt to transition to the more traditional structure of an embassy. The OPLAN called for civilians to be "embedded" in military commands in five regions. They would serve with the military civil affairs units supporting reconstruction and capacity-building initiatives. These early attempts at civil-military cooperation would evolve into the Provincial Reconstruction Team program under Ambassador Khalilzad.

On June 8, 2004, UNSCR 1546 endorsed the formation of the Iraqi Interim Government and approved the timetable for elections and the referendum on Iraq's new constitution. The UNSCR also noted the presence of the multinational force in Iraq, authorizing it to take all necessary measures to preserve the security and stability of Iraq.[31]

The End of the CPA

The CPA, which the UN had recognized in UNSCR 1483 as an "occupation authority," had several missions assigned to it by the U.S. government and the international community, including: the administration of Iraq; the reform of the country's bureaucratic, security, and economic institutions; the repair of Iraq's infrastructure; and the establishment of a democratic foundation for a constitutional government that would represent all of the country's people.[32] Each of these missions required a mammoth effort; tackling them all simultaneously, as the CPA had sought to do, called for a level of operational synchronization that was simply beyond the CPA's capacity.

When the CPA came into being, it did not have the staff or resources to lead a comprehensive rebuilding program in Iraq. The Defense Department, which was given the lead over postwar Iraq by NSPD 24, had failed to provide the CPA with sufficient numbers of qualified staff and an integrated overarching plan that articulated achievable objectives for the rebuilding of Iraq. Operating in a crisis environment, the CPA had no time to deliberate or develop alternative implementation plans. Ambassador Bremer made quick decisions that responded to changing circumstances on the ground. This process yielded some ill-advised orders that undermined the CPA's capacity to achieve its very ambitious reconstruction goals.

In 14 months, the CPA promulgated more than 100 orders, numerous regulations, memoranda, and public notices addressing everything from de-

Ba'athification and reforming the criminal justice system to disbanding the Iraqi army and amending trade laws. It stood up new security organizations, including a new Iraqi army, the Iraq Civil Defense Corps, and the Facilities Protection Service. It created new departments and ministries for Iraq, including the Ministry of Electricity, the Department of Border Enforcement, the Ministry of Science and Technology, the Ministry of Environment, the Ministry of Human Rights, and the Ministry of Defense. To fight endemic corruption, the CPA established an Iraqi inspector general system, based on the U.S. model, and the Commission on Public Integrity. It appointed an independent electoral commission to ensure free and fair elections and promulgated regulations seeking to decentralize the authority of Baghdad by devolving power to local government. The CPA orders also reformed banking laws, the penal code, government salaries, and traffic regulations; opened the country to foreign investment; and established a modern stock exchange.[33]

The CPA helped shape the development of a democratic Iraq, but it never had the organizational capacity to realize many of its goals. It was forced to improvise, creating ad hoc offices such as the PMO to perform vital reconstruction tasks. These offices filled boxes on ever-expanding organizational charts but remained under-staffed and under-resourced from the CPA's inception until its end.

In a hastily arranged ceremony, the CPA folded its tent in the Green Zone on June 28, 2004, returning sovereignty to Iraq two days ahead of schedule. As its senior officials departed, the CPA issued a glowing report card on itself titled, "An Historic Review of CPA Accomplishments." Ambassador Bremer compared the reconstruction of Iraq to the Marshall Plan, and the CPA's self-assessment ended with a list of achievements purporting to show that the CPA had done more in a shorter period of time in Iraq than the United States had accomplished nearly six decades earlier in postwar Germany. For example, Bremer noted, the CPA had created an independent central bank in two months; Germany did not have one for three years. Iraq became independent after one year; German sovereignty did not come for a decade. The CPA had "trained a new military" in three months; in Germany it took ten years. The CPA put together a reconstruction program in just four months; the Marshall Plan was designed over three years.[34]

The CPA's self-assessment missed the mark. The Iraq it left behind was in a perilous state. The Coalition's record on improving security, providing essential services, jumpstarting the economy, and laying the foundation for good governance was very mixed. The CPA concluded that "Iraq has many challenges ahead; however, it is poised to be a nation united, prosperous, and able to take its rightful place as a responsible member of the region and the international community."[35] This was a remarkably optimistic assessment given the environment in which it was issued. Iraq had slipped into the grip of a fierce insurgency, more U.S. troops were dying almost every day, and the occupation had soured many Iraqis on the continuing U.S. presence in their country. It would be up to Ambassador John Negroponte and General George Casey to develop new approaches to address the most serious threat to the continuing reconstruction of Iraq: security.

The Marshall Plan and the Iraq Reconstruction Program

From 1948 to 1951, the Congress appropriated more than $12 billion for the Marshall Plan, equal to about $100 billion in 2008 dollars.[36] The four-year program, a joint U.S.-European venture, provided aid to sixteen countries in the wake of the devastation of Europe caused by World War II.

The most salient difference between the Iraq program and the Marshall Plan was that the latter's aid was conditional, with each recipient country required to deposit money into a counterpart fund. U.S. money spent on rebuilding Iraq was not made contingent on any contribution from Iraq.[37] It effectively was a series of huge grants.

The Marshall Plan's Economic Cooperation Administration (ECA), an independent agency created by the Congress, managed the program for its entire four-year duration.[38] The management of the U.S. reconstruction effort in Iraq, however, changed hands four times in two years—from the NSC to ORHA to the CPA to the U.S. Embassy.

Those who developed the Marshall Plan methodically and successfully cultivated widespread bipartisan congressional and public support, even though opposing parties controlled the White House and the Congress. Secretary of State George C. Marshall made an extensive speaking tour of the country, selling the idea of an enormous foreign aid program for a defeated enemy. The head of the ECA in Washington was auto-industry executive Paul Hoffman, a Republican Party leader; his deputy in Paris was former ambassador and businessman Averill Harriman, a Democratic Party leader. Hoffman gave some 150 speeches about the Marshall Plan's value.[39] In contrast, the CPA's IRRF 2 request was conceived, prepared, and presented in less than three months; the Congress passed it after only four days of debate.

The Marshall Plan recruited a mix of experienced civil servants and professionals from the private sector and academia. Thousands of talented candidates applied for each job opening, with only 1 out of every 200 hired. A streamlined deployment process was able to get prospective employees medically examined, then hired and issued security clearances, passports, and travel vouchers in only two days.[40] The standard tour of service with the ECA was two years.

The CPA staff, cobbled together and roiled by conflicting lines of authority and institutional allegiances, had a very uneven quality. Although some personnel were hired and deployed quickly, others had to wait up to ten months. Turnover was high; most CPA officials served for only a few months.[41] Similar turnover problems afflicted the U.S. Embassy when it took over the management of the reconstruction program.

The Marshall Plan was structured to restore the remnants of a democratic system. In Iraq, the United States sought to implant an entirely new system of government, building democracy where a dictatorship or monarchy had long prevailed. The nations in Western Europe had homogeneous societies, functioning institutions, a tradition of democratic governance, and advanced technical knowledge. They were also at peace. Iraq lacked a history of democratic government, had weak public institutions, and never had a diversified market economy.[42] Violence in Iraq, stemming chiefly from sectarian disputes, undermined every aspect of the reconstruction effort. Above all, the Iraq program, unlike the Marshall Plan, never received adequate resources to match its ambitious vision.

Essential Services Overview– Transition From the CPA to the Embassy

Metric[43]	Pre-invasion	Post-invasion	CPA Transition
Electricity Production			
Megawatts	4,075	711	3,621
Oil Production			
Million Barrels per Day	2.58	0.30	2.16
Iraqi Security Forces			
Soldiers and Police	1,300,000	7,000-9,000	87,000[44]
Telecommunications			
Landline Subscribers	833,000	0	791,000
Mobile Subscribers	80,000	0	461,000
Human Toll			
U.S Troop Fatalities	-	139	862
Civilian Contractors	-	1	46
U.S. Civilians	-	~9	52
Iraqi Civilians	-	7,413	16,848
Financial Cost ($ billions)			
U.S Funding	-	$3.45	$22.93
Iraqi Funding	-	$0.00	$16.00
International Funding	-	$0.00	$13.60
Total Funding	-	$3.45	$52.53

When Ambassador Bremer arrived in May 2003, electricity production averaged just 711 megawatts per day. At the time the CPA transferred sovereignty to the Iraqi Interim Government, production had risen to 3,621 megawatts.[45] This significant improvement in one year was still well below the 6,000 megawatts the CPA had set as its ultimate goal.[46] The CPA effort to get electricity production up to 4,400 megawatts was fleetingly successful in October 2003, but the short-term actions taken to meet that target proved counter-productive to long-term progress.[47]

Oil production increased fairly steadily in 2003 and 2004, but still suffered from the consequences of insufficient maintenance and poor infrastructure security. By the time of Ambassador Bremer's departure, production had reached an average of 2.16 million barrels per day, a significant increase from the immediate postwar output, but still below prewar levels.[48]

PART III
THE U.S. EMBASSY TAKES CHARGE
JUNE 2004 TO JUNE 2005

CHAPTER 16
NEGROPONTE'S REVISIONS

*Security was the paramount issue ... without security, it was going to be impossible to move these economic projects forward ... That was one of the fundamental corrections that had to be made.**

Ambassador John Negroponte
U.S. Ambassador to Iraq (2004-2005)

Ambassador John Negroponte presented his diplomatic credentials to the Iraqi Interim Government on June 29, 2004, the day after the CPA passed sovereignty back to Iraq. The President had placed the new ambassador, who had been serving as the U.S. Permanent Representative to the United Nations, in charge of the largest and most challenging diplomatic mission in the world, which then had a staff of about 900 Americans and 550 Foreign Service Nationals.[1] Negroponte would serve in Iraq for nearly nine months before leaving in March 2005 to become the first Director of National Intelligence.[2]

Shortly after arriving in Baghdad, Ambassador Negroponte put the CPA's reconstruction plans on hold and directed a thorough re-examination of the $18.4 billion program. This review led to a series of IRRF 2 reprogrammings intended chiefly to improve security in Iraq by increasing funding for training and equipping Iraq's security forces, and to strengthen democracy by increasing investment in the preparations for three elections scheduled for 2005. During Negroponte's tenure, the U.S. government reallocated $4.41 billion of IRRF 2.[3]

IRMO vs. PCO
Negroponte took the helm of a reconstruction program in transition. The recently signed National Security Presidential Directive 36 defined the functions of two new offices—the Iraq Reconstruction and Management Office and the Project and Contracting Office. IRMO was a Department of State entity, and PCO was part of the Department of Defense.

NSPD 36 placed IRMO in charge of formulating reconstruction policy, and the CPA's advisors to the Iraqi government continued as ministry "senior advisors" within the new IRMO structure.[4] The senior advisors operated as consultants to Iraqi ministers by helping them coordinate ministry operations and reconstruction projects.[5]

---

* SIGIR interview with Ambassador John Negroponte, former U.S. Ambassador to Iraq, February 12, 2008.

The PCO inherited PMO's duties to provide acquisition and project management support to the U.S. relief and reconstruction program. It also took charge of providing program management services for IRRF projects "to ensure [the] integration of projects within and across infrastructure sectors and within and across other sectors when requested by IRMO or other agencies."[6] USACE provided technical support and quality assurance programs for PCO's projects.

Although NSPD 36 sought to clarify reconstruction roles and responsibilities, its ambiguities actually aggravated the management situation in Iraq, making it more difficult to achieve unity of effort by fragmenting reconstruction responsibilities. IRMO and PCO reported to different masters, the Multi-National Security Transition Command-Iraq managed its own affairs, and USAID continued to control its own programs. In practice, the chief of mission was only nominally in charge of the overall reconstruction program.[7] The diffusion of authority limited Ambassador Negroponte's ability to integrate reconstruction programs, weakened management capacity, and fed interagency tensions, all of which impeded progress.

The PMO's Dave Nash ran both the PCO and IRMO during the first two months after the transition. Ambassador William B. Taylor, a career diplomat with extensive reconstruction experience, replaced Nash as the head of IRMO in late summer 2004. Charlie Hess, who had served as director of the operations and response division of the U.S. Department of Homeland Security, took over as director of the PCO at about the same time.[8] Hess understood that he reported to three different people—the commanding general in Iraq, the secretary of the Army, and the ambassador—but he did not believe that he reported to the IRMO director.[9]

The Strategic Review of IRRF 2

In early July 2004, the MNF-I command was upgraded to a four-star general with General George Casey replacing Lieutenant General Ricardo Sanchez as senior theater commander.[10] General Casey's and Ambassador Negroponte's paramount concern was security. "I felt that we had moved into a reconstruction phase when we were still actually in a conflict phase," said Negroponte. "We were in an insurgency."[11] Negroponte concluded that implementing economic development projects would be fruitless as long as security remained a serious problem.[12] General Casey concurred, noting that the reconstruction program and military operations required integration in a way that was "mutually reinforcing."[13]

Ambassador Negroponte directed IRMO to conduct a complete review of the IRRF 2 program and to develop a new strategic plan that would address the problem that had most bedeviled the CPA—the breakdown of security across Iraq. He asked IRMO to analyze the original CPA spend plan and to provide suggestions for adjusting its budget allocations among the ten reconstruction sectors.[14] IRMO's senior staff worked with USAID, PCO, and the military throughout the summer of 2004, identifying ways to use the IRRF 2 program to bolster Iraqi security capabilities.[15]

In the spring of 2004, OMB had apportioned more than $11 billion of IRRF 2 to four implementing agencies: Defense, State, USAID, and Treasury, with Defense receiving over three-quarters of the funds.[16] By the time the CPA dissolved, only a small portion of IRRF 2 had been spent ($366 million).[17] The Congress had earmarked $5.56 billion for electricity and $4.3 billion for water resources and sanitation. IRRF 2 program managers, however, had not planned to begin construction on major projects in these two sectors until 2005.[18] Ambassador Negroponte seized upon these funds as available capital that he could recommit—with congressional approval—to pressing new priorities, most notably security.

The First Reprogramming

USAID's mission director, Spike Stephenson, was barely on speaking terms with Admiral Nash when the Negroponte/Casey strategic review began. According to Ambassador Taylor, "the relationship between PCO and USAID was not good."[19] USAID, which had been largely ignored during the creation of IRRF 2, welcomed the strategic review because it offered the agency a new opportunity to shape the reconstruction effort. "It gave us a chance to get in on the policy end of it," said Stephenson. "Win or lose, you got to speak your piece."[20]

USAID's piece was a proposed development package for more investment in capacity-building and democracy projects. It also sought an additional $200 million for its Office of Transition Initiatives (OTI). The OTI had been providing expertise to military-led CERP projects, which were increasing Iraqi employment and promoting economic development. Through this program, USAID had helped implement many CERP projects, particularly in Baghdad. "We were doing them literally at the direct request of the major subordinate commanders," particularly Major General Peter Chiarelli (then commanding the 1st Cavalry Division), said Stephenson.[21]

After listening to presentations from all of the major reconstruction and security players, Ambassador Negroponte and General Casey agreed to move $3.46 billion to programs to strengthen Iraq's security forces, promote economic and private-sector development, build democracy, and prepare for the upcoming elections. The security sector alone received an increase of $1.81 billion from reprogrammed funds.[22] At the same time, $1.94 billion was taken from the water sector and $1.07 billion from electricity.[23]

Because the reallocations amounted to a more than ten percent shift in funding within IRRF 2, the State Department had to submit a request for congressional approval. Deputy Secretary of State Richard Armitage made the department's case for the funding shifts before the House Appropriations Committee, stating that "our most urgent priority right now is security. Short-term stability and long-term prospects in Iraq quite simply depend on improving the security situation."[24] The Congress agreed, approving all the changes on September 30, 2004.[25]

The Second Reprogramming

While the Congress evaluated Negroponte's first reprogramming request, the State Department initiated a second review.[26] PCO's new director, Charlie Hess, objected and sent a long email to Ambassador Taylor stating that it was a bad idea to send another group of short-term "helpers" to "squeeze more hypothetical dollars from the IRRF program to accomplish other much-needed program objectives."[27] Hess wanted to avert further delays in starting IRRF projects, which had been frozen during the first reprogramming. He believed that it was time to stop analyzing the program's financial allocations and to start accomplishing rebuilding work. The contractors on the ground were accruing millions of dollars in overhead costs without producing much. "Every day that we rethink what we are all about is one less day of getting on with the job."[28] His complaints fell on deaf ears.

In December 2004, the State Department announced the second reprogramming, moving $457 million in IRRF 2 money, again mostly out of the water sector. The reallocation restored $211 million to the electricity sector for quick-impact projects and transferred $246 million for projects to improve essential services in the embattled cities of Falluja, Samarra, Najaf, and Sadr City. The latter shift sought to mollify restive populations in the most dangerous parts of Iraq.[29]

For the second time in four months, Ambassador Taylor had to tell the Minister of Municipal and Public Works, Nesreen Berwari, that the funding for her water treatment, waste management, and irrigation projects was going to be cut significantly. She had worked closely with the CPA to develop the program, and Taylor, who had previously gone to her office to inform her of the first cut, did not look forward to giving her more bad news. Minister Berwari told Taylor she never wanted to see him in her office again. "She said it with a little bit of a smile," Taylor said, "but not much."[30]

The Third Reprogramming

In the spring of 2005, Charlie Hess again was exasperated to learn that the State Department was planning yet another reprogramming of IRRF 2, this time focusing on new operations and maintenance efforts, the electricity sector, and project cost overruns. Hess complained to his Defense Department boss, Claude Bolton, Assistant Secretary of the Army for Acquisition, Logistics and Technology, stating:

> The impact of incremental reprogramming has a significant detrimental effect on the momentum of program execution (it slows the pace) and consequently results in increased overhead costs while we sort out the skills and contracting staffing levels necessary to execute the remaining work. This is particularly debilitating when accomplished in a series of back-to-back reprogramming exercises where, as we finish dealing with the first reprogramming cycle, it is followed by yet another round of reprogramming reviews. Again, this stifles momentum, generates added costs and typically reduces effectiveness of program dollars.[31]

Hess's complaints again had no effect.

On March 25, 2005, the State Department notified the Congress of its desire to reallocate $832 million.[32] Drawing mostly from pending energy-sector projects and five large water projects, the realignment provided $225 million to bolster the essential services infrastructure in Baghdad, and $607 million to fund operations and maintenance programs.[33] Sustainability had become an increasing concern among U.S. officials, who worried that Iraq did not have the capacity to maintain new or refurbished facilities once transferred.[34] Most of the new sustainment funding went to the electricity sector.[35]

Iraq Relief and Reconstruction Fund Allocations by Sector for June 2004, December 2004, and June 2005 ($ Millions)

Sector	June 2004 Allocation	December 2004 Allocation	June 2005 Allocation	Percent Change from Original
Security & Law Enforcement	$3,235.0	$5,045.0	$5,017.6	55%
Justice, Public Safety Infrastructure, and Civil Society	$1,484.0	$1,953.0	$2,188.5	47%
Electricity Sector	$5,465.0	$4,369.0	$4,318.5	-21%
Oil Infrastructure	$1,701.0	$1,701.0	$1,723.0	1%
Water Resources and Sanitation	$4,247.0	$2,279.0	$2,146.0	-49%
Transportation and Telecommunications Projects	$500.0	$513.0	$508.4	2%
Roads, Bridges, and Construction	$368.0	$360.0	$334.0	-9%
Health Care	$786.0	$786.0	$786.0	0%
Private Sector Employment Development	$183.0	$843.0	$840.0	359%
Education, Refugees, Human Rights, Democracy, and Governance	$259.0	$379.0	$363.0	40%
Administrative Expenses	$213.0	$213.0	$214.0	0%
Total	$18,439	$18,439	$18,439	

Source: OMB, *Section 2207 Report*, Funding Table, July 2004; and DoS, *Section 2207 Report*, Status of Funds, July 2005. Note: Totals may not add up due to rounding.

The Impact of the Reallocations

Negroponte's reallocations reflected the U.S. government's response to changing conditions in Iraq, chiefly the worsening security situation. They also demonstrated recognition of the need to increase investment in Iraq's political process. Each funding shift, however, caused the elimination or curtailment of planned or ongoing infrastructure projects.

The water sector suffered the most, losing nearly 50 percent of its funding (from $4.25 billion to $2.15 billion), which forced the cancellation of numerous projects.[36] The electricity sector was the second-hardest hit, suffering a loss of almost a quarter of its IRRF 2 money (from $5.47 billion to $4.32 billion), resulting in a reduction of proposed power projects. This cut planned increases in electricity capacity from 3,400 megawatts to 2,100 megawatts.[37]

Notwithstanding these infrastructure funding cuts, Negroponte and Casey firmly believed that the reprogrammings were necessary to implement their new strategy. They recognized that the CPA's vision had given inadequate weight to security, democracy, and project sustainment.[38] Along with the security and democracy increases, the reprogrammed funds supported new sustainment programs across the ministries.[39] But these funds, although an important start, addressed only a fraction of Iraq's operation and maintenance needs. As the State Department noted, "the process of capacity development to manage and sustain infrastructure projects will take time."[40]

CHAPTER 17
CONTINGENCY CONTRACTING AND PROGRAM MANAGEMENT

> *I was the deputy prime minister in charge of reconstruction, and I still have difficulty understanding what USAID, IRMO, and GRD-PCO actually do.**

Dr. Barham Salih
Deputy Prime Minister of Iraq (2004-present)

The United States struggled in Iraq to establish integrated contracting and program management systems that could provide effective direction, support, and oversight of the reconstruction program. Beginning with the creation of the CPA's Program Management Office in August 2003, a succession of contracting and program management offices suffered under varying sets of complex contracting regulations, divergent chains of authority, changing program requirements and shifting reconstruction priorities. A shortage of qualified contracting officers, continuous staff turnover, and poor program management practices, particularly regarding quality assurance programs, weakened oversight of reconstruction projects. Finally, contracting officers did not have adequate information systems to track contract activity.

Contracting Shortfalls

Every reconstruction project begins with a contract that defines the government's expectations of a contractor. A good contract clearly describes the work requirements, the construction schedule, and the budget. Contractors perform only what the contract provides, albeit in an environment that anticipates change orders. The government manages quality-assurance programs to ensure contract compliance, and the contractor manages quality-control programs to ensure that its workers accomplish contract requirements effectively.

In February 2004, Brigadier General Stephen Seay took over as CPA's Head of Contracting Activity. Seay brought an extensive Army contracting and program management background to his new job. He inherited an office that was grossly understaffed and completely overwhelmed by hundreds of DFI contracts. The most serious problem was the dearth of qualified contracting personnel who could develop good project requirements and statements of work.

---

* SIGIR interview with Dr. Barham Salih, Deputy Prime Minister of Iraq, June 20, 2006.

Brigadier General Seay concluded that the contracting office could not manage the approaching wave of IRRF 2 contracts. He thus rapidly reorganized and expanded the small office, recruiting a dozen new people, including acquisition professionals who could draft statements of work, thereby free contracting officers to do their job of writing contracts.[1] Seay also requested more lawyers "to troubleshoot solicitations and to support contracting so that procurement and construction delays did not result from disputes relating to the contracting process." He wanted to make sure that each solicitation and contract award process followed the FAR and the IRRF 2 statutory requirements.[2]

Despite implementing many improvements, Brigadier General Seay still struggled with familiar problems: personnel shortages, poor program management, and inadequate information management systems. For example, his staffing chart called for 69 people. Throughout his one year in Iraq, over a third of Seay's staff positions remained vacant.[3]

Contracts and Task Orders

A Pentagon team handled the contract award process for the twelve IRRF 2 contracts but the PMO and then the PCO planned and managed their execution. Under the PMO's organizational structure, the sector program-management contractors—private firms hired to help manage the design-build contractors— were supposed to develop project requirements and prepare them for execution through task orders. They took reconstruction projects identified by the PMO/ PCO and defined the work requirements, schedules, and budgets.[4] Seay's contracting office then took this information and developed task orders, which the PMO/PCO would assign to construction contractors. GRD provided quality assurance for the projects.

Developing and managing task orders in 2004 and 2005 proved to be difficult. The contracting office did not have management or information systems that could effectively track them. The PCO did not have enough information about potential projects to develop good scopes of work; and it had too few career government employees capable of negotiating with contractors to define good requirements. The SPMOs tried to fill this void, but they "were really just construction supervisors, not program managers."[5]

Seay attempted to solve these problems by holding program-wide reviews with all the contracting officers, program managers, and contractors. This remedial measure had some success but Seay still had to contend with PCO program managers who "preferred to build facilities" rather than think through the "preconstruction and task order award process."[6]

Andy Bailey, vice president of the Louis Berger Group, which had the program management contracts for three sectors—Communications and Transportation; Building, Education, and Health; and Security and Justice—thought that the design-build management concept was "brilliant," but the execution poor. He said that the PMO/PCO had neither the systems nor the processes in place to support the effort. Moreover, there were serious disagreements regarding the proper role of contractors who served as program managers. For example, the contracting office and the GRD argued for more government oversight, believing that too many contractors were overseeing other contractors.[7] A SIGIR assessment later noted that "the many layers of management, including program management contractors, made it difficult to determine who had ultimate authority over money, people, and projects."[8]

Information System Challenges
The IRRF 2 legislation required the Administration to submit reports to the Congress every three months updating the use of the funds on a project-by-project basis and including estimates of the costs required to complete each project. The Congress provided $50 million to develop a system to manage the program and track projects, but the PMO failed to create a good information management database for IRRF 2.[9]

When Brigadier General Seay arrived in early 2004, he found no existing information management program to track contracts. "We had to scramble to assemble an automated system," he said. "There was a computer system in boxes, but there was no one who was a qualified system administrator who could set it up for us and keep it running."[10]

In the absence of a single integrated database, each implementing agency established its own. USAID used its proprietary financial and program management system while the Department of Defense used its system to track CERP projects. Because these systems were not compatible, someone from Seay's office had to go to IRMO and PCO every day to ensure that everyone all had the same information on every contract.[11]

In 2004, in response to SIGIR audits criticizing the lack of a single project-management system, the PCO created the Iraq Reconstruction Management System (IRMS), to integrate data on all projects in Iraq.[12] Through IRMS, the PCO sought to reconcile various incompatible information management systems by developing a "PCO Solution" that would assemble essential data and thus allow managers visibility into the entire range of reconstruction activity.[13] But it would be years before the United States had a reasonably integrated system to manage and monitor reconstruction. A subsequent SIGIR review found that the failure to develop a cohesive information management system "hampered the work of others who rely upon the PCO data set for reporting purposes."[14] The IRMS ultimately was able to track only about 70 percent of all reconstruction projects.

Contracting Waste

During the spring of 2004, the IRRF 2 design-build contractors quickly mobilized and deployed to Iraq, but most of the task orders for construction work were not ready. While the PMO and the contracting office struggled to develop task orders, the construction companies, awaiting new work, continued to charge high overhead costs.[15] Five design-build firms during this period submitted invoices totaling $62.1 million in overhead costs and only $26.7 million in construction costs, an example of the scope of waste caused by project delays.[16]

As costs rose, U.S. civilian and military authorities in both Baghdad and Washington became increasingly anxious to see reconstruction projects started. Apart from curbing waste, they wanted to demonstrate the U.S. commitment to Iraq by improving essential services, building the Iraqi Security Forces, and helping the Iraqi Interim Government prepare for the 2005 elections. They also hoped to undercut the insurgency by providing electricity, clean water, and jobs, while simultaneously stimulating economic progress and fostering democratic political processes. This new urgency forced the PCO to issue task orders rapidly, before they had been "definitized"—meaning before the government and the contractor had reached formal agreement on what would be done, how much it would cost, and when it would be completed.[17]

Contracting regulations allow "undefinitized contracts" under two conditions: when there is not enough time to negotiate a definitized contract or when it is imperative to make a binding commitment that allows work to begin immediately. But by law, these contracts must eventually be definitized.[18] A SIGIR audit found that some contracting officials in Iraq erroneously believed that the definitization requirements did not apply to Iraq task orders. This incorrect assumption caused millions of dollars in waste.[19]

The Creation of the Joint Contracting Command-Iraq

In November 2004, CENTCOM formally established the JCC-I to support reconstruction and military contracting in Iraq.[20] The Assistant Secretary of the Army for Acquisition, Logistics, and Technology designated Brigadier General Seay as the new commander of the JCC-I and appointed two Principal Assistants Responsible for Contracting, one to supervise U.S. military contracting and the other to manage reconstruction contracting. JCC-I assumed responsibility for managing all remaining DFI-funded contracts and for developing a training program to help Iraqi ministries strengthen their contracting and procure-ment procedures. USACE still maintained its own contracting office, based in Washington, D.C., with a forward contingent in Iraq.[21] The change also did not affect USAID or the Department of State, which continued to write their own contracts and manage the IRRF 2 funds apportioned to them.[22]

A New Contracting Strategy

During the late summer of 2004, the embassy re-evaluated the wisdom of continu-ing to use the large IRRF 2 design-build contracts. The reconstruction program was shifting emphasis from big infrastructure projects to targeted programs supporting security, governance, and economic development. Moreover, the design-build cost-plus contracts were proving too expensive and difficult to manage.

Task orders were issued under the design-build contracts on either a cost-plus or fixed-price basis, but virtually all were cost plus "incentive fee" contracts. Under cost-plus contracts contractors are reimbursed for all expenses, regard-less of whether projects are successfully completed. The incentive-fee formula determines the contractor's award fee on top of the guaranteed fixed fee. The design-build contractors in Iraq usually received a guaranteed fee of three percent and were eligible for an additional incentive award fee of up to twelve percent. Thus, contractors could earn up to fifteen percent of the costs of any contract in award fees.[23]

In the unstable environment of mid-2004, cost-plus contracts appeared to some to be tantamount to "an open checkbook."[24] The contractors countered these complaints by asserting that running construction programs in Iraq's dan-gerous environment justified the high costs. The government was also negligent in controlling costs. For example, many contracts had clauses that permitted the government to convert them from a cost-plus to a fixed-price contract (after a percentage of design work was completed). But government contracting offices failed to exercise these conversion provisions, and they were frequently excised from contracts after the first year.

High contract costs ultimately led the PCO to stop issuing new task orders under the design-build IDIQ contracts and to begin contracting directly on a fixed-price basis with Iraqi firms.[25] The FAR's "simplified acquisition" rules, which require fewer bids and less cost data for contracts valued under $500,000, allowed contracting officers to rapidly award new work to local contractors. When the Congress increased the threshold for simplified acquisition to $1 million, more direct contracting became possible.[26]

In the fall of 2004, the high costs of the design-build contractors, the de-em-phasis on large infrastructure projects, and a new push to create jobs led embassy officials to urge the PCO to move work from big firms to Iraqi companies. PCO director Charlie Hess opposed the move. "My professional belief is that we are in an extremely precarious acquisition position if we attempt to move more than a modest amount of awarded work to some other contract vehicle (unless the contractor is failing to perform)," he wrote. "Work that has been awarded to the [design-build contractors] under full and open competition in accordance with the criteria established at the time of award should not be moved to accomplish other worthwhile purposes now."[27]

Hess believed that, because of increased security risks, the design-build contractors had opted to work through Iraqi subcontractors anyway. "The [design-build contractors] are on the hook for contract performance whether they subcontract with one firm or many firms," he said. "On the other hand, as we attempt to move to more direct contracting with Iraqi firms, the U.S. government takes on the risk of overseeing many more contractors in terms of execution and contract administration."[28] But the change in reconstruction strategy ultimately proved beneficial and began to reduce costs.

Monitoring Costs and Performance

In the IRRF 2 legislation, the Congress required the Administration to provide continuing analysis on how much it was going to cost to complete each IRRF 2 project. Cost-to-complete estimates determine the amount of work, time, and money needed to finish an ongoing project.[29] But neither the CPA nor the embassy was able to develop a system that provided consistent cost-to-complete analysis.

The lack of an integrated program management system significantly contributed to this shortfall. A 2005 SIGIR audit concluded that "IRMO, as well as GRD-PCO, MNSTC-I, and USAID (the reporting entities), failed to develop methodologies to assure reliable and transparent cost-to-complete reporting."[30]

PCO Merges with GRD

When the PMO was first established, USACE provided construction management and quality assurance for IRRF 2 construction projects. The Defense Department always envisioned that USACE, which had more experience in managing projects during the construction and closeout phases, would eventually assume all program management responsibilities for IRRF 2 infrastructure projects.[31] In March 2005, the PCO submitted a plan to merge with the GRD. On October 14, 2006, the PCO ceased to exist, and the GRD thus became the sole entity responsible for overseeing the completion of the Defense Department's IRRF 2 construction program.[32]

Moving Forward

As the IRRF 2 program matured, the U.S. government reformed and reorganized reconstruction offices in Iraq, seeking to improve coordination within and among agencies. Some changes—such as the formation of JCC-I—incrementally helped. But others—such as the creation of the PCO and IRMO, with their ambiguous lines of authority—perpetuated existing problems.

The various reorganizations invariably created new layers of management, interweaving public- and private-sector program managers. But none of the reforms vested anyone with the ultimate responsibility—and authority—for the entire reconstruction program. As a result, there was plenty of management oversight, but little accountability.[33]

Contracting and program management problems—coupled with the turbulence engendered by constant organizational change—affected the ability of construction firms to build projects on time and within budget. To add to these many troubles, they were building in a war zone.

*I felt that because we instituted the program when we did, we had
to spend a disproportionate amount of the money on security. I
realize that's now accepted as a fact of life, but the cost seemed to
me very, very high.*[*]

Ambassador John Negroponte
U.S. Ambassador to Iraq (2004-2005)

No aspect of the U.S. program to rebuild Iraq was left untouched by the escalating violence of 2004 and 2005. Coalition troops and members of Iraq's security forces were not the only ones dying: insurgent attacks claimed the lives of many reconstruction workers. More than 400 non-Iraqi civilians had died by September 2005. Of the 147 U.S. civilian deaths that had occurred as of October 2005, 117 were contractors killed by insurgents.[1] The number of non-Iraqi contractor deaths would continue to rise, nearing 1,300 by the end of 2008.[2]

Iraq's dangerous environment posed serious challenges for both design-build contractors and the PCO's program managers. It was often impossible to carry out projects in dangerous areas. And it was more difficult to draft contracts with well-defined statements of work when contracting personnel could not visit project sites. Similarly, U.S. government quality-assurance personnel frequently could not monitor project progress because of rising conflict.

Reconstruction Under Fire
Violence also impinged upon the relationships between U.S. reconstruction officials—whose travel outside the Green Zone was increasingly circumscribed—and their Iraqi counterparts. Insurgent attacks on building sites and on the convoys carrying supplies to them delayed construction work. Intimidation of Iraqi employees caused frequent work stoppages. And the design-build firms and their subcontractors experienced a high turnover in Iraqi staff, as personnel were killed or fled to escape the violence. By the end of 2005, deteriorating security conditions had severely slowed work and driven costs higher in every reconstruction sector, threatening the entire effort.

The increasing conflict altered the reconstruction program in two significant ways. First, the United States had to reprogram resources within IRRF 2

---

[*] SIGIR interview with Ambassador John Negroponte, former U.S. Ambassador to Iraq, February 12, 2008.

to fund the massive expansion of Iraq's security forces. These reprogrammings had the effect of canceling hundreds of planned and ongoing projects, causing what came to be termed a "reconstruction gap"—the difference between what was intended and what was actually built.[3] Second, the direct security costs for every reconstruction contract escalated. A 2005 SIGIR examination of nine major construction firms that were awarded IRRF 2 contracts found that security costs accounted for up to 16.7 percent of the contract price, more than double the original estimates by PMO.[4]

The U.S. military's mission did not include providing security protection for U.S. civilian government agencies and contractors. These organizations consequently hired private security companies to protect their employees.[5] By December 2004, government agencies and reconstruction contractors had obligated more than $766 million for private security firms.[6] Despite this large expenditure, neither the State Department nor the Pentagon had complete data in 2005 for what these companies actually cost or on the number of people they employed in Iraq. The Defense Department could only estimate that at least 60 private security providers employed as many as 25,000 people.[7] But without the protection provided by these firms, neither the U.S. civilian agencies nor the con- tractors they employed would have been able to perform their missions. In 2008, a SIGIR review found that $5.3 billion had been obligated to 77 private security contractors to provide security services in support of U.S.-funded projects and programs since 2003.[8]

In the face of growing violence, the U.S. government pressed ahead with major infrastructure projects to improve the provision of essential services. Both the U.S. military and civilian leaders hoped the enhancements would help sustain military successes in the fight against the insurgency. But SIGIR audits of key programs in the oil, electricity, water/sewerage, and health sectors revealed that, between June 2004 and July 2005, the United States reconstruction program made only limited progress because of the unstable security environment.

The Oil Sector

Under the IRRF 2 program, two design-build firms—Parsons Iraq Joint Venture (PIJV) in the north and KBR in the south—worked on oil projects to rehabili- tate pipelines, refineries, gas-oil separation plants, and export facilities. KBR, as part of Task Force RIO, had operated in the southern oil sector since the March 2003 invasion.[9] By July 2005, the United States had provided about $2.7 billion in U.S.-appropriated funds and another $2.7 billion in Iraqi funds—much of it going to KBR—to rebuild Iraq's oil infrastructure, import refined fuels, develop oil security and pipeline repair teams, and provide technical assistance.[10]

Despite this significant U.S. investment in the oil sector, Iraq's production fell after reaching a peak of 2.54 million barrels per day (MBPD) in September 2004. From June 2004 to June 2005, Iraq averaged less than 2.2 MBPD and exported only about 1.4 MBPD.[11] The worsening security environment, inadequate contractor performance, and frequent program changes accounted for the decline in oil production.[12] In October 2004, the State Department reported that security had driven cost estimates higher and caused delays in projects to repair oil export terminals, pump-compressor stations, and gas-oil separation plants.[13]

In January 2005, a significant decrease in the levels of oil production and exports stemmed from "the number and locations of pipelines sabotaged, combined with an inability to secure some strategic pipelines."[14] Attacks on the northern pipeline brought all pipeline exports from the Kirkuk oil fields to a halt in December 2004.[15] Iraq's Ministry of Oil reported that insurgents launched 186 attacks during 2004, causing more than $6 billion in damage to oil fields and pipelines. At least 138 oil-security and technical employees were also killed during this period.[16]

The Qarmat Ali Water Treatment Plant

Security was the largest but not the only problem afflicting the oil sector. Reconstruction planners frequently failed to coordinate oil sector projects sufficiently, making it difficult to achieve production objectives. In Iraq's southern oil fields, for example, years of underinvestment and poor maintenance made it impossible to sustain the underground pressure needed to pump oil out of the ground. Clean water had to be pumped into the fields to produce sufficient pressure. But the only source of clean water was the Qarmat Ali water treatment plant and the collection of 48-inch pipes that carried its water to eight pump stations.[17]

Task Force RIO contracted with KBR for a $225 million project to refurbish the Qarmat Ali water treatment plant. By August 2004, KBR had completed much of the work, and six of the eight water-injection pump stations were operational. But repeated breakdowns of the corroded pipes prevented the system from injecting the necessary amounts of water into the oil fields. KBR's contract did not include repair of the field-pipes, so the PCO issued another task order to repair the pipes.[18] This project was still ongoing in mid-2006 because of delays due to the degraded state of the delivery systems.[19] The failure to complete the Qarmat Ali project significantly limited the productivity of the southern oil fields.

In late 2004, the PCO became increasingly concerned about KBR's "failure to adequately control and report costs" of its rehabilitation work in the southern oil fields. The PCO issued a "cure notice"—or intention to terminate the contract—unless KBR provided a more detailed explanation of costs by January

29, 2005.[20] Six months later, KBR finally convinced the PCO that it had satisfactorily addressed the cost issues. But during this period, the PCO decided to begin shifting work to PIJV, which had the oil sector contract for the north. In the spring of 2005, PIJV mobilized its resources southward to conduct facilities assessments, and the PCO eventually gave it much of the southern oil sector work originally intended for KBR.[21]

The Al Fatah Pipeline Crossing
The oil sector problems in northern Iraq were also challenging. During the invasion that toppled Saddam Hussein, the United States inadvertently bombed the Al Fatah Bridge, destroying the fifteen oil and gas pipelines it carried across the Tigris River. The damaged lines included the major crude-oil pipeline that originated in the rich Kirkuk oilfields and angled 100 kilometers southwest to Al Fatah, where it crossed the Tigris to supply Iraq's largest refinery and the power plant at Baiji.[22] Al Fatah also connected the oil fields to the Ceyhan pipeline, the direct avenue for oil export to Turkey. The loss of this important connection cost Iraq at least $5 million per day and contributed to keeping export levels below prewar levels.[23]

On June 8, 2003, a group of Task Force RIO engineers, along with representatives from KBR, USAID, and Bechtel, visited the Al Fatah project site and concluded that the easiest way to repair the pipelines was to restore the bridge and install new pipes across it. The engineers recommended that USAID use its Bechtel contract to rebuild the bridge and that Task Force RIO use its KBR contract for the pipe installation. Task Force RIO engineers estimated the project's total cost at about $5 million and calculated that it would take two to four months to complete.[24]

The first delay occurred when Bechtel said it could not start the job for two months. The CPA and Iraq's Ministry of Oil, concerned that the site was vulnerable to insurgent attacks, looked for an alternative solution. One of the CPA's oil experts suggested using a technique called "horizontal directional drilling," which entailed excavating a tunnel under the river for the placement of pipes. With CPA approval, the advisor contacted Laney, Inc., an American company that specialized in horizontal drilling. Laney advised that a 40-inch crude-oil pipe could be installed in as little as six weeks, depending on soil conditions.[25]

The CPA considered awarding a sole-source contract to Laney so work could proceed quickly but instead authorized KBR to manage a competitive subcontracting process for the project.[26] KBR posted the Al Fatah job, received responses from four qualified bidders, and awarded the subcontract, valued at nearly $50 million, to a joint venture of Wilbros, Inc., and Laney. KBR also awarded a $10,000 contract to Fugro, Inc., to do a geotechnical analysis of the Al Fatah soil. The Fugro report described the geology in the area as complex and recommended that KBR do further field exploration before beginning horizontal drilling.[27] KBR instead opted against doing the field studies—a fatefully expensive decision, as time would reveal.

The subcontractors on the project mobilized in October 2003 but refused to begin work until a secure camp was established at Al-Fatah. Insurgent activity had made the area increasingly dangerous. By the end of January 2004, the contractors finally began horizontal drilling only to discover that the riverbed's loose subsurface made it impossible to tunnel a hole large enough to accommodate a 40-inch pipe.[28] For the next five months, the contractors drilled unsuccessfully into the crumbling shale and loose gravel, with tunnels repeatedly collapsing. USACE finally cancelled the project in August 2004, a year after it had started. KBR attributed the failure to unforeseen subsurface geologic conditions. But the Fugro report had raised exactly this issue.[29]

A SIGIR inspection found that USACE and KBR failed to ensure that the necessary engineering studies were completed before the project began. "The government and the contractor failed to adequately research, plan, design, and manage the project," the SIGIR assessment concluded, and thus "$75.7 million allocated to the project was exhausted, while only 28 percent of the drilling scope was completed."[30] Because this was a cost-plus contract, the government was unable to recover the taxpayer dollars that KBR unwisely spent—and thus wasted—on this project.

Oil Sector Challenges
Partly as a result of continuing cost problems with KBR, the PCO restructured the way it managed projects in the oil sector, melding the resources of the oil ministry's state-owned enterprises with the expertise of design-build contractors. The design-build companies provided engineering, procurement, and technical support, while the Iraqi companies supplied labor and equipment for construction. This collaborative approach allowed the PCO to stretch the remaining IRRF 2 funds for the oil sector and to complete repairs on more gas-oil separation plants than would have been otherwise possible.[31]

By the spring of 2005, the PCO had definitized task orders for 82 oil sector projects worth $781 million and was negotiating another 55 projects worth $323 million. The delay in finalizing the 55 pending projects arose from a change in contracting strategy as well as an "insufficient staff to execute the workload."[32]

The U.S. emphasis on increasing oil production meant that two important and related issues were left largely unaddressed: increasing the supply of refined petroleum products and reforming Iraq's subsidy system for those products. With little money in IRRF 2 for refineries, the embassy encouraged Iraq to invest in upgrading them.[33] Estimates for rehabilitating the country's existing refinery system ranged as high as $7 billion.[34]

The shortage of refined fuels in Iraq presented a conundrum. Iraq needed to boost its supplies of refined fuels and increase its production and export of crude oil. But projects to increase refinery capacity and those to improve production competed for the same limited ministry funds. Oil production projects, which quickly put cash in the government's coffers, usually trumped refining. But that outcome limited Iraq's capacity to meet its own refining needs, which made it more difficult to rebuild another vital sector that depended heavily on these fuels: electricity.

The Electricity Sector

From the start of the reconstruction program, increasing Iraq's electricity production to prewar levels was a top U.S. priority. When Ambassador Negroponte initiated his strategic review in mid-2004, the sector's $5.54 billion allocation—amounting to nearly one-third of IRRF 2—was divided among generation ($2.79 billion), transmission ($1.55 billion), distribution ($998 million), an automated monitoring and control system ($150 million), and security ($50 million).[35] Negroponte's reprogrammings first reduced and then restored IRRF 2 funds for electricity projects, so that by July 2005, the sector was down about twenty percent from its original IRRF 2 allocations.[36] By the end of March 2005, about $5.7 billion in U.S. appropriations and Iraqi funds had been allocated to improve the electricity infrastructure across Iraq.[37] Only the security sector would get more money—in fact, five times more.

Although the U.S. reconstruction program made progress in rebuilding the electricity sector during the two years following the 2003 invasion, by the spring of 2005, Iraq's average daily power output was still below prewar levels.[38] U.S. officials attributed the shortfall to a litany of familiar problems: security, sabotage, shortages of appropriate fuels for generating facilities, limited ministerial capacity, inadequate operations and maintenance, poor program management, and project cancellations caused by cost overruns and realignments.[39]

The government had awarded contracts to four design-build firms to rehabilitate and rebuild the electricity grid in Iraq. Through the PCO, the Defense Department managed three of the firms: FluorAMEC Joint Venture for nationwide generation projects, Washington Group International for transmission and distribution projects in the north, and Perini Corporation for transmission and distribution projects in the south.[40]

About $1.1 billion in USAID money was contracted to Bechtel for the electricity sector work.[41] Bechtel was supposed to implement 22 electricity projects during the 2003 to 2005 period, but SIGIR and USAID Inspector General audits found that Bechtel's projects frequently failed to meet their objectives.[42] The Bechtel effort at the Doura Power Plant, one of the main facilities providing electricity for Baghdad, illustrates the problems that design-build contractors encountered in the electricity sector.

The Doura Power Plant

USAID tasked Bechtel to rehabilitate two of the four steam turbines at the Doura power plant. The two turbines were designed to produce 160 MW each, but—because of poor maintenance—neither was operational at the time of the 2003 invasion. Bechtel began work at the plant on August 1, 2003, planning to complete the project within nine months. A series of delays pushed the completion date to the end of 2005, more than a year overdue, and the final cost was more than four times greater than planned (rising from $34.1 million to $121.1 million).[43]

The security situation at the project site had deteriorated in late 2003, and ministry employees and Bechtel's subcontractors refused to go to work. The contractor camp at Doura "was a shoot 'em up place."[44] Bechtel beefed up security, and the U.S. military agreed to guard the gate to the project, a rare example—during this period—of U.S. forces providing infrastructure security. Nevertheless, by the summer of 2004, several subcontractors had pulled out, and Bechtel had to employ new support for the project.

The two Doura turbines were reported substantially complete by June 2005, but only one had been commissioned by February 2006.[45] The other was almost ready, needing only a process called steam blowing before becoming fully operational. Because the project was over budget, USAID decided to turn it over to the ministry to complete the finishing touches.[46] But the ministry was not ready to operate or maintain it.

In August 2006, one of the Doura units experienced "catastrophic failure" because of poor maintenance of the "exciter," a key component that supplies power to the generator's rotor. The ministry removed an exciter from another unit to replace the broken one, and the repaired unit operated until April 2007, when another major failure occurred. USACE/GRD then stepped in and took over the project, eventually bringing both units online by the end of the summer.[47] But more U.S. money had to be expended on this project after it had been turned over to the Iraqis.

Case Studies in Waste

During 2004 and 2005, rising costs and the re-allocation of IRRF 2 funds forced the embassy to cancel or reduce the scope of several large projects undertaken by Bechtel and Perini in the electricity sector. These included building new power generation plants, as well as restoring transmission and distribution lines.

Bechtel: As part of the first realignment of IRRF 2 resources, USAID cancelled the $100.6 million Bechtel project to rehabilitate Units 4 and 5 of the Baiji Thermal Power Plant. The project would have increased the plant's output by 275 MW, but USAID halted the project in late September 2004, just three months after it began. At that time, Unit 4 was producing about 125 MW, just 57 percent of its design capacity. About $7 million was spent on the project before its cancellation.[48]

USAID terminated another large Bechtel effort—the $381 million Mansuria Natural Gas Power Plant project—after very substantial U.S. investment. Bechtel was contracted to build two new electric plants about 65 miles northeast of Baghdad. The site was selected so that the plant could use the natural gas in the Mansuria fields to power its turbines. In February 2004, after an urgent request from CPA for a quick increase in the Baghdad electricity supply, USAID fast-tracked the project, increasing costs. But it was halted in the summer of 2004 in the wake of the first IRRF 2 reprogramming.[49]

The Mansuria power plant project was finally cancelled in the spring of 2005, but not before Bechtel had billed the government for $62.7 million for a base camp and for the purchase of turbines, generators, transformers, and other equipment. In June 2005, USAID transferred much of the Mansuria equipment to the Ministry of Electricity, which said it would install all of it at projects in the Najaf area.[50]

Perini: In March 2004, the Defense Department awarded Perini a $500 million IRRF 2 contract to repair the electrical transmission and distribution lines in southern Iraq. By late 2004, however, the PCO concluded that Perini's overhead costs—which included security costs—were too high and began to cut back on issuing task orders. The PCO eventually terminated half of Perini's task orders because of its cost proposals that "significantly exceeded budgets and available funding," and "concerns about the company's management of project schedules."[51]

Perini's Basrah substation task orders illustrate the cost problem. Perini had received a task order in May 2004 for eight projects to improve Basrah's electricity-distribution network. The PCO budgeted $36 million to rebuild five substations and to rehabilitate the distribution network. Substations convert high-voltage electricity from transmission lines to low-voltage electricity that feeds distribution lines, which carry power to local communities. In July 2004, Perini submitted a $105 million cost proposal for these projects. The PCO then reduced the project's scope to just the substation work, and Perini consequently dropped its price to about $44 million. By October 2004, further negotiations brought the cost down to about $23 million and work began. Perini completed the substations in September 2005, at a cost of $28.8 million.[52]

A March 2006 SIGIR inspection of the substations reported that, although the construction met the "standards of the design," they were not operating because the Ministry of Electricity had failed to install transmission and distribution lines as agreed.[53] A follow-up visit by SIGIR found the substations finally operational in October 2006—more than a year and a half after Perini completed them.

Between June and October 2004, the PCO issued additional task orders to Perini to build more substations and distribution networks in Babil, Anbar, Thi-Qar, Najaf, Umm Qasr, and Basrah. But by the end of the year, the PCO had terminated much of this work. A SIGIR audit found that Perini completed five of the ten task orders issued under the $500 million contract, and that the PCO cancelled the remainder. The U.S. government ultimately paid $123 million to Perini—including its mobilization costs and its $8 million award fee—on a contract that produced just $26 million in finished projects.[54]

An Evolving Reconstruction Strategy

In late January 2004, the embassy used money freed up by de-scoping design-build contracts to initiate a new Rapid Recovery Program with the Ministry of Electricity. The program sought to increase the hours of available power in advance of the January 2005 elections by completing projects begun during the CPA period that had been turned over to the ministry before completion because of cost overruns.[55] Recognizing that the Iraqis did not have the capacity to manage and maintain new infrastructure, IRMO and PCO continued the shift away from the "design-build-handover" model, moving toward inculcating a "build-train-handover" approach, which emphasized not just project completion, but also the need for Iraq to invest in operations and maintenance programs.[56]

The Water and Sewerage Sector

The original IRRF 2 plan earmarked $4.33 billion for the water sector, giving it the second-highest infrastructure priority, behind electricity, but Negroponte's strategic reviews cut $2.2 billion from the sector.[57] Nearly $1.5 billion of the remaining funds went to projects to provide clean drinking water for Iraq's population. The rest was used to build sewerage systems, improve irrigation, and repair the 149-mile Sweetwater Canal in southern Iraq, which delivered fresh water to Basrah.[58]

Three design-build contractors worked on U.S. water projects: Bechtel, FluorAMEC, and a joint venture between Washington Group International and Black & Veatch. By the summer of 2005, USAID had assigned 34 water and sanitation rehabilitation projects worth $369 million in IRRF 1 money to Bechtel.[59] Meanwhile, the PCO issued task orders funded by IRRF 2 to FluorAMEC and to Washington Group to provide potable water, build sewage systems, and help Iraq manage its water resources.[60]

As of June 2005, Bechtel had completed eighteen task orders, repairing six sewage treatment facilities, rehabilitating two water treatment plants, and constructing a large water-supply system for a city in southern Iraq. But a dozen of Bechtel's water projects suffered significant delays.[61]

A GAO assessment identified several reasons for the delays. GAO found that, in addition to ubiquitous security challenges, the CPA's initial assessments for the sector had underestimated water-project costs by 25 to 50 percent, thus requiring the re-scoping of many projects and the cancellation of others. High staff turnover and poor project-site selection also created delays.[62]

A SIGIR audit of the $500 million FluorAMEC contract found that, of four water sector task orders awarded to FluorAMEC in 2004, the PCO had terminated two by July 2005 because of funding constraints caused by project delays.[63] The other two were significant projects, including the largest single IRRF 2 project, which was supposed to provide water to 300,000 Iraqis in the Nassriya area.

The Nassriya Water Supply System

The PCO awarded the task order for the Nassriya water supply project in April 2004, estimating then that it would cost between $90 million and $120 million. But shortly after FluorAMEC began construction in August 2004, the PCO's water-sector manager realized that the project's cost would be much higher, and would exceed the available budget. He recommended merging two nearby water projects into the Nassriya project. In January 2005, the PCO definitized the task order for the merged projects at $172 million. Five separate modifications over the next year increased the price tag to just over $244 million. By October 2007, FluorAMEC had finished the Nassriya project and turned it over to the Iraqis, at a final cost of $277 million—almost three times the estimated cost, and about two years late.[64]

Sustaining this complex water treatment facility became an issue. A September 2005 GAO report concluded that "the long-term outlook for sustaining re-constructed Iraqi [water] facilities remains unclear."[65] GAO's concerns were substantiated in late 2007, when SIGIR inspectors visited the Nassriya water project to find it operating at just twenty percent of capacity, three months after being commissioned and transferred to Iraqi control.

The Falluja Wastewater Treatment System

Fierce fighting between Sunni-backed insurgents and Coalition forces erupted in Falluja in the spring of 2004 and continued through November when U.S. military officials finally secured the city. Although the fighting had forced many residents to flee, Falluja's population was still around 180,000. With no existing wastewater treatment system, much of the city's raw sewage was dumped directly into the Euphrates River. Sewage ran in the streets, exposing the city's residents to serious public health problems.[66]

Seeing Falluja as a "hub for the campaign of violence aimed at destabilizing Iraq's interim government and driving foreign military forces from the country," the embassy wanted to launch a project that would benefit the city's population and demonstrate the U.S. commitment to enhancing life in that beleaguered Sunni bastion.[67] In June 2004, the PCO issued a $32.5 million task order to FluorAMEC to design and construct a new wastewater treatment system that would serve most of the city. The embassy prioritized the project, identifying it as a "key national reconciliation issue."[68] The task order provided a completion date eighteen months out.[69] Four years later, when SIGIR inspectors visited Falluja to assess the project, work was still ongoing.

FluorAMEC experienced a series of security problems as it attempted to build the Falluja wastewater treatment system. Insurgent activity prevented it from conducting proper site evaluations. One member of a survey team was wounded by gunfire. Contractors also had to deal with unexploded ordnance, improvised explosive devices, and intimidation.[70]

But security was not the only obstacle. The contractor had based its design on an Iraqi engineering firm's plans for a typical wastewater stabilization pond—known as a lagoon system—that recycles water, which is then used for irrigation. The system's principal advantages were "simplicity, low cost, and high efficiency."[71] But in August 2005, the new Iraqi Ministry of Municipalities and Public Works notified the embassy that the lagoon system was unacceptable; it wanted a system of more-sophisticated compact sewage-treatment units.[72] IRMO and PCO spent the next three months negotiating with ministry officials about which system best suited Falluja. Finally, in November 2005, the United States abandoned the lagoon-system design, with all of the investment that had already gone into building it, and agreed to build the more modern system that the minister wanted.[73] This change caused substantial cost increases and more delay. Whether the Iraqis could operate so modern a water treatment system also became an issue.

Because of slow progress, the U.S. government terminated FluorAMEC's task order for the Falluja project in September 2005, after expending $18.7

million—more than half the cost of the original task order. Then, between 2005 and 2008, the U.S. government spent an additional $79.3 million—drawn from IRRF, CERP, and DFI funds—on 45 other contracts, mostly with Iraqi firms, in an attempt to complete the system.

SIGIR's 2008 inspection of the Falluja project found that, when finally finished, the wastewater treatment system, which was supposed to serve the entire population of Falluja, will serve a little more than a third of the city's population, will have cost three times its original price, and will have been completed four years later than originally planned. Moreover, serious questions remain about whether the Iraqis can sustain the system once it becomes operational in the spring of 2009.[74]

The Health Sector

IRRF 2 allocated $786 million for Iraq's health sector. The CPA designated $439 million of that money for a program to build 150 new primary healthcare centers (PHCs) across Iraq and to renovate 17 hospitals. Another $297 million was allocated for procuring medical equipment for the clinics and hospitals, setting up a mobile blood collection program, rebuilding the Academy of Health Science, training PHC staff, and providing technical assistance to the Ministry of Health. Fifty million dollars supported construction of a modern pediatric hospital in Basrah.[75] None of the Negroponte reprogrammings affected these allocations. Nevertheless, no single U.S. construction program encountered more problems than the health sector's effort to construct 150 PHCs across Iraq.

Fundamental disagreements between U.S. officials and the Iraqi Ministry of Health about the approach to health care stymied sector progress from the outset. U.S. experts wanted to move Iraq away from its hospital-based national health care system to one emphasizing preventive care delivered at local clinics. This change was necessary, U.S. experts believed, to ensure health care delivery in rural areas, where access to basic medical services did not exist.[76] The Iraqi medical community resisted this change, urging reconstruction officials to put U.S. money into renovating hospitals rather than into a new chain of rural clinics. Their complaints had no effect.

The Primary Health Clinic Program

In March 2004, the Defense Department awarded a $243 million design-build contract to Parsons Delaware to upgrade 17 hospitals, repair 3 ministry buildings, and build 150 new primary healthcare centers across Iraq.[77] The contract also required Parsons to provide and install medical and dental equipment for each of the primary healthcare centers.[78] In May 2004, Parsons received three task orders from PMO, initially valued at $88 million, to build 41 healthcare centers in central Iraq, 49 in the northern region and 60 in the south. The equipment was to cost an additional $70 million.

For a variety of reasons, the program fell far short of meeting its goals. A SIGIR audit concluded that Parsons and the U.S. government agencies in charge of managing the contract—IRMO, PCO, and USACE—shared responsibility for the program's failure. SIGIR cited the high turnover in personnel, poor program management, and weak quality assurance as the primary factors that caused the program to fail.[79] From May 2004 to the end of 2005, eight different contracting officers, six different program managers, and five different PCO sector leads worked on the clinic program.[80] This constant turnover made it difficult to resolve the many problems that arose among the contractor, the U.S. government, Parsons, and the Iraq Ministry of Health.

SIGIR auditors found that the U.S. government's program managers lost track of program costs and schedules. In September 2005, the JCC-I reduced the scope of the project and formally notified Parsons that it had lost confidence in the company's ability to deliver the projects on schedule and within budget.[81] The PCO terminated the contract because Parsons had completed only six clinics, while spending $186 million on the program (about 77 percent of the definitized costs).[82] After the termination of the Parsons contract, over 100 of the partially built clinics were completed through direct contracts with Iraqi firms.

SIGIR inspections of five primary healthcare centers in Kirkuk revealed that the clinics' construction was so shoddy that it "raised questions as to the safety of occupancy of the structures." The inspections concluded that "inadequate quality control and quality assurance on the part of the contractor and the U.S. government, respectively, resulted in not properly identifying and correcting construction deficiencies."[83]

Parsons also had a $70 million contract for the delivery and installation of medical equipment to each of the primary healthcare centers, including X-ray machines, exam tables, patient beds, ventilators, defibrillators, incubators, dental chairs, lights, and cabinets.[84] The clinic supplies began arriving in Baghdad in the spring of 2006, long before any clinic was open, but the U.S. government did "not fully know the type, quantities, and condition of the equipment" it received. By June 2006, Parsons had delivered 115 "full or partial medical equipment sets to the warehouse in Abu Ghraib."[85] Jack Holly, a retired Army colonel who was asked by CPA to manage its logistics operation, said he had to build a new climate-controlled storage facility to house the medical supplies.[86] He cited the Parsons equipment-delivery fiasco as a prime example of poor coordination in Iraq reconstruction operations.[87]

The Demise of Design-Build Contracts

During 2004 and 2005, reconstruction efforts across the sectors faced many challenges: deteriorating security, poor project integration, insufficient collaboration with and acceptance by Iraqis, weak Iraqi capacity to sustain projects, and poor U.S. contract and program management. Overhead costs skyrocketed as all reconstruction contracts required increasing security. Many projects were descoped and then declared complete, while others were simply cancelled. Virtually every project ended up over budget and behind schedule.

But there was some progress in the program as well. By June 2005, PCO, IRMO, and the JCC-I had decisively moved away from the design-build model, which would yield cost savings and build Iraqi capacity. Reallocated funds frequently went to support security initiatives, operations and maintenance, and programs promoting democracy. But Iraq's security forces were far from ready for the task that confronted them.

CHAPTER 19
IRAQI SECURITY FORCES AND COUNTERINSURGENCY

> In the fall of 2004, it was very difficult. I remember a day of 55
> dead bodies of [Iraqi] soldiers who were trying to go on leave
> from Mosul... Ambushes of three minibuses full of recruits who
> had just completed basic training and going home. Just endless
> challenges during that time on the security front.*
>
> **Lieutenant General David Petraeus**
> Commander of MNSTC-I (2004-2005)

The scope and nature of U.S. support to Iraq's security forces changed dramatically after the June 2004 transfer of sovereignty. By Presidential order, the Multi-National Force-Iraq was assigned responsibility for building the Iraqi security forces and it designed an ambitious new program to train, equip, employ, and support Iraq's forces. Faced with escalating violence across the country, MNF-I aimed to boost the Iraqi Security Forces' capacity and effectiveness, so that the Iraqi government eventually could assume control of security in all eighteen provinces.

MNF-I divided responsibilities for Iraq's security forces between two subordinate commands. The Multi-National Security Transition Command-Iraq was responsible for training and equipping Iraqi security forces; the Multi-National Corps-Iraq was responsible for the operational control of trained and equipped units.[1]

Iraq's Growing Security Needs
In July and August 2004, a formal "troops-to-task" assessment was conducted by a team of senior military officers under the leadership of MNF-I's commander, General George Casey and the commander of MNSTC-I, Lieutenant General David Petraeus. "We started by figuring out what we wanted those forces to do," Lieutenant General Petraeus said. "What are their tasks and purposes? Number two, based on certain assumptions, what types of forces do you need? How are you going to organize them?"[2]

The assessment concluded that the Iraqi forces were not prepared to combat the violent insurgency then threatening the fledgling democracy. The country urgently needed more forces—both police and military—trained, equipped, and prepared for counterinsurgency operations.

---

* SIGIR interview with General David Petraeus, Commander of MNF-I and former Commander of MNSTC-I, March 2, 2008.

The CPA designed the Iraqi police and military forces to deal with the mundane missions of domestic law enforcement and national defense; they had not trained and equipped the police to face heavily armed and well-organized insurgents, nor had they prepared Iraq's army to provide internal security. The April 2004 uprisings made clear that Iraq's security forces did not have the capacity to successfully combat the growing insurgency.[3] Significant change was needed immediately.

MNF-I called for three major initiatives to bolster the Iraqi Security Forces (ISF) structure. The Iraqi Police Service would expand from 90,000 to 135,000; the Iraqi Civil Defense Corps—renamed the Iraqi National Guard—would add 20 battalions, for a total of 65; and the number of border patrol officers would double to 32,000.[4] In all, the plan called for bringing the number of trained and equipped personnel to approximately 271,000.[5] Virtually all Iraq's security forces—from the local police to the special operations forces—would receive counterinsurgency training.

General Casey's and Lieutenant General Petraeus's conclusion that the growing insurgency required a substantially larger Iraqi force heavily influenced Ambassador Negroponte's strategic review of reconstruction funds.[6] The IRRF 2 legislation provided $3.24 billion of its total $18.44 billion to support the ISF, but the expansions to meet the security requirement proposed by MNF-I's troops-to-task assessment immediately created additional funding needs.[7] Ambassador Negroponte's first reallocation included $1.81 billion to strengthen Iraq's forces.[8]

Building Iraqi Capacity

In preparing the ISF for its many missions, MNSTC-I faced enormous challenges: equipment procurement lagged behind training and logistical support was nonexistent. MNSTC-I commander Lieutenant General Petraeus knew that building institutions to enable the ISF to prevail in the field would be "very, very painful and very difficult."[9] Petraeus began by improving MNSTC-I's flexibility, funding, and contracting capacity, allowing it to increase quickly the ISF's rate of expansion.[10] MNSTC-I first established flexible contracting mechanisms for procurement and construction, working with an array of military agencies, such as the Joint Contracting Command-Iraq, USACE, the Defense Logistics Agency, and the Air Force Center for Engineering and the Environment.[11] This contracting flexibility was complemented by an increase in capacity as MNSTC-I bypassed PCO and IRMO to get more contracting officers and purchasing agents from CENTCOM.[12] As Lieutenant General Petraeus would later note, this strategy also saved money.

By October 2004, security construction was booming. Work rapidly progressed at Al Kasik, An Numaniyah, Tallil, and Kirkuk military bases, and was completed at Umm Qasr Naval Base. Police academies were built or refurbished in Mosul, Baghdad, Al Sulaymaniyah, Hilla, Al Kut, Al Asad, and Basrah. The camp at Taji was expanded to accommodate the new elite Special Police Forces, and hundreds of police stations across the country were under construction.[13]

The equipping of Iraq's security forces similarly accelerated. Contracts awarded in early 2004 finally began to deliver. The Iraqi National Guard received 310 vehicles, nearly 30,000 AK-47s, 969 PKM machine guns, and other much-needed equipment in summer 2004.[14] The Ministry of Interior forces began receiving equipment as well, including trucks, sport-utility vehicles, AK-47 assault rifles, Glock pistols, radios, and body armor.[15]

Transforming the ISF
Through the second half of 2004 and into 2005, the Iraqi Armed Forces (IAF) and the Iraqi Police Service grew rapidly. MNSTC-I developed new units with greater capabilities, making possible Iraqi participation in counterinsurgency activities.

Ministry of Interior
The CPA had envisioned the IPS as a traditional law-and-order police force accountable to local authorities. This vision reflected a community-policing model, where the primary police task is upholding the rule of law by conducting criminal investigations, questioning witnesses, and arresting suspects.[16] As in most insurgencies, however, the police bore the brunt of the violence. Pitted against heavily armed and motivated foes, the IPS experienced high casualty and desertion rates in 2004. The insurgency also undermined the IPS in other ways: training was disrupted, morale was low, and increasing attacks kept many officers confined to their stations.[17]

One of the main conclusions of MNSTC-I's troops-to-task assessment was that the Iraqi police needed better training and equipment. This required more funding, so Petraeus recommended moving more IRRF 2 funds to support MNSTC-I.[18] In June 2004, $849.3 million was reprogrammed to supplement the $1.04 billion already shifted to improve police training, equipping, and employment.[19] MNSTC-I also added specialized courses in leadership, internal affairs, negotiation, investigation, and crowd control.[20] The new programs combined counterinsurgency training with courses in survival skills and counterterrorism.[21]

The CPA's efforts to create Ministry of Interior (MoI) paramilitary units for special operations achieved minimal results. The Emergency Response Units—based on U.S. SWAT teams—were well trained and equipped, but only

40 personnel were operationally ready by July 2004.[22] MNSTC-I and the MoI thus created additional heavily armed and specially trained police units called the Special Police Forces, consisting of the Special Police Commandos, Mechanized Police, and the Public Order Battalions. In April 2006, these forces were reorganized into the National Police.[23]

In September 2004, Iraq's Minister of Interior, Bayan Jabr, created the Special Police Commandos, an elite paramilitary force for indigenous counterinsurgency support.[24] When Lieutenant General Petraeus was given a demonstration of their abilities, he was impressed and committed more MNSTC-I funds to support them, developing a six-week intensive training course at the Special Police Commando Academy in northern Baghdad.[25]

The MoI also created the Mechanized Police for rapid response deployment, fixed-site security, and cordon-and-search operations. Training in operations, communications, and maintenance began at Taji Military Base in November 2004.[26] Once trained, these forces were stationed mostly in and around Baghdad, where they conducted vehicle-mounted operations to secure high-value routes, such as "Route Irish," the road to Baghdad International Airport.[27] MNSTC-I awarded a $43.9 million contract to build permanent facilities for the Mechanized Police.[28]

Public Order Battalions rounded out the MoI's elite civil-security forces. They were a lighter force intended for situations not requiring the greater combat power of the Special Police Commandos and the Mechanized Police.[29] Although Public Order Battalions conducted counterinsurgency operations, they primarily performed traditional police functions in very hostile environments.[30] Their first training program began in late September 2004 at An Numaniyah military base, and nearly 1,110 students graduated in mid-November, comprising the first three Public Order Battalions.[31]

Ministry of Defense

The size and capability of the security forces under the Ministry of Defense increased dramatically during late 2004 and 2005. The IAF grew from three divisions to ten, incorporating the Iraqi National Guard (ING)—formerly the Iraqi Civil Defense Corps—and developing new specialized counterinsurgency units. The Iraqi special operations forces attained more proficiency, and the Iraqi navy and air force took their first formative steps. The ICDC had been a key Combined Joint Task Force-7 initiative, but it performed disastrously during the April 2004 uprisings, when almost half its personnel deserted. Local commanders reconstituted much of the force as the ING, and implemented new vetting and training procedures to make it a more reliable and effective force.[32]

The 2004 troops-to-task assessment pointed to the ING as critical to the counterinsurgency effort. The Congress—at Ambassador Negroponte's request—reallocated $442 million in IRRF 2 funds to support its growth.[33] By January 2005, 42 of the 45 ING battalions were manned above 70 percent—a major recovery from their April 2004 collapse.[34] The increasing professionalism of the ING was recognized on January 6, 2005, when the Iraqi Interim Government announced that it would be integrated into the Iraqi army.[35]

Like the MoI, the MoD developed new special counterinsurgency units following the April 2004 uprisings, calling them the Iraqi Intervention Force (IIF), which began operating in Baghdad in June 2004.[36] Although smaller than the ING, the IIF was designed specifically for counterinsurgency operations. Its members received an extra five weeks of training, better equipment, and more tactical support from MNC-I.[37]

The nascent Iraqi Air Force and Navy were the weakest components of the IAF. MNSTC-I, following the CPA's original plan, did not equip the Air Force with fixed-wing fighters or bombers—considering them "unnecessary and incapable of influencing the counterinsurgency fight"—and instead favored aerial reconnaissance and transport aircraft.[38] By August 2004, two Iraqi Air Force reconnaissance aircraft were conducting airborne assessments of damage to Iraqi oil-pipelines. The fledgling Iraqi Navy policed Iraq's waterways to deter smuggling and other illicit activities and to protect Iraq's port and oil assets in the Persian Gulf.[39] Like the Air Force, Iraq's Navy had limited operational capacity.[40]

In July 2004, the MoD established the Iraqi Special Operations Force (ISOF) as an elite force operating outside the Iraqi Armed Forces chain of command.[41] The ISOF consisted of a Commando Battalion, which was trained to conduct raids and seize airfields, and the Iraqi Counter-Terrorism Force (ICTF), which was trained to fight high-threat terrorist organizations.[42] U.S. Special Forces provided instruction to the ISOF, using the U.S. Ranger program for the Commando Battalion and U.S. elite counterterrorism forces programs for the ICTF. In time, the ISOF became the most effective counterinsurgency force in Iraq.[43]

Training Adapts

After being trained and equipped by MNSTC-I, Iraqi units were transferred to the control of MNC-I, which deployed them in support of the counterinsurgency campaign. In the fall of 2004, Special Police Commandos acquitted themselves well in offensive operations in Baghdad, Falluja, Samarra, Mosul, North Babylon, and elsewhere.[44] An ISF high-water mark came on January 30, 2005, when 130,000 security force personnel provided security at more than 5,200 polling sites throughout the country so that more than 8 million Iraqis could vote.[45]

U.S. commitment to training also increased. From November 2003 to November 2004, the number of U.S. soldiers whose primary mission was to advise Iraqi units grew from 350 to 1,200.[46] Many of these new advisors came from the Army Reserve 98th Division, an institutional-training division known as the "Iroquois Warriors," which had been filling many of MNSTC-I's headquarters billets.[47]

MNSTC-I designed new advisory programs to partner U.S. teams with Iraqi units in basic training, and then to stay together during deployments.[48] Between ten and fifteen U.S. military personnel comprised each team. The advisory teams mentored their Iraqi counterparts and served as a critical link to U.S. logistics, communications, medical, and fire-support capabilities.[49]

Retired General Gary Luck's early 2005 assessment reaffirmed the importance of these embedded advisory teams. He advocated doubling or tripling the number of advisors partnering with Iraqi units, believing that this increase would allow Iraqi units to take the lead sooner in the counterinsurgency campaign.[50] In response to Luck's assessment, MNSTC-I expanded the embedded advisors program. In the late spring of 2005, MNSTC-I changed the name of the partnered advisory teams to Military Transition Teams to reflect more accurately MNF-I's goal of transitioning security responsibility to Iraq.[51]

Measuring Progress

During the CPA's tenure, the primary metric used to measure the ISF's progress was the number of security force personnel "on duty." But this metric obscured the distinction between trained and untrained personnel, leading to exaggerated expectations, constantly changing force-size numbers, and consequent credibility problems regarding these numbers.[52] For example, of the 83,789 IPS personnel reportedly on duty shortly before the transition of sovereignty in June 2004, only 26,876 (32 percent) had received any training. Of those trained, more than three-quarters had received just the short Transition Integration Program training, meaning that only 5,857 academy-trained personnel were in the IPS.[53] MoI manning data were further skewed because personnel who were absent without leave or deceased were not removed from the "on duty" rolls. Corrupt Iraqi officials collected the payments to these "ghost employees," who accounted for 20 to 30 percent of the MoI staff.[54]

During 2004, MNSTC-I made a number of important reforms that improved U.S. policymakers' ability to measure progress. Immediately after the transition, MNSTC-I replaced the "on duty" metric with a "trained and equipped" personnel metric.[55] The net result was that the report showed a 75 percent drop in MoI force totals, from 181,297 "on duty" personnel on June 15, 2004, to 47,255 "trained and equipped" personnel on August 25, 2004.

In the winter of 2004-2005, MNSTC-I developed a Transition Readiness Assessment (TRA), based on the U.S. military's readiness-reporting system, to measure both training and equipping status, as well as operational effectiveness.[56] MNC-I Transition Teams administered the TRAs every month, reflecting MNF-I's belief that "the best measure of the capabilities of Iraqi units and improvements in the security situation comes from commanders on the ground."[57]

The TRAs graded units on a four-level scale, assessing their ability to conduct counterinsurgency operations. At level one, they could operate independently. At level two, Iraqi units needed MNC-I "enablers"—such as medical evacuation, transport, and fire support—to operate. At level three, Iraqis could operate only alongside MNC-I forces. And at level four, ISF units were still in training or otherwise not capable. Transition teams used the TRAs to estimate how many months it would take a unit to advance to the next level.[58] By July 2005, only one IAF unit was rated at level one, although 24 were judged at level two.[59]

Iraq Security Forces Fund

National Security Presidential Directive 36 resolved many of the ISF training and equipping problems by authorizing the Defense Department to take charge of all security force development in Iraq. But it did not solve the resource problem. MNF-I still depended on IRRF 2 to fund most of its training programs.[60] The $1.81 billion reallocation approved by the Congress in September 2004 had helped, but MNSTC-I needed more.

By January 2005, MNSTC-I had obligated $1.44 billion of the $2.32 billion available in IRRF 2 funds for the Ministry of Interior security forces. It also had obligated $1.69 billion of the $2.64 billion available to the MoD security forces.[61] Even with this new investment, the expanding ISF were unable to stem the rising violence, and the Iraqi Ministries of Defense and Interior could not sustain and support the forces without U.S. assistance.[62]

It was clear that transitioning security responsibilities would cost much more than IRRF 2 could provide. Thus, in November 2004, MNSTC-I began developing its own supplemental request for the specific purpose of increasing U.S. investment in training and equipping the ISF.[63] After months of negotiation, OMB submitted a congressional budget request on February 14, 2005.[64]

On May 11, 2005, the Congress approved the request, appropriating $5.39 billion to the newly created Iraq Security Forces Fund (ISFF). The Congress provided the Defense Department flexibility on the use of the funds, allowing it to reallocate large amounts of money for different ISF purposes without seeking congressional approval, as was required under IRRF 2.[65] Additional appropriations through 2008 would bring the total value of ISFF appropriations to $17.9

billion.[66] Coupled with nearly $5 billion in IRRF 2 allocations, investment in Iraq's security sector was by far the single largest Iraq reconstruction expense.[67]

Perilous Progress
By the end of June 2005, MNSTC-I had spent $544 million on construction projects for the IAF, up from $57 million a year earlier. It also had spent $346 million on military equipment, compared to just $11 million the previous year.[68] But even with these dramatic increases, new problems surfaced regarding ISF equipment accountability, logistics capability, and sectarian infiltration of the forces.

Logistics
In June 2004, the capacity of Iraq's Ministries of Interior and Defense to support security forces in the field was very weak. "There wasn't even a Ministry of Defense building, much less something that you would call a Ministry of Defense," said Lieutenant General Petraeus. Only "about five guys with cell phones and a couple of old generals" remained.[69] Petraeus added that the Ministry of Interior "was nascent, to put it mildly."[70]

Iraqi Army units could not sustain independent operations for any significant period of time without U.S. support.[71] The police struggled with vehicle maintenance and equipment distribution.[72] As a consequence, the ISF remained heavily dependent on MNF-I funding, logistics, transportation, and fire support as their mission evolved and as they became more proficient in counterinsurgency operations.[73]

Continuing security problems across Iraq meant that, for MNSTC-I, strengthening the ministries' logistical capabilities was secondary to equipping and training security forces. Unfortunately, this caused MNSTC-I to overlook oversight functions necessary to account for all equipment. For example, it failed to implement a tracking system for weapons issued to the ISF. As a SIGIR audit concluded, MNSTC-I should have appointed, at its inception, an officer accountable for property (including weapons). It finally did appoint one in the spring of 2005, but the absence of an effectively managed distribution system hindered MNSTC-I's ability to track equipment provided to the Iraqi forces.[74]

In response to the audit, MNSTC-I developed a tracking system that catalogued equipment by serial number, vehicle identification number, or some other unique identifying number. When MNSTC-I issued the equipment to the Iraqis, the Iraqi recipient had to sign for it.[75] But even with these new policies, security problems prevented MNSTC-I staff from consistently collecting physical records, which led to accountability weaknesses. As a consequence of these shortfalls, MNSTC-I could not properly account for many of the weapons it issued, both before and after implementing the new tracking system. Thus, too many U.S.-supplied weapons intended for ISF use may have ended up in militia or insurgent hands.[76]

Regarding logistics, MNSTC-I established a fixed-base logistics doctrine for supporting the ISF.[77] This meant that Iraqi supply, transportation, and maintenance capabilities above the unit level would be centrally located and directed to units as needed. In support of the program, MNSTC-I constructed a logistics depot for weapons and equipment at the Taji Army Base and started training a transportation regiment to deliver equipment to the Iraqi security forces.[78] But authority to advise the Ministries of Defense and Interior on logistics and other issues still resided with IRMO and the U.S. mission. It was not until October 1, 2005, that MNSTC-I became responsible for institution-building at the ministerial level, thus ending a bifurcated approach that had hindered progress.[79]

Sectarianism

As the ISF grew, a number of serious recruiting and manning problems also arose. MNSTC-I recruited nationally for the Iraqi Army, with the goal of creating a diverse security force whose personnel were not tied to a particular province, sect, ethnicity, or tribal group.[80] Recruiting was more complicated for the police because it was difficult for MNSTC-I to vet recruits for the IPS.[81] It consequently relied on Iraqis, especially community leaders, for vetting, but this approach opened the IPS manning process to politicization. The huge expansion of the police payroll during Ambassador Negroponte's tenure and beyond stemmed in part from the growth of new IPS patronage networks.[82]

The CPA's Transitional Administrative Law outlawed militias, and CPA Order 91, issued in March 2004, established a process to integrate them into the ISF. But the program was underfunded and understaffed.[83] The larger sectarian militias, particularly the Kurdish Peshmerga and the Shi'a Badr Corps, remained largely intact. Muqtada al-Sadr's Mahdi Army—one of the main adversaries during the April 2004 uprisings—was also not part of the integration plan.[84] Compounding the problem, many Iraqis viewed militias as the primary guarantors of security in certain areas, and some members of the Iraqi parliament depended on militias for protection.[85]

Some militia members who integrated into the ISF retained their old loyalties; their sectarian agendas undermined certain segments of the ISF, especially within the Ministry of Interior.[86] The Special Police Force proved most problematic regarding infiltration. The Ministry of Interior's desperate need for experienced recruits forced them to piece together units from Saddam-era commando units and Shi'a militia, each of which were likely to have their own sectarian agendas.[87] The result was a force "riddled with corruption and sectarian influence," whose members engaged in routine shakedowns for private gain and committed appalling human rights abuses.[88] These elite Iraqi units, trained and equipped by MNSTC-I for counterinsurgency, were regularly accused of human rights abuses. The sectarian and militia influences in Iraq's security forces fed the country's growing communal violence and threatened the return of abuses commonplace under Saddam.[89]

Security Redux

In its first year of existence, MNF-I made significant progress in training, equipping, and employing the ISF. MNF-I and the Iraqi Ministries of Interior and Defense expanded the size of the various Iraqi forces and added new counterinsurgency units that could better address Iraq's security needs. Improved measures of training and equipping and unit effectiveness helped MNF-I, CENTCOM, and the Pentagon track progress, adjust policy, and allocate resources. During the year, MNF-I also initiated a large-scale advisory program to mentor and support Iraqi forces in the field and took critical first steps in developing Iraq's logistical capabilities, so that security responsibilities could eventually be transferred.

Progress was expensive. But the additional resources improved the ability of the Iraqi security forces to fight the insurgency. Under the command of MNC-I, Iraqi units performed well in Falluja in November 2004, across the country in late January 2005, and in May 2005, when Iraqi forces engaged in their first coordinated counterinsurgency operation without significant U.S. assistance. During "Operation Lightning," the ISF operations across Baghdad resulted in the capture of 108 suspected insurgents.[90]

Problems nonetheless remained. Iraqi ministerial capacity continued to be weak.[91] MNC-I commanders reported that some Iraqi units who assumed control over their own territory subsequently collapsed. In March 2005, for example, an Iraqi unit that deployed to the border "virtually disintegrated, allowing foreign fighters to enter Iraq from over the Syrian border."[92] The new counterinsurgency mission assigned to the ISF placed them in direct contact—and often confrontation—with the Iraqi populace, and they increasingly became the target of insurgent attacks. Service in the ISF was dangerous: a total of 296 Iraqi police and military personnel were killed in June 2005—nearly ten per day.[93]

The ISF was not yet the professional force that the CPA had envisioned. Many of the elite forces created to fight the insurgency were increasingly infiltrated by sectarian elements and implicated in human rights abuses.[94] Factions within the ISF became politicized, feeding the growing conflict.[95] MNF-I faced a moving target: as it trained and equipped Iraqi security forces for counterinsurgency, it was unwittingly feeding the sectarianism that would rack Iraqi society in 2005 and 2006.

Chapter 20
Elections, Rule of Law, and Fighting Corruption

> *Corruption is a disease which is connected with many aspects of the government and in this society. It has become now a social phenomenon from the low rank and class to the higher rank in government... and for that reason there is no remedy for that except privatization. I think the government failed to defeat the corruption.* *

Ali Baban
Minister of Planning, Government of Iraq (2006-present)

The United States intended to build strong and democratic national and local governments in Iraq. Notwithstanding this noble goal, the original IRRF 2 plan allocated relatively few resources for governance and democracy programs.

The original plan divided support for democracy, rule of law, anticorruption, and governance programs in Iraq between two sectors: $1.3 billion went to the Justice, Public Safety Infrastructure, and Civil Society sector, while $280 million went to the Education, Refugees, Human Rights, and Governance sector. Most of the money in the justice sector was allocated for physical infrastructure projects, including courts and prisons. Democracy-building activities initially received $100 million—about one-half of one percent of the $18.4 billion IRRF 2.[1] Just $10 million in IRRF 2 funding went to civil-society programs. Almost no money was designated for anticorruption programs.[2]

Although the new constitution and the 2005 elections were signal achievements for Iraq, sustaining democratic institutions required a strong foundation in the rule of law. But, as with many U.S. programs in Iraq, several government agencies engaged in the effort, with none in charge. Moreover, support for Iraq's anticorruption entities—necessary to protecting Iraq's resources from waste or theft—was very weak.

Building Democracy
In 2003 and 2004, the CPA and then the U.S. Embassy recognized the need for more money to support the political process outlined in the Transitional Administrative Law.[3] The CPA moved money into democracy projects just after

---

* SIGIR interview with Ali Baban, Minister of Planning, November 23, 2008.

the November 15, 2003 agreement to return sovereignty to Iraqis. It also reprogrammed $358 million from infrastructure projects to efforts aimed at establishing the democratic foundations for a new Iraq. OMB divided these reprogrammed funds among the Defense Department, the State Department, and USAID to support a wide range of new projects, including developing political parties, building governance capacity, and promoting transparency in political and civic life.[4]

Following Ambassador Negroponte's mid-2004 strategic review, the State Department shifted another $380 million into democracy building, pushing the total reallocation to this sector above $830 million. This new money included $100 million to strengthen local and provincial governments and $200 million to help reduce sectarian conflict.[5] By the summer of 2005, total funding adjustments had increased U.S. investment in democracy building to $942 million.[6]

In late 2004 and 2005, the United States obligated approximately $130 million for non-security assistance to support two national elections and the constitutional referendum in 2005. The Department of State awarded $30 million to the National Democratic Institute and the International Republican Institute to organize political parties and provide training to build their capacity.[7] But almost a third of this money—$41.1 million—supported the work of the new Independent Electoral Commission as it readied Iraq for the three elections.

The Independent Electoral Commission
At the end of May 2004, the CPA established the Independent Electoral Commission of Iraq to "organize, oversee, conduct, and implement all elections" required by the TAL.[8] A week later, it promulgated Order Number 96, delineating the "legal framework for genuine and credible elections" to elect the members to a new Transitional National Assembly (TNA), which would eventually follow the CPA and Iraqi Interim Government as the third temporary governing body ruling Iraq in less than a year. CPA Order 96 further provided that the elections,which would be for provincial councils and the Kurdistan Regional Government, as well as the TNA, had to take place by the end of January 2005. Any "political entity" could present a list of candidates to the electoral commission for approval, but one-third of the candidates on any submitted list had to be women.[9]

The UN team that advised the Iraqi government on voter registration and other electoral issues recommended treating the entire country as a single voting district. There was not enough time to draw a system of geographical districts for the 275 assembly seats before the mandated election date.[10] Although easier to organize, the single-district approach had inherent problems. The most significant was that members elected to the assembly would primarily be accountable to their parties—not the voters.

With $40 million in U.S. funding, the International Foundation for Election Systems helped the Independent Electoral Commission prepare for the January 30, 2005 elections by drafting regulations, training staff, planning logistics, and procuring voter registration forms.[11] The electoral commission began distributing voter registration materials in October 2004 and registered more than 14 million Iraqis by January 2005. The ballot offered 256 political entities from which to choose, representing nearly 19,000 candidates running for the Transitional National Assembly, the provincial councils, and the Kurdistan National Assembly.[12]

Elections and Increasing Violence

During the summer and fall of 2004, the Iraqi Interim Government and the Coalition faced renewed conflicts with the followers of Shi'a leader Muqtada al-Sadr in Najaf, as well as with insurgents in the Sunni cities of Falluja and Samarra. Grand Ayatollah Sistani stepped in again to end a tense standoff in Najaf between Muqtada al-Sadr and the Coalition-backed ISF.[13] In the wake of the Najaf crisis, Sistani forged a new coalition—the United Iraqi Alliance, combining the major Shi'a parties—to compete for seats in the January 2005 elections. Meanwhile, continuing battles against extremists in Samarra and Falluja hardened Sunni sentiment against the Coalition.

On November 9, 2004, in the wake of the Coalition attacks on Falluja, Iraq's most prominent Sunni political party—the Iraqi Islamic Party—announced its withdrawal from the Iraqi Interim Government, having decided against participating in the January 2005 elections.[14] Sunni Arabs—who had dominated Iraq's governing and economic institutions under Saddam Hussein and who comprised about twenty percent of Iraq's population—had the most to lose from a single-list election.[15] Some predicted that if elections took place without Sunni participation, they "would be cut out of the process of governing and constitution-making for the duration of the transition, leaving them little option but violent resistance."[16]

The elections occurred as scheduled on January 30, 2005. About 130,000 members of Iraq's security forces, with U.S. support, guarded polling stations across the country. The Iraqi Interim Government had banned vehicular traffic and closed the borders two days before the election. On election day, insurgents launched about 300 attacks, killing at least 35 people and wounding more than 100. Despite this violence, attacks were fewer than anticipated.[17]

Some 8.5 million Iraqis, nearly 60 percent of the registered electorate, cast ballots. President Bush hailed the results: "Today, the people of Iraq have spoken to the world, and the world is hearing the voice of freedom from the center of the Middle East."[18]

Twelve political groups won seats in the Transitional National Assembly. The United Iraqi Alliance, with its coalition of predominantly Shi'a groups, received more than 50 percent of the vote, giving it 140 of the 275 seats. The Kurdish bloc earned 27 percent of the vote, giving it 75 seats. Ayad Allawi's Iraqi List, with about 14 percent of the vote, garnered 40 seats.[19] Only 17 Sunni Arabs were elected, giving them about six percent of the seats in the new body.[20]

Six weeks later, the TNA met for the first time in the heavily fortified Green Zone, but factional disputes delayed the formation of the government until April 2005 when the Presidency Council finally took shape. Kurdish leader Jalal Talabani was named president, and Sunni Sheikh Ghazi al-Yawar and Shi'a Adel Abdel Mahdi were named vice presidents. The Presidency Council then named Shi'a leader Ibrahim al-Ja'afari as Prime Minister.[21]

At the end of April, the TNA approved a cabinet that still needed ministers for five critical ministries: Defense, Oil, Electricity, Industry, and Human Rights. Even with some of these key cabinet positions vacant, Iraq's first elected government was sworn into office on May 3, 2005. A week later, the TNA named a 55-member committee to draft the country's permanent constitution.[22] Only two of the committee's members were Sunnis, sowing yet another seed of dissension that would burst forth in 2006's sectarian violence.[23]

Although many Iraqis and international observers called for extending the deadline for producing a new constitution, the United States pushed the drafting committee to meet the August 15 deadline provided by the TAL. To speed the process, Shi'a and Kurdish leaders removed the negotiations from the drafting committee, placing them instead in the hands of a new Leadership Council. By the end of August, the new council formally submitted a draft constitution to the TNA, just two weeks overdue.[24]

The Sunnis, who had been largely cut out of negotiations by the Shi'a alliance and the Kurds, strongly opposed the constitution. Former Prime Minister Ayad Allawi, a Sunni, and Muqtada al-Sadr, a Shi'a, criticized the content and the hurried, secretive process by which the document was drafted.[25] Sunnis objected to the federal model, favoring instead a stronger central government.[26]

The Rule of Law

As the United States sought to help Iraq form a representative government based on a constitution that protected the rights of all Iraqis, it also used reconstruction dollars to try to rebuild Iraq's justice system. A mix of U.S. government agencies—the Department of Defense, the Department of State, USAID, and the Department of Justice—bore responsibility for various aspects of the rule-of-law program in Iraq, but none was in charge of coordinating their disparate efforts.

The lack of any concentrated responsibility for this critical area meant that there was no coordinated leadership on rule-of-law initiatives and a paucity of personnel devoted to the effort. For example, only in June 2005 would the embassy, in response to SIGIR audits, appoint a rule-of-law coordinator for Iraq initiatives.[27]

A State Department Inspector General review of the rule of law in Iraq, issued two and a half years after Coalition forces toppled Saddam Hussein, found an absence of coordination "among U.S. elements in Iraq, between Washington and the field, and between the United States and coalition partners and potential donors or NGO implementers."[28] The report concluded that the government had been very slow to disburse the few funds allocated for rule-of-law projects, particularly regarding capacity building.[29] Most of the funds obligated in 2004 and 2005 in the justice sector went for infrastructure projects, which were supposed to be carried out under the $900 million IRRF 2 contract awarded to Parsons Delaware for border-control posts, police and civil defense facilities, fire stations, and courthouses and prisons.[30] Parsons fell far short of fulfilling its obligations, and the United States terminated the contract in 2007, after expending $333 million.

Rebuilding Prisons

In May and June 2003, a Department of Justice team surveyed 21 of Iraq's 151 prisons and detention facilities, finding that almost all had "been looted, trashed, burned, and everything of any value either destroyed or stolen."[31] The CPA estimated that the total cost of rehabilitating the prisons would range from $50 million to $100 million.[32]

Despite its history as a brutal detention center under Saddam, Abu Ghraib, the country's largest prison, was the only maximum-security facility capable of housing dangerous inmates.[33] During the first months after the invasion, the Coalition housed prisoners in temporary facilities—tents or plywood buildings—and in hastily rehabilitated detention centers. In July 2003, the CPA re-opened Abu Ghraib, which had the capacity to hold 400 people.[34]

From March to November 2004, the PMO/PCO issued 53 task orders to Parsons Delaware for construction projects, including prisons, in the security and justice sector. By December 2004, due to Parsons poor progress, the U.S. government cancelled 26 of the task orders, most before much work had been accomplished. A SIGIR audit found that of the 53 original task orders assigned to Parsons, the contractor successfully completed only eighteen, which included the construction of border posts, courts, fire stations, and military or police academies.

The government terminated nine of the 53 task orders, seven for convenience and two for default. The two terminated for default involved two

Western-style prisons—the Nassriya Corrections Facility and the Khan Bani Sa'ad Corrections Facility. SIGIR's audit of Parsons concluded that "terminated and canceled task orders accounted for approximately $142 million of the $366 million disbursed to Parsons."[35]

Before its contract was terminated, Parsons had completed about 45 percent of the work on two security buildings at the Nassriya prison but much less was accomplished at the Khan Bani Sa'ad prison north of Baghdad. While the Nassriya prison was eventually finished by a follow-on contractor, the Khan Bani Sa'ad story—perhaps the single greatest project failure in the U.S. reconstruction program—illustrates many of the problems the government and its contractors faced in Iraq.[36]

The Khan Bani Sa'ad Prison

In May 2004, the CPA awarded a task order for $73 million to Parsons to build a maximum-security prison in Diyala Province. The project, scheduled to begin immediately and be finished by November 2005, had problems from the start.[37] Construction did not begin until November 2004 and progressed very slowly, chiefly because of poor security conditions and weak subcontractor performance.

In the spring of 2006, Parsons notified USACE-GRD that the prison would not be completed until September 2008, three years late. The U.S. government promptly terminated the contract for default, noting that "Parsons has endangered completion both by continued schedule slips and by incurring massive cost overruns that cannot be sustained by the Government … The circumstances that have caused the vast majority of the schedule slips have, in fact, been within Parsons' control."[38]

Parsons attributed the many delays to poor security, contending that when the contract was awarded the U.S. government indicated that Iraq would be relatively stable. The U.S government disagreed, pointing out that neither the original contract nor the task order suggested that Parsons would be working in a permissive environment.[39]

The government continued work on the prison, awarding a fixed-price bridging contract to an Iraqi subcontractor of Parsons. In September 2006, the GRD awarded two contracts to an Iraqi contractor for further construction on the prison and one to a U.S. contractor to rehabilitate the prison's electrical system. None of these contractors made significant progress. In March 2007, GRD sent the Iraqi company a list of items it had failed to deliver and, in June 2007, GRD terminated the contract.

At this point, the U.S. government stopped all work, having spent three years and approximately $40 million on the project, with just 52 percent of it finished.

Moreover, the completed work had major structural problems, including improperly laid concrete floors and poorly built walls. GRD informed Iraq's Deputy Minister of Justice that it would turn the incomplete Khan Bani Sa'ad prison over to the Iraqi government on August 1, 2007, but the deputy minister refused to accept it, stating that the ministry had no plans to "complete, occupy, or provide security for this facility."[40]

When SIGIR inspectors visited Khan Bani Sa'ad in June 2008, they found an unoccupied, unsecured site with numerous construction problems; $1.2 million worth of material was missing.[41] Ultimately, the U.S. program spent $40 million on the project, terminating it in 2007—without any prospect of return on the investment. Khan Bani Sa'ad will probably never house an inmate. The Iraqis in Diyala derisively referred to the skeletal, half-built prison on the flatlands north of Baghdad as "the whale."[42]

Building Courts

The Ba'athist constitution consolidated Iraq's civilian court system in the Ministry of Justice, giving Saddam strict executive control over the judicial system. Saddam tightened his stranglehold on the legal system by creating military and security courts.[43] CPA Order Number 2, which disbanded the Iraqi military and intelligence services, abolished these courts as well.[44] An array of other courts—appellate, criminal, civil, and juvenile—continued under the jurisdiction of the Ministry of Justice.

In mid-2003, the CPA and the Department of Justice estimated that the country had 130 courthouses, 570 courts, and 710 judges.[45] Early U.S. judicial reform initiatives foundered, in part because some in the Iraqi legal establishment felt detached from the planning and rehabilitation process. Sermid Al-Sarraf, a member of the Iraqi Jurists Association, testifying before the U.S. Congress at the end of June 2003, said that the CPA had largely left Iraqi lawyers and judges out of discussions about how to reform the country's legal system. He pointed out that a Department of Justice assessment team failed to include a single Iraqi legal professional and that the CPA had inexperienced people making arbitrary decisions affecting Iraqi law. "Iraqis are feeling like strangers in their own country," Al-Sarraf said. "Either through neglect, lack of understanding, or for the sake of expediency, current efforts seem to be avoiding direct Iraqi involvement and their opinions in important decisions."[46]

The CPA created a critically important new legal institution—the Central Criminal Court of Iraq (CCCI)—empowering it to try serious offenses committed since the invasion and giving it jurisdiction over "any and all criminal violations," regardless of where they occurred within Iraq. By August 2003, the new court was open in the Green Zone and trying its first cases. The CCCI concentrated its limited resources on offenses involving "terrorism, organized crime, government corruption, and acts intended to destabilize democratic institutions."[47]

To ensure that justice was administered fairly in the new Iraq, the CPA first had to resolve the issue of whether judges who had served under the Saddam regime, and had been Ba'athists, could continue in office. In one of its first orders, the CPA created a Judicial Review Committee to vet former judges and prosecutors for connections to the Ba'ath Party, vesting it with the power to remove those with significant connections.[48] Over the next year, the committee removed about 180 judges.[49]

By the fall of 2003, too few Iraqi courts were up and running. At the end of November, Judge Daniel Rubini, a senior advisor to the Ministry of Justice, sent a memo to CPA's leadership noting that there had only been twenty criminal convictions in Baghdad since the criminal courts re-opened in May and only 80 trials nationwide. Many investigative judges feared bringing cases to trial because of potential attacks. Corruption was also a major problem. "Police, court investigators, and investigating judges hold out for bribes before acting upon a defendant's case," said Rubini.[50]

The CPA also sought to construct courthouses, but did not devote sufficient resources to the effort, partly because the IRRF 2 money was not available until the end of its tenure. In April 2004, the OMB allocated $135 million for the construction and repair of courthouses, as well as for increasing their security.[51] This funding sought to address the very serious problem of judicial security in Iraq. In November 2003, gunmen kidnapped and killed Muhan Jabr al-Shuwaili, the top judge in Najaf, who had supported the creation of a judicial commission to investigate former Ba'ath Party officials.[52] A month later, insurgents killed Youssef Khoshi, a senior judge in Mosul, firing six bullets into his back.[53] Attacks on judges have plagued the reconstruction program since its inception. By the end of 2008, more than 40 judges or their family members had been murdered in Iraq since the 2003 invasion. Many more had quit their jobs and fled the country because of threats.[54]

Anticorruption Initiatives

Corruption permeated Saddam Hussein's Iraq. Although it infected every level of Iraq's government, it was concentrated chiefly among the ruling elite of the Ba'ath Party and those who served them. The fact that the problem of corruption persisted after the U.S. invasion is no surprise because, as scholars have noted, "Corruption thrives in the environment of post-conflict reconstruction," which combines "large public procurement projects, major funding infusions, and inadequate government economic management."[55] Throughout the life of the U.S.

reconstruction program, Iraqi corruption "exerted a corrosive force upon [the] fledgling democracy," contributing to a flight of capital that "directly harmed the country's economic viability."[56]

Corruption in Iraq's government, which Prime Minister Maliki has referred to as a "second insurgency," fundamentally impeded U.S. efforts to develop ministry capacity.[57] Institutions of government were "undermined by the widespread association of political elites with corrupt activities."[58] The oil sector's corrupt practices were particularly egregious.

A 2006 GAO report noted that "about 10 percent of refined fuels are diverted to the black market, and about 30 percent of imported fuels are smuggled out of Iraq and sold for a profit."[59] Some oil-smuggling money reportedly ended up in the hands of insurgents.[60] Failing to exert effective oversight came at a high price: the cost of corruption to Iraq during 2004 and 2005 was estimated at $4 billion per year.[61]

Developing a New Anticorruption System

To combat this "second insurgency," U.S. officials implemented comprehensive reforms of Iraq's anticorruption system, setting up new institutions and drafting new laws. But the U.S. efforts to help develop effective Iraqi oversight institutions, begun under the CPA and continued by the embassy, produced mixed results, primarily because of underfunding and a lack of coordination among the U.S. agencies administering various initiatives.

Before the U.S. invasion, the Board of Supreme Audit (BSA) served as Iraq's primary government oversight agency. Created by Great Britain during its occupation of Iraq in the 1920s, the BSA had become a paper tiger under Saddam. To augment the BSA's efforts, the CPA established two new anticorruption institutions: the Commission on Public Integrity (CPI) and the ministry inspectors general (IGs) system.[62]

The CPA's conception of how these new entities should function was simple and quintessentially American. An IG would notice something amiss that could be the result of corruption and would forward to the CPI a file documenting his suspicions, along with whatever evidence he managed to gather. The CPI then would conduct a criminal investigation, much as the FBI does upon receiving a referral from a U.S. inspector general. After completing the investigation, the CPI would deliver its findings to the CCCI's investigative judges. The judges, functioning much like U.S. prosecutors, would decide whether to bring the case to trial, close it, or send it back to the CPI for further investigation.[63]

In practice, things rarely ran this smoothly. To begin with, the CPA failed to provide adequate resources to the two institutions it created. Ambassador

Bremer authorized a budget of just $35 million—$20 million from the DFI and $15 million from IRRF 2.[64] Most of these funds went to the CPI, with the IGs receiving nothing until the very end of the CPA's tenure.

Compounding these funding troubles was the fact that nothing like either institution had previously existed in Iraq. This led to misunderstandings and suspicions about them among ministry officials. Modeled on Hong Kong's much-lauded Independent Commission Against Corruption, the CPI was intended to be Iraq's primary corruption-fighting agency. The IGs were modeled on the U.S. system of federal inspectors general and were designed to be frontline anticorruption watchdogs in every ministry.[65] But the perception of foreign taint burdened both the CPI and the IGs from their inception.

High-ranking Iraqi officials expressed confusion about where these two institutions fit within the country's highly formalized legal hierarchy. Many mistakenly believed that the CPI had independent arrest authority. Similarly, many GOI ministers mistrusted their IGs and perceived them as spies for either the Prime Minister's Office or the Americans. Grafted onto the existing Iraqi legal system and inadequately supported by their U.S. creators, the CPI and the IGs struggled to find their footing in a new, corrupt, and dangerous Iraq.[66]

The Commission on Public Integrity

On January 28, 2004, CPA Order Number 55 established the CPI, giving it statutory authority to investigate allegations of corruption against Iraqi governmental officials and to forward cases meriting judicial action to the CCCI. Order 55 further charged the CPI with educating the Iraqi populace about the dangers of corruption, drafting and administering financial disclosure regulations for government employees, and revising Iraq's Code of Conduct for public servants.[67]

Although established in January 2004, the CPI remained leaderless until the waning days of the CPA. Finally, in June 2004, the last month of the CPA's existence, Ambassador Bremer appointed Judge Radhi Hamza al-Radhi as CPI's first Commissioner. Radhi had served as a judge during Saddam's regime. Because of his independence and integrity, he had been imprisoned and tortured.[68]

Almost from the first day of its existence, American advisors were involved with the CPI's operations. The State Department's Bureau of International Narcotics and Law Enforcement Affairs committed $11 million to train the CPI's investigators and to purchase equipment. The CPA allocated this money to the U.S. Department of Justice's International Criminal Investigative Training Assistance Program, which provided a handful of trainers.[69] By the summer of 2005, more than 150 CPI investigators were being trained by 20 ICITAP advisors.[70] Significant INL-funded training programs for the CPI continued until

2008, when the embassy scaled them back, partly because of the CPI's diminishing effectiveness as a law enforcement institution.

During the eighteen months following its formation, the CPI filed 541 cases with the CCCI, including 42 against ministers, their deputies, and ministerial directors general. Judge Radhi later told a U.S. congressional oversight committee that, for perhaps the first time in Middle East history, "a minister was arrested, in accordance with the rule of law, in a non-political, non-sectarian manner on corruption charges." He noted, however, that early cases like this inflamed strong opposition to the CPI, resulting in efforts to limit its powers.[71]

The CCCI, which received all corruption case referrals, proved an unsatisfactory vehicle for prosecuting them. The overburdened court—charged with prosecuting terrorism, organized crime, and ethnic and sectarian violence—was either unwilling or unable to devote adequate attention to corruption cases.[72] Of the 3,000 cases forwarded to the court by the CPI between 2004 and 2007, the CCCI adjudicated and rendered only 241 guilty verdicts—about 8 percent. "However, the cost of corruption that my Commission has uncovered so far across all ministries in Iraq has been estimated to be as high as $18 billion," Judge Radhi said.[73]

Article 136(b) of the Iraqi Penal Code—first enacted in 1971— also hampered the CPI's ability to investigate corruption. This law provides that no case against a ministry official or former official can go to trial without the permission of the minister of the agency involved. In June 2004, the CPA suspended the law, but the Iraqi government later reinstated it.[74] In the six months from September 2006 to February 2007, Article 136(b) was invoked to block investigations by the CPI in 48 cases involving 102 defendants.[75] CPI Commissioner Radhi believed that the use of Article 136(b) "prevented CPI from transmitting many corrupt employees' cases to court until CPI received permission of the agency it was investigating…presenting obvious problems." In the spring of 2007, Prime Minister Maliki issued an executive order similarly providing that no action could be taken against any minister without permission of the Prime Minister's Office. Radhi stated that this official action blocked many corruption cases, "at an estimated worth of 100 billion Iraqi dinar [approximately $80 million]."[76]

Despite often being stymied by these and many other roadblocks, the CPI's modest efforts to enforce the law soon made it a target. Between 2004 and 2007, 31 CPI employees were assassinated, and 12 family members were murdered. Judge Radhi himself lived under constant threat. He ultimately had to flee Iraq, seeking political asylum in the United States in August of 2007.[77] Since then, the CPI has struggled to open new investigations and has been unable to establish a true nationwide presence. It remains an open question whether the CPI is rooted firmly enough in the Iraqi political structure to survive the eventual withdrawal of U.S. support.

Iraq's Inspectors General

CPA Order 57, signed by Ambassador Bremer on February 10, 2004, "established within each Iraqi ministry an Office of Inspector General... headed by an Inspector General [IG]."[78] The IGs were initially appointed by Ambassador Bremer to serve a five-year term, which could be renewed for an additional five-year period. By the time the CPA closed its doors in June 2004, Bremer had named 29 IGs to five-year terms. When sovereignty was returned to the Iraqis in 2004, the power to appoint and re-appoint IGs shifted to the prime minister's office.[79]

The duties of Iraqi IGs, virtually identical to those of their American counterparts, include auditing ministry records and activities; conducting administrative investigations; addressing allegations of waste, fraud, and abuse; recommending corrective actions to the minister; and cooperating with investigative agencies and the judiciary on cases.[80] To accomplish these many tasks, the Government of Iraq is supposed to accord the IGs "full and unrestricted access to all [ministerial] offices." Order 57 also gave the IGs the power to subpoena witnesses and documents. The IGs are supposed to report their findings to their minister and to issue an annual report to the Iraqi public.[81]

Today, more than 30 IGs serve in the Government of Iraq. Most of them are housed within its ministries, with the remainder working at quasi-ministerial government entities, such as the Shi'a, Sunni, and Christian Endowments. Each IG's staff ranges in size from the very small (the Ministry of Foreign Affairs IG has approximately 20 employees) to the very large (the Ministry of Defense IG is authorized a staff of several thousand). The budget to pay staff and fund other expenses comes from the IG's parent ministry through the Ministry of Finance.[82]

The perception of the IGs as a foreign antibody inserted into Iraq's body politic by the Americans persists. Many IGs believe that "everyone assumes we're just spies for the Americans." One IG noted: "If we're too active, our minister will fire us." Another said, "If I do my job, they'll kill me."[83]

Since 2004, the U.S. government has provided limited support to build the capacity of Iraq's IG system. CPA Order 57 stated that "to be effective" the IGs required "adequate resources."[84] The CPA, however, budgeted no DFI funds for the IGs, nor was any money forthcoming from the Departments of State or Justice. It fell to the Department of Defense to lead the way.

In March 2004, a Department of Defense Inspector General (DoD IG) official detailed to SIGIR, Dr. Charles Johnson, arrived in Iraq to help the new IGs. He quickly developed good relations with the beleaguered and ill-trained group, providing them their first instruction on oversight. Johnson soon submitted a request for $11 million for the IGs to the CPA's Program Review Board, but the proposal lost by one vote. However, on June 27, 2004—the day before the CPA closed shop—Ambassador Bremer overturned the vote, directing that $11 million in Iraqi funds be allocated to support the IG system. But, Johnson recounted, "the IG offices were anything but operational at the time of the transition" to Iraqi sovereignty on June 28, 2004.[85]

In 2005, a team from the DoD IG Investigations and Evaluations Directorate traveled to Baghdad to train and advise the IGs in the government's two largest ministries: the Ministry of Interior and the Ministry of Defense. To this day, the Defense Department, through MNSTC-I, continues to train, mentor, and advise the IGs and their staffs in these ministries. Scant U.S. assistance has been provided to any of the other Iraqi IGs. While the State Department was pouring millions of dollars and dozens of personnel into capacity building efforts at the CPI, it offered almost nothing to the IGs. Finally, in February 2007, State appointed a senior consultant to Iraq's Inspectors General. He alone—with no budget—was responsible for training, mentoring, and advising the non-security ministry IGs.[86]

The Board of Supreme Audit

CPA Order Number 77, signed by Ambassador Bremer in April 2004, reconstituted the BSA, the oldest and most highly regarded anticorruption institution in Iraq and the analogue to the U.S. Government Accountability Office.[87] The CPA's creation of the CPI and the IG system removed and redistributed some of the BSA's responsibilities, but it still remained the sole government-wide auditing agency in Iraq, with "jurisdiction to oversee all public contracts."[88] Mindful of its 70-year history, the BSA guards "jealously what it perceives as its prerogatives." It has been a reluctant player in the "U.S.-imposed anticorruption structure ... often hesitant about providing its audit findings to the two other anticorruption agencies."[89]

When the CPA ceased operations, the BSA was still "severely antiquated in terms of its methodology, in terms of its requirements, and in terms of its abilities." With a staff of 1,200, it had only five computers and "only between 100 and 150 real ... auditor[s]—for an entire nation."[90] The first head of the BSA, Dr. Ihsan Karim Ghanem, appointed by Ambassador Bremer, was killed by a suicide bomber on the streets of Baghdad in 2004.[91]

U.S. support for the BSA has been meager. INL allocated money to the GAO for an Arabic translation of its Government Auditing Standards. The GAO also trained a small number of mid-level auditors, but very little capacity-building funding was allocated to the BSA.[92] International funding was also limited.[93] Today, the BSA is functional, but its capacity to provide effective oversight of the Iraqi government's expenditures needs bolstering.

An Uphill Battle

A 2006 joint survey by SIGIR and the State Department Inspector General found that the institutional framework for Iraqi anticorruption activities that the CPA put in place was "fragile." The absence of adequate financial support further weakened that framework. The survey also found that, "despite the fact that attacking corruption is among the top U.S. priorities in Iraq," the total amount allocated through June 15, 2006, was only $65 million, "less than .003 percent of the total IRRF funding to date." Furthermore, these very modest funds were poorly managed.[94]

SIGIR's subsequent reviews of the Anti-Corruption Working Group, formed by the embassy to oversee U.S. anticorruption programs, found that it suffered from a lack of consistent leadership and interagency coordination. In 2008, a SIGIR audit noted that, despite an articulated commitment to improving the U.S. anticorruption program, much more "remains to be accomplished to establish and implement a comprehensive and effective program."[95]

CHAPTER 21
INVESTIGATING FRAUD

*If an IG team was in there from the get-go, we may have had free rein, but it would not be the Wild West. They could have told us, if you do A, B, C, D, you won't get in trouble. It might have been a pain in the butt, but we would live with it.**

Robert J. Stein
Comptroller, CPA South-Central Region (2003-2004)
(now serving nine years in prison)

Since April 2003, hundreds of thousands of U.S. civilian and military personnel have participated in the Iraq reconstruction effort. The vast majority of them served honorably, but some did not. During the CPA's existence, when there was little oversight of the reconstruction effort and no fraud-fighting presence in Iraq, an unscrupulous few took advantage of the chaotic circumstances to enrich themselves. Not until SIGIR (then operating as the CPA Inspector General) began to deploy to Baghdad in March 2004, did the United States have meaningful numbers of auditors and investigators permanently based in Iraq to pursue allegations of fraud, waste, and abuse.

As the chart at the end of this chapter shows, there have been at least 35 convictions resulting from criminal misconduct committed during the U.S. reconstruction program. Although this amounts to a small percentage of the total number of Americans who have served in Iraq, the egregious acts by those who chose to break the law harmed the rebuilding effort in two important ways. First, their criminal activity diverted funds from important projects, sidetracking the programs in which those projects played a part. Second, their criminality tarnished the reputation of the United States in the eyes of many Iraqis. Although the scope of the fraud was relatively small, the brazen nature of many of the crimes underscores the importance of maintaining a strong oversight presence from the beginning of any contingency relief and reconstruction operation.

The Bloom-Stein Conspiracy
During the U.S. occupation's first months in 2003, rumors of theft and fraud were rife throughout the CPA and contractor communities. Once SIGIR established a presence in the Republican Palace in March 2004, whistleblowers had a place

---

* SIGIR interview with Robert Stein, former Defense Department contractor, Federal Penitentiary, Petersburg, VA, June 13, 2007.

to report alleged crimes. In April 2004, one such individual told SIGIR auditors about troubling financial practices he had witnessed—and, in fact, had participated in—as a member of the CPA Comptroller's office. He specifically raised concerns about the regional comptroller for the CPA's South-Central Region.

The Scheme Unfolds

Robert J. Stein, Jr., served as Comptroller for the CPA's South-Central Region in late 2003 and 2004. Stein, who liked to dress in black and tell people he had been a member of the U.S. Army's elite Delta Force (one of many lies he told), was hired by S&K Technologies, a company with a $5 million contract to provide administrative support services to the CPA. Despite a federal credit-card fraud conviction in 1996—for which he served eight months in prison—Stein was cleared to serve in Iraq. He also had been sued for embezzling $750,000 from a previous employer.[1] SIGIR auditors later learned that Stein reportedly had an accomplice who helped him hide these potentially disqualifying facts.[2]

Stein arrived in Iraq in November 2003, and was sent to the South-Central Region headquarters in Hilla, about an hour's drive southwest of Baghdad and the site of the ancient city of Babylon and Nebuchadnezzar's palace. Stein's first assignment was as director of security, logistics, and re-supply operations. In December 2003, when the sergeant then serving as the South-Central Region's comptroller went on leave, Stein was placed in the position, making him responsible for overseeing, disbursing, and accounting for millions of reconstruction dollars. "I was supposed to be the operations specialist," Stein later said, "I wasn't there to be comptroller."[3]

Almost immediately upon assuming his new office, Stein entered into a criminal conspiracy with Philip Bloom, a corrupt American contractor with burgeoning businesses in Iraq. From December 2003 to June 2004, Stein rigged bids for and funneled contracts to Bloom, who received more than $8.6 million in cash from this fraudulent activity. Bloom repaid Stein and other complicit CPA employees with a variety of kickbacks, including jewelry, deluxe cars, weapons, business-class airline tickets, and cash. Bloom also laundered more than $2 million in stolen funds for Stein and his fellow CPA South Central criminals, using bank accounts in Iraq, Switzerland, and Romania (of which he was a dual citizen).[4]

The Scheme Unravels

On the day the SIGIR (then the CPA-IG) was appointed—January 20, 2004—Stein emailed Bloom: "I love to give you money."[5] The Bloom-Stein conspiracy was, at that moment, in full tilt. But its unraveling began in April 2004, when complaints about Stein came to SIGIR's attention. In response to these allegations, SIGIR immediately deployed auditors to Hilla to investigate.[6]

SIGIR's auditors met in Hilla with Lieutenant Colonel Deborah Harrison, the South-Central Region's deputy comptroller. Harrison—known as the "bird lady of Hilla" because of the large bird cage in her office populated by more than twenty birds—told the auditors that regional comptroller Robert Stein was on emergency leave in the United States because his son had brain cancer. The auditors later would learn that Stein was actually on a trip to Disneyland with his son, for which Bloom had paid all expenses.[7]

The auditors pressed Harrison for documentation on the South-Central Region's use of money on reconstruction projects. She was unable to provide any records, but attempted to allay concerns by assuring the auditors that she would get all the documents from Stein when he returned. Harrison then emailed Stein, warning him that the SIGIR auditors were onto his criminal scheme. "Don't worry," Stein retorted, "[SIGIR] will never figure it out."[8]

The Audits Begin

The auditors were now highly suspicious that significant fraud was occurring in the CPA office at Hilla. They initiated an audit to track every dollar spent by the South-Central Region and to determine how much money the CPA's Comptroller had disbursed to Stein to fund reconstruction activities.

The CPA Comptroller's documents indicated that Stein had received three disbursements totaling $57.8 million in cash.[9] But the lead SIGIR auditor found a picture in Hilla showing Stein surrounded by a mountain of cash, with a sign saying, "$58.8 million." When the auditors alerted the CPA Comptroller to this fact, the Comptroller responded, "I have no idea how much [money] Stein got." The auditors found other incriminating photos, including one showing several hands reaching into a suitcase containing millions of dollars in cash, with one hand—Stein's—sporting an expensive Breitling watch, which he had recently received from Bloom.[10]

After Stein returned to Hilla, SIGIR's auditors confronted him about the fund discrepancies they had found. Stein recounted that he had traveled to Baghdad in January 2004 with three others from Hilla in two unarmored SUVs to pick up tens of millions of dollars in cash for reconstruction from the CPA Comptroller's vault. He said he met with the CPA Comptroller's staff, signed a receipt (which the CPA Comptroller could not produce for SIGIR's auditors), backed up his SUV to the palace entrance, and loaded more than $58 million in cash into the back. "It's amazing," he later said. "The vault had pallet upon pallet of hundred dollar bills. This was more cash than Donald Trump had ever seen in his life. When you work around money like that, it becomes 'so what, it's just paper.'

The procedures were so lax it was unbelievable. I worked government contracts before in the States, so I know."[11]

After their meeting with Stein, the auditors called the IG with troubling news—there was evidence of rampant fraud in Hilla. The IG promptly deployed a team of investigators to support the auditors' work. SIGIR's lead auditor had documented a litany of various acts of alleged fraud, waste, and abuse by Stein and Bloom. The most flagrant examples involved two pet projects of Stein's: the Babylon Police Academy and the Kerbala Library.

The Babylon Police Academy

The Babylon Police Academy was intended to be the leading police training institute for the South-Central Region. Stein awarded eleven contracts and four grants to Bloom for demolition work, barracks and classroom construction, and the purchase of generators and other equipment. Upon review of the contracts and grants, the auditors found that Stein had kept the costs of each contract and grant below $500,000—the ceiling above which he would have had to seek approval from the CPA's Comptroller before award.[12] The auditors further discovered that Stein had disbursed most of the contract and grant money before any contracts had been signed. When SIGIR auditors visited the police academy, they saw that much of the work was incomplete or had not begun.

The contracts and grants for the police academy totaled $7.3 million. Of that, SIGIR concluded that CPA officials "needlessly expended almost $1.3 million in contract funds for duplicate construction" and for "equipment not needed, not delivered, and overpriced." Moreover, Stein "could not account for more than $2 million of disbursed grant funds." The auditors were also "unable to clearly determine" whether the remaining $4 million had been used to meet contract obligations.[13]

The Kerbala Library

Located 45 kilometers south of Hilla, the Kerbala Library houses southern Iraq's most important collection of Arabic translations of western literature—as well as books on history, philosophy, politics, and science. Stein awarded five contracts to Bloom's companies, ostensibly to repair the aged library, to purchase furniture and new bookcases, to provide Internet services and landscaping, and to train librarians. Stein also approved a $210,000 grant to pay librarian salaries and issued 33 micro-contracts—worth approximately $535,000—to purchase 30,000 books. The total outlays came to $2,128,916.[14]

When SIGIR auditors visited the library, they found the same problems they had seen at the police academy: circumvention of regulations, improper disbursements, and the failure to monitor contracts. The quantity and quality of equipment delivered was far below the requirements stipulated in the contract. For example, the contractor provided only 14 personal computers and desks, not the 68 computers and 60 desks required by the contract. There were no Internet connections. Flimsy plastic patio chairs, not the upholstered metal ones specified in the contract, sat in the hall. The library's manager said he had received no grant money for salaries or books.

SIGIR's auditors concluded that CPA officials had needlessly disbursed more than $1.8 million on the project to rehabilitate the library. Of this, about $1.6 million was spent on work that was never done.[15]

End Game

During 2004 and 2005, several auditors from SIGIR spent many months in Hilla, carefully reviewing documentation, visiting project sites, and interviewing CPA South-Central Region personnel. A series of audits issued in 2005 detailed numerous findings of egregious misconduct, mismanagement, and potential fraud, concluding that the CPA's "controls" of cash disbursements were so weak that "the South-Central Region paying agents and the DFI Account Manager could not properly account for or support $96.6 million in cash and receipts."[16]

SIGIR's investigators, along with partners from the Internal Revenue Service and Immigration and Customs Enforcement, soon pieced together this spectacular array of incriminating evidence, bringing into relief the complex Bloom-Stein conspiracy and implicating a handful of senior officials in Hilla. SIGIR took the case to Department of Justice prosecutors, who presented it to a grand jury. Subpoenas were issued and, in November 2005, Robert Stein was arrested at his home in Fayetteville, North Carolina.[17]

Six people were eventually convicted for their roles in the Bloom-Stein criminal scheme; another was charged and is awaiting trial. Stein, convicted on money laundering and fraud charges, received a prison sentence of nine years. Bloom pleaded guilty to three counts of conspiracy, bribery, and money laundering, and received a sentence of 46 months. Lieutenant Colonel Bruce Hopfengardner, who conspired to direct contracts to Bloom and received $100,000 in kickbacks, was convicted and sentenced to 21 months in prison. Lieutenant Colonel Harrison, the deputy comptroller at the South-Central Region headquarters, pleaded guilty to fraud after admitted to receiving a Cadillac Escalade from Bloom and stealing more than $300,000 from the CPA. She awaits sentencing.[18]

After a lengthy trial in October 2008, Colonel Curtis Whiteford, once the second-most senior official in Hilla, and Lieutenant Colonel Michael Wheeler, an advisor on South-Central Region reconstruction projects, were convicted of conspiracy to commit bribery and for interstate transportation of stolen property. Whiteford and Wheeler also await sentencing.[19]

Although federal prosecutors proved beyond a reasonable doubt that the Bloom-Stein criminals stole at least $8.6 million, the full extent of their fraud was probably greater. How much they actually stole will probably never be known.

The Cockerham Case

In mid-2006, agents from SIGIR and the Departments of Defense, Treasury, Homeland Security, and Justice initiated a lengthy joint investigation that broke up a multi-million-dollar bribery scheme at Camp Arifjan, Kuwait. On July 22, 2007, U.S. Army Major John Cockerham, the chief perpetrator of the scheme, was arrested at his home in San Antonio, Texas, by SIGIR and other federal agents for bribery, money laundering, and conspiracy. While serving as a contracting officer in Kuwait, Cockerham solicited and received more than $9 million in bribes from Defense Department contractors in exchange for awarding them contracts for bottled water and other goods and services funded in part by money from the Iraq Relief and Reconstruction Fund. Cockerham's wife and sister were also charged for their money-laundering activities. Cockerham and his wife pleaded guilty on January 31, 2008. They await sentencing. Cockerham's sister was scheduled for trial in March 2009.[20]

Major James Momon, Jr., the officer who replaced Cockerham in Kuwait and who continued the crime scheme, also pleaded guilty to bribery and conspiracy to commit bribery. According to his plea agreement, entered on August 13, 2008, Momon accepted $5.8 million in bribes from five Defense Department contractors supplying goods and services to U.S. military bases in Kuwait. He also awaits sentencing.[21]

Investigative Results

From 2004 to 2008, SIGIR has built a robust investigative capacity, with 26 investigators on staff, including 6 stationed in Iraq. SIGIR's investigations, which frequently have involved teaming with other law enforcement organizations, have produced eighteen indictments, thirteen convictions, five imprisonments, and more than $17 million in fines, forfeitures, and restitution payments as of December 31, 2008.

SIGIR and the other law enforcement agencies operating in Iraq have obtained at least 35 convictions. The following table provides an overview of those cases.

Name	Charges	Date of Conviction	Sentence
Maj. Theresa Baker, USAR Contracting Officer	Conspiracy and bribery	12/22/2008	Pending
Col. Curtis Whiteford, USAR Senior Official, CPA South-Central Region	Conspiracy, bribery, and wire fraud	11/7/2008	Pending
Lt. Col. Michael Wheeler, USAR CPA Reconstruction Advisor	Conspiracy, bribery, wire fraud, interstate transportation of stolen property, and bulk cash smuggling	11/7/2008	Pending
David Ramirez Contractor, Readiness Support Management, Inc.	Bulk currency smuggling and structuring transactions	10/9/2008	Pending
Lee Dubois Contractor, Future Services General Trading and Contracting Company	Theft of government property	10/7/2008	Pending
Robert Bennett Contractor, KBR	Violating the Anti-Kickback Act	8/28/2008	Pending
Maj. James Momon, Jr., USA Contracting Officer	Conspiracy and bribery	8/13/2008	Pending
Lt. Col. Debra M. Harrison, USA Acting Comptroller for CPA South-Central Region	Conspiracy, bribery, money laundering, wire fraud, interstate transportation of stolen property, smuggling cash, and preparing false tax returns	7/28/2008	Pending
Maj. John Lee Cockerham, Jr., USA Contracting Officer	Bribery, conspiracy, and money laundering	6/24/2008	Pending
Melissa Cockerham Wife of Maj. John Cockerham	Conspiracy and money laundering	6/24/2008	Pending
Lt. Col. Levonda Selph, USAR Contracting Officer	Conspiracy and bribery	6/10/2008	Pending
Raman International Corp.	Conspiracy and bribery	6/3/2008	$500,000 fine and $327,192 restitution
Michael Carter Project Engineer, Force Protection Industries	Violating the Anti-Kickback Act	1/25/2008	Pending
Capt. Austin Key, USA Contracting Officer	Bribery	12/19/2007	Pending
Maj. John Rivard, USAR Contracting Officer	Bribery, conspiracy, and money laundering	7/23/2007	10 years in prison; 3 years supervised release; $5,000 fine; and $1 million forfeiture order
Kevin Smoot Managing Director, Eagle Global Logistics, Inc.	Violating the Anti-Kickback Act and making false statements	7/20/2007	14 months in prison; 2 years supervised release; $6,000 fine; and $17,964 restitution

Name	Charges	Date of Conviction	Sentence
Anthony Martin Subcontractor Administrator, KBR	Violating the Anti-Kickback Act	7/13/2007	1 year and 1 day in prison; 2 years supervised release; and $200,504 restitution
Jesse Lane, USAR 223rd Finance Detachment	Conspiracy and honest services wire fraud	6/5/2007	30 months in prison and $323,228 restitution
Steven Merkes DoD Civilian, Operational Support Planner	Accepting illegal gratuities	2/16/2007	12 months and 1 day in prison and $24,000 restitution
Chief Warrant Officer Peleti Peleti, Jr., USA Army's Food Service Advisor for Kuwait, Iraq, and Afghanistan	Bribery and smuggling cash	2/9/2007	28 months in prison and $57,500 fine and forfeiture
Jennifer Anjakos, USAR 223rd Finance Detachment	Conspiracy to commit wire fraud	11/13/2006	3 years probation; $86,557 restitution; and $100 assessment
Sgt. Lomeli Chavez, USAR 223rd Finance Detachment	Conspiracy to commit wire fraud	11/13/2006	3 years probation; $28,107 restitution; and $100 assessment
Sgt. Derryl Hollier, USAR 223rd Finance Detachment	Conspiracy to commit wire fraud	11/13/2006	3 years probation; $83,657.47 restitution; and $100 assessment
Sgt. Luis Lopez, USAR 223rd Finance Detachment	Conspiracy to commit wire fraud	11/13/2006	3 years probation; $66,865 restitution; and $100 assessment
Bonnie Murphy Contracting Officer	Accepting unlawful gratuities	11/7/2006	1 year supervised release and $1,500 fine
Samir Mahmoud Employee of U.S. construction firm	Making false statements	11/3/2006	1 day credit for time served; and 2 years supervised release
Gheevarghese Pappen USACE Civilian	Soliciting and accepting illegal gratuities	10/12/2006	2 years in prison; 1 year supervised release; and $28,900 restitution
Lt. Col. Bruce Hopfengardner, USAR Special Advisor to CPA South-Central Region	Conspiracy, conspiring to commit wire fraud and money laundering, and smuggling currency	8/25/2006	21 months in prison; 3 years supervised release; $200 fine; and $144,500 forfeiture
Faheem Mousa Salam Interpreter, Titan Corp.	Violating the Foreign Corrupt Practices Act's Anti-Bribery Provisions	8/4/2006	3 years in prison; 2 years supervised release; 250 hours community service; and $100 special assessment
Mohammad Shabbir Khan Director of Operations for Kuwait and Iraq, Tamimi Global Co. Ltd.	Violating the Anti-Kickback Act	6/23/2006	51 months in prison; 2 years supervised release; $10,000 fine; $133,860 restitution; and $1,400 assessment

Name	Charges	Date of Conviction	Sentence
Philip Bloom Owner - Global Business Group, GBG Holdings, and GBG-Logistics Division	Conspiracy, bribery, and money laundering	3/10/2006	46 months in prison; 2 years supervised release; $3.6 million forfeiture; $3.6 million restitution; and $300 special assessment
Stephen Seamans, Subcontracts Manager, KBR	Wire fraud, money laundering, and conspiracy	3/1/2006	12 months and 1 day in prison; 3 years supervised release; $380,130 in restitution; $200 assessment
Christopher Cahill Regional Vice President, Middle East and India, Eagle Global Logistics, Inc.	Major fraud against the United States	2/16/2006	30 months in prison; 2 years supervised release; $10,000 fine; and $100 assessment (a civil settlement with EGL arising from the same facts resulted in a settlement of $4 million)
Robert Stein CPA South-Central Comptroller and Funding Officer	Felon in possession of a firearm, possession of machine guns, bribery, money laundering, and conspiracy	2/2/2006	9 years in prison; 3 years of supervised release; $3.6 million forfeiture; $3.5 million restitution; and $500 special assessment
Glenn Powell Subcontracts Manager, KBR	Major fraud and violating the Anti-Kickback Act	8/1/2005	15 months in prison; 3 years supervised release; $90,973.99 restitution; and $200 assessment

Source: SIGIR, *Quarterly Report to the United States Congress*, January 2009, Section 4.

Fighting Fraud in Contingency Operations

In the first year of the reconstruction experience in Iraq, weak or absent oversight permitted unscrupulous individuals to commit fraud and other crimes. This hard lesson underscores the need to ensure that future contingency operations include strong oversight from their outset so that U.S. taxpayers' dollars are kept as safe as possible from criminal abuse, and that when crimes do occur, the perpetrators are caught and brought to justice. Although maintaining the proper balance between operational effectiveness and strong oversight will always be challenging in a contingency operation, ensuring a robust inspector general presence from an operation's inception must never again be overlooked as it was in Iraq.

Essential Services Overview – Transition from Negroponte to Khalilzad

Metric[22]	Pre-invasion	Post-invasion	CPA Transition	Negroponte Era
Electricity Production				
Megawatts	4,075	711	3,621	4,262
Oil Production				
Million Barrels per Day	2.58	0.30	2.16	2.13
Iraqi Security Forces				
Soldiers and Police	1,300,000	7,000-9,000	87,000	171,300
Telecommunications				
Landline Subscribers	833,000	0	791,000	998,000
Mobile Subscribers	80,000	0	461,000	2,422,000
Human Toll				
U.S Troop Fatalities	-	139	862	1,745
Civilian Contractors	-	1	46	217
U.S. Civilians	-	~9	52	113
Iraqi Civilians	-	7,413	16,848	29,155
Financial Cost ($ billions)				
U.S Funding	-	$3.45	$22.93	$29.21
Iraqi Funding	-	$0.00	$16.00	$21.03
International Funding	-	$0.00	$13.60	$13.87
Total Funding	-	$3.45	$52.53	$64.11

In June 2005, Iraq's average daily electricity production was 4,262 megawatts, an increase of approximately 600 megawatts from the year before.[23] A variety of problems—including security, cuts in IRRF 2 funding, and decisions to defer maintenance in favor of short-term generation initiatives—made these levels of production unsustainable.

More than $5 billion was drawn from IRRF 2, Defense Department funds, and Iraqi money to support oil sector reconstruction, but Iraq's unstable security environment—including numerous attacks on pipelines and other oil facilities—delayed projects and reduced production and exports. Thus, oil production had not returned to prewar levels by the time Ambassador Negroponte left Iraq in mid-2005.[24]

Part IV
Overcoming Roadblocks to Reconstruction
June 2005 to October 2008

KHALILZAD'S ADAPTATIONS

The Khalilzad approach was very much a systems-management RAND-style approach, which is come in, assume nothing… and take a new look from the ground up. What are the mission tasks? What are the mission resources? And what are the structures to apply those resources most effectively?*

Ambassador David Satterfield
Deputy Chief of Mission (2005-2006)

The Iraq that Zalmay Khalilzad left in the spring of 2003—after serving as Special Presidential Envoy and Ambassador-at-large to the Free Iraqis—was not the country to which he returned as the new U.S. Ambassador in June 2005. Khalilzad's April 2003 attempt to piece together an interim Iraqi government with Jay Garner had been superseded by a fourteen- month occupation during which the CPA assumed all governing responsibilities. Iraqi factions reacted violently to the occupation, turning against each other and the Coalition. Two years later, the violence had claimed the lives of nearly 25,000 Iraqi civilians, 1,328 Coalition soldiers, and 330 contractors.[1] "Security," Ambassador Khalilzad said, "was a defining issue, shaping everything, and it got more complicated over time."[2]

Khalilzad—the Bush Administration's highest-ranking Muslim official—is an American who was born in Afghanistan and raised as a Sunni. He watched Iraq's descent into violence from the country of his birth, where he had served as ambassador since November 2003. During his ambassadorship, Khalilzad succeeded in helping Afghan leaders draft a constitution, strengthen their new democratic government, and develop their economy. Most notably, Khalilzad pioneered Provincial Reconstruction Teams (PRTs), a novel approach to stabilizing Afghan provinces that placed civilian development experts in military units.[3]

The U.S. reconstruction program that Khalilzad took over in Iraq was several orders of magnitude larger than the effort in Afghanistan. In the economy-of-force operation that Khalilzad led in Kabul, all the relevant high-level military and civilian staff could fit around a single table. In Baghdad, he arrived to an immense, sprawling enterprise, with separate military and civilian headquarters on opposite sides of the city managing separate—and frequently disconnected—reconstruction missions.

---

* SIGIR interview with Ambassador David Satterfield, former Deputy Chief of Mission, April 14, 2008.

Iraq's desperate political and security situations required Khalilzad's immediate intervention. The Sunni boycott of the January 2005 elections left the Iraqi Interim Government dominated by Shi'a and Kurdish factions, which maneuvered to consolidate control over federal and provincial institutions. The ensuing polarization fueled an escalation in sectarian violence that slowed the pace of reconstruction and dimmed prospects for national reconciliation. Khalilzad needed a new strategy.

Strategic Reassessment

Before the new ambassador's arrival, the Departments of Defense and State had begun independent reviews of reconstruction strategy. Secretary Rumsfeld dispatched retired General Gary Luck to Iraq to review security force training. Luck's call to expand in-the-field training of Iraq's army and police seconded an emerging consensus in Washington for increased investment in the security sector.[4] The new Iraq Security Forces Fund (ISFF), with its $5.7 billion for ISF support, opened a new stream of significant reconstruction funding that, in time, would rival the IRRF in size.[5]

In early February 2005, newly confirmed Secretary of State Condoleezza Rice sent a team to Iraq led by Ambassador Richard Jones, the former CPA deputy administrator.[6] Jones concluded that violence and fragmentation had caused the Iraqi state to fail and called for the reconstruction effort to pivot from a capital-investment approach to a capacity-building focus. The Jones report reached troubling conclusions about the civilian element of the program, finding that reconstruction efforts as then configured—with personnel generally restricted to the Green Zone and only four regional outposts—was ill suited to reviving Iraq's provincial and local governments. Jones called for new joint civil-military teams to deploy into the provinces, possibly placing one in every combat brigade.[7] The Jones team also found that the lack of on-the-job mentoring of police forces led to poor neighborhood policing, a critical weakness in a country in the grip of an insurgency.[8]

Ambassador Khalilzad used these and other reviews to develop a new strategy.[9] First, he sought to broaden Sunni participation in the political process, hoping to convince Sunni insurgents to view the United States as an "honest broker" and thus to encourage them to lay down their arms. Khalilzad believed that only if Sunnis reengaged with the government could he shepherd the country's leaders through the difficult process of writing a constitution.[10]

Khalilzad's second priority was to defeat the insurgency, a task that demanded close collaboration with General George Casey, commanding general of MNF-I. After considering several counterinsurgency strategies, Khalilzad favored the "oil-spot" approach advocated by defense policy analyst Andrew Krepinevich, which called for the targeted application of military force to create safe havens from which stability could be extended.[11] The success of the oil-spot approach hinged upon the delivery of reconstruction aid immediately after military clearing operations that suppressed violence. Local populations would support Coalition efforts only if they saw tangible, sustainable improvements in their quality of life. Whether to adopt a more aggressive country-wide counterinsurgency posture or keep the military mission focused on the transition to Iraqi security forces would later become the subject of intense debate between Secretaries Rumsfeld and Rice. Rumsfeld favored the transitional approach.[12]

Finally, Khalilzad had to reevaluate the complex and disjointed reconstruction effort.[13] Upon his arrival in Baghdad, his first act—like Negroponte's before him—was to freeze all IRRF 2 obligations while he conducted a bottom-up review. "He was not convinced that the decisions of 2002 and 2003 were relevant to the world of summer 2005," said Ambassador David Satterfield, Khalilzad's deputy chief of mission.[14] Khalilzad wanted to move funding into civilian stability operations that would help support a counterinsurgency campaign and emphasize IRRF projects that would have an immediate impact. "I came to do a job," said Khalilzad of his IRRF 2 review, "And the question was really, 'how much did I have of the $18 billion?'"[15]

Reconstruction at an Impasse

Khalilzad landed in Iraq as the actual rebuilding work under IRRF 2 peaked. By the end of June 2005, the Congress had appropriated almost $30 billion in taxpayer dollars for Iraq's reconstruction to an alphabet soup of funding accounts, including IRRF 1, IRRF 2, ESF, CERP, and ISFF.[16] The DFI and international donors also funded reconstruction, but only a small percentage of the international pledges had been kept.[17]

After a long planning and mobilization phase, the sweeping reconstruction program initiated by Ambassador Bremer's CPA—and modified by Ambassador Negroponte's re-programming—was in high gear, with a thousand projects finished and a thousand more underway. Tens of thousands of private contractors from hundreds of firms now worked across Iraq, employing an estimated 180,000 Iraqis on U.S.-funded projects.[18] Of the $18.4 billion IRRF 2 appropriation, nearly three-quarters had been obligated and a third disbursed.[19] Under the structure set up in Baghdad, State Department officials directed most programs, while the Defense Department officials executed the lion's share of their funding, managing seventy cents of every U.S. dollar spent. The rest was divided among USAID, the Department of State, and Treasury.[20]

Despite extraordinary outlays of cash and other resources, the IRRF 2 program had not achieved its goal of stabilizing Iraq or significantly improving infrastructure outputs. Delivery of essential services continued to lag behind targets established by reconstruction managers.[21] Oil revenues were not yet sufficient to fund all Iraqi government operations and a nationwide reconstruction program.[22] The power grid remained unreliable; fuel shortages, sabotage, and a fragile distribution system caused frequent blackouts, including a nationwide one in August 2005.[23] Rising security costs and the cancellation or delay of dozens of water-sector projects made it unlikely that the Coalition's original goals for potable water and sewage would be met.[24]

In all sectors, rebuilding was more difficult, more expensive, and more time consuming than anticipated, primarily because of continuing violence, but also because of contracting snarls and quality-control shortfalls. Maintaining what the United States built—what officials called the challenge of sustainment—emerged as yet another problem for reconstruction managers. Some completed projects transferred to Iraqi control were falling apart, raising concerns that Iraqi administrators—with their outmoded technical skills, limited management capacity, and uneven access to spare parts and supplies—would be unable to maintain new U.S.-provided facilities.[25]

Despite some significant local successes, the reconstruction effort had yet to generate the hoped-for nationwide goodwill that might temper attacks against Coalition forces and calm tensions among Iraq's rival groups. Most Iraqis perceived their lives as no better than under Saddam; for some, life seemed worse.[26]

Reconstruction Gaps

By the spring of 2005, policymakers were beginning to identify internal weaknesses in the reconstruction program. Poor interagency cooperation across the vast enterprise was plainly evident. At least a dozen offices representing six U.S. agencies directly spent IRRF 2 funds. According to a SIGIR report, there was "minimal, if any, integration among the various systems that these offices used to manage information on contracting, finance, and projects."[27]

Incompatible data systems made generating a reliable, consolidated view of all activities a virtually impossible task. The reconstruction program lacked the basic elements of integrated program management, including a database that could match projects with the contracts that fund them and estimate how much their completion would cost. The organizational fragmentation made it difficult to present an accurate picture of progress.[28]

How the institutions that managed reconstruction interfaced with each other was also a leading cause for concern. The July 2003 decision by the CPA to create an ad hoc contracting and management structure—the PMO—had by 2005 led to many degrees of separation among Coalition officials, contractors, and the mid- and lower-level Iraqi officials who would inherit what had been built or rebuilt.

At the very bottom of this administrative ladder was an army of contractors who actually did the brick-and-mortar work. The project scopes and requirements to which they built frequently were not determined in partnership with the ultimate customer—the Iraqis—as should ordinarily happen. Instead, the attempt by U.S. program officers to work on the Iraqis' behalf frequently ran afoul of what they wanted. By 2005, most U.S. reconstruction managers were concentrated in the PCO. But USAID, State, MNF-I, JCC-I, and USACE also had contracting and program officers; and for almost all rebuilding projects, the GRD provided quality assurance and independent verification of results.[29]

IRMO was yet another player. The Ambassador made IRMO responsible for overall policy guidance on reconstruction and granted its director the additional title of "Strategic Director of Economics and Governance," with broad responsibilities for ensuring program coordination.[30] In the opinion of Lieutenant General Peter Chiarelli, who returned to Iraq as MNC-I commander in November 2005, IRMO "became another layer that I felt, in many instances, was detached from reality."[31] To Ambassador Khalilzad, however, IRMO was a central node that helped him manage the massive reconstruction enterprise.[32]

The complex of administrative structures that managed Iraq's reconstruction in 2005 and 2006 would have been difficult to navigate in peacetime. But Iraq was not safe, and the violence was killing more contractors each month. MNF-I did not have enough forces to provide fixed security for Iraq's critical infrastructure—oil pipelines, refineries, and electrical substations—and still conduct its other counterinsurgency operations. Contractors and civilian government officials continued to rely heavily on the private sector for security.

Private security services, provided by dozens of companies, protected reconstruction people and programs; security costs could increase a typical project's price tag by up to 22 percent.[33] The need to guard Coalition advisors as they worked within Iraqi ministries drove security costs for capacity-building projects higher still, ranging from 24 to 53 percent.[34] Because contracts let under IRRF 2 assigned responsibility for security to the contractor, expenses for guards and hardening facilities were taken directly from funds that would otherwise have been used for brick-and-mortar work. To make up the difference, mangers had to de-scope projects or provide additional funds.

The insurgency had a powerful second-order effect. By restricting most reconstruction personnel to the Green Zone, the violence disrupted the oversight relationships necessary to ensure a project's successful completion. Program managers, contracting officers, contractors, and the engineers who conduct quality assurance normally work together in the field, but insurgent activity made such face-to-face collaboration impossible. Oversight ordinarily done on site was now done via email, sometimes through hired Iraqi surveyors using digital cameras to take pictures—or not done at all. Teams from GRD continued conducting missions from their offices in south, central, and northern Iraq, but security conditions drastically curtailed their size and number.[35]

Although a number of Iraqis found employment as subcontractors, IRRF 2 did not bring about the large-scale job creation originally envisioned. Rather than hiring local firms directly, IRRF 2 introduced a competitive contracting process similar to that used in the United States. Letting contracts under the FAR was a roadblock for many Iraqi firms, most of whom knew nothing about federal contracting. The acquisition regulations mandated by U.S. law thrust Web-based personal identification numbers and thousand-page rulebooks on family-run businesses that had yet to join the global business environment. Online contracting, which frequently entailed bids of more than a hundred pages, bewildered Iraqi contractors who were used to sealing a business deal with just a handshake. Ruth-Ann Ijames, a senior advisor to JCC-I, described the challenge as "trying to make U.S. rules work in a non-U.S. country to mobilize a non-U.S. economy."[36]

A second roadblock for Iraqi contractors was the difficulty of obtaining start-up capital. IRRF 2 contracting used a purchase-order system in which payment was rendered upon delivery of services, not in advance. As a result, Iraqi contractors who had performed satisfactory work on a pay-as-you-go cash basis for military contracting officials in the pre-IRRF 2 days were relegated to the role of subcontractors, working for other firms—often from Gulf States—who had mastered the art of bidding on projects and possessed sufficient capital to cover start-up costs.[37] This subsidiary position, combined with their unfamiliarity with the complexities of modern contracting, left Iraqi companies vulnerable to predatory business partners from the United States and elsewhere.[38]

Ambassador Daniel Speckhard, IRMO's second director, explained that "layers of middlemen" emerged as large multinationals "tried to find local partners to be able to implement their programs."[39] Even as the U.S. objective to "employ Iraqis" grew more pressing, the Coalition's actual capacity to do so trended in the opposite direction. The U.S. program was allowing too many reconstruction dollars to exit Iraq into the coffers of non-Iraqi firms.

IRRF 2 emphasized capital expenditures—the building of new facilities—rather than improving existing infrastructure and the ability of Iraqis to sustain it. The end result was that the U.S. invested billions of dollars for only marginal gains in essential services. In the view of one assessment, Iraq was a bleeding patient, hemorrhaging at an alarming rate, kept alive only by expensive American transfusions.[40]

When Khalilzad arrived, many planned reconstruction projects had yet to start and a significant number that were underway would not be finished, giving rise to what became known as the "reconstruction gap."[41] Increased spending on security needs, higher costs for materials, project delays, cost overruns, multiple reprogrammings, and added expenses for maintenance all contributed to the gap between the number of projects promised and the number actually completed.[42] All of this left Khalilzad with a stark bottom line: "There was very little money left," he said, to meet ambitious reconstruction goals.[43]

The program of infrastructure reconstruction set in motion by Bremer, and amended by Negroponte, had yet to achieve its goal of giving Iraq a reasonably modern infrastructure upon which a stable economy could be built. It had produced neither a reduction in sectarian conflict nor a decrease in attacks against Coalition forces.

Devising a New Strategy

To assess the situation and propose a way forward, Khalilzad formed the Joint Civil-Military Strategic Planning Group, known informally as the Red Cell. "I took a couple of months to take a top-to-bottom look," Khalilzad said.[44] The current strategy was based on the Joint Mission Plan issued by Ambassador Negroponte and General Casey in February 2005, and a cable sent in April by the Secretary of State.[45]

Khalilzad asked the Red Cell to devise a plan that would break the back of the insurgency in one year and defeat it in three. The Red Cell assessment was more pessimistic: it would take three years to break the insurgency and five years to defeat it.[46] Moreover, the current strategy—overly focused on transitioning security responsibilities to the Iraqis—would fail if it was followed. A new approach was needed, one that recognized that it was unwise to hand off security responsibilities to provinces that were at best only marginally ready to perform them. A different way of linking security and reconstruction was also necessary, one that would require tighter integration of civil and military efforts and greater focus on civilian stability operations in support of a counterinsurgency campaign.[47]

The heavy reliance on private-sector firms to carry out civilian operations meant that major change would come slowly. "The instruments were pretty constrained," one senior advisor to Khalilzad recalled. "On the civilian side, almost nothing is done directly: virtually everything is done through a contractor. It's much tougher. If we didn't have a primary contractor on the scene, you can imagine the delay that there would be to put a bid out and get someone over. It's a very tough way to do business."[48]

Ambassador Khalilzad's first impulse was to request a new appropriation from the Congress for civilian stabilization operations. While he was exploring this option, Hurricane Katrina struck New Orleans. After the scale of the devastation became apparent, Khalilzad realized it was unlikely that the Congress would fund new civilian programs for Iraq and instructed his staff to craft a strategy based on the appropriations that had already been made.[49] The strategy they produced focused on three crucial areas: integrating military and civilian activities, achieving the right balance of reconstruction programs, and returning a civilian presence to the provinces.

Military and Civilian Integration

Like Ambassador Negroponte before him, Khalilzad recognized the fundamental imbalance between civilian and military assets. Civilian agencies, because of their comparatively small size and concentration in the Green Zone, had limited insight into Iraqi society. On the other hand, military personnel at the brigade level ventured daily into Iraqi neighborhoods, but were not as cognizant of the political process playing out in Baghdad or as expert in economic and political development as their civilian colleagues.[50] This mismatch of expertise and reach, along with poor agency integration, persisted from the occupation's earliest days. As in 2003, the challenge in 2005 was to pair the knowledge of civilian experts with the military's on-the-ground presence.

The concerted movement toward greater integration of civilian and military reconstruction began in mid-2004, when military representatives were encouraged to attend meetings of the embassy country team and the Joint Steering Committee. After General Casey's arrival, a new Deputy Chief of Staff for Political-Military-Economics at MNF-I worked closely with the embassy's Political-Military Counselor and the Director of IRMO on economics, governance, and reconstruction issues. General Casey also established an interagency Strategic Operations Center, which hosted regular briefings for senior military and civilian staff.[51]

Khalilzad and Casey further augmented these joint staff structures. In 2005, IRMO established "post-kinetic" coordinators whose job was to bring civilian reconstruction resources to bear once military operations had stabilized an area. Key civilian and military staff met weekly in core groups on reconstruction, economic policy, political issues, and public communications, each of which became part of an integrated line of operation and reporting in support of goals established in the campaign plan.[52] Joint participation was nurtured, to a degree, in the standing committees that the military uses to evaluate effects, including the Effects Synchronization Board. Khalilzad also created the Joint Strategic Planning and Assessment office (JSPA) to conduct strategic planning, provide independent analysis, and act as a liaison to the MNF-I planning and assessment offices.[53] JSPA gave civilian analysts more scope to evaluate strategy options in partnership with the military, whose planning staff dwarfed that of their civilian counterparts. "As Zal always said," Ambassador Speckhard remembers, "he wanted to talk about integration, not coordination."[54]

Balancing Reconstruction Programs
"Jointness" was not an end in itself. Above all, U.S. policymakers were asking what combinations of civilian and military operations would produce the desired effects. The Jones assessment team, and later Khalilzad, examined how the panoply of individual reconstruction projects, stovepiped under various categories, could work better as an integrated whole. Military and civilian strategists pushed for an examination of the approaches underlying reconstruction and how civilian operations could be better incorporated into overall strategy.

By mid-2005, five functional types of reconstruction projects were being executed: public infrastructure; quick-impact, high-visibility; democracy building; transitional stabilization; and capacity building. Each had a role in seeking to pacify Iraq and enabling its newly elected government to function independently of Coalition support.

Public infrastructure projects: Public infrastructure projects, underwritten largely by IRRF 2, are generally quite complex. With the exception of road building and other simple construction, they require specialized engineering and design capabilities that call for international firms that generally employ non-Iraqi workers. Although a boon to economic development over the long term, upgrades to the water, sewer, electricity, transportation, communication, and oil sectors are expensive, take a long time to complete, usually generate little local employment, and often are invisible to the public.

Quick-impact, high-visibility projects: Small, quick-impact projects undertaken by military commanders are at the other end of the reconstruction spectrum. The military has long used "walking around money" to help tactical units on the ground gain community support, improving public perceptions of the Coalition ("winning hearts and minds") and enhancing troop safety (force protection). In Iraq, CERP fulfilled this purpose. Typical projects included trash cleanups—which improve local sanitation, but also can eliminate hiding places for improvised explosive devices—constructing soccer fields, and building health clinics.[55] Although many of these projects were congruent with broad Coalition goals, when implemented they often were not coordinated with IRRF 2 programs or the Iraqi government.[56] CERP projects generally did not foster long-term change on their own, but rather served as vehicles for allowing the military to operate with greater local cooperation in the short-term.

Democracy-building projects: A small portion of IRRF 1 and IRRF 2 funds went to programs to build democracy and civil society, and to foster reconciliation. The community action and local governance programs developed by USAID specifically for post-conflict situations were the primary instruments supporting this approach. They encouraged participatory politics at the community level, with the goal of helping a viable democratic infrastructure take root. The goal of these "soft" programs was to help Iraqis develop a process for managing their affairs in a democracy and to train civil servants and political leaders at all levels. It was hard to measure the impact of programs that sought to instill an understanding of, and allegiance to, the principles of participatory democracy. Evaluating their success or failure posed challenges for both embassy management and oversight organizations.[57]

Transitional stabilization projects: The Coalition pioneered another type of intervention. Aimed at stabilizing violent cities, transitional stabilization projects sought to bridge quick-impact projects with longer-term development efforts. In a prototypical partnership in the spring of 2004, USAID's OTI worked with the 1st Cavalry Division in Baghdad's Sadr City—a key stronghold of the militant Shi'a cleric Muqtada al-Sadr—to repair battle damage and jump-start economic rebuilding in the wake of major clearing operations.[58] On-the-spot grant-making authority and the ability to let contracts without having to comply with some of the more cumbersome parts of the FAR—mostly for projects employing people in the neighborhood—led to quick results.[59] These projects, which ranged from sewer repair to grants to local businesses, were typically initiated and monitored exclusively by Iraqi employees of the Coalition, who operated with relative freedom. Keeping the Iraqi employees who spearheaded these collaborations safe from insurgent attack often meant disguising the project's source of funding; keeping the projects themselves safe meant not advertising their location, even within the Coalition. The full impact of USAID transitional stabilization projects thus remained hidden from both Iraqis and many U.S. officials.[60]

Capacity-building projects: For infrastructure projects to produce the desired essential services and for the Iraqi government to function effectively, personnel at all levels had to be properly trained and supported with effective planning, budgeting, and operations. Some IRRF 2 projects aimed to build this "capacity" where it did not exist and to strengthen existing administrative systems. Capacity-building programs undertaken with IRRF funds ranged from classroom training for operators of electrical power plants to installation of accounting and information management systems inside government ministries. The U.S. investment in Iraq could be sustained only by building institutional capacity within Iraqi ministries and the infrastructure they oversaw.

Ambassador Khalilzad's advisors concluded that they needed a framework for determining the right mixture of these approaches to apply and how to match funding and support for them in the constituent parts of the reconstruction effort.[61] IRMO senior advisors to Iraqi ministries, USAID program managers, MNF-I personnel, and soldiers on the ground each worked according to their own priorities, using their own funding streams, and were only loosely coordinated by an overarching plan.

Focusing on Provincial Support

Ambassador Khalilzad moved to expand civilian operations in the provinces, reversing a trend begun after June 2004, when concerns about deteriorating security and budget shortfalls led the State Department to close most CPA provincial offices. The 2004 pullback reflected the views of incoming State personnel who argued for the development of a normal embassy structure, in which fewer Coalition personnel would be involved in Iraqi affairs. In the prevailing State Department view, this would push the Iraqi Interim Government to assume more responsibility. It was also thought that consolidating advisors within the embassy's political and economic sections would enhance the ambassador's in-house capacity to support the management of political and economic affairs. "The State Department tried to make it a normal mission," strategic analyst Andrew Rathmell said, but "quickly discovered this would not be possible."[62]

Hopes of returning to a normal embassy stayed alive, however. Khalilzad had to rebut calls for implementing traditional State Department structures and protocols so often that he came up with a one-line riposte: "As soon as we have a normal mission," Khalilzad would shoot back, "we'll have a normal embassy."[63]

In contrast to the embassy's June 2004 pullback from the provinces, the number of U.S. military personnel assisting in developing Iraqi Security Forces across Iraq had increased over the previous year as MNSTC-I embedded teams of advisors in Iraqi units down to the battalion level. The opportunity to forge enduring relationships between Coalition and Iraqi personnel and fine-tune operations from within the system proved to be "a formula for success" in the eyes of its practitioners.[64]

In reconstruction, the strategy of "pulling back to let the Iraqis do it themselves" failed to stabilize Iraq.[65] Iraqi provincial governments remained weak and disconnected from the central government. Improving the delivery of essential services and the credibility of Iraq's government would occur only if provincial institutions were strengthened.

By the late spring of 2005, the embassy reached consensus on two courses of action: to reconstitute its ability to influence and monitor provincial affairs, and to expand on the concept of embedding U.S. personnel in Iraqi institutions in order to develop their capacity for self-rule. Khalilzad seized on the consensus that more should be done locally by launching two far-reaching initiatives: Provincial Reconstruction Development Councils (PRDCs) and Provincial Reconstruction Teams.

Provincial Reconstruction Development Councils: In the spring of 2005, the U.S. Embassy reinforced the PRDCs, the first joint Iraqi-American vehicle explicitly aimed at building capacity in regional governing institutions.[66] The councils, which had existed in fifteen provinces in various forms since the CPA days, became an important instrument of coordination that brought together local Iraqi officials and the Coalition personnel overseeing reconstruction in their provinces. Everyone had a seat at the table: elected Iraqi officials and their municipal staffs, USAID representatives, civil affairs soldiers, and embassy representatives. The development councils became a forum where these stakeholders could collectively evaluate provincial needs and match them with available U.S. and Iraqi resources.[67]

In most provinces, PRDCs drew up prioritized lists of projects in line with national and provincial development plans. They then worked to secure funding. In June 2005, IRMO allocated $241 million to the PRDC partnership—$80 million through CERP and $161 million through USAID's Community Action Program and Local Governance Program.[68] Councils also had their own funding provided by the Iraqi government, which, together with U.S. funding, eventually amounted to about $10 million per province.[69] This was a relatively modest amount, but it marked the start of a trend toward greater spending and control by provincial governments.

Provincial Reconstruction Teams: Khalilzad's introduction of PRTs in Iraq—a concept he brought from Afghanistan—would be his most enduring contribution to the reconstruction program.[70] Building on the PRDC concept and recommendations of the Jones review to project civilian power beyond the Green Zone, he and General Casey deployed mixed teams of military and civilian reconstruction personnel in the regions. Their mission was to work directly with provincial governments and military brigades. Some advisors—including Lieutenant General Raymond Odierno and Dr. Philip Zelikow, the State Department's Counselor—called for small teams to be embedded in every brigade. But Khalilzad preferred fielding fewer larger teams that remained under embassy control and maintained their own arrangements for basing and support.[71]

The PRT initiative in Iraq was originally conceived as a two-phase program over four years. It was to have a complement of ten PRTs, seven led by the United States and one each by the United Kingdom, Italy, and Korea.[72] The PRTs' mission, set forth in a joint cable to the Secretary of State, was to "assist Iraq's provincial governments with developing a transparent and sustained capability to govern, promote increased security and rule of law, promote political and economic development, and provide the provincial administration necessary to meet the basic needs of the population."[73] PRTs harkened back to the CORDS program in Vietnam, in which USAID and military personnel worked on rural development as part of a counterinsurgency campaign.[74]

Secretary of State Rice delayed announcing the PRT program until the Iraqi constitution was ratified by national referendum on October 15, 2005. She did not want to give the impression that the U.S. government presumed the existence of the regional governance structure before the Iraqis had approved it. In a surprise visit to Iraq, she inaugurated the first PRT in Mosul on November 11, 2005.[75]

The PRT program established a formal framework in which military and civilian personnel could work as an integrated team, rather than as a partnership between separate military and civilian offices. Coaxing the Departments of State and Defense to set the terms of their first major operational collaboration in Iraq required a herculean effort that touched off frequent arguments between MNF-I, the embassy, and Washington. A patchwork quilt of memoranda of agreement, cables, and military orders—many of them at cross-purposes—evolved to codify policy for PRTs. More than a year elapsed before basic issues of budgets, the provision of security, and command and control relationships were resolved, delaying full deployment of the PRTs and limiting their early effectiveness in the field.[76]

PRT control and support: The PRT command structure put the Department of State in charge of the program. A military deputy was assigned to each civilian team leader. The chain of command and the legalities of program support, however, were ambiguous. By law, State Department officials do not have a place in the military's chain of command. Some Defense Department officials thought the PRT guidelines gave the State Department more control over military assets than was permitted under Title 10 of the U.S. Code.[77]

The exceptionally high cost of providing security for PRTs led to a second disagreement. Throughout Iraq, civilians and their movement teams donned armor-plated vests when they ventured "outside the wire," traveling on roads that at times were mined with explosives and through neighborhoods where ambushes sometimes occurred. Only when supported by platoon- and company-level firepower could the PRTs carry out their mission in an active combat zone. The question of whether PRTs were to be supported by military units, as the Department of State wanted, or by private security details, as the Department of Defense advocated, remained unsettled for some time.[78] Early consideration was given to the use of civilian security contractors for all PRTs, but the notion was abandoned because of the unsustainable price tags.[79]

Debates also raged over budget resources. According to the original agreement reached in Baghdad, the Department of State would pay for establishing and hosting PRTs at Regional Embassy Office (REO) sites, and MNF-I would fund those located on forward operating bases.[80] In April 2006, the MNC-I Judge Advocate General ruled that the Department of State was responsible for the mission and that Department of Defense operation and maintenance funds could not be used to support PRTs.[81]

The operational impact of this administrative stalemate was immediate. When the REO in Mosul closed, the Mosul PRT suddenly had no security or housing, forcing the team to relocate to Forward Operating Base Marez. The first PRT, personally launched by the Secretary of State, lost its dedicated budgetary and movement support, forcing it to rely on the support of the base commander, who redirected funds intended for other purposes as a stop-gap. For months the PRT had no budget for office supplies or for maintaining its network of computers, and no dedicated funds of its own for reconstruction.[82]

The unexplored frontier of civil-military operations in Iraq was the root problem, leading to shortfalls in financial and policy support by two departments unaccustomed to working together. "The PRT policy emerged well before resources started flowing," Andrew Rathmell explained.[83] Thus began what one officer called "the REO-PRT shell game."[84] To end the impasse, Major General Bill Caldwell, the MNF-I Deputy Chief of Staff for Strategic Effects, proposed that Ambassador Khalilzad and General Casey sign a memorandum declaring PRTs a joint mission. The draft included a cost-sharing formula that increased the burden on the Department of State. State officials in Washington sought redress from the NSC and the Joint Staff, who left it to the embassy and MNF-I to negotiate a solution. It took nearly a year before government lawyers negotiated a cooperative security agreement for the PRTs.[85]

PRT personnel: Staffing the PRTs proved another enormous challenge. Finding individuals with the right combination of experience, expertise, and judgment was difficult. The Department of State and other civilian agencies struggled to field adequate numbers of civilian advisors, leaving many PRTs at half capacity and forcing the military to fill positions with soldiers who did not have the right expertise or experience.[86]

The mismatch of needs and staff had significant consequences in the field. A SIGIR review of the PRTs' first year of operation found that a veterinarian was developing agriculture programs, an aviation maintenance manager was a PRT co-leader, and advisors to Iraqi provincial governors included a Navy submariner, an ultrasound technician, and an infantry drill sergeant.[87] On the whole, PRTs were short of personnel who could best assist Iraqis in developing the capacity to administer the economy, establish the rule of law, and foster good governance. Staffing challenges, the unresolved budget issue, and troop shortages at prospective PRT sites hindered the operations of several PRTs and canceled the deployment of another. SIGIR's 2006 audit found that of the nine PRTs and four satellite offices reviewed, four were "generally able," four were "somewhat able," three were "less able," and two were "generally unable" to carry out their mission.[88]

Iraq and Afghanistan: A Brief Comparison

Early success in Afghanistan in 2002 suggested a model that might work in Iraq in 2003. The U.S. goals in the two countries were similar—to establish democracy and defeat terrorism. But their geopolitical, economic, historical, and cultural differences complicated applying the Afghan model to Iraq.

Soon after Afghanistan's Taliban government was toppled in late 2001, the U.S. installed a new government led by Afghan expatriate Hamid Karzai. Under Karzai's leadership, the Afghan Transitional Authority sought to set the country on a path toward democratic stabilization. Karzai was formally elected president on November 3, 2004, and was still holding that office at the end of 2008.[89]

ORHA's director Jay Garner and Special Presidential Envoy to Iraq Zalmay Khalilzad aimed to replicate the Afghan model by rapidly transferring power to an interim Iraqi authority. But no "Karzai-like" figure emerged. For a variety of reasons, the plan to quickly create a sovereign interim government in Iraq was abandoned. After more than a year of a CPA-led occupation, the U.S. transferred sovereignty to the Iraqi Interim Government in late June 2004. Iraq has since been successively led by Prime Ministers Ayad Allawi, Ibrahim Ja'afari, and Nouri al-Maliki.[90]

In 2002, the vast majority of Afghans had no access to essential services such as water and electricity. By contrast, Iraqi citizens were accustomed to such services under Saddam and expected them to continue after his fall. Afghanistan's literacy rate was less than 30 percent when the Coalition invaded, and Iraq's was 74 percent (though it fell during Saddam's rule).[91] Twenty-five years of conflict had driven educated Afghans abroad, but Iraq retained a large professional class and a capable workforce during Saddam's reign (although many left during the violence that followed his fall).[92]

After the U.S. invasion of Afghanistan, U.S. military forces added to the existing Afghan forces, aiming to develop an army of about 70,000 soldiers.[93] In Iraq, the CPA disbanded the Iraqi Army shortly after the 2003 invasion and began to build a New Iraqi Army of 40,000.[94] Initially, the CPA, not the U.S. military, oversaw the training of the New Iraqi Army. That changed in 2004 when MNSTC-I took the lead in building the Iraqi Security Forces. By late 2008, MNSTC-I had trained well over 200,000 soldiers for Iraq's military.[95]

Ambassador Khalilzad developed PRTs in Afghanistan and adapted the concept to Iraq in late 2005, with a different mission and organizational structure. In Afghanistan, the PRTs sought to "extend the authority of the Afghan government into the provinces in order to develop a stable and secure environment, enable security sector reform and economic and social development." In Iraq, the PRTs worked with Iraqi provincial and municipal councils and civil-society groups to build local governance capacity, carry out reconstruction projects, and improve security in the provinces.[96] In both countries, the PRTs were staffed by civilian and military personnel, but in Afghanistan staffing was weighted toward the military, while in Iraq it was mostly civilian.

Since 2001, the Congress has appropriated about $50 billion for Iraq's relief and reconstruction, while just over $30 billion was appropriated for Afghanistan.[97] About half of the money provided to each country was spent on developing security forces.

Clear-Hold-Build

By the fall of 2005, many of the threads of civil-military operations were coming together. The growing recognition in military circles that reconstruction is a tactically useful "non-lethal effect" was expressed in a handbook for commanders, "Money as a Weapons System (MAAWS)." Published by MNC-I in October 2005 and distributed widely across Iraq, MAAWS embraced reconstruction as a "critical enabler of everything we do on the battlefield." "Effective application of all available resources," the handbook begins, "is vital to the success of our mission."[98]

At the same time, MNF-I and the embassy made progress employing civilian reconstruction resources in the military counterinsurgency campaign. Using the partnership between USAID's OTI and the military in Falluja, Najaf, Samarra, and Baghdad as a model, officials developed a more robust package of civilian stability operations for the Strategic Cities Initiative.[99] In the initiative, MNF-I coordinated with the NSC to periodically designate Iraqi cities for targeted intervention.[100] Now, civilian resources would play a major role in what had been a primarily military-led operation.

While the use of reconstruction resources as part of a military-led campaign gained traction with lower-level ground commanders in Iraq, a debate erupted in Washington. High-level backing for a robust counterinsurgency strategy that blended military and civilian resources materialized in the NSC and in the Office of the Secretary of State. It became known as "Clear-Hold-Build," an apt description of the succession of clearing and stability operations undertaken in some of the strategic cities.[101] But Secretary Rumsfeld and General Casey initially opposed this strategy because it would shift the military focus from transitioning security responsibilities to the Iraqis and preparing to draw down U.S. forces.

The rift broke into public view after Secretary Rice testified in favor of the Clear-Hold-Build approach before the Senate on October 19, 2005, only to be rebuffed by Secretary Rumsfeld, who disavowed the strategy in favor of continuing the emphasis on transition.[102] "Anyone who takes those three words and thinks it means the United States should clear and the United States should hold and the United States should build," Rumsfeld said, "doesn't understand the situation. It is the Iraqis' country. They've got 28 million people there. They are clearing, they are holding, they are building. They're going to be the ones doing the reconstruction in that country."[103]

Settling the argument in Rice's favor, the President publicly put his seal of approval on Clear-Hold-Build in a Veterans Day speech on November 11, 2005.[104] Two weeks later, the White House announced "Clear-Hold-Build" as official policy in the document "National Strategy for Victory in Iraq."[105] The strategy's integration of military, political, and economic lines of operation was a notable milestone in the evolution of the U.S. approach to Iraq. However, critics inside and outside the government asked whether the strategy was sufficiently resourced—with adequate numbers of troops and funding for civilian operations—to be effective. Disagreements between the President's key advisors in the Departments of State and Defense soon appeared to be impeding the execution of the new strategy.[106]

Within six months of Ambassador Khalilzad's arrival in Iraq, the U.S. reconstruction program moved beyond its original emphasis on infrastructure construction. Bringing to the table experts in development and counterinsurgency refocused the debate on how reconstruction dollars could support political transition and reduce violence. From spring 2005 forward, the reconstruction effort began to shift. Now the emphasis was on modest Iraqi-led projects designed to deliver jobs and services to the most vulnerable, violent, and strategically significant neighborhoods, and on working as much as possible through municipal and provincial institutions.

In engineering this shift, MNF-I and embassy officials forged a more comprehensive model of civil-military integration that returned U.S. civilian personnel to the regions and put them back inside Iraqi institutions. The gradual acceptance of the need to integrate civilian and military efforts, and to embed coalition personnel with Iraqis at every level, amounted to a rejection of CPA's approach to nation-building, which relied primarily on infrastructure construction and did not sufficiently focus on building capacity inside Iraqi institutions.[107] Although the Rumsfeld-Rice debate on overall strategy continued, leaving the Clear-Hold-Build strategy under-resourced for over a year, the utility of its approach became increasingly apparent. Nevertheless, forging cooperative relationships with Iraqis and between U.S. civil and military personnel below the level of the Ambassador and the Commanding General remained a major challenge.

Although Khalilzad and a series of strategic review teams succeeded in reconfiguring reconstruction in accordance with a more sophisticated approach to nation building and the ongoing counterinsurgency campaign, a signal challenge awaited the nascent strategy. The movement of reconstruction personnel out to the provinces and back into Iraqi regional institutions brought to light the deeply dysfunctional relationship between officials in Iraq's central and provincial governments. By 2006, reconstruction managers would come to see that U.S. efforts to make Iraq into a federal democratic state had actively undermined the country's public institutions.

CHAPTER 23
RETURNING TO THE PROVINCES

*We must not forget the importance of ... improving Iraqi lives
in their communities across the country. Iraq requires not
only good government at the center, but also effective local
government and strong coordination between the provincial and
central governments.*

Ambassador Zalmay Khalilzad
U.S. Ambassador to Iraq (2005-2007)

"Go out Assassin's Gate, over the 3rd ID bridge, onto the highway of death, left down through the overpass of assault, and then turn right," Lieutenant Colonel Otto Busher said.[1] It was Sunday, June 25, 2006, and members of the Baghdad PRT were on their way to a meeting of the city's Water and Sewer Board. Their convoy of Humvees plowed through Baghdad's crowded streets, sirens blaring, for the short but dangerous trip from the Green Zone to the Amanat—or city hall—whose 14,000-man workforce provides basic services to Baghdad residents. With weapons ready, the team entered a conference room and waited for Iraqi engineers to filter past the armed sentries Busher placed at the door. Tea was served before the meeting began.[2]

The Army Reservist from New Hampshire was on his third tour in Iraq. Using skills honed as a city manager in civilian life and as a civil affairs officer in Kosovo, he was known in reconstruction circles for his dogged pursuit of water projects across Baghdad. With Busher as essential services lead, the Baghdad PRT had forged links with the Iraqi engineers working to repair Baghdad's sewer and water system. Only with the Iraqis' active cooperation would Coalition-sponsored projects be successful. Since their weekly meetings began several months before, the team had helped the Baghdad Water and Sewer Board make progress toward self-governance; the board's deputy director general for water, not Busher, chaired meetings.[3]

The Politics of Service Delivery
At the Amanat that morning, Baghdad's plumbing was not the only item for discussion: politics were also on the agenda. The struggle for power between Iraq's warring factions had by now engulfed municipal institutions across Iraq. Assassinations were an all too common occurrence. More than 50 members of

* Ambassador Zalmay Khalilzad, "Remarks by Ambassador Zalmay Khalilzad for the Inauguration of the Salah ad Din PRT," Baghdad embassy Press Release, October 12, 2006.

• 247 •

the assorted Baghdad councils—city, district, sub-district, neighborhood—had been struck down.[4] The Amanat itself had been the site of a sectarian "municipal coup." On August 8, 2005, members of the Badr militia, the armed wing of the Shi'a Supreme Council for the Islamic Revolution in Iraq (SCIRI), deposed the mayor, a secular technocrat who had been appointed by the central government. SCIRI replaced him with the man whom the newly elected and SCIRI-dominated provincial council had also appointed governor of Baghdad Province.[5]

One of the first agenda items for the meeting concerned what Busher called "the water pipe to nowhere."[6] An enterprising district council in a Sunni neighborhood had convinced a civil affairs company to build a pipe connecting their constituents, then without fresh water, to a nearby water plant under construction. The plan sounded reasonable to the civil affairs team, which used CERP funds to initiate construction through a local contractor.

There was, however, a technical stumbling block. The plant pumped water at far higher than household pressures. Had the lines been connected, "everyone's faucets would have ended up in their backyards," Busher said.[7] Worse yet was a political issue: the construction commissioned by the civil affairs team crossed a de facto sectarian boundary. The Shi'a who held sway over city government took a "Shi'a first" view of service delivery. Even if the pipes were completed, city officials would not allow the connection to a Sunni neighborhood to be activated.[8]

Next on the agenda was a bigger problem—a water treatment plant in the city's Karkh neighborhood that was being refurbished by the Coalition—the same plant whose generator Task Force Fajr used to turn on Baghdad's lights after the invasion. When finished, the plant and its adjacent reservoir would hold a week's worth of fresh water for Baghdad's seven million residents, a vital supply that would help blunt the insurgents' efforts to sabotage the city's essential services. Engineers on the water board, however, had identified a potential showstopper. A contractor on the project had purchased a PVC reservoir liner that was not certified for human use. The Iraqi water engineers were outraged and threatened to reject the project unless the liner was replaced.[9]

As Busher worked to address these and other problems, a car bomb exploded two blocks up the street, sending black smoke billowing skyward. Amanat security guards had witnessed insurgents casing Busher's convoy from nearby rooftops, and now an Iraqi police checkpoint had been attacked by a vehicle-borne IED.[10]

Busher's meeting at the Amanat demonstrates many of the issues the reconstruction effort faced in 2006. Projects had to pass through a maze of Iraqi and Coalition institutions before they even began. Coordination was a perennial challenge, in part because it was not always clear who was in charge on either side. To corral the disparate players, the PCO mandated in June 2006 that all relevant

Iraqi and Coalition authorities sign a memorandum of agreement before moving forward with any project.[11] Even when this rudimentary level of coordination was achieved, political agendas often intervened. Sorting out who was Shi'a and who was Sunni was hard enough; discerning who was following a sectarian agenda and who was impartially carrying out the job was almost always impossible.

As PRTs penetrated the institutions of the Iraqi state, they discovered that sectarianism and the battle for control between provincial and ministerial officials had crippled once-functioning organs of public administration. The never-ending stream of minor catastrophes that resulted made some reconstruction officials compare their lives to the movie *Groundhog Day*, in which the protagonist suffers through a bad day he is condemned to repeat perpetually.[12] The cycle's root causes were apparent. The struggle for power in Iraq's new electoral system, hurriedly arranged in the last days of the CPA, had overwhelmed the public institutions that manage reconstruction. The seeds of this tangled story were planted in 2003, matured in 2004, and finally burst open in 2005.

Reconstructing Governance in Iraq

After the 2003 invasion, Coalition military units across Iraq worked to restore local government. They did so under a loose plan, developed after the invasion started, in which Governorate Support Teams composed of civil affairs personnel and USAID contractors assisted military commanders in forming local councils. The plan, however, reflected an unresolved tension in U.S. policy over how to connect the councils formed in neighborhoods, cities, and provinces to the national government in Baghdad. The United States had begun the war without any notion of how the new councils it was installing—and attempting to empower—at the community level of Iraqi society would integrate with existing institutions at the top.[13] The councils immediately found themselves at odds with the provincial directors general, who reported to national ministries in Baghdad and jealously guarded their prerogative to oversee public services and disburse funding.[14]

The debate over how to make central ministries accountable to local communities, and thereby decentralize the power of a formerly tyrannical regime, played out during the CPA era. As Ambassador Bremer sought to usher Iraq into a democratic era, the extent to which Iraq's central and provincial governments would share power remained contested. The CPA put enormous resources into electing councils across Iraq, envisioning a system in which they held most of the power in each province.[15]

Iraqis were divided over Bremer's plan to radically devolve power from Baghdad to the provinces. The Shi'a in the south and the Kurds in the north wanted an even greater devolution of power, one that maximized local control in regions with Kurdish and Shi'a majorities. Sunnis and many leaders in the national ministries in Baghdad, however, preferred continued concentration of power in the central government. This struggle was at the heart of what the new Iraqi state was to be. Bremer's actions—including enshrining the decentralization of power in the TAL—marked the opening gambit in what became an extended imbroglio over Iraqi federalism.[16]

Ministry Politicization

As the Iraqi debate over federalism unfolded in the occupation's first three years, Iraq's political parties battled not only for victory in the country's first democratic elections, but also for control of the central ministries and their powerful chains of directors general. Under the CPA, members of the Iraqi Governing Council were able to exploit what control Bremer allowed them over the ministries. Each council member was permitted to appoint a minister and thereby control a ministry.[17] This undisguised power grab continued under the Iraqi Interim Government established after the return of sovereignty on June 28, 2004. Given the traditional mores of Arab culture and widespread nepotism under Saddam, IGC members—and many of the interim ministers who followed them—appointed their sons, cousins, and other members of their own families, tribes, or parties to ministry positions, establishing a ruling clique that further stocked ministerial ranks with political loyalists.[18]

Almost overnight, a majority of the ministries of Iraq's central government—once controlled by the Ba'ath Party, but largely staffed by technocrats—became aligned with, and then dominated by, competing political parties. Sadrists seized the Health and Education ministries. Employing the model of service delivery embraced by Hezbollah—the radical Islamic Shi'a group based in Lebanon—they openly deployed ministry resources to build support among the Shi'a underclass. At the same time, SCIRI, the largest Shi'a political party, took control of the Ministry of the Interior—and its powerful internal security apparatus—and later the Ministry of Finance. The major Sunni party, the Iraqi Accord Front, would exert a lesser degree of control over the newly formed Ministry of Defense. Who received services and who did not was increasingly decided on the basis of political allegiance and sectarian identity.[19]

The capture of central ministries by political parties had enduring consequences for reconstruction and for the development of a functioning Iraqi state. A new cadre of directors general was selected for party loyalty rather than technical competence. As parties put their people in power, political rivalries affected relations among ministries and between national and provincial governments. Ministerial appointments of provincial officials injected national party politics into local affairs. The result was, at times, a significant breakdown in local order. In several instances, the Minister of Interior refused to assent to the dismissal of police chiefs by provincial authorities and insisted that party loyalists remain in the job—exactly the kind of central-government control Ambassador Bremer's reforms had sought to reverse.[20]

Another dynamic eroded ministry competence. Each time the cabinet was reshuffled and ministers changed, a whole new clique moved into the upper echelons of ministry staff. Institutional knowledge of ministry operations, as well as training paid for by U.S. capacity-development programs, went out the door with their predecessors.

Local-National Disconnect

After the January 2005 elections, the Shi'a parties took full advantage of the Sunni boycott to consolidate their influence, especially in the capital. A primer on city politics written by the Baghdad PRT chronicles what happened next. "The lopsided nature of political power, with SCIRI/Badr domination, has created a desperate chemistry for the province," it states. A "political Darwinism" prevailed in which the Shi'a party elite centralized authority.[21] The result of the Sunni boycott was that Iraq's capital was ruled by what one official characterized as a "Shi'a dictatorship."[22] During this period, SCIRI deposed Baghdad's mayor and took over the Amanat.

The Shi'a takeover opened rifts between provincial councils, stacked with SCIRI supporters, and many of the 437 neighborhood, 195 sub-district, and 96 district councils that USAID had established across Iraq as part of its LGP.[23] Although provincial councils were supposed to represent a province's entire population, the Sunni boycott of the 2005 election yielded Sunni-majority provinces ruled by Shi'a councils. Projects and services came to be distributed along sectarian lines, reflecting the "Shi'a first" mentality that Lieutenant Colonel Busher witnessed at the Amanat. By mid-2006, the party grip was entrenched. "SCIRI/Badr has worked diligently to maintain and increase their hold on power," the primer continues, "trying to delay new elections or any structural changes that might weaken their position."[24]

One of USAID's local governance advisors took an even bleaker view of the effect of the elections. During 2004, the LGP had worked to "solidify and extend the role of sub-national governmental institutions to prevent, or at least discourage, a recentralization of power."[25] "The party list system sabotaged [the LGP]," the advisor said, laying waste to two years of diligent work fostering authentic local governance in Iraq.[26] USAID had helped create a mechanism in Iraq for local representation that was undermined both by the electoral formula and a disregard for decentralization that dated back to the CPA.[27]

Issues of federalism and provincial government that would directly impact reconstruction were again on the negotiating table when the constitution was drafted during the late spring and summer of 2005. Ambassador Khalilzad pressured the constitutional drafting committee to clearly demarcate federal from provincial responsibilities, but the issue proved too explosive to settle.[28] The draft constitution deferred until a later time the question of provincial powers—and thereby how public administration would be controlled at the local level.

The continuing disagreements between Iraq's Shi'a, Sunni, and Kurdish populations, over how much power the central government should have nearly caused the constitutional referendum to fail. In the electoral formula governing the referendum process, a simple majority was required for approval, but the constitution could also have been defeated by a "no" vote with a two-thirds majority in three or more governorates.[29] When Iraqis went to vote on October 15, 2005, Kurdish- and Shi'a-dominated provinces supported the constitution by overwhelming margins, while Sunni-dominated provinces voted against it in equal measure.[30] A simple nationwide majority was achieved, but the constitution narrowly missed defeat by the governorate rule. Two predominantly Sunni provinces—Anbar and Salah Al-Din—voted against the constitution by more than the required two-thirds majority. Although a majority of voters in a third province—Ninewa—rejected the constitution, it fell short of the two-thirds majority required to qualify as a "no" vote, allowing the constitution to be passed.[31]

Under the new constitution, national elections were held two months later, on December 15, 2005, to select members of Iraq's first permanent legislature. This time, Iraq was divided into electoral districts by province, although the party-list system remained in force.[32] Sunni participation in the elections brought some balance to the distribution of power in the National Assembly, but elections for local and provincial offices were postponed repeatedly, perpetuating the Shi'a over-representation on provincial councils. The failure to hold provincial elections complicated reconstruction efforts at the local level. Who held government office did not necessarily reflect who held power in the province. As a result, provincial elections remained a political grievance held by almost all non-Shi'a parties, as well as those Shi'a parties not aligned with the ruling coalition.

Three years would pass before the issue was resolved. Provincial elections planned for September 2006 were postponed until March 2007 after the Shi'a-majority parliament failed to appoint an electoral commission and draft election bylaws. Soon another delay was announced, putting off still further the prospect of a democratic rebalancing of Iraq's provincial and local governments. Throughout

2007, parliament refused even to consider implementing legislation on provincial powers. A law eventually passed in February 2008 but was then vetoed by the Presidency Council. Although the veto was later rescinded, the law would not come into effect until a law on national elections was fashioned.[33] On September 24, 2008, the Provincial Election Law was finally passed, mandating national elections before January 31, 2009.[34]

The long delay in holding competitive local elections left political conflicts simmering across the country, complicating efforts of reconstruction personnel to work at the local level. Despite the approval of the new constitution and the seating of an elected national parliament, the organization of Iraq's local governments, as specified in CPA Order 71, was by now a poor guide to who actually wielded control. In the absence of a clear legal framework, power fell to those best positioned to seize it, both inside and outside institutions of government. The resulting breakdown between the central government and provincial councils—and in turn between the provincial governments and neighborhood and district councils—crippled the administration of public services the U.S. reconstruction program was trying to rebuild.

Regional Responses

In response to the fragmentation of the Iraqi state, military and civilian officials used USAID soft programs, PRTs, and brigade combat teams to strengthen local administrative capacities and connect provincial governments with national ministries. The sheer logistics of setting up the PRTs and assessing the status of reconstruction and institutional development in each province was difficult. All PRTs were explicitly tasked to bridge the local-national disconnect, but it was often the larger and more powerful brigade combat teams who made the most difference. By 2006, brigade commanders came to see improving local governance as an essential part of their mission. In addition to their primary tasks of securing the battle space, brigades often would provide security for local government facilities and at times for local officials. They also used their CERP funds and civil affairs brigades to support local government initiatives.

Both brigade commanders and PRT leaders found that pushing past Ba'athist practices and transforming the roles and responsibilities of local officials was difficult. One PRT official commented, "It's still 'big man' diplomacy," in which people rather than institutions wield power.[35] Provincial council members, not used to discretionary authority, were often reluctant to act independently on behalf of their constituencies. "In a post-authoritarian society, where you have to be told what you are allowed to do (not what you aren't), provincial and local government leaders are not going to be risk takers," a PRT political officer explained.

"In the end, if people do not know what they are allowed to do, or what they are supposed to do—they will end up either doing nothing, or they will do what is in their best interest."[36]

In Diyala province, relations deteriorated so badly that the governor resorted to arresting directors general to force them to attend council meetings. Despite the trying conditions, PRTs and brigade commanders helped create legitimacy for the provincial governments and had some success at uniting officials from different sects. One PRT leader said, "Without our presence you would have a full-scale civil war."[37]

Coaxing local officials to work together productively was only half the battle. Relations had to be nurtured between municipal governments and the provinces, and between the provinces and Baghdad. In many places, relationships were so lacking that provincial leaders wanting to meet with ministerial officials transmitted their requests through the embassy.[38] Many also relied on Coalition commanders for transportation to and from Baghdad, a practice that military commanders came to call "helicopter diplomacy." "Making the lack of ground rules even worse," a political officer remarked, "is the incredibly poor communication between and among all levels of the Iraqi government. If, by some stroke of luck or hard work, there are clear and comprehensive rules for something, it is highly likely that they have not been transmitted to all of the appropriate people in an effective or open manner."[39]

The efforts of the PRTs and brigades slowly opened a conversation between provincial and national officials. In the late summer of 2007, five governors from the northern non-Kurdish provinces arrived in Baghdad to attend a conference arranged by the office of the Deputy Prime Minister. It was one of the first meetings of its kind. Governors from some of the most violent provinces of Iraq were allowed to air their concerns. They complained that some ministry directors general were operating in the provinces outside the control of provincial authorities. The governor of Diyala stood up and said that he did not even have the phone numbers for ministry officials in Baghdad.[40] It was clear that provincial and local governments were not yet ready to govern, and that focused PRT support to build local and provincial capacity would be necessary for an extended period.

USAID Expands Local Governance Program
Operating in parallel with the PRTs, USAID soft programs also played an essential role in helping local governments improve. The LGP began a $350 million initiative on October 1, 2005, which aimed to join the citizen councils it formed across Iraq into an integrated network and build their capacity for local administration. Democracy advisors from the LGP also worked at the national level as

advocates for writing clearly stated powers, roles, and responsibilities for local governments into Iraqi law.[41] The challenge was to provide a forum and a legal framework in which a fledgling cadre of Iraqi civil servants and elected officials could bridge the institutional gaps that had resulted from the Coalition's remaking of the Iraqi political system into federal, provincial, and local institutions.[42]

The LGP was unlike the Coalition's other methods of assistance. Its physical isolation from other U.S. government agencies, its predominantly Iraqi face, and its work at political levels far removed from national government created what was in effect a parallel reconstruction effort. Four USAID regional offices—in Baghdad, Hilla, Erbil, and Basrah—were embedded in local neighborhoods, rather than being housed on forward operating bases. When the compounds needed food, they sent Iraqi employees, many of whom lived in surrounding neighborhoods, to purchase it at nearby markets. The compounds' outer rings of security were manned by Iraqi details, not U.S. military or international guard forces. One compound shared a wall and part of its security detail with a next-door mosque.[43] For every international advisor staffing the program, more than ten fulltime Iraqi professionals provided management training and assisted with projects.[44]

USAID's emphasis on distancing themselves from the embassy and blending with local communities was met with dismay in some corners of the U.S. mission. A huge American purse was being emptied in parts of Iraq about which the State Department knew little, and the success in realizing its goal—developing a functional local government—was hard to measure.

An audit of the LGP program by the USAID Inspector General in 2007 found that "the local governance activities did not have intended outputs or baselines to measure progress against because USAID/Iraq failed to enforce contract requirements." The inspector general's office also stated, "In our view, [USAID's contractor] reported only on successful achievements rather than progress achieved toward specified targets."[45] A subsequent SIGIR audit raised similar concerns, noting that although program outcomes appeared to be positive, identifying and tracking project funds and outcomes required improvement.[46]

The LGP's high-water mark of institution building was the creation of the Iraq Local Government Association in August 2006. Council members across Iraq recognized the need for a local government advocacy group within Iraq's developing political framework. With USAID support, members of the Baghdad provincial council worked throughout the summer of 2006 to plan a conference in Baghdad that would be a vehicle for provincial authorities to lobby the national government, which was attempting to draft a provincial powers law. Council members from around the country wanted to make sure that the process of political decentralization would not be derailed. Conference attendees included 110 representatives from all of Iraq's 18 provincial councils. They unanimously adopted a draft local government code and moved to form a permanent Local Government Association, electing a member of the Baghdad Provincial Council as its chair.

The Local Government Association became a single voice speaking at the national level for local institutions and built a caucus of support in the Council of Representatives.[47] It was an impressive opening of a dialogue between Iraq's local and national leaders over how the devolution of power would proceed and how the capacities of local government would develop.

Barriers to Progress

Despite the Coalition's best efforts, the provision of government services became more rather than less politicized in the years following the CPA. By 2006, the U.S. approach to democratizing Iraq, while simultaneously federalizing its government structures, yielded mixed results. The local and district councils created immediately after the invasion had not become formally linked to the directors general who administered services using funding provided by the central government. Soon, ministries were deeply riddled with partisan infighting. The elections that were to be the capstone of a new democracy were based on a formula that only increased the forces driving Iraqis apart. The failure to hold new provincial elections also compromised the legitimacy of provincial councils through with which power was to be shared.

Even though Iraq's constitution ostensibly defined the framework for a unified state, political authority had fragmented into Kurdish, Arab Shi'a, and Arab Sunni constituencies, themselves split by deep and violent divisions. Rival Shi'a parties, each with their own militias, fought over key government positions in the south and over the central question of federal unification. In the Sunni areas, a combustible mix of terrorists, insurgents, and powerful rural tribes rejected Shi'a dominance in a government that was the inevitable result of nominally democratic elections. Despite the deployment of substantial Coalition resources beyond the Green Zone, there seemed to be an unbridgeable gap between provincial governments and the increasingly isolated national government.

By the end of 2006, U.S. officials agreed that the single most important governance challenge was to strengthen the connection between Iraq's national and provincial institutions, so services could be delivered and government properly administered in the new decentralized framework. "Capacity building"—ensuring the ability of the Iraqi government to handle its own affairs—became the catchword for reconstruction's next phase. Doing this would require the

Coalition to continue stitching together its "top-down" efforts in Baghdad with the "bottom-up" efforts in the provinces, linking all levels of the Iraqi government and the reconstruction. While this effort was underway, a series of failures in reconstruction projects turned over to Iraqi control underlined how important Iraqi capacity would be. The sustainment of facilities had fallen into crisis, yet another casualty of Iraq's failed administrative state.

CHAPTER 24
THE PRIMACY OF CAPACITY DEVELOPMENT

*Our job is not to build it for them, our job is to help them build
the capacity so that they can use their own substantial resources
to do things for themselves.* *

Ambassador Joseph Saloom
Director, Iraq Reconstruction Management Office (2006-2007)

On most days in Baghdad, plumes of black smoke from at least one of the Doura power plant smokestacks are visible in the southwest sky—a sign that the generators beneath them are turning, putting a few dozen megawatts each on the grid. Blue sky over Doura almost always means that something is wrong, as was the case in August 2006, when an electrical surge disabled the plant. Despite a three-year, $90-million project to restore it, the plant that supplied much of Baghdad's power ground to a halt.[1]

Doura's failure had many causes. Plant technicians had overlooked dust and debris collecting in the generators' cooling systems. The debris should have been discovered by a routine check, but plant managers had yet to establish a formal maintenance program for Doura's equipment. They had also followed orders from directors general at the Ministry of Electricity to swap critical components between the generators, which caused parts to deteriorate faster and break down more frequently. The directors general themselves were hamstrung by a ministry policy that forbade plant-level employees from purchasing replacement parts before emergencies occurred.[2] The minister was under pressure from the Prime Minister, who gave continuous power-generation precedence over scheduled shut-downs for repairs.[3] Ultimately, this chain of failures was a product of U.S. reconstruction policy that emphasized rebuilding Iraq's physical infrastructure but not the institutions to maintain it.

All across Iraq in late 2005 and beyond, a series of SIGIR inspections discovered that physical infrastructure put in place by U.S.-funded reconstruction was breaking down and coming off-line.[4] Failures plagued both refurbished and new facilities in the water, electrical, sewer, and oil sectors. It was not just a question of maintaining individual plants and teaching Iraqi engineers who run them to master more advanced machinery. It was about building the systems and processes within Iraq's government to sustain the infrastructure it had just received.

---

* SIGIR interview with Ambassador Joseph Saloom, former IRMO director, April 21, 2008.

Unless the government could manage these necessary operations, the Doura power plant and facilities like it would continue to fall apart.

From the beginning, reconstruction policymakers knew it would be a challenge to build capacity inside Iraq's government and marshal it to sustain reconstruction facilities.[5] A variety of U.S. agencies and organizations made efforts to develop functioning institutions within Iraq's ministries, but—despite millions of dollars in contracts and, at times, furious activity—the embassy failed to create large-scale capacity-building programs until late 2006. Even then, the effectiveness of the U.S. strategy was mixed.

Iraq's Capacity Crisis

In Iraq, the story of capacity development—the ability of the government to operate effectively—begins with Saddam Hussein. Iraq's government did function before the 2003 invasion. Despite significant deficiencies on every front, some three dozen ministries controlled virtually every factory, warehouse, administrative office, and service facility in the Iraqi inventory, as well as the distribution of essential commodities, including fuel and food. Even after the imposition of international sanctions choked the flow of spare parts and cash, the Saddam regime expected its ministries to perform as usual.

To meet Saddam's demands, officials became "entrepreneurial" and, at times, draconian. Ministries made shadowy credit arrangements so that ledgers would remain in the black; raw materials produced within Iraq were stockpiled and often withheld from other ministries; ministries imported materials in contravention of international sanctions; and a climate of fear kept workers in line.[6] Power over the ministries was jealously guarded by Iraqi officials at the highest ranks, many of whom sought to profit from their positions.[7] All these practices left a legacy of corruption for the embassy to try to overcome.

Looting following the 2003 invasion dealt the first major blow to government capacity. Next came the exodus of both people and property from Iraq's government offices, effectively redefining reconstruction from restarting a government to building one anew. The goal was to restore the core capacities of government—its strategic and policy-planning ability, as well as its financial, information, and human resources management. To this end, USAID contracted in July 2003 with BearingPoint to give Iraq's Ministry of Finance the tools to start collecting, tracking, and disbursing state revenue.[8] Part of the BearingPoint contract required the provision of a state-of-the-art financial management information system, which turned out to be unworkable. It was a harbinger of the challenges to come: having been built with U.S. rather than Iraqi accounting practices in mind, it was rejected by the Iraqi civil servants who were to use it.[9]

In the summer of 2003, three major funding streams—CERP, IRRF 1, and the DFI—were available for capacity-building efforts. Working independent of U.S. government agencies, CPA senior advisors drew on what they could get from the military and USAID, as well as on funds for projects approved by the Program Review Board. Most funds came from Iraqi money in the DFI. More than $10 billion was set aside during the first year for ministerial operations; $1.2 billion came from U.S. funds.[10]

Down in the trenches of reconstruction, U.S. military engineers and international contractors were in a position to develop sustainment programs for the effective operations and maintenance of the infrastructure projects they were building. But the IRRF 1 contract with Bechtel, like the other infrastructure contracts, did not emphasize sustainment. A short paragraph in the contract required Bechtel to "provide technical assistance and training to build the capacity for effective operation and maintenance."[11] What the sustainment programs might include or how their success would be measured was not specified.

USAID officials in charge of administering the IRRF 1 contracts assumed that a core cadre of ministry employees would carry over the maintenance practices of the old era.[12] The CPA, however, had dismissed many of those ministry employees in the de-Ba'athification process, and those that remained found it difficult to push past the culture of centralized management and take responsibility for maintaining local facilities.[13] Even if Iraqi officials had taken the initiative, few in the summer of 2003 had functioning procurement systems or even regular communication with ministry offices in Baghdad. USAID's second Bechtel contract, reflecting the expansion of reconstruction's scope and duration under IRRF 2, placed greater emphasis on maintenance and sustainability. It required that every job order written under the contract specify the level of technical capacity that would be passed to the Iraqis.[14]

As the CPA's PMO grew to administer the larger part of IRRF 2 funding, it too approached capacity building and sustainability with greater purpose. PMO internal guidelines suggested that contracting officers use Iraqi services "to the greatest extent practicable," and that design-build contractors collaborate with ministries in drafting project requirements. As much as 16 percent of a contractor's award fee became dependent on the ability to train local staff and transition projects effectively to the Iraqis.[15]

Simply writing language into IRRF 2 contracts, however, did not constitute a true sustainability program. There was no U.S. commitment to fund projects aimed exclusively at maintenance objectives, an oversight that troubled USAID officials experienced with infrastructure construction in the developing world. In their view, PMO's staff, largely composed of engineers without development experience, tended to issue infrastructure contracts without attention to follow-on maintenance.[16] USAID's own infrastructure cell was acutely aware of the problem by late winter 2004, but the agency's loss of influence during the early CPA period marginalized its ability to advocate for sustainability contracts.[17] "Bremer," according to USAID Mission Director Spike Stephenson, "was not interested in anything but construction."[18] The CPA went so far as to remove $50 million from an operations and maintenance budget that USAID proposed.[19] Although specific task orders would allow training at the ministry level to continue, the lack of dedicated sustainability contracts left it to the Iraqis to make critical purchases for maintaining facilities—which most ministries were unable to do.[20]

Despite the lack of emphasis on sustainability and capacity building, some international contractors found that the professional development of Iraqi subcontractors was in their own best interests. They went beyond what was required by their contracts to establish substantial training programs. One example, "Bechtel University," introduced a cadre of Iraqi contractors to international procurement policies, safety routines, and quality assurance practices.[21] The theory was that if Iraqi firms were taught these skills, they would effectively use them in the future. Graduates of Bechtel University later took leadership roles in other reconstruction projects.[22]

Widespread success in IRRF-sponsored training programs at the plant level, however, was elusive in 2003 and 2004. Thomas Wheelock, who helped lead USAID's management of the Bechtel IRRF contracts, noted that there was such a range of competence among Iraqi technicians that it was difficult to design any universally applicable curricula. Some of the greatest challenges to facility-level sustainability were found in the management ranks at central ministries, where maintenance programs were designed and critical spare parts were procured. The PMO could require sustainment measures in the task orders it issued to contractors, but without a program to link them to efforts at the ministry level, there was little chance for long-term, effective management.[23] In the reconstruction program's first two years, there was no coordinated effort among the U.S. organizations working in Iraq to draft and implement strategies for interagency capacity building or sustainment that would reach all parts of the reconstruction effort.

The Problem of Sustainability

In the fall of 2004, Bruce Parmelee, a program officer in USAID's Community Action Program, discovered a rehabilitated water-treatment plant on the outskirts of Hilla sitting idle after repairs costing $5 million. Work on the plant had been completed, but there was no effective effort to transfer the facility to local Iraqi authorities. Because the job order focused only on the facility, contractors did not connect the plant to the city's network of water-pipes and sewers or teach Iraqi employees how to use it. Few people in Hilla even knew it existed, and the facility had already started to decay. It was a perfect example of the failure to incorporate an adequate plan for transfer and sustainability.[24]

A similar set of sustainment issues arose across the reconstruction effort in 2004 and 2005.[25] Contracts written for physical reconstruction frequently left out the crucial next step of ensuring that the new facilities would be used and maintained. A policy of keeping international contractors on hand for 90 days to assist with early operations was seen by IRMO as woefully insufficient.[26] The security situation compounded the challenge, with targeted attacks on infrastructure, the withdrawal of international engineers, and widespread attrition among Iraqi technicians. The effort was also affected by Iraq's political process, which led to constant changes in ministries' leadership in the three years before the installation of a permanent government in 2006.[27]

All of these factors hampered the delivery of essential services that reconstruction was supposed to provide. The major indicators of government performance in 2004 and 2005 were generally flat.[28] "It became clear," Ambassador David Satterfield said, "that we ran the real risk of huge multi-million dollar projects … sitting alone, non-operative, because we had not put the same focus on sustainability as we have on building it." Satterfield added, "It had been assumed that Iraqis would take on the last-mile connectivity but they never did."[29]

PCO Addresses Capacity Development

Working closely with contractors building essential services facilities, PCO took the earliest steps to prioritize sustainability efforts. Much of the initiative began in the water sector where, by the late summer of 2004, the sheer number of projects outlined by the IRRF 2 spending plan convinced water-sector program managers that a separate capacity-development program was necessary. The 79-page Management and Interface Plan, which PCO briefed to agencies, think-tanks, congressional staff, and contractors, outlined five critical levels at which the embassy could help develop the Iraqi government's capacity to sustain reconstruction.[30]

The PCO focused on level 5 of this framework—infrastructure—while encouraging other parts of the U.S. mission to engage further upstream. By early 2005, the mission had established an internal office, staffed by two people in Baghdad and two in Washington, specifically charged with coordinating PCO's capacity-development initiatives. In March 2005, PCO modified statements of work for the IRRF 2 sector program-manager support contractors to include key sustainability objectives.[31]

PCO's Five-Level Approach

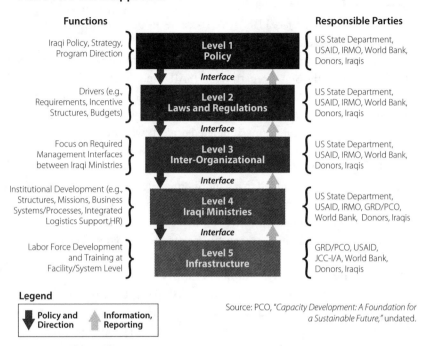

| Functions | | Responsible Parties |

Source: PCO, *"Capacity Development: A Foundation for a Sustainable Future,"* undated.

The PCO sustainability office also created reporting systems that tracked the new contract requirements, ranging from the number of Iraqi technicians trained on a project to documenting overall lessons learned by contractors working in the field. One result was a new set of confidential PCO databases that tracked the effectiveness of all Iraqi subcontractors hired by the design-build contractors, as well as the progress of PCO-sponsored capacity-development activities.[32] Training programs run by prime contractors ultimately reached 509,000 Iraqis and comprised more than a million hours of training.[33]

The focus on sustainability by the PCO eventually led it to look beyond the infrastructure level. In 2005, it established eight technical learning centers in seven provinces.[34] The centers offered hands-on training in equipment maintenance and engineering innovations that had been unknown in sanctions-era Iraq. Six focused on the water sector, the first sector to embrace all aspects of PCO's sustainment strategy, and two were established for workers in oil and electricity.[35]

Further up the ladder, a new PCO grant program encouraged ministries to shoulder a larger portion of the management of reconstruction. The PCO would reimburse ministries for the costs of projects if they agreed to manage their planning, solicitation, bidding, financing, and construction. The entire capacity-building effort, from vocational training to ministerial agreements, was encapsulated in an IRMO white paper in May 2005. The paper praised the "PCO Management and Interface Plan," which became the basis of the first interagency capacity development strategy in Iraq reconstruction.[36]

However, this strategy—and, in particular, the cooperation it presumed between IRMO, the State Department, USAID, and PCO—did not take hold in 2005. Events quickly overtook the white papers circulating in the embassy. During Ambassador Khalilzad's tenure, failures in infrastructure sustainment became more significant. More completed projects were not operating, and essential service benchmarks in key sectors like electricity and oil remained unmet.[37] Nearly a year after the PCO introduced its interagency engagement strategy, the State Department concluded that a more "integrated approach was essential." Agencies had implemented reconstruction programs "without a clear understanding of the programs' objectives or their contribution to the larger goal of transferring responsibility for reconstruction to the Iraqi government."[38]

Reorganizing Capacity-Development Efforts

The Department of State initiated a "National Capacity Development Program" in late 2005. The plan focused on the twelve key ministries that accounted for 65 percent of Iraq's government workforce of 2.2 million people, and oversaw 74 percent of the national budget. Instead of assigning responsibility for the ten civilian ministries to one organization or agency—as had been done for the Ministries of Interior and Defense—the embassy asked USAID to focus on medium-term capacity issues while IRMO and the Departments of State looked after immediate needs.[39] "We tried to build on the senior consultants," recalled Ambassador Speckhard, who served first as IRMO director and then as deputy chief of mission under Ambassador Khalilzad. "The first step was to go out and have each one of them do an intensive survey of their own ministries to make judgments on how they were doing on strategic planning, on leadership and personnel, on budget and finance, and on public communications."[40]

The Embassy tapped IRMO to coordinate the new capacity-building effort, but overseeing the capacity-development activities of so many permanent and semi-permanent agencies in the U.S. government proved too tall an order for an ad hoc group of senior consultants.[41] The consultants' principal charge had always been to maintain relationships with key Iraqi officials—including the minister— in each ministry, allowing the exchange of information and resources between the embassy and the Iraqi government. Many senior consultants focused on keeping these crucial connections going and simply did not have the time to deal with all the other U.S. agencies who were supposed to be involved in capacity building.

IRMO was itself burdened with developing its own capacity—that is, recruiting enough qualified advisors to replace those who were leaving. "Every year," Ambassador Speckhard said, "you're turning over some 90 percent."[42]

In March 2006, when it became apparent that IRMO alone could not effectively coordinate the initiative, the deputy chief of mission ordered the creation of a Ministerial Capacity Team. The idea was to link the work of senior consultants with other efforts in the Green Zone by bringing everyone together in a coordinating body. Vested with a $15 million dollar budget, the Ministerial Capacity Team began a series of efforts to build capacity into the ministries. It constructed a new press room for the office of the prime minister, created a digitized copy of the Iraqi legal code, and assembled a much-needed survey of Iraq's health infrastructure. Projects like this, however, did not amount to a systemic strategy for correcting plant-level failures by redressing ministerial deficits at the top.[43]

By summer 2006, the formula changed yet again. Thirty officers from Coalition forces and a similar number of reporting officers from the State Department joined IRMO senior advisors in what were called Ministerial Assistance Teams.[44] The teams developed one-year programs designed to jump-start capacity just as ministries received permanent ministers for the first time. By early 2007, twenty advisors worked in the Ministry of Oil, eighteen in the Ministry of Finance, and eighteen in the Ministry of Electricity.[45]

The introduction of new faces into a tightly knit group of advisors and ministers—one that already had to work around language barriers, cultural differences, and gaps in technical knowledge—disrupted the solid relationships that had been established. For this reason, the ministry assistance teams failed to gain the necessary momentum. Neither IRMO's senior consultants nor the Iraqi ministry officials who for three years had built very specific partnerships wanted others to intrude.[46]

The failure of Ministerial Assistance Teams in 2006 opened again the question of who was in control. In 2006, the embassy created a Joint Task Force for Capacity Development that included representatives from USACE, USAID, MNSTC-I, the embassy, and IRMO.[47] For the first time in more than three years, a central body met to oversee the agencies and organizations that had significant relationships with various components of the Iraqi government. Unfortunately, the task force was yet another meeting of men and women in the Green Zone who lacked the authority to mandate action by their constituent agencies.[48]

The task force coincided with a new initiative by USAID to provide medium-term capacity assistance to Iraqi ministries. The $165 million *Tatweer* program—Arabic for "development"—focused initially on enhancing the professional qualifications of civil servants at the ministries of Planning, Finance, Oil,

Electricity, and Water Resources. Management Systems International (MSI), USAID's implementing partner, intended to attach its own training programs to Iraq's National Center for Consultation and Management Development, a training academy in Baghdad's suburbs run by the Ministry of Planning. MSI also sought to establish its own ministry assistance teams staffed by Arabic-speaking advisors.[49]

Implementation of the *Tatweer* program was slow. By December 2006, MSI had positioned advisors in only the Ministries of Oil and Electricity, even though the other ten civilian ministries mentioned in the National Capacity Development Plan were scheduled for assistance. The lack of MSI advisors and the limited reach of the Ministerial Coordination Team over USAID programs seriously compromised the overall effort. The Center for Consultation and Management Development did not fare much better. By December 2006, USAID reported that the center's ability to host and expand on MSI training programs was limited.[50] Two subsequent audits found that implementers were having difficulty finding Iraqis who were willing to participate in the training programs, and that the center prohibited foreign advisors from visiting its premises because their presence would draw attention to the compound and create a security risk to Iraqi attendees.[51]

To direct these myriad activities, the embassy turned finally to the Joint Executive Steering Committee. With high-ranking representatives from MNF-I, USAID, GRD, MNSTC-I, IRMO, and each embassy section, the steering committee had originally served as the policy planner for the emergent PRT program. In late summer 2006, the steering committee's mandate was enlarged to make it the strategic hub for all joint efforts among agencies in Iraq, including capacity-building programs.[52] The Joint Task Force on Capacity Development now reported to the steering committee, which was chaired by the deputy chief of mission.[53] Although this structure in theory brought the ambassador into closer contact with the capacity-development program, policy influence remained with IRMO, whose director frequently chaired steering committee meetings in the absence of the deputy chief of mission.[54]

An imminent deadline soon complicated these arrangements. In the continuing effort to "normalize" operations, the embassy set IRMO's demise as an organization for early 2007. IRMO's last director, Ambassador Joe Saloom, arrived in May 2006 to begin shutting down the three-year-old organization.[55] His own perception was that the State Department wanted to create a year-long "glide-path" for senior consultants, who would continue overseeing reconstruction in their ministries, but increasingly under the direction of section heads at the embassy.[56] It was all part of a trend to bring the functions of many ad hoc offices created to manage reconstruction together under the traditional embassy structure, with its political and economic sections.

The transition to Saloom's leadership in IRMO revived the search for adequate measures of success in capacity development. IRMO's initial effort—started in September 2006 to measure core indicators of Iraqi ministry capacity—quickly ran out of steam and failed to produce further findings.[57] Nevertheless, the assessment confirmed that most ministry staff lacked sufficient training to do their jobs, and that a quarter of all ministerial functions depended on Coalition or other foreign support.[58]

The Rise of Budget Execution

By late 2006, a growing awareness that the Iraqi government was ill-prepared to move money from its treasury to the many offices that actually spend the budget helped bring focus to the capacity-building program. Iraq's capital reserves were growing, and much of the money was not being spent. Embassy officials wanted to prepare for the day when Iraqi revenues alone would carry reconstruction forward.[59] Exasperated with the scope of ongoing capacity-building efforts, IRMO leaders were happy to narrow their focus. "It became obvious, once again," Ambassador Speckhard said, "that we bit off more than we could chew, in the timeframes we were talking about." "To make noticeable differences in the short-term," he said, "you really need to focus on a few things."[60]

With new input from the Ambassador and a working group established on budget execution, U.S. officials zeroed in on the failure of Iraqi institutions to spend their capital budgets, citing it as "the most important capacity restraint to the Government of Iraq's performance."[61] Improving the ability of the Iraqi government to spend its own revenue became the keystone in a new arc of capacity-development activities. It was all part of a shift in the reconstruction program to supporting Iraqi priorities with Iraqi resources. Iraqi budget performance would be tracked daily on both the civilian and military side of the U.S. program, and all efforts would be made to increase the rate at which Iraqi money flowed from ministry budgets to reconstruction contracts.

Once the embassy identified budget execution as a clear measure of progress, it marshaled nearly every agency at its disposal to improve it. IRMO, JCC-I, the Department of the Treasury, USACE, the embassy economic section, and the ambassador's front office all became deeply involved in providing program management and contracting assistance to Iraqi ministries. The Iraqi Prime Minister's office and the office of Deputy Prime Minister Barham Salih also engaged in the effort. Salih convened weekly meetings on procurement and spending approval processes with the Ministers of Planning and Finance and officials in provincial and city government.[62] It was an "all-government approach," according to Ambassador Saloom. [63]

The Ministry of Planning was one of the weak links in the chain. Iraqi law requires the Ministry of Planning to approve all requests for funding by other parts of the Iraqi government. Only after receiving Ministry of Planning approval can the Ministry of Finance disburse funds to ministries or provinces. A Ministry of Planning "fusion cell" was created. Dozens of Americans, many of them of Iraqi origin, took desks next to ministry employees in order to coach them at every step. In some cases, they even answered the phones. The support of Iraqi bureaucrats, often untrained and not used to making major funding decisions, accelerated the pace at which the Iraqi government increased its capital expenditures.[64]

These innovative efforts yielded modest results at first. Before budget execution was identified as a priority, the Iraqi government as a whole spent just 17 percent of its capital budgets, meaning that badly needed infrastructure projects had either not begun or were being executed entirely with U.S. funds.[65] In 2007, the government substantially improved budget execution at the ministerial level, spending $4 billion of its $7.9 billion capital budget for an execution rate of just over 51 percent. Results in the provinces, however, were mixed. Rates varied from a high of 64 percent in Najaf to zero in Diyala province. Strategically crucial Anbar province reported spending only $4 million of the $107 million available—an execution rate of less than 4 percent.[66]

Violence was also a major impediment. "The bread and butter of a director general's job is dealing with his superiors in Baghdad," Treasury attaché Jeremy Pam explained. "Without a war on, he would go back to Baghdad every two weeks. But if he can't drive on the roads, you have the different levels of government increasingly cut off from each other." "Imagine," Pam said, "if the Internet went down, and you didn't have email. Our budget execution would go down, too."[67]

The U.S. mission's focus on budget execution raised two fundamental issues. The first was whether it was wise to be so concerned about the Iraqi capacity to spend money quickly.[68] The second had to do with the long-term value of the more intensive capacity-building approaches directed at the security ministries and the Ministry of Planning. In 2007, a GAO audit of the capacity-development program concluded that with so many international advisors in effect "sitting in" for Iraqi government employees, "the Coalition's involvement in [Iraq's] budgeting and procurement processes may have hindered the ministries' capacity to improve their own procurement and contracting systems and perform other vital services."[69] "We were not convinced that ministries actually were building their own capacity to do those things that we were doing for them," Ambassador Satterfield said.[70]

Transferring Completed Projects

As the United States worked to enhance ministerial capacity, the process for transferring completed reconstruction projects to the Iraq government broke down. Beginning in 2006, a series of SIGIR audits revealed that the process of asset transfer—as project handover is formally called—was not ensuring that the Iraqi government was capable and willing to assume responsibility for maintaining U.S.-built facilities.[71] Transferring responsibility for sophisticated facilities, such as electrical or water treatment plants worth tens of millions of dollars, was a difficult task by any measure. Detailed operational and maintenance procedures had to be drawn up. Manuals and technical documentation had to be handed over. Most critically, the Iraqis had to be adequately trained to operate and maintain the facilities on their own, a task that would require careful planning and budgeting skills in perpetuity, at both the facility and the ministry responsible for it.

The breakdown between Iraq's central and local governments made asset transfer an especially arduous task. A municipality's pledge to care for a facility was no guarantee that the central ministry actually responsible for its upkeep was prepared to support it over the long term—or even knew it existed. Handing over smaller projects, such as schools and clinics, was also fraught with difficulty. Although not necessarily difficult to maintain or operate, smaller projects still needed to be kept supplied and staffed year after year to realize the full value of U.S. investment.

The asset transfer process was the ultimate test of Iraqi buy-in to the U.S. reconstruction effort. If done properly, it would provide three crucial checks. First, it would ensure formal recognition by the Iraqi government that a project was satisfactorily complete and ready for transfer. Second, it would provide an opportunity for the Iraqi ministries involved in operating and maintaining the facility to acknowledge their technical readiness and show that they had dedicated adequate budgetary and personnel resources for all future operations, maintenance, and capital-replacement costs. Third, and most important, it would provide an occasion for the United States and the Iraqi government to certify that the U.S. investment would be cared for responsibly in the years to come.[72]

The scope of asset transfer, like the reconstruction itself, was enormous and involved many projects that the Iraqis never agreed to or wanted in the first place. By the middle of 2006, 579 IRRF projects, valued at $765 million, had been officially transferred to the Iraqi Ministry of Finance. However, this was only 18 percent of the total number of completed IRRF projects. Still more projects would come from the other reconstruction funds, including CERP and the ISFF. The cost of maintaining IRRF projects alone was estimated in 2006 at approximately $1.2 billion annually. As that year drew to a close, the United

States planned to have the Iraqis shoulder most of this burden. An estimated $372 million in sustainment funds would be available within IRRF for short-term operations, spare parts, consumables, and contracted support during 2007. The government of Iraq would fund the remaining $828 million.[73]

One of the flaws of the asset transfer approach as it was structured in 2006 was that each U.S. agency working in Iraq had different procedures, levels of detail, and due diligence requirements for transferring projects. A sampling showed that one agency provided an exhaustive accounting of asset values and maintenance requirements in its transfer package while another provided no information at all.[74] Procedures differed even within agencies for separate reconstruction funds.

SIGIR's asset transfer audits found that the lack of uniformity confused Iraqis and caused some assets to be transferred to Iraqi control with insufficient technical documentation. SIGIR recommended that, at a minimum, U.S. managers provide formal notification of a project's transfer to the Iraqi Ministry of Planning, Ministry of Finance, and the appropriate operating ministry. The notification should list all relevant data and specifications that would allow the Iraqis to plan better for long-term upkeep, including the start date, asset cost, estimated short-term and long-term sustainability costs, terms of warranties, and the location of maintenance and systems manuals.[75]

The lack of one centralized authority to manage asset transfer for the entire U.S. reconstruction effort was problematic. Policy guidance issued by the embassy's Asset Transfer Working Group in April 2006 was not binding. Agencies were pursuing different and uncoordinated approaches to transferring completed assets to Iraqi control.

In mid-2008, a SIGIR audit found that U.S. agencies continued to develop their own transfer procedures—confusing the government of Iraq in the process. USAID, for instance, elected not to use the process established by the Asset Transfer Working Group. MNSTC-I took a different approach altogether, trying to develop the capacity within the MoI to sustain all transferred projects.[76] MNSTC-I unilaterally transferred 388 projects to the government of Iraq even though they did not obtain formal assent—thus putting a billion dollars of U.S. investment at potential risk.[77]

Unilateral transfers caused many problems. A report in 2007 by the BSA, Iraq's audit agency, found that many Iraqi ministries did not have records showing the U.S.-funded reconstruction projects supposedly under their control.[78] Later modifications to the asset transfer policy addressed some of the issues identified by the reviews, but these modifications did not apply to all projects provided by U.S. reconstruction funds and did not centralize the management of the asset transfer process. The Iraqi government also failed to respond to a memorandum of agreement forwarded by the United States, leaving any policy agreement between the two governments at an impasse into the fall of 2008.[79]

Beyond the Green Zone

By late 2005, nurturing capacity at the provincial and municipal levels had become a strategic objective. Four Coalition entities were at work supporting the development of capacity in local and provincial governments: Provincial Reconstruction Development Councils, Provincial Reconstruction Teams, Brigade Combat Teams, and USAID's Local Governance Program. In 2006, policymakers used each of these institutions to help link the capacity development underway in Baghdad with efforts in the provinces.

PRDCs became a way to tutor Iraqi officials in program and project management while at the same time increasing the Iraqis' commitment to maintaining U.S. projects. "We were dissatisfied with what appeared to be a disconnect between our projects and Iraqi sense of ownership and buy-in," Ambassador Satterfield explained. "We were creating white elephants that did not have Iraqi buy-in or training to keep going." PRDCs fostered joint decision making between American and Iraqi officials and helped harness Iraqi government capacity in the ongoing reconstruction. "The skills gained in doing [the PRDC process]," Satterfield said, "would then translate into the ability to use Iraqi funds when the provinces were funded."[80]

PRTs also played a leading role. Having existed principally as capacity-building institutions, PRTs were staffed to provide guidance to provincial councils, governors, directors general, and other local officials. As violence increased across Iraq in 2006, new tasks were given to the PRTs, including the execution of economic components of counterinsurgency programs. Becoming an important link between provincial reconstruction efforts and the military's counterinsurgency strategy, however, risked undermining PRTs' original capacity-building mission.[81] At first, they were not equipped to become project and program managers in their own right.[82] The solution was more staff and support from Baghdad, but the National Coordination Team, which came to supplant the role of IRMO's Directorate of Operations in overseeing PRTs, was unable to keep pace with the increased demands.

In the spring of 2007, with the PRTs fully deployed, the embassy attempted to address staffing and capability shortages for both the teams and the offices that supported them from Baghdad by developing a new organization, the Office of Provincial Affairs (OPA), with a "direct-report" to the ambassador. This bureaucratic restructuring, along with the appointment of a more senior official to head the office, gave the PRT program a greater opportunity to help lead capacity-development efforts in the provinces. OPA, however, was not well staffed, and at first was overwhelmed with carrying out basic reporting and support functions.[83]

Capacity Building: A Missed Opportunity

Despite the importance of comprehensive capacity-development and sustainment programs to the long-term success of the U.S. mission in Iraq, the United States failed to develop them in the initial years after the invasion. This did not mean that reconstruction officials completely ignored the problem. In the first year of occupation, the CPA expended more than $10 billion of Iraqi and U.S. funds on ministry operations.[84] In 2004, the PCO modified contracts and introduced a series of programs designed to address emerging sustainability challenges in infrastructure rebuilding. By the end of 2006, the U.S. government allocated $169 million to build Iraq's governing capacity, and many sustainment efforts began.[85]

A unified effort to coordinate capacity-building activities proved to be elusive. Officials concentrated on what they knew: diplomats focused on political reform, businesspeople on the Iraqi private sector, and engineers on sustaining facilities. As a result, many of the weak links in the chain of Iraqi institutions were neither understood nor properly addressed, leading to a crisis of Iraqi government mismanagement. Efforts to address this crisis have had only partial success. Years after some capacity-building programs began, it was not clear whether they had any lasting effect, and no overall strategy had been put in place until the end of 2007.[86]

A look at Diyala province four years after the invasion illustrates how slowly Iraq's governing capacity had developed. None of Diyala's service directorates had a dedicated maintenance budget. Although central-government ministries still controlled 80 percent of Iraq's capital budgets in 2007, the local government in Diyala knew no more about ministry projects planned in its territory than it did in 2004.[87]

These shortfalls raise hard questions about how capacity-development programs in Iraq should have been managed. While MNSTC-I flooded the ministries of Interior and Defense with more than 200 advisors, each working hand-in-hand with Iraqi counterparts, the ten other major civilian ministries had only a handful of advisors, except for those involved in the Ministry of Planning effort to increase budget execution.

Finally, the lack of security threatened all capacity-development efforts. Iraqi officials often had to limit their days at the office to just two or three hours because of threats from insurgents and warring sects and the length of time it took to navigate safely the checkpoints between home and workplace. By 2007, the kidnapping and killing of capacity-development advisors when they left the Green Zone led to restrictive policies that limited contacts between Coalition and Iraqi officials, sometimes preventing interaction altogether.[88] Raising a new system of government and endowing it with the capacity to sustain its infrastructure effectively was a never-ending challenge, one that still had not been overcome toward the end of 2008.

RECONSTRUCTION AMID SECTARIAN VIOLENCE

> *To provide security you need to engage people. You need to tackle*
> *unemployment. You need to create job opportunities, substantial*
> *opportunity so people would be more involved in their well-being*
> *rather than explosives and insurgency.**

Dr. Ayad Allawi
Prime Minister of Iraq (2004-2005)

Hope that Iraq's democratic elections would defuse sectarian tensions unraveled on the morning of February 22, 2006. At five minutes before seven, al-Qaeda terrorists in Samarra destroyed the golden dome of the al-Askari mosque, the revered Shi'a holy site on the east bank of the Tigris River, 60 miles north of Baghdad. Desecrating the gravesite of the Tenth and Eleventh Imams was a psychic blow to Iraq's Shi'a and accelerated the pace of sectarian killing that had been rising steadily for months. At least 1,300 Iraqis, mostly Sunni, were murdered in the next four days, many slain in the streets by organized killing squads associated with the militia of Muqtada al-Sadr.[1]

The humanitarian and political crisis precipitated by the Samarra bombing forced reconstruction policymakers to shift course on a number of fronts. Refugees posed the first problem. A quarter-million Iraqis fled their homes, hastening the segregation of Baghdad and south-central Iraq into Sunni and Shi'a enclaves.[2] By the end of 2006, one out of every eight Iraqis had left the country or became displaced within it.[3] Tent cities sprouted to accommodate the most desperate homeless, triggering food and water shortages that exacerbated already poor conditions.

In keeping with previous trends, attacks were concentrated in Baghdad and the provinces of Anbar, Diyala, and Salah Al-Din.[4] The difference was that in the month after Samarra, execution-style killings claimed eight times more Iraqi lives than insurgent attacks, indicating a shift from insurgency to civil conflict.[5] Iraq's history could be seen in the patterns of violence. Tribal codes drove revenge killings between Sunni and Shi'a, while the methods of torture and execution—power drills and severed heads—echoed Ba'athist practices.[6]

The mass violence between Iraq's sects came amid a deadlock over seating the new government. Members of the Shi'a, Sunni, and Kurdish factions—elected

---

* SIGIR interview with Dr. Ayad Allawi, former Prime Minister of Iraq, February 25, 2008.

to parliament under Iraq's newly ratified constitution—could not agree who should be named ministers. The United States lobbied against nominating the incumbent Prime Minister, Ibrahim Ja'afari, to that post again, viewing his divisiveness and political wavering as profoundly unhelpful to reconciliation.[7] With government at a standstill, the killing continued.

The Iraqi government's inability to contain the flow of displaced persons within Iraq further radicalized the population. With the Ministry of Displacement and Migration and the Red Crescent unable to meet their basic needs, displaced Iraqis turned to neighborhood mosques and the religious offices that supported them. SCIRI's charitable organization, Shahid al-Mihrab, and the offices of Grand Ayatollah Sistani and Muqtada al-Sadr distributed cash and material assistance to Shi'a refugees, while the Association of Muslim Scholars and the Islamic Party aided displaced Sunnis.[8]

In response to the security vacuum, the Mahdi Army and the Badr Brigade manned hundreds of informal checkpoints to stem the incursion of Sunni terrorists in Shi'a neighborhoods, while a parallel network of Sunni militiamen attempted to stop Shi'a killing squads from infiltrating Sunni areas. Numerous militia barricades slowed the flow of goods, disrupting Baghdad's economy. The market soon adapted. Informal exchange points on the city's west side let Sunni drivers off-load their wares to Shi'a trucks.[9]

When government forces could not stop the killing, refugees also became increasingly dependent on sectarian militias for their safety. The militias that came to rule whole sections of Baghdad also penetrated the state security apparatus. In 2006, the United States discovered evidence of Shi'a death squads operating from the Ministry of Interior, and a secret network of prisons across Baghdad.[10] Rival Shi'a factions asserted claims to the spoils of government, commandeering floors of the MoI and appropriating U.S.-purchased weapons and vehicles for militia activity.[11] Shi'a militias in particular successfully placed large numbers of their fighters on the government payroll. The National Police became so compromised that Sunnis began calling it a "Shi'a militia in uniform."[12]

The Balkanization of Baghdad ushered in a new calculus of risk, in which moving between neighborhoods became a kind of Russian roulette. A fake ID card bearing a Shi'a name was no longer good enough to get Sunnis through Shi'a checkpoints. Websites also advised Sunnis to play Shi'a devotional music and hang pictures of Imam Ali, considered the founding leader of the Shi'a, from the rear-view mirror.[13]

Reconstruction Under Fire

The volatile conditions undermined the ability of the United States to carry out reconstruction activities at construction sites and to visit government offices in central and south-central Iraq. Baghdad was especially dangerous. The segregation of Sunni and Shi'a neighborhoods became so pervasive that color-coded maps charted sectarian contours and relative levels of violence with block-by-block accuracy.[14] The U.S. military office overseeing security for reconstruction produced its own version of these maps, replete with "no-go" zones that were off-limits to reconstruction convoys. Taken collectively, these maps constitute a cartographic history of the reach of U.S. power in Iraq, showing the extent to which sectarian violence prevented Coalition contractors from working on reconstruction.[15] "I had gotten security-related delays on projects down to under five percent by the February [2006] timeframe," said Major General McCoy, in command of USACE-GRD. "We were actually into a fairly permissive environment for us to do construction, and then it started to back away."[16]

To coordinate security for construction activities, the GRD relied on its regional offices, which were co-located with military units. "We very conscientiously tried to make that coordination a part of the daily battle rhythm for the maneuver unit," McCoy said. "We needed them to either directly or indirectly put eyes on those projects to make sure things were continuing." During the year following Samarra, McCoy found himself railing at contractors who often failed to account for the delays. "If there are security issues, we'll accommodate those," he found himself saying, "but you're a professional contractor, and you ought to be managing the labor, the materials, [and] the construction quality that ensures we get the construction done on time as much as we can."[17]

Government oversight of three of McCoy's priorities—public health clinics, prisons, and border forts—was affected by the ongoing violence. Violence, however, was not the only impediment to effective monitoring. The complicated relationships between the various U.S. reconstruction offices were also at fault.[18]

In McCoy's assessment, the presumption that reconstruction contracts could be managed centrally from Baghdad was part of the problem. "You can't do construction remotely," McCoy said. "You have to put your eyes on it to see it. That's why we never knew if a project was on time or not. And it was a perfect environment for design-build contractors, because they get paid whether it's on time or not."

The convoluted management structure also prevented reconstruction managers from holding contractors accountable. "I was up outside Erbil, looking at a health clinic," he said. "There were seven or eight safety violations. I looked over at the District Commander and I said, 'Why aren't we having a cease work here?'

He said, 'We don't have the authority to do that. That's PCO's call.' I was finding contractors who were like kids playing Mom and Dad," McCoy said. "They'd go to PCO and ask a question, and if they didn't get the answer they liked, they'd go to GRD and ask a question, and they'd keep playing this Mom-and-Dad thing back and forth until they got the answer they were looking for."[19]

The new wave of violence caused a tide of Iraqi officials to leave the country. Although no sources fully document the emigration of the Iraqi professional class, one estimate suggests that more than 12,000 doctors fled the country since the war began.[20] The attenuation of state capacity undermined the effort to rebuild. One PRT political officer explained that his province had no "bench," no backup team of capable, educated citizens able to step in and run the government.[21] In Baghdad, senior advisors searched in vain for young energetic "champions" to help them carry out crucial tasks. They found instead "a bunch of people who were too old and too locked into the system to leave," as one senior advisor said. "Everyone else is in Jordan."[22]

The naming of the Dawa Party's Nouri al-Maliki as the compromise choice for Prime Minister on May 28, 2006, did not ease the violence. Daily attacks against U.S. and Iraqi soldiers increased by 44 percent from June 2005 to June 2006, with IEDs at four times the recorded levels of January 2004.[23] Civilian deaths proved harder to measure; the estimates range from tens of thousands to hundreds of thousands.[24]

Maliki's appointment soon sparked more discontent. "By the middle of July," MNC-I Commander Lieutenant General Peter Chiarelli said, "it was clear that his government ... wasn't a government of national reconciliation. The Sunnis felt they'd been sold a bill of goods." Chiarelli believed that "Samarra was an accelerator, but nothing near Maliki coming into power."[25] Sunni ministers would later pull out of Maliki's government in protest of unmet political demands and not rejoin the government for more than a year.[26]

Amid the violence, infrastructure attacks skyrocketed. "The insurgents figured out that the best way to fight back against the government of Maliki," Ambassador Khalilzad explained, "was to try and strangle Baghdad on the infrastructure side." Rapid-response teams created within the Ministry of Electricity struggled to undo damage and stay ahead of the sabotage. Water treatment plant workers and garbage collectors also become targets. Infrastructure security, Khalilzad said, was an "uphill battle."[27]

In early summer 2006, U.S. military and Iraqi security forces mobilized to quell the violence. Operation Together Forward deployed 49,000 Iraqi soldiers and police and 7,200 Coalition troops to patrol Baghdad's most insecure neighborhoods, enforce nighttime curfews, and continue a Friday vehicle ban.[28] To coordinate the application of reconstruction resources for the security plan, a Joint Planning Commission, which included representatives from U.S. agencies and the government of Iraq, met weekly. MNC-I also established a Joint Reconstruction Operations Center under the auspices of the GRD.[29]

When violence levels did not drop significantly, the Americans and Iraqis initiated a second phase of the operation in August 2006. More troops were redeployed from Anbar province to the capital, in effect giving up ground to one enemy to fight another. In September, military officials announced their intention to construct a series of trenches and berms around Baghdad's 60-mile circumference and control entry to the city through 28 checkpoints.[30]

Drawing Down IRRF 2

The violence triggered by Samarra reached its highest pitch just as the primary program of infrastructure reconstruction drew to a close. Ambassador Khalilzad's concern that IRRF 2 would not achieve its goal of pacifying Iraq proved well founded. As the last IRRF 2 dollars were being obligated, Iraqi popular support for attacks against American troops became a majority position: six in ten Iraqis viewed attacks on Coalition forces favorably.[31]

The reconstruction program funded by IRRF made its final project allocations in as much haste as it had been formulated by CPA officials. The Congress had appropriated IRRF 2 in 2003 as "three-year money." All funds not obligated to a specific project or re-obligated to specific sectors by September 30, 2006, could be used only to pay adjustments toward existing contracts. In a move reminiscent of the rush to spend DFI funds in 2004, the PCO launched a drive to meet the deadline, raising concerns in the Congress that the "race to obligate" would lead to waste and extravagance.[32] "Obligator" posters, in which PCO sector heads superimposed their photographs on a picture of Arnold Schwarzenegger's *Terminator* movie character, adorned the office's halls, and a massive banner hung in PCO's main workroom: "Obligating 'R' Us: Getting 'Er Done (by 30 Sep 2006)."[33]

The irony was not lost on those working on reconstruction. "The goal of PCO isn't to complete projects—it's to obligate the money," Lieutenant Colonel Busher said. "Do you see on the walls, 'Quality Projects for the Iraqi People by September 30'? No—you see the 'obligator' posters."[34] The review of IRRF projects and programming holds imposed by Ambassador Khalilzad had shortened the timeframe in which PCO had to work.[35] Despite the rush, PCO generally succeeded in awarding contracts in the largest program of reconstruction since the Marshall Plan, although a later SIGIR audit faulted it for improperly shifting some funds into holding accounts.[36] On the day PCO fully obligated the last of the IRRF funds, 88 percent of the IRRF projects had been completed; most of the rest would be finished by the end of 2007.[37] The problem was what had been left undone in Iraq.

When night fell on September 30, 2006, much of Baghdad was still dark. Attacks on power lines and substation failures left the capital with only three hours of government-provided electricity per day, although some parts of the city were lit at night by private generators.[38] The rest of the country was faring better: most provinces received fourteen hours. Although average peak generation surpassed prewar levels for the first time, demand still outstripped supply by a factor of two.[39]

Iraq's other sectors showed uneven progress. Oil production, the government's predominant source of revenue, averaged 2.2 million barrels per day.[40] A worrisome internal assessment written by the Ministry of Oil advisor warned that "inadequate expenditures for maintenance and lack of replacement of critical parts" threatened to undo recent production gains.[41] The water sector lagged most of all. U.S.-funded projects were on track to bring access to potable water to 8.2 million Iraqis.[42] Although this met the goal set by IRMO after water funds had mostly been reprogrammed to security, only one in three Iraqis had regular access to fresh water.[43]

The lack of essential services depressed the economy. Half the adult population was unemployed or underemployed, and the country's manufacturing and agricultural sectors were mostly in a state of collapse.[44] This was not the Iraq that Ambassador Bremer envisioned as the legacy of IRRF 2. Speaking to the dramatically scaled-back ambitions, GRD's Major General Bill McCoy said that the United States "never intended to completely rebuild Iraq."[45]

The Rise of CERP

As IRRF funds began to wind down, reconstruction entered a new phase. The PCO stood down after two years as the primary reconstruction executing agency. Most of its personnel moved seamlessly to the GRD, which thereafter became the leading project contracting office for ongoing construction in Iraq. The drawdown of IRRF also marked a shift in the U.S. approach to reconstruction.

As a result of changes made by Ambassador Khalilzad in his initial months as Chief of Mission, reconstruction became more defined in purpose even as it grew more diffuse in execution. With the massive upgrade of Iraq's physical infrastructure drawing to a close, the design-build contractors that executed IRRF 2 began packing up. Bechtel, the first large contractor on the ground in 2003, removed all but two of its 200 employees by November 2006.[46] It had been a harrowing three years for the construction firm. Fifty-two people working on Bechtel projects had been killed, and another 49 had been seriously wounded.[47] In place of the design-build contractors, Iraqi firms that had served as subcontractors assumed increasingly prominent roles. GRD often contracted with them directly to finish projects not completed under design-build contracts.[48]

The focus shifted from building new facilities to maintaining the new infrastructure's more complex systems, which overextended Iraqi engineers, who lacked technical skills and reliable supply chains. Targeted sustainment and capacity-development programs launched by USAID and PCO/GRD brought technical assistance into all levels of the Iraqi government. At the same time, the PRDCs and PRTs developed by Ambassador Khalilzad moved reconstruction money and expertise farther into the provinces to sustain and expand the delivery of essential services.

In this new post-IRRF phase, the military oversaw a significant evolution of the Commander's Emergency Response Program.[49] Lieutenant General Peter Chiarelli had pioneered stability operations in Sadr City while leading the 1st Cavalry in 2004, and he returned to Iraq in January 2006 as MNC-I commander. The many rounds of de-scoping had left Iraq littered with half-finished projects—a power plant that ran at partial capacity here, a waste treatment facility left unconnected to the sewer system there.

Chiarelli saw an opportunity, realizing that a creative application of CERP funds—a $510 million program that supported 3,800 projects in fiscal year 2006—could wring more from what was already constructed.[50] Power lines, which are comparatively inexpensive to construct, could connect under-utilized power plants to Iraqi homes. The same could be done for sewer and water treatment plants. The "invisible capacity" that existed in a variety of sectors could make an enormous difference in the lives of the Iraqi people, if only production and distribution networks finally meshed.[51] What had begun as "walking around money" for soldiers became a powerful tool for linking IRRF-constructed infrastructure with the people it was designed to serve. "Our commanders will tell you that CERP is probably the most important 'bullet' they have," said Deputy Secretary of Defense Gordon England. "I mean, you can help somebody instantly."[52]

Rather than fixing on the number of projects started or completed, as embassy reconstruction accounting practices did, officials began to define success as the delivery of services to the Iraqi people. Putting their day-to-day needs first was part of a larger recognition of the need to reorient U.S. strategy around counterinsurgency goals—the "winning of hearts and minds" through quality-of-life improvements. "I made it a purpose of every one of my troops out to brigade commanders to not only be briefed on what they were doing kinetically [on the battlefield], but what they were doing non-kinetically," Chiarelli said. "As part of my battlefield tour I always make them take me to a project that was going on."[53]

A transformation in military thinking was underway. "The CERP program grew as the military really got into the role of post-kinetic stabilization," Ambassador David Satterfield said. "You had a succession of people like Pete Chiarelli who really believed in the value of civil-military work—buying people out of violence, out of conflict."[54] The increasing use of CERP for infrastructure construction and other large-scale projects brought new challenges. Although small humanitarian relief applications for which the program was originally conceived constitute almost half of CERP projects in numerical terms, only four percent of total expenditures went to support them. From fiscal year 2004 through 2006, more than a third of the budget went to CERP projects that cost more than $500,000, although these comprised only three percent of all projects.[55]

Efficiently managing these projects and ensuring their sustainment by the government of Iraq was difficult. The military officers who initiated them often lacked a background in project management. Occasionally, project documentation lagged or was missing altogether. Although the Joint Reconstruction Operations Center tracked CERP projects in Baghdad, no similar centrally administered repository tracked them in the rest of the country.[56] Nevertheless, CERP functioned in 2006 for brigades, PRTs, and PRDCs as an essential bridge linking the capital expenditures made by IRRF 2 to real gains in essential services and quality of life for Iraqis.

Hitches and Roadblocks

As Chiarelli refocused CERP, he found himself managing an unexpected decrease in the civilian programs the military needed most. USAID's OTI, whose pioneering collaboration with the 1st Cavalry Division in 2004 served as a model for Clear-Hold-Build, was being moved out of the country. The office's mandate normally permits it to remain active for three years in any one country; at the military's request, this had been extended twice.[57] To replace the office, the USAID country director began developing other long-term programs, first called "Focused Stabilization," but subsequently renamed "Community Stabilization."[58]

The transition to focused stabilization would strengthen the ability of USAID and other civilian organizations to contribute to counterinsurgency operations in the "strategic cities" designated by MNF-I and the NSC.[59] The operational concept for this unique mix of civilian and military assets was published in MNF-I's Joint Campaign Plan. To coordinate its implementation, MNC-I established the Interagency Stabilization Task Force.[60] This steering body brought Iraqi officials from the ministerial and provincial governments together with embassy and military personnel at all levels—from IRMO and USAID down to PRTs and NGOs.[61] Beginning with the task force's first meeting on May 28, 2006, the military's counterinsurgency campaign would be much better coordinated with civilian and Iraqi efforts.

There was, however, a "small" hitch. "[Focused stabilization] didn't get funded," Chiarelli said.[62] USAID was able to obligate only $30 million of IRRF funding to International Relief and Development, the contractor that was to replace OTI.[63] Budgeting and acquisition delays also slowed the program's deployment.[64] A strategy that called for mounting significant civilian-led reconstruction operations in at least nine cities appeared in the summer of 2006 to have funding for merely three or four.

The shaky transition to a new vehicle for rapid assistance caused intermittent slowdowns in high-performing programs funded by USAID. At the same time, the challenges of staffing and funding PRTs delayed their full deployment. The White House had issued its *National Strategy for Victory in Iraq*, but the Department of State and USAID seemed unable to follow through with the Clear-Hold-Build strategy it prescribed.[65] A lack of capacity was only part of the problem. Disagreements continued among the President's advisors on whether the U.S. military should assume a different counterinsurgency posture.[66]

The partial implementation of Clear-Hold-Build exacerbated a structural weakness in the reconstruction program. Although the U.S. capacity to undertake rapid, localized interventions through projects funded by CERP and OTI could deliver immediate results, the benefits of longer-term development and capacity-building efforts pioneered by IRRF often took years to be seen.

The need for "middle-range" interventions was acutely felt in violent provinces like Anbar, where counterinsurgency operations were underway. Lieutenant Colonel Christian Shomber, a Reservist on his second tour in the violent Sunni-dominated province, served as an economics liaison officer for the Marine command. Since his first tour, the situation had grown dire. Shomber saw no purpose in continuing approaches to reconstruction that had already failed in the province. "If it wasn't working," he said, "doing more won't help." In place of existing programs, he proposed the kind of interventions that fell outside IRRF 2's focus on infrastructure construction, but beyond CERP's purview. "We need local community action plans—livestock vaccines, seed distributions, housing funds," Shomber said, projects that could jump-start Anbar's idle factories and farms.[67] USAID programs could provide some of these, but it was for the most part too dangerous for them to operate in the province.

Other roadblocks existed. Advisors in the embassy, including several who had been architects of the CPA's free-market policies, refused to support Shomber's requests. Shomber, who in civilian life worked as an investment banker on Wall Street, was struck by the embassy's continued reliance on market mechanisms to drive recovery in a province where violence made a "normal" market impossible. It was not the first time that embassy advisors were reluctant to support short-term projects that they did not think were likely to be catalysts of long-term growth. OTI's withdrawal from Iraq further hamstrung Shomber's efforts to deliver economic and political gains that met Iraqi needs and supported the counterinsurgency campaign. "Anybody who says [the troops] are getting what we need is not listening," he said.[68]

Neglecting Agriculture

Shomber was right to notice that U.S.-funded reconstruction programs had overlooked the agriculture sector. Although agriculture was Iraq's second-largest economic activity, with the potential to employ an estimated 25 to 30 percent of the population, the IRRF 2 supplemental did not fund any agriculture programs in 2003.[69] The CPA ultimately stepped back from its initial policy and tasked USAID to work with the Ministry of Agriculture to develop a plan. Three years later, activity levels were still low. In 2006, the primary instrument was still the "Agricultural Reconstruction and Development Program for Iraq," which USAID had launched with $5 million in October 2003.[70] During the November 2004 IRRF 2 reprogramming, Ambassador Negroponte increased its funding to $72 million, but even this amounted to an investment of only $3 per Iraqi.[71]

In the wake of decades of inefficient central planning and the systemic underinvestment of the Saddam years, advisors faced difficult decisions to make the U.S. agriculture investment stretch as far as possible. The last major infusion of agricultural technology had come in the late 1980s, when the United States sold Iraq $800 million worth of goods, part of which was an aid package to support Iraq's war against Iran.[72] Since then, agricultural production had mostly collapsed as a result of dilapidated irrigation systems and limited water supply, as well as the high salinity that affected 75 percent of Iraq's arable land. By 2004, production had dipped below pre-war levels.[73]

Development Alternatives Incorporated, the contractor implementing the USAID agriculture program, produced an assessment in April 2004 calling for short-term job creation measures to be paired with longer-term reform.[74] The master plan, developed in coordination with the Ministry of Agriculture, called for a two-phase recovery targeted on physical, human, and institutional resources. Raising the availability of agricultural inputs was among the most crucial short-term measures. In the winter of 2003, farmers in Iraq's non-Kurdish provinces had access to only eight percent of the nitrogen fertilizer they needed.[75] Pesticides, seeds, diesel for machinery, and spare parts were necessary to help spur production and re-establish the domestic market for wheat and other high-value crops.

A subsidy fund of $200 million of Iraqi funds in the custody of the Ministry of Finance helped purchase some of these agriculture inputs. Livestock improvement was also planned, with poultry and sheep a priority.

In addition to these short-term measures, fundamental reforms were also started, including land and water reclamation and privatizing state-owned farms. The USAID plan envisioned that the Ministry of Agriculture would be transformed from its historical role as a manager of production to a regulatory body that would facilitate a free-market agricultural economy. The U.S. Department of Agriculture was also enrolled to help modernize Iraq's agricultural science base and the country's capacity to engage in regional trade. In 2006, a consortium of U.S. universities helped revamp the Iraqi university curricula used to train farmers and veterinarians. The Agriculture Department also supplied a handful of advisors who worked at the embassy, Ministry of Agriculture, and on PRTs. However, only two agriculture advisors were on PRTs at the end of 2006.[76]

By the end of 2006, when the program shut down, the outputs of USAID's agricultural program appeared impressive: it had helped repair more than 3,000 tractors, delivered 4,000 tons of wheat seed to a storage facility in Mosul, restored 70 veterinarian clinics, and distributed 169 seed-cleaning machines.[77] In addition, longer-term planning had begun: the Ministry of Water joined with the Ministry of Agriculture to develop an integrated approach to land and water reclamation.[78] Other IRRF 2 funds for water and irrigation projects contributed to the agriculture sector, as did smaller expenditures from CERP and other USAID programs.

On the whole, though, this was not enough to transform Iraq's beleaguered agricultural sector into a modern, market-based system able to produce enough for domestic consumption and compete in the regional market. Even if the United States had invested more heavily, the failure to deliver reliable essential services would have undercut commercial farms. Commercial poultry operations, for instance, require stable electric power to see chicks through their fourth week of life. Power and affordable diesel fuel are also essential to operate the pumps that irrigate field crops.[79] Agriculture, like Iraq's other economic enterprises, was in need of both modernization and the basic services typically supplied by the state.

For these reasons, in May 2007, USAID provided $343 million for a three-year modernization program called *Inma*—Arabic for growth—targeted on the development of agribusiness and agricultural markets.[80] The program aimed to forge stronger linkages among farmers, agribusinesses, and markets—both domestic and international. *Inma*'s implementers would work closely with PRTs and continue the technology transfer and modernization programs begun under the earlier agricultural effort. It was an aggressive approach in keeping with the sector's potential, but one that came years too late for Shomber and his fellow soldiers in Anbar.

Standing Up the Iraqi Security Forces

As in many reconstruction sectors, investment in agriculture had been diverted to an even more pressing need—Iraq's security forces. It was part of the U.S. approach, announced by Prime Minister Ja'afari and MNF-I in June 2005, to transition security responsibilities to the Iraqis through a process known as provincial Iraqi control (PIC).[81] President Bush succinctly stated the strategy in a June 2005 address. "As Iraqis stand up," he said, "we will stand down."[82]

With the new focus on transitioning security responsibilities, the ISFF surpassed IRRF 2 as the primary reconstruction fund. Appropriations through 2008 brought the total value of ISFF to $17.94 billion.[83] Coupled with $4.97 billion in IRRF 2 allocations, spending on the Iraqi security sector was larger than U.S. spending on all other sectors combined.[84]

Iraq Security Forces Fund Appropriations ($ Millions)		
Appropriation	Public Law	Amount
Emergency Supplemental Appropriations Act for Defense, the Global War on Terror, and Tsunami Relief, 2005	P.L. 109-13	$5,391
Emergency Supplemental Appropriations Act for Defense, the Global War on Terror, and Hurricane Recovery, 2006	P.L. 109-234	$3,007
Department of Defense Appropriations Act, 2007	P.L. 109-289	$1,700
U.S. Troop Readiness, Veterans' Care, Katrina Recovery, and Iraq Accountability Appropriations Act, 2007	P.L. 110-28	$3,842
Consolidated Appropriations Act, 2008	P.L. 110-161	$1,500
Supplemental Appropriations Act, 2008	P.L. 110-252	$2,500
Total		$17,940

Source: SIGIR, *Quarterly Report to the United States Congress*, October 2008, 26.

MNSTC-I used ISFF to organize, train, equip, and sustain the Iraqi security forces. In addition, more than 4,000 U.S. personnel served in MNC-I transition teams, which lived, worked, and fought alongside Iraqi battalions. This constituted an enormous investment of resources that had produced an impressive new force, at least on paper. Tens of thousands of police and soldiers had been trained, and more than 1,200 facilities were built.[85]

Despite the outlay of U.S. human and financial resources, Iraqi forces were mostly unable to contain the rising violence in 2006. They were extremely vulnerable to sectarian and insurgent attack and also stretched thin, with fewer members in per capita terms than security forces in other countries facing similar challenges.[86] In the year and a half following the Samarra bombing, three times as many Iraqi army and police were killed than Coalition forces in Iraq.[87]

The sectarian conflict gripping Iraq also played out inside its government. Soldiers, police, and judges could not easily shed their sectarian identities when on the job. For many, loyalties to sect or tribe competed with their willingness to serve the Iraqi state. The police and military also depended on the support of a set of institutions that were not yet competent to manage the various forces as they confronted the insurgency.

When June 2006 arrived, not one province had attained what Iraqi and U.S. officials considered the requisite degree of stability for the transition to provincial control to proceed.[88] Target dates for the PIC process shifted five more times over the next year and a half. By the end of 2007, handoff had occurred in only nine of eighteen provinces, and three of those handed off had long been under de facto Kurdish control.[89]

Ministry of Defense

The Ministry of Defense was one of the relatively better functioning parts of the Iraqi government, although it too suffered from rampant corruption.[90] The army as a whole, however, underperformed in a number of key areas just when its services were needed most. Few units were operationally ready and able to conduct missions in tandem with U.S. forces or on their own. A byzantine and reportedly corrupt contracting and procurement system meant that soldiers lacked the guns, body armor, radios, and vehicles to take on the militias and insurgents they were fighting—who often had heavy weapons of their own.

In October 2005, formal responsibility for building capacity in the Ministries of Interior and Defense shifted from IRMO to MNSTC-I, ratifying the shift that began with the creation of the CPATT and the CMATT in 2004. To help develop Iraq's capacity to equip its own troops, MNSTC-I fielded a team of 68 advisors, mostly civilian contractors, to assist the ministry's civilian leadership. A separate Joint Headquarters Transition Team of about 50 personnel, also mostly contractors, worked with the Iraqi military staff to improve command and control and to train and equip the nascent forces.[91] The purpose of both teams was to mentor their Iraqi colleagues while at the same time strengthening capacity inside the ministry.

Their work yielded mixed results. They first tried to bypass the Iraqi procurement system altogether, but attempts to use the U.S. Foreign Military Sales system turned into what one senior U.S. commander lamented as "a national embarrassment" for the United States. Of $1.7 billion in acquisitions made by the government of Iraq in 2006, only $300 million had arrived by mid-2007.[92] "We overwhelmed the system," said Lieutenant General Martin Dempsey, MNSTC-I commander. "There was a period of time when we had one desk officer in the Department of Defense watching the Iraqi account. Of course, that was just not going to work."[93] Although deliveries eventually improved, unexpected delays in the U.S. system hamstrung Iraqi forces at a critical moment.

By October 2006, the CPA or MNSTC-I had trained more than 115,000 Ministry of Defense personnel.[94] Ninety-two Iraqi Army and Special Operations battalions were deemed capable of operating independently or "in the lead," a nearly four-fold increase since July 2005.[95] These units increasingly took "primary area security responsibility" in many parts of the country, and in September 2006, Thi-Qar Province became the second province to transfer to PIC.[96] The most significant continuing shortcomings were the ISF's logistics and sustainment capabilities.[97]

Coalition advisors also pursued longer-term solutions, including the installation of a new financial management and accounting system. As with the unsuccessful effort to install a government-wide financial management system in the Ministry of Finance, the design of the Defense Ministry system was ill-suited to Iraqi norms and experience.[98] Logistics capability nevertheless slowly improved, and by 2007 Iraqi expenditures on its security services would exceed those of the U.S. government.[99]

Ministry of Interior

Iraq's police, even more than the army, were deeply divided by sectarian rivalry and hobbled by administrative malaise. The fragmentation of police training identified in reviews of the program in 2005—which faulted a lack of cohesion among the civilian trainers, MNSTC-I advisors, and MNC-I officials—had been partially addressed.[100] A three-phase training program had been introduced by MNSTC-I—which named 2006 the "Year of the Police"—and more U.S. forces were now mentoring Iraqi police after their graduation. A planned total of 750 State Department contractors and 2,250 U.S. military personnel would be deployed in police training teams.[101]

By August 2006, 160 Coalition police transition teams circulated among Iraqi police in the field, while an additional 38 teams worked with the Iraqi National Police.[102] Modules on detecting suicide bombers were added to the training courses for new recruits, and local intelligence collection—a key element of the counterinsurgency campaign—gradually improved. However, in 2006, the Coalition had enough personnel to monitor only a quarter of the 1,200 police stations across Iraq. Two hundred stations were considered too dangerous for U.S. personnel even to visit.[103]

Like the army, the Iraqi police were supported by a ministry that was not yet entirely functional. The Ministry of the Interior, described by some as an "eleven-story powder keg of factions," was viewed by many as a protector of Shi'a interests.[104] It was also a key site of intra-Shi'a rivalry. Political parties, religious groups, tribes, families, and members of the government each struggled to bolster their authority over forces in the provinces. The Ministry became notorious for discriminating by sect in its hiring practices. At times, who got paid came down to ethnicity.[105]

After the Samarra bombing, Ministry of Interior leadership hastened the integration of a Shi'a militia into the force. Bayan Jabr, who served as Minister of Interior from April 2005 to May 2006 and thereafter as Minister of Finance, appointed members of the Badr Organization, the armed wing of the political party SCIRI, to key ministerial posts. Much of the controversy centered on the Iraqi National Police, an elite counterterrorism force that was 85 percent Shi'a. In 2005, units had been implicated in a prison torture scandal. Sunni communities violently rejected the National Police, seeing it as an extension of Shi'a militia killing squads.[106]

Jawad al-Bolani, who followed Jabr as Minister of Interior, ultimately removed commanders from 7 of 9 National Police brigades and 17 of 26 National Police battalions, but even this failed to curb sectarian infiltration. A later review found the National Police so riddled with sectarian influences that it recommended disbanding it altogether—a suggestion disregarded by Lieutenant General Petraeus, who viewed the force as redeemable. Al-Bolani himself was only partially successful in taking the reins. The Interior Ministry's proximity to Sadr City made travel there exceptionally dangerous. On most days, he ran the ministry from an office just outside the Green Zone. So many officials were assassinated on their way to work that many started sleeping in their offices.[107]

To help establish capacity within the Ministry of Interior, MNSTC-I assembled a 90-person transition team. The danger forced Coalition officials to move around inside the ministry with body armor and heavily armed escorts. Although the provision of equipment reached rates of 70 to 80 percent of assessed needs in some places, the police—like the military—were still frequently outgunned. Ill-trained police patrolling in soft-sided trucks with AK-47s and pistols were little match for militias attacking with heavy weapons, rocket-propelled grenades, and mortars. As was the case in the Ministry of Defense, the Ministry of Interior's budget execution was a perennial problem. Two years after MNSTC-I assumed responsibility for capacity development, one third of the ministry's $3 billion budget remained unspent.[108]

Sectarian rivalry and an open power struggle between provincial and central authorities were often the root cause of poor performance. Once the power to hire police devolved to the provinces, tribal sheikhs—who asserted an increasing influence over local government—placed tribal members on the job rolls. Although it was expected and often helpful for the police to mirror the sectarian character of the neighborhoods they patrolled, payroll remained under control of the central ministry, opening the door to favoritism and abuse. A separate system for new recruits complicated matters further. Rather than being disbursed through the Ministry of Interior payroll system, pay was distributed by provincial police chiefs, whom the Ministry of Finance supplied directly with funds. "Ghost employees" were a constant concern.[109]

The attempts to vet police and rid the system of sectarianism and corruption, first begun by the qualifying committees in early 2005, grew ever more sophisticated.[110] New recruits were made to submit to a retinal scan and fingerprinting, which were crosschecked against criminal databases and allowed for more rigorous scrutiny of payroll and rosters. All through 2006 and 2007, purges of the police force occurred when the will of local political authorities overcame the coercive power of factions controlling the force.[111]

The militarization of the police was also a growing concern. One review found that MNSTC-I's assumption of leadership over police training inadvertently marginalized the civilian police advisors best positioned to teach Iraqis policing skills. The Bureau of International Narcotics and Law Enforcement Affairs trainers were older—and therefore more respected in Iraqi culture—than the younger MNC-I soldiers who manned police training teams. They were also professional law enforcement officers with experience in civilian policing. Fielding sufficient numbers of them was the problem. Although the police command with MNSTC-I requested 6,000, the Congress authorized only 1,000. A year and a half after Samarra, 900 were in Iraq, along with some 3,500 military personnel. By 2007, they oversaw a police force of more than 230,000—a ratio of 1 to 50.[112]

Expanding Rule of Law Programs
The range of activities falling under the rubric "rule of law" included everything from digitizing the Iraqi legal code to training judges, securing court houses, and building prisons. Even getting fuel oil to the generators so the courts could operate with air-conditioning and light was part of the job. By the end of 2005, the United States had expended more than $400 million for law- and security-related programs other than police training, $300 million of which went toward brick-and-mortar projects and $100 million to capacity building.[113]

The sheer number of agencies and funding streams involved in rule-of-law activities gave rise to all sorts of bureaucratic complications. Funding for resident legal advisors from the Department of Justice came through the State Department's Bureau of International Narcotics and Law Enforcement Affairs. Military officials overseeing detainees relied upon prison funds under the control of the embassy, and State Department officials on PRTs used the military's CERP funds to support courts. Coordination was a constant challenge on both the Iraqi and American side.

Ambassador Khalilzad instituted a Rule of Law Task Force in 2005, but an overall coordinator was not named until 2006. Only in 2007 did Ambassador Crocker delegate real authority to the position. "We were sometimes our own worst enemies because we did not talk to each other and did not coordinate with each other," said James Santelle, the embassy's third rule-of-law coordinator.[114] The Iraqis were equally disorganized. To promote the integration of police, courts, and prisons, INL facilitated the Iraqi Integration Commission, comprising the ministers of interior and justice and the chief justice, which first met on July 26, 2005.[115] A second committee, the Ministerial Committee on Rule of Law and Detention, with even wider participation from Iraqi ministries, began meeting in 2007. "It was the first time [Iraqi] agencies involved in the rule of law sat down at the same table in the Ministry of Justice and talked about these issues," Santelle said.[116]

The whole effort had many moving parts, the largest of which was the Central Criminal Court of Iraq, originally established by the CPA to prosecute terrorism and corruption cases. The CCCI had twelve panels operating at secure sites throughout Iraq, but most of the work took place in Baghdad. During 2006, the CCCI processed 118 insurgency cases per month.[117] Support for a number of high-level prosecutions came from the Major Crimes Task Force—a team of twelve American law enforcement agents and eleven Iraqi officers, as well as five translators—established after a series of bombings went uninvestigated in 2004 and 2005.[118]

Processing detainees, whether arrested by U.S. forces or Iraqi authorities, was a bottleneck. "It's bad to have someone in jail for eighteen months without seeing a judge," Santelle said. However, bringing together judges, case files, and detainees for hearings that would rule on release or continued incarceration was a monumental effort.[119] The lack of a developed penal system of jails and prisons was part of the problem. Initial designs by design-build contractor Parsons for the major prison complexes at Nassriya and Khan Bani Sa'ad included air-conditioning—a luxury few Iraqis could afford—and were constructed to U.S. standards rather than Middle Eastern norms. "Iraqi penal theory calls for prisons to be less comfortable than the inmate's home," a State Department review found. The air-conditioning units stood "a good chance of being unplugged once the Americans leave."[120]

The large U.S. investment in the CCCI had effectively created a two-tiered Iraqi justice system. "For the average Iraqi," Santelle said, "day-to-day justice being doled out is not at the CCCI." Rather, people were getting divorced, suing each other, and working out other legal problems in provincial courts.[121] The United States was seen to have invested heavily in the CCCI, which served its own national interest by prosecuting terrorism cases, but to have done little for the courts that Iraqis use most. "We have co-opted the Iraqi justice system for our own use and left ordinary Iraqis with nothing," said Stephen Andersson, a resident legal advisor in the Baghdad PRT.[122] To the average Iraqi, the CCCI courts are an American creation. "We call them the Potemkin Courts," one former judge said.[123]

In the courts where ordinary Iraqis sought justice, the insecure environment took its toll on the judiciary. The Islamic State of Iraq, an umbrella organization of insurgent groups, mounted continual attacks on Baghdad courthouses. The chief judge at the al-Rusafa Appellate District Court kept bullets fired at his office stacked in his ashtray.[124] The danger extended beyond the courthouses themselves. Unlike the CCCI judges, who were granted secure housing in the Green Zone or on U.S.-protected rule-of-law compounds, the vast majority of Iraq's judges lived in their own homes with no protection. "Judges are living in places like Doura and Kadhamiya," Santelle said, "and they've got to go home at night and live amongst the other communities where they are not protected ... That's tough for anyone to do."[125]

The judges' vulnerability may have compromised their ability to render impartial verdicts. One former Iraqi judge estimated that nine of every ten decisions in the common court system are shaped by extra-judicial considerations, in contrast to four to seven out of ten in the CCCI courts—both unacceptable ratios by Western standards.[126] Corruption had always been a part of judicial practice under Saddam, but after the invasion its motivating factor changed from money to safety. "It's for keeping their life, and keeping their job," one former judge said. The result is that "the courts are functioning but the system is not."[127]

Iraq Policy in Crisis

The country had begun coming together again—however slightly—during Ambassador Khalilzad's early tenure, but sectarian violence, accelerated by the Samarra bombing, blew it back apart. As summer 2006 turned to fall, U.S. Iraq policy fell into crisis. The stalled deployment of the PRTs and slow establishment of the focused stabilization effort undercut the President's Clear-Hold-Build strategy. Chiarelli's push to use CERP funds for "last-mile" construction could not by itself make up for the under-performance of IRRF 2. Enormous capacity-building and sustainability challenges loomed, but efforts to address them were still unformed.[128] Those programs that seemed to work were spread too thinly across the war-torn country. Sectarian violence escalated: more than 1,000 Iraqis died at the hands of their countrymen every month.[129]

The day after congressional elections in 2006, the White House announced the resignation of Secretary of Defense Donald Rumsfeld. The man who oversaw the planning and management of the war for more than three years, and who opposed some of the White House's most recent policies, would be replaced by Robert Gates, who had directed the CIA in the early 1990s. Gates was then serving on the bipartisan review of Iraq policy led by former Secretary of State James Baker and former Congressman Lee Hamilton.[130]

The Iraq Study Group, commissioned by the Congress and eventually welcomed by the White House, was given access to all intelligence and information on Iraq.[131] In anticipation of its report and at the direction of the President, Deputy National Security Advisor J.D. Crouch began a review of Iraq options. The Joint Chiefs of Staff also undertook their own assessment, as did a number of think-tanks in Washington. Plans under consideration ranged from a complete pull-out to a major escalation.[132]

Issued on December 6, 2006, the Iraq Study Group report argued that continuing the current course would lead to failure. Its 79 recommendations addressed the full spectrum of policy issues: geopolitics, political dynamics at work in Iraq, and the performance of U.S. institutions assisting the Iraqi government.

To resolve sectarian aggression, the study group set out specific milestones. One of the most important was holding local elections to break the monopoly on service delivery held by what one official called a "Shi'a dictatorship" that ruled most of Iraq's provincial governments.[133] The study group also called for reordering the responsibility for Iraq's security forces and shifting the U.S. role to that of training and equipping the Iraqi army and police so that U.S. troops could begin to withdraw. The 4,000 American troops now serving in this role were seen as inadequate; the study group called for the number to be increased to a total of 10,000 to 20,000.[134]

To ready the Iraqi government for its transition to self-reliance, the study group recommended a further $5 billion in economic assistance per year focused on capacity development and job creation. The study group also criticized the poor coordination between USAID and the Departments of State and Defense. "There are no clear lines establishing who is in charge of reconstruction," the report stated. It prescribed a major overhaul of the U.S. effort, calling for the appointment of a reconstruction coordinator reporting directly to the President, authorizing the ambassador to provide or rescind funding on a project-by-project basis, and for the takeover of rule-of-law programs by the Department of Justice.[135]

Some observers thought the Iraq Study Group members had not fully appreciated the effectiveness of the Clear-Hold-Build strategy or what a possible increase in troop strength could achieve, and had instead bought into the prevailing thinking of General Casey and supporters of the "transition to Iraqis" approach.[136] It would be up to the President to decide between the competing military strategies. By the end of the year, the White House would make its decision.

ESSENTIAL SERVICES OVERVIEW – TRANSITION
FROM KHALILZAD TO CROCKER

Metric[137]	Pre-invasion	Post-invasion	CPA Transition	Negroponte Era	Khalilzad Era
Electricity Production					
Megawatts	4,075	711	3,621	4,262	3,475
Oil Production					
Million Barrels per Day	2.58	0.30	2.16	2.13	1.95
Iraqi Security Forces					
Soldiers and Police	1,300,000	7,000-9,000	87,000	171,300	328,700
Telecommunications					
Landline Subscribers	833,000	0	791,000	998,000	1,111,000
Mobile Subscribers	80,000	0	461,000	2,422,000	8,720,000
Human Toll					
U.S Troop Fatalities	-	139	862	1,745	3,248
Civilian Contractors	-	1	46	217	916
U.S. Civilians	-	~9	52	113	224
Iraqi Civilians	-	7,413	16,848	29,155	72,858
Financial Cost ($ billions)					
U.S Funding	-	$3.45	$22.93	$29.21	$36.96
Iraqi Funding	-	$0.00	$16.00	$21.03	$37.27
International Funding	-	$0.00	$13.60	$13.87	$15.20
Total Funding	-	$3.45	$52.53	$64.11	$89.43

During Khalilzad's tenure, project delays and increasing security costs limited improvements in essential service delivery. The output increases of the Negroponte era were short-lived, especially in the oil and electricity sectors. Insurgent attacks and a lack of fuel drove average levels of electricity generation down below prewar levels, and power outages again became common. Attacks on critical infrastructure increased in 2006, causing electricity production to fall to a daily average of 3,475 megawatts by March 2007.[138]

The oil sector continued to be plagued by corruption and smuggling. Between 10 and 30 percent of refined fuels was diverted to the black market or smuggled out of Iraq.[139] Although the oil sector's capacity was estimated at 3 million barrels per day, only about 2 million barrels per day were produced during 2005-2006.[140]

CHAPTER 26
THE CIVILIAN SURGE

2006 was a bad year in Iraq. The country came close to unraveling politically, economically, and in security terms. 2007 has brought improvement. Enormous challenges remain. Iraqis still struggle with fundamental questions about how to share power, accept their differences and overcome their past. The changes to our strategy last January—the surge—have helped change the dynamics in Iraq for the better. *

Ambassador Ryan Crocker
U. S. Ambassador to Iraq (2007-present)

President Bush unveiled his new Iraq strategy on January 10, 2007, a day after fierce fighting broke out in Baghdad off Haifa Street, a thousand yards from the Green Zone.[1] In a nationally televised speech, the President announced a "surge" of more than 20,000 troops whose primary mission would be to reduce violence nationwide.[2] The new focus on civilian security was premised on the notion that stemming sectarian violence would enable Iraq's leaders to reach reconciliation.[3] When complete, the surge would add two Marine battalions in Anbar province and five Army brigades in Baghdad province.[4]

The surge in troops would be coupled with an intensive focus on neighborhood reconstruction by joint civilian and military teams and by an expansion of USAID programs. The President announced that smaller "embedded" Provincial Reconstruction Teams (ePRTs) would place development experts directly inside brigade combat teams. More of the larger "traditional" PRTs would also be added.[5] This "civilian surge" would double the number of reconstruction advisors serving outside the Green Zone, bringing the total to 700 by the end of a 9-month build-up.[6]

USAID's Community Stabilization Program (CSP), which operated through Iraqi intermediaries with little visible association with U.S. civilian or military forces, would expand to work with all PRTs.[7] Iraqi neighborhoods would be flooded with modest infrastructure projects that hired unskilled labor for trash pickups, awarded grants to invigorate small businesses, and provided vocational training and youth programs.[8] It would be an "all-hands-on-deck" approach to reversing the acceleration of violence that followed the Samarra bombing.[9]

---

* Ambassador Ryan Crocker, U.S. Ambassador to Iraq, Testimony before the House Committee on Foreign Affairs and the Committee on Armed Services, September 10, 2007.

A New Military Strategy

The surge plan pushed back the possibility of a phased withdrawal of U.S. forces for 12 to 18 months. Although it incorporated many of the Iraq Study Group's performance benchmarks, the plan departed from the policies of General George Casey, the outgoing commander, and the Iraq Study Group's call for gradual disengagement.[10] Like many members of the group, Casey viewed an intrusive American presence as counterproductive to solving Iraq's underlying political and security problems and therefore advocated a rapid hand-off to Iraqi forces.[11]

To carry out the surge, the President nominated—and the Senate unanimously confirmed—General David Petraeus as MNF-I's new Commanding General in Iraq. After his command of MNSTC-I in 2005, which followed his 2003-04 command of the 101st Airborne in Mosul, Petraeus had directed the first rewrite of the Army and Marine Corps' counterinsurgency manual since the Vietnam War. The revised doctrine called for increased use of forces to protect the population, even if that put soldiers at greater risk of attack. It also suggested that a focus on quality-of-life improvements could help turn the population against insurgents.[12] Stationing troops in neighborhoods in small combat outposts and stepping up patrols would reverse the trend, begun in 2005, of consolidating the U.S. presence on large forward operating bases.[13] To teach counterinsurgency tactics, the U.S. Army erected a mock Iraqi village at Ft. Irwin, California, complete with 400 native Arabic speakers playing insurgents, shopkeepers, and security forces. The training course, built at a facility originally used for mock tank battles, aimed to replicate the dilemmas that soldiers would face on patrol in Iraq.[14] The military also mandated that officers rotating into Iraq attend a one-week course on counterinsurgency, known as "the COIN Academy."[15]

Change-of-command ceremonies took place on February 10, 2007, a month after the President's speech. Four days later, General Petraeus and the commander of MNC-I, Lieutenant General Raymond Odierno, presented eight slides to President Bush showing how they intended to implement the surge.[16] Petraeus put the third iteration of the Baghdad Security Plan into effect quickly. By the end of February, 2,700 new U.S. troops had arrived in the capital. By June, that number reached 16,700—enough for 400 to 600 combat troops to secure each security district established under the plan.[17]

The troop increases enabled a strategy that Major General Joe Fil, commanding Coalition forces in Baghdad, described as "clear, control, and retain." U.S. forces and capable Iraqi Security Forces would continue to hold territory rather than turning it over to ill-prepared Iraqi forces. After mounting clearing operations to drive out insurgents, troops found houses and public buildings to use as combat outposts, creating a permanent presence in neighborhoods that had been only occasionally patrolled.[18] As soon as security was established, USACE moved in to restore water and electricity service.[19] The military also strengthened existing population control measures to separate Shi'a and Sunni enclaves. Many of Baghdad's districts were cordoned off by multiple series of twelve-foot-high concrete walls, the longest of which ran for three miles.[20]

Negotiating with what the campaign plan termed "reconcilable elements" was also a key component of the surge.[21] A realignment of Sunni tribes in Anbar was underway, and their loyalty was up for grabs. Ambassador Khalilzad had been quietly talking to them for months; Marine Corps officers had been doing so for years. Now it looked as if popular dissatisfaction with al-Qaeda's brutal tactics, along with its infringement on traditional tribal prerogatives, might drive them to forge an alliance with the Coalition.

In one of the war's most extraordinary stories, small special operations teams had been escorting Lieutenant General Graeme Lamb, a British officer familiar with the peacemaking negotiations with the Irish Republican Army, to secret meetings with insurgent leaders. The response to Lamb's initiative, which began before Petraeus arrived, was promising. Petraeus and his advisors moved to expand this engagement strategy by having brigade and battalion commanders reach out to insurgents in their area. "Come in, let's talk about what it would take, and figure it out," was the rubric.[22] The Sunni tribes eventually formed U.S.-funded security forces, known in turn as Awakening Councils, Concerned Local Citizens, or Sons of Iraq, which would also contribute significantly to the success of the surge. Eventually, similar groups were established within some Shi'a communities.

A New Reconstruction Strategy

The surge also ushered in new diplomatic leadership. Ambassador Ryan Crocker, the State Department's senior Arabist, replaced Zalmay Khalilzad as U.S. Ambassador to Iraq. At the time of his appointment, Crocker was Ambassador to Pakistan. He had previously served as ambassador to Syria, Kuwait, and Lebanon; his prior experience in Iraq included a posting there in the late 1970s and a short tour with CPA in 2003 as the director of governance.[23] The Secretary of State also appointed Ambassador Timothy Carney as Coordinator for Economic Transition in Iraq, a new position designed to centralize authority for reconstruction and economic affairs.[24] A veteran diplomat, Carney had initially served with ORHA in 2003, but left Iraq, as did Crocker, soon after Ambassador Bremer took charge.[25]

The diplomatic and economic elements of the surge were slower to materialize. Petraeus arrived to find a collection of reconstruction programs that ran mostly independent of one another. In the words of his economic advisor,

Colonel Michael Meese, reconstruction consisted of "stovepiped programs out of specific appropriation and oversight lines with specific purposes that have a logic of their own." The categorization of funding and authorities, while undertaken for "all the right legal reasons," meant that the Commanding General and the Ambassador had little ability to allocate resources among competing programs without first returning to the Congress. "What you did as a commander is pull on all these strings," Meese explained. "The answer was full speed ahead on all these things."[26]

With funding streams essentially fixed until the Congress passed the 2008 supplemental later in the spring of 2007, Petraeus and Crocker focused on how the reconstruction was administered in concert with combat operations and how the military itself conceived of its mission. They convened a group of advisors with broad expertise in counterinsurgency and political science, dubbed the Joint Strategic Assessment Team. After a period of study, they recommended in April that political accommodation become the goal of all lines of operation. Every tool in the Coalition arsenal—including the use of force, but also political negotiation and economic aid—would be used to foster accommodation between warring groups. Although falling well short of true reconciliation, this would at least bring about local ceasefires that could subsequently be expanded across Iraq.[27]

The campaign plan later developed on the basis of the JSAT report incorporated several new ideas that would guide the actions of commanders and reconstruction personnel. In the previous campaign plan, preparing Iraqis for the transition to self-rule was seen as a separate activity. Transition remained an important future goal for Petraeus, but he viewed it as inherent in every line of operation. The new standard, Meese explained, was "if it can't be done by the Iraqis, we probably shouldn't do it." "What is better is a project that takes 60 days instead of 30 days—but is done by the Iraqi manager and is sustainable by the Iraqis [and] that their operations can support."[28] Nevertheless, Petraeus's advisors understood that economic incentives would have little traction in a sectarian conflict. "People who are killing for political reasons or to ethnically cleanse an area are rarely going to stop because of a new job opportunity," stated one memorandum to the commanding general.[29]

Ambassador Carney largely concurred with Petraeus's assessment. "On the overall policy, we were continuing to proceed without sufficient Iraqi participation," he said. "I was appalled when I learned that Iraqis were simply not signing off to accept huge numbers of projects." In Carney's view, the problem began in 2003. "We got an insurgency because we didn't have Iraqis completely with us on the effort to move the country forward after we destroyed Saddam Hussein's regime," he said in 2008. According to his assessment, the endgame was by now completely in Iraqi hands. "We essentially wound up in the position, as we are in today, of being able to act as a shield and to provide resources, but we are much less of an accepted mentor than we might have been if we had taken Iraqis into our counsel from the outset," Carney said. "This is a position of great weakness because we are vulnerable to Iraqi bad decisions."[30]

To redress the lack of Iraqi participation, the embassy moved to coordinate all U.S. economic and reconstruction actions with Deputy Prime Minister Barham Salih, Minister of Planning Ali Baban, and Minister of Finance Bayan Jabr. Together with National Security Advisor Mowaffak al-Rubaie, the trio said they would do their best to ensure that Iraq's ministries made use of their capital budgets and that provincial governments spent funds allotted to them.[31] It would be an essential step toward fiscal self-reliance, one that now seemed within reach.

Between existing ministry budgets, central government grants to provinces in 2006, and provincial line-item funds in the 2007 Iraqi budget, Iraqis "had more than $5 billion to spend." Spending this Iraqi money became an essential political benchmark in the eyes of U.S. lawmakers. "If the Iraqis remained unable or unwilling to spend their own capital investment budget, there was certainly no reason for the Congress of the United State to appropriate money for Iraq," Carney said.[32]

By late spring, Petraeus, Crocker, and their advisors were still waiting for the economic surge to take shape. Although Petraeus arrived in Baghdad early in February 2007, the rest of the civilian leadership appeared much later. Ambassador Crocker did not assume chief of mission duties until March 29.[33] The team that Crocker selected to take over key positions in the embassy came still later, in early summer. The staggered arrival hampered coordination between the military and civilian leadership, and slowed the implementation of surge policies on the civilian side.[34]

Delays in the deployment of rank-and-file civilian personnel slowed the transition still further. Carney was surprised to find it just as difficult to bring people into Iraq in 2007 as it had been in 2003. He resorted to hiring his deputy as a contractor when the State Department was unable to add him to the rolls quickly. "The recruitment process is in sclerosis," Carney said. "We are not responsive to the President's policy for Iraq if we cannot get people hired in fewer than six weeks."[35]

A funding slowdown further complicated matters. Supplemental funds appropriated by the Congress for fiscal year 2006 did not reach Iraq for a longer-than-usual period, forcing programs to scale back activity temporarily. From the date when the Congress authorized its spending, money contained in the supplemental took between 62 and 218 days to be disbursed in Iraq.[36] When combined with the longer-than-anticipated time for contractors associated with the economic surge to set up in country, the effects were significant. "Ensuring that the non-DoD organizations have the resources provided to do what is necessary is of enormous importance," Petraeus said later.[37]

Embedding Reconstruction
As the Baghdad Security Plan was put into effect, the ePRT and PRT teams started arriving at posts across Iraq. Three waves of PRT staff would provide almost every brigade with a dedicated staff of development experts, realizing the original vision advanced nearly two years before by Lieutenant General Raymond Odierno and Dr. Philip Zelikow, the State Department's Counselor.[38] Led primarily by State Department officials, and staffed in part by USAID and reservists and civilians from the Department of Defense, ePRT teams of four to eight people would help brigades leverage their resources in new ways.

The expansion of the PRT program was a landmark event in the reconstruction effort. For the first time in four years, a formal civil-military structure enabled civilian reconstruction experts to work side-by-side with maneuver commanders who were prosecuting the war. The experiment in civil-military relations that Ambassador Khalilzad saw to an uneasy start in 2005 was taking hold. Reconstruction became embedded in brigades and in Iraqi society and focused as much on building capacity inside Iraqi institutions as infrastructure construction.[39]

The brigades, whose substantial resources were increasingly applied to the reconstruction and capacity-building missions, welcomed the arrival of ePRTs. "You can tell when you walk in, when the PRT chief is finishing the Battalion Commander's sentences, that's a great relationship," Meese said. On the other hand, "if the PRT chief can't find the bathroom because he hasn't been to the HQ often enough," the relationship has not developed.[40] Most of all, ePRTs augmented the capability of brigades to engage with local governments.

Nowhere in a normal brigade staff structure could "you find people that are organized and trained to go help municipal governance and reconstruction issues," explained Lieutenant Colonel Douglas Winton, Executive Officer of the First Brigade Combat Team, Third Infantry Division. By helping brigades integrate their use of CERP funds with embassy reconstruction plans and tying the actions of civil affairs teams to the development of local and provincial governments, ePRTs were helping brigades take "essential services to the next level." The war had evolved so that reconstruction, the functioning of local government, and security reinforced each other. "Gains in governance and gains in reconstruction are linked," Winton said.[41]

The PRTs' daily contact with municipal and provincial officials allowed them to gain a level of insight into Iraqi affairs unreachable inside the embassy, which usually dealt with Iraq in a more detached fashion. "We are here on the ground, face to face, every day, with the mayor, [directors general], sheiks," one ePRT member commented.[42] The relationships developed by PRT and civil affairs team members allowed them to gauge what interventions would be most effective, and allowed Iraqis, rather than Americans, to take the lead in articulating Iraqi needs. "We've got to start listening to the Iraqis. That's Development 101," said David Atteberry, the USAID representative on the Rasheed ePRT, located in one of the most dangerous neighborhoods in Baghdad. "The answer to most of your questions can be found by talking to the people you are working with."[43]

To help manage their relationships with Iraqis, many PRTs and Civil Affairs teams compiled "facebooks" with digital pictures of directors general and neighborhood and district council members, their mobile phone numbers, and short biographical sketches. More sophisticated techniques were sometimes used. Wall-sized diagrams mapping relationships among sheiks, provincial council members, and municipal officials were updated to reflect assassinations and changing loyalties. Some PRTs even kept detailed logbooks, with entries for each encounter with an Iraq official, including notes on their moods and personality quirks.[44] This social network analysis gave PRT members a better sense of the complexity of the society in which they were working and a greater ability to pass that knowledge to replacements when unit rotations occurred every nine to twelve months.

The military's acceptance and support of the reconstruction mission, more widespread in 2007 than any other previous year of the war, provided the biggest boost to PRT and Civil Affairs efforts. The brigades' wider reach had a multiplier effect in achieving reconstruction goals that was an essential part of the surge strategy. Lieutenant Colonel Winton explained:

> When an NGO shows up and says, I want to establish some agriculture programs, we think we have the ability to put fish farms in along the Euphrates. Does anybody know of a good place to establish a fish farm? The brigade commander turns to his battalion commanders, who turn to the company commanders, who turn to their platoon commanders. In 96 hours you get the data back. Here are ten historic fish farms. Here are their locations. And oh by the way, we have a relationship with the guy that owns this one, and we trust him. And oh by the way, this one over here has been used as a mortar firing point. Don't go there. We can flood the zone and bring back the information.[45]

This was exactly the dynamic envisioned by earlier assessments that suggested the key to success in Iraq would be marrying civilian development expertise to the military's circulation within local communities.[46]

PRT Problems

The extensive insight ePRTs gained into the communities they served highlighted dilemmas that had plagued reconstruction from the beginning. One of the biggest challenges was figuring out whom to trust. With money flooding in, some Iraqi government offices took on the atmosphere of the proverbial "smoke-filled back room," where unsavory business was conducted. "My favorite description is the bar scene of Star Wars," one ePRT member recalled. "When you go to a [district advisory council] meeting, it's just a parade of characters."[47] The characters were assembled in part to divide up the spoils handed out by the PRT and military. "Our district council chairman has become the Tony Soprano of Rasheed, in terms of controlling resources," Atteberry said.[48] "You will use my contractor, or your work will not get done," the chairman told the PRT.[49]

The cozy relationships between Iraqi officials and the contractors employed through reconstruction programs attracted allegations of fraud and waste that were hard to verify. An audit of USAID's Community Stabilization Program, which made extensive use of Iraqi intermediaries to implement short-term employment projects, discovered that program funds might have been diverted to militia activity in one Baghdad district.[50] It was the worst fear of any development officer, and also an inevitable risk of pushing large sums of money into a warzone.

The need to keep the loyalty of fledgling local governments in effect left PRTs, soldiers using CERP funds, and USAID programs vulnerable to over-pricing of materials and services. The PRTs and military units channeling development and CERP funds were frequently paying for more than the costs of material in construction. "We're pumping over $1 million just to renovate the [district advisory council] hall," Atteberry said. "We're building a farmer's market across from the Doura market, and we're spending over a million dollars. It's just a concrete slab and a tin roof. And the contract is $900,000."[51]

Dealing with local powerbrokers sometimes put the PRTs' long-term development goals in conflict with the brigades' immediate needs. On the one hand, many of the powerbrokers could make good on their promises to "make things happen," an important skill to soldiers whose first interest is security. Brigades taking casualties often resorted to CERP "fast cash" projects that pay Iraqis to administer services that local municipalities should already have been providing. However, using Coalition cash rather than Iraqi institutions set back efforts to foster self-reliance.

Trash pickup was the archetypal municipal service in which the brigade's security needs were in opposition with the traditional development approach. "The XO [Executive Officer] of a battalion comes in here," one ePRT leader recalls. "'If the trash isn't picked up,' the XO will say, 'somebody will put an IED in it and one of my guys will go down. I'm not going to get my guys killed. I'm going to pay someone to pick up the trash.'"[52] It was a pragmatic approach to security, but one that provided a disincentive for municipalities to discharge their responsibilities promptly. Complicating matters further, the contractors the Coalition employed often distorted local labor markets. The USAID Inspector General found that wages paid for trash pick-up by the CSP were higher than the average for skilled laborers, which put pressure on local officials to continue employing them rather than transition to other forms of development.[53]

In the view of some civilians on PRTs, the set of metrics used by the military to measure CERP progress placed too much emphasis on spending money and not enough on achieving the right effects. "They are being graded on how many projects are being carried out, how much money is flowing to the districts," said Tim Zuniga-Brown, team leader of the Rasheed ePRT. "They should be graded on how many projects are being turned over to the Iraqis and how much less money they are spending. That would be a better indicator of success." "Success," Zuniga-Brown said, "is getting Iraqis to deliver their own services using their own funds and their own people."[54] Still other PRT officials viewed this type of Coalition assistance as wholly counterproductive. "The best thing we could do," one ePRT official said, "is cut off CERP money," adding that the Iraqis are less likely to "spend their money when we're just pumping in ours."[55]

Balancing the brigade's short-term imperative of force protection against the PRT's longer-term development goals was difficult. Because of the party-list electoral structure and the failure to hold new provincial elections, the provincial and district councils through which PRTs and ePRTs worked were to some extent a theater for decisions made elsewhere—in party structures that operated outside Iraqi government institutions. Making sense of this murky world was mostly beyond the PRTs' abilities. "It's so presumptuous to think we have any idea what's going on," David Atteberry said. "We are continually stumbling around in the dark blind. We're worse than the blind because at least the blind know they are blind."[56] Linguistic and cultural expertise had always been in short supply and still was. Only 29 of the 610 PRT personnel deployed by mid-2007 were Arabic-speaking cultural advisors, and several of them, including highly effective Kurds, subsequently quit in protest of the Coalition alliance with Sunni tribes.[57] "If you don't have an interpreter," a military officer serving on an ePRT said, "it's like Wimbledon. You just watch it go from side to side."[58]

Some PRT members doubted that the assistance they provided would affect Iraqi politics. It was the same worry that Petraeus's economics advisor expressed when he wrote that economic incentives carried limited currency in a civil conflict. One ePRT member said, "Through the delivery of essential services, we might extend legitimacy to the local government, but I don't know if that's necessarily true." When asked what motivated the focus on essential services, the official replied, "Out of a sense of moral imperative, out of a sense of wanting to do the right thing." "I know the Iraqis appreciate that we are doing this," the official said, "but it might not translate into strategic success for us."[59]

The other main reservation voiced by PRT leaders concerned the daunting scope of their mission. The area of operations of the East Rasheed ePRT had as many people in it as the city of Detroit. To advise the brigade on how best to serve these 800,000 people and to carry out its own projects, the ePRT had a staff of six.[60]

Boosting Iraq's Manufacturing Base

As ePRT staff moved out into local neighborhoods and PRTs continued their work with provincial governments, reconstruction entities in the Green Zone began implementing the economic surge with newly available funding and personnel. Steering reconstruction and military procurement contracts to viable Iraqi businesses became a key U.S. objective. The idea was straightforward. Sustaining the Coalition's presence in Iraq cost more than twice Iraq's gross domestic product.[61] The military spent a significant portion of these costs on goods and services that could be procured locally. If properly channeled, military needs could drive job creation in the Iraqi industrial base and thus help end the insurgency soldiers were there to fight.

During the transition to direct, fixed-price contracting in late 2006 and 2007, USACE-GRD moved diligently to "Iraqify" their workforce, relying as much as possible on Iraqi contractors and vendors, many of whom had been trained by Bechtel University and other multinational firms.[62] A special effort called the "Iraqi First" program was begun in mid-2006 by Major General Darryl Scott, head of JCC-I.[63] From October 2006 to September 2007, JCC-I awarded $2.7 billion in contracts to Iraqi firms who collectively employed an estimated 75,000 Iraqis. In the first half of 2007 alone, it provided Iraqi businesses with more than a billion dollars of business.[64] By early 2008, more than 4,100 Iraqi companies were registered with the Coalition, which awarded 85 percent of them at least one contract. Overall, 90 percent of reconstruction projects awarded by USACE-GRD were going to Iraqi firms.[65] It was the latest of many attempts by the Coalition to involve Iraqi firms in the reconstruction of their country.[66]

An effort to revive Iraqi factories also got underway. Deputy Under Secretary of Defense Paul Brinkley led a task force to explore what it would take to breathe life into a sector of the economy that had employed an estimated 500,000 Iraqis in 2003.[67] "Frankly, we had exported a lot of our business processes to Iraq, and they were inappropriate," said Deputy Secretary of Defense Gordon England, who recruited Brinkley to go to Iraq.[68]

Brinkley became convinced that the CPA-era decision to close Iraq's state-owned enterprises should be reversed.[69] There were an unknown number of shuttered factories that could put Iraqis back to work. With private investment not yet entering the country, Brinkley advocated using Coalition funds to pay start-up and capital improvement costs that would bring these enterprises back online. Many in the State Department doubted the wisdom of this initiative. Although State Department officials had resisted Defense Department plans to decommission the state-owned enterprises in 2003, by 2007 the embassy's economics section was skeptical that reviving long-closed factories would be the best use of U.S. resources.

Once again, the U.S. failed to achieve a unified policy on what role state-owned industries should play in Iraq's economic recovery. The debates became so vituperative that Brinkley moved his staff from the embassy to separate quarters in the Green Zone. He also drew his budget exclusively from Defense Department funding, over which State personnel had little or no say.[70] Deputy Secretary of Defense England later said "that the whole Brinkley operation was also part of the interagency confusion in terms of who is responsible for what."[71]

By March 2007, Brinkley had selected 140 factories as candidates for Coalition assistance.[72] The factories manufactured everything from farm equipment to pharmaceuticals. Brinkley based decisions on how to allocate assistance on the potential speed and economic impact of a factory's restart.[73] By September 2007, he had succeeded in opening 17 of them. Brinkley intended his $200 million budget for assistance to be the catalyst for eventually creating 150,000 Iraqi jobs.[74]

The End of IRRF 2

Elsewhere around the embassy, programs that had existed since 2003 and 2004 were in a state of transition. Most remaining IRRF 2 projects were closed out during 2007. About 450 were still on the books in 2008.[75] GRD personnel anticipated that only fifteen to twenty of the largest and most complicated among them would still be underway by mid-2009.[76] Although the drawdown of IRRF 2 had led most large design-build contractors to pack up, new projects and ongoing military construction needs kept more than a thousand GRD employees working across Iraq's three regions. The 2008 supplemental budget also provided $285 million for sustainment programs and $60 million for capacity development, which the GRD used to fund vocational training of young apprentices and on-the-job training for more experienced workers at both infrastructure sites and in ministries.[77]

The focus of reconstruction shifted overwhelmingly to supporting Iraqi initiatives, in national as well as local ventures. In this new phase, Ambassador Crocker said, "You have to listen as much as you talk. Let them tell you the problem and then use ways they think it can be fixed with our help. It is not going to resemble how the Walla Walla, Washington City Council deals with Olympia, but it may work in Iraqi terms. So we talk about Iraqi solutions....It has to work for them."[78]

Reorganizing the Embassy

Just as the civilian surge reached its highest point, Ambassador Crocker reorganized the embassy, strengthening his ability to give high-level direction for the reconstruction program.[79] The IRMO had housed the senior advisors who worked with Iraqi ministries and oversaw reconstruction in the various sectors. Of its 258 positions, 147 moved to embassy sections, and 44 others were eliminated. The remaining 67 became the staff of the embassy's Iraq Transition Assistance Office (ITAO), which retained responsibility for the Ministries of Electricity and Water, as well as residual ministerial capacity-building efforts.[80]

The reorganization further realized the desire of State Department management to bring reconstruction more directly under the embassy's control. The embassy's economics section assumed responsibility for the Ministries of Oil, Agriculture, Trade, Transportation, and Communication. The Rule-of-Law Task Force took the Ministries of Justice and Interior. The Health and Human Services section took on the Ministry of Health, and Treasury attachés had the Ministry of Finance. The National Coordination Team, which directed the PRTs, became the Office of Provincial Affairs. The Public Affairs section assumed responsibility for the Ministries of Education and Culture. At times, these shifts were confusing. The formal point of contact for the Ministry of Planning, for instance, was at first unclear. Initially, representatives of the embassy's political and economic sections and ITAO disavowed their assigned role.[81]

The new staffing structure was devised by Patrick Kennedy, the State Department's Undersecretary for Management, whom Crocker had invited to review embassy operations. Kennedy's report aimed to prepare officials for the move to the new embassy complex, still under construction, where space would be at a premium.[82] The Kennedy Report also recommended increased staffing in the embassy's economic and political sections, lengthening tours to eighteen months, and ensuring at least one-week overlaps during personnel rotations. Wider dissemination of PRT weekly reports were also needed, in part because State Department personnel paid less attention to dispatches not distributed in cable form.[83]

Embassy 2007 Organizational Chart
USG Funds Flow for Iraq

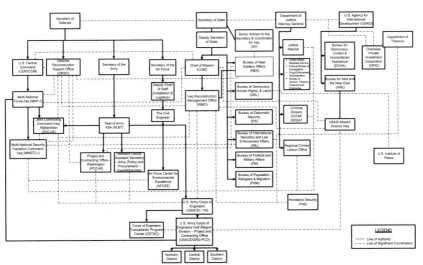

Source: SIGIR Audit 07-008, "Fact Sheet on the Roles and Responsibilities of U.S. Government Organizations Conducting IRRF-Funded Reconstruction Activities," July 26, 2007, i.

To many, the embassy reorganization made reporting chains more complex than before. The cadre of U.S. personnel in IRMO whose primary job was to travel "outside the wire" to interface with senior managers in the Iraqi government was now dispersed through multiple offices. Its convoluted organizational chart depicts the complexity inherent in an effort that by July 2007 involved at least 62 agencies or sub-agency offices in reconstruction alone.[84]

When Petraeus arrived, his advisors identified eight major coordination bodies.[85] "We have an underdeveloped Iraqi bureaucracy and an overdeveloped U.S. bureaucracy," Colonel Meese observed, "and the two of them [make] each other [stagnate]."[86] By 2007, spending too much time dealing with the Coalition bureaucracy—and not enough meeting with Iraqis—was a frequent complaint of officials based in the Green Zone. It was a far cry from the CPA period, where individuals could more easily take the initiative. "We so rapidly went from … the Wild West days," one senior advisor lamented, "to a different kind of waste."[87]

The lack of executive authority was apparent everywhere. Even though Crocker and Petraeus assigned coordinators to the political, economic, military, communication, and rule-of-law lines of operation, the coordinators in most cases did not have tasking or budget authority over the offices they were responsible for managing. A truly joint command structure never evolved. To Crocker and Petraeus, achieving unity of effort, in which everyone worked toward common goals, was more important than unity of command, where action was not always predicated upon achieving consensus. This arrangement worked well enough when the military and civilian leadership saw eye to eye, but when they disagreed, the civilian and military arms of the U.S. government would at times work at cross-purposes.[88]

The complexity of the Coalition effort and its chain of command was especially difficult for the Iraqis to understand. Figuring out whom to contact for help was often the first problem. Frustration at the ever-growing Green Zone staff evoked suggestions for radical change. "If I were you," USAID's acting-Deputy Administrator James Kunder advised Ryan Crocker, "I'd reduce the embassy presence to a hundred people and give everybody else two choices: they can either go to a PRT, or they can go home."[89]

Crocker and Petraeus were acutely aware of the management challenge that faced them. "You have to be joined at the hip," Petraeus said. "That's why the Ambassador and I have offices next to each other." "If all else fails," Petraeus said, "once a week, the ambassador and the MNF-I commander get to sit down with the President of the United States and the NSC. And you can again cut through quite a few layers of bureaucracy in a real hurry in that kind of situation."[90] The physical proximity maintained by Crocker and Petraeus, however, did not always extend to their staffs, who continued working in separate office space, frequently attending separate morning meetings, and reporting through separate chains of command.[91] Despite this litany of challenges, the civil-military relationship between the embassy and MNF-I improved steadily during 2007.

Social Capital and the Civilian Surge

Relationships with Iraqis that often eluded embassy personnel flourished just miles away in compounds maintained by USAID contractors, and to a lesser extent on PRTs. The Community Stabilization Program, the Community Action Program, and the Local Governance Program employed Iraqis to work in neighborhoods not far from the Green Zone, as well as in other places across Iraq. By 2007, this approach to reconstruction—the strengthening of Iraqi civil society by operating within it—was viewed as a crucial tool.[92]

Through interventions large and small, in places from community halls to main street businesses, the CAP and LGP continued to reinforce democratic processes, build capacity, and spur commerce in more than a hundred neighborhoods across Iraq. The CSP, designed in 2005 to execute the civilian component of Clear-Hold-Build, mounted the largest effort in monetary terms.[93] By providing short-term employment and vocational training programs, as well as micro-grants and youth activities, the $544 million program harnessed underemployed populations in the wake of clearing operations—a cohort that would otherwise be vulnerable to the cash-for-violence scheme of insurgents and militias.[94]

The program operated in tandem with military campaigns in Baghdad, Kirkuk, Mosul, Falluja, Ramadi, Al Qaim, Habaniyah, Ba'quba, Basrah, and eventually nine other cities, often gaining access to neighborhood leaders and organizations through relationships established by other USAID initiatives.[95] By the end of 2007, it employed 319,583 Iraqis in short-term labor projects and provided 13,275 with vocational training for a total of 260,000 man-months of employment.[96] More than 260,000 man-months of short-term employment helped make visible community improvements, many of which were overseen by municipal governments in places just swept by violent clearing operations.[97] The role of this economic stimulus in solidifying security gains, although hard to measure, was seen by its implementers and military personnel as an essential element of the surge's success.[98]

All of these programs were carried out with little overt evidence of U.S. funding. The low-profile facilities maintained by USAID, along with the outreach it did in local neighborhoods, meant its people were rarely attacked. USAID, perhaps more than other reconstruction entities, believed that security could be achieved by muting the association with the Coalition and by gaining community trust and cooperation.

It was a sociological, rather than an exclusively physical conception of security. The office of Grand Ayatollah Sistani, for instance, issued a carefully worded *fatwa* permitting Shi'a to work with USAID implementing partners, but not the Coalition military. Sistani's office even issued identification cards to Iraqi workers hired by one of the USAID programs, giving them safe passage through militia checkpoints when collaborating with the Coalition would have meant certain death.[99]

The Security Net

USAID's compounds constituted a parallel reconstruction apparatus that in 2007 many embassy personnel did not know existed. The secrecy was in part by design to keep the Iraqis who worked there safe, but it was also because the embassy's regional security officer deemed these compounds unsafe for government personnel. According to standing Regional Security Office rules, they were off-limits to civilian officials. At a time when mentoring was essential, one of the few venues in which Western advisors and their Iraqi protégés could build solid relationships was walled off in the name of security.[100]

The security office's restrictions gave rise to a curious asymmetry. During the surge, the military, State officials in ePRTs, and USAID contractors exposed themselves to greater risk by frequently meeting with Iraqis in their communities, while other civilian personnel, under more restrictive Chief of Mission security protocols, were prevented from holding or attending such meetings.[101] If the State Department's conservative protocol for measuring danger had been strictly observed, the embassy in Baghdad itself would have closed.[102] The ePRTs were able to achieve the high degree of engagement enjoyed by USAID contractors because the military brigades they worked with assumed responsibility for their security, and the units had a higher acceptance of risk in allowing site visits.[103]

By mid-2007, the Regional Security Office sought to extend its control to vetting assistance provided to Iraqis. In the process, the office nearly smothered the PRT Quick Response Program before it began. Since their creation in 2005, PRTs had lobbied for a CERP-like fund so they could sponsor small and medium-sized projects autonomously. Eighteen months later, the embassy developed the Quick Response Fund, funded by ESF. With an initial tranche of over $100 million, the QRF program was to be the surge's signature civilian resource—the primary financial means by which PRTs could independently undertake short-term capacity-development projects in their areas.[104]

The initial procedures that governed the fund's distribution for projects larger than $25,000 entailed three stages of review.[105] After the PRT completed a seven-page grant application and a five-page summary, a technical committee at the embassy reviewed the proposal.[106] From there, proposals went to Washington, where a separate technical committee evaluated them. Once these two operational hurdles were cleared, a new requirement mandated that they be sent for review by the Regional Security Office, which had never before played an active role in vetting recipients of grant funds.[107] The QRF funds thus were initially saddled with administrative requirements that far exceeded the military's parallel CERP program, in which a brigade commander could unilaterally approve expenditures up to $200,000.

PRT members were flabbergasted when they received an email in September 2007 from a mid-level staffer in the Office of Provincial Affairs detailing these extensive vetting procedures.[108] Rather than checking potential grant recipients against a government database of terrorist suspects, as had been the original policy, the Regional Security Office requested Iraqi applicants to list their associations and life histories on a multipage form similar to that used for U.S. government security clearances.[109] In addition, the Iraqis were required to submit fingerprints and agree to have their information stored in a database. Forms could not be faxed or scanned; the security office required an original signature.[110]

Although the danger of money falling into the wrong hands was real, PRT members knew that if the new rules were followed, the fund would be unusable. Iraqis, wary of who would have access to information about their whereabouts and associations, would not consent to the security review. It would be humiliating for grant recipients, usually esteemed members of their communities, to submit fingerprints as though they were common criminals. Finally, no PRT leaders would be willing to send their personnel into the Red Zone for the sake of chauffeuring paperwork. PRT personnel began calling the program the "Quagmire Response Fund."[111]

The rules were eventually streamlined. Micro-purchases would not need prior approval, and the embassy could approve projects up to $25,000. Only those larger than $25,000 would be sent to Washington for review. Nevertheless, the dispute over procedures limited total disbursements in the program's first five months to just $3.5 million.[112] As a consequence, PRTs initially lost much of their "surge" capacity to engage provincial governments, missing opportunities for progress during early lulls in violence. As of late September 2008, 2,065 programs have been approved through QRF grants, and almost 50 percent of funds have been disbursed.[113]

Status of the Sectors

As the civilian surge developed more effective tools, reconstruction went on in each of the major sectors: electricity, oil and gas, water and sewer, security, and justice. The IRRF program had essentially ended. By the end of 2007, just under four percent of the IRRF 2 monies had yet to be obligated; only six percent was unexpended.[114] Security and justice was ultimately the largest sector of the IRRF reconstruction program, constituting 40 percent of its expenditures. Electricity was next at 23 percent, water at 11 percent, and oil and gas at 9 percent. Of the contractors responsible for the program's execution, Bechtel expended more than $1.1 billion, followed closely by FluorAMEC, Parsons, KBR, and the Washington Group International.[115]

In the new post-IRRF phase, Iraqi expenditures began to rival and then exceed U.S. funding in many areas. Provincial and ministerial budget execution, although still low in absolute terms, nevertheless pushed increasing amounts of Iraqi revenues into capital projects. On the U.S. side, reconstruction was mostly funded by CERP, ESF, and ISFF, with much of new construction occurring in the security sector and through efforts in the provinces.[116] PRDCs were increasingly active in developing ESF-funded and embassy-approved projects in the provinces.

In 2006 and 2007, funding for PRTs and PRDC projects totaled $790 million, and PRDCs managed more than 400 projects, with a cumulative value of $495 million. In addition, $217 million went to the Infrastructure Security Program, which spent $110 million constructing pipeline exclusion zones—essentially large berms and other obstacles blocking access to the major oil pipelines—designed to prevent illegal tapping and sabotage. Another $51 million was spent hardening critical sites and making improvements to the facilities used by Strategic Infrastructure Battalions, the main Iraqi force responsible for infrastructure security.[117]

But it was not an easy time. The heightened levels of violence following the Samarra bombing continued well into the first half of 2007. Reconstruction personnel faced extraordinarily trying conditions, and many lost their lives. From January 2006 until March 2007, 418 contractors working on reconstruction or for the military were killed.[118]

In some places, contractors continued their work, often at great risk, while others suspended operations altogether, leading to high overhead costs as contractors sat idle waiting for projects to resume or be re-scoped. A SIGIR audit found that for reasons of security, mismanagement, and cost overruns, the U.S. government terminated 1,262 contracts and task orders, either for default or convenience, during the course of the reconstruction program. Of the nearly $1 billion value of these contracts and task orders, the government had already paid $600 million. Although a few of these projects were near completion, the vast majority were not.[119]

Electricity

In the electricity sector, the push continued to raise generation capacity and put more megawatts on the grid, as did the efforts to stabilize and expand the distribution networks that carried power to Iraqi homes and businesses. In the transition from the IRRF-funded effort, the scope of activities pursued by the embassy broadened to include training of personnel at generation plants and at the Ministry of Electricity. On the generation side, connecting to the right fuel sources remained problematic. In 2007, 16 of the 35 gas turbines built by the United States were using diesel, crude oil, or heavy fuel instead of the natural gas they were designed for, resulting in higher maintenance costs and the loss of an estimated 2,000 MW of daily production. Improving access of these turbines to natural gas and to reliable fuel sources at generation plants nationwide was linked to ongoing work in the oil and gas sector, as well as Coalition efforts to interdict oil smuggling.[120]

Meanwhile, the Iraqi government struggled to gain control over the many substations responsible for routing power across the grid, which remained unstable and prone to insurgent attack. In June 2007, eight of the twelve major transmission lines feeding Baghdad were out of service. Coalition and Iraqi forces moved to improve security along these lines while constructing dozens more transmission lines and substations. Average daily output, however, was still 1,740 megawatts below the CPA's 6,000 megawatt goal.[121]

Oil and Gas

Increasing capacity in the oil and gas sector remained linked to progress in the electricity sector and to the overall security situation: refineries need reliable power to function, and the network of pipes was vulnerable to attack and criminal tapping. For almost all of 2007, interdiction of the northern pipelines left the southern oil terminal at Basrah as the only node for oil export.

Output hovered at just over two million barrels per day, even though the system's capacity—if free from attacks and without maintenance shutdowns—by now reached three million. Ongoing facility upgrades included installing communication links at oil terminals, repairing multiple liquid-natural-gas plants, and installing oil-metering equipment at the terminal. Sustainability and capacity-building challenges remained a high priority.[122]

Water

By mid-2007, the 1,095 water projects funded by IRRF were 90 percent complete. Although the revised targets for increasing access to potable water and sewage were largely met, cutbacks dating from the 2004 reprogrammings, which removed more than a billion dollars from the sector to fund pressing security needs, meant that the Coalition's original ambitions in the water sector would not be realized. In Baghdad, only 30 percent of homes were connected to distribution lines. Sewer service reached 40 percent in Najaf and 50 percent in Basrah, but remained essentially nonfunctional in Kirkuk, Samarra, and Falluja.[123]

The challenges that plagued the water sector nationwide could be seen in the $277 million Nassriya water delivery system. Designed to produce potable water for a half-million Iraqis in five cities, the plant suffered from a long list of problems that curbed output: the lack of a reliable power supply, a weakened pipe system unable to withstand the plant's higher pressure flow, illegal taps on the transmission lines, and poorly qualified staff unwilling to attend contractor-provided training.[124] Ambassador Crocker's personal intervention in the failing project spurred performance improvements in the months after it was found to be operating substantially below capacity. "The Nassriya water treatment plant is not going to be the largest monument to American folly in decades out here," Crocker said. His focus was on helping the Iraqis reach solutions on their own. "How can we help the Iraqis complete the Nassriya main drain?" he said. "We put so much money into sustainment. Don't let it go to waste."[125]

Security and Justice

Throughout 2007, re-training of National Police brigades—a process known as "re-bluing"—continued, as did the training and equipping of Iraq's other security forces, which now numbered more than 350,000.[126] The decline in violence was especially helpful to the court system.[127] The construction of the Rusafa rule-of-law complex, bringing together multiple parts of the justice system in one place, greatly facilitated the processing of cases in Baghdad.[128] Although coaxing judges to use modern investigative methods—including forensic evidence— and to eschew sectarian influences remained a challenge, progress in the judicial system continued.[129]

By mid-2008, 655 courts operated in Iraq. Major Crimes Courts—regional branches of the Central Criminal Court of Iraq—were being established in all 18 provinces. The 567 judges, 281 investigative judges, 312 assistants, and 645 judicial investigators working nationwide were protected by a force of more than 5,000 guards.[130] Nonetheless, just under half of all inmates in Iraqi detention were awaiting trial, contributing to overcrowding in four of the six prison facilities transferred to Iraqi control.[131]

The Surge in Late 2007

The surge brought more personnel and funds into Iraq, but more important, it redefined the terms of reconstruction. Brigades became a center of gravity in the reconstruction effort in a new way: brigade commanders and ePRTs each viewed capacity as a top priority. No longer was transition, the Casey-era watchword, the primary goal. The surprising agility with which the military embraced the economic and reconstruction missions was made possible by the wide support in its ranks for the counterinsurgency doctrine articulated and implemented by Petraeus. What was resisted in 2003 and 2004 was seen as absolutely necessary by 2007. Using brigades as "landlords" for the ePRT program yielded the intended multiplier effect on capacity building and reconstruction. Through these innovations, civil-military cooperation reached new heights.

Despite significant progress in specific places, Iraq in 2007 proved stubbornly resistant to many of the surge's political and economic innovations and to the Coalition effort overall. In July 2007, the new Prime Minister of Britain, Gordon Brown, proposed a host of policy initiatives in a letter to Iraqi Prime Minister

Nouri al-Maliki. These included "an integrated energy strategy," "banking reform," and possibly a "National Investment Commission"—ideas that had been minted by the Coalition back in 2003 and were still relevant only because they had not been fulfilled.[132] In August 2007, Minister of Finance Bayan Jabr announced that completing Iraq's reconstruction would require an additional investment of $100 billion to $150 billion—an amount equal to what had already been spent.[133] It was a sobering reminder of how the continuing violence had undone so much of the infrastructure investments made by the United States and Iraq.

Targeted killings also continued. On the first day of Ramadan, Sheikh Abd al-Sattar, leader of the Anbar awakening, was assassinated just a week after President Bush, during a September 2007 visit, personally commended his efforts at fighting al-Qaeda.[134]

By fall 2007, the surge and other political developments in Iraq, including the Sunni awakening, brought about a modest reduction in violence, with total attacks trending downward across Iraq.[135] Calmer conditions did not immediately translate into progress on reconciliation or passage of the legislative articles the Congress had hoped Iraqi leaders would tackle.[136]

The Congress wrote eighteen benchmarks into the 2007 emergency supplemental appropriations act that funded the surge; the President had to certify that the Iraqi government was making progress toward meeting the benchmarks before it could receive further support from the Economic Support Fund, absent a Presidential waiver of the requirement.[137] An initial White House assessment in July 2007 found that few of the benchmarks had been fulfilled, but that satisfactory progress was being made.[138]

A later GAO audit, released in advance of the September 15, 2007 testimony of General Petraeus and Ambassador Crocker before the Congress, found that the Iraqi government had met three, partially met four, and had not met eleven of the eighteen benchmarks.[139] Petraeus and Crocker acknowledged in their testimony that few of the benchmarks had been met, but cited continued Iraqi progress toward achieving them as reason enough for the Coalition to continue the surge.[140]

A second set of benchmarks came into play in the International Compact with Iraq, a framework negotiated in 2007 through which international donors and aid organizations, including the World Bank, United Nations, and International Monetary Fund, pledged support in return for progress in bringing Iraq's laws and economy in line with international best practices.[141] Along with the standby arrangement negotiated with the International Monetary Fund, the International Compact with Iraq was another step toward reintegrating Iraq into the regional and international economy.

Although signs of progress could be discerned, the road ahead remained long. Iraq in 2007 was rated by analysts at the World Bank in the bottom 10 percent of all countries in measures of corruption and accountability, political stability, government effectiveness, regulatory quality, and rule of law.[142] In December 2008, the International Monetary Fund agreed to cancel 80 percent of Iraq's foreign debt.[143]

The Surge and Its Aftermath in 2008

As 2008 dawned, violence continued to recede. The military effort to pacify first Baghdad and then western and north central Iraq paid off, but at great cost to U.S. and Iraqi troops. Attacks against Coalition forces during the initial phases of the surge reached their highest level since 2003. However, relative calm returned to large parts of the country, partly because of the surge, but also because of the organization of Sunni groups—and eventually Shi'a groups—into local security forces. Neighborhoods gripped by near-constant violence since the increase in attacks after Samarra returned to something like normalcy, and levels of ethno-sectarian violence fell precipitously.

During 2008, the Iraqi Army demonstrated increasing ability as it performed clearing operations in Basrah and Sadr City with limited U.S. support. Although fierce fighting persisted in parts of Ninewa, Diyala, Salah Al-Din, and Basrah provinces, overall attacks in late 2008 fell to their lowest level since 2003.[144] The improving security situation was a boon to civilian programs. In the summer of 2008, a USAID contractor estimated that with fewer cancellations of meetings and convoys, the LGP was achieving a 25 percent higher mission-accomplished rate.[145]

More than any year since the 2003 invasion, 2008 produced a gradual and persistent transition to Iraqi leadership in reconstruction and security. Establishing uniform contracting and funds-disbursal regulations by the Ministries of Planning and Finance enabled directors general across Iraq's government to execute their budgets more easily. The existence of clear rules and a national budget passed by Iraq's parliament meant that U.S. reconstruction officials increasingly worked to reinforce Iraqi priorities, rather than retrofitting U.S. projects into the Iraqi system. "You don't have to worry about getting post-hoc buy-in," said the Treasury attaché, when "things originate in the Iraqi system."[146]

In April, Ambassador Crocker testified before the Congress that "the era of U.S. major infrastructure projects is over."[147] Although some new construction continued, the effort to build capacity was in full swing; 238 Coalition employees worked in the non-security ministries, and many large sustainment programs were being carried out across the country.[148]

The global economy provided an unexpected boost to Iraq's reconstruction. Record oil prices—which peaked at over $140 per barrel during the summer of 2008—and sustained export production buoyed Iraq's coffers and continued the trend toward greater capital expenditures by its ministries and provincial governments.[149] A subsequent decline in prices, however, constrained Iraq's burgeoning reconstruction plans, forcing budgetary revisions upon the government.

Political progress was uneven in 2008. Passage of the important hydrocarbons law remained elusive, but the parliament did pass provincial powers and provincial elections laws that would lay the foundation for eventual provincial elections in January 2009.[150] Although the Iraqi government began performing at ever higher levels, the U.S. presence still remained large, with 164,000 contractors and 157,000 troops seemingly an enduring feature of the political and security landscape.[151]

Despite the continued engagement of so many soldiers and advisors, care was not always taken to ensure Iraqi input and acceptance. Officials conducting a review of PRTs—now the signature reconstruction program—were astonished to learn that Prime Minister Maliki had never been fully briefed on the program's details. The teams of U.S. advisors interacted with an entire swath of the Iraqi government without having formally sought the Prime Minister's permission.[152]

The Ultimate Impact of Reconstruction

Toward the end of 2008, there were few direct ways to take a final measure of the impact of U.S. reconstruction programs. U.S. goals went beyond putting megawatts on the grid or providing more gallons of treated water. Using reconstruction as a tool, the goal was to create a self-reliant Iraqi government and a satisfied population, and to increase trust between Iraqis and the United States and among Iraqis themselves.

Only recently have nationwide surveys measuring satisfaction rates with essential services been undertaken with any degree of consistency. The data suggest that, broadly speaking, a majority of Iraqis remain unsatisfied with the delivery of basic services, including electricity, water and sewer, and trash removal. More significantly, these satisfaction rates tend to vary by location and sectarian identity. Rates in Baghdad, for instance, are markedly lower than many other areas in the country, especially the Kurdish region. Interestingly, the rates of satisfaction with essential service delivery during the surge have been broadly similar among Sunnis and Shi'a for potable water, sewage, food, and trash, but divergent for electricity, fuel delivery and, to a lesser extent, health.[153] For electricity in particular, this is counterintuitive, because Sunni-majority provinces typically enjoyed more hours of power per day than almost all Shi'a-majority provinces during the same time period.[154] Actual differentials in service delivery thus do not alone account for the differing rates of satisfaction among sectarian communities. Historical entitlements, perceived political disenfranchisement, and expectations raised by early Coalition pledges also likely affected satisfaction rates.

Even with Iraqi levels of satisfaction trending upward and violence trending downward, the United States was still caught in a nation-building effort it had not anticipated and still did not fully understand. In 2000, future Secretary of State Condoleezza Rice articulated her belief that the U.S. military should focus primarily on combat operations. "Carrying out civil administration and police functions is simply going to degrade the American capability to do the things America has to do," she said, adding, "We don't need to have the 82nd Airborne escorting kids to kindergarten."[155] Eight years later, during the surge, the 82nd Airborne, serving its second Iraq deployment, was helping oversee the construction of greenhouses outside Tikrit.[156]

More than five years after the overthrow of Saddam Hussein, the ultimate success of the reconstruction program and the future of Iraq were still unresolved. The Joint Campaign Plan that Crocker and Petraeus promulgated was predicated on the belief that stopping openly violent clashes would allow Iraqis gradually to resolve their conflicts through elections rather than militias. Such a transformation was both elusive and extraordinarily costly—for Americans and Iraqis—in lives and national treasure.

Even as the security situation improved dramatically through the second half of 2008, potentially violent rivalries between political groups competing for power still threatened Iraq's fragile government structures. "SCIRI is fighting Sadr is fighting Fadhila," said an Iraqi whose home is in Basrah, where clashes have frequently taken place. The social effects of violence have taken their toll on family life. For most of the past four years, he said, "it is too dangerous for my kids to play outside the house. They have bicycles; they are walking on the roof. They play football inside the house." Even as violence recedes, and life regains a degree of normalcy in many provinces, the new realities of post-Saddam life bring their own complications. Before, he said, many Iraqis could remain largely ignorant of politics. "Now it's a truth for all life."[157]

ESSENTIAL SERVICES OVERVIEW – AFTER THE SURGE

Metric[158]	Pre-invasion	Post-invasion	CPA Transition	Negroponte Era	Khalilzad Era	Surge Ends
Electricity Production						
Megawatts	4,075	711	3,621	4,262	3,475	4,400
Oil Production						
Million Barrels per Day	2.58	0.30	2.16	2.13	1.95	2.43
Iraqi Security Forces						
Soldiers and Police	1,300,000	7,000-9,000	87,000	171,300	328,700	478,500
Telecommunications						
Landline Subscribers	833,000	0	791,000	998,000	1,111,000	1,200,000
Mobile Subscribers	80,000	0	461,000	2,422,000	8,720,000	~13,000,000
Human Toll						
U.S Troop Fatalities	-	139	862	1,745	3,248	4,115
Civilian Contractors	-	1	46	217	916	1,229
U.S. Civilians	-	~9	52	113	224	271
Iraqi Civilians	-	7,413	16,848	29,155	72,858	95,236
Financial Cost ($ billions)						
U.S Funding	-	$3.45	$22.93	$29.21	$36.96	$50.46
Iraqi Funding	-	$0.00	$16.00	$21.03	$37.27	$50.33
International Funding	-	$0.00	$13.60	$13.87	$15.20	$17.00
Total Funding	-	$3.45	$52.53	$64.11	$89.43	$117.79

By mid-2008, daily electricity production had edged up above prewar levels, with outputs averaging 4,400 megawatts per day. The third quarter of 2008 showed postwar highs, averaging over 4,900 megawatts per day. But Iraqi demand still far outpaced production. The electricity distribution system improved too, but equitable allocations among the provinces and major cities remained a problem.[159]

Oil production continued to rise through 2008, falling just short of prewar levels of 2.58 million barrels per day by mid-year. The July 2008 production rate reached 2.43 million barrels per day—the highest since the 2003 invasion. Because of the success of infrastructure security measures, no successful pipeline attacks occurred in 2008.[160]

PART V
LESSONS LEARNED

CHAPTER 27
HARD LESSONS

I don't think we had the right structure... We tried in Iraq to give it to a single department, the Department of Defense. That's why the President has now said that we need a civilian response corps that can do those activities. But clearly, we didn't have the right structure. *

Dr. Condoleezza Rice
Secretary of State (2005-2009)

In March 2003, the United States invaded Iraq, made short work of its armed forces, and easily toppled Saddam Hussein's government. A well-trained and properly equipped force achieved a quick and efficient military victory. But the United States was unprepared and ill-equipped to deal with what came next: a "post-conflict" environment torn by violence, looters, criminals, and a nascent insurgency; a governmental system in a state of complete collapse; and an economy that had slipped into idle and then switched off.

With no established plans to manage the increasing chaos it faced, no developed doctrine of nation building to rely on, and no existing governmental structures through which to carry out contingency relief and reconstruction operations, policymakers struggled to respond to a broken Iraq. They abandoned the hoped-for quick transfer of power to an interim Iraqi authority and entered into an occupation. Thrust into this deepening crisis, Ambassador L. Paul Bremer III and the Coalition Provisional Authority were asked to do the virtually impossible: restore order, restore governance, restore the economy, and restore basic services—quickly, with limited resources, and little capacity to act.

Focusing on the economy, Bremer improvised an infrastructure-heavy reconstruction program that became the largest foreign assistance effort undertaken by the United States since the Marshall Plan. Although a short period of shaky peace followed Saddam's fall, the rapidly growing problems in Iraq—especially in the security sector—were beyond the CPA's capacity to solve. The formal dissolution of Iraq's military and a more extensive de-Ba'athification effort than anticipated aggravated matters by sidelining two expected sources of Iraqi assistance.

The United States struggled over the next six years to develop and implement a strategy for reconstructing Iraq as a stable and democratic nation on

---

* Fox News interview with Dr. Condoleezza Rice, Secretary of State, December 7, 2008.

the path to prosperity. Deteriorating security both informed and complicated every decision. Employing a variety of tactics to address the growing violence, the United State poured money and—finally—more troops into the country, all while trying to rebuild Iraq's physical infrastructure, its security forces, and its capacity to govern. U.S. governmental agencies, military units, nongovernmental organizations, international groups, and private-sector firms engaged in the massive effort.

Through trial and error, the U.S. strategy moved away from the CPA's large infrastructure approach to a more modest, Iraqi-driven program focused on developing the fledgling government's capacity for self-rule. Along the way, the U.S. government created a series of ad hoc offices and systems as it moved from crisis to crisis. The government and the private contractors it employed adapted as they learned hard lessons from the rebuilding program, gradually becoming more effective in an exceedingly lethal environment. Notwithstanding this progress, the United States still struggled in late 2008 to make Iraq's reconstruction a success.

Each of the four periods of reconstruction chronicled in *Hard Lessons* yields unique conclusions. Taken collectively, they underscore the need for the U.S. government to reform its approach to contingency relief and reconstruction operations and to develop greater capacity to execute them.

Prewar Planning and ORHA (September 2001-April 2003)
The U.S. approach to Iraq reconstruction had its origins in the fall of 2001, when the President and the Secretary of Defense began fashioning the Iraq war plan according to a "liberation" model. From the outset, the Pentagon's leadership believed that victory would be swift and that a new interim Iraqi authority would quickly assume power. They planned on Iraq's police providing postwar security and anticipated that Iraqi oil revenues would fund most relief and reconstruction projects. When Iraq's withering post-invasion reality superseded these expectations, there was no well-defined "Plan B" as a fallback and no existing government structures or resources to support a quick response.

During prewar preparations, certain officials at the Department of State and the U.S. Agency for International Development argued that the postwar reconstruction of Iraq would be more difficult, would take more time, and would require an extraordinary commitment of financial and human resources. But even veteran development experts misjudged what would be necessary to rebuild the country's physical, security, and governmental infrastructure. "We needed to be thinking at a much different order of magnitude [about] what is required to reconstruct a failed state, in the context of a U.S. military invasion," USAID's Deputy Administrator James Kunder later said.[1]

Force size was a central issue. Planners across the government and within the military disagreed on how many troops would be necessary. Prewar analyses of post-conflict situations suggested that at least 300,000 troops—and perhaps as many as 500,000—would be required to maintain post-invasion order in a country with the size and population of Iraq. But the President and his advisors, both military and civilian, decided against deploying so large a number and chose not to prepare for large-scale reconstruction operations. Instead, the invasion plan called for deploying a light and agile force. Post-conflict efforts focused on averting humanitarian disasters like those that followed the first Gulf War. The plan assumed the best-case reconstruction scenario and the worst-case humanitarian scenario.

Historically rooted conceptions of defense, diplomacy, and development shaped the content of prewar reconstruction discussions. Military planners excluded post-conflict experts from early deliberations that determined the scope of U.S. policy. USAID Administrator Andrew Natsios, the highest-ranking Administration official with both development and combat experience, was not invited to NSC meetings until long after the war began.

The way the U.S. government is structured facilitated this exclusion. Since 1947, the Departments of Defense and State—and later USAID—have operated mostly independently of one another, even though in today's world overseas missions usually require a blending of each one's strengths, along with those of other U.S. government agencies. Integrating their various capabilities was left to the President's war cabinet and the NSC staff, where joint planning is difficult to manage and tends to be subject to the personalities of those who inhabit key posts. "Don't try to use Iraq as the model [for reform]," Secretary of State Colin Powell cautioned, "without recognizing and acknowledging that it was as much a process and personality as it was a structural problem."[2]

The government's lack of strong mechanisms to integrate the work of separate departments led the White House to delegate interagency missions to a lead agency just months before the invasion. The battle over whether the liberation model would guide Administration policy in Iraq became, in truth, a battle over which department would control reconstruction itself. In the absence of a clear precedent on how to coordinate postwar operations of this magnitude, the President decided, in late 2002, to hand operational control for planning and managing post-invasion Iraq to the Department of Defense, sidelining the only interagency system—the NSC—designed to orchestrate the government's actions in international security matters.

Secretary of Defense Donald Rumsfeld recognized that this was not a perfect solution. "The U.S. government has had to rely on quickly assembled, ad hoc efforts, such as [the Office of Reconstruction and Humanitarian Assistance], to coordinate reconstruction," he later wrote.[3] "The truth is," Secretary of State Condoleezza Rice would later say, "we really did not have, either in any department or in the U.S. government as a whole, an institution that could really deal with post-conflict stabilization."[4] "A lot of it wasn't handled very well," Rice added. "There are a lot of things, if I could go back and do them differently, I would."[5]

The Coalition Provisional Authority (May 2003-June 2004)

The liberation model—in which a rapid transfer of power to Iraqi authorities would enable U.S. troops to depart 90 days after the regime's fall—broke down almost immediately after the invasion. Neither the U.S. military nor the civilian leadership was prepared for the complete disintegration of Iraq's government and the subsequent loss of law and order. The looting and the chaos it engendered destroyed plans for a rapid transfer of power. With public institutions and critical infrastructure crippled, the mission of ORHA's successor agency—the Coalition Provisional Authority—turned from restoring essential services to rebuilding from scratch the ministries that provided them.

The CPA adopted a maximalist approach to reconstruction, developing plans to transform every aspect of Iraqi society, from the banking system to traffic laws. But the CPA—and the U.S. government agencies that supported it—demonstrated an inadequate understanding of both Iraqi culture and the complicated internal political relationships that existed among and within various Iraqi groups.

During the first weeks of its existence, the CPA issued momentous orders— de-Ba'athification and disbanding the military—with insufficient interagency debate. Although there may have been sound reasons for removing members of the Ba'ath party from senior government positions and for dissolving the army, both decisions added considerably to the difficulty of reconstruction and establishing a functioning government. Had these issues been fully discussed by the war cabinet and within the CPA, the United States might have acted differently. Instead, the U. S. rebuilding program was left to deal with the instant loss of many of the Iraqi technocrats it would later need. It also had to build entirely new Iraqi security forces, a task that would ultimately consume more than half of all U.S.-appropriated reconstruction dollars.

In 2003, the United States lacked an accepted doctrine for contingency relief and reconstruction operations that could inform how decision-makers should address the complex array of problems then at play in Iraq. There was no agreed-upon approach to Iraq's reconstruction, little understanding of the dynamics of post-conflict rebuilding, and no structure for the rapid provision of resources to the CPA. Moreover, those at the head of what quickly became the largest overseas rebuilding effort in U.S. history struggled to differentiate between the pursuit of transformational goals for their own sake and what it would take to achieve rapidly the U.S. national objective of a stable Iraq. Efforts across many sectors were poorly conceived, overambitious, and often at cross-purposes. Part of the problem was that the CPA failed to consult sufficiently with Iraqis to understand what they really wanted from the reconstruction program. Consequently, the CPA made decisions that often undercut the goals they were trying to reach.

The reform of Iraq's economy was a striking example of how the lack of an accepted doctrine undermined U.S. objective. The CPA decided, over considerable internal opposition, to discontinue support to Iraq's state-owned enterprises. Its senior economic advisor apparently did not appreciate the interdependence among factories producing chlorine, agricultural fertilizer, and cement and the impact their closing would have on Iraq's oil, electricity, water, and agricultural sectors. Rather than committing resources to their continued existence, the CPA hoped that an emergent private-sector in Iraq would generate a new manufacturing sector, employ large numbers of people, and produce the goods the country needed. But Iraq's harsh postwar reality quickly trumped economic theories that suggested a market solution was possible.

By mid-summer 2003, the CPA had settled on a strategy to spur growth by rebuilding infrastructure, focusing particularly on the electricity, oil, and water sectors. The CPA hoped that these projects, once completed, would energize the economy and supply Iraqis with needed essential services. The Administration persuaded the U.S. Congress to appropriate $18.4 billion to fund this grand vision, and the CPA created the first of what would be several ad hoc organizations to manage reconstruction—the Program Management Office. Like the organizations that came before and after, the PMO did not have the personnel and the systems to administer so large a program effectively.

Believing that conditions in Iraq demanded speed, the CPA developed its reconstruction program in great haste, missing opportunities to integrate adequately the views of Iraqis and implementing agencies—USAID, the State Department, and the military—in the process that led to the creation of the second Iraq Relief and Reconstruction Fund. Many of the program's infrastructure projects also suffered from inadequate design, weak government oversight, and a lack of planning for Iraqis to sustain them.

Growing Iraqi opposition to the prolonged transition to self-rule—complemented by the U.S. desire to disengage from a lengthening occupation—resulted in the announcement on November 15, 2003, to transfer sovereignty from the

CPA to Iraq by June 30, 2004. Reconstruction plans that had just been devised on a two-year timetable now had to shift, and the rush began to prepare Iraq's government to stand on its own in seven months. The announcement also meant that U.S. appropriations for reconstruction—slowed by the NSC's high-level review in Washington—would not arrive until the very end of the CPA's tenure. Ambassador Bremer had to fund most of the CPA's early reconstruction projects, as well as Iraqi government operations, with Iraqi funds held in trust by the UN and the United States. But the CPA failed to keep detailed accounts of how most of this money was spent. Expenditures of the roughly $20 billion in DFI money used by the CPA were initially tracked on an Excel spreadsheet—hardly a sufficient control. At its end, the CPA had barely begun to execute the grand reconstruction program it had designed.

An even more fundamental problem plagued the CPA's efforts. Its reconstruction strategy was premised on a "permissive" environment, meaning one generally free from violence; but most of Iraq was racked by violence for most of the CPA's existence. Almost immediately after the invasion, many in Iraq—from the CPA Administrator and the Commanding General of Coalition forces to Iraqis in the ministries and on the streets—recognized that security was the most compelling issue confronting the country. Lieutenant General Sanchez, the man in charge of the U.S. military in Iraq, requested more troops in May 2003. Until mid-July, though, the United States stuck to its original plan to reduce troop strength as quickly as possible. The troop withdrawal stopped only when General Abizaid replaced General Franks as CENTCOM commander.[6]

With the increase in violence, planners confronted a political and economic landscape that was evolving faster than they could adapt to or understand. All the while, the magnitude of what needed to be done was overwhelming. The absence of a well-defined doctrine or an effectively coordinated strategy caused the CPA's approach to reconstruction to have a disjointed and ad hoc quality: Get the oil flowing. Stop the smugglers. Get the electricity up and running. Clean out the sewers. Re-write the textbooks. Change the currency. Employ more Iraqis. Focus on the cities. Focus on agriculture. Focus on security.

The U.S. Embassy under Negroponte (July 2004-June 2005)
When the new U.S. Embassy in Iraq inherited the CPA's reconstruction program in July 2004, the U.S. ambassador faced two critical problems. First, the United States had to adjust the reconstruction program to address the deteriorating security conditions in Iraq. Second, more capabilities needed to be mobilized to implement the rebuilding program. The U.S. reconstruction management structure was overwhelmed by the challenges of building in a war zone. Contractors found it difficult

to carry out projects in the dangerous environment, and the lack of adequate oversight by government contracting officers, program reviewers, and other agencies permitted wasteful spending to career out of control. Safeguarding reconstruction personnel, equipment, and work sites against insurgent attacks further drove up costs. The violence also prevented managers and quality control engineers from visiting projects to check progress. The system of oversight so crucial to effective reconstruction had collapsed. The United States had to change course.

Immediately after his arrival in Iraq, Ambassador John Negroponte ordered a review of all reconstruction priorities, which led to a reprogramming of $3.46 billion, with most of the shifted funds going to the security sector. More reprogramming followed and, by September 2005, U.S. officials had shifted a total of $5.59 billion—nearly a third of reconstruction appropriations—to support security, job creation, and economic reform projects, drawing the money chiefly from the water and electricity sectors. The CPA designed its program to be executed in a secure postwar environment, but the rise of a violent insurgency forced the reconstruction effort to change course from laying the foundation for long-term economic growth to producing short-term results in support of a counterinsurgency campaign. The challenge was to achieve security gains while fostering economic and democratic development.

By the middle of 2005, the United States had completed a thousand projects using IRRF 2 funding and had another thousand underway. Hundreds of firms were active across the country, employing tens of thousands of foreign contractors and an estimated 180,000 Iraqis. The rebuilding effort, however, proved to be more expensive and time consuming than planners anticipated. Power generation and distribution continued to fall short of Coalition goals, as did oil production, chiefly because so much of Iraq's critical infrastructure was vulnerable to sabotage and in poor condition.

Project management systems remained problematic. In late 2005, the embassy still could not match projects with the contracts that funded them, nor could it estimate how much they would cost to complete. Completed projects also were failing after being turned over to Iraqis who were unable to properly maintain and operate the facilities. These failures highlighted the need to build capacity in Iraqi institutions so the country could manage the new infrastructure the United States was providing.

The U.S. Embassy under Khalilzad and Crocker (June 2005-2008)

U.S. reconstruction strategy continued to evolve during the tenure of Ambassador Zalmay Khalilzad, who arrived in Baghdad in June 2005. A new approach for counterinsurgency operations, called Clear-Hold-Build, further integrated military and civilian efforts. Khalilzad deployed Provincial Reconstruction Teams across Iraq, adapting a concept that he developed during his tenure as ambassador to Afghanistan. The PRTs, together with Provincial Reconstruction Development Councils, helped Iraq's provincial governments improve their working relationships with Iraq's central government and strengthened the coordination of Iraqi and Coalition resources.

From Khalilzad forward, the reconstruction effort moved quickly away from the large infrastructure approach and toward more modest projects designed to deliver jobs and services to the most vulnerable, violent, and strategically consequential Iraqi cities and towns, and to do this, as much as possible, through provincial, municipal, and local institutions. By going through official Iraqi institutions instead of around them, U.S. reconstruction expenditures directly served the goal of building a functioning Iraqi state.

As the U.S. ability to deliver reconstruction resources improved, the amount of money it had left to spend diminished. Meanwhile, Iraq fell further into chaos. As many as 300 companies provided security services to the U.S. reconstruction effort, increasing costs on some large reconstruction contracts by 24 to 53 percent.[7]

The Samarra bombing in February 2006 exacerbated sectarian tensions, overlaying the insurgency with civil conflict among Iraq's sects. The resulting political fragmentation complicated efforts to build capacity in ministries held captive by political parties with sectarian or regional agendas. As the nature of the violence evolved from a traditional insurgency to a sectarian struggle, economic incentives proved less and less effective and military force became more necessary.

The 2007 surge of troops and the complementary civilian effort—driven by a revised counterinsurgency strategy formulated by General David Petraeus and Ambassador Ryan Crocker—ushered in a new era. As the major program of U.S. infrastructure rebuilding began drawing to a close, emphasis moved to building capacity inside Iraqi institutions and using direct contracts with Iraqi firms to help the country's economy recover.

As the surge of troops and civilian resources peaked, the U.S. investment in Iraq's security forces also began to pay dividends. In 2005, the Congress had authorized the Iraq Security Forces Fund, a major new appropriation that eventually matched the IRRF in size. During the following three years, the ISFF channeled more than $18 billion into training and equipping Iraq's police and soldiers, building the facilities they used, and developing the Ministries of Defense and Interior. The increase in the size, reliability, and readiness of Iraqi forces contributed to a significant reduction in violence that began in the summer of 2007 and was sustained through 2008.

The surge's hard-won security gains led to a more secure reconstruction environment. With the accumulation of oil revenues in Iraqi capital budgets, the Government of Iraq now had in its coffers the resources necessary to pursue its own relief and reconstruction program. Helping Iraq execute this new budget emerged as a key objective. By the end of 2008, the reconstruction program was many orders of magnitude more Iraqi-driven and Iraqi-funded than when it had begun in 2003.

Over nearly six years, the U.S. program had undergone an extraordinary evolution. What was originally conceived as a modest program to repair war damage and treat refugees had ballooned into an expansive and expensive nation-building effort. This in turn was supplanted by a counterinsurgency campaign and then a countrywide initiative to build Iraqi capacity. Constant re-evaluations of how U.S. resources could be employed to achieve the desired result of a stable Iraq led to a shift from large infrastructure reconstruction to a program that combined "soft" and "hard" projects aimed at mitigating security problems and building capacity.

Of the many lessons to be drawn from Iraq reconstruction, the most compelling speak to the need to develop an agreed-upon doctrine and structure for contingency relief and reconstruction operations to guide the use of military and economic power so that the United States is ready when it next must intervene in a failed or failing state. The Iraq reconstruction experience chronicled in this report, in hundreds of audits and inspections, and in three previous Lessons Learned reports led SIGIR to identify these most significant hard lessons:[8]

First Principles for Contingency Relief and Reconstruction Operations

- **Security is necessary for large-scale reconstruction to succeed.** A successful reconstruction program requires a balancing of security, political, and economic interests. Reconstruction cannot proceed on a large scale without the requisite security to protect those carrying out the projects and those overseeing them. In Iraq, the scope of reconstruction was too often unmatched by available security resources. To this day, Iraq's reconstruction environment has never been truly "post-conflict." Endlessly rebuilding in the wake of sustained attacks on reconstruction personnel and critical infrastructure proved to be a demoralizing and wasteful proposition. To guide decisions on funding projects facing security threats, the U.S. government should analyze whether and at what costs those security risks can be mitigated. Projects should only proceed when senior leaders determine that the strategic objective they fulfill outweighs the risk of failure and the costs of mitigating security risks.

- **Developing the capacity of people and systems is as important as bricks and mortar reconstruction.** The CPA's reconstruction program focused chiefly on large infrastructure projects aimed at improving service delivery. Little of its money was set aside to boost government capacity. The failure to pursue capacity-building efforts alongside infrastructure construction led to a crisis in sustainability that continues to this day. The deterioration of poorly maintained infrastructure projects after transfer to Iraqi control could end up constituting the largest source of waste in the U.S. reconstruction program. A robust capacity-development program implemented from the outset of the reconstruction effort could have helped obviate this circumstance. Such a program should be an essential component of future contingency relief and reconstruction operations.

- **Soft programs serve as an important complement to military operations in insecure environments.** An emerging lesson from Iraq is that when violence is pervasive, soft programs—like those orchestrated by USAID and Provincial Reconstruction Teams—are especially important in advancing U.S. goals. Operating through Iraqi intermediaries reduced the exposure of reconstruction personnel to violent attack and helped deliver economic stimuli to local communities even when Coalition military forces were engaged in clearing operations. The apparent success of these programs, although often hard to quantify, highlights the extent to which social capital matters. Working through indigenous networks seems to increase community acceptance and provide a higher and more lasting degree of local security than military or private-security protection alone could achieve. Especially because many such programs operate out of view of most U.S. personnel, the selection of metrics and careful monitoring of expenditures are critical to ensuring value for the U.S. taxpayer.

- **Programs should be geared to indigenous priorities and needs.** Host country buy-in is essential to reconstruction's long-term success. Much of the early and some later efforts in Iraq focused on large projects that were meant to benefit Iraqis directly. Other projects devised new and more efficient systems for conducting business inside the Iraqi government. In many cases, there was a lack of sufficient Iraqi participation in deciding how or what to reconstruct and ensuring that projects could be maintained afterwards. Detailed joint planning with Iraqi officials—perhaps the most important prerequisite for success after security—only gradually improved over time.

- **Reconstruction is an extension of political strategy.** The reconstruction experience in Iraq revealed deficiencies in how the U.S. government understands the dynamics of societies it seeks to influence through military and non-military means. War, politics, and reconstruction are linked in ways that individuals within the government failed to appreciate in the opening years of the Iraq conflict. If war, as Clausewitz said, is an extension of politics by other means, so too is relief and reconstruction an extension of political, economic, and military strategy. In this regard, there is a distinct difference between pursuing reconstruction to catalyze long-term economic growth and deploying reconstruction to support a counterinsurgency campaign.

Organizing the Interagency System for Contingency
Relief and Reconstruction Operations

- **Executive authority below the President is necessary to ensure the effectiveness of contingency relief and reconstruction operations.** The role of executive authority—and the lack thereof—over interagency coordination lies at the heart of the failures in the Iraq reconstruction program. The question of who was in charge, both in Washington and in Baghdad, was fiercely contested throughout the reconstruction effort. Was the CPA Administrator the President's envoy or an employee of the Secretary of Defense? Was the ambassador to Iraq the President's personal representative, with authority over all U.S. personnel and resources, or merely the chief State Department official? Do personnel on detail report through their agency chain of command or to the heads of embassy sections? To what extent can the "lines-of-operation" coordinators designated by the ambassador and the commanding general task agencies under their purview for support? The lack of unity of command in Iraq meant that unity of effort was seldom achieved. Too often, programs were designed to meet agency goals, rather than U.S. national interests. Stronger integration was needed not only between the military and civilian agencies but also among the civilian agencies themselves. With weak interagency cooperation an endemic feature of the U.S. national security system, reform efforts should press for structures that will promote the development of a unifying strategy with clearly delineated agency responsibilities and adequate authority to enforce its execution.

- **Uninterrupted oversight is essential to ensuring taxpayer value in contingency operations.** In the absence of effective management by government officials, contractors in Iraq were often left in dangerous circumstances to carry out insufficiently defined contracts written by inexperienced contracting officers who lacked situational awareness. In this chaotic environment, it was, at times, difficult to differentiate between reliable contractors who could carry out good work and those whose ad hoc operations and lack of experience pointed to failure. As a result, contractors fell into two clusters. Most companies responsibly complied with the requirements of their contracts, even if the U.S. administrative apparatus did not make the best use of their capabilities. A relative few took advantage of the situation by committing fraud. In this context, uninterrupted oversight by inspectors general and the Congress—accompanied by adequately staffed quality-control and quality-assurance programs—is essential to ensuring the efficient and effective use of taxpayer dollars.

- **An integrated management structure is necessary to ensure effective interagency reconstruction efforts.** After the reconstruction program got underway in 2003, at least 62 offices and agencies ultimately became involved in managing IRRF-funded projects.[9] There were no interagency project management and information systems that could coordinate the activities of the hundreds of firms and subcontractors performing construction work orders at thousands of sites across Iraq. An integrated management structure—coupled with an interoperable information system—could have helped to ensure that programs and projects were planned and executed with effective communication, control, and cooperation.

- **Outsourcing management to contractors should be limited because it complicates lines of authority in contingency reconstruction operations.** By law, contractors report solely to the government contracting officers or the designated representatives of the agency that awarded the contract. In Iraq, authority for reconstruction plans and policy was given to the IRMO, under control of the ambassador. At the same time, contracting officers operating out of the PCO were under Defense

Department supervision and thus only nominally under the authority of the ambassador. The proliferation of contractors serving as managers and advisors in each of the offices raised questions regarding what constituted inherently governmental activity, and the extent to which oversight authority can be delegated to a contractor.

Contracting Mechanisms and Human Resources
in Contingency Relief and Reconstruction Operations

- **The U.S. government should develop new wartime contracting rules that allow for greater flexibility**. The United States needs contracting reform that enables U.S. dollars to be more effectively used in contingency relief and reconstruction operations. A "Contingency FAR" should be developed by the Congress and the executive branch. The Federal Acquisition Regulation's complicated contracting regulations, which can be modified by agency rules, should be knitted into a single set of simplified, uniform rules for conflict environments that all contracting agencies would have to use. A much larger corps of well-trained and experienced contracting officers must also be developed and then maintained for deployment during all phases of contingency operations, including planning. Similarly, a diverse pool of contractors with expertise in post-conflict reconstruction should be pre-competed and pre-qualified to be available when a contingency operation begins.

- **The U.S. government needs a new human-resources management system capable of meeting the demands of a large-scale contingency relief and reconstruction operation.** Supplying adequate numbers of personnel with the requisite expertise emerged as a critical bottleneck early in the reconstruction effort. Employing experts to work temporarily in Iraq often entailed long delays before their deployment, and many of those who finally arrived stayed for only three to six months. Although personnel recruitment improved somewhat as the reconstruction enterprise matured, at no time were there sufficient numbers of experienced advisors to meet Iraq's critical capacity-building needs. Washington was unable to draw effectively on the extraordinary talent available in America to form a cadre of workers that combined private-sector expertise with academic knowledge and bureaucratic skill. Further, the failure to provide unambiguous authority to the Chief of Mission in NSPD 36 and the reluctance of the several chiefs of mission to exercise that authority made the effective cross-jurisdictional management of personnel almost impossible. A uniform set of human resource rules that would apply to all federal personnel deployed for contingency operations is needed, as are stronger recruiting mechanisms and a large stable of ready-to-deploy personnel.

- **The U.S. government must strengthen its capacity to manage the contractors that carry out reconstruction work in contingency relief and reconstruction operations.** Once Baghdad fell and the looting began, the scope of reconstruction quickly overwhelmed the U.S. government's standing capacity to respond. The post-Cold War downsizing of USAID and military construction capacities increased reliance on the private sector. Neither the NSC, the CPA, nor the Pentagon could mobilize contractors fast enough as they struggled to comply with complex FAR regulations while awarding large cost-plus contracts. Nor were they able to provide the degree of government oversight that was necessary. The decision to reduce the number of warranted contracting officers during the ten years preceding the Iraq invasion proved particularly consequential.[10] It became clear that the U.S. and international contractors hired by the CPA were not ready to quickly mount a large-scale reconstruction operation in a dangerous security environment.

- **Diplomatic, development, and area expertise must be expanded to ensure a sufficient supply of qualified civilian personnel in contingency reconstruction operations.** Despite the crucial need for diplomatic skills and development expertise in contingency relief and reconstruction operations, as well as for area experts fluent in local culture and politics, the civilian agencies that provide them proved unable to staff the number of positions needed in Iraq. The Iraq reconstruction experience illustrates the extent to which civilian agencies do not have the capacity to project power abroad. Cuts at USAID have halved the number of permanent government employees at that agency, severely attenuating its technical competence and managerial facility.[11] To remedy this weakness, Secretary of Defense Robert Gates has called for a "dramatic increase in spending on the civilian instruments of national security."[12] The Congress and the President should consider a long-term strategy for building technical and area expertise in the government's civilian diplomatic and development agencies and creating mechanisms for deploying such capabilities abroad in times of crisis and peace.

• • •

The following Afterword suggests ways the hard lessons of Iraq reconstruction can be addressed further, focusing on the Reconstruction and Stabilization Civilian Management Act of 2008, which the Congress recently passed to enhance the ability of the United States to carry out contingency relief and reconstruction operations abroad.

REFORMING CONTINGENCY RELIEF AND RECONSTRUCTION OPERATIONS

> *History will judge the war against Iraq not by the brilliance of its military execution, but by the effectiveness of the post-hostilities activities.* *

Lieutenant General Jay Garner
Director of ORHA (2003)

Since the Marshall Plan transformed Europe after World War II, the United States has undertaken large and small contingency relief and reconstruction operations in countries from Bosnia and Haiti to Sri Lanka and Somalia. Every President since Harry Truman has faced at least one contingency requiring the deployment of civilian and military resources abroad. Even so, the government as a whole has never developed a legislatively sanctioned doctrine or framework for planning, preparing, and executing contingency operations in which diplomacy, development, and military action all figure.

On October 14, 2008, the President signed into law "The Reconstruction and Stabilization Civilian Management Act of 2008" (RSCMA), as part of the Duncan Hunter National Defense Authorization Act for 2009. It is the most significant congressional legislation ever passed regarding the structure of and planning for contingency relief and reconstruction operations.[1]

RSCMA addresses a number of recommendations for contingency operations reform that SIGIR put forward in its three previous lessons learned reports.[2] Most notably, the Act creates a structure to address planning, personnel, and program management needs. The Act places responsibility for preparing the civilian side of contingency relief and reconstruction operations within the Department of State and directs the Secretary of State—in consultation with the Administrator of USAID—to develop an interagency strategy for executing reconstruction and stabilization operations.[3]

RSCMA provides for a presidentially appointed, Senate-confirmed Coordinator for Reconstruction and Stabilization, whose significant duties and responsibilities include:

- coordinating the development of interagency contingency plans and procedures to mobilize and deploy civilian personnel

---

* ORHA, "A Unified Mission Plan for Post-Hostilities Iraq," April 2003.

and conduct reconstruction and stabilization operations for various types of crises

• identifying personnel in state and local governments and in the private sector who are available to participate in the Civilian Reserve Corps or otherwise participate in reconstruction and stabilization activities

• taking steps to ensure that training and education of civilian personnel to perform reconstruction and stabilization activities are adequate and are carried out, as appropriate, with other agencies involved with stabilization operations

• planning, in conjunction with USAID, to address requirements, such as demobilization, disarmament, rebuilding of civil society, policing, human rights monitoring, and public information, that commonly arise in reconstruction and stabilization crises

• maintaining the capacity to field on short notice an evaluation team consisting of personnel from all relevant agencies to undertake on-site needs assessments[4]

The Act further states that the Secretary of State, in consultation with the USAID Administrator, may create a Response Readiness Corps and a Civilian Reserve Corps. The Response Readiness Corps, if formed, "shall be composed of active and standby components consisting of United States Government personnel, including employees of the Department of State, the United States Agency for International Development, and other agencies." The Civilian Reserve Corps, if formed, shall employ and train "individuals who have the skills necessary for carrying out reconstruction and stabilization activities, and who have volunteered for that purpose."[5]

A Giant First Step

The new architecture created by RSCMA establishes in U.S. law reforms that the President set in motion when he signed NSPD 44, which assigned the State Department the lead in managing government-wide civilian preparation for contingency operations.[6] The duties that must now be carried out by the State Department's Coordinator for Reconstruction and Stabilization (S/CRS) are monumental. The coordinator's office must monitor activities worldwide, prepare contingency plans, coordinate the development of relief and reconstruction strategy across the government, and perform human-resources functions (recruitment, training, equipping) on a grand scale. But without adequate funding and a large staff, S/CRS will not be able to accomplish all these tasks. Three things are necessary to fulfill the Act's purpose.

First, the Congress must provide appropriations suitable to meet the RSCMA mandate. Some of the necessary funding may come from the President's Fiscal Year 2009 Budget Request to the Congress, which included $249 million for a Civilian Stabilization Initiative that would vastly improve the civilian partnership with United States Armed Forces in post-conflict stabilization situations.[7] But the new Congress should address the funding mandates contained in RSCMA with all due speed.

Second, more must be done to ensure that the interagency coordination and integration required by RSCMA actually occurs. The State Department's S/CRS office was initially created in June 2004 to lead civilian planning for contingency operations, but it has been hamstrung both by weak budgets and a lack of authority. Only in late 2008, more than four years after its creation, were the office's proposals for government-wide reform beginning to gain any traction.[8] Even though the Congress has now written the roles of S/CRS fully into law, its ability to foster change across the government remains unproven, and many of the same structural obstacles remain. Contingency relief and reconstruction operations are not inherently the function of any single department, and the concept has no single constituency in the Congress, whose oversight committees are organized along departmental lines.[9]

The Department of Defense, usually the largest player in contingency relief and reconstruction operations, has pursued its own course toward enhancing its capacities for such operations. DoD Directive 3000.05, issued in November 2005, provided that "stability operations are a core U.S. military mission" that "shall be given priority comparable to combat operations and be explicitly addressed and integrated across all DoD activities." The directive assigns the military departments responsibility to conduct contingency relief and reconstruction operations if civilian agencies cannot.[10] In response to this directive, USACE has strengthened its engineering support to combatant commands and enhanced its own capacity to deploy divisions specializing in post-conflict reconstruction.[11] In addition, the Army has made stability operations a central part of its doctrine.[12] However, progress toward meeting the goals of directive 3000.05 has been uneven, as noted by many reports, including the Gansler Commission on Contracting.[13]

Third, the Administration should work to revise and integrate the civilian and military components of contingency relief and reconstruction operations. The President and the relevant cabinet secretaries should ensure that all agencies—especially Defense and State—better integrate the structure and resources for contingency relief and reconstruction operations. The Iraq reconstruction experience was characterized by a continuing and disabling lack of coordination among the government agencies, contractors, and other organizations involved. As much as any other factor, this lack of coordination—arising from weak integration—kept the U.S. program from achieving its objectives. Only by strengthening agency integration and preparation can the United States move toward the "jointness" necessary for successful contingency operations.

Unity of Command and Unity of Effort

The Iraq reconstruction experience makes clear that contingency relief and reconstruction operations are inherently complicated, and that they require coordinated and cross-jurisdictional structures, planning, resources, and management. This broaches a difficult conundrum—finding a way to achieve unity of command in a multi-agency operation. The military has the security role; State has the diplomatic mission; USAID provides humanitarian relief and development expertise; and other agencies have specific missions. Although roles may adjust as conditions change, agency personnel always report to their department heads in Washington. This chain of command, as it currently stands, will inevitably exert a countervailing force on interagency coordination.

As General Petraeus said:

> State is never going to put an ambassador under a general, and DoD is never going to put a general under an ambassador. So you have to resolve to work together. You have to make way and pull together and be joined at the hip. You have to have unity of purpose is the bottom line.[14]

When unity of command is missing and unity of purpose does not foster unity of effort, a solution can only be implemented at the top. Interagency working groups operating at several levels across the government can and do make decisions that affect many departments and agencies. But under the current system, only the President has the decisive authority necessary to require interagency coordination for contingency relief and reconstruction operations.

The Iraq endeavor fell short on many occasions because the absence of unity of command prevented unity of effort. Too often, agencies and offices worked in their respective stovepipes without ensuring that their activities fully supported U.S. goals and objectives and avoided duplicating other agencies' efforts. The NSC apparently was powerless to break many of the logjams that occurred.

The Project on National Security Reform, under the auspices of the Center for the Study of the Presidency, recently issued a report that noted: "Presidential intervention to compensate for the systematic inability to integrate or resource missions well centralizes issue management and burdens in the White House." The fact that "integration across disciplines is left to the President" has serious consequences; the government often cannot coordinate its own actions in a contingency environment.[15] A new integrated interagency management system for contingency relief and reconstruction operations is necessary to ensure their future success.

As the Iraq reconstruction experience demonstrates, the U.S. government was neither prepared for nor able to respond to the ever-changing demands of the contingency relief and reconstruction mission it faced in Iraq. Reform of U.S. policy for contingency operations—embodied in RSCMA—is a prerequisite for future success. As Secretary of Defense Robert Gates observed, "In recent years the lines separating war, peace, diplomacy, and development have become more blurred, and no longer fit the neat organizational charts of the 20th century."[16] The inevitability of future contingency relief and reconstruction operations after or during conflict, disaster, or political chaos demands that the U.S. government develop new ways of preparing for and managing the projection of civil-military power.

The President and the Congress should take further steps toward achieving this goal. Time and resources must be devoted to assembling a sound doctrine for contingency relief and reconstruction operations and for developing the capabilities throughout the government to carry them out. Great effort, reflection, and imagination could put the Iraq reconstruction experience to good use, yielding new structures, resources, and approaches that apply and build on the hard lessons learned in Iraq.

ANNEXES

Annex A
The Genesis and Methodology of *Hard Lessons*

Genesis of the Project

The Special Inspector General for Iraq Reconstruction (SIGIR) is the successor to the Coalition Provisional Authority Inspector General (CPA-IG), which was created by the Congress in November 2003. The Congress created SIGIR in October 2004 by amendment to Public Law 108-106. The agency's mandate, expanded several times by the Congress, is the oversight of the use of reconstruction funds for Iraq, most notably the two Iraq Relief and Reconstruction Funds (IRRF 1 and 2) and the Iraq Security Forces Fund, the Commander's Emergency Response Program, and the Economic Support Fund. To carry out this mandate, SIGIR conducts audits, inspections, reviews, and investigations.[1]

SIGIR's work is embodied in quarterly reports to the Congress, audit reports, project assessment reports, congressional testimony given by the Special Inspector General, and the SIGIR Lessons Learned Initiative. SIGIR's lessons learned reports capture and apply the lessons learned from the Iraq reconstruction experience, comporting with SIGIR's congressional mandate to provide advice and recommendations that "promote economy, efficiency, and effectiveness in the administration of [reconstruction] programs and operations" in Iraq.[2]

The SIGIR lessons learned initiative began with "Lessons Learned in Human Capital Management" (released in February 2006), the development of which included a day-long forum at Johns Hopkins University on September 20, 2005, where more than 30 experts, many of whom served in Iraq, discussed issues of human capital policy, recruitment, retention, and continuity of staff, among other issues that related to personnel in Iraq reconstruction programs. Similar sessions were part of SIGIR's two subsequent lessons learned reports: Contracting and Procurement (released in July 2006) and Program and Project Management (released in March 2007).[3] Shortly after the second report's release, SIGIR began work on a more-comprehensive narrative of the reconstruction effort, focusing on the major events that shaped its course and the central themes that emerged from the program, aiming to produce a cumulative report on lessons learned from Iraq reconstruction.

Hard Lessons is that report, capping SIGIR's Lessons Learned Initiative. It seeks to answer the following questions:

- How—and how well—did the U.S. government meet its mission to restore Iraq's infrastructure and economy, rebuild the country's military, foster civil society, and establish democratic institutions?

- What lessons have been learned that can guide the United States in making future contingency relief and reconstruction operations more coordinated, efficient and thus successful?

Methodology

The *Hard Lessons* team drew on SIGIR's audits, investigations, inspections, and other reports to root the book's findings in the broader context of the U.S. mission in Iraq. Its members used government archives, including the unclassified documentary record from ORHA, the CPA, and the U.S. Embassy Baghdad, as well as those records in the Departments of Defense and State, USAID, and the White House that relate to Iraq reconstruction. Further documentary resources included USAID contractor reports and data from the Project Contracting Office and the U.S. Army Corps of Engineers Gulf Region Division.

It should be noted that this report is not an audit product. Its methodology differs from the standards set for audit reports, which use generally accepted government auditing norms, issued by the Comptroller General of the United States—the head of the U.S. Government Accountability Office. SIGIR's historical account of reconstruction is also drawn from a wider range of source material, including books, articles, and reports by scholars, think tanks, and individuals who were participants in the effort.

This documentary evidence, however useful, can tell only part of the story of Iraq's reconstruction. The account was greatly strengthened by hundreds of interviews conducted by SIGIR staff and the Special Inspector General. These provided a great deal of information on when key decisions were made, why they were made, and what their consequences were. Efforts were made to interview key Iraqi officials, as well as American and Coalition participants. The writers made every attempt to balance the statements of individual interviewees with other sources, so that conclusions were not based solely on the memory or opinion of one person.

Research was conducted mainly in SIGIR's offices in Arlington, Virginia, but also included several staff trips to Iraq between 2006 and 2008. These trips yielded many interviews with U.S. and Coalition personnel, contractors, Iraqi government officials, and Iraqi private citizens.

The Special Inspector General interviewed key civilian and military leadership, including virtually all of the high-ranking officials from the Departments of

State and Defense, the U.S. Agency for International Development, and the U.S. Army Corps of Engineers involved in Iraq reconstruction. Among these were the current and former commanding generals of Multi-National Force-Iraq and the current and former U.S. ambassadors to Iraq.

While in Iraq, team members observed reconstruction first-hand as they visited military civil affairs units, the Army Corps of Engineers, military brigades, NGOs, and contractors working on behalf of the U.S. mission. Team members, along with staff from SIGIR's audits, inspections, and investigations directorates, conducted site visits at major reconstruction institutions and projects in cities across Iraq.

In addition, SIGIR researchers consulted scholars who are conducting similar projects. Dr. Gordon Rudd, the ORHA/CPA historian, graciously agreed to provide access to his many interviews of key officials. The United States Institute of Peace, the Center for Strategic and International Studies, and the Center for Army Lessons Learned also provided interview transcripts and other documentation.

The report's major conclusions were presented to and discussed by a diverse group of experts on April 30, 2008, at a peer roundtable hosted by the Center for Strategic and International Studies. Participants included experts on Iraq and reconstruction from academia, major Washington think tanks, nonprofit organizations, and U.S. government agencies. Representatives attended from the Departments of State and Defense, USAID, the U.S. Institute of Peace, the U.S. Army Corps of Engineers, the Government Accountability Office, the Army's Peacekeeping and Stability Operations Institute, and the National Defense University.

The project was also ably served by the ongoing advice of outside reviewers. Several editorial advisors—all experts in the field of post-conflict operations—commented on drafts at various points in the project and met four times in 2007 and 2008 to review chapter drafts and provide advice on the project's direction. This project also had the benefit of insights from individuals both inside and outside of government who made helpful comments on early drafts. In addition, officials from SIGIR's audits, investigations, and inspections divisions provided the writing team with invaluable help at various stages of the drafting process.

Lastly, SIGIR asked stakeholder agencies to vet a final draft. Copies were sent to the Departments of State and Defense, USAID, and the U.S. Army Corps of Engineers. While this occurred formally near the end of the editing process, all of these agencies were involved in the project at various times along the way. Their staffs provided helpful technical and analytical observations that were subsequently integrated into the text.

Annex B
Oversight of Reconstruction
Programs and Expenditures

Since 2003, the U.S. Congress has appropriated more than $50 billion for the support of relief and reconstruction efforts in Iraq, including the restoration of the country's oil and electricity sectors, the establishment of new security forces, and the strengthening of Iraq's capacity to govern itself.[1] A number of federal agencies—including SIGIR, the U.S. Army Audit Agency, the Inspectors General of the Departments of Defense, State, and USAID, and the Government Accountability Office—have conducted oversight of and reporting on the expenditure of funds for Iraq relief and reconstruction activities.[2]

This extensive body of work is available in studies, reports, audits, inspections, and congressional testimony covering issues that arose during the expenditure of U.S. government funds for or in Iraq. They range from the meticulous analysis of specific projects to broad overviews of entire programs and sectors. Most included recommendations for improving the management of reconstruction efforts now and in the future.

In 2008, the Congress established the independent, bipartisan Commission on Wartime Contracting to study U.S. wartime contracting in Iraq and Afghanistan. Its mandate is to study, assess, and make recommendations concerning contracting for "the reconstruction, logistical support, and performance of security functions" in both theaters from 2003 to the time of the commission's final report in 2010. Its objectives include assessing "the systemic problems identified with interagency wartime contracting," identifying instances of waste, fraud, and abuse and "ensuring accountability for those responsible.[3]

The tension inherent in maintaining financial accountability while achieving foreign policy objectives has long had a place in the history of nations. In an iconic letter, the Duke of Wellington asked the British Foreign Office in 1812 if he was to "train an army of uniformed clerks in Spain for the benefit of the accountants ... in London or, perchance, to see to it that the forces of Napoleon are driven out of Spain." He had, he said, accounted for every farthing, "with two regrettable exceptions." One, he claimed, was a "hideous confusion as to the number of jars of raspberry jam issued to a cavalry regiment during a sandstorm in Western Spain," and the other a shilling-and-nine-pence unaccounted for in a battalion's petty cash. "This reprehensible carelessness," Wellington wrote, "may be related to a pressure of circumstance, since we are at war with France, a fact which may come as a bit of surprise to you gentlemen in Whitehall."[4]

Those overseeing and reporting on the expenditure of billions of U.S. dollars appropriated for the reconstruction of Iraq had to face many of the same challenges faced by the reconstruction managers themselves, particularly in providing an adequate number of personnel to accomplish oversight work. Given the vicissitudes of the reconstruction effort—which was dogged from the start by persistent violence, shifting goals, constantly changing contracting practices, and undermined by a lack of unity of effort—a complete accounting of all reconstruction expenditures is impossible to achieve.

Oversight of the Iraq reconstruction program began slowly. No oversight plan accompanied either Lieutenant General Garner or Ambassador Bremer as they went to Baghdad to head the Office of Reconstruction and Humanitarian Assistance and the Coalition Provisional Authority, in April and May of 2003. During the run-up to war and the initial months following the invasion, oversight did not exist, with the notable exception of limited efforts by the USAID OIG. USAID included an IG as part of the Iraq Task Force set up within the agency during the planning phase in advance of combat operations.

USAID OIG staff went into Iraq ahead of other federal oversight agencies, establishing a Baghdad office in the early summer of 2003. At first, the office was staffed by assignments on a three-month temporary duty (TDY) rotation basis until July 2004; at that point, it became permanent and tour length became more regular.[5]

During its short duration, ORHA had no IG dedicated to provide oversight of its reconstruction programs. For the CPA, Ambassador Bremer, in June of 2003, appointed an interim IG—a single official on loan from the DoD OIG—but he had no staff and the IG had very little effect. An Iraq-specific oversight presence, with a clear mandate, was not created until passage of the law that funded the second tranche to the Iraq Relief and Reconstruction Fund in November 2003—the CPA-IG, which later became SIGIR.[6]

The Federal Oversight Agencies in Iraq

USAID

Until the March 2004 arrival in Baghdad of CPA-IG's first auditors, inspectors, and investigators, the USAID OIG was the only IG to house a fully staffed in-country office in Baghdad. The USAID OIG had institutional experience in conducting oversight abroad. Since 2008, the office has conducted audits of the contracts comprising most of the USAID-based effort in Iraq. The USAID OIG released its first Iraq audit in March 2004, followed by audits of the first ten Iraq reconstruction contracts issued by the agency. Although the audits identified some minor irregularities, they found no substantial problems and lauded USAID staff for their performance under the trying circumstances in which contracts were awarded and executed. As of the end of 2008, the office had released a total of 28 Iraq audits reporting on both "hard" and "soft" infrastructure programs.[7]

Government Accountability Office

The Government Accountability Office (GAO) is charged with enabling the Congress to meets its constitutional responsibility to ensure that federally programmed funding is expended properly for its legislated purpose and used for the benefit of the American people. By 2008, GAO's responsibilities in Iraq had substantially increased since the planning stages of the Iraq war. Since January 2002, GAO has produced more than 160 testimonies and reports on the Iraq war. More than 100 of these reports specifically targeted reconstruction issues. The agency's remaining reports on Iraq focused heavily on military or veterans' affairs.[8]

Department of State Office of the Inspector General

DoS OIG conducted five Iraq reconstruction-related reviews in 2004; three of them addressed routine aspects of embassy operations. In 2005, DoS OIG issued fourteen Iraq-related reports on topics ranging from a review of the U.S. Embassy in Baghdad to Iraqi police training. Seven reports were released in 2006, five of which dealt with indirect cost rates (such as the costs of operating and maintaining facilities and equipment and administrative salaries). The other two focused on Department of State contracting procedures. In 2007, the office released three Iraq reports, examining the Iraqi Police contract with the Bureau of International Narcotics and Law Enforcement (a joint audit with SIGIR), the delivery of security services by DynCorp International, and projects conducted by the National Endowment for Democracy. By the end of 2008, the DoS OIG had issued 33 Iraq audits.[9]

Department of Defense Office of the Inspector General

The DoD OIG role in oversight of Iraq reconstruction, governance, and security efforts included supporting other DoD audit and investigative organizations. DoD OIG did the first auditing on Iraq contracting.[10] Between 2004 and the end of 2008, DoD OIG produced 46 audits relating to Iraq reconstruction, and many others related to military operations in Iraq.[11] In July 2008, a DoD OIG report on recommendations made by the panoply of audit agencies regarding oversight in Iraq identified the "most prevalent" systemic management and performance challenges. These included: contract management and resource limitations; asset accountability; and financial management, including accuracy of cost reporting and accountability.[12]

U. S. Army Audit Agency

Between May 2004 and the end of 2008, USAAA—which effectively serves as the internal auditor for the Secretary of the Army— released 61 Iraq reports or audits. The major focus of the agency's oversight efforts has been various aspects of the Logistics Civil Augmentation Program (LOGCAP), which was the contracting mechanism for approximately half the Army's Iraq reconstruction-related work. The agency has also examined various other programs, such as the Commander's Emergency Response Program, as well as the procurement and repair of military and logistical equipment.[13]

Like many other agencies, USAAA did not initially send auditors to Iraq and when they were finally deployed, their numbers fluctuated. By the fall of 2005, nine were working in Iraq and six in Kuwait. In April 2006, fourteen were assessing LOGCAP contracts in both places; that number fell to eleven by July 2006 and was down to four at the end of 2006, although it increased to 29 following the holiday season.[14] During the summer of 2007, USAAA had seven auditors working in Iraq and six others working on LOGCAP in Kuwait. As of September 30, 2008, a staff of seventeen auditors worked in Iraq and seven in Kuwait.[15]

Defense Contract Audit Agency

With a staff of more than 4,000 in 300 field offices across the world, the Defense Contract Audit Agency (DCAA)—which effectively serves as internal auditor for the Comptroller of the Department of Defense—is a major force for accountability of contracts awarded by the Department of Defense.[16] Although the audits are not generally public documents, DCAA has conducted thousands of audits on Iraq reconstruction, including some undertaken in coordination with SIGIR.

Early in the reconstruction program, the DCAA alerted the DoD OIG to irregularities it had noticed in contracts awarded by the Defense Contracting Command-Washington for ORHA and CPA. A subsequent review found that, although procedural shortcuts had led to less than full accountability, contracting officers had not acted in bad faith. The commander of Defense Contracting Command-Washington wrote that it would be "unconscionable to recommend that administrative action be taken against the contracting officials and not hold senior officials responsible for generating the demands."[17]

Later DCAA reviews identified more serious problems. In early 2006, a controversy arose over the near-full payment of fees of $263 million billed by the contractor KBR for oil-sector work, including what appeared to be exorbitant charges for transporting fuel to Iraq from Turkey and Kuwait. DCAA auditors raised serious questions about these charges.[18] Although a 2004 audit reported that the costs were inflated and not supported by documentation, the Army decided to pay KBR all but $10.1 million of those contested costs. That meant the Army withheld payment on just 3.8 percent of the charges questioned by the Pentagon audit agency, far below the rate at which the agency's recommendation is usually followed or sustained by the military.[19]

The Special Inspector General for Iraq Reconstruction
Some six months after the CPA took over the reconstruction mission in Iraq, the Congress created the office of the CPA-IG, through the November 2003 IRRF 2 legislation.[20] Had an operational IG been in place from the start of CPA, irregularities discovered post hoc might have been prevented. During the ORHA and early CPA periods, there were frequent uses of procedural shortcuts and liberal interpretation of federal acquisition regulations, leading to contracting irregularities. Some—but not all—of these can be understood in light of the exigencies associated with jump-starting Iraq's reconstruction program in a wartime environment. An audit criticizing the CPA oversight of $8.8 billion in Development Fund for Iraq money provided to Iraqi ministries was challenged by Ambassador Bremer on exactly those grounds, arguing that it was unrealistic to demand anything else in the midst of a country in chaos.[21]

During the process leading to passage of IRRF 2 legislation, a lively debate in the Senate followed the introduction by Senator Robert Byrd (D-WV) of an amendment proposing that the GAO audit the CPA. Although some senators thought that enough oversight already existed, and that the GAO would serve as the default oversight agency, a number were in favor of even more stringent oversight to be conducted by a Special Inspector General. Senator Russ Feingold (D-WI) introduced an amendment that proposed setting aside $10 million for the creation of the Office of Inspector General for the CPA. When the bill went to conference, the Feingold amendment was ultimately adopted.[22]

The legislation gave the CPA-IG the same powers as other federal agency inspectors general, but President Bush, in his signing statement, added some restrictions. He said that the IG was to refrain from "initiating, carrying out, or completing an audit or investigation, or from issuing a subpoena, which requires access to sensitive operation plans, intelligence matters, counterintelligence matters, ongoing criminal investigations by other units of the Department of Defense related to national security, or other matters the disclosure of which would constitute a threat to national security." The statement added, however, that the Secretary of Defense "may make exceptions to the foregoing direction in the public interest."[23] The restrictions never impeded CPA-IG or SIGIR's work.

The IG was appointed on January 20, 2004, and the first CPA-IG auditors arrived in Baghdad in mid-March 2004, just over three months before the CPA was to close its doors. The transfer of sovereignty to the Iraqi Interim Government, which took place on June 28, 2004, started the clock toward the sunset of the CPA-IG—which was scheduled to occur six months after the CPA's demise.[24]

In June 2004, Robin Cleveland, Deputy Director of the Office of Management and Budget, put forward a plan to transfer the CPA-IG's oversight responsibilities to the IGs of USAID, the Department of State, and the Department of Defense. However, in October 2004, again at Senator Feingold's impetus, the Congress took oversight in a different direction by passing a new law that transformed the CPA-IG into the Special Inspector General for Iraq Reconstruction and giving it oversight responsibilities for all IRRF 2 relief and reconstruction dollars.[25]

SIGIR initiated new oversight activities under its mandate to report on IRRF 2. Independent accountability in Iraq was buttressed by the full-scale staffing of SIGIR, the development of innovative oversight practices by a new staff of inspectors, a focus on timely performance auditing rather than ex post facto financial review, and on increased coordination among executive-branch audit and investigative agencies overseeing Iraq.

Audits and Inspections: SIGIR has produced more than 250 audits and inspections since 2004, covering a range of reconstruction issues, including contracting, anticorruption, funding obligations, asset transfers, and the Iraqi Security Forces. The purpose of SIGIR audits has been to determine whether programs and operations funded by the United States are being managed efficiently and effectively and to promote effective change through "real time" reporting.[26]

SIGIR's inspections focus on the construction and/or sustainment of specific projects. Assessments determine if project components were adequately designed before construction or installation, if construction or rehabilitation adequately met the standards of the design, if the contractor's quality-control plan and the U.S. government's quality-assurance program were adequately carried out, if project sustainability and operational effectiveness were adequately addressed, and if project results were consistent with the original objectives.[27]

In July 2008, SIGIR issued a capping report prepared by its audits directorate that identified key recurring systemic management issues identified in the agency's audits of Iraq reconstruction efforts. Four broad issues, which fed into and are widely evinced in *Hard Lessons*, were seen as central contributing causes to the deficiencies noted in the body of SIGIR's audit work:

> • The difficulty of implementing reconstruction programs
> in an insecure environment points to the need for a better

understanding of the potential impact of the lack of security on contingency reconstruction efforts.

- The lack of an integrated management structure that provides clear lines of authority, interagency coordination, and program accountability impacted the successful delivery of projects.

- The need to attract, develop, and retain qualified program and contract-management personnel was not anticipated and worked against the effective implementation of reconstruction programs.

- Working closely with host-country government officials and other groups is essential in developing reconstruction projects and programs that will—and can be—accepted and maintained.

Understanding these issues, the report states, is "critical to avoid repeating them in the future." Their prevalence in Iraq "contributed significantly to reduced program effectiveness and increased the potential for fraud, waste, and abuse."[28]

Investigations: In addition to audits, inspections, and the lessons learned initiative, SIGIR undertook a number of criminal investigations, with more than 370 cases opened between the agency's inception and the end of 2008. At that time, SIGIR had 67 open investigations, more than 30 of which had been assigned to prosecutors at the Department of Justice. The investigatory work of SIGIR had also resulted in eighteen arrests, seventeen indictments, thirteen convictions, and five imprisonments. The investigators' work yielded fines, forfeitures, recoveries, and restitution of more than $17 million.[29]

Lessons Learned Initiative: SIGIR's Lessons Learned initiative first focused on three main areas of Iraq reconstruction: human capital management, contracting and procurement, and program and project management. Three reports were issued in February 2006, July 2006, and March 2007—the latter two at hearings before the Senate Homeland Security and Governmental Affairs Committee. The initiative's purpose was to identify significant challenges in reconstruction and to identify actionable recommendations to improve the overall reconstruction effort. Much of the data, documentation, and personal observations supporting the lessons-learned conclusions were gleaned from a series of forums which brought together experts representing the full spectrum of agencies, organizations, and individuals participating in the reconstruction of Iraq.[30]

The reports have led to legislative and executive action to improve both Iraq's ongoing reconstruction and the government's approach to managing contingency contracting and operations. For example, the Office of Federal Procurement Policy adopted SIGIR's contracting recommendation as guidance for contingency situations. The Accountability in Government and Contracting Act, introduced by Senator Susan Collins (R-ME) and unanimously approved by the Senate in 2007, proposed implementation of a number of SIGIR's recommendations.[31]

Quarterly Reports: SIGIR's quarterly reports to the Congress provide a snapshot of the current state of Iraq reconstruction. Twenty reports have been issued between March 2004 and January 2009. They break down reconstruction progress by sector and funding stream, with a focus on IRRF-funded programs and projects. Published 30 days following the end of each quarter of the fiscal year, the reports summarize SIGIR findings, including audits, inspections, investigations, and analysis of data and developments related to Iraq reconstruction progress, as well as a summary of oversight conducted by other agencies. The activities of the IG during each quarter and updates on various SIGIR initiatives are also reported.[32]

Interagency Initiatives
As the number of oversight agencies deploying auditors and inspectors to Iraq increased after 2003, SIGIR spearheaded several coordinating bodies to ensure that duplicate work did not take place and to provide additional support to incoming agencies. These include: the Iraq Inspectors General Council, the Iraq Accountability Working Group, the Special Investigative Task Force for Iraq Reconstruction, and the International Contract Corruption Task Force. Each body has a specific purpose, but all provide a forum for discussion and collaboration on oversight efforts in Iraq. For example, the Iraq Inspectors General Council—based in Arlington, Virginia—is a vehicle for collaboration among the IGs and staff of the many agencies involved in using and overseeing IRRF 2; the Iraq Accountability Working Group also coordinates audit efforts in Baghdad. The Special Investigative Task Force for Iraqi Reconstruction—a partnership including the IRS, FBI, Department of Homeland Security, and the Department of State IG—pursued the Bloom/Stein conspiracy and followed a number of leads arising from that case. The International Contract Corruption Task Force is a group of federal agencies that combines resources to investigate and prosecute cases of contract fraud and public corruption in U.S. government spending

on Iraq reconstruction. In addition to SIGIR, it includes the Defense Criminal Investigate Service, U.S. Army Criminal Investigations, and the IGs of the State Department and USAID.

Oversight of contingency operations is important and must begin early in their planning. Although there is a trade-off between operational necessity and accounting accuracy during conflict, the danger that huge amounts of money may be potentially wasted or stolen makes it essential to provide a meaningful and robust oversight presence in contingency operations. All future post-conflict reconstruction plans should include a strong oversight function to make sure American taxpayers' money is properly used to achieve the nation's objectives.

ACKNOWLEDGEMENTS

A word of heartfelt thanks to all the SIGIR staff who helped plan, develop, and compile *Hard Lessons*. I especially commend my two senior writers, Victoria Butler and Christopher Kirchhoff, who shouldered virtually all the writing burden, which included research travels to Iraq. Thanks to Executive Editor Colonel (Ret.) John R. Martin and Senior Editor Barbara Wolfson for good insight and guidance. I thank the researchers—Jennifer McGee, Bradley Larson, and Gwendolyn Toops—for thousands of hours of detail work to help ensure the report's accuracy. I thank our editorial advisors for their invaluable assistance: Dr. Philip D. Zelikow of the University of Virginia; Fredrick D. Barton of the Center for Strategic and International Studies; Dr. Dana Eyre of the U.S. Institute for Peace; Dr. Terrence K. Kelly of RAND Corporation; Dr. Ernest R. May of Harvard University; and Dr. Gordon W. Rudd of the U.S. Marine Corps School of Advanced Warfighting.

Each of these advisors provided consistently helpful advice and insights, but one deserves special recognition. Dr. Rudd, the ORHA/CPA Historian, conducted hundreds of nearly contemporaneous interviews with key reconstruction figures during the early stages of the program, and he provided them all to SIGIR. Our report is stronger and deeper for his diligent work and generous spirit.

I also thank the many SIGIR staff-members who supported the research, writing, and review of *Hard Lessons,* including: Ginger Cruz, Brian Flynn, Dave Warren, Jon Novak, Hillel Weinberg, Lynne Halbrooks, Danny Athanasaw, Glenn Furbish, Barry Holman, Karl Tool, Dan Willkens, Paul Cooksey, Christopher Griffith, Andrea Bernardo, Kristine Belisle, Bill Maly, Joan Hlinka, Kevin O'Connor, Christopher Williams, Dena Nevarez, Sandy Keith, Rick Olson, Mike Boisvenue, Scott Michaud, Robin Raphel, Hunter Keith, Roger Williams, Kirk Johnson, Rick Whitaker, and David Gandle. Thanks also to Ed Gold, Christine Bath-Zachery, Barbara Lewis, and Nell Todd. Tender thanks to my wife, Adriana Sanchez Bowen, who put up with my many hours away working on this project.

Finally, I sincerely thank the hundreds of people who contributed to *Hard Lessons* by giving of their time, talent, and knowledge in interviews, written responses, or comments on early drafts. Their service and sacrifice in supporting Iraq's reconstruction—and in telling its story—made this report possible.

Stuart W. Bowen, Jr.
Inspector General

ENDNOTES

Chapter 1

1 For an account of the September 13, 2001, National Security Council (NSC) meetings and several follow-on sessions concerning the debate over Iraq war plans, see Douglas Feith, War and Decision: Inside the Pentagon at the Dawn of the War on Terror (New York: HarperCollins, 2008), 13-15, 47-49.

2 SIGIR interviews with Brigadier General (Ret.) Mark Scheid, former CENTCOM logistics planner; Colonel John Agoglia, former CENTCOM planner; and Colonel (Ret.) Michael Fitzgerald, former CENTCOM J5 Chief of War Plans.

3 SIGIR interview with General (Ret.) Colin Powell, former Secretary of State and Richard Armitage, former Deputy Secretary of State, February 4, 2008; and Karen DeYoung, Soldier: The Life of Colin Powell (New York: Alfred A. Knopf, 2006), 401-403.

4 Christopher Catherwood, Churchill's Folly: How Winston Churchill Created Modern Iraq (New York: Carroll & Graf, 2004), 74.

5 Judith S. Yaphe, "The View from Basra: Southern Iraq's Reaction the War and Occupation, 1915-1925," in The Creation of Iraq, 1914-1921, ed. Reeva Spector Simon and Eleanor H. Tejirian (New York: Columbia University Press,2004), 28-30.

6 Phebe Marr, The Modern History of Iraq, 2nd edition, (Boulder, CO: Westview Press, 2003), 12-19.

7 Christopher Catherwood, Churchill's Folly: How Winston Churchill Created Modern Iraq (New York: Carroll & Graf, 2004), 19, 44, 74.

8 Christopher Catherwood, Churchill's Folly: How Winston Churchill Created Modern Iraq, (New York, NY: Carroll & Graf, 2004), 7, 123, 130, 217, 221.

9 Phebe Marr, The Modern History of Iraq, 2nd edition, (Boulder, CO: Westview Press, 2003), 113-116.

10 Phebe Marr, The Modern History of Iraq, 2nd edition, (Boulder, CO: Westview Press, 2003), 177-178, 207-208, 217-259.

11 Kuwaiti political structures remained intact after the nation's leadership fled in 1990. This enabled negotiations with the United States before military action restored the Kuwaitis to power, a very different situation than in 2002 and early 2003 when the Iraqi exile leadership was fractious and could not provide a unified front with which to negotiate plans. Nevertheless, the condition of Kuwait's infrastructure proved worse than anticipated, just as would happen in Iraq in 2003. Sewage, water, and electricity plants in Kuwait failed in 1991. The effort ultimately repaired 10,000 kilometers of electrical lines and restored more than 145 schools, 1,000 public buildings, and hundreds of other facilities. The Army Corps of Engineers alone completed 1,200 task orders with the help of international contractors. Janet A. McDonnell, After Desert Storm: The United States Army and the Rebuilding of Kuwait (Washington, DC: Department of the Army, 1999), 31, 129-131, 176-185.

12 See: United Nations Security Council Resolutions (UNSCRs) 661, 687, 706, 712, 986, and 1051. UNSCR 661 of August 6, 1990, imposed comprehensive economic sanctions on Iraq, exempting food and medicine, and established a committee to oversee implementation of the sanctions; UNSCR 687 of April 3, 1991, set terms for a cease-fire and maintained the terms of the embargo; UNSCR 706 of August 15, 1991, set out a mechanism for an oil-for-food program and authorized an escrow account to be established by the Secretary-General (to fund an oil-for-food program, $1.6 billion was to be raised in six months by the sale of Iraqi oil); UNSCR 712 of September 19, 1991, confirmed the sum of $1.6 billion to be raised by the sale of Iraqi oil in a six-month period to fund the Oil-for-Food program; UNSCR 986 of April 14, 1995, enabled Iraq to sell oil worth up to $1 billion every 90 days and use the proceeds for humanitarian supplies (it also set terms of reference for the Oil-for-Food program); and UNSCR 1051 of March 27, 1996, established the export/import monitoring system for Iraq.

13 Independent Inquiry Committee, "The Impact of the Oil-for-Food Programme on the Iraqi People," September 7, 2005, 8, 16.

14 Organization of the Petroleum Exporting Countries, "Annual Statistical Bulletin 2001," 2001, 3.

15 United Nations Security Council S/1999/356, "Annex II: Report of the Second Panel Established Pursuant to the Note by the President of the Security Council of 30 January 1999 (S/1999/100), Concerning the Current Humanitarian Situation in Iraq," March 30, 1999; and Independent Inquiry Committee, "The Impact of the Oil-for-Food Programme on the Iraqi People," September 7, 2005, 10.

16 To make up the additional intake necessary to survive, the very poor relied on wheat flour and bread, the only foodstuff whose prices remained low. Independent Inquiry Committee, "The Impact of the Oil-for-Food Programme on the Iraqi People," September 7, 2005, 18, 20.

17 UN Secretariat Memorandum S/1996/356, "Memorandum of Understanding between the Secretariat of the United Nations and the Government of Iraq on the Implementation of Security Council Resolution 986 (1995)," May 20, 1996.

18 UN Office of the Iraq Programme: Oil-for-Food, "Background Brief: Food Basket," February 26, 2003, http://www.un.org/Depts/oip/food-facts.html; and GAO Testimony 04-651T, "United Nations: Observations on the Oil for Food Program," April 7, 2004.

19 Independent Inquiry Committee, "Manipulation of the Oil-for-Food Programme by the Iraqi Regime," October 27, 2005, 1-9; and Iraq Survey Group, "Comprehensive Report of the Special Advisor to the DCI on Iraq's WMD with Addendums," September 30, 2004, 8-9, http://www.gpoaccess.gov/duelfer/index.html.

20 For an overview of international aid provided to Iraq in the 1990s, see GAO Report 03-792R, "Rebuilding Iraq," May 15, 2003.

21 SIGIR interview with William Orme, Director of Communications, UN Development Program, September 8, 2006.

22 Douglas Feith, *War and Decision: Inside the Pentagon at the Dawn of the War on Terror* (New York: HarperCollins, 2008), 219.

23 The cell's members included Major General Victor Renuart, CENTCOM Director of Operations (J3); Brigadier General John F. Kimmons, CENTCOM Director of Intelligence (J2); Colonel David D. Halverson, Chief of Operations Plans Division, CENTCOM (J3); and Colonel Mark Scheid, Chief of Logistics Plans Division, CENTCOM (J4). SIGIR interview with Brigadier General (Ret.) Mark Scheid, former CENTCOM logistics planner, September 20, 2006.

24 SIGIR interview with Colonel (Ret.) Michael Fitzgerald, former CENTCOM J5 Chief of War Plans, May 30, 2008; SIGIR interview with Brigadier General (Ret.) Mark Scheid, former CENTCOM logistics planner, September 20, 2006; and SIGIR interview with Colonel John Agoglia, former CENTCOM planner, May 22, 2008. Secretary Rumsfeld later stated, "I do not recall, nor do others present in the numerous discussions with General Franks, giving any guidance that could be interpreted as requesting CENTCOM not plan for Phase IV postwar operations, as General Franks will attest. Nor would I have minimized its importance." Donald Rumsfeld, written comments to SIGIR, November 5, 2008. Michael Fitzgerald, CENTCOM Chief of War Plans, attests that, "We, CENTCOM, were not in charge of designating and developing the government, determining who would be responsible in immediate post-conflict." Michael Fitzgerald, former CENTCOM J5 Chief of War Plans, May 30, 2008.

25 SIGIR interviews with Brigadier General (Ret.) Mark Scheid, former CENTCOM logistics planner, September 20, 2006; and Colonel John Agoglia, former CENTCOM planner, May 22, 2008. The notation used for campaign phases changes over the years as military doctrine evolves. From 2001 to 2006, the phases were: 1-Deter/Engage; 2-Seize; 3-Decisive Operations; and 4-Transition. Joint Chiefs of Staff Joint Publication 3-0, "Joint Operations," III-18-III-21, http://www.bits.de/NRANEU/others/jp-doctrine/jp3_0(01).pdf. In 2006, the phases were changed to 0-Shape; 1-Deter; 2-Seize Initiative; 3-Dominate; 4-Stabilize; and 5-Enable Civil Authority. Joint Chiefs of Staff Joint Publication 3-0, "Joint Operations," IV-26-IV-30, http://www.dtic.mil/doctrine/jel/new_pubs/jp3_0.pdf. The phases represent general guidance to combatant commanders and may be changed for specific plans. For purposes of this book, Phase IV refers to the establishment of self-sustaining peace, civil control, and the rule of law.

26 For popular accounts, see Michael R. Gordon and General Bernard E. Trainor, *Cobra II: The Inside Story of the Invasion and Occupation of Iraq* (New York: Pantheon Books, 2006); Thomas E. Ricks, *Fiasco: The American Military Adventure in Iraq* (New York: Penguin Group, 2007); Bob Woodward, *State of Denial: Bush at War, Part III* (New York: Simon & Schuster, 2006); and Bob Woodward, *Plan of Attack* (New York: Simon & Schuster, 2004).

27 Warrick initially discussed this evaluation with State Department officials Steve Beecroft, Alan Limpert, and others from the Iraq desk. ORHA/CPA Historian interview with Thomas S. Warrick, former Senior Advisor to the Assistant Secretary of State for Near Eastern Affairs, November 10, 2004. Dr. Gordon Rudd was the staff historian for both the Office of Reconstruction and Humanitarian Assistance (ORHA) and the Coalition Provisional Authority (CPA). All of Rudd's interviews will be identified as "ORHA/CPA Historian." The groups were: Democratic Principles and Procedures; Economy and Infrastructure; Defense Policy and Institutions; Education; Public Health and Humanitarian Needs; Civil Society Capacity Building; Transitional Justice; Water, Agriculture and Environment; Preserving Iraq's Cultural Heritage; Public Finance; Oil and Energy; Local Government; Anti-Corruption Measures; Foreign and National Security; Free Media; Migration; and Public Outreach. DoS, "Future of Iraq Project," May 12, 2003, Overview, 4, http://www.gwu.edu/~nsarchiv/NSAEBB/NSAEBB198/FOI%20Overview.pdf.

28 These meetings, held in the White House situation room, included Deputy Secretary of State Richard Armitage, Under Secretary of State Marc Grossman, Under Secretary of Defense Douglas Feith, Vice Chairman of the Joint Chiefs of Staff General Peter Pace, Chief of Staff to the Vice President I. Lewis "Scooter" Libby, Deputy Director of Central Intelligence John McLaughlin, and Deputy National Security Advisor Steven Hadley. General Wayne Downing—then Zalmay Khalilzad and later Frank Miller—attended as staff representatives from the NSC. The internal NSC calendar referred to the Deputies gatherings as "regional affairs" meetings, obscuring their purpose from the wider NSC staff. ORHA/CPA Historian interview with Douglas Feith, Under Secretary of Defense for Policy, December 17, 2004. For a general description of the "Deputies Lunches," see Douglas Feith, *War and Decision: Inside the Pentagon at the Dawn of the War on Terror* (New York: HarperCollins, 2008), 237-298.

29 Douglas Feith, *War and Decision: Inside the Pentagon at the Dawn of the War on Terror* (New York: HarperCollins, 2008), 237-298; and SIGIR interview with Douglas Feith, Under Secretary of Defense for Policy, March 21, 2008.

30 ORHA/CPA Historian interview with Douglas Feith, Under Secretary of Defense for Policy, December 17, 2004; and Richard Armitage, "The Future of Iraq," Department of State policy paper distributed to the Deputies Committee on July 25, 2002, as quoted in Douglas Feith, *War and Decision: Inside the Pentagon at the Dawn of the War on Terror* (New York: HarperCollins, 2008), 277-78.

31 Donald Rumsfeld, "Beyond Nation Building," DoD speech, February 14, 2003.

32 For an analysis of the Afghan campaign, see Stephen Biddle, "Afghanistan and the Future of Warfare: Implications for Army and Defense Policy," Strategic Studies Institute, November 2002.

33 It was only later that the initial gains in Afghanistan unraveled with the resurgence of the Taliban. David Rohde and David E. Sanger, "How a 'Good War' in Afghanistan Went Bad," *New York Times*, August 12, 2007; and Center for the Study of the Presidency, "Afghanistan Study Group Report," January 30, 2008.

34 Richard Armitage, "The Future of Iraq," Department of State policy paper distributed to the Deputies Committee on July 25, 2002, as quoted in Douglas Feith, *War and Decision: Inside the Pentagon at the Dawn of the War on Terror* (New York: HarperCollins, 2008), 277-78.

35 SIGIR interviews with Douglas Feith, former Under Secretary of Defense for Policy, March 21, 2008; SIGIR interview with Colonel (Ret.) Michael Fitzgerald, former CENTCOM (J5) Chief of War Plans, May 30, 2008; and SIGIR interview with Colonel John Agoglia, former CENTCOM planner, May 22, 2008.

36 Bob Woodward, *Plan of Attack* (New York: Simon & Schuster, 2004), 154-56; and NSC briefing, "Iraq: Goals, Objectives, Strategy," circulated by National Security Advisor Condoleezza Rice, October 29, 2002.

37 Douglas Feith, *War and Decision: Inside the Pentagon at the Dawn of the War on Terror* (New York: HarperCollins, 2008), 281-83.

38 ORHA/CPA Historian interview with Colonel John Agoglia, former CENTCOM planner, June 28, 2003.

39 ORHA/CPA Historian interview with Major Thomas Fisher, former CENTCOM planner, August 27, 2003; and ORHA/CPA Historian interview with Major Ray Eiriz, former CENTCOM planner, December 7, 2006.

40 SIGIR interviews with Frank Miller, former Chairman of the Executive Steering Group of the NSC, June 26, 2008; and February 4, 2008; and Douglas Feith, *War and Decision: Inside the Pentagon at the Dawn of the War on Terror* (New York: HarperCollins, 2008), 276-77.

41 ORHA/CPA Historian interview with Douglas Feith, Under Secretary of Defense for Policy, December 17, 2004.

42 Lieutenant General (Ret.) Jay Garner, multiple interviews with ORHA/CPA Historian and SIGIR; and DoD IG Report 07-INTEL-04, "Report on the Pre-Iraqi War Activities of the Office of the Under Secretary of Defense for Policy," February 9, 2007. Douglas Feith disputes the assertion that the name of the office was chosen as a deliberate deception and that its products were not widely shared, saying that "The Office of Special Plans was one of the most transparent offices in the United States Government." Douglas Feith, former Under Secretary of Defense for Policy, written comments to SIGIR, January 7, 2009.

43 SIGIR interview with Frank Miller, former Chairman of the Executive Steering Group of the NSC, August 19, 2008.

44 SIGIR interview with Wendy Chamberlin, former USAID Assistant Administrator, Near East Bureau, May 3, 2006.

45 ORHA/CPA Historian interview with Major Ray Eiriz, former CENTCOM planner, December 7, 2006.

46 SIGIR interview with Jonathan Dworken, former Director for Humanitarian Assistance and Disaster Response for the NSC, October 11, 2006.

47 Colin H. Kahl, "In the Crossfire or the Crosshairs? Norms, Civilian Casualties, and U.S. Conduct in Iraq," *International Security* 32, no. 1 (Summer 2007), 16.

48 According to Frank Miller, to whom the Humanitarian Working Group reported, it was not originally charged to do any reconstruction planning. SIGIR interview with Frank Miller, former Chairman of the Executive Steering Group of the NSC, June 26, 2008.

49 SIGIR interview with Wendy Chamberlin, former USAID Assistant Administrator, Near East Bureau, May 3, 2006.

50 SIGIR interview with Jonathan Dworken, former Director for Humanitarian Assistance and Disaster Response for the NSC, October 11, 2006; and SIGIR interview with Frank Miller, former Chairman of the Executive Steering Group of the NSC, June 26, 2008.

51 ORHA/CPA Historian interview with Colonel (Ret.) Joseph J. Collins, former Deputy Assistant Secretary of Defense for Stability Operations, August 29, 2006.

52 SIGIR interview with Jonathan Dworken, former Director for Humanitarian Assistance and Disaster Response for the NSC, October 11, 2006.

53 SIGIR interview with Jonathan Dworken, former Director for Humanitarian Assistance and Disaster Response for the NSC, October 11, 2006.

54 ORHA/CPA Historian interview with Colonel (Ret.) Joseph J. Collins, former Deputy Assistant Secretary of Defense for Stability Operations, August 29, 2006.

55 ORHA/CPA Historian interview with Colonel (Ret.) Joseph J. Collins, former Deputy Assistant Secretary of Defense for Stability Operations, August 29, 2006.

56 SIGIR interview with Jonathan Dworken, former Director for Humanitarian Assistance and Disaster Response for the NSC, October 11, 2006.

57 The "Karzai" comment refers to how Hamid Karzai emerged in Afghanistan as a national leader around whom the nation could generally rally. Karzai, an Afghan exile leader, was named as the country's president after the overthrow of the Taliban.

58 ORHA/CPA Historian interview with Colonel (Ret.) Joseph J. Collins, former Deputy Assistant Secretary of Defense for Stability Operations, August 29, 2006.

59 SIGIR and ORHA/CPA Historian interviews with Douglas Feith, Under Secretary of Defense for Policy, December 17, 2004, January 27, 2005, and March 21, 2008; and Douglas Feith, *War and Decision: Inside the Pentagon at the Dawn of the War on Terror* (New York: HarperCollins, 2008), 315-317, 544-45.

60 SIGIR interview with General George Casey, former Director of the Joint Staff and former Commander of MNF-I, July 30, 2008.

61 This subdivision of Phase IV had long been CENTCOM's preferred concept of operations, and was taken from OPLAN 1003-98, a standing plan for war in Iraq that had been approved by the Secretary of Defense in 1998. SIGIR interview with Colonel (Ret.) Michael Fitzgerald, former CENTCOM J5 Chief of War Plans, May 30, 2008.

62 SIGIR interview with Colonel (Ret.) Michael Fitzgerald, former CENTCOM J5 Chief of War Plans, May 30, 2008.

63 SIGIR interview with Douglas Feith, former Under Secretary of Defense for Policy, March 21, 2008; and Douglas Feith, *War and Decision: Inside the Pentagon at the Dawn of the War on Terror* (New York: Harper Collins, 2008), 316-317.

64 ORHA/CPA Historian interview with Douglas Feith, Under Secretary of Defense for Policy, December 17, 2004.

65 The strategy paper was circulated on October 29, 2002. Condoleezza Rice, National Security Advisor, Memorandum to the Vice President, the Secretary of State, the Secretary of Defense, Chief of Staff to the President, Director of Central Intelligence, Chairman of the Joint Chiefs of Staff, "Principals' Committee Review of Iraq Police Paper," October 29, 2002, as reproduced in Douglas Feith, *War and Decision: Inside the Pentagon at the Dawn of the War on Terror* (New York: HarperCollins, 2008), 541-43.

66 SIGIR interview with Douglas Feith, former Under Secretary of Defense for Policy, January 27, 2005.

67 SIGIR interview with Donald Rumsfeld, former Secretary of Defense, December 12, 2008.

68 Assistant Secretary of State William Burns and his deputy, Ryan Crocker, worked to produce a twelve-page, single-spaced analysis of political risks they titled "The Perfect Storm." Karen DeYoung, *Soldier: The Life of Colin Powell* (New York: Alfred A. Knopf, 2006), 459; and SIGIR interview with Ambassador Ryan Crocker, United States Ambassador to Iraq, February 24, 2008.

69 SIGIR interview with General (Ret.) Colin Powell, former Secretary of State and Richard Armitage, former Deputy Secretary of State, February 4, 2008; and SIGIR interview with Frank Miller, former Chairman of the Executive Steering Group of the NSC, August 19, 2008.

70 For an overview of the literature, see, for instance: James Dobbins, et al., *America's Role in Nation-Building: From Germany to Iraq* (Santa Monica, CA: RAND, 2003); and Stephen Kinzer, *Overthrow: America's Century of Regime Change from Hawaii to Iraq* (New York: Times Books, 2006). For an opposing view, see Justin Logan and Christopher Preble, "Failed States and Flawed Logic: The Case Against a Standing Nation-Building Office," CATO Institute Policy Analysis, no. 560 (January 11, 2006).

71 Minxin Pei and Sara Kasper, "Lessons from the Past: The American Record on Nation Building," Carnegie Endowment for International Peace Policy Brief, no. 24 (May 2003), 2, 4.

72 See: Charles Tripp, "Iraq: The Imperial Precedent," *Le Monde Diplomatique*, January 13, 2003; and Brent Scowcroft, "Don't Attack Saddam," Op-Ed, *Wall Street Journal*, August 15, 2002.

73 For perspectives on the Germany case study and how historians viewed its relevance to Iraq, see Charles S. Maier, Seminar, "Comparative Insights: Marshall Plan, Japan, and Iraq," Seminar at Massachusetts Institute of Technology, Cambridge, MA, March 7, 2005, http://mitworld.mit.edu/video/255/. On the use of historical analogy between Japan and Iraq, see John W. Dower, "A Warning from History: Don't Expect Democracy in Iraq," *Boston Review*, February 2003; John W. Dower, "The Other Japanese Occupation," *The Nation*, July 7, 2003; and John W. Dower, "Lessons from Japan about War's Aftermath," Op-Ed, *New York Times*, October 27, 2002. These analyses are drawn from a larger body of scholarship, including: John W. Dower, *Embracing Defeat: Japan in the Wake of WWII* (New York: W.W. Norton & Company, 2000).

74 National Intelligence Council, "Principal Challenges in Post-Saddam Iraq," January 2003, as reproduced in: U.S. Senate Select Committee on Intelligence, "Prewar Intelligence Assessments about Postwar Iraq," May 25, 2007, 56-94.

75 SIGIR interview with Frank Miller, former Chairman of the Executive Steering Group of the NSC, August 19, 2008.

76 The Institute for National Strategic Studies at the National Defense University in November 2002 hosted a meeting of more than 70 scholars, experts, and practitioners from inside and outside the government to discuss post-intervention reconstruction and political stabilization of Iraq. A 41-page proceeding of the workshop, "Iraq: Looking Beyond Saddam's Rule," was circulated across the government, including to the office of Douglas Feith. National Defense University, "Workshop Report: Iraq: Looking Beyond Saddam's Rule," National Defense University Institute for National Strategic Studies in collaboration with the Naval Postgraduate School, November 20-21, 2002; Edward P. Djerejian and Frank G. Wisner, co-chairs, *Guiding Principles for U.S. Post-Conflict Policy in Iraq* (New York: Council on Foreign Relations, 2003); Richard W. Murphy and C. Richard Nelson, "Winning the Peace: Managing a Successful Transition in Iraq," The Atlantic Council Policy Paper, January 2003; William D. Nordhaus, "Iraq: The Economic Consequences of War," *The New York Review of Books* 49, no. 19, December 5, 2002; and Bob Davis, "Cost of Iraq War May Top $100 Billion," *Wall Street Journal*, September 16, 2002. For subsequent news accounts, see Carl Kaysen, Steven E. Miller, Martin B. Malin, William D. Nordhaus, and John D. Steinbruner, *War with Iraq: Costs, Consequences and Alternatives*, (Cambridge, MA: American Academy of Arts, 2002); Frederick D. Barton and Bathsheba N. Crocker, "A Wiser Peace: An Action Strategy for Post-Conflict Iraq," Center for Strategic and International Studies, January 2003; and Anthony Cordesman, "Planning for a Self-Inflicted Wound: U.S. Policy to Reshape a Post-Saddam Iraq," Center for Strategic and International Studies, December 31, 2002.

77 Conrad C. Crane and W. Andrew Terrill, "Reconstructing Iraq: Insights, Challenges, and Missions for Military Forces in a Post-Conflict Scenario," U.S. Army War College Strategic Studies Institute, February 1, 2003.

78 Sinan Al-Shabibi, Colonel (Ret.) Scott Feil, Rend Rahim Francke, and Phebe Marr testified before the Senate Foreign Relations Committee on August 1, 2002, as part of a multi-day hearing on Iraq. Their panel focused specifically on post-Saddam Iraq. U.S. Senate Committee on Foreign Relations, "Hearings to Examine Threats, Responses, and Regional Considerations Surrounding Iraq," July 31 and August 1, 2002. Also see Phebe Marr's subsequent writings, especially Phebe Marr, "Iraq 'The Day After': Internal Dynamics in Post-Saddam Iraq," *Naval War College Review* LVI, no. 1 (Winter 2003); P.L. 107-243, Authorization for Use of Military Force against Iraq Resolution of 2002, October 16, 2002; and White House Press Release, "Statement by the President," October 16, 2003.

79 GPO Access, "Congressional Hearings," 107th Congress (2001-2002), 108th Congress (2003-2004), http://www.gpoaccess.gov/chearings/.

80 The project's first meetings, held April 9 and 10, 2002, under the auspices of the Middle East Institute, a nonpartisan research center in Washington, DC, opened with the discord that was to mark its findings and Iraqi exile politics more generally. Ahmed Chalabi, the prominent Iraqi exile and leader of the Iraqi National Congress, raised concerns about the Middle East Institute's participation. He viewed the think tank as an unnecessary intermediary between the Iraqi National Congress and the State Department. Acceding to Chalabi's concerns, the State Department agreed to be the project's sole sponsor, with meetings resuming in early July. ORHA/CPA Historian interview with Thomas S. Warrick, former Senior Advisor to the Assistant Secretary of State for Near Eastern Affairs, November 10, 2004. The three groups that did not meet were Refugees and Internally Displaced Persons; Foreign and National Security Policy; and Preserving Iraq's Cultural Heritage. DoS, "The Future of Iraq Project," May 12, 2003, http://www.gwu.edu/~nsarchiv/NSAEBB/NSAEBB198/index.htm.

81 Four of the groups (Education; Free Media; Transparency and Anti-Corruption Measures; and Civil Society Capacity Building) did not begin meeting until after the start of the new year. DoS, "Future of Iraq Project," Overview, 7-8, May 12, 2003, http://www.gwu.edu/~nsarchiv/NSAEBB/NSAEBB198/FOI%20 Overview.pdf. For details on updates sent to the Executive Steering Group, see ORHA/CPA Historian interview with Thomas S. Warrick, former Senior Advisor to the Assistant Secretary of State for Near Eastern Affairs, November 10, 2004.

82 ORHA/CPA Historian interview with Thomas S. Warrick, former Senior Advisor to the Assistant Secretary of State for Near Eastern Affairs, November 10, 2004.

83 SIGIR interview with Frank Miller, former Chairman of the Executive Steering Group of the NSC, August 19, 2008.

84 For the edited volumes of the Future of Iraq Project, see DoS, "The Future of Iraq Project," May 12, 2003, http://www.gwu.edu/~nsarchiv/NSAEBB/NSAEBB198/index.htm.

85 SIGIR interview with Frank Miller, former Chairman of the Executive Steering Group of the NSC, August 19, 2008.

86 SIGIR interview with Ambassador Ryan Crocker, United States Ambassador to Iraq, February 24, 2008.

87 NSC briefing, "Iraq: Goals, Objectives, Strategy," circulated by National Security Advisor Condoleezza Rice, October 29, 2002; and Douglas Feith, *War and Decision: Inside the Pentagon at the Dawn of the War on Terror* (New York: HarperCollins, 2008), 541-543.

Essential Services Overview – Prewar Levels in Iraq
88 International Monetary Fund, "Iraq: Statistical Appendix," August 2007; Energy Information Administration, Department of Energy, "Iraq Country Analysis Brief," December 2005, as cited in SIGIR, *Quarterly Report to the United States Congress*, July 2006, 34; Kenneth M. Pollack, *The Threatening Storm: The Case for Invading Iraq* (New York: Random House, 2002), 116-117; and Economist Intelligence Unit, "Country Profile: Iraq," 2005, 34; International Telecommunication Union, "World Telecommunication/ICT Indicators," no date, A-30m, http://www.itu.int/ITU-D/ict/statistics/at_glance/cellular03.pdf.

89 There were an estimated 500,000 people working in various intelligence, security and police organizations. With the inclusion of the armed forces and paramilitary units, the estimate for the total Iraqi Security Forces is 1.3 million. Kenneth M. Pollack, *The Threatening Storm: The Case for Invading Iraq* (New York: Random House, 2002), 116-117.

90 Bechtel National, Inc., "Iraq Infrastructure Reconstruction Program," Assessment Report submitted to USAID, June 2003; and Paul Wolfowitz, Deputy Secretary of Defense, Testimony before the Senate Foreign Relations Committee, May 22, 2003.

91 International Monetary Fund, "Iraq: Statistical Appendix," August 2007. Pre-war estimates of electricity production ranged from 3,250 to 4,500 megawatts per day. The 2003 UN/World Bank estimated production at 4,500 MW. United Nations/World Bank, "Joint Iraq Needs Assessment," October 2003, 28. The Gulf Region Division later noted, "4,500 MW represents a short-term peak before the war. The full prewar average for 2002 was 4,300MW." GRD, response to SIGIR vetting for the *Quarterly Report to the United States Congress*, April 18, 2007. Iraq Transition Assistance Office reports that data from the Ministry of Electricity "suggest that prewar high levels of production... never exceeded 70,000 MWhr [megawatt hours]" which translates into 3,250 MW. ITAO-Electricity response to SIGIR Vetting for the *Quarterly Report to the United States Congress*, January 13, 2008.

92 DoS Briefing by U.S. Embassy Baghdad, November 30, 2005, as cited in SIGIR, *Quarterly Report to the United States Congress*, July 2006, 25.

93 Energy Information Administration, Department of Energy, "Country Analysis Brief: Iraq," December 2005, as cited in SIGIR, *Quarterly Report to the United States Congress*, July 2006, 34.

Chapter 2

1 USAID, "2002 Congressional Budget Request," http://www.usaid.gov/pubs/cbj2002/request.html.

2 USAID, "Primer: What We Do and How We Do It," revised January 2006, http://www.usaid.gov/about_usaid/PDACG100.pdf. In 2002, only 1,985 of USAID's workforce were government employees; more than two-thirds of the workforce of 7,741 was made up of contractors. GAO Testimony 03-117T, "Foreign Assistance: USAID Needs to Improve Its Workforce Planning and Operation Expense Accounting," September 23, 2003, 1-2.

3 SIGIR interview with Andrew Natsios, former USAID Administrator, April 17, 2006.

4 SIGIR interview with Ross Wherry, former USAID Director of the Office of Iraq Affairs, April 5, 2006; and SIGIR interview with Wendy Chamberlin, former USAID Assistant Administrator, Near East Bureau, May 3, 2006.

5 Chamberlin had just stepped down as Ambassador to Pakistan, and knew White House planners from her long career at the Department of State. SIGIR interviews with Wendy Chamberlin, former USAID Assistant Administrator, Near East Bureau, April 18, 2007 and May 3, 2006.

6 The Asia and Near East Bureau was headed by Chamberlin. USAID Press Release, "Wendy Chamberlin Sworn in as Head of USAID's Asia and Near East Bureau," December 2, 2002.

7 Andrew Natsios, former USAID Administrator, email to SIGIR, October 25, 2008.

8 SIGIR interview with Jonathan Dworken, former Director for Humanitarian Assistance and Disaster Response for the NSC, March 29, 2007.

9 SIGIR interviews with Christopher Milligan, USAID Deputy Director of Iraq, February 9, 2006 and March 27, 2007.

10 SIGIR interviews with Wendy Chamberlin, former USAID Assistant Administrator, Near East Bureau, May 3, 2006 and April 18, 2007.

11 SIGIR interview with Andrew Natsios, former USAID Administrator, April 17, 2006.

12 USAID, *Vision for Post-Conflict Iraq*, February 19, 2003. Although not released to the public until February 2003, a working draft of this document was produced by members of the Humanitarian Working Group in the fall of 2002.

13 SIGIR interview with Andrew Natsios, former USAID Administrator, April 17, 2006.

14 USAID Fact Sheet, "USAID Contingency Plans for Humanitarian Assistance to Iraq," February 24, 2003.

15 SIGIR interview with Lauren Barbour, former Iraq Team Leader, USAID Office of Transition Initiatives, December 20, 2005; USAID, "Transition Initiatives," http://www.usaid.gov/our_work/cross-cutting_programs/transition_initiatives/.

16 USAID memorandum, "USAID Consultations on Iraq Contingency Plans," February 24, 2003, http://pdf.dec.org/pdf_docs/PDABY342.pdf.

17 SIGIR interview with Jonathan Dworken, former Director for Humanitarian Assistance and Disaster Response for the NSC, March 29, 2007.

18 USAID memorandum, "USAID Consultations on Iraq Contingency Plans," February 24, 2003, http://pdf.dec.org/pdf_docs/PDABY342.pdf.

19 SIGIR interview with Jonathan Dworken, former Director for Humanitarian Assistance and Disaster Response for the NSC, March 29, 2007; USAID memorandum, "USAID Consultations on Iraq Contingency Plans," February 24, 2003, http://pdf.dec.org/pdf_docs/PDABY342.pdf; USAID Press Release, "USAID Announces $200 Million in Emergency Food Assistance to Iraq," April 2, 2003; and World Food Program Press Release, "WFP Welcomes International Response to Iraq Appeal," April 4, 2003.

20 SIGIR interview with Jonathan Dworken, former Director for Humanitarian Assistance and Disaster Response for the NSC, March 29, 2007.

21 Interestingly, the group was not directed to meet by the Joint Staff Political-Military Cell, but rather arose more spontaneously from contacts of lower and mid-level staff members on the NSC and at CENTCOM. ORHA/CPA Historian interview with Major Ray Eiriz, former CENTCOM planner, December 7, 2006.

22 SIGIR and ORHA/CPA Historian interviews with CENTCOM planners Colonel (Ret.) Michael Fitzgerald, Colonel John Agoglia, Major Thomas Fisher, and Major Ray Eiriz.

23 SIGIR interview with Ross Wherry, former USAID Director of the Office of Iraq Affairs, April 5, 2006.

24 SIGIR interview with Christopher Milligan, USAID Deputy Director of Iraq, March 27, 2007.

25 SIGIR interview with Christopher Milligan, USAID Deputy Director of Iraq, February 9, 2006. Joshua B. Bolten, OMB Director, Testimony before the Senate Foreign Relations Committee, July 29, 2003; and USAID, "Vision for Post-Conflict Iraq," February 19, 2003. Shelter and payroll management assistance sectors had been considered but were ultimately dropped.

26 Milligan, a USAID official, had worked in Ecuador, Zimbabwe, and finally Indonesia, where Agency personnel were evacuated after the Bali bombing. Shortly thereafter, Wendy Chamberlin included him in planning.

27 Jock Covey, Michael J. Dziedic, and Leonard R. Hawley, eds., *The Quest for Viable Peace: International Intervention and Strategies for Conflict Transformation* (Washington, DC: USIP, 2005).

28 SIGIR interviews with Ross Wherry, former USAID Director of the Office of Iraq Affairs, April 5, 2006; Christopher Milligan, USAID Deputy Director of Iraq, March 27, 2007; Jonathan Dworken, former Director for Humanitarian Assistance and Disaster Response for the NSC, March 29, 2007; and Wendy Chamberlin, former USAID Assistant Administrator, Near East Bureau, April 18, 2007.

29 Condoleezza Rice, National Security Advisor, Memorandum to the Vice President, the Secretary of State, the Secretary of Defense, Chief of Staff to the President, Director of Central Intelligence, Chairman of the Joint Chiefs of Staff, "Principals' Committee Review of Iraq Police Paper," October 29, 2002, as reproduced in Douglas Feith, *War and Decision: Inside the Pentagon at the Dawn of the War on Terror* (New York: HarperCollins, 2008), 541-43.

30 USAID, "Vision for Post-Conflict Iraq," February 19, 2003.

31 See: "Electricity" in USAID, "Vision for Post-Conflict Iraq," February 19, 2003.

32 See: "Food, Agriculture, and Rural Economy" in USAID, "Vision for Post-Conflict Iraq," February 19, 2003.

33 See: "Education" and "Electricity" in USAID, "Vision for Post-Conflict Iraq," February 19, 2003.

34 SIGIR interview with Ross Wherry, former USAID Director of the Office of Iraq Affairs, April 5, 2006.

35 SIGIR interview with Christopher Milligan, USAID Deputy Director of Iraq, February 9, 2006.

36 See: "Transportation" in USAID, "Vision for Post-Conflict Iraq," February 19, 2003.

37 The CORDS pacification program in rural Vietnam is an interesting precursor to Provisional Reconstruction Teams used in Afghanistan and Iraq. See: R. W. Komer, RAND Report R-967-ARPA, "Bureaucracy Does Its Thing: Institutional Constraints on U.S.-GVN Performance in Vietnam," August 1972; Lewis Sorley, *A Better War: The Unexamined Victories and Final Tragedy of America's Last Years in Vietnam* (New York: Harcourt Brace & Company, 1999); and Neil Sheehan, *A Bright Shining Lie: John Paul Vann and America in Vietnam* (New York: Vintage, 1989).

38 SIGIR interview with Christopher Milligan, USAID Deputy Director of Iraq, March 27, 2007.

39 SIGIR interviews with Christopher Milligan, USAID Deputy Director of Iraq, April 14, 2006; and March 27, 2007.

40 SIGIR interview with Frank Miller, former Chairman of the Executive Steering Group of the National Security Council, August 19, 2008.

41 SIGIR interview with Wendy Chamberlin, former USAID Assistant Administrator, Near East Bureau, April 18, 2007. The military also uses this term to denote large depictions of plans, schedules or programs.

42 SIGIR interview with Ross Wherry, former USAID Director of the Office of Iraq Affairs, April 5, 2006; and SIGIR interview with Wendy Chamberlin, former USAID Assistant Administrator, Near East Bureau, April 18, 2007.

43 SIGIR interview with Jonathan Dworken, former Director for Humanitarian Assistance and Disaster Response for the NSC, March 29, 2007; and SIGIR interview with Ross Wherry, former USAID Director of the Office of Iraq Affairs, November 2, 2005.

44 SIGIR interview with Ross Wherry, former USAID Director of the Office of Iraq Affairs, April 5, 2006.

45 GAO Testimony 03-1171T, "Foreign Assistance: USAID Needs to Improve Its Workforce Planning and Operation Expense Accounting," September 23, 2003, 1-5.

46 SIGIR interview with Andrew Natsios, former USAID Administrator, April 17, 2006.

47 For current provisions for the FAR, see Acquisition Central, "Federal Acquisition Regulation (FAR)," http://www.acqnet.gov/FAR/.

48 James Q. Wilson, *Bureaucracy: What Government Agencies Do and Why They Do It* (New York: Basic Books, 1991 reprint edition), 126-127.

49 USAID Acquisition Regulation (AIDAR), Subpart Level 48, CFR 706.302-70, October 18, 2007, http://www.usaid.gov/policy/ads/300/aidar.pdf. A good overview of contracting procedures can be found in: Valerie Bailey Grasso, Congressional Research Service Report RL32229, "Iraq: Frequently Asked Questions about Contracting," updated March 18, 2005; and John R. Luckey, Congressional Research Service Report RS21555, "Iraq Reconstruction: Frequently Asked Questions Concerning the Application of Federal Procurement Statues," June 23, 2003. For an overview of budget mechanisms for humanitarian assistance, see Rhoda Margesson, Congressional Research Service Report RL33769, "International Crisis and Disasters: U.S. Humanitarian Assistance, Budget Trends, and Issues for Congress," updated May 3, 2007; and SIGIR Lessons Learned Forum: Contracting and Procurement, Washington, DC, December 5, 2005.

50 Authority comes from Public Law 87-195 which amended the Foreign Assistance Act (FAA). P.L. 87-195, Foreign Assistance Act of 1961, Section 491, September 4, 1961. The FAA of 1961 releases the agency from some of the more stringent requirements for domestic acquisition. The conditions under which exemptions may be invoked are outlined in an addendum specific to each agency. USAID implements the procurement aspects of the FAA under AIDAR provision 48 CFR 701.601. AIDAR, Subpart Level 48, CFR 701.601, October 18, 2007, http://www.usaid.gov/policy/ads/300/aidar.pdf.

51 Under a pre-authorization letter, contractors proceed "at risk," which means that they will only be reimbursed for expenses later deemed by USAID to have been appropriate given the nature of the pending task.

52 Bruce N. Crandlemire, USAID Assistant Inspector General for Audit, Memorandum to Wendy Chamberlin and Timothy T. Beans, "USAID's Compliance with Federal Regulations in Awarding the Iraq Education Sector Contract, (AIG/A Memorandum 03-001)," June 6, 2003, http://www.usaid.gov/oig/iraq_doc/memorandum_03-001_6-06-03.pdf. Seven exemptions in the FAR allow contracting officers to hold shorter bid periods, use a pre-selected list of bidders, or award a contract outright without competition. (The latter is known as no-bid or sole-source contracting.) Thorough justification must accompany these awards and the FAR prescribes that they be re-competed as soon as practical. The FAR requires a written, certified justification before any exemption to full and open competition is used. The FAR Subpart 6.3 governs the applicability. FAR, Subpart 6.3, "Other Than Full and Open Competition," June 12, 2008, http://www.arnet.gov/far/current/html/Subpart%206_3.html#wp1086841. The AIDAR provides regulations for USAID. AIDAR, Subpart Level 48, CFR 706.302-70, October 18, 2007, http://www.usaid.gov/policy/ads/300/aidar.pdf.

53 USAID IG Audit A-000-04-003-P, "Capping Report on the Audit of USAID's Compliance with Federal Regulations in Awarding the Iraq Phase I Contracts," May 19, 2004.

54 SIGIR interview with Bruce Spake, Vice President of DAI, November 2, 2006.

55 USAID, "Funding Summary #3, Fiscal Year (FY) 2003," April 2, 2003.

56 USAID memorandum, "USAID Consultations on Iraq Contingency Plans," February 24,2003, http://pdf.dec.org/pdf_docs/PDABY342.pdf.

57 SIGIR interview with Christopher Milligan, USAID Deputy Director of Iraq, March 27, 2007. On January 24, 2003, USAID issued IRG a request for proposal, giving the organization three days to respond. On February 7, 2003, USAID subsequently issued the firm the Agency's first sole-source contract in the reconstruction effort. USAID Press Release, "USAID Reconstruction Efforts in Iraq," May 1, 20003. See also: IRG Press Release, "IRG will support USAID in the overall planning, monitoring, coordination, management, and reporting on reconstruction and rehabilitation activities across a variety of sectors including health, agriculture, civil society strengthening, and infrastructure." IRG, "IRG Selected to Implement Key Post-War Reconstruction," March 13, 2003. "Only one of the first eight contracts was sole-sourced by USAID, for personnel support, which was awarded to IRG." USAID Fact Sheet, "Contracting by USAID for Reconstruction of Iraq, Questions and Answers," May 2, 2003, http://www.usaid.gov/press/factsheets/2003/fs030508.html.

58 For examples of USAID's Statements of Work see RTI, USAID contract EDG-C-00-03-00010-00, Section C, April 11, 2003; Abt Associates, USAID contract RAN-C-00-03-00010-00, Section C, April 30, 2003; and CAI, USAID contract EDG-C-00-03-00011-00, Section C, April 11, 2003.

59 SIGIR interview with Wendy Chamberlin, former USAID Assistant Administrator, Near East Bureau, May 3, 2006.

60 SIGIR interview with Ross Wherry, former USAID Director of the Office of Iraq Affairs, April 5, 2006.

61 SIGIR, "Iraq Reconstruction: Lessons in Contracting and Procurement," July 2006, 29.

62 For final amounts of USAID contracts, several of which were increased multiple times, see USAID, "Assistance for Iraq Contracts and Grant," http://www.usaid.gov/iraq/contracts/.

63 SIGIR interview with Ross Wherry, former USAID Director of the Office of Iraq Affairs, April 5, 2006.

64 P.L. 108-11, Emergency Wartime Supplemental Appropriations Act for Fiscal Year 2003, and for other purposes," April 16, 2003; and SIGIR Lessons Learned Forum: Contracting and Procurement, Washington, DC, December 5, 2005, 29-30.

65 SIGIR, "Iraq Reconstruction: Lessons in Contracting and Procurement," July 2006, 30; and Bruce N. Crandlemire, USAID Assistant Inspector General for Audit, Memorandum to Gordon West and Timothy T. Beans, "USAID's Compliance with Federal Regulations in Awarding the Iraq Infrastructure Reconstruction Program Phase II Contract (AIG/A Memorandum 04-006)," April 20, 2004, http://www.usaid.gov/oig/iraq_doc/memo04_006.pdf. USAID eventually increased the contract's ceiling to $1.03 billion in September 2003.

66 USAID Press Release, "USAID Awards Iraq Infrastructure Contract," April 17, 2003.

67 USAID Bechtel Contract EEE-C-00-03-00018-00, Section C, http://www.usaid.gov/iraq/contracts/pdf/BechtelSecC.pdf.

68 SIGIR, "Iraq Reconstruction: Lessons in Contracting and Procurement," July 2006, 30.

69 "There's a lot of money to pay for this that doesn't have to be U.S. taxpayer money … the oil revenues of that country could bring between $50 billion and $100 billion over the course of the of the next two or three years … We're dealing with a country that can really finance its own reconstruction, and relatively soon." Paul Wolfowitz, Deputy Secretary of Defense, in a hearing before the House Appropriations Committee, March 27, 2003.

70 Iraq contains 115 billion barrels of proven oil reserves, the third largest in the world. Since only 10 percent of the country has been explored, analysts believe that there is much more to be found. Energy Information Administration, Department of Energy, "Country Analysis Briefs: Iraq," August 2007.

71 Eliot A. Cohen, Director, "Gulf War Air Power Survey," U.S. Air Force, 1993; and ORHA/CPA Historian interview with Gary Vogler, Senior Advisor to the Ministry of Oil, June 18, 2003.

72 The resolution authorized expanding sales from $2.1 billion to $5.256 billion in a six-month period. UN Press Release SC/6492, "Security Council Authorizes Sale of Iraq Oil to Offset Shortfall in Revenues Resulting from Delay in Oil Sales, Drop in Oil Prices," March 25, 1998; and United Nations Security Council Resolution 1153, February 20, 1998.

73 Michael H. Mobbs, "Memorandum for the Record: Potential for Competition in Obtaining Contractor Services Required by the Energy Infrastructure Planning Group (EIPG)," November 8, 2002.

74 Members included Mike Mackowski, Senaca Johnston from State, Barbara Glotfelty from DoD Contracting, Matt Armitrano, a consultant, and a CIA representative. SIGIR interview with Gary Vogler, CPA Senior Advisor to Oil, May 10, 2006.

75 Michael H. Mobbs, "Memorandum for the Record: Potential for Competition in Obtaining Contractor Services Required by the Energy Infrastructure Planning Group (EIPG)," November 8, 2002; and SIGIR Lessons Learned Forum: Contracting and Procurement, Washington, DC, December 5, 2005.

76 SIGIR Lessons Learned Forum: Contracting and Procurement, Washington, DC, December 5, 2005.

77 Donald L. Trautner, "A Personal Account and Perspective of the U.S. Army Logistics Civil Augmentation Program (LOGCAP)," 2004 Conference of Army Historians, July 15, 2004.

78 Donald L. Trautner, "A Personal Account and Perspective of the U.S. Army Logistics Civil Augmentation Program (LOGCAP)," 2004 Conference of Army Historians, July 15, 2004.

79 Lieutenant Colonel Steven T. Mitchell, "Targetable Logistics: Contractors in Zones of Conflict-Backbone or Underbelly?" U.S. Army War College Strategy Research Paper, March 18, 2005, 4.

80 T. Christian Miller, *Blood Money: Wasted Billions, Lost Lives, and Corporate Greed in Iraq* (New York: Little, Brown and Company, 2006), 76.

81 For a detailed analysis of contractors in the Iraq theater, see Congressional Budget Office, "Contractors' Support of U.S. Operations in Iraq," August 2008.

82 Michael H. Mobbs, "Memorandum for the Record: Potential for Competition in Obtaining Contractor Services Required by the Energy Infrastructure Planning Group (EIPG)," November 8, 2002. In this memorandum Mobbs identifies Bechtel and Fluor as among other contractors who have the technical capacity but not an existing connection to CENTCOM. See: SIGIR Lessons Learned Forum: Contracting and Procurement, Washington, DC, December 5, 2005.

83 SIGIR Lessons Learned Forum: Contracting and Procurement, Washington, DC, December 5, 2005.

84 SIGIR Lessons Learned Forum: Contracting and Procurement, Washington, DC, December 5, 2005.

85 John L. Long, Associate General Counsel, Acquisition and Logistics, Memorandum to Barbara Glotfelty, Energy Infrastructure Planning Group, "Legal Position on LOGCAP Scope of Work," November 8, 2002.

86 SIGIR Lessons Learned Forum: Contracting and Procurement, Washington, DC, December 5, 2005.

87 USACE, "Frequently Asked Questions: Engineer Support to Operation Iraqi Freedom," USACE Missions—Oil Fire Suppression and Restoration of Production, updated September 5, 2007.

88 "The resulting contingency plan was used as justification for subsequently awarding a sole-source contract to Kellogg Brown & Root for restoring the oil infrastructure, for which nearly $1.4 billion was obligated during fiscal year 2003." GAO Report 04-605, "Rebuilding Iraq: Fiscal Year 2003 Contract Award Procedures and Management Challenges," June 2004, 14, 16, 19-20. The contract was replaced by competitively procured contracts in January 2004. KBR was awarded a contract capped at $1.2 billion to repair the oil infrastructure of Southern Iraq. Parsons Iraqi Joint Venture was awarded a contract capped at $800,000 to carry out repairs in Northern Iraq. USACE, "Frequently Asked Questions: Engineer Support to Operation Iraqi Freedom. USACE Missions—Oil Fire Suppression and Restoration of Production," updated January 20, 2004, http://www.hq.usace.army.mil/cepa/iraq/faq.htm (accessed April 24, 2006).

89 Although the contingency plan that violated contracting regulations was used as justification for the sole-source contract to Kellogg Brown & Root, GAO found that the award of the contract generally complied with applicable legal standards. GAO Report 04-605, "Rebuilding Iraq: Fiscal Year 2003 Contract Award Procedures and Management Challenges," June 2004, 19-21.

90 SIGIR Lessons Learned Forum: Contracting and Procurement, Washington, DC, December 5, 2005.

91 ORHA/CPA Historian interview with Brigadier General Robert Crear, Commander of Task Force RIO, June 25, 2003.

92 SIGIR interview with Frank Miller, former Chairman of the Executive Steering Group of the National Security Council, August 19, 2008.

93 For an overall account of Treasury's activities, see Chapters 7, 8 and 9 in John B. Taylor, *Global Financial Warriors: The Untold Story of International Finance in the Post-9/11 World* (New York: W.W. Norton & Company, 2007); and U.S. Treasury, "Contingency Plans for Reconstruction of Iraq's Financial Institutions and Financial Markets," April 28, 2003.

94 Iraqi currency printed before 1990 in Switzerland is referred to as the Swiss dinar, which was still used in the Kurdish region at the time of the 2003 invasion even though the Iraqi Central Bank began printing a new currency, known as the Saddam dinar, in 1991. Iraq, as a result, had two systems of currency, one of which—the Saddam dinar—had been subject to inflation, and another—the Swiss dinar—which had not lost nearly as much of its value, even though it had technically ceased to be legal tender. For a description of how the Treasury team approached this problem, see Chapters 7, 8 and 9 in John B. Taylor, *Global Financial Warriors: The Untold Story of International Finance in the Post-9/11 World* (New York: W.W. Norton & Company, 2007).

95 For supplementary accounts, see USIP and ORHA/CPA Historian interviews with David Nummy, former Senior Advisor to the Ministry of Finance, October 14, 2004, and June 23 and 27, 2003.

96 GAO Testimony 04-579T, "Recovering Iraq's Assets: Preliminary Observations on U.S. Efforts and Challenges," March 18, 2004; Roger H. Bezdek, "Using Vested Assets for the Reconstruction of Iraq," *Public Fund Digest* 5, no. 2 (2005); and Executive Order 13290, "Confiscating and Vesting Certain Iraqi Property," March 20, 2003.

97 SIGIR interview with Christopher Milligan, USAID Deputy Director of Iraq, April 14, 2006.

98 SIGIR interview with Frank Miller, former Chairman of the Executive Steering Group of the NSC, June 26, 2008.

99 SIGIR interview with Jonathan Dworken, former Director for Humanitarian Assistance and Disaster Response for the NSC, March 29, 2007.

Chapter 3

1 SIGIR interview with Douglas Feith, former Under Secretary of Defense for Policy, March 21, 2008; and Douglas Feith, *War and Decision: Inside the Pentagon at the Dawn of the War on Terror* (New York: HarperCollins, 2008), 316-317.

2 SIGIR interview with Douglas Feith, former Under Secretary of Defense for Policy, March 21, 2008.

3 SIGIR interview with Colonel John Agoglia, former CENTCOM planner, May 22, 2008.

4 SIGIR interview with Colonel (Ret.) Michael Fitzgerald, former CENTCOM J5 Chief of War Plans, May 30, 2008; SIGIR interview with Colonel John Agoglia, former CENTCOM planner, May 22, 2008; and Michael R. Gordon and General Bernard E. Trainor, *Cobra II: The Inside Story of the Invasion and Occupation of Iraq* (New York: Pantheon Books, 2006), 140-46.

5 SIGIR interview with Colonel (Ret.) Michael Fitzgerald, former CENTCOM (J5) Chief of War Plans, May 30, 2008; and SIGIR interview with Colonel John Agoglia, former CENTCOM planner, May 22, 2008.

6 Lieutenant Colonel Thomas Fisher, former CENTCOM planner, email to SIGIR, October 20, 2008.

7 ORHA/CPA Historian interview with Major Thomas Fisher, former CENTCOM planner, August 27, 2003.

8 SIGIR interview with General George Casey, former Director of the Joint Staff and former Commander of MNF-I, July 30, 2008. For an early history of JTF-4, see Chapter 4 of Nora Bensahel et. al., *After Saddam: Prewar Planning and the Occupation of Iraq* (Santa Monica, CA: RAND Corporation, 2008).

9 SIGIR interview with Douglas Feith, former Under Secretary of Defense for Policy, March 21, 2008; and Douglas Feith, *War and Decision: Inside the Pentagon at the Dawn of the War on Terror* (New York: HarperCollins, 2008), 347.

10 Powell explained his concurrence in the following terms: "People say, 'Well it should have been State.' State does not have the personnel, the capacity, or the size to deal with an immediate postwar situation in a foreign country that's eight thousand miles away from here, so there was never a disagreement about this. It made sense. I point out to people that Douglas MacArthur was not a Foreign Service Officer ... neither was Lucius Clay a Foreign Service Officer." SIGIR interview with Colin Powell, former Secretary of State, February 4, 2008.

11 SIGIR interview with Colin Powell, former Secretary of State, February 4, 2008.

12 SIGIR interview with Douglas Feith, former Under Secretary of Defense for Policy, March 21, 2008; and Douglas Feith, *War and Decision: Inside the Pentagon at the Dawn of the War on Terror* (New York: HarperCollins, 2008), 347-50. Frank Miller disputes that the discussion of the Defense Department's takeover of the reconstruction mission was as clear as Feith characterized it. SIGIR interview with Frank Miller, former Chairman of the Executive Steering Group of the NSC, February 4, 2008.

13 National Security Archive, "New State Department Releases on the 'Future of Iraq' Project," September 1, 2006, http://www.gwu.edu/~nsarchiv/NSAEBB/NSAEBB198/index.htm. National Security Presidential Directive 24, "Post-War Iraq Reconstruction," January 20, 2003, is not publicly available. Information about NSPD 24 was obtained through: DoD IG Audit D-2004-057, "Contracts Awarded for the Coalition Provisional Authority by the Defense Contracting Command-Washington," March 18, 2004, 1.

14 SIGIR interview with Andrew Natsios, former USAID Administrator, April 17, 2006.

15 SIGIR interview with James Kunder, USAID Acting Deputy Administrator, February 15, 2008.

16 SIGIR interview with Frank Miller, former Chairman of the Executive Steering Group of the NSC, February 4, 2008.

17 ORHA/CPA Historian interview with Major Ray Eiriz, former CENTCOM planner, December 7, 2006.

18 For an overview of how the war plan developed, see Michael R. Gordon and General Bernard E. Trainor, *Cobra II: The Inside Story of the Invasion and Occupation of Iraq* (New York: Pantheon Books, 2006).

19 SIGIR interview with Colonel (Ret.) Michael Fitzgerald, former CENTCOM (J5) Chief of War Plans, May 30, 2008; and Michael R. Gordon and General Bernard E. Trainor, *Cobra II: The Inside Story of the Invasion and Occupation of Iraq* (New York: Pantheon Books, 2006), 48-51, 52-54, 66-67.

20 SIGIR interview with Colonel (Ret.) Michael Fitzgerald, former CENTCOM (J5) Chief of War Plans, May 30, 2008.

21 SIGIR interview with Colonel (Ret.) Michael Fitzgerald, former CENTCOM (J5) Chief of War Plans, May 30, 2008.

22 ORHA/CPA Historian interview with Lieutenant General (Ret.) Jay Garner, former Director of ORHA, September 14-15, 2005. For an overview of how force levels evolved, see Michael R. Gordon and General Bernard E. Trainor, *Cobra II: The Inside Story of the Invasion and Occupation of Iraq* (New York: Pantheon Books, 2006), 95-105.

23 SIGIR interview with Frank Miller, former Chairman of the Executive Steering Group of the NSC, December 12, 2005.

24 SIGIR interview with Colonel (Ret.) Michael Fitzgerald, former CENTCOM J5 Chief of War Plans, May 30, 2008.

25 ORHA/CPA Historian interview with Major Thomas Fisher, former CENTCOM Planner, August 27, 2003.

26 ORHA/CPA Historian interview with Lieutenant General (Ret.) Jay Garner, former Director of ORHA, September 14-15, 2005. An account of Lieutenant General (Ret.) Jay Garner's involvement in ORHA is to be published in 2009 by Gordon Rudd, the ORHA/CPA Historian.

27 SIGIR interview with Douglas Feith, former Under Secretary of Defense for Policy, March 21, 2008.

28 ORHA/CPA Historian interview with Lieutenant Colonel Jeffrey S. Kojac, NSC military aide, October 19, 2007.

29 DoD News Transcript, "DoD News Briefing-Secretary Rumsfeld and Gen. Myers," March 20, 2003.

30 SIGIR interview with Wendy Chamberlin, former USAID Assistant Administrator, Near East Bureau, April 18, 2007.

31 ORHA/CPA Historian interview with Lieutenant General (Ret.) Jay Garner, former Director of ORHA, March 30, 2004.

32 ORHA/CPA Historian interview with Lieutenant General (Ret.) Jay Garner, former Director of ORHA, March 30, 2004. Douglas Feith asserts that his office provided Garner with both written and oral briefings. Feith also asserts that Garner must have known about the office of Special Plans. Douglas Feith, former Under Secretary of Defense for Policy, written comments to SIGIR, January 7, 2009.

33 ORHA/CPA Historian interview with Lieutenant General (Ret.) Jay Garner, former Director of ORHA, March 30, 2004.

34 ORHA/CPA Historian interview with Lieutenant General (Ret.) Jay Garner, former Director of ORHA, March 30, 2004; and ORHA/CPA Historian interview with Colonel (Ret.) Paul Hughes, former ORHA/CPA Director of Strategic Policy, June 29, 2006.

35 ORHA/CPA Historian interview with Lieutenant General (Ret.) Jay Garner, former Director of ORHA, March 30, 2004; and ORHA, "Contracting Support for ORHA, Office of Reconstruction and Humanitarian Assistance (ORHA) Operational Structure," March 28, 2003.

36 SIGIR interview with Christopher Milligan, USAID Deputy Director of Iraq, February 9, 2006.

37 ORHA/CPA Historian interview with Lieutenant General (Ret.) Jay Garner, former Director of ORHA, March 30, 2004.

38 ORHA/CPA Historian interview with Lieutenant General (Ret.) Jay Garner, former Director of ORHA, September 14-15, 2005. Douglas Feith recalls contention only over the Civil Affairs pillar Douglas Feith, former Under Secretary of Defense for Policy, written comments to SIGIR, January 8, 2009.

39 Secretary Rumsfeld characterizes this exchange differently. "As I recall, the issue with General Garner was not whether Defense should staff every position at ORHA, but over several individuals whom the White House believed would not be a good fit with ORHA." Donald Rumsfeld, former Secretary of Defense, written comments to SIGIR, November 5, 2008.

40 USAID Assistant Administrator Wendy Chamberlin had called Lucke—formerly AID's mission director in Jordan, the agency's second largest mission—out of retirement in October when she learned he spoke some Arabic. SIGIR interview with Wendy Chamberlin, former USAID Assistant Administrator, Near East Bureau, April 18, 2007.

41 ORHA/CPA Historian interview with Lieutenant General (Ret.) Jay Garner, former Director of ORHA, March 30, 2004.

42 Mobbs was not Feith's first choice. Feith's first candidate was ineligible to serve. His second, David Kay, was appointed to ORHA, but resigned after two days. Kay would eventually lead the Iraq Survey Group, a task force that searched for weapons of mass destruction at the war's end. Although Mobbs had served in the U.S. Arms Control and Disarmament Agency in the 1980s, much of his professional experience was as a lawyer specializing in corporate and commercial matters in Russia and Eastern Europe. Fox News, "Bio: Michael H. Mobbs," provided by ORHA, April 23, 2003.

43 ORHA/CPA Historian interview with Lieutenant General (Ret.) Jay Garner, former Director of ORHA, September 14-15, 2005.

44 ORHA/CPA Historian interview with Lieutenant General (Ret.) Jay Garner, former Director of ORHA, September 14-15, 2005; and ORHA/CPA Historian interview with Colonel Thomas Baltazar, C3 Operations Officer for ORHA, June 10, 2003.

45 ORHA/CPA Historian interview with Lieutenant General (Ret.) Jay Garner, former Director of ORHA, September 14-15, 2005.

46 ORHA/CPA Historian interview with George F. Ward, former Head of Humanitarian Pillar of ORHA, June 29, 2006.

47 ORHA/CPA Historian interview with Brigadier General Steven Hawkins, former Commander, JTF-4, June 23, 2003.

48 ORHA/CPA Historian interview with Major Thomas Fisher, former CENTCOM Planner, August 27, 2003.

49 ORHA/CPA Historian interview with Brigadier General Steven Hawkins, former Commander, JTF-4, June 23, 2003; and SIGIR interview with Brigadier General Mike Jones, Director of J-5 Middle East Affairs, April 13, 2007.

50 ORHA/CPA Historian interview with Brigadier General Steven Hawkins, former Commander, JTF-4, June 23, 2003.

51 SIGIR interview with Douglas Feith, Under Secretary of Defense for Policy, December 17, 2004.

52 ORHA/CPA Historian interview with Brigadier General Steven Hawkins, former Commander, JTF-4, June 23, 2003.

53 SIGIR interview with Colonel (Ret.) Michael Fitzgerald, former CENTCOM J5 Chief of War Plans, May 30, 2008.

54 SIGIR interview with Colonel (Ret.) Michael Fitzgerald, former CENTCOM J5 Chief of War Plans, May 30, 2008.

55 SIGIR interview with Brigadier General Mike Jones, Director of J-5 Middle East Affairs, April 13, 2007. Title X of the U.S. Code obliges the Joint Chiefs to provide military advice to the President. A staff larger than that working for the Secretary of Defense backs the Joint Chiefs. These different echelons of planning—the Joint Staff in Washington, combatant commanders in the field, and civilian staff in the Office of the Secretary of Defense—are collaborative, at least in theory. Some analysts note that Rumsfeld's tenure strained this system of civil-military cooperation. Michael C. Desch, "Bush and the Generals," *Foreign Affairs* 86, no. 3 (May/June 2007). Secretary Rumsfeld himself, however, disputes this characterization. "Relationships with the Joint Chiefs during my tenure were professional. As is their statutory obligation, they provided useful and constructive advice to the President and to me." Donald Rumsfeld, former Secretary of Defense, written comments to SIGIR, November 5, 2008. Rumsfeld notes that Chairman of the Joint Chiefs of Staff Richard Meyers and Richard H. Kohn wrote a rebuttal to Desch's article. See: Richard B. Myers and Richard H. Kohn, "The Military's Place," *Foreign Affairs* 86, no. 5 (September/October 2007).

56 ORHA/CPA Historian interview with Brigadier General Steven Hawkins, former Commander, JTF-4, June 23, 2003.

57 ORHA/CPA Historian interviews with Lieutenant General (Ret.) Jay Garner, former Director of ORHA, April 5, 2006, and September 14-15, 2005.

58 ORHA/CPA Historian interview with Lieutenant General (Ret.) Jay Garner, former Director of ORHA, September 14-15, 2005.

59 ORHA/CPA Historian interview with Lieutenant General (Ret.) Jay Garner, former Director of ORHA, September 14-15, 2005.

60 SIGIR interview with Colonel (Ret.) Michael Fitzgerald, former CENTCOM J5 Chief of War Plans, May 30, 2008.

61 SIGIR interview with General (Ret.) Colin Powell, former Secretary of State, February 4, 2008.

62 SIGIR interview with Bob Gersony, former Advisor to the USAID Administrator, January 16, 2007; and ORHA/CPA Historian interview with Lieutenant General (Ret.) Ronald E. Adams, former Deputy Director of ORHA, September 29, 2006.

63 Milligan sent a memorandum to Lieutenant General (Ret.) Garner summarizing progress across eleven sectors and highlighting outstanding issues for his action. Christopher Milligan, Reconstruction and Humanitarian Assistance Group, memorandum to Lieutenant General (Ret.) Jay Garner, Director of ORHA, "Status of Reconstruction and Humanitarian Assistance Preparations," January 26, 2003.

64 SIGIR interview with Thomas Wheelock, former Chief of Party for USAID's contractor International Resources Group, January 5, 2006.

65 ORHA/CPA Historian interview with Lieutenant General (Ret.) Carl A. Strock, former Commanding General of USACE, October 30, 2006. Bernoulli's equation is used by engineers to describe the relationship between air pressure and velocity in fluid dynamics.

66 ORHA/CPA Historian interview with Lieutenant General (Ret.) Jay Garner, former Director of ORHA, March 30, 2004.

67 ORHA/CPA Historian interview with Colonel Robert D. Costello, Jr., ORHA Chief of Logistics, June 15, 2003.

68 Douglas Feith disputes this characterization. Douglas Feith, former Under Secretary of Defense for Policy, written comments to SIGIR, January 7, 2009.

69 Dayton Maxwell, "Deliberate and Development Post-Conflict Planning in Iraq: The Office of Policy, Planning, and Analysis, Coalition Provisional Authority, A USAID Perspective," unpublished manuscript, July 23, 2004, 9.

70 Leonard Hawley, "Urgent Policy Issues and Capability Needs: U.S. Interim Civilian Transitional Administration (ICTA) in Iraq," written analysis to Lieutenant General (Ret.) Jay Garner, March 10, 2003.

71 SIGIR interview with Leonard Hawley, former Deputy Assistant Secretary of State for Peacekeeping, February 12, 2008.

72 SIGIR, "Iraq Reconstruction: Lessons in Human Capital Management," January 2006, 7-9.

73 An inherently governmental activity involves: (1) binding the United States to take or not to take some action by contract, policy, regulation, authorization, order, or otherwise; (2) determining, protecting, and advancing economic, political, territorial, property, or other interests by military or diplomatic action, civil or criminal judicial proceedings, contract management, or otherwise; (3) significantly affecting the life, liberty, or property of private persons; or (4) exerting ultimate control over the acquisition, use, or disposition of United States property (real or personal, tangible or intangible), including establishing policies or procedures for the collection, control, or disbursement of appropriated and other federal funds. White House Office of Management and Budget Circular A-76 (Revised), "Performance of Commercial Activities," May 29, 2003; and FAR, Subpart 7.5, "Inherently Governmental Functions," http://www.acquisition.gov/far/current/html/Subpart%207_5.html.

74 SIGIR, "Iraq Reconstruction: Lessons in Human Capital Management," January 2006, 10.

75 The statutory provision used was Title 5, Section 3161, of the U.S. Code, under 5 CFR 213.3199.

76 ORHA, "Staffing for the Office of Reconstruction and Humanitarian Assistance (ORHA)," Attachment to email from Larry Hanauer, Special Assistant to the Director of ORHA, to Gretchen Anderson, Office of the Under Secretary of Defense (Comptroller), "ORHA Personnel Growth," April 18, 2003.

77 ORHA/CPA Historian interview with Colonel Thomas Baltazar, C3 Operations Officer for ORHA, June 10, 2003.

78 General Garner dictated notes for the record on February 28, March 3, and March 10, 2003 about the general status of ORHA preparations and his meetings with Secretary Condoleezza Rice, President Bush, and the United Nations. ORHA/CPA Historian and SIGIR interviews with Lieutenant General (Ret.) Jay Garner.

79 ORHA/CPA Historian interview with Lieutenant General (Ret.) Jay Garner, former Director of ORHA, September 14-15, 2005.

80 ORHA/CPA Historian interview with Lieutenant General (Ret.) Jay Garner, former Director of ORHA, April 5, 2006.

81 A spreadsheet of Rock Drill attendees was maintained by ORHA staff. ORHA, "Rock Drill," undated. During military operations undertaken with other countries, officers from the coalition countries typically join the headquarters staff in various capacities.

82 The Political-Military and Near East Affairs bureaus did not dispatch their senior officers handling the Iraq portfolio. ORHA, "Interagency Rehearsal and Planning Conference: Summary and Analysis," February 21-22, 2003.

83 Dayton Maxwell, "Deliberate and Development Post Conflict Planning in Iraq: The Office of Policy, Planning, and Analysis, Coalition Provisional Authority, A USAID Perspective," unpublished manuscript, July 23, 2004, 23-24; and ORHA, "Interagency Rehearsal and Planning Conference: Summary and Analysis," February 21-22, 2003.

84 ORHA, "Interagency Rehearsal and Planning Conference: Summary and Analysis," February 21-22, 2003.

85 ORHA, "Interagency Rehearsal and Planning Conference: Summary and Analysis," February 21-22, 2003.

86 ORHA/CPA Historian interview with George F. Ward, former Head of Humanitarian Pillar of ORHA, June 29, 2006.

87 ORHA, "Interagency Rehearsal and Planning Conference: Summary and Analysis," February 21-22, 2003.

88 ORHA, "Interagency Rehearsal and Planning Conference: Summary and Analysis," February 21-22, 2003.

89 SIGIR interview with Ross Wherry, former USAID Director of the Office of Iraq Affairs, April 5, 2006.

90 ORHA/CPA Historian interview with Lieutenant General (Ret.) Jay Garner, former Director of ORHA, March 30, 2004.

91 Lieutenant General (Ret.) Jay Garner, follow-up interview notes to ORHA/CPA Historian, March 10, 2003; and SIGIR and ORHA/CPA Historian interviews with Lieutenant General (Ret.) Jay Garner.

92 ORHA/CPA Historian interview with Lieutenant General (Ret.) Carl A. Strock, former Commanding General of USACE, October 30, 2006.

93 Lieutenant General (Ret.) Jay Garner, follow-up interview notes to ORHA/CPA Historian, March 3, 2003; and SIGIR and ORHA/CPA Historian interviews with Lieutenant General Garner.

94 SIGIR interview with Frank Miller, former Chairman of the Executive Steering Group of the NSC, December 12, 2005; and Michael R. Gordon and General Bernard E. Trainor, *Cobra II: The Inside Story of the Invasion and Occupation of Iraq* (Pantheon Books, 2006), 160-63.

95 SIGIR interview with Douglas Feith, former Under Secretary of Defense for Policy, March 21, 2008; and Douglas Feith, *War and Decision: Inside the Pentagon at the Dawn of the War on Terror* (New York: HarperCollins, 2008), 402-11.

96 Lieutenant General (Ret.) Jay Garner, follow-up interview notes to ORHA/CPA Historian, March 10, 2003.

97 SIGIR interview with General (Ret.) Colin Powell, former Secretary of State, February 4, 2008; and ORHA/CPA Historian interview with Lieutenant General (Ret.) Jay Garner, former Director of ORHA, March 30, 2004.

98 ORHA/CPA Historian interview with Lieutenant General (Ret.) Jay Garner, former Director of ORHA, September 14-15, 2005.

99 Douglas Feith asserts that Rumsfeld wanted to institute a "proper analysis and process" to "find the best candidates in the United States, not just the best ones in the U.S. government. See Douglas Feith, *War and Decision: Inside the Pentagon at the Dawn of the War on Terror* (New York: HarperCollins, 2008), 387.

100 ORHA/CPA Historian interview with Lieutenant General (Ret.) Jay Garner, former Director of ORHA, March 30, 2004.

101 ORHA/CPA Historian interview with Lieutenant General (Ret.) Jay Garner, former Director of ORHA, March 30, 2004.

102 Lieutenant General (Ret.) Jay Garner, follow-up interview notes to ORHA/CPA Historian, March 10, 2003.

Chapter 4

1 SIGIR interview with Colonel (Ret.) Paul Hughes, former ORHA/CPA Director, Strategic Policy Office, May 2, 2007.

2 ORHA/CPA Historian interview with Lieutenant General (Ret.) Jay Garner, former Director of ORHA, September 14-15, 2005.

3 Gordon Rudd, ORHA/CPA Historian, compiled a list of language skills of ORHA personnel. SIGIR conversations with Gordon Rudd, ORHA/CPA Historian, Summer 2007.

4 ORHA/CPA Historian interview with Colonel Robert D. Costello, Jr., ORHA Chief of Logistics, June 15, 2003.

5 SIGIR interview with Colonel (Ret.) Paul Hughes, former ORHA/CPA Director, Strategic Policy Office, May 2, 2007.

6 ORHA/CPA Historian interview with Colonel Robert D. Costello, Jr., ORHA Chief of Logistics, June 15, 2003; and SIGIR and ORHA/CPA Historian interview with Lieutenant General (Ret.) Jay Garner, former Director of ORHA, October 27, 2008.

7 SIGIR interview with Colonel (Ret.) Paul Hughes, former ORHA/CPA Director, Strategic Policy Office, May 2, 2007.

8 SIGIR, "Iraq Reconstruction: Lessons in Contracting and Procurement," July 2006, 21.

9 ORHA/CPA Historian interview with Lieutenant Colonel Stephen M. Elliott, Contracting Officer for ORHA as part of DCMA's Contingency Contracting Administration Services Mission, July 12, 2003.

10 Some question remains about the purpose of this funding. Some say it was strictly for the ORHA staff and translators; the ORHA/CPA comptroller says the purpose was more expansive. Gary Minor, "Financing the Fight—From the Front," *Air Force Comptroller* (January 2004).

11 The war started on March 20 in Iraq, late evening on March 19 in the United States. The date of the event in local time is used for this report.

12 ORHA/CPA Historian interview with Lieutenant General (Ret.) Ronald E. Adams, Deputy Director of ORHA, September 29, 2006.

13 SIGIR interview with Lieutenant General (Ret.) Jay Garner, former Director of ORHA, April 5, 2006. For a chronology of JTF-4's dissolution, see Nora Bensahel et al., *After Saddam: Prewar Planning and the Occupation of Iraq* (Santa Monica, CA: RAND Corporation, 2008), 51-52.

14 Dayton Maxwell, "Deliberate and Development Post Conflict Planning in Iraq: The Office of Policy, Planning, and Analysis, Coalition Provisional Authority, A USAID Perspective," unpublished manuscript, July 23, 2004, 24.

15 ORHA's leaders did not give it credence, and it was never formally issued. ORHA/CPA Historian interview with Lieutenant General (Ret.) Ronald E. Adams, Deputy Director of ORHA, September 29, 2006.

16 Dayton Maxwell, "Deliberate and Development Post Conflict Planning in Iraq: The Office of Policy, Planning, and Analysis, Coalition Provisional Authority, A USAID Perspective," unpublished manuscript, July 23, 2004, 23-24.

17 Lieutenant General (Ret.) Jay Garner, Director of ORHA, memorandum to Secretary of Defense Donald Rumsfeld, passed through Larry Hanauer, Special Assistant to the Director of ORHA, March 21, 2003.

18 OSD, "Policy, Governance & External Relations in Post War Iraq, Ministry Candidates," March 25, 2003.

19 Colin Powell, Secretary of State, memorandum to Donald Rumsfeld, Secretary of Defense, untitled, March 26, 2003.

20 USAID Press Release, "Food and Non-Food Relief Supplies to Iraq," April 10, 2003.

21 SIGIR interview with Sloan Mann, USAID/OTI DART team member, August 10, 2007; and USAID, "A Year in Iraq," May 2004, 4.

22 For background on the Humanitarian Operations Center (HOC) and for an articulation of NGO reticence, see Refugees International, "Humanitarian Coordination for Iraq: A Job for the United Nations," April 9, 2003. The article notes that, "Even as they rely on the HOC for access, the view of most aid agencies is that close association with the military forces of a belligerent compromises the impartiality that lies at the core of their mission. The aid agencies provide humanitarian assistance based on need, not politics; the idea of using aid strategically to win "hearts and minds" is anathema to the humanitarian community. Yet while the principles espoused by most aid organizations would seem to dictate distance from the HOC, pragmatism seems to have dictated association."

23 Dayton Maxwell, "Deliberate and Development Post Conflict Planning in Iraq: The Office of Policy, Planning, and Analysis, Coalition Provisional Authority, A USAID Perspective," unpublished manuscript, July 23, 2004, 18.

24 USIP interview with Thomas Wheelock, Chief of Party for USAID's contractor International Resources Group, September 8, 2004.

25 ORHA/CPA Historian interview with Brigadier General Steven Hawkins, former Commander, JTF-4, June 23, 2003.

26 SIGIR interview with Bruce Spake, Vice President of DAI, and Steve Connolly, Task Order Manager, DAI, November 2, 2006.

27 Dayton Maxwell, "Deliberate and Development Post Conflict Planning in Iraq: The Office of Policy, Planning, and Analysis, Coalition Provisional Authority, A USAID Perspective," unpublished manuscript, July 23, 2004, 40.

28 CENTCOM, "Governorate Support Team (GST) Concept," briefing slides; and Lieutenant Colonel Thomas Fisher, former CENTCOM planner, email to SIGIR, October 20, 2008.

29 Christopher Milligan, "Bottom Up Governance: For a Democratic Iraq," briefing slides, April 2, 2003, 11, 14.

30 Jon Wegge and T. Christopher Milligan, "Regime Change and Local Government: A Strategy for a Stable Iraq, with Lessons from Indonesia," November 2002.

31 SIGIR interview with Christopher Milligan, USAID Deputy Director of Iraq, March 27, 2007, and Christopher Milligan, "Bottom Up Governance: For a Democratic Iraq," briefing slides, April 2, 2003.

32 ORHA/CPA Historian interview with Lieutenant General (Ret.) Jay Garner, former Director of ORHA, September 14-15, 2005.

33 Larry Hanauer, Special Assistant to the Director of ORHA, email to Gretchen Anderson, Office of the Under Secretary of Defense (Comptroller), "ORHA Personnel Growth," April 18, 2003.

34 Some of that staff included personnel who provided security but were not assigned specifically to ORHA. ORHA/CPA Historian interview with Lieutenant Colonel Stephen M. Elliot, Contracting Officer for ORHA as part of DCMA's Contingency Contracting Administration Services Mission, July 12, 2003; and Director for Operations and Personnel memorandum to Under Secretary of Defense (Comptroller), "Questions from Jaymie Durnan—Why the Huge Increase in [ORHA] Staff?" attachment to email from Larry Hanauer, Special Assistant to the Director of ORHA, to Gretchen Anderson, of the Under Secretary of Defense (Comptroller), "ORHA Personnel Growth," April 18, 2003.

35 Dov S. Zakheim, Under Secretary of Defense and Comptroller, memorandum to Special Assistant to the Deputy Secretary of Defense, "Response to Your Question on Increased Staffing Level for the Office of Reconstruction and Humanitarian Assistance," April 14, 2003.

36 Two could write them for up to $5 million; the other could write contracts for up to $1 million. SIGIR, "Iraq Reconstruction: Lessons in Contracting and Procurement," July 2006, 21; and ORHA/CPA Historian interview with Lieutenant Colonel Stephen M. Elliot, Contracting Officer for ORHA as part of DCMA's Contingency Contracting Administration Services Mission, July 12, 2003.

37 ORHA/CPA Historian interview with Lieutenant Colonel Stephen M. Elliot, Contracting Officer for ORHA as part of DCMA's Contingency Contracting Administration Services Mission, July 12, 2003.

38 ABC News, "Project Iraq," *Nightline*, April 23, 2003.

39 Dr. Condoleezza Rice, National Security Advisor, "Dr. Condoleezza Rice Discusses Iraq Reconstruction," White House Press Release, April 4, 2003.

40 Dr. Condoleezza Rice, National Security Advisor, "Dr. Condoleezza Rice Discusses Iraq Reconstruction," White House Press Release, April 4, 2003.

Chapter 5

1 Kathleen T. Rhem, "Security Still Most Serious Concern for U.S. Forces in Iraq," *American Forces Press Service*, May 15, 2003; and ORHA/CPA Historian interview with Michael Kelly, Australian Army Colonel, June 12, 2004.

2 SIGIR interview with Sinan al-Najaar, former senior manager in an Iraqi ministry, November 30, 2006.

3 The Saddam memorandum was published in Arabic by *Al-Hayat* (London) on July 12, 2003. For a translated version, see Middle East Media Research Institute, Special Dispatch Series no. 538, "A Top Secret Document Dated January 23, 2003 from Iraqi Intelligence: A Plan for Action in the Event of a Regime Downfall," July 17, 2003.

4 ORHA/CPA Historian interview with Colonel Glenn Collins, ORHA/CPA Facility Manager, July 17, 2003.

5 SIGIR conversations with Barbara Lewis, former Senior Advisor to the Rafidain Bank, Summer 2007.

6 Robin Raphel, former Senior Advisor to the Ministry of Trade, email to SIGIR, April 11, 2007.

7 The Independent High Electoral Commission, "Fact Sheet: Voter Registration Update in the International Zone," June 25, 2008.

8 For a description of ordinary life in Iraq in the weeks preceding the invasion, see Anthony Shadid, *Night Draws Near: Iraq's People in the Shadow of America's War*, Part One: Before (New York: Henry Holt, 2005).

9 ORHA/CPA Historian interview with Brigadier General Steven Hawkins, former Commander, JTF-4, June 23, 2004.

10 CNN, "Ground Troops Clash Over Baghdad Airport," April 4, 2003.

11 For an account of the war plan, see Michael R. Gordon and General Bernard E. Trainor, *Cobra II: The Inside Story of the Invasion and Occupation of Iraq* (New York: Pantheon Books, 2006).

12 Anthony Shadid, *Night Draws Near: Iraq's People in the Shadow of America's War* (New York: Henry Holt, 2005), 67, 96-97.

13 For a representative account of a clash between coalition and irregular forces, see Michael R. Gordon and General Bernard E. Trainor, *Cobra II: The Inside Story of the Invasion and Occupation of Iraq* (New York: Pantheon Books, 2006), 217-221.

14 Colin H. Kahl, "COIN of the Realm: Is There a Future for Counterinsurgency?" *Foreign Affairs* 86, no.6 (November/December 2007); and Bernard Weinraub and Thom Shanker, "A Nation at War: Under Fire; Rumsfeld's Design for War Criticized on the Battlefield," *New York Times*, April 1, 2003.

15 SIGIR interview with Lieutenant General (Ret.) Jay Garner, former Director of ORHA, April 1, 2006.

16 USAID, "A Year in Iraq," May 2004, 4.

17 ORHA/CPA Historian interview with Brigadier General David Blackledge, Commander of the 354th Civil Affairs Brigade, January 2, 2004; ORHA/CPA Historian interview with Mike Gfoeller, former Deputy Director of ORHA Region-South, August 10, 2003; and USAID, "Assistance for Iraq: DART Assessment of Umm Qasr and Relief Efforts," March 27, 2003.

18 USAID, "Assistance for Iraq: DART Assessment of Umm Qasr and Relief Efforts," March 27, 2003. A month later, on April 26, another DART team based in Jordan crossed into al-Anbar province to monitor conditions in western Iraq. USAID, "Assistance for Iraq: DART Ar Rutbah Assessment," April 26, 2003.

19 ORHA/CPA Historian interview with Lieutenant Colonel (Ret.) Schappi Marsh, FEST team member, July 30, 2003.

20 During the invasion's initial phase, FEST teams helped shut down a hydroelectric dam that would have impacted the operations of the Third Infantry Division if it had failed. The FEST teams also ensured bridges over the Euphrates River could support M-1 tanks waiting to cross. Tele-engineering kits enabled them to relay real-time images to the reach-back center in the United States, where Farsi and Arabic-speaking engineers stood ready to translate diagrams and control panel labels. This capacity to draw on reach-back expertise brought new levels of engineering know-how to the battlefield. Once combat needs were met, the FEST teams moved on to assessing oil, water and electricity infrastructure. Two fully outfitted FEST-Main teams, larger units augmented with more engineers, worked with Task Force Restore Iraqi Oil. As the restoration of power became a major need, FEST teams later assisted Task Force Restore Iraq Electricity. By the end of May, eighteen teams were in country working for ORHA through a USAID-USACE agreement. SIGIR interview with William Fritz, USACE Assistant Deputy G-3 (Operations), Chief, Concepts, Plan and Doctrine Branch, March 1, 2006.

21 The USACE operations center and Infrastructure Assessment Team completed the assessment in the fall of 2002. Estimates for three scenarios were drawn: no damage, middle-range damage, extensive damage. $35 billion was the middle-range scenario. SIGIR interview with William Fritz, USACE Assistant Deputy G-3 (Operations), Chief, Concepts, Plans and Doctrine Branch, March 1, 2006.

22 ORHA/CPA Historian interview with Lieutenant General (Ret.) Jay Garner, former Director of ORHA, April 22, 2004.

23 Only a two-man contingent from the DART team remained in Umm Qasr after March 27, 2003. The rest of the team made follow-up trips from Kuwait on April 2 and April 5, 2003. USAID, "Assistance for Iraq: DART Assessment of Umm Qasr and Relief Efforts," April 7, 2003.

24 SIGIR interview with Bob Gersony, former Advisor to the USAID Administrator, January 16, 2007.

25 ORHA/CPA Historian interview with Lieutenant General (Ret.) Jay Garner, former Director of ORHA, April 22, 2004.

26 SIGIR interview with Andrew Natsios, former USAID Administrator, April 17, 2006.

27 In a letter to Secretary Rumsfeld on the relationship between DART and ORHA, Secretary Powell wrote, "if operational disagreements arise between DART and ORHA and cannot be resolved … the final resolution of the matter will come to us." Later that day, Powell wrote another letter regarding the selection of ORHA staff, claiming "these individuals may not be acceptable to you and that you have your own list of candidates to fill these positions. We have frozen these assignments until you and I deal with this." Colin Powell, Secretary of State, letters to Donald Rumsfeld, Secretary of Defense, March 26, 2003. In response Rumsfeld wrote, "If you agree to this common sense approach, our involvement in subsequent disputes will be kept to a minimum." Donald Rumsfeld, Secretary of Defense, letter to Colin Powell, Secretary of State, "Disaster Assistance Response Team and the Garner Group," March 31, 2003.

28 ORHA/CPA Historian interview with Lieutenant General (Ret.) Jay Garner, former Director of ORHA, April 22, 2004.

29 USAID, "Assistance for Iraq: DART Assessment of Umm Qasr and Relief Efforts," April 4, 2003.

30 ORHA/CPA Historian interview with Mike Gfoeller, former Deputy Director of ORHA Region-South, August 10, 2003.

31 DoD News Transcript, "DoD News Briefing-ASD PA Clarke and Major General McChrystal," April 10, 2003.

32 ORHA/CPA Historian interview with Lieutenant General (Ret.) Jay Garner, former Director of ORHA, September 14-15, 2005.

33 ORHA/CPA Historian interview with Brigadier General David Blackledge, Commander of the 354th Civil Affairs Brigade, January 2, 2004.

34 For contemporaneous accounts of Garner's visits to Umm Qasr and developments there, see CNN, "U.S. Interim Administrator Visits Iraq," April 12, 2003.

35 DoD News Transcript, "DoD News Briefing-Secretary Rumsfeld and General Myers," April 7, 2003; and David L. Phillips, *Losing Iraq: Inside the Postwar Reconstruction Fiasco* (New York: Basic Books, 2005), 8.

36 Anthony Shadid, *Night Draws Near: Iraq's People in the Shadow of America's War* (New York: Henry Holt, 2005), 378-380.

37 SIGIR interview with Lieutenant General David McKiernan, former Commander of Coalition Forces Land Component Command, December 5, 2006.

38 SIGIR interview with Lieutenant General David McKiernan, former Commander of Coalition Forces Land Component Command, December 5, 2006.

39 Public Broadcasting Service, "Interview with Laith Kubba," *FRONTLINE*, September 11, 2003.

40 ORHA/CPA Historian interview with Lieutenant General (Ret.) Carl A. Strock, former Commanding General of USACE, October 30, 2006.

41 The military grid used by NATO militaries is based on the Universal Transverse Mercator coordinate system, not longitude and latitude. SIGIR interview with Dustin Felix, Civil Affairs Officer in the 5th Brigade, 1st Cavalry Division, December 21, 2005.

42 ORHA/CPA Historian interview with Lieutenant General (Ret.) Jay Garner, former Director of ORHA, September 14-15, 2005.

43 SIGIR interview with Colonel John Agoglia, former CENTCOM planner, May 22, 2008; and SIGIR interview with Colonel (Ret.) Michael Fitzgerald, former CENTCOM (J5) Chief of War Plans, May 30, 2008.

44 ORHA/CPA Historian interview with Lieutenant General (Ret.) Jay Garner, former Director of ORHA, September 14-15, 2005.

45 ORHA/CPA Historian interview with Lieutenant General (Ret.) Jay Garner, former Director of ORHA, September 14-15, 2005.

46 Lieutenant General Garner recalls that Colonel Colin Boag, a British colonel, informed him of two possible locations to house ORHA: the Rashid Hotel or the Republican Palace. Since the media was already in the hotel, and Garner was concerned about the security risks of a vertical structure, he elected to house ORHA in the palace. SIGIR and ORHA/CPA Historian interview with Lieutenant General (Ret.) Jay Garner, former Director of ORHA, October 27, 2008.

47 ORHA/CPA Historian interview with Lieutenant General (Ret.) Jay Garner, former Director of ORHA, September 14-15, 2005.

48 ORHA/CPA Historian interview with Colonel Glenn Collins, ORHA/CPA Facility Manager, July 17, 2003.

49 Dayton Maxwell, "Deliberate and Development Post Conflict Planning in Iraq: The Office of Policy, Planning, and Analysis, Coalition Provisional Authority, A USAID Perspective," unpublished manuscript, July 23, 2004, 10-17.

50 Richard Miller, "A Brief History of CPATT," unpublished manuscript, May 15, 2005, 1. CPATT stands for the Coalition Police Assistance Training Team. Chapter 12 explains the creation of CPATT and other Iraqi security forces, both police and military.

51 ORHA/CPA Historian interview with Timothy Carney, Senior Advisor to the Ministry of Industry and Minerals, June 12, 2003.

52 ORHA/CPA Historian interview with Lieutenant General (Ret.) Jay Garner, former Director of ORHA, September 14-15, 2005.

53 SIGIR interview with Bruce Spake, Vice President of DAI, and Steve Connolly, QRF Coordinator, DAI, November 2, 2006.

54 ORHA/CPA Historian interview with Christopher Spear, Senior Advisor to the Ministry of Labor and Social Affairs, July 15, 2003; and SIGIR interview with James Haveman, former Senior Advisor to the Ministry of Health, and Robert Goodwin, former Chief of Staff, Ministry of Health, December 22, 2005.

55 ORHA/CPA Historian interview with Christopher Spear, Senior Advisor to the Ministry of Labor and Social Affairs, July 15, 2003.

56 SIGIR conversations with Barbara Lewis, former Senior Advisor to the Rafidain Bank, Summer 2007.

57 SIGIR interview with Samir Sumaida'ie, Iraqi Ambassador to the United States, March 11, 2008.

58 ORHA/CPA Historian interview with Major General Donald F. Campbell, Senior Advisor to the Ministry of Justice, July 14, 2003.

59 ORHA/CPA Historian interview with Major Lyn S. Brown, Advisor to the Ministry of Youth and Sport, June 22, 2004.

60 ORHA/CPA Historian interview with Lieutenant General (Ret.) Jay Garner, former Director of ORHA, September 14-15, 2005.

61 ORHA/CPA Historian interview with Gary Vogler, Senior Advisor to the Ministry of Oil, June 18, 2003.

62 USACE, "Iraqi Oil Infrastructure Restoration Strategic Plan: Rough Order of Magnitude," June 3, 2003; and ORHA/CPA Historian interview with Gary Vogler, Senior Advisor to the Ministry of Oil, June 18, 2003.

63 USACE, "Iraqi Oil Infrastructure Restoration Strategic Plan: Rough Order of Magnitude," June 3, 2003.

64 ORHA/CPA Historian and SIGIR interviews with Steven Browning, Task Force RIO Advisor, June 21, 2003 and April 26, 2006.

65 Dept. of the Army Memorandum to CJTF-7 C9, "Information Paper: Religious Groups in Iraq," June 24, 2003, 5.

66 ORHA/CPA Historian interview with Gary Vogler, Senior Advisor to the Ministry of Oil, June 18, 2003.

67 Peter W. Galbraith, National Defense University, Testimony before the Senate Foreign Relations Committee, June 12, 2003. One estimate of looting circulating among CPA officials was $12 billion. L. Paul Bremer, James Dobbins, and David Gompert, "Early Days in Iraq: Decisions of the CPA," Survival, August 2008, 23, 46.

68 Colonel (Ret.) Gregory Fontenot, Lieutenant Colonel E.J. Degen, and Lieutenant Colonel David Tohn, On Point: The United States Army in Operation Iraqi Freedom (Fort Leavenworth, KS: Center for Army Lessons Learned, 2005).

69 GAO Report 07-444, "Operation Iraqi Freedom: DoD Should Apply Lessons Learned Concerning the Need for Security over Conventional Munitions Storage Sites to Future Operations Planning," March 2007, 1, 5.

70 USAID, "Iraq – Humanitarian and Reconstruction Assistance," Fact Sheet #16, Fiscal Year (FY) 2003, April 21, 2003, 3. The 1st Cavalry division turned around en route. Rumsfeld also elected to remove the Third Infantry Division from the theater as soon as the 1st Armored Division, commanded by then-Major General Ricardo Sanchez, arrived—making for a net gain of zero troops. Lieutenant General Ricardo S. Sanchez, Wiser in Battle: A Soldier's Story (New York: HarperCollins, 2008); Michael R. Gordon and General Bernard E. Trainor, Cobra II: The Inside Story of the Invasion and Occupation of Iraq (New York: Pantheon, 2006); Thomas E. Ricks, Fiasco: The American Military Adventure in Iraq (New York: Penguin Group, 2006); and ORHA/CPA Historian interview with Colonel John Agoglia, former CENTCOM planner, September 22, 2006.

71 ORHA/CPA Historian interview with Colonel John Agoglia, former CENTCOM planner, September 22, 2006.

72 SIGIR interview with Lieutenant General (Ret.) Jay Garner, former Director of ORHA, April 1, 2006.

73 P.L. 108-11, Emergency Wartime Supplemental Appropriations Act, 2003, April 16, 2003.

74 General Tommy R. Franks, "Freedom Message to the Iraqi People," April 16, 2003.

75 SIGIR, "Iraq Reconstruction: Lessons in Contracting and Procurement," July 2006, 27.

76 For an account of the Nassriya conference and early political events, see Douglas Feith, War and Decision: Inside the Pentagon at the Dawn of the War on Terror (New York: HarperCollins, 2008), 416-26; and Kenneth Katzman, Congressional Research Services Report RL31339, "Iraq: U.S. Regime Change Efforts and Post-Saddam Governance," January 7, 2004, 22-23.

77 BBC, "Key Shia Leader Returns to Iraq," April 16, 2003.

78 SIGIR interview with Lieutenant General (Ret.) Carl Strock, former Commanding General of USACE, May 13, 2008.

79 Karen DeYoung, *Soldier: The Life of Colin Powell* (New York: Alfred A. Knopf, 1995), 463.

80 SIGIR and ORHA/CPA Historian interview with Lieutenant General (Ret.) Jay Garner, former Director of ORHA, October 27, 2008.

81 Different iterations of this list exist. See: annotated briefing slide, "ORHA's Key Tasks (Complete by 15 Jun 03)," undated; and another annotated slide by the same title, also undated.

82 ORHA/CPA Historian interview with Gary Vogler, Senior Advisor to the Ministry of Oil, June 18, 2003.

83 ORHA/CPA Historian interview with Lieutenant Colonel Joseph Morgan, JTF-4 Chief of Public Works, August 12, 2003.

84 Michael Mobbs left ORHA shortly after its arrival in Baghdad. SIGIR conversations with Gordon Rudd, ORHA/CPA Historian, Summer 2007.

85 Lieutenant General Garner notes that Iraqis and the military were cooperative, and that the coordination between Washington and ORHA was most problematic. SIGIR and ORHA/CPA Historian interview with Lieutenant General (Ret.) Jay Garner, former Director of ORHA, October 27, 2008.

86 SIGIR interview with Douglas Feith, former Under Secretary of Defense for Policy, March 21, 2008; and Douglas Feith, *War and Decision: Inside the Pentagon at the Dawn of the War on Terror* (New York: HarperCollins, 2008), 421.

87 General Tommy R. Franks, "Freedom Message to the Iraqi People," April 16, 2003.

88 For Bremer's own account of his selection, see L. Paul Bremer III, *My Year in Iraq, The Struggle to Build a Future of Hope* (New York: Simon & Schuster, 2006).

89 Garner notes that he asked Rumsfeld to consider delaying Bremer's arrival until July 1, 2003, by which time he felt he could prepare for a transition. Rumsfeld disagreed. SIGIR interview with Lieutenant General (Ret.) Jay Garner, former Director of ORHA, April 1, 2006; and SIGIR and ORHA/CPA Historian interview with Lieutenant General (Ret.) Jay Garner, former Director of ORHA, October 27, 2008.

90 SIGIR interview with Ambassador Zalmay Khalilzad, former Presidential Envoy to the Free Iraqis, March 19, 2008.

Essential Services – The Effects of Invasion

91 International Monetary Fund, "Iraq: Statistical Appendix," August 2007; and DoD, *Iraq Status Update*, August 28, 2003. Scott Wilson, "Bremer Shifts Focus to New Iraqi Economy; U.S. Occupation Chief Cites Progress on Restoring Order," *Washington Post*, May 27, 2003. USAID noted that 95 percent of landlines were down and cell phone service was only provided in Basrah. USAID: Assistance for Iraq, "NGO Pre-Bid Conference," April 17, 2003. Iraq Coalition Casualty Count; "US Deaths By Month," updated September 2008; Iraq Coalition Casualty Count, "Iraq Coalition Casualties: Contractors,", updated July 2008; Ariana Eunjung Cha, "Peril Follows Contractors in Iraq; Tennessee Pair Killed Despite Precautions," *Washington Post*, November 14, 2003; Iraq Body Count, "Documented civilian deaths from violence," updated August 24, 2008; P.L. 108-7, Consolidated Appropriations Resolution for Fiscal Year 2003, February 20, 2003; and P.L. 108-11, Emergency Wartime Supplemental Appropriations Act for Fiscal Year 2003, and for other purposes," April 16, 2003.

92 CPA Orders 1 and 2 greatly impacted the security forces as the Army was disbanded and many others loyal to Saddam deserted. The Iraqi Army post-invasion did not exist. The numbers available for the Iraq Security Force only includes the Iraqi Police. CPA Order Number 1, "De-Ba'athification of Iraqi Society," May 16, 2003; and CPA Order Number 2, "Dissolution of Entities," May 16, 2003.

93 The exact number of civilian contractor deaths are unknown and only include those which have been reported to the Department of Labor and the Iraq Coalition Casualty Count. This probably underestimates civilian casualties.

94 International Monetary Fund, "Iraq: Statistical Appendix," August 2007.

95 CPA, "A Free Iraq's Vision for the Future," October 23, 2003.

96 DoD, *Iraq Status Update*, August 28, 2003, 14.

Chapter 6

1 CPA, "Biography: Ambassador L. Paul Bremer," undated; and L. Paul Bremer III, *My Year in Iraq, The Struggle to Build a Future of Hope* (New York: Simon and Schuster, 2006), 3-5, About the Authors.

2 Peter W. Galbraith, *The End of Iraq: How American Incompetence Created a War Without End,* (New York: Simon and Schuster, 2007), 118.

3 L. Paul Bremer III, *My Year in Iraq, The Struggle to Build a Future of Hope* (New York: Simon and Schuster, 2006), 6.

4 L. Paul Bremer III, *My Year in Iraq, The Struggle to Build a Future of Hope* (New York: Simon and Schuster, 2006), 11-12.

5 SIGIR interview with General (Ret.) Colin Powell, former Secretary of State, February 4, 2008.

6 Donald Rumsfeld, for Secretary of Defense, written comments to SIGIR, January 7, 2009.

7 White House Press Release, "President Names Envoy to Iraq," May 6, 2003.

8 Donald Rumsfeld, Secretary of Defense, memorandum to L. Paul Bremer, Presidential Envoy to Iraq, "Designation as Administrator of the Coalition Provisional Authority," May 13, 2003.

9 L. Paul Bremer III, *My Year in Iraq: The Struggle to Build a Future of Hope* (New York: Simon & Schuster, 2006), 12.

10 Donald Rumsfeld, Secretary of Defense, memorandum to L. Paul Bremer, Presidential Envoy to Iraq, "Designation as Administrator of the Coalition Provisional Authority," May 13, 2003.

11 Two international laws—The 1907 Hague Regulation and the Geneva Conventions of 1949—pertain to occupations. Article 42 of the 1907 Hague Regulations states that a "territory is considered occupied when it is actually placed under the authority of the hostile army. The occupation extends only to the territory where such authority has been established and can be exercised." According to their common Article 2, the four Geneva Conventions of 1949 apply to any territory occupied during international hostilities. They also apply in situations where the occupation of state territory meets with no armed resistance.

12 CPA Regulation Number 1, "The Coalition Provisional Authority," May 16, 2003.

13 CPA Regulation Number 1, May 16, 2003.

14 Office of the Secretary of Defense, "Iraqi Interim Authority Overview," April 28, 2003.

15 Office of the Secretary of Defense, "Iraqi Interim Authority Overview," April 28, 2003.

16 Douglas Feith, Under Secretary of Defense for Policy, Testimony before the House Committee on International Relations, May 15, 2003.

17 L. Paul Bremer, III, former CPA Administrator, written comments to SIGIR, December 19, 2008.

18 L. Paul Bremer, III, former CPA Administrator, written comments to SIGIR, December 19, 2008.

19 Lieutenant General Ricardo S. Sanchez, *Wiser in Battle: A Soldier's Story* (New York: HarperCollins, 2008), 168.

20 Major General Sanchez had been nominated for appointment to the grade of Lieutenant General on May 5, 2003. His appointment was for the command of V Corps in Europe. DoD Press Release, "Flag and General Officer Announcements," May 5, 2003. A Corps headquarters, which would be the basis for CJTF-7, is much smaller and more tactically oriented than an Army headquarters, which was the basis for the Coalition Forces Land Component Command.

21 SIGIR interview with Lieutenant General (Ret.) Ricardo Sanchez, former CJTF-7 Commander, October 26, 2007; and ORHA/CPA Historian interview with L. Paul Bremer III, former CPA Administrator, January 7, 2008.

22 SIGIR interview with Major General William H. McCoy, former Commander of USACE-GRD, June 5, 2008.

23 Ali A. Allawi, *The Occupation of Iraq: Winning the War, Losing the Peace* (New Haven, CT: Yale University Press, 2007), 105.

24 United Nations Security Council Resolution 1483, May 22, 2003; and L. Elaine Halchin, "The Coalition Provisional Authority (CPA): Origin, Characteristics, and Institutional Authorities," Congressional Research Service Report RL32370, updated September 21, 2006.

25 General Tommy R. Franks, "Freedom Message to the Iraqi People," April 16, 2003. Two million members: Sharon Otterman, "IRAQ: De-Ba'athification," *Council on Foreign Relations*, April 7, 2005.

26 "Senior Party Members" were Regional Command Members, Branch Members, Section Members, and Group Members. CPA Order Number 1, "De-Ba'athification of Iraqi Society," May 16, 2003.

27 More junior ranks included Member and Active Member. CPA Order Number 1, May 16, 2003.

28 ORHA/CPA Historian interview with J. Scott Carpenter, Governance Director of the CPA, June 18, 2004.

29 L. Paul Bremer III, *My Year in Iraq, The Struggle to Build a Future of Hope* (New York: Simon & Schuster, 2006), 40.

30 ORHA/CPA Historian interviews with Lieutenant General (Ret.) Jay Garner, Director of ORHA; Robin Raphel, Coordinator for Civil Administration; David Nummy, Senior Advisor to the Ministry of Finance; Gary Vogler, Senior Advisor to the Ministry of Oil; and Major General David Petraeus, Commander of the 101st Airborne Division .

31 ORHA/CPA Historian interview with Lieutenant General (Ret.) Jay Garner, former Director of ORHA, September 14-15, 2005.

32 SIGIR interview with Nazar Janabi, former Director General, Ministry of Defense, July 2, 2008.

33 SIGIR interview with Frank Miller, former Chairman of the Executive Steering Group of the NSC, February 4, 2008.

34 Lieutenant General Ricardo S. Sanchez, *Wiser in Battle: A Soldier's Story* (New York: HarperCollins, 2008), 184.

35 SIGIR interview with Samir Sumaida'ie, Iraqi Ambassador to the United States, March 11, 2008.

36 CPA Order Number 5, "Establishment of the Iraqi De-Ba'athification Council," May 25, 2003.

37 Lieutenant General Ricardo S. Sanchez, *Wiser in Battle: A Soldier's Story* (New York: HarperCollins, 2008), 185.

38 CPA Memorandum Number 7, "Delegation of Authority Under De-Ba'athification Order No. 1," November 4, 2003.

39 Sharon Otterman, "IRAQ: De-Ba'athification," *Council on Foreign Relations*, April 7, 2005.

40 CPA Order Number 2, "Dissolution of Entities," May 23, 2003.

41 SIGIR interview with Frank Miller, former Chairman of the Executive Steering Group of the NSC, February 4, 2008.

42 SIGIR interview with General (Ret.) Colin Powell, former Secretary of State, February 4, 2008.

43 SIGIR interview with General (Ret.) Colin Powell, former Secretary of State, February 4, 2008.

44 SIGIR interview with L. Paul Bremer III, former CPA Administrator, March 18, 2008.

45 SIGIR interview with Douglas Feith, former Under Secretary of Defense for Policy, March 21, 2008.

46 ORHA/CPA Historian interview with Meghan O'Sullivan, CPA Governance Team Member, December 29, 2003.

47 SIGIR interview with Lieutenant General (Ret.) Ricardo Sanchez, former CJTF-7 Commander, October 26, 2007.

48 SIGIR interview with Lieutenant General David McKiernan, former Commander of Coalition Forces Land Component Command, December 5, 2006; SIGIR interview with Lieutenant General (Ret.) Ricardo Sanchez, former CJTF-7 Commander, October 26, 2007; and ORHA/CPA Historian interview with Major General David Petraeus, Commander of the 101st Airborne Division, July 28, 2003.

49 L. Paul Bremer III, *My Year in Iraq, The Struggle to Build a Future of Hope* (New York: Simon & Schuster, 2006), 55.

50 Lieutenant General Ricardo Sanchez, former CJTF-7 Commander, written comments to SIGIR, October 26, 2008.

51 ORHA/CPA Historian interview with Walter B. Slocombe, Senior Advisor for Defense and Security Affairs, July 18, 2003.

52 Ali A. Allawi, *The Occupation of Iraq: Winning the War, Losing the Peace* (New Haven, CT: Yale University Press, 2007), 157.

53 Public Broadcasting Service, "Interview with Laith Kubba," *FRONTLINE*, September 11, 2003.

54 Kirsten Lundberg, "The Accidental Statesman: General Petraeus and the City of Mosul, Iraq," *Kennedy School of Government Case Program*, 2006, 41.

55 ORHA/CPA Historian interview with Major General David Petraeus, Commander of the 101st Airborne Division, July 28, 2003.

Chapter 7

1 P.L. 108-11, Emergency Wartime Supplemental Appropriations Act for Fiscal Year 2003, April 16, 2003.

2 Most contracts were indefinite delivery/indefinite quantity (IDIQ) contracts. U.S. government agencies use IDIQ contracts when exact quantities of supplies and/or services to be obtained through the contract cannot be precisely determined. Task orders are then issued as more detail becomes available. FAR, Subpart 16.5, "Indefinite-Delivery Contracts," June 12, 2008, http://www.arnet.gov/far/current/html/Subpart%2016_5. html.

3 This estimate includes cumulative deposits to fund Iraqi government operations and reconstruction programs. CPA-IG, *Quarterly Report to the United States Congress*, July 2004, 59-60. A smaller portion of these funds, approximately $7 billion, was allocated for relief and reconstruction projects. GAO Report 05-876, "Rebuilding Iraq: Status of Funding and Reconstruction Efforts," July 2005, 2.

4 The humanitarian and reconstruction sectors established by the legislation were: (1) Water/sanitation infrastructure; (2) feeding and food distribution; (3) supporting relief efforts related to refugees, internally displaced persons, and vulnerable individuals, including assistance for families of innocent Iraqi civilians who suffer losses as a result of military operations; (4) electricity; (5) health care; (6) telecommunications; (7) economic and financial policy; (8) education; (9) transportation; (10) rule of law and governance; (11) humanitarian demining; (12) agriculture. P.L. 108-11, Emergency Wartime Supplemental Appropriations Act for Fiscal Year 2003, April 16, 2003. The Department of Health and Human Services never received any IRRF 1 funding.

5 SIGIR, "Iraq Reconstruction: Lessons in Contracting and Procurement," July 2006, 32.

6 SIGIR interview with Christopher Milligan, Deputy Director of USAID in Iraq, February 9, 2006; and ORHA/CPA Historian interview with Christopher Milligan, Deputy Director of USAID in Iraq, August 13, 2003.

7 Joshua B. Bolten, Director of the Office of Management and Budget, Testimony before the Senate Foreign Relations Committee, July 29, 2003; and Executive Order 13290, "Confiscating and Vesting Certain Iraqi Property," March 20, 2003.

8 United Nations Security Council Resolution 1483, May 22, 2003.

9 United Nations Security Council Resolution 1483, May 22, 2003.

10 United Nations Security Council Resolution 1483, May 22, 2003; International Advisory and Monitoring Board (IAMB), Press Release, "Establishment of the International Advisory and Monitoring Board," October 24, 2003; and IAMB, "Minutes of the organizational meeting held at the United Nations Headquarters, New York," December 5, 2003.

11 United Nations Press Release, "Oil-for-Food Programme: Status of Funds 19 November 2003," November 19, 2003; DoS Fact Sheet, "UN Security Council Resolution 1483 Lifts Sanctions on Iraq; International Community Pledges Assistance for People of Iraq," May 22, 2003; and Timothy Carney, "We're Getting in Our Own Way," *Washington Post*, Op-Ed, June 22, 2003.

12 CPA, Program Review Board Minutes, June 7, 2003.

13 ORHA/CPA Historian interview with James D. Warlick, Consular for Oil-for-Food program, June 13, 2004.

14 CPA Regulation Number 2, "The Development Fund for Iraq," June 10, 2003.

15 CPA Regulation Number 2, June 10, 2003.

16 CPA Regulation Number 3, "Program Review Board," June 18, 2003.

17 McPherson had taken leave from his job as president of Michigan State University to serve with the CPA. He chaired the PRB for the first two months and then turned over chairmanship to Oliver. Dave Oliver, "Restarting the Economy in Iraq," November 2003, 9.

18 CPA Regulation Number 3, June 18, 2003.

19 CPA Public Notice, "Managing Financial Resources for Iraq," June 18, 2003; and KPMG, "Development Fund for Iraq: Report of Factual Findings in Connection with Disbursements: For the Period from 1 January 2004 to 28 June 2004," October 14, 2004, 2.

20 CPA Regulation Number 3, June 18, 2003.

21 CPA Memorandum Number 4, "Contract and Grant Procedures Applicable to Vested and Seized Iraqi Property and the Development Fund for Iraq: Implementation of Regulation Number 3, Program Review Board," August 19, 2003.

22 CPA Memorandum Number 4, August 19, 2003.

23 SIGIR Audit 05-004, "Oversight of Funds Provided to Iraqi Ministries through the National Budget Process," January 30, 2005, 18; KPMG, "Development Fund for Iraq Appendix: Matters Noted Involving Internal Controls and Other Operations Issues During the Audit of the Fund: For the Period to 31 December 2003," June 2004; and IAMB, Report of the International Advisory and Monitoring Board of the Development Fund for Iraq, "Covering the Period from the Establishment of the DFI on May 22, 2003 until the Dissolution of the CPA on June 28, 2004," December 14, 2004, 4.

24 Mark S. Martins, "The Commander's Emergency Response Program," *Joint Force Quarterly* 37 (2nd Quarter 2005). Martins was deputy legal counsel to the Chairman of the Joint Chiefs of Staff at the time he wrote this article. A Fragmentary Order (FRAGO) is a change or amendment to a previous operational order.

25 SIGIR, *Quarterly Report to the United States Congress*, October 2008, 16.

26 Mark S. Martins, "The Commander's Emergency Response Program," *Joint Force Quarterly* 37 (2nd Quarter 2005), 48.

27 SIGIR, "Iraq Reconstruction: Lessons in Contracting and Procurement," July 2006, 88.

28 SIGIR Lessons Learned Forum: Human Capital Management, Washington, DC, September 20, 2005, 56.

29 ORHA was mentioned in the memorandum, but it had already been subsumed by CPA by this time. The executive agency for ORHA was transferred seamlessly to CPA until ORHA officially dissolved in mid-June. SIGIR, "Iraq Reconstruction: Lessons in Contracting and Procurement," July 2006, 24.

30 SIGIR refers to HCA as the "HCA office" when speaking of HCA as an organization and "HCA" when referring to the person in charge of the HCA office. The HCA office acted as the contracting organization for the CPA, and later for the CPA's Project Management Office (PMO) after the PMO was created in the fall of 2003. When the CPA dissolved, the HCA office continued its contracting support for the Project and Contracting Office (PCO), which took over many of the PMO's responsibilities. This distinction is noted in SIGIR, "Iraq Reconstruction: Lessons in Human Capital Management," January 2006, 119.

31 SIGIR, "Iraq Reconstruction: Lessons in Contracting and Procurement," July 2006, 25-26, 48-51.

32 SIGIR, "Iraq Reconstruction: Lessons in Human Capital Management," January 2006, 13-14.

33 CPA-IG Audit 04-002, "Management of Personnel Assigned to CPA in Baghdad," June 25, 2004, 1, 4.

34 SIGIR, "Iraq Reconstruction: Lessons in Human Capital Management," January 2006, 29; and DoS, comments to SIGIR, October 28, 2008.

35 SIGIR Lessons Learned Forum: Human Capital Management, Washington, DC, September 20, 2005; and ORHA/CPA Historian interview with Colonel Dennis J. DeGraff, CPA Director of Personnel, June 25, 2004.

36 SIGIR, "Iraq Reconstruction: Lessons in Human Capital Management," January 2006, 14.

37 ORHA/CPA Historian interview with Colonel Dennis J. DeGraff, CPA Director of Personnel, June 25, 2004.

38 DoD Personnel Assessment Team, "Report to the Secretary of Defense," February 11, 2004, 3.

39 CPA-IG Audit 04-002, "Management of Personnel Assigned to CPA in Baghdad," June 25, 2004, 1, 3.

40 GAO Report 04-902R, "Rebuilding Iraq: Resource, Security, Governance, Essential Services, and Oversight Issues," June 2004, 37. Other analysis suggests the CPA never had more than 55 percent of its staffing requirement. Terrence K. Kelly, Ellen E. Tunstall, Thomas S. Szayna, and Deanna Weber Prine, *Stabilization and Reconstruction Staffing: Developing U.S. Civilian Personnel Capabilities* (Santa Monica, CA: RAND Corporation, 2008).

41 SIGIR Lessons Learned Forum: Human Capital Management, Washington, DC, September 20, 2005, 73-74.

42 SIGIR, "Iraq Reconstruction: Lessons in Human Capital Management," January 2006, 10. According to Colonel DeGraff, the U.S. government relied on the 3161 special hiring authority because most federal agencies did not respond to repeated requests for personnel. The Secretary of Defense sent letters to his cabinet-level counterparts asking them to help staff the CPA, but by late fall 2003, few had provided adequate numbers of personnel. In November 2003, the NSC appealed to the federal agencies for assistance, but this plea was similarly ineffective. ORHA/CPA Historian interview with Colonel Dennis J. DeGraff, CPA Director of Personnel, June 25, 2004.

43 SIGIR, "Iraq Reconstruction: Lessons in Human Capital Management," January 2006, 21.

44 GAO Report 04-902R, "Rebuilding Iraq: Resource, Security, Governance, Essential Services, and Oversight Issues," June 2004, 39. The number of military and civilian staff provided to the CPA by the Defense Department varied from month to month. For example, in March 2004, the Defense Department provided 293 military and 168 civilian personnel, or 461 of the 1,196 on the CPA personnel roster. When the CPA ended, 384 of the CPA's 1,050 staff were either members of the U.S. military or civilians from the Defense Department.

45 ORHA/CPA Historian interview with Colonel Dennis J. DeGraff, CPA Director of Personnel, June 25, 2004.

46 SIGIR Lessons Learned Forum: Human Capital Management, Washington, DC, September 20, 2005, 132.

47 USIP interview with Rodney Bent, former OMB Director, September 14, 2004.

48 SIGIR, "Iraq Reconstruction: Lessons in Human Capital Management," January 2006, 22; and Nora Bensahel et al., "After Saddam: Prewar Planning and the Occupation of Iraq," (Santa Monica, CA: RAND Corporation, 2008), 118, 184.

49 Ali A. Allawi, *The Occupation of Iraq: Winning the War, Losing the Peace* (New Haven, CT: Yale University Press, 2007), 100.

50 SIGIR, "Iraq Reconstruction: Lessons in Human Capital Management," January 2006, 22.

51 GAO Report 04-902R, "Rebuilding Iraq: Resource, Security, Governance, Essential Services, and Oversight Issues," June 2004, 39.

52 SIGIR, "Iraq Reconstruction: Lessons in Human Capital Management," January 2006, 22; and DoD IG Audit D-2004-057, "Contracts Awarded for the Coalition Provisional Authority by the Defense Contracting Command-Washington," March 18, 2004, 10-11, 28-29. The costs of the contract soon rose. For example, one third of the subject-matter experts demanded life insurance, and SAIC requested the use of higher labor rates than originally negotiated "because the subject matter experts required higher compensation." The value of the contract grew from $7.7 million when it was awarded on March 5, 2003, to $24.8 million by the end of November.

53 DoS, comments to SIGIR, October 28, 2008.

Chapter 8

1 SIGIR conversations with Barbara Lewis, former Senior Advisor to the Rafidain Bank, Summer 2007.

2 John B. Taylor, Under Secretary of the Treasury for International Affairs, Testimony before the Senate Committee on Foreign Relations, June 4, 2003. The Treasury team found that looters, frustrated by their inability to break into the vaults, had opened a sewer main and flooded the central bank. ORHA/CPA Historian interview with David Nummy, Senior Advisor to the Ministry of Finance, June 23, 2003.

3 ORHA/CPA Historian interview with David Nummy, Senior Advisor to the Ministry of Finance, June 27, 2003.

4 John B. Taylor, "Billions Over Baghdad," *New York Times*, Op-Ed, February 27, 2007.

5 ORHA/CPA Historian interview with David Nummy, Senior Advisor to the Ministry of Finance, June 27, 2003.

6 Joseph A. Christoff, GAO Director of International Affairs and Trade and Davi M. D'Agostino, GAO Director of Financial Markets and Community Investment, Testimony before the House Committee on Financial Services Subcommittee on Oversight and Investigations, March 18, 2004; and ORHA/CPA Historian interview with George B. Wolfe, Deputy General Counsel, U.S. Treasury Department, June 13, 2004.

7 House Committee on Oversight and Government Reform Memorandum, "Cash Transfers to the Coalition Provisional Authority," February 6, 2007, 6.

8 SIGIR interview with George "Ged" Smith, U.S. Treasury attaché, August 20, 2007.

9 Timothy Carney, We're Getting in Our Own Way," *Washington Post*, Op-Ed, June 22, 2003; and Timothy Carney, Senior Advisor to the Ministry of Industry and Minerals, written comments to SIGIR, November 16, 2008.

10 SIGIR conversations with Barbara Lewis, former Senior Advisor to the Rafidain Bank, Summer 2007.

11 SIGIR conversations with Barbara Lewis, former Senior Advisor to the Rafidain Bank, Summer 2007.

12 John B. Taylor, Under Secretary of the Treasury for International Affairs, Testimony before the Senate Committee on Foreign Relations, June 4, 2003.

13 Dave Oliver, "Restarting the Economy in Iraq," November 2003, 23.

14 CPA Order Number 30, "Reform of Salaries and Employment Conditions of State Employees," September 8, 2003.

15 House Committee on Oversight and Government Reform Memorandum, "Cash Transfers to the Coalition Provisional Authority," February 6, 2007, 6.

16 Henry A. Waxman, Chairman, Statement before the House Committee on Oversight and Government Reform, February 6, 2007; and Robert Kraus email to Joseph Botta, "DFI-Cash00220," December 12, 2003, as cited in: House Committee on Oversight and Government Reform Memorandum, "Cash Transfers to the Coalition Provisional Authority," February 6, 2007, 6-7.

17 John B. Taylor, *Global Financial Warriors: The Untold Story of International Finance in the Post-9/11 World* (New York: W.W. Norton, 2007), 200-210; and CPA Press Release, "Iraq Currency Exchange Begins," October 15, 2003.

18 John B. Taylor, Under Secretary of the Treasury for International Affairs, Testimony before the Senate Committee on Foreign Relations, June 4, 2003.

19 CPA Press Release, "Text of Ambassador Bremer's Address to the Iraqi People: Budget and Banknotes," no. 0014, July 7, 2003.

20 CPA Order Number 43, "New Iraqi Dinar Banknotes," October 14, 2003.

21 CPA, "Iraq Currency Exchange," http://www.iraqcoalition.org/budget/IraqCurrencyExchange.html.

22 USIP interview with Brigadier General Hugh Tant, former Director of Iraqi Currency Exchange Program, October 22, 2004.

23 John B. Taylor, "Billions Over Baghdad," New York Times, February 27, 2007; and John B. Taylor, *Global Financial Warriors: The Untold Story of International Finance in the Post-9/11 World* (New York: W.W. Norton, 2007), 225-245.

24 George W. Bush, "President Holds Press Conference," White House Press Release, October 28, 2003.

25 John B. Taylor, *Global Financial Warriors: The Untold Story of International Finance in the Post-9/11 World* (New York: W.W. Norton, 2007), 243.

26 John B. Taylor, Under Secretary of the Treasury for International Affairs, Testimony before the Senate Committee on Foreign Relations, June 4, 2003.

27 John B. Taylor, "Billions Over Baghdad," New York Times, February 27, 2007; and John B. Taylor, *Global Financial Warriors: The Untold Story of International Finance in the Post-9/11 World* (New York: W.W. Norton, 2007), 250-273.

28 John B. Taylor, *Global Financial Warriors: The Untold Story of International Finance in the Post-9/11 World* (New York: W.W. Norton, 2007), 250, 260-262.

29 John B. Taylor, *Global Financial Warriors: The Untold Story of International Finance in the Post-9/11 World* (New York: W.W. Norton, 2007), 263.

30 John B. Taylor, *Global Financial Warriors: The Untold Story of International Finance in the Post-9/11 World* (New York: W.W. Norton, 2007), 250-273. The Paris Club is an informal group of financial officials from 19 creditor nations that helps debtor countries restructure their debts; the London Club is a similar group of private international creditors. On November 21, 2004, long after the CPA was gone, the London Club members agreed, in the light of "the exceptional situation of the Republic of Iraq and of its limited repayment capacity over the coming year" on "exceptional treatment" that significantly reduced Iraq's external debt. See Paris Club Press Release, "The Paris Club and the Republic of Iraq Agree on Debt Relief," November 21, 2004.

31 Dave Oliver, "Restarting the Economy in Iraq," November 2003, 23.

32 SIGIR interview with George "Ged" Smith, U.S. Treasury Attaché, August 20, 2007; Christopher Foote, William Block, Keith Crane, and Simon Gray, "Economic Policy and Prospects in Iraq," *Journal of Economic Perspectives* 18, no. 3 (Summer 2004); and Nora Bensahel et al., *After Saddam: Prewar Planning and the Occupation of Iraq* (Santa Monica, CA, RAND Corporation, 2008), 195-208.

33 International Monetary Fund, "Iraq: Macroeconomic Assessment," October, 21, 2003.

34 Peter McPherson, former CPA director of Economic Policy, written comments to SIGIR, January 7, 2009.

35 Zoubida Allaoua, et al., "State Owned Enterprises Reform in Iraq," World Bank: Reconstructing Iraq Working Paper no. 2, July 26, 2004.

36 Zoubida Allaoua, et al., "State Owned Enterprises Reform in Iraq," World Bank: Reconstructing Iraq Working Paper no. 2, July 26, 2004.

37 Peter McPherson, former CPA director of Economic Policy, written comments to SIGIR, January 3, 2009.

38 Peter McPherson, former CPA director of Economic Policy, written comments to SIGIR, January 3, 2009.

39 Peter McPherson, former CPA director of Economic Policy, written comments to SIGIR, January 3, 2009 and August 19, 2008.

40 The $2 billion in recorded deposits included $1 billion from SOEs and $1billiion from private depositors. Peter McPherson, former CPA director of Economic Policy, written comments to SIGIR, January 7, 2009.

41 Peter McPherson, former CPA director of Economic Policy, written comments to SIGIR, January 7, 2009.

42 Peter McPherson, former CPA director of Economic Policy, written comments to SIGIR, January 3, 2009.

43 Peter McPherson, former CPA director of Economic Policy, written comments to SIGIR, January 3, 2009.

44 Peter McPherson, former CPA Director of Economic Policy, written comments to SIGIR, August 19, 2008.

45 Peter McPherson, former CPA Director of Economic Policy, written comments to SIGIR, August 19, 2008.

46 The Geneva Conventions require an occupying power to protect the assets of the state, but there is little precedent for determining if state-owned industries are included in this provision of the Conventions. Christopher Foote, William Block, Keith Crane, and Simon Gray, "Economic Policy and Prospects in Iraq," *Journal of Economic Perspectives* 18, no. 3 (Summer 2004).

47 Timothy Carney, Senior Advisor to the Ministry of Industry and Minerals, memorandum to Peter McPherson, CPA Director of Economic Policy, "Fatal Flaws in Budget Policy towards State-Owned Enterprises," June 15, 2003. Timothy Carney was Ambassador to Sudan (1995–1997) and Haiti (1998–1999) and served with UN peacekeeping missions in Cambodia, Somalia and South Africa. State Department Biography, "Timothy M. Carney, Chargé d'Affaires," http://haiti.usembassy.gov/timothy_m4._carney.

48 International Monetary Fund, "Iraq: Macroeconomic Assessment," October 21, 2003, 9.

49 SIGIR interview with Dr. Sami Al-Araji, Deputy Minister of Industry and Minerals, May 2007.

50 John B. Taylor, Under Secretary of the Treasury for International Affairs, Testimony before the Senate Committee on Foreign Relations, June 4, 2003.

51 USAID IG Audit E-266-04-004-P, "Audit of USAID/Iraq's Economic Reform Program," September 20, 2004; and SIGIR interview with Gareth Davies, Chief of Party, Bearing Point, May 15, 2007.

52 CPA Order Number 18, "Measures to Ensure the Independence of the Central Bank of Iraq," July 7, 2003.

53 CPA Order Number 20, "Trade Bank of Iraq," July 14, 2003

54 Peter McPherson, former CPA director of Economic Policy, written comments to SIGIR, January 3, 2009.

55 CPA Order Number 40, "Bank Law," September 19, 2003.

56 SIGIR interview with Gareth Davies, Chief of Party, Bearing Point, May 15, 2007.

57 Peter McPherson, former CPA Director of Economic Policy, written comments to SIGIR, August 19, 2008.

58 Christopher Foote, William Block, Keith Crane, and Simon Gray, "Economic Policy and Prospects in Iraq," *Journal of Economic Perspectives* 18, no. 3 (Summer 2004).

59 Anne Ellen Henderson, USIP Special Report 138, "The Coalition Provisional Authority's Experience with Economic Reconstruction in Iraq," April 2005. Under the Oil-for-Food program, the United Nations assisted the government of Iraq in providing a "food basket" for all Iraqis. An estimated 60 percent of the population depended on the food and supplies provided by the UN. This social safety net cost the Iraqi government about $4.9 billion per year. International Monetary Fund, "Iraq: Macroeconomic Assessment," October, 21, 2003.

60 Ali A. Allawi, *The Occupation of Iraq: Winning the War and Losing the Peace* (New Haven, CT: Yale University Press, 2007).

Chapter 9

1 Dave Oliver, "Restarting the Economy in Iraq," November 2003, 23.

2 Bechtel National, Inc, "Iraq Infrastructure Reconstruction Program," Assessment Report submitted to USAID, June 2003, 4.4.

3 Bechtel National, Inc, "Iraq Infrastructure Reconstruction Program," Assessment Report submitted to USAID, June 2003, 3.1.

4 Bechtel National, Inc, "Iraq Infrastructure Reconstruction Program," Assessment Report submitted to USAID, June 2003, 3.1.

5 USACE, "Iraqi Oil Infrastructure Restoration Strategic Plan, Rough Order of Magnitude," June 3, 2003, ii, 5, 6.

6 USACE, "Iraqi Oil Infrastructure Restoration Strategic Plan, Rough Order of Magnitude," June 3, 2003, 1.

7 USACE, "Iraqi Oil Infrastructure Restoration Strategic Plan, Rough Order of Magnitude," June 3, 2003; and Joint Planning Workshop, "Restoration of Iraqi Oil Infrastructure Final Work Plan," July 24, 2003, http://www.energyintel.com/resources/workplan.pdf.

8 United Nations/World Bank, "Joint Iraq Needs Assessment," October 2003.

9 United Nations/World Bank, "Joint Iraq Needs Assessment," October 2003, v, 55-56.

10 United Nations/World Bank, "Joint Iraq Needs Assessment," October 2003, 3.

11 United Nations/World Bank, "Joint Iraq Needs Assessment," October 2003, 56.

12 Frederick Barton, Bathsheba N. Crocker, John J. Hamre, Johanna Mendelson-Forman, and Robert C. Orr, "Iraq's Post-Conflict Reconstruction: A Field Review and Recommendations," July 17, 2003, foreword, iii.

13 Frederick Barton, Bathsheba N. Crocker, John J. Hamre, Johanna Mendelson-Forman, and Robert C. Orr, "Iraq's Post-Conflict Reconstruction: A Field Review and Recommendations," July 17, 2003, 2, 5-7.

14 The Office of Strategic Planning was later renamed the Office of Policy, Planning, and Analysis. Dayton Maxwell, "Deliberate and Development Post-Conflict Planning in Iraq: The Office of Policy, Planning and Analysis, Coalition Provisional Authority, A USAID Perspective," unpublished manuscript, July 23, 2004, 5.

15 ORHA/CPA Historian interview with Dayton Maxwell, USAID official assigned to the CPA Office of Policy, Planning, and Analysis, and Lieutenant Colonel Robert B. Polk, ORHA Director of Plans, August 14, 2003.

16 Dayton Maxwell, "Deliberate and Development Post Conflict Planning in Iraq: The Office of Policy, Planning and Analysis, Coalition Provisional Authority, A USAID Perspective," unpublished manuscript, July 23, 2004, 9-10; and ORHA/CPA Historian interview with Dayton Maxwell, USAID official assigned to the CPA Office of Policy, Planning, and Analysis, and Lieutenant Colonel Robert B. Polk, ORHA Director of Plans, August 14, 2003.

17 CPA, *A Vision for Iraq*, July 11, 2003.

18 L. Paul Bremer III, CPA Administrator, memorandum to President Bush, "Iraqi Strategy," July 21, 2003.

19 Dayton Maxwell, "Deliberate and Development Post-Conflict Planning in Iraq: The Office of Policy, Planning and Analysis, Coalition Provisional Authority, A USAID Perspective," unpublished manuscript, July 23, 2004, 27.

20 Dayton Maxwell, "Deliberate and Development Post Conflict Planning in Iraq: The Office of Policy, Planning and Analysis, Coalition Provisional Authority, A USAID Perspective," unpublished manuscript, July 23, 2004, 27-28.

21 ORHA/CPA Historian interview with Dayton Maxwell, USAID official assigned to the CPA Office of Policy, Planning, and Analysis, and Lieutenant Colonel Robert B. Polk, ORHA Director of Plans, August 14, 2003.

22 CPA, "Achieving the Vision to Restore Full Sovereignty to the Iraqi People," October 1, 2003.

23 CPA, "Republic of Iraq Budget Revenues and Expenses: 2003 July-December," 2003, 3, 5-6.

24 Dave Oliver, "Restarting the Economy in Iraq," November 2003, 24-25.

25 Dave Oliver, "Restarting the Economy in Iraq," November 2003, 20, 24-25.

26 Dave Oliver, "Restarting the Economy in Iraq," November 2003, 20, 30.

27 SIGIR interview with Rear Adm. (Ret.) David Nash, former Director of the Iraq PMO, January 13, 2006.

28 ORHA/CPA Historian interview with Rear Adm. (Ret) David Nash, Director of the Iraq PMO, July 1, 2004; and Design-Build Institute of America, "Leadership and Staff: David Nash," http://www.dbia.org/about/staff/bod/nash.htm.

29 Tom C. Korologos, CPA congressional liaison, memorandum to L. Paul Bremer III, CPA Administrator, "Supplemental Memo Rebuttal," August 17, 2003.

30 Tom C. Korologos, CPA congressional liaison, memorandum to L. Paul Bremer III, CPA Administrator, "Supplemental Memo Rebuttal," August 17, 2003.

31 CPA, "Program/Integration Management Plan Recovery, Reconstruction and Redevelopment of Iraq," August 29, 2003, 1.

32 CPA, "Request to Rehabilitate and Reconstruct Iraq," September 2003, 2.

33 George W. Bush, "Address of the President to the Nation," White House Press Release, September 7, 2003.

34 SIGIR interview with Christopher Milligan, USAID Deputy Director of Iraq, February 9, 2006.

35 SIGIR interview with Andrew Natsios, former USAID Administrator, March 17, 2008.

36 SIGIR interview with Andrew Natsios, former USAID Administrator, March 17, 2008.

37 SIGIR interview with Christopher Milligan, USAID Deputy Director of Iraq, February 9, 2006.

38 Lewis Lucke, USAID mission director in Iraq, email to Rear Adm. (Ret.) David Oliver, CPA Director, Management and Budget Office, "RE: Final Draft Info Paper on Execution of the FY04 Supplemental for Iraq Relief Reconstruction Fund2," October 21, 2003.

39 USAID, "Priorities for USAID under FY04 Supplemental," October 2003.

40 SIGIR interview with Rear Adm. (Ret.) David Nash, former Director of the Iraq PMO, March 3, 2006; SIGIR interview with Christopher Milligan, USAID Deputy Director of Iraq, February 9, 2006; and SIGIR interview with Dayton Maxwell, USAID Official assigned to the CPA Office of Policy, Planning and Analysis, November 3, 2005.

41 Representative Nita M. Lowey, Testimony before the House Appropriations Subcommittee on Foreign Operations, Export Financing, and Related Programs, September 24, 2003.

42 Representative David R. Obey, Testimony before the House Appropriations Subcommittee on Foreign Operations, Export Financing and Related Programs, September 30, 2003.

43 Questions from the House and Senate Staffs and Answers attached to an email to Adm. (Ret.) David Oliver, CPA Director, Management and Budget Office, October 4, 2003.

44 Questions from the House and Senate Staffs and Answers attached to an email to Adm. (Ret.) David Oliver, CPA Director, Management and Budget Office, October 4, 2003.

45 Questions from the House and Senate Staffs and Answers attached to an email to Adm. (Ret.) David Oliver, CPA Director, Management and Budget Office, October 4, 2003.

46 CPA Regulation Number 5, "Regarding the Council for International Coordination," June 18, 2003.

47 ORHA/CPA Historian interview with Peter Andrew Bearpark, CPA Director of Operations, December 18, 2003; and ORHA/CPA Historian interview with Andrew L.J. Goledzinowski, Deputy Chairman, Council for International Coordination, January 1, 2004. Marek Belka became Prime Minister of Poland in June 2004 after serving with the CPA. UN, "Marek Belka, Executive Secretary of the United Nations Economic Commission for Europe," http://www.un.org/sg/senstaff_details.asp?smgID=3.

48 United Nations, "In Memoriam," September 4, 2003, http://www.un.org/staff/condolence/inmemoriam.html.

49 UN Press Release, "Annan to Withdraw UN Staff from Iraq," March 17, 2003.

50 United Nations Security Council Resolution 1511, October 16, 2003.

51 Joseph A. Christoff, GAO Director of International Affairs and Trade, Testimony before the House Committee on Foreign Affairs Subcommittee on International Organizations, Human Rights, and Oversight, May 9, 2007.

52 United Nations Assistance Mission for Iraq, "Trust Fund Facility," http://www.uniraq.org/donors/irffi.asp.

53 Congress added two important oversight mechanisms to the legislation. Section 2207 of the law required the Office of Management and Budget to produce quarterly reports documenting how the money was being spent. Section 3001 created the Office of the Inspector General of the CPA. It required the Inspector General to produce quarterly reports to the Congress on the "obligations, expenditures, and revenues associated with reconstruction and rehabilitation activities in Iraq." P.L. 108-106, Emergency Supplemental Appropriations Act for Defense and for the Reconstruction of Iraq and Afghanistan for Fiscal Year 2004, November 6, 2003.

54 P.L. 108-106, Emergency Supplemental Appropriations Act for Defense and for the Reconstruction of Iraq and Afghanistan for Fiscal Year 2004, November 6, 2003.

55 P.L. 108-106, Emergency Supplemental Appropriations Act for Defense and for the Reconstruction of Iraq and Afghanistan for Fiscal Year 2004, November 6, 2003.

Chapter 10

1 OMB, *Section 2207 Report*, January 2004; and SIGIR Lessons Learned Forum: Program and Project Management, April 12, 2006.

2 SIGIR, "Iraq Reconstruction: Lessons in Program and Project Management," March 2007, 48-49, 53-54.

3 ORHA/CPA Historian interview with Steve Browning, former Task Force RIO Advisor, July 21, 2007.

4 Dov S. Zakheim, former Under Secretary of Defense and DoD Chief Financial Officer, email to SIGIR, "Re: An Iraq-related question for SIGIR Lessons Learned," June 30, 2008.

5 Rear Adm. (Ret.) David Nash, Director of the Iraq PMO, email to Peter Andrew Bearpark, CPA Director of Operations, "Re: Establishing Communications," September 18, 2003.

6 DoD Cover Brief, "Project from the Coalition Provisional Authority (CPA)—Iraq Project Management Office (PMO)," September 9, 2003; and SIGIR interview with Craig Johnson, Stanley Consultants, spokesman for the "Baker-Stanley" team and former PMO Program Engineer, March 9, 2006.

7 CPA/Department of the Army, letter to Principal Assistant Responsible for Contracting (PARC), September 15, 2003.

8 SIGIR interview with Craig Johnson, Stanley Consultants, spokesman for the "Baker-Stanley" team and former PMO Program Engineer, March 9, 2006; and Craig Johnson, Stanley Consultants, spokesman for the "Baker-Stanley" team and former PMO Program Engineer, written comments to SIGIR, November 4, 2008.

9 SIGIR, "Iraq Reconstruction: Lessons in Program and Project Management," March 2007, 56; and SIGIR interview with Rear Adm. (Ret.) David Nash, former Director of the Iraq PMO, March 3, 2006.

10 USACE, comments to SIGIR, November 4, 2008. A design-build contractor is responsible for every phase of a project from design to completion, although it may subcontract pieces of a project to other contractors. SIGIR, "Iraq Reconstruction: Lessons in Program and Project Management," March 2007, 56.

11 SIGIR, "Iraq Reconstruction: Lessons in Program and Project Management," March 2007, 53; and ORHA/CPA Historian interview with Major General Ronald Johnson, Deputy Director of the Iraq PMO, June 27, 2004.

12 SIGIR Lessons Learned Forum: Program and Project Management, Washington, DC, April 12, 2006.

13 SIGIR Lessons Learned Forum: Contracting and Procurement, Washington, DC, December 5, 2005; and SIGIR, "Iraq Reconstruction: Lessons in Program and Project Management," March 2007, 52-53, 57-59.

14 SIGIR, "Iraq Reconstruction: Lessons in Program and Project Management," March 2007, 53.

15 SIGIR, "Iraq Reconstruction: Lessons in Contracting and Procurement," July 2006, 55; and DoD, "Iraq Reconstruction Pre-Proposal Conference Briefing, Program Management and Design-Build Construction," January 21, 2004, 10, 27, 32.

16 Dov S. Zakheim, former Under Secretary of Defense and DoD Chief Financial Officer, email to SIGIR, "Re: An Iraq-related question for SIGIR Lessons Learned," June 30, 2008.

17 SIGIR interview with Rear Adm. (Ret.) David Nash, former Director of the Iraq PMO, January 13, 2006.

18 SIGIR Lessons Learned Forum: Program and Project Management, Washington, DC, April 12, 2006.

19 SIGIR Lessons Learned Forum: Program and Project Management, Washington, DC, April 12, 2006; and SIGIR Lessons Learned Forum: Contracting and Procurement, Washington, DC, December 5, 2005.

20 PMO/PCO Historian interview with Tina Ballard, Deputy Assistant Secretary of the Army, November 17, 2004.

21 SIGIR, "Iraq Reconstruction: Lessons in Contracting and Procurement," July 2006, 54-56.

22 PMO/PCO Historian interview with Tina Ballard, Deputy Assistant Secretary of the Army, November 17, 2004.

23 Paul Wolfowitz, "Determination and Findings," December 5, 2003; and GAO Report 04-605, "Rebuilding Iraq: Fiscal Year 2003 Contract Award Procedures and Management Challenges," June 2004, 28-46. GAO identified two issues with the memorandum. First, GAO concluded that the memorandum constituted a class determination and finding, which is prohibited by the Federal Acquisition Regulation. Additionally, GAO noted that the waiver to competition requirements was based on a public interest exception, which can only be issued by the Secretary of Defense. GAO noted that while the Deputy Secretary has broad authority to act on behalf of the Secretary of Defense, he did not have authority to do so in this instance.

24 CPA-IG Audit 04-005, "Award of Sector Design-Build Construction Contracts," July 23, 2004, 6.

25 SIGIR, "Iraq Reconstruction: Lessons in Program and Project Management," March 2007, 64-65; and PMO/PCO Historian interview with Tina Ballard, Deputy Assistant Secretary of the Army, November 17, 2004.

26 CPA, "Rebuilding Iraq: Prioritized Supplemental Project List," December 1, 2003; and SIGIR interview with Craig Johnson, Stanley Consultants, spokesman for the "Baker-Stanley" team and former PMO Program Engineer, March 9, 2006.

27 SIGIR interview with Craig Johnson, Stanley Consultants, spokesman for the "Baker-Stanley" team and former PMO Program Engineer, March 9, 2006; and Craig Johnson, Stanley Consultants, spokesman for the "Baker-Stanley" team and former PMO Program Engineer, written comments to SIGIR, November 4, 2008.

28 SIGIR interview with Craig Johnson, Stanley Consultants, spokesman for the "Baker-Stanley" team and former PMO Program Engineer, March 9, 2006.

29 SIGIR interview with James Haveman, former Senior Advisor to the Ministry of Health, December 22, 2005; and SIGIR interview with Craig Johnson, Stanley Consultants, spokesman for the "Baker-Stanley" team and former PMO Program Engineer, March 9, 2006.

30 SIGIR interview with Craig Johnson, Stanley Consultants, spokesman for the "Baker-Stanley" team and former PMO Program Engineer, March 9, 2006.

31 Craig Johnson, Stanley Consultants, spokesman for the "Baker-Stanley" team and former PMO Program Engineer, written comments to SIGIR, November 4, 2008.

32 SIGIR interview with Rear Adm. (Ret.) David Nash, former Director of the Iraq PMO, March 3, 2006.

33 SIGIR Lessons Learned Forum: Program and Project Management, Washington, DC, April 12, 2006.

34 SIGIR interview with Rear Adm. (Ret.) David Nash, former Director of the Iraq PMO, January 13, 2006.

35 SIGIR interview with Andrew Natsios, former USAID Administrator, March 17, 2008.

36 SIGIR interview with Andrew Natsios, former USAID Administrator, April 17, 2006.

37 SIGIR interview with Andrew Natsios, former USAID Administrator, April 17, 2006.

38 SIGIR interview with Andrew Natsios, former USAID Administrator, April 17, 2006.

39 OMB, *Section 2207 Report*, January 2004. The decision to transfer sovereignty earlier than originally envisioned by Ambassador Bremer is discussed in detail in subsequent chapters. The CPA—and the U.S. Embassy that replaced it in June 2004—repeatedly re-aligned money in the supplemental to meet changing needs on the ground in Iraq. Part III of this book looks at re-programming in more depth.

40 OMB, *Section 2207 Report*, January 2004.

41 OMB, *Section 2207 Report*, January 2004.

42 SIGIR Audit 05-026, "Fact Sheet on the Use of the $50 million Appropriation to Support the Management and Reporting of the Iraq Relief and Reconstruction Fund," January 27, 2006; and SIGIR interview with Rear Adm. (Ret.) David Nash, former Director of the Iraq PMO, March 3, 2006.

43 CPA, "Program Management Plan," October 15, 2003, Figure 2 as cited in: SIGIR, "Iraq Reconstruction: Lessons in Program and Project Management," March 2007, 60.

44 SIGIR interview with Rear Adm. (Ret.) David Nash, former Director of the Iraq PMO, March 3, 2006.

45 SIGIR Lessons Learned Forum: Program and Project Management, Washington, DC, April 12, 2006.

46 SIGIR, "Iraq Reconstruction: Lessons in Contracting and Procurement," July 2006, 66; SIGIR interview with James "Spike" Stephenson, USAID Iraq Mission Director, January 19, 2006; and SIGIR interview with Andrew Natsios, former USAID Administrator, April 17, 2006.

47 James Stephenson, *Losing the Golden Hour, An Insider's View of Iraq's Reconstruction* (Washington, DC: Potomac Books, 2007).

48 SIGIR interview with Rear Adm. (Ret.) David Nash, former Director of the Iraq PMO, January 13, 2006.

49 SIGIR interview with Rear Adm. (Ret.) David Nash, former Director of the Iraq PMO, March 3, 2006.

50 James Stephenson, *Losing the Golden Hour, An Insider's View of Iraq's Reconstruction* (Washington, DC: Potomac Books, 2007), 33.

51 James Stephenson, *Losing the Golden Hour, An Insider's View of Iraq's Reconstruction* (Washington, DC: Potomac Books, 2007), 32-35.

52 CPA-IG Audit 04-004, "Task Orders Awarded by the Air Force Center for Environmental Excellence in Support of the Coalition Provisional Authority," July 28, 2004, 4-5, 7-8.

53 CPA-IG Audit 04-004, "Task Orders Awarded by the Air Force Center for Environmental Excellence in Support of the Coalition Provisional Authority," July 28, 2004, 4-5.

54 John Daley, U.S. Army Corps of Engineers, written comments to SIGIR, June 26, 2008.

55 SIGIR, "Iraq Reconstruction: Lessons in Contracting and Procurement," July 2006, 60.

56 OMB, *Section 2207 Report*, July 2004, Funding Table.

Chapter 11

1 SIGIR interview with Vijay Samaraweera, Senior Policy Advisor for Regional Government, RTI International, August 16, 2007.

2 For Umm Qasr and South-Central, see ORHA/CPA Historian interview with Mike Gfoeller, former Deputy Director of ORHA Region-South, August 10, 2003; Amatzia Baram, "Post-Saddam Iraq: The Shiite Factor," The Brookings Institution, April 30, 2003; and Ken Pollack, "The Seven Deadly Sins of Failure in Iraq: A Retrospective Analysis of the Reconstruction," The Brookings Institution, December 1, 2006.

3 Peter W. Brorsen, "Accountability Builds Legitimate Government," *Capacity.org* 32 (December 2007); USAID, "Transcript: Local Governance Update," June 19, 2003; and USAID, "New Freedom and Opportunities: Founding a New Democracy in Iraq", November 18, 2003.

4 ORHA/CPA Historian interview with Major Gen. David Petraeus, Commander of the 101st Airborne Division, July 28, 2003.

5 ORHA/CPA Historian interview with Major General David Petraeus, Commander of the 101st Airborne Division, July 28, 2003.

6 ORHA/CPA Historian interview with J. Scott Carpenter, CPA Director of Governance, June 18, 2004.

7 L. Paul Bremer, III, former CPA Administrator, written comments to SIGIR, December 19, 2008.

8 ORHA/CPA Historian interview with J. Scott Carpenter, CPA Director of Governance, June 18, 2004.

9 SIGIR, "Iraq Reconstruction: Lessons in Contracting and Procurement," July 2006, 32; and Research Triangle Institute, USAID contract EDG-C00-03-00010-00, Section C, April 11, 2003.

10 SIGIR interview with Dr. Ronald Johnson, Senior Vice President for International Development, RTI International, March 2, 2006.

11 USIP interview with Aaron Williams, Vice President for International Business Development, RTI International, October 1, 2004.

12 USIP interview with Charles "Chuck" Costello, Deputy Chief of Party in the Local Governance Support Project with RTI International, October 14, 2004.

13 USIP interview with Aaron Williams, Vice President for International Business Development, RTI International, October 1, 2004.

14 USIP interview with Aaron Williams, Vice President for International Business Development, RTI International, October 1, 2004.

15 USIP interview with Charles "Chuck" Costello, Deputy Chief of Party in the Local Governance Support Project with RTI International, October 14, 2004.

16 USIP interview with Aaron Williams, Vice President for International Business Development, RTI International, October 1, 2004; SIGIR interview with Dr. Ronald Johnson, Senior Vice President for International Development, RTI International, March 2, 2006; and USIP interview with Charles "Chuck" Costello, Deputy Chief of Party in the Local Governance Support Project with RTI International, October 14, 2004.

17 RTI International, "Lessons Learned Brief: Military-Civilian Cooperation in Postwar Iraq: Experience with Local Governance Reconstruction," Brief no. 7, May 2005.

18 USAID IG Audit E-267-05-001-P, "Audit of USAID/Iraq's Community Action Program," January 31, 2005, 6.

19 USAID IG Audit E-267-05-001-P, "Audit of USAID/Iraq's Community Action Program," January 31, 2005, 5, 11-12.

20 SIGIR interview with Steve Connolly, QRF Coordinator for DAI, December 21, 2006.

21 SIGIR Audit 05-004, "Oversight of Funds Provided to Iraqi Ministries through the National Budget Process," January 30, 2005, 3, 15.

22 United Nations Security Council Resolution 1483, May 22, 2003.

23 ORHA/CPA Historian interview with J. Scott Carpenter, CPA Director of Governance, June 29, 2004.

24 The English translation of the *fatwa* differs depending on who did the translation. BBC News/Middle East, "Ayatollah Sistani in quotes," August 27, 2004; Babak Rahimi, USIP Report 187, "Ayatollah Sistani and the Democratization of Post-Ba'athist Iraq," June 2007; and Rajiv Chandrasekaran, "How Cleric Trumped U.S. Plan for Iraq: Ayatollah's Call for Vote Forced Occupation Leader to Rewrite Transition Strategy," *Washington Post*, November 26, 2003.

25 According to Carpenter, the Council consisted of 25 members so each could select a cabinet minister. ORHA/CPA Historian interview with J. Scott Carpenter, CPA Director of Governance, June 29, 2004.

26 L. Paul Bremer III, "Iraq's Path to Sovereignty," *Washington Post*, Op-Ed, September 8, 2003.

27 Donald Rumsfeld, former Secretary of Defense, written comments to SIGIR, November 5, 2008.

28 L. Paul Bremer III, "Facts for Feith: CPA History," *National Review*, March 19, 2008; and SIGIR interview with L. Paul Bremer III, former CPA Administrator, July 11, 2008.

29 SIGIR interview with Douglas Feith, former Under Secretary of Defense for Policy, March 20, 2008.

30 L. Paul Bremer III, *My Year in Iraq: The Struggle to Build a future of Hope* (New York: Simon & Schuster, 2006), 167.

31 L. Paul Bremer III, *My Year in Iraq: The Struggle to Build a future of Hope* (New York: Simon & Schuster, 2006), 187.

32 L. Paul Bremer III, *My Year in Iraq: The Struggle to Build a future of Hope* (New York: Simon & Schuster, 2006), 188; and David. E. Sanger, "White House to Overhaul Iraq and Afghan Missions," *New York Times*, October 6, 2003.

33 Public Broadcasting Service, "Interview: Robert Blackwill," *FRONTLINE*, July 25, 2006.

34 SIGIR interview with Richard Armitage, former Deputy Secretary of State, February 4, 2008.

35 Public Broadcasting Service, "Interview: Robert Blackwill," *FRONTLINE*, July 25, 2006.

36 SIGIR interview with Frank Miller, former Chairman of the Executive Steering Group of the NSC, February 4, 2008.

37 United Nations Security Council Resolution 1511, October 16, 2003.

38 Iraqi Governing Council and the Coalition Provisional Authority, "The November 15 Agreement: Timeline to a Sovereign, Democratic and Secure Iraq," November 15, 2003.

39 Iraqi Governing Council and the Coalition Provisional Authority, "The November 15 Agreement: Timeline to a Sovereign, Democratic and Secure Iraq," November 15, 2003.

40 Iraq's eighteen major federal units are called governorates or provinces. The terms are used interchangeably, but this book will exclusively use the term "province." Sharon Otterman, "Iraq: The Changing Plan," Council on Foreign Relations, December 1, 2003.

41 RTI International, "Lessons Learned Brief: Military-Civilian Cooperation in Postwar Iraq: Experience with Local Governance Reconstruction," Brief no. 7, May 2005.

42 Mark Etherington, *Revolt on the Tigris: The al-Sadr Uprising and the Governing of Iraq* (Ithaca, NY: Cornell University Press, 2005), 223-224.

43 USAID IG Audit E-267-06-003-P, "Audit of USAID/Iraq's Local Governance Activities," July 10, 2006, 5.

44 Mark Etherington, *Revolt on the Tigris: The al-Sadr Uprising and the Governing of Iraq* (Ithaca, NY: Cornell University Press, 2005), 133.

45 GAO Report 04-902R, "Rebuilding Iraq: Resource, Security, Governance, Essential Services, and Oversight Issues," June 2004, 32.

46 SIGIR, "Iraq Reconstruction: Lessons in Program and Project Management," March 2007, 70, 101.

47 SIGIR, *Quarterly Report to the United States Congress*, October 2003, 69.

48 CPA Order Number 71, "Local Governmental Powers," April 6, 2004.

49 CPA, "Republic of Iraq: 2004 Budget," October 2003. For all of Iraq's 2003 and 2004 budgets, see http://www.cpa-iraq.org/budget.

50 USIP interview with Charles "Chuck" Costello, Deputy Chief of Party in the Local Governance Support Project with RTI International, October 14, 2004.

Chapter 12

1 Robert Perito, USIP Special Report 137, "The Coalition Provisional Authority's Experience with Public Security in Iraq: Lessons Identified," April 2005, 3; and DoD Briefing, "Rebuilding the Iraqi Military," January 21, 2003, declassified March 12, 2007, 2.

2 Scott Feil, "Building Better Foundations: Security in Postconflict Reconstruction," *The Washington Quarterly* 25, no. 4 (Autumn 2002), 97-98.

3 Michael Gordon, "For Training Iraq's Police, the Main Problem Was Time," *New York Times*, October 21, 2004.

4 SIGIR interview with Frank Miller, former Chairman of the Executive Steering Group of the NSC, February 4, 2008.

5 Even if an organized insurgency had not begun, the Iraqi police would probably have had difficulty maintaining order. At the eve of the invasion, a web of secret police, paramilitary organizations, and intelligence services were the main providers of public order. However, these groups were guilty of many human rights abuses committed under Saddam, and DoD prewar planning called for their dissolution. In contrast, the Iraqi police service only ventured out of their stations "to round up possible suspects, extract confessions by force, and extort bribes from family members for release of the suspects." Seth G. Jones, Jeremy M. Wilson, Andrew Rathmell, and K. Jack Riley, *Establishing Law and Order after Conflict* (Santa Monica, CA: RAND Corporation, 2005), 109-110; and Robert Perito, USIP Special Report 137, "The Coalition Provisional Authority's Experience with Public Security in Iraq: Lessons Identified," April 2005, 2-3. DoD Briefing, "Rebuilding the Iraqi Military," January 21, 2003, declassified March 12, 2007.

6 SIGIR interview with Frank Miller, former Chairman of the Executive Steering Group of the NSC, February 4, 2008. CIA officials denied Frank Miller's claim that they provided intelligence assessments suggesting Iraq's police were capable of maintaining order. Michael Gordon, "For Training Iraq's Police, the Main Problem Was Time," *New York Times*, October 21, 2004.

7 SIGIR interview with Gerald Burke, Advisor to the Baghdad police, June 14, 2007.

8 CPA, "Iraqi Police: An Assessment of the Present and Recommendations for the Future," May 30, 2003, 20, as cited in: House Armed Services Committee Subcommittee on Oversight and Investigations, "Stand Up and Be Counted: The Continuing Challenge of Building the Iraqi Security Forces," July 2007, 55.

9 Robert Perito, USIP Special Report 137, "The Coalition Provisional Authority's Experience with Public Security in Iraq: Lessons Identified," April 2005, 5. Police trainers conduct classroom instruction on human rights, investigations, and rule of law, in addition to firing range and other practice exercises. Police advisors conduct follow-up training and mentorship in the field, where they coach and support new police officers as they apply their new methods and techniques.

10 SIGIR interview with Gerald Burke, Advisor to the Baghdad police, June 14, 2007.

11 Robert Perito, USIP Special Report 137, "The Coalition Provisional Authority's Experience with Public Security in Iraq: Lessons Identified," April 2005, 6.

12 White House Press Release, "President Bush, Police Commissioner Kerik Discuss Police Force in Iraq," October 3, 2003; and SIGIR interview with Major General Paul Eaton, former Commander of CMATT and OSC, May 28, 2008.

13 Lieutenant General Ricardo Sanchez quoted in: Stephanie Gaskell, "Former Iraq Commander: Bernard Kerik Was 'A Waste of Time' in Iraq," *New York Daily News*, May 5, 2008. See also Lieutenant General Ricardo S. Sanchez, *Wiser in Battle: A Soldier's Story* (New York: HarperCollins, 2008), 249-251.

14 Lieutenant General Ricardo S. Sanchez, *Wiser in Battle: A Soldier's Story* (New York: HarperCollins, 2008), 191; and Kristopher Joseph, "18th Military Police Brigade helps Iraqis Restore Law and Order," USAREUR News Release, May 16, 2003.

15 L. Paul Bremer III, *My Year in Iraq: The Struggle to Build a Future of Hope* (New York: Simon & Schuster, 2006), 19.

16 DoS IG Report ISP-IQO-05-72 and DoD IG Report IE-2005-002, "Interagency Assessment of Iraq Police Training," July 15, 2005, 19.

17 SIGIR interview with John Meiklejohn, Advisor for police academies and curriculum, June 14, 2007.

18 SIGIR interview with John Meiklejohn, Advisor for police academies and curriculum, June 14, 2007; and L. Paul Bremer III, *My Year in Iraq: The Struggle to Build a Future of Hope* (New York: Simon & Schuster, 2006), 168.

19 SIGIR interview with John Meiklejohn, Advisor for police academies and curriculum, June 14, 2007.

20 DoS IG Report ISP-IQO-05-72 and DoD IG Report IE-2005-002, "Interagency Assessment of Iraq Police Training," July 15, 2005, 39-40, 55.

21 Initial allocations from the Iraqi budget for the Ministry of Interior totaled $22.9 million, including $2.4 million for operational expenses and $20.5 million for capital expenditures. CPA, "Republic of Iraq Budget Revenues and Expenses: 2003 July-December," 2003. Capital expenditures were reduced with the revision, to $16.5 million. CPA, "Summary of Changes to Ministry Budgets Arising from 30 Day Review," July 2003.

22 L. Paul Bremer III, *My Year in Iraq: The Struggle to Build a Future of Hope* (New York: Simon & Schuster, 2006), 168-170; and GAO Report 04-902R, "Rebuilding Iraq: Resource, Security, Governance, Essential Services, and Oversight Issues," June 2004, 57.

23 Andrew Rathmell, Olga Oliker, Terrence K. Kelly, David Brannan, and Keith Crane, *Developing Iraq's Security Sector: The Coalition Provisional Authority's Experience* (Santa Monica, CA: RAND Corporation, 2005), 46.

24 CPA Order Number 26, "Creation of the Department of Border Enforcement," August 24, 2003.

25 U.S. troops deployed as immigration inspectors received a three-hour training module. In the United States, training for immigration duties takes four months, followed by extensive field training, and an immigration officer in the United States would not be considered proficient at reviewing documents for at least three years. USIP interview with Larry G. Hines, Advisor for customs and border enforcement, October 3, 2004.

26 Robert Perito, USIP Special Report 137, "The Coalition Provisional Authority's Experience with Public Security in Iraq: Lessons Identified," April 2005, 9.

27 CPA Order Number 27, "Establishment of the Facilities Protection Service," September 4, 2003.

28 Sharon Otterman, "Iraq: Security Forces," Council on Foreign Relations , March 16, 2004; and Walter Slocombe, "Iraq's Special Challenge: Security Sector Reform 'Under Fire,'" in *Reform and Reconstruction of the Security Sector*, ed. Alan Bryden and Heiner Hänggi (Geneva, Switzerland: Geneva Centre for the Democratic Control of Security Forces, 2004), 244.

29 DoD, *Measuring Stability and Security in Iraq*, June 2007, 36.

30 CPA Order Number 2, "Dissolution of Entities," May 23, 2003.

31 CPA Order Number 22, "Creation of a New Iraqi Army," August 7, 2003.

32 Combat Studies Institute interview with Major General Paul Eaton, former Commander of CMATT and OSC, August 3, 2006; and CPA Order Number 22, August 7, 2003.

33 Combat Studies Institute interview with Major General Paul Eaton, former Commander of CMATT and OSC, August 3, 2006.

34 Combat Studies Institute interview with Major General Paul Eaton, former Commander of CMATT and OSC, August 3, 2006.

35 USIP interview with Colonel P.J. Dermer, former CPA governance advisor, August 22, 2004.

36 SIGIR interview with Major General Paul Eaton, former Commander of CMATT and OSC, May 20, 2008.

37 L. Paul Bremer III, *My Year in Iraq: The Struggle to Build a Future of Hope* (New York: Simon & Schuster, 2006), 150.

38 Combat Studies Institute interview with Major General Paul Eaton, former Commander of CMATT and OSC, August 3, 2006.

39 ORHA/CPA Historian interview with Major General Paul Eaton, former Commander of CMATT and OSC, January 1, 2004.

40 Combat Studies Institute interview with Major General Paul Eaton, former Commander of CMATT and OSC, August 3, 2006.

41 SIGIR interview with General John Abizaid, former CENTCOM Commander, February 4, 2008.

42 Walter Slocombe, "Iraq's Special Challenge: Security Sector Reform 'Under Fire,'" in *Reform and Reconstruction of the Security Sector*, ed. Alan Bryden and Heiner Hänggi (Geneva, Switzerland: Geneva Centre for the Democratic Control of Security Forces, 2004), 241; and GAO Report 04-902R, "Rebuilding Iraq: Resource, Security, Governance, Essential Services, and Oversight Issues," June 2004, 57.

43 Lieutenant General Ricardo S. Sanchez, *Wiser in Battle: A Soldier's Story* (New York: HarperCollins, 2008), 254; Lieutenant General (Ret.) Ricardo Sanchez, former CJTF-7 Commander, written comments to SIGIR, October 26, 2008; and CPA Order Number 28, "Establishment of the Iraqi Civil Defense Corps," September 3, 2003.

44 Combat Studies Institute interview with Lieutenant Colonel Blaise Cornell-d'Echert, former CMATT official, October 31, 2006.

45 Lieutenant General Ricardo S. Sanchez, *Wiser in Battle: A Soldier's Story* (New York: HarperCollins, 2008), 254-255.

46 Anne Ellen Henderson, USIP Special Report 138, "The Coalition Provisional Authority's Experience with Economic Reconstruction in Iraq: Lessons Identified," April 2005, 9.

47 Celeste Ward, USIP Special Report 139, "The Coalition Provisional Authority's Experience with Governance in Iraq," May 2005, 6.

48 OMB, *Section 2207 Report*, January 2004, 18.

49 CPA Office of Policy Planning, "Iraqi Security Sector Reform Action Memo," November 14, 2003.

50 CPA, "Draft Framework for Iraqi National Security Institution Building," December 10, 2003.

51 Andrew Rathmell, Olga Oliker, Terrence K. Kelly, David Brannan, and Keith Crane, *Developing Iraq's Security Sector: The Coalition Provisional Authority's Experience* (Santa Monica, CA: RAND Corporation, 2005), 27-28; and USIP interview with Frederick Smith, former Deputy Senior Advisor for National Security Affairs, August 4, 2004.

52 USIP interview with Colonel P.J. Dermer, former CPA governance advisor, August 22, 2004. The reforms made Iraq one of the only Arab countries with a civilian-led defense ministry. Arnold Luethold, "Security Sector Reform: the Arab Middle East," in *Reform and Reconstruction of the Security Sector*, ed. Alan Bryden and Heiner Hänggi (Geneva, Switzerland: Geneva Centre for the Democratic Control of Security Forces, 2004), 103.

53 The concern for ethnic balance also extended to the other "power ministries" involved in national security, including the Ministries of Interior, Finance, Foreign Affairs, and Justice. USIP interview with Frederick Smith, former Deputy Senior Advisor for National Security Affairs, August 4, 2004.

54 Andrew Rathmell, Olga Oliker, Terrence K. Kelly, David Brannan, and Keith Crane, *Developing Iraq's Security Sector: The Coalition Provisional Authority's Experience* (Santa Monica, CA: RAND Corporation, 2005), 30.

55 SIGIR interview with Major General Paul Eaton, former Commander of CMATT and OSC, May 28, 2008.

56 Colonel P.J. Dermer, CPA governance advisor, memorandum to Frederick Smith, Deputy Senior Advisor for National Security Affairs, "Thoughts on Choosing the Iraqi Minister of Defense," December 5, 2003.

57 USIP interview with Frederick Smith, former Deputy Senior Advisor for National Security Affairs, August 4, 2004.

58 ORHA/CPA Historian interview with Steven Casteel, Senior Advisor to the Ministry of Interior, July 3, 2004.

59 SIGIR Audit 07-016, "Interim Review of DynCorp International, LLC, Spending Under Its Contract for the Iraqi Police Training Program," October 23, 2007.

60 Gerald Burke, Advisor to the Baghdad police, Testimony before the House Armed Services Committee Subcommittee on Oversight and Investigations, April 25, 2007.

61 The relative peace, however, was short-lived. Fewer in number, the 101st Airborne Division's successors could not prevent Mosul from succumbing to increased violence. Amatzia Baram, USIP Special Report 134, "Who Are the Insurgents? Sunni Arab Rebels in Iraq," April 2005, 7-9.

62 Public Broadcasting Service, "Interview: General Jack Keane (Ret.)," *FRONTLINE*, February 8, 2007, and May 1, 2007.

63 OMB, *Section 1506 Report*, October 2003, 3.

64 SIGIR interview with General (Ret.) Colin Powell, former Secretary of State, February 4, 2008.

65 Former Secretary of Defense Donald Rumsfeld, SIGIR interview, December 12, 2008.

66 L. Paul Bremer III, *My Year in Iraq: The Struggle to Build a Future of Hope* (New York: Simon & Schuster, 2006), 157.

67 Lieutenant General Ricardo S. Sanchez, *Wiser in Battle: A Soldier's Story* (New York: HarperCollins, 2008), 316.

68 SIGIR interview with General John Abizaid, former CENTCOM Commander, February 4, 2008.

69 Robert Perito, USIP Special Report 137, "The Coalition Provisional Authority's Experience with Public Security in Iraq: Lessons Identified," April 2005, 11.

70 SIGIR interview with Major General Paul Eaton, former Commander of CMATT and OSC, May 28, 2008.

71 Lieutenant General Ricardo S. Sanchez, *Wiser in Battle: A Soldier's Story* (New York: HarperCollins, 2008), 315; and Andrew Rathmell, Olga Oliker, Terrence K. Kelly, David Brannan, and Keith Crane, *Developing Iraq's Security Sector: The Coalition Provisional Authority's Experience* (Santa Monica, CA: RAND Corporation, 2005), 51-52.

72 Operational control was ceded to the military, although the CPA retained administrative control of budgets and policy direction came from CPA advisors. SIGIR interview with Major General Paul Eaton, former Commander of CMATT and OSC, May 28, 2008.

73 Gerald Burke, Advisor to the Baghdad police, Testimony before the House Armed Services Committee, Subcommittee on Oversight and Investigations, April 25, 2007.

74 Lieutenant General Ricardo Sanchez, "Combined Joint Task Force 7 Briefing from Baghdad," DoD News Transcript, February 26, 2004.

75 Lieutenant General Ricardo Sanchez, "Combined Joint Task Force 7 Briefing from Baghdad," DoD News Transcript, February 26, 2004; and Sharon Otterman, "Iraq: Security Forces," Council on Foreign Relations, March 16, 2004.

76 Lieutenant General Ricardo S. Sanchez, *Wiser in Battle: A Soldier's Story* (New York: HarperCollins, 2008), 329-331; and GAO Report 04-902R, "Rebuilding Iraq: Resource, Security, Governance, Essential Services, and Oversight Issues," June 2004, 49, 58.

77 Andrew Rathmell, Olga Oliker, Terrence K. Kelly, David Brannan, and Keith Crane, *Developing Iraq's Security Sector: The Coalition Provisional Authority's Experience* (Santa Monica, CA: RAND Corporation, 2005), 36.

78 GAO Report 04-902R, "Rebuilding Iraq: Resource, Security, Governance, Essential Services, and Oversight Issues," June 2004, 59.

79 Lawrence Korb, "Five Steps To a More Stable Iraq," *Star-Ledger*, April 11, 2004.

80 GAO Report 04-902R, "Rebuilding Iraq: Resource, Security, Governance, Essential Services, and Oversight Issues," June 2004, 56.

81 CPA Order Number 22, August 7, 2003.

82 SIGIR interview with Major General Paul Eaton, former Commander of CMATT and OSC, May 28, 2008.

83 Lieutenant General Ricardo S. Sanchez, *Wiser in Battle: A Soldier's Story* (New York: HarperCollins, 2008), 317.

84 ORHA/CPA Historian interview with Steven Casteel, Senior Advisor to the Ministry of Interior, July 3, 2004.

85 SIGIR interview with Major General Paul Eaton, former Commander of CMATT and OSC, May 28, 2008.

86 ORHA/CPA Historian interview with David Gompert, Senior Advisor for National Security Affairs, June 13, 2004.

87 SIGIR interview with General John Abizaid, former CENTCOM Commander, February 4, 2008.

88 CPA, *A Vision for Iraq*, July 11, 2003.

89 DoD, *Iraq Status Working Papers*, July 13, 2004.

90 DoD, "Transition Update to the Secretary of Defense," Iraq Interagency Transition Planning Team, June 23, 2004, 5, 11.

91 DoD, *Iraq Status Working Papers*, July 13, 2004; Anthony Cordesman, *Iraqi Security Forces: A Strategy for Success* (Westport, CT: Praeger Security International, 2006), 85; and Lieutenant General Ricardo S. Sanchez, *Wiser in Battle: A Soldier's Story* (New York: HarperCollins, 2008), 317.

92 Independent Institute for Administration and Civil Security Studies, "Public Opinion in Iraq: First Poll Following Abu Ghraib Revelations," May 14-23, 2004, http://www.globalpolicy.org/security/issues/iraq/poll/2004/06iiacss.pdf.

93 Gilbert Burnham, Riyadh Lafta, Shannon Doocy, and Les Roberts, "Mortality after the 2003 Invasion of Iraq: A Cross-Sectional Cluster Sample Survey," *The Lancet* 368, no. 9545 (October 21, 2006); and The Brookings Institution, "Iraq Index: Tracking Variables of Reconstruction and Security in Post-Saddam Iraq," July 23, 2004, 5.

Chapter 13

1 Energy Information Administration, Department of Energy, "Country Analysis Briefs: Iraq," August 2007, 2.

2 Lawrence Kumins, "Iraq Oil: Reserves, Production, and Potential Revenues," Congressional Research Service Report RS21626, updated April 13, 2005, 1-2.

3 Energy Information Administration, Department of Energy, "Country Analysis Briefs: Iraq," August 2007.

4 Norm Kent, ITAO Senior Advisor to the Ministry of Oil, written comments to SIGIR, June 4, 2008.

5 USACE, "Iraqi Oil Infrastructure Restoration Strategic Plan, Rough Order of Magnitude," June 3, 2003, 1.

6 ORHA/CPA Historian interview with Gary Vogler, Senior Advisor to the Ministry of Oil, June 18, 2003.

7 ORHA/CPA Historian interview with Brigadier General Robert Crear, Commander of Task Force RIO, June 25, 2003.

8 USACE, "Iraqi Oil Infrastructure Restoration Strategic Plan, Rough Order of Magnitude," June 3, 2003.

9 Energy Information Administration, Department of Energy, "Country Analysis Briefs: Iraq," August 2007, 14.

10 ORHA/CPA Historian interview with Gary Vogler, Senior Advisor to the Ministry of Oil, June 18, 2003.

11 ORHA/CPA Historian interview with Gary Vogler, Senior Advisor to the Ministry of Oil, June 18, 2003; and ORHA/CPA Historian interview with Brigadier General Robert Crear, Commander of Task Force RIO, June 25, 2003.

12 GAO Report 04-605, "Rebuilding Iraq: Fiscal Year 2003 Contract Award Procedures and Management Challenges," June 2004, 19, 36.

13 ORHA/CPA Historian interview with Gary Vogler, Senior Advisor to the Ministry of Oil, June 18, 2003.

14 ORHA/CPA Historian interview with Brigadier General Robert Crear, Commander of Task Force RIO, June 25, 2003.

15 ORHA/CPA Historian interview with Gary Vogler, Senior Advisor to the Oil Ministry, June 18, 2003.

16 ORHA/CPA Historian interview with Gary Vogler, Senior Advisor to the Ministry of Oil, June 18, 2003.

17 ORHA/CPA Historian interview with Clark D. Turner, Member of the Energy Infrastructure Planning Group in the Pentagon and Advisor to the Ministry of Oil, June 24, 2003.

18 ORHA/CPA Historian interview with Clark D. Turner, Member of the Energy Infrastructure Planning Group in the Pentagon and Advisor to the Ministry of Oil, June 24, 2003.

19 ORHA/CPA Historian interview with Clark D. Turner, Member of the Energy Infrastructure Planning Group in the Pentagon and Advisor to the Ministry of Oil, June 24, 2003.

20 ORHA/CPA Historian interview with Clark D. Turner, Member of the Energy Infrastructure Planning Group in the Pentagon and Advisor to the Ministry of Oil, June 24, 2003.

21 ORHA/CPA Historian interview with Gary Vogler, Senior Advisor to the Ministry of Oil, June 18, 2003.

22 ORHA/CPA Historian interview with Clark D. Turner, Member of the Energy Infrastructure Planning Group in the Pentagon and Advisor to the Ministry of Oil, June 24, 2003.

23 ORHA/CPA Historian interview with Clark D. Turner, Member of the Energy Infrastructure Planning Group in the Pentagon and Advisor to the Ministry of Oil, June 24, 2003.

24 SIGIR interview with Thamir al-Ghadban, Advisor to the Ministry of Oil, July 7, 2007.

25 ORHA/CPA Historian interview with Clark D. Turner, Member of the Energy Infrastructure Planning Group in the Pentagon and Advisor to the Ministry of Oil, June 24, 2003.

26 USACE, "Iraqi Oil Infrastructure Restoration Strategic Plan, Rough Order of Magnitude," June 3, 2003, 2.

27 ORHA/CPA Historian interview with Clark D. Turner, Member of the Energy Infrastructure Planning Group in the Pentagon and Advisor to the Ministry of Oil, June 24, 2003.

28 Energy Information Administration, Department of Energy, "Iraq Energy Chronology: 1980-November 2005," December 2005.

29 ORHA/CPA Historian interview with Gary Vogler, Senior Advisor to the Ministry of Oil, June 18, 2003.

30 ORHA/CPA Historian interview with Gary Vogler, Senior Advisor to the Ministry of Oil, June 18, 2003.

31 GAO Report 07-839, "Defense Contract Management: DOD's Lack of Adherence to Key Contracting Principles on Iraq Oil Contract Put Government Interests at Risk," July 2007, 17.

32 GAO Report 07-839, "Defense Contract Management: DOD's Lack of Adherence to Key Contracting Principles on Iraq Oil Contract Put Government Interests at Risk," July 2007, 5-7, 17.

33 Joint Planning Workshop, "Restoration of Iraqi Oil Infrastructure Final Work Plan," July 24, 2003, http://www.energyintel.com/resources/workplan.pdf.

34 Joint Planning Workshop, "Restoration of Iraqi Oil Infrastructure Final Work Plan," July 24, 2003, http://www.energyintel.com/resources/workplan.pdf.

35 Kenneth Katzman, "Iraq: Oil-for-Food Program, International Sanction, and Illicit Trade," Congressional Research Service Report EL30472, April 16, 2003, Summary.

36 United Nations Security Council Resolution 1483, May 22, 2003.

37 Steve Wright, "Iraqi Oil Exports Increasing," *USACE Engineer Update* 27 no.8 (August 2003).

38 Energy Information Administration, Department of Energy, "The Iraq Energy Chronology: 1980-November 2005," December 2005.

39 ORHA/CPA Historian interview with Gary Vogler, Senior Advisor to the Ministry of Oil, June 18, 2003.

40 International Monetary Fund, "Iraq: Macroeconomic Assessment," October 21, 2003, 10.

41 The Brookings Institution, "Iraq Index: Tracking Variables of Reconstruction & Security in Post-Saddam Iraq," June 29, 2006; and United Nations Security Council Resolution 1483, May 22, 2003.

42 Energy Information Administration, Department of Energy, "Iraq Energy Chronology: 1980-November 2005," December 2005.

43 Energy Information Administration, Department of Energy, "Iraq Energy Chronology: 1980-November 2005," December 2005; and ORHA/CPA Historian interview with Gary Vogler, Senior Advisor to the Ministry of Oil, June 18, 2003.

44 CPA, Program Review Board Minutes, July 12, 2003.

45 CPA Contracting Action, Contract DABV01-03-C-0007, awarded to Erinys, August 6, 2003; and Erinys, "The Erinys Iraq Oil Protection Force: Infrastructure Security in a Post-Conflict Environment," October 2005. The company's name is the Greek word for Fury, the mythological personification of vengeance.

46 SIGIR Audit 06-009, "Review of Task Force Shield Programs," April 28, 2006, 10.

47 SIGIR Audit 06-009, "Review of Task Force Shield Programs," April 28, 2006, i, 1.

48 SIGIR Audit 06-009, "Review of Task Force Shield Programs," April 28, 2006, 5-15.

49 Erinys, "The Erinys Iraq Oil Protection Force: Infrastructure Security in a Post-Conflict Environment," October 2005.

50 Institute for the Analysis of Global Security (IAGS), "Iraq Pipeline Watch," http://www.iags.org/iraqpipelinewatch.htm.

51 Erinys, "The Erinys Iraq Oil Protection Force: Infrastructure Security in a Post-Conflict Environment," October 2005, 23.

52 Erinys, "The Erinys Iraq Oil Protection Force: Infrastructure Security in a Post-Conflict Environment," October 2005.

53 Institute for the Analysis of Global Security (IAGS), "Iraq Pipeline Watch," http://www.iags.org/iraqpipelinewatch.htm.

54 Institute for the Analysis of Global Security (IAGS), "Iraq Pipeline Watch," http://www.iags.org/iraqpipelinewatch.htm.

55 ITAO, *Monthly Import, Production and Export,* response to SIGIR data call for the *Quarterly Report to the United States Congress,* April 2008; and SIGIR, *Quarterly Report to the United States Congress,* July 2006, 34.

56 ORHA/CPA Historian interview with J. Michael Stinson, Senior Advisor to the Ministry of Oil, June 12, 2004.

Chapter 14

1 ORHA/CPA Historian interview with Brigadier General Steven Hawkins, former Commander, JTF-4, June 23, 2003.

2 ORHA/CPA Historian interview with Brigadier General Steven Hawkins, former Commander, JTF-4, June 23, 2003.

3 Brigadier General Steven R. Hawkins and Colonel (Ret.) Gordon M. Wells, "Nation-Building in Mesopotamia: U.S. Military Engineers in Iraq," *ARMY* 55, no. 2 (February 2005).

4 Brigadier General Steven R. Hawkins and Colonel (Ret.) Gordon M. Wells, "Nation-Building in Mesopotamia: U.S. Military Engineers in Iraq," *ARMY* 55, no. 2 (February 2005).

5 Major General Carl Strock, USACE Director of Civil Works, Testimony before the House Committee on Government Reform, March 11, 2004. Strock was one of the original members of ORHA and became Deputy Director for Operations and Infrastructure for the CPA. He later served as Commanding General of the U.S. Army Corps of Engineers.

6 Brigadier General Steven R. Hawkins and Colonel (Ret.) Gordon M. Wells, "Nation-Building in Mesopotamia: U.S. Military Engineers in Iraq," *ARMY* 55, no. 2 (February 2005).

7 Brigadier General Steven R. Hawkins and Colonel (Ret.) Gordon M. Wells, "Nation-Building in Mesopotamia: U.S. Military Engineers in Iraq," *ARMY* 55, no. 2 (February 2005).

8 International Monetary Fund, "Iraq: Statistical Appendix," August 2007.

9 Republic of Iraq, Ministry of Electricity, "About the Minister," Biography of Dr. Kareem Waheed al-Aboudi. He became Minister of Electricity under Prime Minister Maliki.

10 GAO-04-902R, "Rebuilding Iraq: Resource, Security, Governance, Essential Services, and Oversight Issues," June 2004, 85.

11 Bechtel National, Inc., "Iraq Infrastructure Reconstruction Program," Assessment Report submitted to USAID, June 2003.

12 Colonel Mike Moon, USACE, formerly with GRD, email to SIGIR, July 3, 2008.

13 Bechtel National, Inc., "Iraq Infrastructure Reconstruction Program," Assessment Report submitted to USAID, June 2003.

14 Nameplate capacity is the maximum amount of electricity a facility can generate. Bechtel National, Inc., "Iraq Infrastructure Reconstruction Program," Assessment Report submitted to USAID, June 2003. One megawatt provides enough power to service an estimated 3,000 homes. USACE-GRD, "Restore Iraqi Electricity," http://www.grd.usace.army.mil/news/factsheets/docs/USACE-RIE%20factsheet.pdf.

15 World Bank, "Republic of Iraq: Emergency Electricity Project," Project Information Document, October 4, 2004.

16 United Nations/World Bank, "Joint Iraq Needs Assessment," October 2003, 28.

17 World Bank, "Republic of Iraq: Emergency Electricity Project," Project Information Document, October 4, 2004; and Isam Al Khalisi, "Decentralizing and Restructuring of Iraq's Electricity Supply System," Middle East Economic Survey XLVIII, no. 1 (January 3, 2005).

18 Bechtel National, Inc., "Iraq Infrastructure Reconstruction Program," Assessment Report submitted to USAID, June 2003, 2.4.

19 Bechtel National, Inc., "Iraq Infrastructure Reconstruction Program," Assessment Report submitted to USAID, June 2003, 2.4-2.9.

20 Bechtel National, Inc., "Iraq Infrastructure Reconstruction Program," Assessment Report submitted to USAID, June 2003.

21 Major General Carl Strock, USACE Director of Civil Works, Testimony before the House Committee on Government Reform, March 11, 2004.

22 USIP interview with Thomas Wheelock, Chief of Party for USAID's contractor International Resources Group, September 8, 2004.

23 Bechtel National, Inc., "Bechtel, USAID, and the Iraq Infrastructure Program: Accomplishments and Challenges," 2, http://www.bechtel.com/assets/files/projects/Accomplishments_and_Challenges.pdf.

24 Major General Carl Strock, USACE Director of Civil Works, Testimony before the House Committee on Government Reform, March 11, 2004; and Bechtel National, Inc., "Iraq Infrastructure Reconstruction Program," Assessment Report submitted to USAID, June 2003.

25 USIP interview with Thomas Wheelock, Chief of Party for USAID's contractor International Resources Group, September 8, 2004.

26 Bechtel National, Inc., "Bechtel, USAID, and the Iraq Infrastructure Program: Accomplishments and Challenges," http://www.bechtel.com/assets/files/projects/Accomplishments_and_Challenges.pdf.

27 Brigadier General Steven R. Hawkins and Colonel (Ret.) Gordon M. Wells, "Nation-Building in Mesopotamia: U.S. Military Engineers in Iraq," ARMY 55, no. 2 (February 2005).

28 Major General Carl Strock, USACE Director of Civil Works, Testimony before the House Committee on Government Reform, March 11, 2004.

29 Tom Wheelock and Robyn McGuckin, "Iraqi Power Sector: CPA's Legacy and Lessons," Middle East Economic Survey XLVIII, no. 29 (July 18, 2005).

30 SIGIR Audit 06-009, "Review of Task Force Shield Programs," April 28, 2006.

31 Tom Ochs, et.al., "Fuels and Power Generation: Lessons Learned and a Path Forward," February 12, 2007; Bechtel National, Inc., "Iraq Infrastructure Reconstruction Program," Assessment Report submitted to USAID, June 2003, 2.4-3.0; and ORHA/CPA historian interview with Gary Vogler, advisor to the Ministry of Oil, June 18, 2003.

32 ORHA/CPA historian interview with Gary Vogler, advisor to the Ministry of Oil, June 18, 2003.

33 Issam Chalabi, "Iraq's Uncertain Oil and Political Prospects," *Middle East Economic Survey* L, no. 48 (November 26, 2007).

34 Tom Ochs, et.al., "Fuels and Power Generation: Lessons Learned and a Path Forward," February 12, 2007, 13-35; SIGIR interview with Bob Krause, advisor to the Ministry of Electricity, May 20, 2007

35 Colonel Mike Moon, USACE, formerly with GRD, email to SIGIR, July 3, 2008; and Energy Information Administration, Department of Energy, "Country Analysis Brief: Iraq," August 2007, 6-10.

36 SIGIR interview with Dick Dumford, Program Manager for USAID, May 18, 2007; and SIGIR interview with Stephen Browning, former Deputy Director of Infrastructure, October 3, 2007.

37 SIGIR interview with Dick Dumford, Program Manager for USAID, May 18, 2007; and ORHA/CPA Historian interview with Brigadier General Steven Hawkins, former Commander, JTF-4, June 23, 2003.

38 SIGIR interview with Dick Dumford, Program Manager for USAID, May 18, 2007.

39 CPA, "Republic of Iraq Budget Revenues and Expenses: 2003 July–December," 2003, 6.

40 CPA, Program Review Board Minutes, August 19, 2003.

41 Bechtel, USAID contract EEE-C-00-03-00018-00, 12, http://www.usaid.gov/iraq/contracts/pdf/Bechtel.pdf; and SIGIR, "Iraq Reconstruction: Lessons Learned in Contracting and Procurement," July 2006, 32.

42 Bechtel National, Inc. "Iraq Infrastructure Reconstruction Program, Recommended Implementation Plan," June 2003, 1-1.

43 Bechtel National, Inc., "Iraq Infrastructure Reconstruction Program," Assessment Report submitted to USAID, June 2003, 2.4-2.7.

44 Bechtel National, Inc., "Iraq Infrastructure Reconstruction Program," Assessment Report submitted to USAID, June 2003.

45 DoD News Transcript, "Ambassador Paul Bremer Interview on CBS Face the Nation," July 20, 2003. On the same day, Bremer also told Fox News, "We are expecting to be back at prewar levels in the next six weeks or so." Ambassador Bremer, "Ambassador L. Paul Bremer Interview with Fox News Sunday," DoD News Transcript, July 20, 2003.

46 ORHA/CPA Historian interview with Peter Andrew Bearpark, CPA Director of Operations, December 18, 2003.

47 Browning was the Senior Advisor to the Ministries of Health; Religious Affairs; and Transportation and Communications. MWH Press Release, "Stephen Browning Joins MWH Executive Team," April 25, 2006; and SIGIR interview with Stephen Browning, former Task Force RIO Advisor, October 3, 2007.

48 SIGIR interview with Stephen Browning, former Deputy Director of Infrastructure, October 3, 2007; and SIGIR interview with Dick Dumford, Program Manager for USAID, May 18, 2007.

49 SIGIR interview with Dick Dumford, Program Manager for USAID, May 18, 2007.

50 SIGIR interview with Stephen Browning, former Deputy Director of Infrastructure, October 3, 2007.

51 Tom Wheelock and Robyn McGuckin, "Iraqi Power Sector: CPA's Legacy and Lessons," *Middle East Economic Survey*, XLVIII, no. 29 (July 18, 2005); SIGIR interview with Stephen Browning, former Deputy Director of Infrastructure, October 3, 2007; and SIGIR interview with Dick Dumford, Program Manager for USAID, May 18, 2007.

52 SIGIR interview with Dick Dumford, Program Manager for USAID, May 18, 2007.

53 SIGIR interview with Dick Dumford, Program Manager for USAID, May 18, 2007.

54 SIGIR interview with Stephen Browning, former Deputy Director of Infrastructure, October 3, 2007.

55 L. Paul Bremer III, "Broadcast to the Iraqi People," August 29, 2003.

56 USAID Fact Sheet, "Upgrading Electricity in Iraq," August 15, 2003.

57 SIGIR interview with Stephen Browning, former Deputy Director of Infrastructure, October 3, 2007

58 USACE, "Major Effort Restoring Iraq Electricity," *Engineer Update* 28, no.2 (February 2004).

59 USACE, "Major Effort Restoring Iraq Electricity," *Engineer Update* 28, no.2 (February 2004).

60 OMB, *2207 Report*, April 2004, Appendix 3.

61 USACE, "Major Effort Restoring Iraq Electricity," *Engineer Update* 28, no. 2 (February 2004).

62 P.L. 108-106, Emergency Supplemental Appropriations Act for Defense and for the Reconstruction of Iraq and Afghanistan for Fiscal Year 2004, November 6, 2003.

63 CPA Electricity Advisory Team, "Meeting Agenda: Project Review for the IIRO – 2004 Supplemental Budget," email from Robyn McGuckin, November 13, 2003.

64 GAO Report 04-902R, "Rebuilding Iraq: Resource, Security, Governance, Essential Services, and Oversight Issues," June 28, 2004, 92-93.

65 Jamie Wilson, "Attacks Halt Rebuilding of Iraq," *The Guardian*, April 27, 2004.

66 GAO Report 04-902R, "Rebuilding Iraq: Resource, Security, Governance, Essential Services, and Oversight Issues," June 28, 2004, 91.

67 GAO Report 04-902R, "Rebuilding Iraq: Resource, Security, Governance, Essential Services, and Oversight Issues," June 28, 2004, 88.

Chapter 15

1 Iraqi Governing Council and the Coalition Provisional Authority, "The November 15 Agreement: Timeline to a Sovereign, Democratic and Secure Iraq," November 15, 2003.

2 Ali A. Allawi, *The Occupation of Iraq: Winning the War, Losing the Peace* (New Haven, CT: Yale University Press, 2007), 215.

3 UN News Centre, "Summary of Press Briefing by Lakhdar Brahimi, Special Advisor to the Secretary-General," March 16, 2004.

4 Ali A. Allawi, *The Occupation of Iraq: Winning the War, Losing the Peace* (New Haven, CT: Yale University Press, 2007), 228-232.

5 Ali A. Allawi, *The Occupation of Iraq: Winning the War, Losing the Peace* (New Haven, CT: Yale University Press, 2007), 230-232.

6 George W. Bush, "President Bush Congratulates Iraq for Transitional Administrative Law," White House Press Release, March 8, 2004; and Iraqi Governing Council, "Law of Administration for the State of Iraq for the Transitional Period," Articles 55-56, March 8, 2004.

7 Iraqi Governing Council, "Law of Administration for the State of Iraq for the Transitional Period," Article 7, March 8, 2004.

8 Iraqi Governing Council, "Law of Administration for the State of Iraq for the Transitional Period," Articles 55-56, March 8, 2004.

9 Iraqi Governing Council, "Law of Administration for the State of Iraq for the Transitional Period," Article 61, March 8, 2004.

10 CPA Transcripts, "Statements by United Nations Envoy Lakhdar Brahimi, Iraqi President Ghazi al-Yawar, and Iraqi Prime Minister Ayad Allawi, Topic: The New Interim Government for Iraq," June 1, 2004. Also named was a deputy prime minister for security affairs.

11 GAO Report 05-876, "Rebuilding Iraq: Status of Funding and Reconstruction Efforts," July 2005, 2.

12 SIGIR Audit 05-004, "Oversight of Funds Provided to Iraqi Ministries through the National Budget Process," January 30, 2005, 5; and SIGIR Audit, 04-009, "Coalition Provisional Authority Comptroller Cash Management Controls Over the Development Fund for Iraq," July 28, 2004, 5.

13 SIGIR Audit 05-004, "Oversight of Funds Provided to Iraqi Ministries through the National Budget Process," January 30, 2005, 5.

14 SIGIR Lessons Learned Forum: Contracting and Procurement, Washington, DC, December 5, 2005.

15 IAMB, "Report of the International Advisory and Monitoring Board of the Development Fund for Iraq: Covering the Period from the Establishment of the DFI on May 22, 2003, until the Dissolution of the CPA on June 28, 2004," 2-3. Almost $6 million in DFI funds was committed by the CPA to pay for the audit.

16 OMB, *Section 2207 Report*, July 2004, 70.

17 James Stephenson, *Losing the Golden Hour: An Insider's view of Iraq's Reconstruction* (Herndon, VA: Potomac Books, 2007), 68.

18 CPA, Program Review Board Minutes, May 15, 2004.

19 ORHA/CPA Historian interview with Neil Hawkins, CPA's Director of Development Coordination and Senior Advisor to the Ministry of Planning, June 21, 2004.

20 James Stephenson, *Losing the Golden Hour: An Insider's view of Iraq's Reconstruction* (Herndon, VA: Potomac Books, 2007), 69.

21 Rep. Henry Waxman, Ranking Minority Member, Statement before the House Committee on Government Reform, June 21, 2005.

22 National Security Council, Interagency Transition Planning Team, "Operation Plan Sovereign Iraq," Draft, version 1.3, April 2004.

23 GAO Report 05-737, "Rebuilding Iraq: Actions Needed to Improve Use of Private Security Providers," July 2005, 13.

24 National Security Council, Interagency Transition Planning Team, "Operation Plan Sovereign Iraq," Draft, version 1.3, April 2004, K-2

25 National Security Council, Interagency Transition Planning Team, "Operation Plan Sovereign Iraq," Draft, version 1.3, April 2004.

26 National Security Presidential Directive 36, "United States Government Operations in Iraq," May 11, 2004.

27 National Security Council, Interagency Transition Planning Team, "Operation Plan Sovereign Iraq," Draft, version 1.3, April 2004, D-3,4.

28 National Security Council, Interagency Transition Planning Team, "Operation Plan Sovereign Iraq," Draft, version 1.3, April 2004, A-10

29 GAO Report 05-876, "Rebuilding Iraq: Status of Funding and Reconstruction Efforts," July 2005, 4.

30 National Security Council, Interagency Transition Planning Team, "Operation Plan Sovereign Iraq," Draft, version 1.3, April 2004, G-3.

31 United Nations Security Council Resolution 1546, June 8, 2004.

32 United Nations Security Council Resolution 1483, May 22, 2003.

33 A complete listing of the various orders, regulations and memoranda promulgated by CPA can be found at www.cpa-iraq.org.

34 CPA, "An Historic Review of CPA Accomplishments," June 2004, 71.

35 CPA, "An Historic Review of CPA Accomplishments," June 2004, 71.

The Marshall Plan and Iraq Reconstruction

36 Barry Eichengreen and Marc Uzan, "The Marshall Plan: Economic Effects and Implications for Eastern Europe and the Former USSR," *Economic Policy* 7 no. 14, (April 1992); and Greg Behrman, *The Most Noble Adventure: The Marshall Plan and the Time When America Helped Save Europe* (New York: Free Press, 2007), 4-5.

37 Barry Machado, *In Search of a Usable Past: The Marshall Plan and Postwar Reconstruction Today*," (Lexington, VA: George C. Marshall Foundation, 2007), 34; and Greg Behrman, *The Most Noble Adventure: The Marshall Plan and the Time When America Helped Save Europe* (New York: Free Press, 2007), 179-180.

38 Greg Behrman, *The Most Noble Adventure: The Marshall Plan and the Time When America Helped Save Europe* (New York: Free Press, 2007), 165.

39 Barry Machado, *In Search of a Usable Past: The Marshall Plan and Postwar Reconstruction Today*," (Lexington, VA: George C. Marshall Foundation, 2007), 8, 15-22, 129.

40 Barry Machado, *In Search of a Usable Past: The Marshall Plan and Postwar Reconstruction Today*," (Lexington, VA: George C. Marshall Foundation, 2007), 35-37.

41 SIGIR, "Iraq Reconstruction: Lessons in Human Capital Management," January 2006, 25-29, 34-37.

42 Barry Machado, *In Search of a Usable Past: The Marshall Plan and Postwar Reconstruction Today*," (Lexington, VA: George C. Marshall Foundation, 2007), 117-18.

Essential Services Overview – Transition from CPA to the Embassy

43 International Monetary Fund, "Iraq: Statistical Appendix," August 2007; ITAO, Monthly Import, Production and Export, response to SIGIR data call for the *Quarterly Report to the United States Congress*, April 2008; DoD, Iraq Status Report, June 15, 2004, and July 6, 2004; Iraq Coalition Casualty Count, "U.S. Deaths By Month," updated September 2008; SIGIR, Quarterly Report to the United States Congress, October 2005, 12; Iraq Body Count, "Documented civilian deaths from violence," updated August 24, 2008; P.L. 108-106, Emergency Supplemental Appropriations Act for Defense and for the Reconstruction of Iraq and Afghanistan for Fiscal Year 2004, November 6, 2003; CPA, "Republic of Iraq Budget Revenues and Expenses: 2003 July–December," 2003; CPA, "Republic of Iraq: Revisions to 2004 Budget," March 2004; and GAO Report 05-876, "Rebuilding Iraq: Status of Funding and Reconstruction Efforts," July 2005, 10.

44 This estimate only includes the number of trained personnel. Although an estimated 74,000 Facilities Protection Service members were listed as part of the security forces, in August 2004 they were deemed unfit as a whole and no longer included in estimates. DoD, *Iraq Status Report,* June 15, 2004, 29-30; and DoS, *Weekly Status Report,* August 25, 2004, 24.

45 International Monetary Fund, "Iraq: Statistical Appendix," August 2007.

46 USAID Press Release, "Upgrading Electricity in Iraq," August 15, 2003.

47 Joint Staff and CPA, "Iraq Fact Sheet," October 21, 2003.

48 ITAO, *Monthly Import, Production and Export,* July 2007 as cited in: SIGIR, *Quarterly Report to the United States Congress,* July 2007, 81.

Chapter 16

1 Baghdad embassy, "Statement by Ambassador John D. Negroponte at Presentation of Credentials Ceremony," June 29, 2004; and OMB, *Section 2207 Report,* July 2004, 14. A career Foreign Service officer, Negroponte had served as ambassador to Honduras, Mexico, and the Philippines before retiring in 1997 to become Executive Vice President for Global Markets of the McGraw-Hill publishing company in New York. He returned the State Department in 2001 as the United States Permanent Representative to the United Nations before his assignment to Iraq. DoS, "Biography of John Negroponte," http://www.state.gov/r/pa/ei/biog/80476.htm.

2 White House Press Release, "President Holds Press Conference," February 17, 2005.

3 SIGIR Audit 05-029, "Challenges Faced in Carrying Out Iraq Relief and Reconstruction Fund Activities," January 26, 2006, 4-6.

4 SIGIR, "Iraq Reconstruction: Lessons in Program and Project Management, March 2007, 10, 82-83; and OMB, *Section 2207 Report*, July 2004, 14-15.

5 SIGIR interview with William B. Taylor, former Director of IRMO, April 3, 2008.

6 OMB, *Section 2207 Report*, July 2004, 15.

7 SIGIR, "Iraq Reconstruction: Lessons in Program and Project Management, March 2007, 84-86.

8 SIGIR interview with William B. Taylor, former Director of IRMO, April 3, 2008; and PCO, "PCO Iraq Reconstruction Update," December 15, 2004.

9 OMB, *Section 2207 Report*, July 2004, 15; Claude M. Bolton, Jr., Assistant Secretary of the Army for Acquisition, Logistics, and Technology, Testimony before the Senate Committee on Armed Services Subcommittee on Readiness and Management Support on Iraq Reconstruction and Contracting, February 7, 2006; and SIGIR interview with Charles Hess, former Director of PCO, April 24, 2006.

10 DoD News Release, "Casey Takes Over Iraq Commander's Reins from Sanchez," July 1, 2004.

11 SIGIR interview with Ambassador John Negroponte, former U.S. Ambassador to Iraq, February 12, 2008.

12 SIGIR interview with Ambassador John Negroponte, former U.S. Ambassador to Iraq, February 12, 2008.

13 SIGIR interview with Gen. George Casey, former Director of the Joint Staff and former MNF-I Commander, July 30, 2008.

14 The ten sectors were: Security and Law Enforcement; Justice, Public Safety Infrastructure, and Civil Society; Electricity; Oil Infrastructure; Water Resources and Sanitation; Transportation and Telecommunications; Roads, Bridges, and Construction; Health Care; Education, Refugees, Human Rights, Democracy and Governance; and Private Sector Development. For an overview of the changes, see: OMB, *Section 2207 Report*, July 2004, 17-20

15 SIGIR interview with Ambassador William B. Taylor, former Director of IRMO, April 3, 2008.

16 CPA-IG, *Quarterly Report to the United States Congress*, July 2004, 55-56.

17 OMB, *Section 2207 Report*, July 2004, 20.

18 OMB, *Section 2207 Report*, January 2004, 19; and Richard Armitage, Deputy Secretary of State, Testimony before the House Appropriations Committee, Foreign Operations Subcommittee, September 24, 2004.

19 SIGIR interview with Ambassador William B. Taylor, former Director of IRMO, April 3, 2008.

20 SIGIR Lessons Learned Forum: Program and Project Management, Washington, DC, April 12, 2006.

21 SIGIR Lessons Learned Forum: Program and Project Management, Washington, DC, April 12, 2006.

22 DoS, *Section 2207 Report*, October 2004, 2.

23 DoS, *Section 2207 Report*, October 2004, 2-4.

24 Richard Armitage, Deputy Secretary of State, Testimony before the House Appropriations Committee, Foreign Operations Subcommittee, September 24, 2004.

25 Section 133 of P.L. 108-309 amended P.L. 108-106. P.L. 108-309, Making Continuing Appropriations for the Fiscal Year 2005, September 30, 2004.

26 SIGIR interview with Charles Hess, former Director of PCO, April 24, 2006.

27 Charles Hess, Director of PCO, email to William B. Taylor, Director of IRMO, September 5, 2004.

28 Charles Hess, Director of PCO, email to William B. Taylor, Director of IRMO, September 5, 2004.

29 DoS, *Section 2207 Report*, January 2005, 8.

30 SIGIR interview with Ambassador William B. Taylor, former Director of IRMO, April 3, 2008.

31 Charles Hess, Director of PCO, memorandum to Claude M. Bolton, Assistant Secretary of the Army for Acquisition, Logistics and Technology, March 2005.

32 DoS, *Section 2207 Report*, April 2005, 5.

33 GAO Report 05-876, "Rebuilding Iraq: Status of Funding and Reconstruction Efforts," July 2005, 8; and DoS, *Section 2207 Report*, April 2005, 6-7; and DoS, *Section 2207 Report*, April 2005, 6-7.

34 IRMO, "Iraq Reconstruction Program: Framework for Sustainable Operations," May 18, 2005; and PCO, "Iraq Capacity Development: PCO Management and Interface Plan," November 22, 2004; and PCO, "Program Management Plan," Section 10, Capacity Development, October 7, 2004.

35 DoS, *Section 2207 Report*, April 2005, 7.

36 OMB, *Section 2207 Reports*, Funding Table, July 2004; DoS, *Section 2207 Report*, Status of Funds, July 2005; and SIGIR Audit 05-029, "Challenges Faced in Carrying Out Iraq Relief and Reconstruction Fund Activities," January 26, 2006, 21-23.

37 OMB, *Section 2207 Reports*, Funding Table, July 2004; DoS, *Section 2207 Report*, Status of Funds, July 2005; and SIGIR Audit 05-029, "Challenges Faced in Carrying Out Iraq Relief and Reconstruction Fund Activities," January 26, 2006, 18.

38 SIGIR Audit 05-029, "Challenges Faced in Carrying Out Iraq Relief and Reconstruction Fund Activities," January 26, 2006, 7.

39 DoS, *Section 2207 Report*, July 2005, 7.

40 DoS, *Section 2207 Report*, July 2005, 5, 7.

Chapter 17

1 Brig. Gen. Stephen Seay, Head of Contracting Activity, comments to SIGIR, October 23, 2008.

2 Brig. Gen. Stephen Seay, Head of Contracting Activity, comments to SIGIR, October 23, 2008.

3 SIGIR interview with Brig. Gen. Stephen Seay, Head of Contracting Activity, November 2-3, 2005.

4 USACE, comments to SIGIR, November 4, 2008.

5 SIGIR interview with Brig. Gen. Stephen Seay, Head of Contracting Activity, June 29, 2006.

6 SIGIR interview with Brig. Gen. Stephen Seay, Head of Contracting Activity, November 2-3, 2005.

7 SIGIR interview with Andy Bailey, Vice President of Louis Berger, March 14, 2006.

8 SIGIR, "Iraq Reconstruction: Lessons in Program and Project Management," March 2007, 85.

9 SIGIR Audit 06-001, "Management of Iraq Relief and Reconstruction Fund Program: The Evolution of the Iraq Reconstruction Management System," April 24, 2006, 1.

10 SIGIR interview with Brig. Gen. Stephen Seay, Head of Contracting Activity, November 2-3, 2005.

11 SIGIR interview with Brig. Gen. Stephen Seay, Head of Contracting Activity, November 2-3, 2005.

12 SIGIR Audit 06-001, "Management of Iraq Relief and Reconstruction Fund Program: The Evolution of the Iraq Reconstruction Management System," April 24, 2006, 3.

13 SIGIR Audit 06-001, "Management of Iraq Relief and Reconstruction Fund Program: The Evolution of the Iraq Reconstruction Management System," April 24, 2006, 17.

14 SIGIR Audit 06-001, "Management of Iraq Relief and Reconstruction Fund Program: The Evolution of the Iraq Reconstruction Management System," April 24, 2006, 4.

15 The PMO and the succeeding PCO had tried to simplify tracking of design-build contractors' overhead costs through administrative task orders. These task orders were supposed to capture all the administrative costs separately from the direct costs of the task orders for project construction. Administrative task orders were only issued to five of the design-build firms, though, and "only one of the contractors had adequate accounting and billing systems to capture administrative costs." SIGIR Audit 06-028, "Review of Administrative Task Orders for Iraq Reconstruction Contracts," October 23, 2006, ii.

16 SIGIR Audit 06-028, "Review of Administrative Task Orders for Iraq Reconstruction Contracts," October 23, 2006, iii.

17 The Defense FAR Supplement defines "undefinitized contract action" as "any contract action for which the contract terms, specifications, or price are not agreed upon before performance is begun under the action." Defense FAR Supplement (DFARS), Subpart 217.7401 (d), revised May 12, 2006.

18 DFARS, Subpart 217.74, "Undefinitized Contract Actions," revised May 12, 2006.

19 SIGIR Audit 06-019, "Review of the Use of Definitization Requirements for Contracts Supporting Reconstruction in Iraq," July 28, 2006, 5-6.

20 CFC FRAGO 09-668, "Contracting and Organizational Changes," 122143Z, November 12, 2004, as cited in: SIGIR, "Iraq Reconstruction: Lessons in Contracting and Procurement," July 2006, 76.

21 SIGIR, "Iraq Reconstruction: Lessons in Contracting and Procurement," July 2006, 77.

22 SIGIR, "Iraq Reconstruction: Lessons in Contracting and Procurement," July 2006, 76-77.

23 SIGIR, "Iraq Reconstruction: Lessons in Program and Project Management," March 2007, 117.

24 See, for example: Miriam Pemberton and William D. Hartung, eds. *Lessons From Iraq: Avoiding the Next War* (Boulder, CO: Paradigm, 2008).

25 The DoD estimates that the shift from design-build to direct contracting with Iraqis saved between 20 to 50 percent in the electricity distribution area. GAO Report 07-30R, "Rebuilding Iraq: Status of DOD's Reconstruction Program," December 15, 2006, 9; and SIGIR, "Iraq Reconstruction: Lessons in Contracting and Procurement," July 2006.

26 P.L. 108-375, Ronald W. Reagan National Defense Authorization Act for Fiscal Year 2005, October 28, 2004.

27 Charles Hess, Director of PCO, email to William B. Taylor, Director of IRMO, September, 5, 2004.

28 Charles Hess, Director of PCO, email to William B. Taylor, Director of IRMO, September, 5, 2004.

29 SIGIR, "Iraq Reconstruction: Lessons in Program and Project Management," March 2007, 106, 108.

30 SIGIR Audit 05-027, "Methodologies for Reporting Cost-to-Complete Estimates", January 27, 2006, 9.

31 USACE, comments to SIGIR, November 4, 2008.

32 SIGIR, "Iraq Reconstruction: Lessons in Program and Project Management," March 2007, 84.

33 SIGIR interview with Linda Allen, Senior Consultant for Environment, Municipalities, Public Works, and Water, May 12, 2007.

Chapter 18

1 SIGIR, *Quarterly Report to the United States Congress*, October 2005, 12. The Defense Base Act provides disability compensation and medical benefits to employees and death benefits to eligible survivors of employees of U.S. government contractors who perform work overseas. For contractors working overseas, the Defense Base Act requires contractors to provide insurance coverage for employees performing work on contracts funded by the U.S. government. The insurance provides lost wages and survivor benefits for death, injury, or other work interruptions, such as kidnapping. If war risk is found, the U.S. government reimburses insurance carriers for their costs and assumes responsibility for future payments. Defense Base Act death and injury claims are filed with the Department of Labor. Department of Labor, "Defense Base Act (DBA) Frequently Asked Questions (FAQ)," May 2005.

2 SIGIR, *Quarterly Report to the United States Congress*, October 2008, 14.

3 SIGIR Audit 08-020, "Key Recurring Management Issues Identified in Audits of Iraqi Reconstruction Efforts," July 27, 2008, 4-7.

4 SIGIR Audit 08-020, "Key Recurring Management Issues Identified in Audits of Iraqi Reconstruction Efforts," July 27, 2008, 6.

5 SIGIR Audit 09-005, "Agencies Need Improved Financial Data Reporting for Private Security Contractors," October 30, 2008, 1-2; and GAO Report 05-737, "Rebuilding Iraq: Actions Needed to Improve the Use of Private Security Providers," July 2005, 3.

6 GAO Report 05-737, "Rebuilding Iraq: Actions Needed to Improve the Use of Private Security Providers," July 2005.

7 GAO Report 05-737, "Rebuilding Iraq: Actions Needed to Improve the Use of Private Security Providers," July 2005, 3, 8. By 2008, SIGIR identified 322 companies who provided security services with contracts totaling more than $6 billion. SIGIR Audit 09-005, "Agencies Need Improved Financial Data Reporting for Private Security Contractors," October 30, 2008, 3.

8 More than $662 million was obligated to contracts for another 233 companies for tasks that could have included physical security, but the descriptions of work were too general to ensure that the funds did not go for other services. SIGIR Audit 09-005, "Agencies Need Improved Financial Data Reporting for Private Security Contractors," October 30, 2008, i-ii, 3.

9 SIGIR, "Iraq Reconstruction: Lessons in Contracting and Procurement," 19, 60.

10 GAO Report 05-876, "Rebuilding Iraq: Status of Funding and Reconstruction Efforts," July 2005, 14.

11 DoS, Section 2207 Reports, July 2005, 11-12; April 2005, 9-10; and January 2005, 4-5.

12 GAO Report 05-876, "Rebuilding Iraq: Status of Funding and Reconstruction Efforts," July 2005, 13, 17.

13 DoS, Section 2207 Report, October 2004, I-47; and GAO Report 05-876, "Rebuilding Iraq: Status of Funding and Reconstruction Efforts," July 2005, 14. The gas-oil separation plants, or GOSPs, separate crude oil from natural gas liquids at well sites. Some of these liquids are processed to produce liquefied petroleum gas, used primarily for cooking and heating in Iraq.

14 DoS, Section 2207 Report, January 2005, I-79.

15 Lawrence Kumins, Congressional Research Service Report RS21626, "Iraq Oil: Reserves, Production, and Potential Revenues," updated April 13, 2005, 4-5.

16 Ariel Cohen, "Reducing U.S. Dependence on Middle Eastern Oil," Heritage Foundation backgrounder no. 1926, April 7, 2006, 5-6.

17 DoS, Section 2207 Report, April 2005, I-55; and DoS, Section 2207 Report, January 2005, I-80.

18 DoS, Section 2207 Report, January 2005, I-80.

19 SIGIR, Quarterly Report to the United States Congress, October 2006, 34.

20 DoS, Section 2207 Report, April 2005, I-55.

21 DoS, Section 2207 Report, July 2005, I-57.

22 SIGIR Inspection SA-05-001, "Pipeline River Crossing: Al Fatah, Iraq," January 27, 2006, 2.

23 SIGIR Inspection SA-05-001, "Pipeline River Crossing: Al Fatah, Iraq," January 27, 2006, 2.

24 SIGIR Inspection SA-05-001, "Pipeline River Crossing: Al Fatah, Iraq," January 27, 2006, 4.

25 SIGIR Inspection SA-05-001, "Pipeline River Crossing: Al Fatah, Iraq," January 27, 2006, 4-5.

26 SIGIR Inspection SA-05-001, "Pipeline River Crossing: Al Fatah, Iraq," January 27, 2006, 5.

27 SIGIR Inspection SA-05-001, "Pipeline River Crossing: Al Fatah, Iraq," January 27, 2006, 5-6.

28 SIGIR Inspection SA-05-001, "Pipeline River Crossing: Al Fatah, Iraq," January 27, 2006, 8.

29 SIGIR Inspection SA-05-001, "Pipeline River Crossing: Al Fatah, Iraq," January 27, 2006, 8.

30 SIGIR Inspection SA-05-001, "Pipeline River Crossing: Al Fatah, Iraq," January 27, 2006, i, 8.

31 DoS, Section 2207 Report, April 2005, I-55.

32 DoS, Section 2207 Report, April 2005, I-56.

33 ORHA/CPA historian interview with Michael Stinson, senior advisor to the Minister of Oil 2003- 2004, June 12, 2004.

34 GAO Report 05-876, "Rebuilding Iraq: Status of Funding and Reconstruction Efforts," July 2005, 19.

35 OMB, Section 2207 Report, April 2004, 45-49.

36 DoS, *Section 2207 Report*, July 2005, 48-56.

37 GAO Report 05-876, "Rebuilding Iraq: Status of Funding and Reconstruction Efforts," July 2005, 20.

38 GAO Report 05-876, "Rebuilding Iraq: Status of Funding and Reconstruction Efforts," July 2005, 20.

39 Compiled from DoS, *Section 2207 Reports*, October 2004, January 2005, April 2005, and July 2005; and GAO Report 05-876, "Rebuilding Iraq: Status of Funding and Reconstruction Efforts," July 2005, 20.

40 American Military Engineers, "Engineering and Construction Efforts to Rebuild Iraq," August 19, 2004.

41 USAID Audit E-267-05-003-P, "Audit of USAID/Iraq's Electrical Power Sector Activities," June 29, 2005, 3.

42 USAID Audit E-267-05-003-P, "Audit of USAID/Iraq's Electrical Power Sector Activities," June 29, 2005, 4.

43 USAID Audit E-267-05-003-P, "Audit of USAID/Iraq's Electrical Power Sector Activities," June 29, 2005, 8-9.

44 SIGIR interview with Dick Dumford, Program Manager for USAID, May 18, 2007.

45 SIGIR Report PA-07-103, "Doura Power Station Units 5 and 6, Baghdad, Iraq," July 18, 2007, 7.

46 SIGIR interview with Dick Dumford, Program Manager for USAID, May 18, 2007.

47 SIGIR Inspection PA-07-103, "Doura Power Station Units 5 and 6, Baghdad, Iraq," July 18, 2007, i.

48 USAID Audit E-267-05-003-P, "Audit of USAID/Iraq's Electrical Power Sector Activities," June 29, 2005, 7.

49 USAID Audit E-267-05-003-P, "Audit of USAID/Iraq's Electrical Power Sector Activities," June 29, 2005, 7; and SIGIR Audit 05-024, "Management of the Mansuria Electrical Reconstruction Project," January 23, 2006, 2-4.

50 SIGIR Audit 05-024, "Management of the Mansuria Electrical Reconstruction Project," January 23, 2006, 3.

51 SIGIR Audit 08-011, "Outcome, Cost, and Oversight of Electricity-Sector Reconstruction Contract with Perini Corporation," April 29, 2008, iii-iv.

52 SIGIR Audit 08-011, "Outcome, Cost, and Oversight of Electricity-Sector Reconstruction Contract with Perini Corporation," April 29, 2008, 5, 23.

53 SIGIR Inspection PA-05-008, "Al Seraji Substation, Basrah, Iraq," March 10, 2006; SIGIR Inspection PA-05-007, "Al Kaffat Substation, Basrah, Iraq," March 10, 2006; SIGIR Inspection PA-05-006, "Hamdan Substation, Basrah, Iraq," March 10, 2006; and SIGIR Inspection PA-05-005, "Al Hakamia Substation, Basrah, Iraq," March 10, 2006.

54 SIGIR Audit 08-011, "Outcome, Cost, and Oversight of Electricity-Sector Reconstruction Contract with Perini Corporation," April 29, 2008, ii, 1, 3-4. SIGIR auditor Paul Converse provided significant work on this audit before he was killed in Iraq on March 24, 2008.

55 DoS, *Section 2207 Report*, January 2005, I-65-67.

56 DoS, *Section 2207 Report*, April 2005, I-43.

57 OMB, *Section 2207 Report*, January 2004, Funding Table; and DoS, *Section 2207 Report*, July 2005, Funding Table.

58 DoS, *Section 2207 Report*, July 2005, I-62-70.

59 USAID Audit E-267-05-004-P, "Audit of USAID/Iraq's Water and Sanitation Rehabilitation Activities," June 30, 2005, 17.

60 SIGIR Audit 08-018, "Outcome, Cost, and Oversight of Water Sector Reconstruction Contract with FluorAMEC, LLC," July 15, 2008; and GAO Report 05-872, "Rebuilding Iraq: U.S. Water and Sanitation Efforts Need Improved Measures for Assessing Impact and Sustained Resources for Maintaining Facilities," September 2005, 11.

61 GAO Report 05-872, "Rebuilding Iraq: U.S. Water and Sanitation Efforts Need Improved Measures for Assessing Impact and Sustained Resources for Maintaining Facilities," September 2005, 2, 11.

62 GAO Report 05-872, "Rebuilding Iraq: U.S. Water and Sanitation Efforts Need Improved Measures for Assessing Impact and Sustained Resources for Maintaining Facilities," September 2005, 21-25.

63 SIGIR Audit 08-018, "Outcome, Cost, and Oversight of Water Sector Reconstruction Contract with FluorAMEC, LLC," July 15, 2008, ii.

64 SIGIR Audit 08-018, "Outcome, Cost, and Oversight of Water Sector Reconstruction Contract with FluorAMEC, LLC," July 15, 2008, 5-6.

65 GAO Report 05-872, "Rebuilding Iraq: U.S. Water and Sanitation Efforts Need Improved Measures for Assessing Impact and Sustained Resources for Maintaining Facilities," September 2005, 28.

66 SIGIR, PA 08-144, PA08-145, PA08-146, PA08-147, PA 08-148, "Fallujah Waste Water Treatment System, Falluja, Iraq," October 27, 2008, 1-2, 13-14.

67 SIGIR, PA 08-144, PA08-145, PA08-146, PA08-147, PA 08-148, "Fallujah Waste Water Treatment System, Falluja, Iraq," October 27, 2008, 7.

68 SIGIR, PA 08-144, PA08-145, PA08-146, PA08-147, PA 08-148, "Fallujah Waste Water Treatment System, Falluja, Iraq," October 27, 2008, 4.

69 The initial completion date was set to three and a half years but the CPA chose to accelerate the date to eighteen months. SIGIR Inspections PA 08-144, PA08-145, PA08-146, PA08-147, PA 08-148, "Fallujah Waste Water Treatment System, Falluja, Iraq," October 27, 2008, 9.

70 SIGIR Inspections PA 08-144, PA08-145, PA08-146, PA08-147, PA 08-148, "Fallujah Waste Water Treatment System, Falluja, Iraq," October 27, 2008, 8-9.

71 SIGIR Inspections PA 08-144, PA08-145, PA08-146, PA08-147, PA 08-148, "Fallujah Waste Water Treatment System, Falluja, Iraq," October 27, 2008, 11, 14.

72 SIGIR Inspections PA 08-144, PA08-145, PA08-146, PA08-147, PA 08-148, "Fallujah Waste Water Treatment System, Falluja, Iraq," October 27, 2008, 11-12.

73 SIGIR Inspections PA 08-144, PA08-145, PA08-146, PA08-147, PA 08-148, "Fallujah Waste Water Treatment System, Falluja, Iraq," October 27, 2008, 16.

74 SIGIR Inspections PA 08-144, PA08-145, PA08-146, PA08-147, PA 08-148, "Fallujah Waste Water Treatment System, Falluja, Iraq," October 27, 2008, i.

75 DoS, *Section 2207 Report*, April 2005.

76 DoS, *Section 2207 Report*, July 2005, I-81.

77 SIGIR Audit 06-011, "Management of the Primary Healthcare Centers Construction Projects," April 29, 2006, i, 1.

78 SIGIR Audit 06-025, "Review of the Medical Equipment Purchased for the Primary Healthcare Centers Associated with Parsons Global Services, Inc." July 28, 2006.

79 SIGIR Audit 06-011, "Management of the Primary Healthcare Centers Construction Projects," April 29, 2006, 5.

80 SIGIR Audit 06-011, "Management of the Primary Healthcare Centers Construction Projects," April 29, 2006, 7.

81 SIGIR Audit 06-011, "Management of the Primary Healthcare Centers Construction Projects," April 29, 2006, 14.

82 SIGIR Audit 06-011, "Management of the Primary Healthcare Centers Construction Projects," April 29, 2006, i, 1, 5.

83 SIGIR Inspections PA-06-042, SIGIR PA-06-043, SIGIR PA-06-044, SIGIR PA-06-045, SIGIR PA-06-046, "Primary Health Care Centers Numbered KE-01, KE-02, KE-03, KE-04, and KE-05, Kirkuk, Iraq," April 25, 2006, i-ii.

84 SIGIR Audit 06-025, "Review of the Medical Equipment Purchased for the Primary Healthcare Centers Associated with Parsons Global Services, Inc.," July 28, 2006, 34.

85 SIGIR Audit 06-025, "Review of the Medical Equipment Purchased for the Primary Healthcare Centers Associated with Parsons Global Services, Inc.," July 28, 2006, ii.

86 SIGIR interview with Jack Holly, Project and Contracting Office logistics, May 2007.

87 SIGIR interview with Jack Holly, Project and Contracting Office logistics, May 2007.

Chapter 19

1 House Armed Services Committee Subcommittee on Oversight and Investigations, "Stand Up and Be Counted: The Continuing Challenge of Building the Iraqi Security Forces," July 2007, 93-94.

2 Combat Studies Institute interview with Lt. Gen. David Petraeus, former commander of MNSTC-I, December 11, 2006.

3 SIGIR interview with Col. Chris King, former MNSTC-I Deputy J5, June 12, 2008.

4 DoS Report ISP-IQO-05-72 and DoD IG Report IE-2005-002, "Interagency Assessment of Iraq Police Training," July 15, 2005, 9; and DoS, *Section 2207 Report*, October 2004, I-1.

5 House Armed Services Committee Subcommittee on Oversight and Investigations, "Stand Up and Be Counted: The Continuing Challenge of Building the Iraqi Security Forces," July 2007, 94.

6 GAO Report 06-788, "Rebuilding Iraq: More Comprehensive National Strategy Needed to Help Achieve U.S. Goals," July 2006, 11.

7 OMB, *Section 2207 Report*, July 2004, 17.

8 P.L. 108-309, Making Continuing Appropriations for the Fiscal Year 2005, and for Other Purposes, September 30, 2004.

9 SIGIR interview with Gen. David Petraeus, Commander of MNF-I, March 2, 2008.

10 Donald. P. Wright and Timothy R. Reese, *On Point II: Transition to the New Campaign* (Ft. Leavenworth, KS: Combat Studies Institute Press, 2008), 453-454; Combat Studies Institute interview with Col. Peter DeLuca, former J7 (Engineer) for MNSTC-I, June 1, 2006; and SIGIR Audit 08-005, "Differences in Services and Fees for Management and Administration of Iraq Reconstruction Contracts," January 29, 2008.

11 SIGIR Audit 08-005, "Differences in Services and Fees for Management and Administration of Iraq Reconstruction Contracts," January 29, 2008; and Combat Studies Institute interview with Col. Peter DeLuca, former J7 (Engineer) for MNSTC-I, June 1, 2006.

12 Donald. P. Wright and Timothy R. Reese, *On Point II: Transition to the New Campaign* (Ft. Leavenworth, KS: Combat Studies Institute Press, 2008), 453-454.

13 DoS, *Section 2207 Report*, January 2005, 5-8; and DoS, *Section 2207 Report*, April 2005, 4-5. SIGIR inspections later revealed improper design practices and poor construction at the Baghdad Police College. SIGIR Inspections PA-06-078.2 and PA-06-079.2, "Baghdad Police College: Baghdad, Iraq," January 29, 2007.

14 DoS, *Section 2207 Report*, July 2004, I-12.

15 DoS, *Section 2207 Report*, October 2004, I-14

16 GAO Report 04-902R, "Rebuilding Iraq: Resource, Security, Governance, Essential Services, and Oversight Issues," June 2004, 56.

17 Donald. P. Wright and Timothy R. Reese, *On Point II: Transition to the New Campaign* (Ft. Leavenworth, KS: Combat Studies Institute Press, 2008), 467.

18 Donald. P. Wright and Timothy R. Reese, *On Point II: Transition to the New Campaign* (Ft. Leavenworth, KS: Combat Studies Institute Press, 2008), 467.

19 DoS, *Section 2207 Report*, October 2004, I-1-3.

20 GAO Report 04-902R, "Rebuilding Iraq: Resource, Security, Governance, Essential Services, and Oversight Issues," June 2004, 60; and DoS, *Section 2207 Report*, October 2004, I-4.

21 Donald. P. Wright and Timothy R. Reese, *On Point II: Transition to the New Campaign* (Ft. Leavenworth, KS: Combat Studies Institute Press, 2008), 467.

22 DoS, *Weekly Status Report*, July 27, 2004, 24.

23 Gen. (Ret.) James L. Jones, Chairman, "Report of the Independent Commission on the Security Forces of Iraq," September 6, 2007, 109.

24 DoD, *Measuring Stability and Security in Iraq*, October 2005, 39; and MNF-I, "Iraqi Special Police," July 22, 2006.

25 DoD, *Measuring Stability and Security in Iraq*, October 2005, 39.

26 DoS, *Section 2207 Report*, January 2005, I-7.

27 MNF-I, "Iraqi Special Police," July 22, 2006; and DoS, *Section 2207 Report*, April 2005, I-2.

28 DoS, *Section 2207 Report*, April 2005, I-5.

29 DoD, *Measuring Stability and Security in Iraq*, October 2005, 39.

30 MNF-I, "Iraqi Special Police," July 22, 2006.

31 DoS, *Section 2207 Report*, January 2005, I-7.

32 DoS, *Section 2207 Report*, July 2004, I-2, I-11.

33 DoS, *Section 2207 Report*, October 2004, 4.

34 DoS, *Section 2207 Report*, January 2005, I-20.

35 DoS, *Section 2207 Report*, April 2005, I-11.

36 House Armed Services Committee Subcommittee on Oversight and Investigations, "Stand Up and Be Counted: The Continuing Challenge of Building the Iraqi Security Forces," July 2007, 93; and DoS, *Section 2207 Report*, July 2004, I-9.

37 By January 2005, the IIF comprised twelve of the army's 27 battalions and was integrated as the 1st Division of the IAF. DoS, *Section 2207 Report*, January 2005, I-3, I-18.

38 House Armed Services Committee Subcommittee on Oversight and Investigations, "Stand Up and Be Counted: The Continuing Challenge of Building the Iraqi Security Forces," July 2007, 98.

39 DoD, *Measuring Stability and Security in Iraq*, July 2005, 16.

40 DoS, *Section 2207 Report*, October 2004, I-2; and House Armed Services Committee Subcommittee on Oversight and Investigations, "Stand Up and Be Counted: The Continuing Challenge of Building the Iraqi Security Forces," July 2007, 99.

41 GlobalSecurity.org, "Iraqi Intervention Force, New Iraqi Army, 1st Division," http://www.globalsecurity.org/military/world/iraq/iif.htm, accessed on April 17, 2008.

42 House Armed Services Committee Subcommittee on Oversight and Investigations, "Stand Up and Be Counted: The Continuing Challenge of Building the Iraqi Security Forces," July 2007, 99-100.

43 Anthony Cordesman, *Iraqi Security Forces: A Strategy for Success* (Westport, CT: Praeger Security International, 2006), 172; and DoD, *Measuring Stability and Security in Iraq*, July 2005, 13.

44 DoS, *Section 2207 Report*, January 2005, I- 2-3.

45 DoS, *Section 2207 Report*, April 2005, I-1.

46 Donald. P. Wright and Timothy R. Reese, *On Point II: Transition to the New Campaign* (Ft. Leavenworth, KS: Combat Studies Institute Press, 2008), 456.

47 Combat Studies Institute interview with Lt. Gen. David Petraeus, former commander of MNSTC-I, December 11, 2006.

48 Donald. P. Wright and Timothy R. Reese, *On Point II: Transition to the New Campaign* (Ft. Leavenworth, KS: Combat Studies Institute Press, 2008), 461.

49 House Armed Services Committee Subcommittee on Oversight and Investigations, "Stand Up and Be Counted: The Continuing Challenge of Building the Iraqi Security Forces," July 2007, 14-15, 130-132. After the transition teams moved under MNC-I control with their Iraqi units, a coordination line was maintained between the advisory teams and MNSTC-I, because MNSTC-I's mission still included recruiting replacement soldiers and providing the bulk of individual equipment for Iraqi personnel. Combat Studies Institute interview with Lt. Gen. David Petraeus, former commander of MNSTC-I, December 11, 2006.

50 Eric Schmitt, "General Seeking Faster Training of Iraq Soldiers," New York Times, January 23, 2005; and DoD News Transcript, "Media Availability with Secretary Rumsfeld; General John Abizaid and General George W. Casey, Jr.," February 11, 2005.

51 Donald. P. Wright and Timothy R. Reese, On Point II: Transition to the New Campaign (Ft. Leavenworth, KS: Combat Studies Institute Press, 2008), 462.

52 Anthony Cordesman, Iraqi Security Forces: A Strategy for Success (Westport, CT: Praeger Security International, 2006), 157.

53 DoD, Weekly Status Report, June 22, 2004, 29.

54 GAO Report 07-308SP, "Securing, Stabilizing, and Rebuilding Iraq: Key Issues for Congressional Oversight," January 2007, 23, 45. SIGIR found that many of these problems persisted in Defense Department reporting on the Iraqi Security Forces as late as October 2008. SIGIR Audit 08-015, "Interim Analysis of Iraqi Security Force Information Provided by the Department of Defense Report, Measuring Stability and Security in Iraq," April 25, 2008; and SIGIR Audit 09-002, "Challenges in Obtaining Reliable and Useful Data on Iraqi Security Forces Continue," October 21, 2008.

55 House Armed Services Committee Subcommittee on Oversight and Investigations, "Stand Up and Be Counted: The Continuing Challenge of Building the Iraqi Security Forces," July 2007.

56 Joseph A. Christoff, GAO Director, International Affairs and Trade, Testimony before the House Committee on Government Reform Subcommittee on National Security, Emerging Threats, and International Relations, March 14, 2005. "Geographic areas secured by ISF forces" was added as a third indicator of progress by October 2005. This came to be known as the Provincial Iraqi Control (PIC) Process. DoD, Measuring Stability and Security in Iraq, October 2005, 27.

57 GAO Report 07-308SP, "Securing, Stabilizing, and Rebuilding Iraq: Key Issues for Congressional Oversight," January 2007, 31.

58 DoD, Measuring Stability and Security in Iraq, July 2005, 13.

59 DoD, Measuring Stability and Security in Iraq, October 2005, 30. DoD provided aggregate information on unit readiness to oversight agencies, but did not release unit-level reports, despite repeated requests by GAO. Questions remained about how TRAs influenced training and equipping policy. GAO Report 07-308SP, "Securing, Stabilizing, and Rebuilding Iraq: Key Issues for Congressional Oversight," January 2007, 31. TRAs were first used to assess the Iraqi Armed Forces, and a law-enforcement analogue was later developed for the Special Police Forces. The lack of consistent MNC-I presence at local police stations prevented systematic operational assessments of the IPS during this period. DoD, Measuring Stability and Security in Iraq, July 2005, 14-19; and DoD, Measuring Stability and Security in Iraq, October 2005, 29.

60 National Security Presidential Directive 36, "United States Government Operations in Iraq," May 11, 2004; and SIGIR interview with Col. John Ferrari, former CJTF-7 strategic planner and OMB program examiner, September 10, 2008.

61 DoS, Section 2207 Report, January 2005, 11.

62 DoD, "FY 2005 Supplemental Request for Operation Iraqi Freedom (OIF), Operation Enduring Freedom (OEF), and Operation Unified Assistance," February 2005, 78.

63 SIGIR interview with Col. Chris King, former MNSTC-I Deputy J5, July 24, 2008.

64 Office of Management and Budget, "FY 2005 Emergency Supplemental Request," February 14, 2005, 25-26, http://www.whitehouse.gov/omb/budget/amendments/supplemental_2_14_05.pdf.

65 P.L. 109-13, Making Emergency Supplemental Appropriations for Defense, the Global War on Terror, and Tsunami Relief, for the Fiscal Year Ending September 20, 2005 and for Other Purposes, May 11, 2005.

66 SIGIR, *Quarterly Report to the United States Congress*, October 2008, 19. ISFF appropriations include: P.L. 109-234, Emergency Supplemental Appropriations for Fiscal Year 2006, June 15, 2006; P.L. 109-289, Department of Defense Appropriations Act for Fiscal Year 2007, September 29, 2006; P.L. 110-28, U.S. Troop Readiness, Veterans' Care, Katrina Recovery, and Iraq Accountability Appropriations Act for Fiscal Year 2007, December 21, 2007; and P.L. 110-161, Consolidated Appropriations Act for Fiscal Year 2008, December 26, 2007.

67 SIGIR, *Quarterly Report to the United States Congress*, October 2008, 19; and DoS, *Section 2207 Report*, July 2008, Status of Funds. When CERP and other Economic Support Fund appropriations are included, total U.S. funding for Iraq security totals more than $27 billion as of July 2008. SIGIR, *Quarterly Report to the United States Congress*, July 2008, 4.

68 DoS, *Section 2207 Report*, July 2004, 17; and DoS, *Section 2207 Report*, July 2005, 18.

69 SIGIR interview with Gen. David Petraeus, Commander of MNF-I, March 2, 2008.

70 Combat Studies Institute interview with Lt. Gen. David Petraeus, former commander of MNSTC-I, December 11, 2006.

71 DoS, *Section 2207 Report*, January 2005, I-4.

72 DoD, *Measuring Stability and Security in Iraq*, October 2005, 38.

73 House Armed Services Committee Subcommittee on Oversight and Investigations, "Stand Up and Be Counted: The Continuing Challenge of Building the Iraqi Security Forces," July 2007, 91.

74 SIGIR interview with Gen. David Petraeus, Commander of MNF-I, March 2, 2008; and GAO Report 07-711, "Stabilizing Iraq: DoD Cannot Ensure that U.S.-Funded Equipment Has Reached Iraqi Security Forces," July 2007, 9.

75 SIGIR Audit 06-032, "Iraqi Security Forces: Review of Plans to Implement Logistics Capabilities," October 28, 2006, 7-8.

76 SIGIR Audit 06-033, "Iraqi Security Forces: Weapons Provided by the U.S. Department of Defense Using the Iraq Relief and Reconstruction Fund," October 28, 2006, 8-10; GAO Report 07-711, "Stabilizing Iraq: DoD Cannot Ensure that U.S.-Funded Equipment Has Reached Iraqi Security Forces," July 2007, 11-12; DoD IG Audit D-2008-026, "Management of the Iraq Security Forces Fund in Southwest Asia-Phase III," November 30, 2007, 9-10; and Claude M. Kicklighter, Department of Defense Inspector General, Testimony before the Senate Appropriations Committee, March 11, 2008. The White House did not certify that a registration and monitoring system for weapons issued to the Iraqi security forces had been established until October 2008. George W. Bush, President of the United States, letter to Chairmen and Ranking Members of the House and Senate Committees on Armed Services, the House Committee on Foreign Affairs, the Senate Committee on Foreign Relations, and the Senate Committee on Banking, Housing, and Urban Affairs, October 23, 2008.

77 Lt. Gen. David Petraeus, "2006 Combat Studies Institute Military History Symposium Keynote Presentation," in Kendall Gott, ed., *Security Assistance: U.S. and International Historical Perspectives* (Ft. Leavenworth: Combat Studies Institute Press, 2006) 6.

78 DoS, *Section 2207 Report*, January 2005, I-4, 15.

79 SIGIR interview with Lt. Gen. Martin Dempsey, former commander of MNSTC-I, April 10, 2008; DoD, *Measuring Stability and Security in Iraq*, October 2005, 27; and SIGIR interview with Gen. David Petraeus, Commander of MNF-I, March 2, 2008.

80 IAF recruits signed a national service contract that required them to serve anywhere they were assigned, although there was no legal penalty for dropping out of the military. DoD, *Measuring Stability and Security in Iraq*, July 2005, 17.

81 DoS Report ISP-IQO-05-72 and DoD IG Report IE-2005-002, "Interagency Assessment of Iraq Police Training," July 15, 2005, 23.

82 Andrew Rathmell, "Fixing Iraq's Internal Security Forces: Why Is Reform of the Ministry of Interior So Hard?," CSIS, November 2007, 10.

83 Iraqi Governing Council, "Law of Administration for the State of Iraq for the Transitional Period," March 8, 2004; and CPA Order Number 91, "Regulation of Armed Forces and Militias Within Iraq," June 2, 2004.

84 DoD, *Measuring Stability and Security in Iraq*, July 2005, 23.

85 Lt. Gen. David Petraeus, "Advance Policy Questions for Lieutenant General David H. Petraeus, Nominee to be General and Commander, Multi-National Forces-Iraq," January 23, 2007, 14,.

86 Andrew Rathmell, "Fixing Iraq's Internal Security Forces: Why Is Reform of the Ministry of Interior So Hard?," CSIS, November 2007, 11.

87 House Armed Services Committee Subcommittee on Oversight and Investigations, "Stand Up and Be Counted: The Continuing Challenge of Building the Iraqi Security Forces," July 2007, 86.

88 House Armed Services Committee Subcommittee on Oversight and Investigations, "Stand Up and Be Counted: The Continuing Challenge of Building the Iraqi Security Forces," July 2007, 71; and Andrew Rathmell, "Fixing Iraq's Internal Security Forces: Why Is Reform of the Ministry of Interior So Hard?," CSIS, November 2007, 10-11.

89 Joseph A. Christoff, GAO Director, International Affairs and Trade, Testimony before the House Armed Services Committee Subcommittee on Oversight and Investigations, March 13, 2007, 11-12.

90 DoS, *Section 2207 Report*, July 2005, I-1.

91 SIGIR interview with Lt. Gen. Martin Dempsey, former commander of MNSTC-I, April 10, 2008.

92 Kenneth Katzman, Congressional Research Service Report RL31339, "Iraq: U.S. Regime Change Efforts and Post-Saddam Governance," July 5, 2005, 32.

93 The Brookings Institution, "Iraq Index: Tracking Variables of Reconstruction and Security in Post-Saddam Iraq," July 11, 2005.

94 DoS, Bureau of Democracy, Human Rights, and Labor, "Country Reports on Human Rights Practices–2005: Iraq," March 8, 2006.

95 James D. Fearon, "Iraq's Civil War," *Foreign Affairs* 86, no. 2 (March/April 2007).

Chapter 20

1 OMB, *Section 2207 Report*, January 2004, 45.

2 OMB, *Section 2207 Report*, January 2004, 102.

3 DoS, *Section 2207 Report*, July 2005, I-31-43.

4 OMB, *Section 2207 Report*, January 2004, 45-47.

5 DoS, *Section 2207 Report*, October 2004, 7, I-30.

6 DoS, *Section 2207 Report*, July 2005, I-31-43.

7 GAO Report 05-932R, "Rebuilding Iraq: U.S. Assistance for the January 2005 Elections," September 7, 2005, 2, 5.

8 CPA Order Number 92, "The Independent Electoral Commission of Iraq," May 31, 2004.

9 CPA Order Number 96, "The Electoral Law," June 15, 2004.

10 United Nations, "Iraq Electoral Fact Sheet, May 17, 2007. For a history of UN involvement, see: United Nations Security Council Report S-2005-585, "Report of the Secretary-General Pursuant to Paragraph 30 of Resolution 1546 (2004)," September 7, 2005.

11 GAO Report 05-932R, "Rebuilding Iraq: U.S. Assistance for the January 2005 Elections," September 7, 2005, 5-6.

12 DoS, Bureau of Public Affairs, "Iraqi Elections: January 30, 2005," January 25, 2005.

13 Council on Foreign Relations, "Iraq Timeline 2004," December 31, 2004.

14 Council on Foreign Relations, "Iraq Timeline 2004," December 31, 2004.

15 Jonathan Morrow, USIP Special Report 155, "Iraq's Constitutional Process II: An Opportunity Lost," November 2005.

16 Larry Diamond, "Not Perfect, but 'Reasonably Credible,'" Op-Ed, *Wall Street Journal*, October 25, 2004.

17 Kenneth Katzman, Congressional Research Service Report RS21968, "Iraq: Government Formation and Performance," updated May 2, 2007, 2; and Council on Foreign Relations, "Iraq Timeline 2005," October 13, 2005.

18 George W. Bush, "President Congratulates Iraqis on Election," White House Press Release, January 30, 2005.

19 GAO Report 05-932R, "Rebuilding Iraq: U.S. Assistance for the January 2005 Elections," September 7, 2005, 3.

20 Jonathan Morrow, USIP Special Report 155, "Iraq's Constitutional Process II: An Opportunity Lost," November 2005.

21 Council on Foreign Relations, "Iraq Timeline 2005," October 13, 2005.

22 Council on Foreign Relations, "Iraq Timeline 2005," October 13, 2005.

23 Ali A. Allawi, *The Occupation of Iraq: Winning the War, Losing the Peace* (New Haven, CT: Yale University Press, 2007), 404.

24 Jonathan Morrow, USIP Special Report 155, "Iraq's Constitutional Process II: An Opportunity Lost," November 2005, 9.

25 Jonathan Morrow, USIP Special Report 155, "Iraq's Constitutional Process II: An Opportunity Lost," USIP Special Report 155, November 2005; and Lionel Beehner and Sharon Otterman, "Iraq: Drafting the Constitution," Council on Foreign Relations, August 23, 2005.

26 Jonathan Morrow, USIP Special Report 155, "Iraq's Constitutional Process II, An Opportunity Lost," USIP Special Report, November 2005, 11.

27 DoS-OIG Report No. ISP-IQO-06-01, "Inspection of Rule-of-Law Programs, Embassy Baghdad," October 2005, 7.

28 DoS-OIG Report No. ISP-IQO-06-01, "Inspection of Rule-of-Law Programs, Embassy Baghdad," October 2005, 15.

29 DoS-OIG Report No. ISP-IQO-06-01, "Inspection of Rule-of-Law Programs, Embassy Baghdad," October 2005, 8.

30 SIGIR, "Iraq Reconstruction: Lessons in Contracting and Procurement," July 2006; and SIGIR Audit 08-019, "Outcome, Cost, and Oversight of the Security and Justice Contract with Parsons Delaware, Inc.," July 28, 2008, 3.

31 CPA Ministry of Justice, "Prisons and Detention Centers in Iraq: An Assessment and Recommendations for Prisons in a Free Society," June 15, 2003, 5.

32 ORHA/CPA Historian interview with Maj. Gen. Donald F. Campbell, Senior Advisor to the Ministry of Justice, July 14, 2003.

33 CPA Ministry of Justice, "Prisons and Detention Centers in Iraq: An Assessment and Recommendations for Prisons in a Free Society," June 15, 2003, 6.

34 ORHA/CPA Historian interview with Maj. Gen. Donald F. Campbell, Senior Advisor to the Ministry of Justice, August 13, 2003.

35 SIGIR Audit 08-019, "Outcome, Cost, and Oversight of the Security and Justice Contract with Parsons Delaware, Inc.", July 28, 2008, 3.

36 SIGIR Audit 08-019, "Outcome, Cost, and Oversight of the Security and Justice Contract with Parsons Delaware, Inc.", July 28, 2008, 8-24.

37 SIGIR Audit 08-019, "Outcome, Cost, and Oversight of the Security and Justice Contract with Parsons Delaware, Inc." July 28, 2008, 17.

38 SIGIR PA-08-138, "Khan Bani Sa'ad Correctional Facility, Khan Bani Sa'ad, Iraq," July 25, 2008, 1.

39 SIGIR Audit 08-019, "Outcome, Cost, and Oversight of the Security and Justice Contract with Parsons Delaware, Inc.," July 28, 2008.

40 SIGIR PA-08-138, "Khan Bani Sa'ad Correctional Facility, Khan Bani Sa'ad, Iraq," July 25, 2008, ii, 3-4, 5-8.

41 SIGIR PA-08-138, "Khan Bani Sa'ad Correctional Facility, Khan Bani Sa'ad, Iraq," July 25, 2008, 22.

42 Senator Bryon L. Dorgan, Chairman, Statement before the Senate Democratic Policy Committee, September 22, 2008, 2.

43 ORHA/CPA Historian interview with Maj. Gen. Donald F. Campbell, Senior Advisor to the Ministry of Justice, July 14, 2003; and Robert Perito, USIP Report 104, "Establishing the Rule of Law in Iraq," April 2003.

44 CPA Order Number 2, "Dissolution of Entities," May 23, 2003.

45 GAO Report 04-902R, "Rebuilding Iraq: Resources, Security, Governance, Essential Services, and Oversight Issues," June 28, 2004, 80.

46 Sermid Al-Sarraf, Board of Directors, Iraqi Jurists' Association, Testimony before the Senate Committees on Foreign Relations and Judiciary, June 25, 2003.

47 CPA Order Number 13, "The Central Criminal Court of Iraq," March 22, 2004.

48 CPA Order Number 15, "Establishment of the Judicial Review Committee," June 23, 2003.

49 United Nations, "The Present Situation of Human Rights in Iraq," June 9, 2004, 34.

50 Judge Daniel L. Rubini, Senior Advisor to the Ministry of Justice, memorandum to Ambassador Richard Jones, Deputy Administrator, November 29, 2003.

51 GAO Report 04-902R, "Rebuilding Iraq: Resources, Security, Governance, Essential Services, and Oversight Issues," June 28, 2004, 82.

52 Agence France Presse (AFP), "Governor Calls Strike in Najaf after Judge Killed," November 6, 2003.

53 Luke Harding, "Judge Shot Dead in Northern Iraq," The Guardian, December 24, 2003.

54 GAO Report 04-902R, "Rebuilding Iraq: Resources, Security, Governance, Essential Services, and Oversight Issues," June 28, 2004, 82-83.

55 Cheryl W. Gray and Daniel Kaufmann, "Corruption and Development," Finance and Development 35 no. 1 (March 1998), 9.

56 Stuart Bowen, Special Inspector General for Iraq Reconstruction, Testimony before the House Committee on Foreign Affairs' Subcommittees on International Relations, Human Rights, and Oversight, and on the Middle East and South Asia, March 27, 2007.

57 Danny L. Athanasaw and Christopher M. Griffith, "Iraq Inspectors General: A Work in Progress," unpublished, 2008, 5. (The authors served with the U.S. Department of State in Embassy Baghdad's anticorruption office, where their portfolio including advising Iraq's Inspectors General.)

58 SIGIR Audit 07-007, "Status of U.S. Government Anticorruption Efforts in Iraq", July 24, 2007, 1.

59 David M. Walker, GAO Comptroller General, Testimony before the House Committee on Government Reform, Subcommittee on National Security, Emerging Threats, and International Relations, July 11, 2006.

60 "The oil is being smuggled from Sunni militias and in Basra through the Shi'ite militia and...they use this to purchase weapons....These monies will target the killing of Iraqis and Americans." Judge Radhi Hamza al-Radhi, former Commissioner, Iraqi Commission on Public Integrity, Testimony before the Senate Committee on Appropriations, March 11, 2008.

61 SIGIR, Quarterly Report to the United States Congress, July 2006, 5.

62 USIP interview with Charles Grinnell, Senior Advisor to the Commission on Public Integrity, October 22, 2004; and Stuart Bowen, Special Inspector General for Iraq Reconstruction, Statement before the House Committee on Foreign Affairs Subcommittees on International Relations, Human Rights, and Oversight and The Middle East and South Asia, March 27, 2007.

63 CPA Order 55, "Delegation of Authority Regarding the Iraq Commission on Public Integrity," January 28, 2004; and CPA Order 57, "Iraqi Inspectors General," February 5, 2004.

64 The money was for "personnel costs and to ramp up its information collection, administration, and community outreach responsibilities." OMB, *Section 2207 Report*, April 2004, 29-30.

65 SIGIR interview with Charles B. Johnson, CPA Trainer and proponent of building the IG system, October 9, 2007; and USIP interview with Charles Grinnell, Senior Advisor to the Commission on Public Integrity, October 22, 2004.

66 Danny L. Athanasaw and Christopher M. Griffith, "Iraq Inspectors General: A Work in Progress," unpublished, 2008.

67 CPA Order 55, "Delegation of Authority Regarding the Iraq Commission on Public Integrity," January 28, 2004.

68 Radhi, a Shi'a, had refused to join the Ba'ath Party. USIP interview with Charles Grinnell, Senior Advisor to the Commission on Public Integrity, October 22, 2004.

69 CPA Order 55, "Delegation of Authority Regarding the Iraq Commission on Public Integrity," January 28, 2004; DoS and the Broadcasting Board of Governors-OIG Report ISP-IQO-06-50, "Survey of Anticorruption Programs: Embassy Baghdad, Iraq," August 2006, 21; and SIGIR Audit 06-021, "Joint Survey of the U.S. Embassy—Iraq's Anticorruption Program," July 28, 2006, 17.

70 Charles B. Johnson and Major Shawn Turner, "Report on Iraqi Anticorruption Systems," October 25, 2007, 27.

71 Judge Radhi Hamza al-Radhi, Commissioner, Iraqi Commission on Public Integrity, Testimony before the House Committee on Oversight and Government Reform, October 4, 2007.

72 DoS, Bureau of Democracy, Human Rights, and Labor, "Country Reports on Human Rights Practices – 2005: Iraq," March 8, 2006.

73 Judge Radhi Hamza al-Radhi, Commissioner, Iraqi Commission on Public Integrity, Testimony before the House Committee on Oversight and Government Reform, October 4, 2007.

74 CPA Memorandum Number 3 (Revised), "Criminal Procedures," June 27, 2004; Stuart Bowen, Special Inspector General for Iraq Reconstruction, Testimony before the House Committee on the Judiciary Subcommittee on Crime, Terrorism, and Homeland Security, June 19, 2007; and SIGIR, *Quarterly Report to the United States Congress*, April 2007, 101.

75 SIGIR, *Quarterly Report to the United States Congress*, April 2007, 101.

76 Judge Radhi Hamza al-Radhi, Commissioner, Iraqi Commission on Public Integrity, Testimony before Senate Committee on Appropriations, March 12, 2007. He added, "There was pressure put on the judiciary not to prosecute cases on behalf of individuals. Many of Iraq's judges live in fear of torture and assassination of themselves and their family members if they adjudicate cases of senior government officials." Currency converted at XE Universal Currency Converter, http://www.xe.com/ucc/convert.cgi, accessed July 2008.

77 Judge Radhi Hamza al-Radhi, Commissioner, Iraqi Commission on Public Integrity, Testimony before the House Committee on Oversight and Government Reform, October 4, 2007.

78 CPA Order 57, "Iraqi Inspectors General," February 5, 2004.

79 Appointment of an Inspector General is subject to confirmation by Iraq's national legislature, the Council of Representatives. CPA Order 57, "Iraqi Inspectors General," February 5, 2004.

80 For a complete list of IG duties see: CPA Order 57, "Iraqi Inspectors General," Section 5, February 5, 2004.

81 CPA Order 57, Section 6(1) details the IGs' powers. CPA Order 57, "Iraqi Inspectors General," February 5, 2004. Subpoena power is better understood as "request" power. Oftentimes, the individual suffers no legal consequences for failing to provide the documents or show up for interviews.

82 Danny L. Athanasaw and Christopher M. Griffith, "Iraq Inspectors General: A Work in Progress," unpublished, 2008.

83 Danny L. Athanasaw and Christopher M. Griffith, "Iraq Inspectors General: A Work in Progress," unpublished, 2008, 1.

84 CPA Order Number 57, "Iraqi Inspectors General," February 10, 2004.

85 SIGIR interview with Charles B. Johnson, CPA Trainer and proponent of building the IG system, October 9, 2007. Johnson later said that the decision to overturn the vote was done literally at the last minute, in an email at 2300 hours to the CPA Treasury Advisor.

86 DoD OIG, "DoD OIG Provides Assistance to Iraqi IGs," http://www.dodig.osd.mil/gwot_iraq/support_iraq_ig.htm.

87 CPA Order Number 77, "Board of Supreme Audit," April 25, 2004.

88 Stuart Bowen, Special Inspector General for Iraq Reconstruction, Testimony before the House Committee on Oversight and Government Reform, October 4, 2007.

89 Danny L. Athanasaw and Christopher M. Griffith, "Iraq Inspectors General: A Work in Progress," unpublished, 2008, 3.

90 USIP interview with Charles Grinnell, Senior Advisor to the Commission on Public Integrity, October 22, 2004.

91 UN, "Iraq: Situation Report," June 28-July 4, 2004.

92 SIGIR, *Quarterly Report to the United States Congress*, October 2006, 114-115.

93 DoS and the Broadcasting Board of Governors-OIG Report ISP-IQO-06-50, "Survey of Anticorruption Programs: Embassy Baghdad, Iraq," August 2006, 9-10.

94 DoS and the Broadcasting Board of Governors-OIG Report ISP-IQO-06-50, "Survey of Anticorruption Programs: Embassy Baghdad, Iraq," August 2006, 17.

95 SIGIR Audit 08-023, "Anticorruption Efforts in Iraq: U.S. and Iraq Take Actions but Much Remains to Be Done," July 29, 2008, 1-2; SIGIR Audit 08-008, "U.S. Anticorruption Efforts in Iraq: Sustained Management Commitment is a Key to Success," January 24, 2008, 2-3; SIGIR Audit 07-007, "Status of U.S. Government Anticorruption Efforts in Iraq," July 24, 2007; and SIGIR Audit 06-021, "Joint Survey of the U.S. Embassy-Iraq's Anticorruption Program, July 28, 2006.

Chapter 21

1 SIGIR Interview with Robert Stein, Federal Penitentiary, Petersburg, VA, June 13, 2007; and SIGIR, *Quarterly Report to the United States Congress*, July 31, 2006, Appendix J-1.

2 SIGIR interviews with Brian Flynn, Assistant Inspector General for Inspections; Kevin O'Connor, SIGIR Auditor; and Special Agent Erick Vail, SIGIR Investigator, May 2007. Brian Flynn was the Assistant Inspector General for Audit from 2004-2005.

3 SIGIR interview with Robert Stein, former DoD contractor, Federal Penitentiary, Petersburg, VA, June 13, 2007.

4 Department of Justice, "U.S. Contractor Sentenced in Case Involving Bribery, Fraud, and Money Laundering Scheme in al-Hillah, Iraq," February 16, 2007.

5 James Glantz, "Wide Plot Seen in Guilty Plea in Iraq Project," *New York Times*, February 2, 2006.

6 SIGIR interviews with Brian Flynn, Assistant Inspector General for Inspections; Kevin O'Connor, SIGIR Auditor; and Special Agent Erick Vail, SIGIR Investigator, May 2007.

7 SIGIR interviews with Brian Flynn, Assistant Inspector General for Inspections; Kevin O'Connor, SIGIR Auditor; and Special Agent Erick Vail, SIGIR Investigator, May 2007.

8 SIGIR interviews with Brian Flynn, Assistant Inspector General for Inspections; Kevin O'Connor, SIGIR Auditor; and Special Agent Erick Vail, SIGIR Investigator, May 2007.

9 SIGIR Audit 05-006, "Control of Cash Provided to South-Central Iraq," April 30, 2005, 6.

10 SIGIR interviews with Brian Flynn, Assistant Inspector General for Inspections; Kevin O'Connor, SIGIR Auditor; and Special Agent Erick Vail, SIGIR Investigator, May 2007.

11 SIGIR interview with Robert Stein, former DoD contractor, Federal Penitentiary, Petersburg, VA, June 13, 2007.

12 SIGIR Audit 05-016, "Management of the Contracts and Grants Used to Construct and Operate the Babylon Police Academy," October 26, 2005, 8-10.

13 SIGIR Audit 05-016, "Management of the Contracts and Grants Used to Construct and Operate the Babylon Police Academy," October 26, 2005.

14 SIGIR Audit 05-020, "Management of Contracts, Grants, and Micro-Purchases Used to Rehabilitate the Kerbala Library," October 26, 2005, 2-3.

15 SIGIR Audit 05-020, "Management of Contracts, Grants, and Micro-Purchases Used to Rehabilitate the Kerbala Library," October 26, 2005, 10-12, 18, 34, Appendix I.

16 SIGIR Audit 05-006, "Control of Cash Provided to South-Central Iraq," April 30, 2005, 4.

17 Department of Justice Press Release, "U.S. Contractor Sentence in Case Involving Bribery, Fraud, and Money Laundering Scheme in Al-Hillah, Iraq," February 16, 2007.

18 Department of Justice Press Release, "Army Lieutenant Colonel Pleds Guilty to Participating in Wire Fraud Scheme Arising out of Al-Hillah, Iraq," July 28, 2008; SIGIR Audit 05-006, "Control of Cash Provided to South-Central Iraq," April 30, 2005, 11; Department of Justice Press Release, "U.S. Contractor Sentence in Case Involving Bribery, Fraud, and Money Laundering Scheme in Al-Hillah, Iraq," February 16, 2007; and SIGIR, Quarterly Report to the United States Congress, July 2006, Appendix J.

19 Department of Justice Press Release, "U.S. Army Colonel and Lt. Colonel Convicted of Conspiracy for Role in Fraud Scheme in Al-hillah, Iraq," November 7, 2008.

20 Department of Justice Press Release, "U.S. Army Major Pleads Guilty to Bribery Scheme Related to Department of Defense Contracts in Kuwait," August 13, 2008.

21 Department of Justice Press Release, "U.S. Army Major Pleads Guilty to Bribery Scheme Related to Department of Defense Contracts in Kuwait," August 13, 2008.

Essential Services Overview - Transition from Negroponte to Khalilzad
22 International Monetary Fund, "Iraq: Statistical Appendix," August 2007; ITAO, Monthly Import, Production and Export, response to SIGIR data call for the Quarterly Report to the United States Congress, April 2008. DoD, Measuring Stability and Security in Iraq, July 2005, 12; DoS, Iraq Weekly Status Report, June 8, 2005; Iraq Coalition Casualty Count, updated September 2008; SIGIR, Quarterly Report to the United States Congress, October 2005, 12; Iraq Body Count, "Documented civilian deaths from violence," updated August 24, 2008; P.L. 108-287, Department of Defense Appropriations Act for Fiscal Year 2005, August 5, 2003; P.L. 109-13, Making Emergency Supplemental Appropriations for Defense, the Global War on Terror, and Tsunami Relief, for the Fiscal Year Ending September 20, 2005 and for Other Purposes, May 11, 2005; Presidency of the Iraqi Interim National Assembly: The State General Budget for 2005; and SIGIR, Quarterly Report to the United States Congress, July 2005, F-3.

23 DoS, Section 2207 Report, July 2005, 10-11; October 2005, 12; and International Monetary Fund, "Iraq: Statistical Appendix," August 2007.

24 GAO Report 05-876, "Rebuilding Iraq: Status of Funding and Reconstruction Efforts," July 2005, 14-17.

Chapter 22

1 In 2005, the U.S. government did not keep official statistics on civilian deaths; these civilian numbers are estimates by the nongovernmental organization Iraq Body Count. See Iraq Body Count, "A Dossier of Civilian Casualties 2003-2005," July 2005. Coalition and contractor death figures come from Hannah Fischer, Congressional Research Service Report RL32492, "American War and Military Operations Casualties: Lists and Statistics," July 13, 2005, 16; and SIGIR, *Quarterly Report to the United States Congress*, July 2005, 4.

2 SIGIR interview with Ambassador Zalmay Khalilzad, former U.S. Ambassador to Iraq, March 19, 2008.

3 Zalmay Khalilzad, "Afghanistan's Milestone," Op-Ed, *Washington Post*, January 6, 2004.

4 Eric Schmitt, "General Seeking Faster Training of Iraq Soldiers," *New York Times*, January 23, 2005.

5 P.L. 109-13, Making Emergency Supplemental Appropriations for Defense, the Global War on Terror, and Tsunami Relief, for the Fiscal Year Ending September 20, 2005 and for Other Purposes, May 11, 2005. By July 2008, ISFF would grow to $17.9 billion. SIGIR, *Quarterly Report to the United States Congress*, July 2008, 4.

6 SIGIR interview with Philip Zelikow, former Counselor, U.S. State Department, June 26, 2008. See also: Robin Wright and Glen Kessler, "Rice Sends Team to Assess Iraq Transition," *Washington Post*, February 15, 2005; and Bob Woodward, *State of Denial: Bush at War, Part III* (New York: Simon & Schuster, 2006), 387-89.

7 SIGIR conversations with Philip Zelikow, former Counselor, U.S. State Department, August and September 2008; and SIGIR interview with Celeste Ward, Deputy Assistant Secretary of Defense for Stability Operations Capabilities, September 9, 2008.

8 SIGIR interview with Philip Zelikow, former Counselor, U.S. State Department, June 26, 2008; and Bob Woodward, *State of Denial: Bush at War, Part III* (New York: Simon & Schuster, 2006), 387-89, 396-97, 412-15.

9 Khalilzad's transition staff cite four milestone documents that articulate his strategy: a 35-slide briefing delivered to the NSC; the written testimony Khalilzad submitted for his Senate confirmation hearing; an op-ed he wrote in *The Wall Street Journal*; and, after the draft Iraqi constitution was written, a speech delivered at CSIS. SIGIR interview with Marin Strmecki, Senior Advisor to Ambassador Khalilzad, January 21, 2008. See Zalmay Khalilzad, U.S. Ambassador to Iraq, Statement before the Senate Committee on Foreign Relations, June 7, 2005; Zalmay Khalilzad, "The Battle of Baghdad: Rampant Insecurity—And a Detailed Plan to Combat It," Op-Ed, *Wall Street Journal*, August 23, 2006; and Zalmay Khalilzad, "Iraq: A Status Report," CSIS Statesmen's Forum, July 11, 2006.

10 Zalmay Khalilzad, U.S. Ambassador to Iraq, Statement before the Senate Committee on Foreign Relations, June 7, 2005.

11 Krepinevich briefed Khalilzad in Washington, D.C. Krepinevich's subsequent article in *Foreign Affairs* was derived from these briefings. Andrew F. Krepinevich, Jr., "How to Win Iraq," *Foreign Affairs* (September/October 2005). Some military officials also refer to this as the "ink-spot" strategy.

12 Public Broadcasting Service, "Interview with Philip Zelikow," *FRONTLINE*, February 6, 2007.

13 SIGIR interview with Ambassador Zalmay Khalilzad, former U.S. Ambassador to Iraq, March 19, 2008.

14 SIGIR interview with David Satterfield, former Deputy Chief of Mission, April 14, 2008.

15 SIGIR interview with Ambassador Zalmay Khalilzad, former U.S. Ambassador to Iraq, March 19, 2008.

16 U.S. Appropriated Funds ($29.1 billion): P.L. 108-11 ($3.34 billion), P.L. 108-106 ($19.48 billion), P.L. 108-287 ($0.14 billion), P.L. 109-13 ($6.136). SIGIR, *Quarterly Report to the United States Congress*, October 2008, 17-18.

17 SIGIR, *Quarterly Report to the United States Congress*, July 2005, Appendix F; and SIGIR, *Quarterly Report to the United States Congress*, October 2008, 17-18.

18 SIGIR, *Quarterly Report to the United States Congress*, July 2005, Introduction, 29-30.

19 SIGIR, *Quarterly Report to the United States Congress*, July 2005, 23.

20 The Office of Management and Budget (OMB) reallocated the $18.44 billion of IRRF 2 funds as follows: DoD, $12.98 billion (70.4%); USAID, $3.10 billion (16.8%) DoS, $1.20 billion (6.5%); Treasury $390 million (2.12%); USIP, $10 million (.05%). SIGIR, *Quarterly Report to the United States Congress,* July 2005, 24-25.

21 For a summary of reconstruction metrics, see SIGIR, *Quarterly Report to the United States Congress,* July 2005, 29-35.

22 Oil production was 16 percent below the Ministry of Oil target of 2.5 million barrels per day. SIGIR, *Quarterly Report to the United States Congress,* July 2005, 30.

23 SIGIR, *Quarterly Reports to the United States Congress,* July 2005, 33, and October 2005, 19-20.

24 For background on progress in the water sector and details about the reprogramming, see GAO Report 05-872, "Rebuilding Iraq: U.S. Water and Sanitation Efforts Need Improved Measures for Assessing Impact and Sustained Resources for Maintaining Facilities," September 2005.

25 SIGIR, *Quarterly Report to the United States Congress,* October 2005, 3-5.

26 ABC News Poll, "Iraq—Where Things Stand," December 12, 2005.

27 SIGIR, *Quarterly Report to the United States Congress,* July 2005, 3.

28 SIGIR, *Quarterly Report to the United States Congress,* April 2005, 3; SIGIR, *Quarterly Report to the United States Congress,* July 2005, 107; SIGIR Audit 05-021, "Management of Iraq Relief and Reconstruction Fund Programs: Cost-to-Complete Estimate Reporting," October 24, 2005, i; and SIGIR Audit 07-003, "Cost-to-Complete Reporting for Iraq Reconstruction Projects," July 26, 2007, 3.

29 For more detail on contracting and program management, see SIGIR, "Iraq Reconstruction: Lessons in Contracting and Procurement," July 2006; and SIGIR, "Iraq Reconstruction: Lessons in Program and Project Management," March 2007.

30 Ambassador Zalmay Khalilzad, vetting comments to SIGIR, October 27, 2008.

31 SIGIR interview with Lieutenant General Peter Chiarelli, former Commander of MNC-I, February 19, 2008.

32 Ambassador Zalmay Khalilzad, comments to SIGIR, October 27, 2008.

33 SIGIR Audit 09-005, "Agencies Need Improved Financial Data Reporting for Private Security Contractors," October 30, 2009, 3; SIGIR Audit 06-044, "Fact Sheet on Major U.S. Contractors' Security Costs Related to Iraq Relief and Reconstruction Fund Contracting Activities," January 30, 2007, 2; and DoS, *Section 2207 Report,* January 2006, 8. The January 2006 *Section 2207 Report* also listed water, health care, and roads/bridges/construction projects that were canceled because funds were shifted to security. In addition to reducing funds available for construction projects, rising security costs made it more challenging to estimate the costs to complete projects. PCO management advised SIGIR that, as of March 31, 2005, the estimated cost for project security had risen from the original program baseline of $1.2 billion to more than $2 billion. SIGIR believes that actual costs (e.g., delays caused by security problems, higher force levels than expected) may be much higher. SIGIR Audit 05-011, "Cost-to-Complete Estimates and Financial Reporting for the Management of the Iraq Relief and Reconstruction Fund," July 26, 2005, 4; and GAO Testimony 06-179T, "Rebuilding Iraq: Enhancing Security, Measuring Program Results, and Maintaining Infrastructure Are Necessary to Make Significant and Sustainable Progress," October 18, 2005.

34 SIGIR Audit 09-005, "Agencies Need Improved Financial Data Reporting for Private Security Contractors," October 30, 2009, 6.

35 SIGIR interview with Major General William H. McCoy, former Commander, USACE-GRD, June 5, 2008; and SIGIR interview with Lieutenant Colonel Otto Busher, Baghdad PRT member, June 25, 2006.

36 SIGIR interview with Ruth-Ann Ijames, Senior Advisor to JCC-I, June 25, 2006.

37 SIGIR interviews conducted in Amman, Jordan, with anonymous Iraqi business owners in June 2006; and multiple interviews in the spring of 2006 with Browning Rockwell, U.S.-Iraqi business consultant. See also: SIGIR interview with Ruth-Ann Ijames, Senior Advisor to JCC-I, June 25, 2006. The PCO developed a web-based management tool, the Subcontracting Excellence Program Database, to monitor the progress of subcontracted work. Ylli Bajraktari, "Economic Empowerment of Women in Iraq: The New Way Forward," USIP Briefing, May 2006; SIGIR, "Iraq Reconstruction: Lessons in Program and Project Management," March 2007, 96; and SIGIR Audit 07-009, "Review of Bechtel's Spending under Its Phase 2 Iraq Reconstruction Contract," July 24, 2007, 23-26.

38 SIGIR interviews with several anonymous Iraqi firms headquartered in Amman, Jordan in June and July 2006.

39 SIGIR interview with Daniel Speckhard, former IRMO Director and former Deputy Chief of Mission, April 29, 2008.

40 SIGIR interview with Philip Zelikow, former Counselor, U.S. State Department, June 26, 2008; and Bob Woodward, *State of Denial: Bush at War, Part III*, (New York: Simon & Schuster, 2006), 387-89.

41 The term "reconstruction gap" denotes the differences between what was expected to be built and what was actually built. It was first discussed in SIGIR, *Quarterly Report to the United States Congress*, October 2005, 3.

42 SIGIR, *Quarterly Report to the United States Congress*, October 2005, 3.

43 SIGIR interview with Ambassador Zalmay Khalilzad, former U.S. Ambassador to Iraq, March 19, 2008.

44 SIGIR interview with Ambassador Zalmay Khalilzad, former U.S. Ambassador to Iraq, March 19, 2008.

45 In addition to the Negroponte-Casey campaign plan, Ambassador Negroponte and General Casey published a second joint mission statement on February 7, 2005, titled "A Plan for the Year Ahead: Transition to Self-Reliance." This, along with a Secretary of State cable "U.S. Government Position on Political/Security Principles and Priorities for Iraq Reconstruction," Cable 061748Z APR 05, SECSTATE 6360, established the strategic direction of U.S. reconstruction policy in early 2005. SIGIR interview with Marin Strmecki, Senior Advisor to Ambassador Khalilzad, January 21, 2008.

46 SIGIR conversations with Dana Eyre, former USAID consultant, Summer 2006; and Terrence K. Kelly, former JSPA director, August 13, 2007.

47 SIGIR conversations with Dana Eyre, former USAID consultant, Summer 2006; and Terrence K. Kelly, former JSPA director, August 13, 2007.

48 SIGIR interview with Marin Strmecki, Senior Advisor to Ambassador Khalilzad, January 21, 2008.

49 SIGIR interview with Marin Strmecki, Senior Advisor to Ambassador Khalilzad, January 21, 2008.

50 This observation was forcefully made by the strategic review performed by Ambassador Negroponte and General Casey in July 2004, and its follow-on analysis by General Luck and members of the Joint Forces Command in August 2004. Leonard R. Hawley, "An Analysis of the DCS for Political and Economic Effects," August 2004; and Henry W. Stratman, "Orchestrating Instruments of Power for Nationbuilding," *Joint Forces Quarterly* 41 (2nd quarter 2006), 33-34.

51 When the strategic communications portfolio was added to PME in 2005, the incumbent became the Deputy Chief of Staff for Strategic Effects. Henry W. Stratman, "Orchestrating Instruments of Power for Nationbuilding," *Joint Forces Quarterly* 41 (2nd quarter 2006), 35.

52 Ambassador Zalmay Khalilzad, comments to SIGIR, October 27, 2007.

53 Although the Joint Strategic Planning and Assessment office was approved in late 2005, it was not fully operational until mid-2006. For details of its formation, see SIGIR interview with Terrence K. Kelly, former JSPA director, August 13, 2007.

54 SIGIR interview with Daniel Speckhard, former IRMO Director and former Deputy Chief of Mission, April 29, 2008.

55 SIGIR, *Quarterly Report to the United States Congress*, January 2008, 35-38.

56 SIGIR Interview with John Bowersox, former Senior Advisor for Health, November 1, 2006.

57 For a description of democracy building programs, see USAID Fact Sheet, "Democracy and Governance: Advancing Freedom Around the World," July 24, 2008.

58 Major General Peter W. Chiarelli and Major Patrick R. Michaelis, "Winning the Peace: The Requirement for Full-Spectrum Operations," *Military Review* (July-August 2005), 4-17.

59 USAID, "Assistance for Iraq: USAID/Military Cooperation," updated June 21, 2006; and James "Spike" Stevenson, "Military-Civilian Cooperation: A Field Perspective," *Foreign Service Journal* (March 2006), 55-62.

60 James Stephenson, *Losing the Golden Hour: An Insider's View of Iraq's Reconstruction* (Washington, DC: Potomac Books, Inc., 2007), 102.

61 SIGIR interview with Marin Strmecki, Senior Advisor to Ambassador Khalilzad, January 21, 2008.

62 SIGIR interview with Andrew Rathmell, former Director of CPA Office of Planning and Analysis and consultant to Joint Strategic Planning and Assessments, June 26, 2006.

63 SIGIR interview with Marin Strmecki, Senior Advisor to Ambassador Khalilzad, January 21, 2008.

64 SIGIR interview with Colonel Kenneth Cox, Engineer Brigade Commander, June 24, 2006.

65 SIGIR interview with Andrew Rathmell, former Director of CPA Office of Planning and Analysis and consultant to Joint Strategic Planning and Assessments, June 26, 2006.

66 SIGIR interview with Calvin Crane, Regional PAO Coordinator, August 12, 2007; and SIGIR, *Quarterly Report to the United States Congress*, October 2005, 7. For background and commentary on PRDCs, see Center for Army Lessons Learned, "Provincial Reconstruction Teams in Iraq Handbook," version 1.5, October 2006, 38; MNF-I, Operation Iraqi Freedom Press Conference, "Provincial Reconstruction," October 2, 2006; MNF-I, Operation Iraqi Freedom Press Briefing, October 9, 2006; and Robert Perito, USIP Report 185, "Provincial Reconstruction Teams in Iraq," March 2007, 8.

67 Plans were also drawn up to create Provincial Support Teams composed of the U.S. Embassy, PCO, and USAID staff, but only three deployed and a later assessment of their performance found them an insufficient vehicle. Inadequacies of the Provincial Support Teams are discussed in Unclassified Baghdad 4045, "Action Plan to Build Capacity and Sustainability within Iraq's Provincial Governments," from embassy Baghdad to SECSTATE, 010330Z October 2005. SIGIR interview with Celeste Ward, political aide to Lieutenant General Peter Chiarelli, and Colonel Kenneth Cox, Engineer Brigade Commander, June 24, 2006.

68 DoS, *Section 2207 Report*, July 2005, 2-3.

69 USACE-GRD, Susan M. Fournier, "Provinces Succeed in Selecting Projects," February 24, 2006.

70 Michael J. McNerney, "Stabilization and Reconstruction in Afghanistan: Are PRTs a Model or a Muddle?" *Parameters* (Winter 2005-2006), 37. For further background on the PRT history and operating concept, see Robert Perito, "Hearts and Minds Model?" *Armed Forces Journal* (December 2005); and Robert Perito, USIP Special Report 152, "U.S. Experience with Provincial Reconstruction Teams in Afghanistan: Lessons Identified," October 2005.

71 SIGIR conversations with Philip Zelikow, former Counselor, U.S. State Department, August and September 2008; and SIGIR interview with Celeste Ward, Deputy Assistant Secretary of Defense for Stability Operations Capabilities, September 9, 2008. With the changing military footprint and eventual transition to Iraqi control, Khalilzad did not want to embed teams in brigades that would soon be withdrawn or repositioned. Ambassador Zalmay Khalilzad, vetting comments to SIGIR, October 27, 2008.

72 Robert Perito, USIP Special Report 185, "Provincial Reconstruction Teams in Iraq," March 2007, 4; and Condoleezza Rice, Secretary of State, Testimony before the Senate Committee on Foreign Relations, October 19, 2005.

73 Unclassified Baghdad 4045, "Action Plan to Build Capacity and Sustainability within Iraq's Provincial Governments," From embassy Baghdad to SECSTATE, 010330Z October 2005.

74 The CORDS (Civil Operations and Revolutionary Development Support) pacification program in rural Vietnam was an interesting precursor to Provisional Reconstruction Teams used in Afghanistan and Iraq. R. W. Komer, RAND Report R-967-ARPA, "Bureaucracy Does Its Thing: Institutional Constraints on U.S.-GVN Performance in Vietnam," August 1972; Lewis Sorley, *A Better War: The Unexamined Victories and Final Tragedy of America's Last Years in Vietnam* (New York: Harcourt Brace & Company, 1999); Neil Sheehan, *A Bright Shining Lie: John Paul Vann and America in Vietnam* (New York: Vintage, 1989); and David Passage, "Speaking Out: Caution: Iraq is Not Vietnam," *Foreign Service Journal* (November 2007).

75 SIGIR interview with Calvin Crane, Regional PAO Coordinator, August 12, 2007; and Condoleezza Rice, "Remarks at the Inauguration of the Provincial Reconstruction Team," November 11, 2005.

76 SIGIR Audit 06-034, "Status of the Provincial Reconstruction Team Program in Iraq," October 29, 2006, 8-11; and SIGIR conversations with Philip Zelikow, former Counselor, U.S. State Department, August and September 2008.

77 Ginger Cruz, Deputy Inspector General for Iraq Reconstruction, Testimony before the House Armed Services Committee, September 5, 2007; and SIGIR Audit 06-034, "Status of the Provincial Reconstruction Team Program in Iraq," October 29, 2006, 9.

78 Joe Saloom, IRMO Director, memorandum to David M. Satterfield, Chargé d'Affaires ad interim, "P.R.T. Support Issues," July 6, 2006.

79 Some PRTs did retain PSD support, but plans for all PRTs to be supported were dropped. DoS Cable, "Estimated Costs for DS PRT Security Recommendations," Ref. Baghdad 2236; Randall Bennett, Regional Security Officer, "PRT PSD Teams discussion between RSO Bennett and Lieutenant General Chiarelli on 07/25/2006," August 10, 2006; and DoS, "DoS Financial Plan to Support PRT Excel," undated.

80 Unclassified Baghdad 4045, "Action Plan to Build Capacity and Sustainability within Iraq's Provincial Governments," From embassy Baghdad to SECSTATE, 010330Z October 2005; and SIGIR Audit 06-034, "Status of the Provincial Reconstruction Team Program in Iraq," October 29, 2006, 8.

81 SIGIR Audit 06-034, "Status of the Provincial Reconstruction Team Program in Iraq," October 29, 2006, 8.

82 SIGIR site visit to Mosul PRT and follow-up correspondence, Forward Operating Base Marez, June 22, 2006.

83 SIGIR interview with Andrew Rathmell, former Director of CPA Office of Planning and Analysis and consultant to Joint Strategic Planning and Assessments, June 26, 2006.

84 SIGIR interview with Rear Admiral Scott R. Van Buskirk, Director, Office of National Unity, Strategic Effects, June 20, 2006.

85 Ginger Cruz, Deputy Inspector General for Iraq Reconstruction, Testimony before the House Armed Services Committee, September 5, 2007; and SIGIR Audit 07-015, "Review of the Effectiveness of Provincial Reconstruction Teams in Iraq," October 18, 2007. See also: Supplemental Agreement to the Memorandum of Agreement between Commander, Multi-National Force-Iraq, and Chief of Mission, U.S. Mission Iraq Regarding Security Responsibility on PRT Security Responsibilities and Requirements, November 9, 2006; and Memorandum of Agreement between the Deputy Secretary of State and the Deputy Secretary of Defense Regarding PRT Support, February 22, 2007.

86 SIGIR Audit 06-034, "Status of the Provincial Reconstruction Team Program in Iraq," October 29, 2006, 15.

87 Ginger Cruz, Deputy Inspector General for Iraq Reconstruction, Testimony before the House Armed Services Committee, September 5, 2007.

88 SIGIR Audit 06-034, "States of the Provincial Reconstruction Team Program in Iraq," October 29, 2006, 5.

89 Bonn Agreement, "Agreement on Provisional Arrangements in Afghanistan Pending the Re-Establishment of Permanent Government Institutions," December 5, 2001.

90 Kenneth Katzman, Congressional Research Service Report RL31339, "Iraq: Post-Saddam Governance and Security," updated November 7, 2006.

91 CIA, "The World Factbook - Afghanistan," January 2008; and CIA, "The World Factbook - Iraq," January 2008.

92 James Kunder, USAID Asst Administrator, Near East Bureau, Testimony before the House Committee on International Relations, March 9, 2006.

93 Decree of the President of the Islamic Transitional State of Afghanistan on the Afghan National Army, December 1, 2002 as cited in: United Nations Assistance Mission in Afghanistan, "Rebuilding Afghanistan: Peace and Stability," December 2, 2002, Annex 1, http://www.unama-afg.org/docs/_nonUN%20Docs/_Internation-Conferences&Forums/Bonn-Talks/decree%20on%20army.pdf.

94 Combat Studies Institute interview with Major General Paul Eaton, former Commander of CMATT and OSC, August 3, 2006; and CPA Order Number 22, August 7, 2003.

95 SIGIR interview with General Paul Eaton, former CMATT Commander, May 20, 2008.

96 Robert Perito, USIP Senior Program Officer, Testimony before the House Armed Services Subcommittee on Oversight and Investigations, October 18, 2007.

97 SIGIR, *Quarterly Report to the United States Congress*, October 2008, 16; SIGAR, *Quarterly Report to the United States Congress*, October 2008, 1.

98 MNC-I, "Money as a Weapons System (MAAWS): MNC-I Smart Book For Resource Managers," MNC-I C8, October 1, 2005, 2.

99 USAID, "Transition Strategy: 2006-2008," PowerPoint Briefing, September 2005; and USAID, "Strategy and Impact of Iraq Transition Initiative: OTI in Iraq (2003-2006), Final Evaluation," September 30, 2006, 15.

100 The list of strategic cities infrequently changed, based on periodic assessments coordinated by the NSC and MNF-I. One list is located at: USAID, "Annex 1- Strategic Cities in Iraq," http://www.usaid.gov/iraq/contracts/pdf/Annex1-StrategicCitiesinIraq.pdf.

101 Clear-Hold-Build is slightly different than the oil-spot strategy, in that it advocates a broader emphasis on creating safe havens simultaneously across all areas of operation by emphasizing civilian security, rather than selecting only some regions for intervention. Public Broadcasting Service, "Interview with Philip Zelikow," *FRONTLINE*, February 6, 2007.

102 Condoleezza Rice, Secretary of State, Testimony before the Senate Foreign Relations Committee, October 19, 2005; DoD News Transcript, "News Briefing with Secretary of Defense Donald Rumsfeld and General Peter Pace," November 29, 2005; and Public Broadcasting Service, "Interview with Philip Zelikow," *FRONTLINE*, February 6, 2007.

103 DoD News Transcript, "News Briefing with Secretary of Defense Donald Rumsfeld and General Peter Pace," November 29, 2005.

104 George W. Bush, "President Commemorates Veterans Day, Discusses War on Terror," November 11, 2005.

105 NSC, "National Strategy for Victory in Iraq," November 30, 2005.

106 Public Broadcasting Service, "Interview with Philip Zelikow," *FRONTLINE*, February 6, 2007; SIGIR interview with Philip Zelikow, former Counselor, U.S. State Department, June 26, 2008; and SIGIR interview with Celeste Ward, political aide to Lieutenant General Peter Chiarelli, and Colonel Kenneth Cox, Engineer Brigade Commander, June 24, 2006.

107 For an elaboration of the conflict transformation approach, see Jock Covey, Michael J. Dziedzic, and Leonard R. Hawley, eds., *The Quest for Viable Peace: International Intervention and Strategies for Conflict Transformation* (Washington, DC: USIP, 2005).

Chapter 23

1 SIGIR interview with Lieutenant Colonel Otto Busher, Baghdad PRT member, June 25, 2006.

2 Sgt. Samson Barini, "Minutes from Meeting with the Water Sector at the Amanat," Baghdad PRT Infrastructure Report, June 25, 2006. Members of SIGIR's lessons learned team observed this meeting. See, also: Baghdad Water Authority, "Minutes of Meeting—The Coordination with USAID," June 11, 2006.

3 SIGIR interview with Lieutenant Colonel Otto Busher, Baghdad PRT member, June 25, 2006.

4 Dan Bisbee, Baghdad PRT, "Baghdad Governance," 3rd ed., April 2007, 10. This manual was written as a primer to city politics for reconstruction personnel working in Baghdad, and is widely circulated among officials and contractors.

5 Dan Bisbee, Baghdad PRT, "Baghdad Governance," 3rd ed., April 2007, 11-12; and James Glanz, "Baghdad Mayor is Ousted by a Shiite Group and Replaced," *New York Times*, August 10, 2005.

6 Sgt. Samson Barini, "Minutes from Meeting with the Water Sector at the Amanat," Baghdad PRT Infrastructure Report, June 25, 2006; and SIGIR interview with Lieutenant Colonel Otto Busher, Baghdad PRT member, June 25, 2006. A SIGIR inspection found similar problems at the Nassriya water treatment plant, where the local distribution system would not be able to withstand increased water pressure and would thus lead to major leakages when the water treatment became operational. SIGIR Inspection PA-07-116, "Nassriya Water Treatment Plant, Nassriya, Iraq," April 28, 2008, 28-29.

7 Sgt. Samson Barini, "Minutes from Meeting with the Water Sector at the Amanat," Baghdad PRT Infrastructure Report, June 25, 2006; and SIGIR interview with Lieutenant Colonel Otto Busher, Baghdad PRT member, June 25, 2006.

8 SIGIR interviews with Lieutenant Colonel Otto Busher, Baghdad PRT member, June 19-28, 2006. See also: Dan Bisbee, Baghdad PRT, "Baghdad Governance," 3rd ed., April 2007, 12; and SIGIR interview with Joseph Gregoire, Baghdad PRT leader, June 20, 2006.

9 Sgt. Samson Barini, "Minutes from Meeting with the Water Sector at the Amanat," Baghdad PRT Infrastructure Report, June 25, 2006; and SIGIR interview with Lieutenant Colonel Otto Busher, Baghdad PRT team member, June 25, 2006.

10 SIGIR interview with Sgt. Timmy R. Rostro, Convoy Commander Red 2, Unit 43029, June 25, 2006, and subsequent correspondence, July 4, 2006.

11 SIGIR interviews with Lieutenant Colonel Otto Busher, Baghdad PRT member, June 19-28, 2006.

12 "Groundhog Day" is a term that some military personnel use to describe "another day in Iraq." SIGIR interview with Lieutenant Colonel Otto Busher, Baghdad PRT member, June 25, 2006.

13 USIP interview with Colonel P.J. Dermer, former CPA governance advisor, August 22, 2004.

14 SIGIR interview with Vijay Samaraweera, Senior Policy Advisor for Regional Government, RTI International, August 16, 2007.

15 This was made explicit in articles 55 and 56 of the Transitional Administrative Law (TAL) and CPA Order Number 71. In theory, these writs empowering local government moved Iraq further toward a decentralized federal republic in which the central government would nominate governors, whose appointment and tenure would be subject to the approval of provincial councils. The councils and the governor would manage ministerial outposts in each province headed by the directors general, thereby putting the resources of national ministries under the direction of local elected officials. Iraqi Governing Council, "Law of Administration for the State of Iraq for the Transitional Period," Articles 55-56, March 8, 2004; and CPA Order Number 71, "Local Governmental Powers," April 6, 2004. SIGIR interview with Vijay Samaraweera, Senior Policy Advisor for Regional Government, RTI International, August 16, 2007.

16 For a discussion of the debate over federalism, see Eric Herring and Glen Rangwala, *Iraq in Fragments: The Occupation and its Legacy* (Ithaca, NY: Cornell University Press, 2006); and Ali A. Allawi, *The Occupation of Iraq: Winning the War, Losing the Peace* (New Haven, CT: Yale University Press, 2007).

17 ORHA/CPA Historian interview with J. Scott Carpenter, CPA Director of Governance, June 29, 2004. For an analysis of how Iraqi factions took control of Iraqi ministries, see Eric Herring and Glen Rangwala, *Iraq in Fragments: The Occupation and Its Legacy* (Ithaca, NY: Cornell University Press, 2006).

18 SIGIR interview with Ali A. Allawi, former Iraqi Minister of Trade and Minister of Defense, September 13, 2007. For an account of nepotism and political capture, see Ali A. Allawi, *The Occupation of Iraq: Winning the War, Losing the Peace* (New Haven, CT: Yale University Press, 2007).

19 Eric Herring and Glen Rangwala, *Iraq in Fragments: The Occupation and its Legacy* (Ithaca, NY: Cornell University Press, 2006), chapters 1-3.

20 Eric Herring and Glen Rangwala, *Iraq in Fragments: The Occupation and its Legacy* (Ithaca, NY: Cornell University Press, 2006), 118, 125.

21 Dan Bisbee, Baghdad PRT, "Baghdad Governance," 3rd ed., April 2007, 10.

22 James A. Baker III and Lee H. Hamilton, co-chairs, "The Iraq Study Group Report," December 6, 2006, 20.

23 USAID, "Local Governance Program," Final Report, June 2005, 12.

24 Dan Bisbee, Baghdad PRT, "Baghdad Governance," 3rd ed., April 2007, 10.

25 USAID, "Local Governance Program," Final Report, June 2005, 9.

26 SIGIR interview with Vijay Samaraweera, Senior Policy Advisor for Regional Government, RTI International, August 16, 2007.

27 Dan Bisbee, Baghdad PRT, "Baghdad Governance," 3rd ed., April 2007.

28 For a detailed history and analysis of Iraq's constitutional negotiations, see Noah Feldman and Roman Martinez, "The International Migration of Constitutional Norms in the New World Order: Constitutional Politics and Text in the New Iraq: An Experiment in Islamic Democracy," *Fordham Law Review* 75, no. 2 (November 2006), 883-920.

29 Iraqi Governing Council, "Law of Administration for the State of Iraq for the Transitional Period," Articles 55-56, March 8, 2004.

30 Noah Feldman and Roman Martinez, "The International Migration of Constitutional Norms in the New World Order: Constitutional Politics and Text in the New Iraq: An Experiment in Islamic Democracy," *Fordham Law Review* 75, no. 2 (November 2006), 900-901.

31 United Nations Security Council Report S-2005-585, "Report of the Secretary-General Pursuant to Paragraph 30 of Resolution 1546 (2004)," September 7, 2005.

32 Dan Bisbee, Baghdad PRT, "Baghdad Governance," 3rd ed., April 2007, 34.

33 SIGIR, *Quarterly Report to the United States Congress*, April 2008, 145-46.

34 SIGIR, *Quarterly Report to the United States Congress*, October 2008, 6.

35 SIGIR interview with John Jones, Diyala PRT member, August 9, 2007.

36 Mat Bouldin, Diyala PRT member, email to SIGIR, August 17, 2007.

37 SIGIR interview with John Jones, Diyala PRT member, August 9, 2007.

38 SIGIR interview with Robert Tillery, former National Coordination Team Chief of Staff, January 11, 2008.

39 Mat Bouldin, Diyala PRT member, email to SIGIR, August 17, 2007.

40 SIGIR site visit to the Northern Governors Conference, Baghdad, August 2007.

41 Not until 2008 was the original CPA Order Number 71, outlining the authorities of local governments, replaced with a formal Provincial Powers Law. The Provincial Powers Law was approved on March 19, 2008. Reuters, "Iraq Presidency Passes Provincial Powers Law," March 19, 2008.

42 For background on the Local Governance Program II, see USAID, "Iraq Strengthening Local and Provincial Governance Program: Annual Report, October 1, 2005-September 30, 2006," December 2006; and USAID, "Assistance for Iraq: "Contracts and Grants," http://www.usaid.gov/iraq/contracts, and USAID, "Iraq Local Governance Program (LGP): 2007 Annual Report," October 1, 2006-December 31, 2007," January 15, 2008.

43 SIGIR interview with Todd Helmeke, RTI regional team leader in Hilla, August 25, 2007.

44 USAID, "Iraq Local Governance Program II (LGP II)," undated, http://www.usaid.gov/iraq/contracts/pdf/AI4-IraqlocalGovernanceProgram_LGPII_FactSheet.pdf.

45 USAID Audit E-267-07-007-P, "Audit of USAID/Iraq's Local Governance Activities," July 31, 2007, 1, 5.

46 SIGIR Audit 09-003, "Cost, Outcome, and Oversight of Local Government Program Contract with Research Triangle Institute," October 21, 2008.

47 SIGIR interview with Vijay Samaraweera, Senior Policy Advisor for Regional Government, RTI International, August 16, 2007.

Chapter 24

1 USAID contracted with Bechtel in 2003 (IRRF 1) and again in 2004 (IRRF 2) to rebuild vast parts of Iraq's electrical infrastructure. The Doura power plant's number 5 and number 6 generators were the objects of two Bechtel job orders under the IRRF 1 and IRRF 2 contracts. The first, amounting to $90.8 million, called for the rehabilitation of the two generators. The second, amounting to an additional $80 million, called for the establishment of operations and maintenance training for personnel at the Ministry of Electricity. Work on the generators was scheduled for completion on April 30, 2004. Actual completion was delayed by almost two years, to April 2006. SIGIR Inspection PA 07-103, "Doura Power Stations 5 and 6, Baghdad, Iraq," July 18, 2007, 3-4.

2 SIGIR Inspection PA 07-103, "Doura Power Stations 5 and 6, Baghdad, Iraq," July 18, 2007, i-ii, 7-10.

3 For instance, the pressure on working-level engineers was so extreme that not only were maintenance periods shortened due to demand, but improper procedures were used after blackouts to restart sensitive components. SIGIR interview with Al Herman, Senior Consultant for Electricity, February 28, 2008.

4 Stuart Bowen, Special Inspector General for Iraq Reconstruction, Testimony before the House Committee on Appropriations Subcommittee on Foreign Operations, Export Financing, and Related Programs, September 7, 2005; and SIGIR, *Quarterly Report to the United States Congress*, January 2006, 4-5. For examples of SIGIR sustainment inspections see SIGIR Inspection PA 07-116, "Nassriya Water Treatment Plant, Nassriya, Iraq," April 28, 2008; and SIGIR Inspection PA 08-137, "Kirkuk to Baiji Pipeline Exclusion Zone – Phase 3, Kirkuk, Iraq," July 24, 2008; and SIGIR Inspections PA 06-082, PA 06-083, PA 06-084, PA 06-085, PA 06-086, "Electrical Substation Sustainment, Basrah, Iraq," January 10, 2007.

5 SIGIR defines sustainment "as the ability of the Iraqi government to support IRRF-funded projects and facilities for an extended period of time after U.S. financial, managerial, and technical assistance is terminated." SIGIR Audit 05-022, "Managing Sustainment for Iraq Relief and Reconstruction Fund Programs," October 24, 2005, i. SIGIR defines capacity development as "an activity or multiple activities that lead to the transfer of knowledge, skills, and abilities across a range of functions over a period of time." SIGIR Audit 06-045, "Status of Ministerial Capacity Development in Iraq," January 30, 2007, 3.

6 One Iraqi employed by the Coalition recalled experiences working for the former regime in which Ba'athist enforcers would identify missing inventory from state factories, and then mete out punishment by shooting employees at random. SIGIR interview with Babil PRT Iraqi employee, August 2008. Individual ministries during the Hussein era also maintained their own prison networks, designed to incarcerate suspected employees and enforce a culture of fear. SIGIR interview with Andrew Natsios, former USAID Administrator, April 17, 2006.

7 For a history of Saddamist management practices, see Kanan Makiya, *Republic of Fear: The Politics of Modern Iraq* (Berkeley: University of California Press, 1998); and Phebe Marr, *The Modern History of Iraq*, 2nd edition (Boulder, CO: Westview Press, 2003).

8 Bearing Point, USAID contract RAN-C-00-03-00043-00, July 18, 2003, http://www.usaid.gov/iraq/contracts/pdf/BearingPoint.pdf.

9 SIGIR Audit 08-007, "Efforts to Implement a Financial-Management Information System in Iraq," January 25, 2008.

10 GAO Report 04-902R, "Rebuilding Iraq: Resource, Security, Governance, Essential Services, and Oversight Issues," June 2004, 14.

11 Bechtel, USAID contract EEE-C-00-03-00018-00, April 17, 2003, 14, http://www.usaid.gov/iraq/con-tracts/pdf/Bechtel.pdf.

12 SIGIR interview with Robert MacLeod, USAID Chief Technical Officer, January 20, 2006.

13 For example, a critical deterioration of the port equipment at Umm Qasr took place between the summer months of 2003, when the port was rehabilitated, and December 2003. Visits by USAID officials revealed that work on maintaining the equipment had been stalled by local managers who were waiting for Baghdad to initi-ate repairs. SIGIR interview with Robert MacLeod, USAID Chief Technical Officer, January 20, 2006.

14 Bechtel, USAID contract SPU-C-00-04-00001-00, January 5, 2004, http://www.usaid.gov/iraq/contracts/pdf/Bechtel_II.pdf.

15 SIGIR, "Iraq Reconstruction: Lessons in Program and Project Management," March 2007, 54-55.

16 James Stephenson, former USAID Mission Director, email to SIGIR, August 2, 2006.

17 SIGIR interview with Robert MacLeod, USAID Chief Technical Officer, January 20, 2006; and James Stephenson, former USAID Mission Director, email to SIGIR, August 2, 2006.

18 James Stephenson, former USAID Mission Director, email to SIGIR, August 2, 2006.

19 SIGIR interview with Andrew Natsios, former USAID Administrator, March 17, 2008.

20 SIGIR interview with Thomas Wheelock, former Chief of Party for USAID's contractor International Resource Group, January 5, 2006.

21 SIGIR interview with Christopher Milligan, USAID Deputy Director of Iraq, February 9, 2006.

22 For example, SIGIR found that, three years after their graduation from Bechtel University, a handful of engineers were leading infrastructure reconstruction programs in Baghdad under the auspices of USAID's second Local Governance Program. SIGIR interviews with members from RTI Baghdad and RTI Green Zone compounds, August and September 2007.

23 SIGIR interview with Thomas Wheelock, former Chief of Party for USAID's contractor International Resources Group, January 5, 2006.

24 SIGIR interview with Bruce Parmelee, Community Action Plan program officer, March 2, 2007. For a more recent example, see SIGIR Inspection PA 07-116, "Nassriya Water Treatment Plant, Nassriya, Iraq," April 28, 2008.

25 SIGIR Audit 05-022, "Managing Sustainment for Iraq Relief and Reconstruction Fund Programs," October 24, 2005.

26 IRMO, "Iraq Reconstruction Program Framework for Sustainable Operations," May 18, 2005, 4.

27 For a discussion of the capacity problems associated with frequent ministry personnel turnover during this period, see SIGIR Audit 06-045, "Status of Ministerial Capacity Development in Iraq," January 30, 2007, 1.

28 Nationwide electricity production in June of 2004, for example, was recorded at approximately 3,900 megawatts, slightly less than Iraq's pre-war generation of 4,400 megawatts, and far below the CPA's goal of 6,000 megawatts by summer. Daily crude export, meanwhile, was at 1.2 million barrels per day, almost half of its pre-war peak. Other services were also underperforming. The Brookings Institution, "Iraq Index: Tracking Variables of Reconstruction and Security in Post-Saddam Iraq," June 21, 2004, 20-21.

29 SIGIR interview with David Satterfield, former Deputy Chief of Mission, April 14, 2008.

30 PCO, "Iraq Capacity Development: PCO Management and Interface Plan," November 22, 2004, 3; and SIGIR, "Iraq Reconstruction: Lessons in Program and Project Management," March 2007, 119-120.

31 SIGIR interview with Sheryl Lewis, PCO Capacity Development officer, December 1, 2007; and SIGIR Inspection PA 07-116, "Nassriya Water Treatment Plant, Nassriya Iraq," April 28, 2008.

32 Most of these tracking data are now held in PCO-GRD capacity development and subcontractor databases. Each database reports on twelve contract deliverables relevant to capacity development, as well as on various general requirements and award fee criteria. See PCO briefing, "Capacity Development and Sustainability Program," March 2007.

33 Department of the Army, PCO/USACE-GRD, "A Report on Iraq Reconstruction," January 2004 - September 2006, 16.

34 PCO briefing, "2005 Capacity Development and Sustainment," PCO Training Center Map, 2005.

35 SIGIR interview with Sheryl Lewis, PCO Capacity Development officer, December 1, 2007.

36 IRMO, "Iraq Reconstruction Program Framework for Sustainable Operations," May 18, 2005.

37 SIGIR, *Quarterly Report to the United States Congress*, October 2005, 16-20.

38 GAO Report 08-117, "Stabilizing and Rebuilding Iraq: U.S. Ministry Capacity Development Efforts Need an Overall Integrated Strategy to Guide Efforts and Manage Risk," October 2007, 14.

39 GAO Report 08-117, "Stabilizing and Rebuilding Iraq: U.S. Ministry Capacity Development Efforts Need an Overall Integrated Strategy to Guide Efforts and Manage Risk," October 2007, 6-7, 14-15.

40 SIGIR interview with Daniel Speckhard, former IRMO Director and Deputy Chief of Mission, April 29, 2008.

41 SIGIR interview with Sheryl Lewis, PCO Capacity Development officer, December 1, 2007.

42 SIGIR interview with Daniel Speckhard, former IRMO Director and Deputy Chief of Mission, April 29, 2008.

43 SIGIR interview with Robert Tillery, former National Coordination Team Chief of Staff, January 11, 2008.

44 SIGIR interview with Robert Tillery, former National Coordination Team Chief of Staff, January 11, 2008.

45 GAO Report 08-117, "Stabilizing and Rebuilding Iraq: U.S. Ministry Capacity Development Efforts Need an Overall Integrated Strategy to Guide Efforts and Manage Risk," October 2007, 8-9.

46 Only the ministry of electricity, which had a long history of working simultaneously with different components of the U.S. mission, successfully integrated the Ministerial Assistance Team concept. SIGIR interview with Robert Tillery, former National Coordination Team Chief of Staff, January 11, 2008.

47 SIGIR Audit 06-045, "Status of Ministerial Capacity Development in Iraq," January 30, 2007, 10-11; and SIGIR interview with Robert Tillery, former National Coordination Team Chief of Staff, January 11, 2008.

48 A SIGIR audit found that, in its first four months of operation, the task force was primarily occupied with cataloging the various capacity-development activities throughout the reconstruction program. It also found that individual relationships with ministries tended to define capacity-development efforts, rather than an overall strategy. SIGIR Audit 06-045, "Status of Ministerial Capacity Development in Iraq," January 30, 2007, 12; SIGIR interview with Robert Tillery, former National Coordination Team Chief of Staff, January 11, 2008; and SIGIR interview with Sheryl Lewis, PCO Capacity Development officer, December 1, 2007.

49 USAID, "Tatweer Project: Developing National Capacity in Public Management," Quarterly Progress Report No.1 (August-October 2006), November 30, 2006, ii, 1.

50 USAID, "Tatweer Project: Developing National Capacity in Public Management," Quarterly Progress Report No. 2 (November-December 2006), January 30, 2007, 7.

51 GAO Report 08-117, "Stabilizing and Rebuilding Iraq: U.S. Ministry Capacity Development Efforts Need an Overall Integrated Strategy to Guide Efforts and Manage Risk," October 2007, 19; and SIGIR Audit 06-045, "Status of Ministerial Capacity Development in Iraq," January 30, 2007, 2.

52 SIGIR conversations with Rick Olson, former Office of Provincial Affairs official, Spring 2008.

53 SIGIR interview with Joseph Saloom, former IRMO Director, April 21, 2008.

54 Rick Olson, former Office of Provincial Affairs official, email to SIGIR, November 19, 2008.

55 IRMO's Presidential charter, National Security Presidential Directive 36, originally defined the office as a temporary organization without an explicit expiration date. National Security Presidential Directive 36, "United States Government Operations in Iraq," May 11, 2004.

56 SIGIR interview with Joseph Saloom, former IRMO Director, April 21, 2008.

57 The U.S. Embassy formally dropped this effort in July 2007. GAO Report 08-117, "Stabilizing and Rebuilding Iraq: U.S. Ministry Capacity Development Efforts Need an Overall Integrated Strategy to Guide Efforts and Manage Risk," October 2007, 16. For a discussion of the difficulty associated with performing capacity building as ministries constantly changed hands, see SIGIR Audit 06-045, "Status of Ministerial Capacity Development in Iraq," January 30, 2007, 1.

58 GAO Report 08-117, "Stabilizing and Rebuilding Iraq: U.S. Ministry Capacity Development Efforts Need an Overall Integrated Strategy to Guide Efforts and Manage Risk," October 2007, 19.

59 SIGIR interview with Jeremiah S. Pam, former Treasury attaché, September 9, 2008.

60 SIGIR interview with Daniel Speckhard, former IRMO Director and Deputy Chief of Mission, April 29, 2008.

61 SIGIR interview with Joseph Saloom, former IRMO Director, December 2, 2007; and Jeremiah S. Pam, former Treasury attaché, September 9, 2008. For further background on Iraq's financial reconstruction, see Jeremiah S. Pam, USIP Special Report 216, "The Treasury Approach to State-Building and Institution-Strengthening Assistance: Experience in Iraq and Broader Implications, October, 2008.

62 Ambassador Zalmay Khalilzad, vetting comments to SIGIR, October 27, 2008.

63 SIGIR interviews with Joseph Saloom, former IRMO Director, December 2, 2007; and Jeremiah S. Pam, former Treasury attaché, September 9, 2008.

64 SIGIR interview with Muhannad Esheiker, Ministry of Planning fusion cell member, August 25, 2007.

65 Conflicting budget execution data exist. SIGIR January 2008 Quarterly Report cites a White House report putting this number at 24 percent, a Treasury Department report showing 15 percent, and a GAO report showing 4.4 percent. SIGIR, *Quarterly Report to the United States Congress,* January 2008, 124.

66 SIGIR, *Quarterly Report to the United States Congress,* April 2008, 142-144.

67 SIGIR interview with Jeremiah S. Pam, former Treasury attaché, September 9, 2008.

68 SIGIR interview with Henry Clarke, former director, Office of Provincial Affairs, August 17, 2007; and Mat Bouldin, Diyala PRT member, August 9, 2007.

69 That many of the advisors had no prior background in development may also be a factor. GAO Report 08-117, "Stabilizing and Rebuilding Iraq: U.S. Ministry Capacity Development Efforts Need an Overall Integrated Strategy to Guide Efforts and Manage Risk," October 2007, 19.

70 SIGIR interview with David Satterfield, former Deputy Chief of Mission, April 14, 2008.

71 SIGIR Audit 06-006, "Multi-National Security Transition Command-Iraq: Management of the Transfer of IRRF-funded Assets to the Iraqi Government," April 29, 2006; SIGIR Audit 06-007, "U.S. Agency for International Development: Management of the Transfer of Iraq Relief and Reconstruction Fund Projects to the Iraqi Government," April 29, 2006; and SIGIR Audit 06-017, "Transition of Iraq Relief and Reconstruction Fund Projects to the Iraqi Government," July 28, 2006. Follow-on audits include SIGIR Audit 07-004, "Transferring Iraq Relief and Reconstruction Fund Capital Projects to the Government of Iraq," July 25, 2007; and SIGIR Audit 08-017, "Transferring Reconstruction Projects to the Government of Iraq: Some Progress Made but Further Improvements Needed to Avoid Waste," April 28, 2008.

72 SIGIR Audit 06-006, "Multi-National Security Transition Command-Iraq: Management of the Transfer of IRRF-funded Assets to the Iraqi Government," April 29, 2006; SIGIR Audit 06-007, "U.S. Agency for International Development: Management of the Transfer of Iraq Relief and Reconstruction Fund Projects to the Iraqi Government," April 29, 2006; and SIGIR Audit 06-017, "Transition of Iraq Relief and Reconstruction Fund Projects to the Iraqi Government," July 28, 2006. Follow-on audits include SIGIR Audit 07-004, "Transferring Iraq Relief and Reconstruction Fund Capital Projects to the Government of Iraq," July 25, 2007; and SIGIR Audit 08-017, "Transferring Reconstruction Projects to the Government of Iraq: Some Progress Made but Further Improvements Needed to Avoid Waste," April 28, 2008.

73 SIGIR Audit 06-017, "Transition of Iraq Relief and Reconstruction Fund Projects to the Iraqi Government," June 28, 2006, ii, 10.

74 SIGIR Audit 08-017, "Transferring Reconstruction Projects to the Government of Iraq: Some Progress Made But Further Improvements Needed to Avoid Waste," April 28, 2008, 7.

75 SIGIR Audit 06-006, "Multi-National Security Transition Command-Iraq: Management of the Transfer of IRRF-funded Assets to the Iraqi Government," April 29, 2006; SIGIR Audit 06-007, "U.S. Agency for International Development: Management of the Transfer of Iraq Relief and Reconstruction Fund Projects to the Iraqi Government," April 29, 2006; and SIGIR Audit 06-017, "Transition of Iraq Relief and Reconstruction Fund Projects to the Iraqi Government," July 28, 2006. Follow-on audits include SIGIR Audit 07-004, "Transferring Iraq Relief and Reconstruction Fund Capital Projects to the Government of Iraq," July 25, 2007; and SIGIR Audit 08-017, "Transferring Reconstruction Projects to the Government of Iraq: Some Progress Made but Further Improvements Needed to Avoid Waste," April 28, 2008.

76 SIGIR Audit 06-017, "Transition of Iraq Relief and Reconstruction Fund Projects to the Iraqi Government," June 28, 2006, 6-7.

77 SIGIR Audit 08-017, "Transferring Reconstruction Projects to the Government of Iraq: Some Progress Made But Further Improvements Needed to Avoid Waste," April 28, 2008, 3.

78 Republic of Iraq, Board of Supreme Audit, "Report on Projects Funded by U.S. Funds," November 25, 2007.

79 SIGIR Audit 08-017, "Transferring Reconstruction Projects to the Government of Iraq: Some Progress Made But Further Improvements Needed to Avoid Waste," April 28, 2008. The State Department notes that, as of October 2008, the asset transfer policy is under active consideration by the Council of Ministers. DoS, written comments to SIGIR, October 28, 2008.

80 SIGIR interview with David Satterfield, former Deputy Chief of Mission, April 14, 2008.

81 SIGIR interview with Joseph Saloom, former IRMO Director, December 2, 2007.

82 SIGIR interview with Joseph Saloom, former IRMO Director, December 2, 2007.

83 SIGIR interview with Henry Clarke, former director, Office of Provincial Affairs, August 17, 2007.

84 GAO 04-902R Report, "Rebuilding Iraq: Resource, Security, Governance, Essential Services, and Oversight Issues," June 28, 2004, 14.

85 GAO Report 08-117, "Stabilizing and Rebuilding Iraq: U.S. Ministry Capacity Development Efforts Need an Overall Integrated Strategy to Guide Efforts and Manage Risk," October 2007, 3, 9.

86 GAO Report 08-117, "Stabilizing and Rebuilding Iraq: U.S. Ministry Capacity Development Efforts Need an Overall Integrated Strategy to Guide Efforts and Manage Risk," October 2007, 1-5.

87 Mat Bouldin, Diyala PRT member, email to SIGIR, August 17, 2007.

88 GAO 08-117 Report, "Stabilizing and Rebuilding Iraq: U.S. Ministry Capacity Development Efforts Need an Overall Integrated Strategy to Guide Efforts and Manage Risk," October 2007, 25-26.

Chapter 25

1 Ellen Knickmeyer and Bassam Sebti, "Toll in Iraq's Deadly Surge: 1,300; Morgue Count Eclipses Other Tallies Since Shrine Attack," *Washington Post*, February 28, 2006; and White House Press Release, "Fact Sheet: Combating Terrorism Worldwide," August 6, 2007.

2 International Committee of the Red Cross, "Civilians without Protection: The Ever-worsening Humanitarian Crisis in Iraq," April 11, 2007.

3 Ron Redmond, "Iraq Displacement," UN High Commissioner for Refugees Briefing Notes, November 3, 2006.

4 DoD, *Measuring Security and Stability in Iraq*, May 2006, 33; and James D. Fearon, "Iraq's Civil War," *Foreign Affairs* 86, no. 2 (March/April 2007).

5 A total of 1,313 murders/executions versus 173 deaths from vehicle-borne improvised explosive devices. Major General Rick Lynch, "Iraq Operational Update Briefing," March 30, 2006; and MNF-I, "Operations Summary 18 Mar-24 Mar 06," March 30, 2006, 5.

6 Victor Tanner and Anonymous, "Revenge Killings in Iraq: Nature and Extent of the Problem," USAID Office of Transition Initiatives, 2004, as cited in: Ashraf al-Khalidi and Victor Tanner, "Sectarian Violence: Radical Groups Drive Internal Displacement in Iraq," Brookings Institution, October 2006; and Kanan Makiya, *Republic of Fear: The Politics of Modern Iraq* (Berkeley: University of California Press, 1998), originally published in 1989 under the pseudonym Samir al-Khalil.

7 "U.S. Envoy 'Calls for New Iraqi PM," *British Broadcasting Corporation*, March 28, 2006.

8 Ashraf al-Khalidi and Victor Tanner, "Sectarian Violence: Radical Groups Drive Internal Displacement in Iraq," Brookings Institution, October 2006, 3.

9 Ashraf al-Khalidi and Victor Tanner, "Sectarian Violence: Radical Groups Drive Internal Displacement in Iraq," Brookings Institution, October 2006, 19.

10 Robert Perito, "Reforming the Iraqi Interior Ministry, Police, and Facilities Protection Service," USIP Briefing, February 2007; and Robert Perito, USIP Senior Program Officer, Testimony before the House Armed Services Committee Oversight and Investigations Subcommittee, March 28, 2007.

11 SIGIR interview with Jon Shumard, Advisor to the Ministry of the Interior, June 21, 2006.

12 General (Ret.) Barry R. McCaffrey, Adjunct Professor of International Affairs, West Point, memorandum to Colonel Michael Meese, U.S. Military Academy Department of Social Sciences, "After Action Report - General Barry R. McCaffrey USA (Ret), Visit Iraq and Kuwait 9-16 March 2007."

13 Institute for War & Peace Reporting, "Checkpoints-Baghdad's Russian Roulette: Security-aware Iraqis try to minimize the risks as they negotiate their way through Baghdad," Iraqi Governance Report, August 2007, 4-6; and Ashraf al-Khalidi and Victor Tanner, "Sectarian Violence: Radical Groups Drive Internal Displacement in Iraq," Brookings Institution, October 2006

14 Many of these maps circulated on websites at different times. See, for example: IraqSlogger, "Baghdad Death Map," 2006, http://www.iraqslogger.com/index.php/post/3398/The_Baghdad_Death_Map, accessed June 30, 2007.

15 Color-coded maps showing safe and unsafe convoy routes, off-limits areas, and significant incident data are produced daily by the Reconstruction Operations Center of the Gulf Region Division, and distributed widely among reconstruction personnel. See for example: USACE-GRD Reconstruction Operations Center, G2 Cell, "Route Status Map," September 22, 2007; USACE-GRD "GRD Battle Update: MNF-I SIGACTS Last 24 Hours – GRN," September 20, 2007; and AEGIS, "Route Status Advisory," August 30, 2007.

16 For then-Brigadier General William McCoy personally, the difference was immediate. Twice in the month after the Samarra bombing, his vehicle was hit by improvised explosive devices, each time as he was on his way to assess progress on a public health clinic. SIGIR interview with Major General William H. McCoy, former Commander, USACE-GRD, June 5, 2008.

17 SIGIR interview with Major General William H. McCoy, former Commander, USACE-GRD, June 5, 2008.

18 SIGIR Audit 06-011, "Management of the Primary Healthcare Centers Construction Projects," April 29, 2006; and SIGIR Project Assessments PA-05-021, PA-05-022, PA-05-023, PA-05-024, "Border Forts Numbered 602, 604, 628, and 634 Sulaymaniyah, Iraq," January 31, 2006.

19 SIGIR interview with Major General William H. McCoy, former Commander, USACE-GRD, June 5, 2008.

20 International Committee of the Red Cross, "Iraq: No Let-up in the Humanitarian Crisis," March 2008, 8; and SIGIR interview with Jon Bowersox, Senior Advisor for Health, November 1, 2006. GRD notes that "while there may have been a question over the timeliness of information, USACE-GRD reports from the period demonstrate that there was awareness of projects that were behind schedule. The security environment did impact the ability to access work sites, however Area and Resident Offices were located across Iraq and it is not correct to say that projects were centrally managed from Baghdad without some oversight in the field." USACE-GRD vetting comments to SIGIR, November 5, 2008.

21 SIGIR interview with Mat Bouldin, Diyala PRT member, August 9, 2007.

22 SIGIR interview with George "Ged" Smith, Director of the U.S. Treasury's Office of Technical Assistance, August 20, 2007.

23 The Brookings Institution, "Iraq Index: Tracking Variables of Reconstruction & Security in Post-Saddam Iraq," June 29, 2006.

24 For estimates of civilian deaths, see Hannah Fischer, Congressional Research Service Report RS22537, "Iraqi Civilian Death Estimates," November 22, 2006; Iraq Body Count, "Incidents," http://www.iraqbodycount.org/database/download/ibc-incidents.php, accessed January 12, 2007; and UN Assistance Mission for Iraq, "Human Rights Report," July 1-August 31, 2006, and September 1-October 31, 2006.

25 SIGIR interview with Lieutenant General Peter Chiarelli, former Commander of MNC-I, February 19, 2008. For a commentary on Maliki's coming to power, see Ali A. Allawi, *The Occupation of Iraq: Winning the War, Losing the Peace* (New Haven, CT: Yale University Press, 2007), 443-54.

26 Sunni ministers engaged in various protests that culminated in members of Tawafiq —the largest Sunni block—leaving government entirely in August 2007. They ultimately re-joined in July 2008. Campbell Robertson and Sabrina Tavernise, "Sunnis End Boycott and Rejoin Iraqi Government," *New York Times,* July 20, 2008.

27 Ambassador Zalmay Khalilzad, vetting comments to SIGIR, October 27, 2008.

28 George W. Bush, "Press Conference of the President," June 14, 2006.

29 For an assessment of how the Joint Reconstruction Operations Center improved the integration of CERP projects with broader reconstruction activities, see SIGIR Audit 07-006, "Management of the Commander's Emergency Response Program in Iraq for Fiscal Year 2006," April 26, 2007.

30 Edward Wong, "Iraqis Plan to Ring Baghdad with Trenches," *New York Times,* September 16, 2006.

31 World Public Opinion, "The Iraqi Public on the U.S. Presence and the Future of Iraq," conducted by Program on International Policy Attitudes, September 1-4, 2006.

32 Senator Susan Collins, Chair, Statement before Senate Committee on Homeland Security and Governmental Affairs, August 2, 2006; and SIGIR, *Quarterly Report to the United States Congress,* October 2006, 3.

33 SIGIR interview with Lieutenant Colonel Otto Busher, Baghdad PRT member, June 25, 2006.

34 SIGIR interview with Lieutenant Colonel Otto Busher, Baghdad PRT member, June 25, 2006.

35 GRD notes that "a critical factor that led to the rush was that the Ambassador had earlier implemented a review of IRRF that lasted over six months and held up a large number of awards and therefore causing a substantial backlog in work." USACE-GRD written comments to SIGIR, November 5, 2008. Ambassador Khalilzad's staff notes that, for his part, he "was not hammering on the obligation side. Quite the contrary, he was arguing for more analysis before funds were obligated on any projects and always questioning the validity of our assumptions on the benefits of our reconstruction program and priorities." He consistently held up programming until he was confident that money was being spent well, and he even ignored those that told him he could not cancel projects and demanded that this be done in cases where cost overruns had become egregious or results inadequate." Ambassador Zalmay Khalilzad, written comments to SIGIR, October 27, 2008.

36 SIGIR Audit 06-037, "Interim Audit Report on Improper Obligations Using the Iraq Relief and Reconstruction Fund (IRRF 2)," September 22, 2006; and SIGIR Audit 06-040, "Improper Obligations Using the Iraq Relief and Reconstruction Fund (IRRF 2)," January 30, 2007.

37 SIGIR, *Quarterly Report to the United States Congress*, October 2006, 3, 18-19.

38 SIGIR, *Quarterly Report to the United States Congress*, October 2006, 17, 21; and IRMO, *Weekly Status Report*, October 3, 2006.

39 IRMO, *Weekly Status Report*, October 3, 2006.

40 SIGIR, *Quarterly Report to the United States Congress*, October 2006, 17.

41 IRMO Action Memorandum, "Recommended Solutions to Relieve the Ministry of Oil from Hampering Budgetary, Spending, and Procurement Constraints," July 29, 2006, 3, as cited in SIGIR, *Quarterly Report to the United States Congress*, October 2006, 35.

42 SIGIR, *Quarterly Report to the United States Congress*, October 2006, 45.

43 Oxfam International, "Rising to the Humanitarian Challenge in Iraq," Briefing Paper, July 2007, 3-4; and Megan Greenwell, "A Dismal Picture of Life in Iraq," *Washington Post*, July 31, 2007.

44 DoD, *Measuring Security and Stability in Iraq*, August 2006, 17.

45 Ellen Knickmeyer, "U.S. Has End in Sight on Iraq Rebuilding," *Washington Post*, January 2, 2006.

46 David Streitfeld, "Iraq: Contractor Bechtel Leaves Disintegrating Iraq Short of Goal," *Baltimore Sun*, November 4, 2006.

47 David R. Baker, "Bechtel Ends Iraq Rebuilding After a Rough 3 Years," *San Francisco Chronicle*, November 1, 2006.

48 SIGIR Inspection PA 06-054, "Nasiriyah Prison Facility: Nasiriyah, Iraq," June 24, 2006, ii.

49 SIGIR Audit 07-006, "Management of the Commander's Emergency Response Program in Iraq for Fiscal Year 2006," April 26, 2007, 1.

50 SIGIR interview with Lieutenant General Peter Chiarelli, former Commander of MNC-I, February 19, 2008. For CERP data from fiscal year 2006, see SIGIR Audit 07-006, "Management of the Commander's Emergency Response Program in Iraq for Fiscal Year 2006," April 26, 2007, 8.

51 SIGIR Audit 07-006, "Management of the Commander's Emergency Response Program in Iraq for Fiscal Year 2006," April 26, 2007, 8. SWET is also variously known as SWET-F (adding fuel) or SWEAT (adding academics).

52 SIGIR interview with Gordon England, Deputy Secretary of Defense, March 28, 2008.

53 SIGIR interview with Lieutenant General Peter Chiarelli, former Commander of MNC-I, February 19, 2008.

54 SIGIR interview with David Satterfield, former Deputy Chief of Mission, April 14, 2008.

55 More than 28 percent of obligated CERP funds—or $537 million of the $2.3 billion Congress appropriated—went to water projects. SIGIR Audit 08-006, "Commander's Emergency Response Program in Iraq Funds Many Large Scale Projects," January 25, 2008, ii.

56 SIGIR Audit 08-006, "Commander's Emergency Response Program in Iraq Funds Many Large Scale Projects," January 25, 2008.

57 SIGIR interview with Heidi Silvey, USAID OTI Chief of Party, June 6 and July 1, 2006; and SIGIR interview with Megan Holleran, OTI Acting Chief of Party, June 19, 2006.

58 USAID, "Focused Stabilization in Strategic Cities Initiative (FSSCI)," http://www.usaid.gov/iraq/contracts/pdf/AI3-FocusedStabilizationofStrategicCitiesInitiative.pdf.

59 DoS, "Advancing the President's National Strategy for Victory in Iraq: Funding Iraq's Transition to Self-Reliance in 2006 and 2007 and Support for the Counterinsurgency Campaign," February 2006.

60 Interagency Stabilization Task Force, "Focused Stabilization: An Interagency Operational Concept," PowerPoint brief, July 4, 2006.

61 Center for Army Lessons Learned, "Provincial Reconstruction Teams in Iraq Handbook," version 1.5, 56.

62 SIGIR interview with Lieutenant General Peter Chiarelli, former Commander of MNC-I, February 19, 2008.

63 USAID Press Release, "USAID Awards Community Stabilization Program in Iraq," August 11, 2006.

64 Dana Eyre, former USAID consultant, comments to SIGIR, October 5, 2008.

65 Public Broadcasting Service, "Interview with Philip Zelikow," *FRONTLINE,* February 6, 2007.

66 Public Broadcasting Service, "Interview with Philip Zelikow," *FRONTLINE,* February 6, 2007; and Dana Eyre, former USAID consultant, comments to SIGIR, October 5, 2008.

67 SIGIR interview with Lieutenant Colonel Christian Shomber, MNF-W Economics Liaison Officer, June 30, 2006.

68 SIGIR interview with Lieutenant Colonel Christian Shomber, MNF-W Economics Liaison Officer, June 30, 2006.

69 Richard Steelman, "USAID Iraq Sectoral Consultation: Agriculture/Marshlands," December 2, 2004; and DoS, comments to SIGIR, October 28, 2008.

70 USAID Press Release, "USAID Awards Contract for Agricultural Reconstruction and Development," October 21, 2003.

71 USAID Audit E-267-07-002-P, "USAID/Iraq's Agriculture Reconstruction and Development Program," January 22, 2007, 2; and USAID Report RAN-C-00-04-00002-00, "Final Report: Agriculture Reconstruction Development Program for Iraq," December 2006.

72 The exported goods included both foodstuff, such as rice, and agricultural technology, such as tractors. See also: Richard Steelman, "USAID Iraq Sectoral Consultation: Agriculture/Marshlands," December 2, 2004.

73 USAID Audit E-267-07-002-P, "USAID/Iraq's Agriculture Reconstruction and Development Program," January 22, 2007, 2; and USAID Report RAN-C-00-04-00002-00, "Final Report: Agriculture Reconstruction Development Program for Iraq," December 2006, 337.

74 USAID, "A Transition Plan for the Agricultural Sector in Iraq," Final Report Vols. I and II, April 2004.

75 USAID, "A Transition Plan for the Agricultural Sector in Iraq," Final Report Vols. I and II, April 2004, ix.

76 U.S. Department of Agriculture, "Fact Sheet: U.S. Agricultural Programs in Iraq," December 2006.

77 USAID, "Assistance for Iraq: Agriculture," updated May 16, 2007; and USAID Audit E-267-07-002-P, "USAID/Iraq's Agriculture Reconstruction and Development Program," January 22, 2007, 4.

78 USAID Audit E-267-07-002-P, "USAID/Iraq's Agriculture Reconstruction and Development Program," January 22, 2007, 4-5.

79 SIGIR, *Quarterly Report to the United States Congress,* April 2008, 130.

80 USAID Press Release, "USAID Awards Inma Agribusiness Program in Iraq," May 16, 2007.

81 MNF-I, "Provincial Iraqi Control," updated January 10, 2008, http://www.mnf-iraq.com/index. php?option=com_content&task=view&id=1469&Itemid=78.

82 President George W. Bush, "President Addresses the Nation, Discusses Iraq, War on Terror," White House Press Release, June 28, 2005.

83 P.L. 109-234, Emergency Supplemental Appropriations for Fiscal Year 2006, June 15, 2006; P.L. 109-289, Department of Defense Appropriations Act for Fiscal Year 2007, September 29, 2006; P.L. 110-28, U.S. Troop Readiness, Veterans' Care, Katrina Recovery, and Iraq Accountability Appropriations Act for Fiscal Year 2007, December 21, 2007; and P.L. 110-161, Consolidated Appropriations Act for Fiscal Year 2008, December 26, 2007.

84 SIGIR, *Quarterly Report to the United States Congress,* October 2008, 19; and DoS, *Section 2207 Report,* July 2008, Status of Funds.

85 SIGIR, *Quarterly Report to the United States Congress,* July 2006, 59.

86 SIGIR conversations with Terrence K. Kelly, former JSPA director, September, 2008.

87 General (Ret.) James L. Jones, Chairman, "Report of the Independent Commission on the Security Forces of Iraq," September 6, 2007, 103.

88 The Joint Committee to Transfer Security Responsibility was set up to develop requirements for readiness for the handover. Members included Iraqi government officials, U.S. and UK embassy staff, and MNF-I leaders. MNF-I, "Provincial Iraqi Control," updated January 10, 2008, http://www.mnf-iraq.com/index.php?option=com_content&task=view&id=1469&Itemid=78.

89 SIGIR, Quarterly Report to the United States Congress, January 2008, 125.

90 General (Ret.) James L. Jones, Chairman, "Report of the Independent Commission on the Security Forces of Iraq," September 6, 2007, 125.

91 General (Ret.) James L. Jones, Chairman, "Report of the Independent Commission on the Security Forces of Iraq," September 6, 2007, 47-48.

92 General (Ret.) James L. Jones, Chairman, "Report of the Independent Commission on the Security Forces of Iraq," September 6, 2007, 50.

93 SIGIR interview with Lieutenant General Martin Dempsey, former commander of MNSTC-I, April 8, 2008.

94 DoS, Section 2207 Report, October 2006, I-2.

95 DoS, Section 2207 Report, October 2006, I-1; and DoD, Measuring Stability and Security in Iraq, October 2005, 30.

96 DoD, Measuring Stability and Security in Iraq, November 2006, 27-29.

97 DoD, Measuring Stability and Security in Iraq, November 2006, 31.

98 General (Ret.) James L. Jones, Chairman, "Report of the Independent Commission on the Security Forces of Iraq," September 6, 2007, 49.

99 SIGIR Audit 08-022, "Government of Iraq Increasingly Funding Iraqi Security Forces Infrastructure Development, but Substantial U.S. Support Remains," July 26, 2008, 12; SIGIR Audit 06-032, "Iraqi Security Forces: Review of Plans to Implement Logistics Capabilities," October 28, 2006; and General (Ret.) James L. Jones, Chairman, "Report of the Independent Commission on the Security Forces of Iraq," September 6, 2007, 36.

100 Bob Woodward, State of Denial: Bush at War, Part III (New York: Simon & Schuster, 2006), 396; and Public Broadcasting Service, "Interview with Philip Zelikow," FRONTLINE, February 6, 2007.

101 Robert Perito, "Policing Iraq: Protecting Iraqis from Criminal Violence," USIP Briefing, June 2006.

102 SIGIR, Quarterly Report to the United States Congress, October 2006, 72.

103 General (Ret.) James L. Jones, Chairman, "Report of the Independent Commission on the Security Forces of Iraq," September 6, 2007, 94-95, 98.

104 Robert Perito, "Iraq's Interior Ministry: Frustrating Reform," USIP Report, May 2008.

105 General (Ret.) James L. Jones, Chairman, "Report of the Independent Commission on the Security Forces of Iraq," September 6, 2007, 44, 88.

106 General (Ret.) James L. Jones, Chairman, "Report of the Independent Commission on the Security Forces of Iraq," September 6, 2007, 43-45, 88, 112.

107 General (Ret.) James L. Jones, Chairman, "Report of the Independent Commission on the Security Forces of Iraq," September 6, 2007, 44, 88, 112-15.

108 General (Ret.) James L. Jones, Chairman, "Report of the Independent Commission on the Security Forces of Iraq," September 6, 2007, 86, 88, 90.

109 General (Ret.) James L. Jones, Chairman, "Report of the Independent Commission on the Security Forces of Iraq," September 6, 2007, 90-91.

110 DoD, Measuring Stability and Security in Iraq, October 2005, 38; DoS Report ISP-IQO-05-72 and DoD-IG Report IE-2005-002, "Interagency Assessment of Iraq Police Training," July 15, 2005, 34; and DoD, Measuring Stability and Security in Iraq, July 2005, 20.

111 General (Ret.) James L. Jones, Chairman, "Report of the Independent Commission on the Security Forces of Iraq," September 6, 2007, 97.

112 General (Ret.) James L. Jones, Chairman, "Report of the Independent Commission on the Security Forces of Iraq," September 6, 2007, 99-101.

113 DoS Audit ISP-IQO-06-01, "Inspection of Rule-of-Law Programs, embassy, Baghdad," October 1, 2005.

114 SIGIR interview with James Santelle, former Rule of Law Coordinator and Resident Legal Advisor, July 22, 2008.

115 DoS, *Weekly Status Report*, August 3, 2005.

116 SIGIR interview with James Santelle, former Rule of Law Coordinator and Resident Legal Advisor, July 22, 2008.

117 SIGIR, *Quarterly Report to the United States Congress*, October 2006, 70.

118 General (Ret.) James L. Jones, Chairman, "Report of the Independent Commission on the Security Forces of Iraq," September 6, 2007, 106.

119 SIGIR interview with James Santelle, former Rule of Law Coordinator and Resident Legal Advisor, July 22, 2008.

120 DoS Audit ISP-IQO-06-01, "Inspection of Rule-of-Law Programs, embassy, Baghdad," October 1, 2005, 48.

121 SIGIR interview with James Santelle, former Rule of Law Coordinator and Resident Legal Advisor, July 22, 2008.

122 SIGIR interview with Stephen Andersson, Baghdad PRT Rule of Law advisor, August 26, 2007.

123 SIGIR interview with former Iraqi judge and Coalition Rule of Law advisor, August 26, 2007. Three days after this interview, the Judge's house was burned to the ground and he was taken to a safe house in the Green Zone. Wilson Myers, Baghdad PRT legal advisor, email to SIGIR, August 31, 2007.

124 SIGIR interview with Chief Judge Kamel Abd Al-Majeed Yousif, al-Rusafa Appellate District Court, August 23, 2007; and Stephen Andersson, Baghdad PRT Rule of Law advisor, "Meeting of Special Inspector General for Iraq Reconstruction (SIGIR) Stuart W. Bowen Jr, and his Deputy, Michael J. Boisvenue, and Chief Judge Kamel Abd Al-Majeed Youisf of the al-Rusafa Appellate District Court," August 23, 2007.

125 SIGIR interview with James Santelle, former Rule of Law Coordinator and Resident Legal Advisor, July 22, 2008.

126 SIGIR interview with former Iraqi Judge and coalition Rule of Law advisor, August 26, 2007.

127 SIGIR interview with former Iraqi Judge and coalition Rule of Law advisor, August 26, 2007.

128 Ministerial Coordination Team, "Ministerial Coordination Team: Briefing for SIGIR," June 2006.

129 DoD, *Measuring Security and Stability in Iraq*, November 2006, 17-18, 24.

130 USIP, "Iraq Study Group," http://www.usip.org/isg/.

131 USIP, "Iraq Study Group Fact Sheet," updated December 20, 2006, http://www.usip.org/isg/fact_sheet.html.

132 Thomas E. Ricks, "Pentagon May Suggest Short-Term Buildup Leading to Iraq Exit," *Washington Post*, November 20, 2006; and Bob Woodward, *The War Within: A Secret White House History 2006-2008* (New York, Simon & Schuster, 2008), 231-247.

133 James A. Baker, III and Lee Hamilton, co-chairs, "The Iraq Study Group Report," December 6, 2006, 20.

134 James A. Baker, III and Lee Hamilton, co-chairs, "The Iraq Study Group Report," December 6, 2006, 49.

135 James A. Baker, III and Lee Hamilton, co-chairs, "The Iraq Study Group Report," December 6, 2006, 23, 57-59.

136 Frederick W. Kagan, "Choosing Victory: A Plan for Success in Iraq: Phase I Report," A Report of the Iraq Planning Group, AEI, January 5, 2007; and Public Broadcasting Service, "Interview with Philip Zelikow," *FRONTLINE*, February 6, 2007.

Essential Services – Transition from Khalilzad to Crocker
137 IRMO, *Electricity Daily Units Performance Report*, March 2007; and ITAO, *Monthly Import, Production and Export*, response to SIGIR data call for the *Quarterly Report to the United States Congress*, April 2008. DoD, *Measuring Stability and Security in Iraq*, March, 2007, 25; IRMO, *Weekly Status Report*, March 13, 2007, 22; Iraq Coalition Casualty Count, "U.S. Deaths By Month," updated September 2008; SIGIR, *Quarterly Report to the United States Congress*, April 2007, 11, 108; Iraq Body Count, "Documented civilian deaths from violence," updated August 24, 2008; P.L. 109-102, Appropriations for the Department of State for Fiscal Year 2006, November 14, 2005; P.L. 109-148, "Appropriations for the Department of Defense for Fiscal Year 2006, December 30, 2005; P.L. 109-234, Emergency Supplemental Appropriations for Fiscal Year 2006, June 15, 2006; P.L. 109-289, Department of Defense Appropriations Act for Fiscal Year 2007, September 29, 2006; and Government of Iraq, "2006 Budget" written into law December 2005; and U.S. Treasury, response to SIGIR data call for the *Quarterly Report to the United States Congress*, January 4, 2008.

138 IRMO, *Electricity Daily Units Performance Report*, March 2007

139 Joseph A. Christoff, GAO International Affairs and Trade Director, Statement before the House Committee on Foreign Affairs Subcommittees on the Middle East and South Asia and International Organizations, Human Rights, and Oversight, July 18, 2007, 13-14.

140 SIGIR, *Quarterly Report to the United States Congress*, July 2007, 79.

Chapter 26

1 Marc Santora, "U.S. and Iraqis Hit Insurgents in All-Day Fight," *New York Times*, January 10, 2007.

2 White House Press Release, "President's Address to the Nation," January 10, 2007.

3 White House Press Release, "Fact Sheet: New Way Forward in Iraq," January 10, 2007; and NSC, "Highlights of the Iraq Strategy Review," January 2007, 11.

4 White House Press Release, "Background Briefing by Senior Administration Officials," January 10, 2007.

5 White House Press Release, "Background Briefing by Senior Administration Officials," January 10, 2007.

6 SIGIR Audit 07-014, "Status of the Provincial Reconstruction Team Program Expansion in Iraq," July 25, 2007, i-ii.

7 DoS, "The New Way Forward: Funding Iraq's Transition to Self-Reliance and Stabilization in the President's 2007 Supplemental and 2008 Requests," February 2007, 5; and USAID, "Assistance for Iraq: Acquisition and Assistance Activities," updated December 17, 2007.

8 USAID, "Assistance for Iraq: Community Stabilization Program," updated November 23, 2007.

9 The President also requested funding for an expansion of existing reconstruction programs in the Fiscal Year 2007 supplemental and regular Fiscal Year 2008 budget request Funding went to Iraqi Provincial Reconstruction Development Councils, USAID's Local Governance and Community Action Programs, the Rule of Law Program, and various ongoing capacity development and sustainability initiatives. DoS, "The New Way Forward: Funding Iraq's Transition to Self-Reliance and Stabilization in the President's 2007 Supplemental and 2008 Requests," February 2007.

10 The plan more closely resembled a strategy advocated by the American Enterprise Institute. See Frederick W. Kagan, "Choosing Victory: A Plan for Success in Iraq: Phase I Report," A Report of the Iraq Planning Group, AEI, January 5, 2007.

11 SIGIR interviews with Colonel John R. Martin, Lieutenant General Peter Chiarelli, Colonel Michael Meese, Dr. Kirk Johnson, and Dr. Terrence K. Kelly. Early in 2007, General Casey reportedly said, "The longer we in the U.S. forces continue to bear the main burden of Iraq's security, it lengthens the time that the government of Iraq has to take the hard decisions about reconciliation and dealing with the militias. And the other thing is that they can continue to blame us for all of Iraq's problems, which are at base their problems." Quoted in David E. Sanger, Michael R. Gordon, and John F. Burns, "Chaos Overran Iraq Plan in '06, Bush Team Says," *New York Times,* January 2, 2007.

12 Department of the Army, *Counterinsurgency,* FM 3-24, MCWP 3-33.5, December 2006.

13 For an articulation of U.S. strategy in 2005, see White House Press Release, "President Outlines Strategy for Victory in Iraq," November 30, 2005.

14 SIGIR interview with General David Petraeus, Commander of MNF-I, March 2, 2008; and Dexter Filkins and John F. Burns, "Mock Iraqi Villages in Mojave Prepare Troops for Battle," *New York Times,* May 1, 2006.

15 Thomas E. Ricks, "U.S. Counterinsurgency Academy Giving Officers A New Mindset: Course in Iraq Stresses the Cultural, Challenges the Conventional," *Washington Post,* February 21, 2006.

16 SIGIR interview with Colonel Michael Meese, Economic and Reconstruction advisor to General David Petraeus, August 30, 2007.

17 Major General William B. Caldwell IV, "MNF-I Situation Update," February 21, 2007; DoD News Transcript, "Joint Press Conference with Secretary Gates, U.S. Ambassador Crocker and General Petraeus," June 16, 2007; and Brookings Institution, "Iraq Index: Tracking Variables of Reconstruction and Security in Post-Saddam Iraq, April 24, 2008, 6.

18 DoD News Transcript, "News Briefing with Major General Fil from Iraq," February 16, 2007.

19 USACE-GRD, comments to SIGIR, November 5, 2008.

20 Edward Wong and David S. Cloud, "U.S. Erects Baghdad Wall to Keep Sects Apart," *New York Times,* April 21, 2007.

21 SIGIR interview with Colonel John R. Martin, Senior Advisor to General David Petraeus; and Ylber Bajraktari, Commander's Initiative Group, August 27, 2007.

22 SIGIR interview with Colonel John R. Martin, Senior Advisor to General David Petraeus; and Ylber Bajraktari, Commander's Initiative Group, August 27, 2007.

23 Condoleezza Rice, "Announcement on Presidential Nominations for U.S. Permanent Representative to the United Nations and U.S. Ambassador to Iraq," January 8, 2007; and Department of State, "Biography: Ryan C. Crocker," March 29, 2007, http://www.state.gov/r/pa/ei/biog/81479.htm.

24 Condoleezza Rice, "Appointment of Tim Carney as Coordinator for Economic Transition in Iraq," January 12, 2007.

25 SIGIR interview with Ambassador Timothy Carney, former Coordinator for Economic Transition in Iraq, April 5, 2008; and Timothy Carney, "We're Getting In Our Own Way," *Washington Post,* June 22, 2003.

26 SIGIR interview with Colonel Michael Meese, Economic and Reconstruction advisor to General David Petraeus, August 30, 2007; Michael Meese, Economic and Reconstruction advisor to General David Petraeus, memorandum for the Commanding General, MNC-I, "How to Think About Current Economic Activity in Iraq," undated; and Michael Meese, Economic and Reconstruction advisor to General David Petraeus, memorandum for the Commanding General, MNC-I, "How to Think About Oil and Electricity in Iraq," February 28, 2007.

27 The Joint Strategic Assessment Team was co-chaired by the State Department's David Pierce, JSPA's Chris Schnaubelt and Colonel H.R. McMaster, who had pioneered the successful retaking of Tal Afar. Other members included Steve Biddle, from the U.S. Council on Foreign Relations; Great Britain's Andrew Rathmell and Toby Dodge; Australian David Kilcullen, on loan from the U.S. State Department; the U.K. Army's Colonel Jim Richardson; and Colonel John R. Martin, late of the Strategic Studies Institute at the U.S. Army War College. SIGIR interview with Colonel John R. Martin, Senior Advisor to General David Petraeus; and Ylber Bajraktari, Commander's Initiative Group, August 27, 2007.

28 SIGIR interview with Colonel Michael Meese, Economic and Reconstruction advisor to General David Petraeus, August 30, 2007.

29 Michael Meese, Economic and Reconstruction advisor to General David Petraeus, memorandum for the Commanding General, MNC-I, "How to Think About Current Economic Activity in Iraq," undated.

30 SIGIR interview with Ambassador. Timothy Carney, former Coordinator for Economic Transition in Iraq, April 5, 2008.

31 SIGIR interview with Ambassador Timothy Carney, former Coordinator for Economic Transition in Iraq, April 5, 2008.

32 SIGIR interview with Ambassador Timothy Carney, former Coordinator for Economic Transition in Iraq, April 5, 2008.

33 DoS, "Biography: Ryan C. Crocker," March 29, 2007, http://www.state.gov/r/pa/ei/biog/81479.htm.

34 SIGIR interview with Ambassador Timothy Carney, former Coordinator for Economic Transition in Iraq, April 5, 2008.

35 SIGIR interview with Ambassador Timothy Carney, former Coordinator for Economic Transition in Iraq, April 5, 2008.

36 SIGIR Audit 07-005, "Fact Sheet on Sources and Uses of U.S. Funding Provided in Fiscal Year 2006 for Iraq Relief and Reconstruction," July 27, 2007, Appendix B.

37 SIGIR interview with General David Petraeus, Commander of MNF-I, March 2, 2008.

38 SIGIR interview with Celeste Ward, Deputy Assistant Secretary of Defense for Stability Operations Capabilities, September 9, 2008.

39 Robert Perito, "Embedded Provincial Reconstruction Teams," USIP Briefing, March 2008.

40 SIGIR interview with Colonel Michael Meese, Economic and Reconstruction advisor to General David Petraeus, August 30, 2007.

41 SIGIR interview with Lieutenant Colonel Douglas Winton, First Brigade Combat Team, Third Infantry Division, September 12, 2007.

42 SIGIR interview with Sgt. Friedman, Ramadi Civil Affairs and ePRT, September 12, 2007.

43 SIGIR interview with David Atteberry, USAID officer, Rasheed ePRT, September 3, 2007.

44 SIGIR site visits to PRTs, 2006-07.

45 SIGIR interview with Lieutenant Colonel Douglas Winton, First Brigade Combat Team, Third Infantry Division, September 12, 2007.

46 The need for a more comprehensive civilian and military integration was highlighted by the strategic review performed by Negroponte and Casey in July 2004, and its follow-on analysis by General Luck in August 2004. See Henry W. Stratman, "Orchestrating Instruments of Power for Nationbuilding," Joint Force Quarterly 41 (2nd quarter 2006), 33-34; and Leonard R. Hawley, "An Analysis of the DCS for Political and Economic Effects," August 2004.

47 SIGIR interview with Mike Antoine, Rasheed ePRT, September 3, 2007.

48 SIGIR interview with David Atteberry, USAID officer, Rasheed ePRT, September 3, 2007.

49 SIGIR interview with Mike Antoine, Rasheed ePRT, September 3, 2007.

50 USAID-IG Audit E-267-08-001-P, "Audit of USAID/Iraq's Community Stabilization Program," March 18, 2008, 6-10.

51 SIGIR interview with David Atteberry, USAID officer, Rasheed ePRT, September 3, 2007.

52 SIGIR interview with Timothy Zuniga-Brown, Team leader, Rasheed ePRT, September 3, 2007.

53 USAID-IG Audit E-267-08-001-P, "Audit of USAID/Iraq's Community Stabilization Program," March 18, 2008, 21.

54 SIGIR interview with Timothy Zuniga-Brown, Team leader, Rasheed ePRT, September 3, 2007.

55 SIGIR interview with David Atteberry, USAID officer, Rasheed ePRT, September 3, 2007.

56 SIGIR interview with David Atteberry, USAID officer, Rasheed ePRT, September 3, 2007.

57 Ginger Cruz, Deputy Special Inspector General for Iraq Reconstruction, Testimony before the House Armed Services Committee, September 5, 2007. For background on the protest by bi-lingual, bi-cultural advisors (BBAs) on alliance with Sunni tribes, see SIGIR interview with Timothy Zuniga-Brown, Team leader, Rasheed ePRT, September 3, 2007.

58 SIGIR interview with Mike Antoine, Rasheed ePRT, September 3, 2007.

59 SIGIR interview with Timothy Zuniga-Brown, Team leader, Rasheed ePRT, September 3, 2007.

60 SIGIR interviews with David Atteberry, USAID officer, Rasheed ePRT; and Timothy Zuniga-Brown, Team leader, Rasheed ePRT, September 3, 2007.

61 Paul A. Brinkley, "Restoring Hope: Economic Revitalization in Iraq Moves Forward," *Military Review* (March-April 2008), 9.

62 SIGIR interview with Christopher Milligan, USAID Deputy Director of Iraq, February 9, 2006; and SIGIR interview with Thomas Wheelock, former Chief of Party for USAID's contractor International Resource Group, January 5, 2006. For background, see DoD News Briefing, "DoD News Briefing with Secretary Gordon England, Paul Brinkley and Minister Fawzi Hariri at the Pentagon, Arlington, VA," September 4, 2007.

63 Joint Contracting Command-Iraq response to SIGIR data call, September 19, 2007.

64 MNF-I Press Release, "MNF-I Iraqi First Program Surpasses $1 Billion for Year," July 16, 2007.

65 MNF-I Press Briefing, "Operational Update: Rear Adm. Smith, Rear Adm. Dussault," February 24, 2008.

66 Early attempts at direct contracting with Iraqi firms include the Accelerated Iraq Reconstruction Program in early 2004, Rapid Construction Initiative and Direct Contracting Initiative in late 2004 and the PW-90 Small Scale Potable Water Program in 2004. John Daley, Gulf Region Division, U.S. Army Corps of Engineers, comments to SIGIR, October 22, 2008.

67 Paul A. Brinkley, "A Cause for Hope: Economic Revitalization in Iraq," *Military Review* (July-August 2007), 2-11; and Paul A. Brinkley, "Task Force to Support Improved Business and Stability Operations in Iraq," DoD Discussion Document, November 18, 2006.

68 SIGIR interview with Gordon England, Deputy Secretary of Defense, March 28, 2008.

69 Paul A. Brinkley, "A Cause for Hope: Economic Revitalization in Iraq," *Military Review* (July-August 2007), 2-11; Paul A. Brinkley, "Restoring Hope: Economic Revitalization in Iraq Moves Forward," *Military Review* (March-April 2008), 8-17; and DoD, "Task Force to Improve Business and Stability Operations-Iraq," http://www.defenselink.mil/tfbso/.

70 SIGIR interview with Ambassador Timothy Carney, former Coordinator for the Economic Transition in Iraq, April 5, 2008; and Rajiv Chandrasekaran, "Defense Skirts State in Reviving Iraqi Industries," *Washington Post*, May 14, 2007.

71 SIGIR interview with Gordon England, Deputy Secretary of Defense, March 28, 2008.

72 SIGIR, *Quarterly Report to the United States Congress*, October 2007, 95.

73 Paul A. Brinkley, "Task Force to Support Improved Business and Stability Operations in Iraq," DoD Discussion Document, November 18, 2006.

74 SIGIR, *Quarterly Report to the United States Congress*, October 2007, 95; and SIGIR Audit 08-024, "Information on a Special Department of Defense Program to Foster Economic Recovery in Iraq," July 29, 2008.

75 USACE-GRD, "Program Review Board," PowerPoint presentation, March 10, 2008.

76 SIGIR interview with David Leach, GRD Deputy Director; and Dennis Plochmeyer, GRD Senior Advisor, March 18, 2008.

77 SIGIR interview with David Leach, GRD Deputy Director; and Dennis Plochmeyer, GRD Senior Advisor, March 18, 2008; and USACE-GRD, comments to SIGIR, November 5, 2008.

78 SIGIR interview with Ambassador Ryan Crocker, U.S. Ambassador to Iraq, February 24, 2008.

79 Executive Order 13431, "Establishment of Temporary Organization to Facilitate United States Government Assistance for Transition in Iraq," May 9, 2007.

80 ITAO, "ITAO Manning Document," January 25, 2008.

81 Correspondence between SIGIR, ITAO, Political and Economic Sections, and the office of the Deputy Chief of Mission, March 2008.

82 Patrick F. Kennedy, "American Embassy Baghdad: Organization and Staffing Report," May 23, 2007, 24.

83 Patrick F. Kennedy, "American Embassy Baghdad: Organization and Staffing Report," May 23, 2007, 18. For further detail about the inadequate circulation of PRT reporting, see SIGIR interview with Allison Monz and Cathy Westley, Political Officers, August 23, 2007.

84 SIGIR Audit 07-008, "Fact Sheet on the Roles and Responsibilities of U.S. Government Organizations Conducting IRRF-Funded Reconstruction Activities," July 26, 2007, 2.

85 Michael Meese, Economic and Reconstruction advisor to General David Petraeus, memorandum for the Commanding General, MNC-I, "How to Think About Current Economic Activity in Iraq," undated.

86 SIGIR interview with Colonel Michael Meese, Economic and Reconstruction advisor to General David Petraeus, August 30, 2007.

87 SIGIR interview with Christopher King, Senior Advisor to the Commission on Public Integrity, June 19, 2006.

88 SIGIR site visit, August-September, 2007.

89 SIGIR interview with James Kunder, USAID Acting Deputy Administrator, February 15, 2008.

90 SIGIR interview with General David Petraeus, Commander of MNF-I, March 2, 2008.

91 Problems in reporting chains on reconstruction projects were noted by a recent SIGIR audit. SIGIR Audit 09-007, "Improvements Needed in Reporting Status of Reconstruction Projects to Chief of Mission," October 28, 2008, i-ii.

92 SIGIR interview with Ambassador Timothy Carney, former Coordinator for Economic Transition in Iraq, April 5, 2008.

93 For a brief description of program activities, see USAID, "Assistance for Iraq: Community Stabilization Program," updated November 23, 2007.

94 USAID-IG Audit E-267-08-001-P, "Audit of USAID/Iraq's Community Stabilization Program," March 18, 2008, 1.

95 SIGIR interview with Joel Sandefur, USAID Regional Legal Advisor, and a panel of staff from the USAID Community Stabilization Program, September 7, 2007.

96 SIGIR, *Quarterly Report to the United States Congress*, January 2008, 52-54; and USAID-IG Audit E-267-08-001-P, "Audit of USAID/Iraq's Community Stabilization Program," March 18, 2008, 13.

97 USAID-IG Audit E-267-08-001-P, "Audit of USAID/Iraq's Community Stabilization Program," March 18, 2008, 13.

98 SIGIR interview with Joel Sandefur, USAID Regional Legal Advisor, and a panel of staff from the USAID Community Stabilization Program, September 7, 2007.

99 SIGIR interview with Vijay Samaraweera, Senior Policy Advisor for Regional Government, RTI International, August 16, 2007.

100 SIGIR site visit, August-September, 2007.

101 SIGIR site visit, August-September, 2007.

102 Patrick F. Kennedy, "American Embassy Baghdad: Organization and Staffing Report," May 23, 2007, 26.

103 SIGIR site visit, August-September, 2007.

104 SIGIR, *Quarterly Report to the United States Congress*, January 2008, 50; and GAO Report 09-86R. "Provincial Reconstruction Teams in Iraq and Afghanistan," October 1, 2008.

105 Stephen D. Andersson, Rule of Law Coordinator, Baghdad PRT, email to SIGIR, September 4, 2007.

106 U.S. Embassy Baghdad memorandum, "Guidelines for Administration of the PRT/ePRT Quick Response Fund," v.1, August 12, 2007; and U.S. Embassy Baghdad memorandum, "Quick Response Fund SOP#1: Grant Submission and Approval Process," v.1, September 3, 2007.

107 SIGIR site visit, August-September, 2007.

108 Stephen D. Andersson, Rule of Law Coordinator, Baghdad PRT, email to SIGIR, September 4, 2007; and SIGIR site visit, August-September, 2007.

109 The original procedures were to check the names against the Office of Foreign Assets Control "Specifically Designated Nationals and Blocked Persons" list. Stephen D. Andersson, Rule of Law Coordinator, Baghdad PRT, email to SIGIR, September 4, 2007.

110 Stephen D. Andersson, Rule of Law Coordinator, Baghdad PRT, email to SIGIR, September 4, 2007; and Regional Security Office, U.S. Embassy Baghdad, official form, "U.S. Embassy Baghdad Security Certification Request," undated. See "Instructions: In order to initiate vetting, complete the following information, attach the requested documents, and make an appointment to submit fingerprints. Failure to provide this information or any supporting documents will result in suspension of action and return of your case."

111 Stephen D. Andersson, Rule of Law Coordinator, Baghdad PRT, email to SIGIR, September 4, 2007.

112 SIGIR interview with Steve Connolly, QRF Coordinator for DAI, March 3, 2008.

113 SIGIR, *Quarterly Report to the United States Congress*, October 2008, 84.

114 An estimated 9 percent of IRRF 1 funds remained unobligated. SIGIR, *Quarterly Report to the United States Congress*, January 2008, 55.

115 Expenditures by each of these contractors through the end of 2007 ranged from $932 million to $501 million, respectively. SIGIR, *Quarterly Report to the United States Congress*, January 2008, 57-58.

116 SIGIR, *Quarterly Report to the United States Congress*, January 2008, 20-22, 122.

117 SIGIR, *Quarterly Report to the United States Congress*, January 2008, 49-52.

118 SIGIR, *Quarterly Reports to the United States Congress*, The Human Toll, April, July, and October 2006, and January and April 2007. A total of $30 million in funds was de-obligated from the Infrastructure Security Program by the State Department in order to pay for refugee assistance, bringing the allocation down from the original $247 million to $217 million. USACE-GRD vetting comments to SIGIR, November 5, 2008.

119 SIGIR Audit 09-004, "Iraq Reconstruction Project Terminations Represent a Range of Actions," October 27, 2008, i, 5.

120 GAO Report 07-677, "Rebuilding Iraq: Integrated Strategic Plan Needed to Help Restore Iraq's Oil and Electricity Sectors," May 2007; and SIGIR, *Quarterly Report to the United States Congress*, July 2007, 34-35.

121 SIGIR, *Quarterly Report to the United States Congress*, July 2007; and DoS, *Section 2207 Report*, July 2007.

122 SIGIR, *Quarterly Report to the United States Congress*, July 2007; and DoS, *Section 2207 Report*, July 2007.

123 SIGIR, *Quarterly Report to the United States Congress*, July 2007; and DoS, *Section 2207 Report*, July 2007.

124 SIGIR Inspection PA-07-116, "Nassriya Water Treatment Plant, Nassriya Iraq," April 28, 2008.

125 SIGIR interview with Ambassador Ryan Crocker, U.S. Ambassador to Iraq, February 24, 2008.

126 SIGIR, *Quarterly Report to the United States Congress*, January 2008, 29-30.

127 SIGIR interview with Colonel Mark Martins, former MNF-I Staff Judge Advocate, July 24, 2008.

128 For a comprehensive account of the building and initial performance of the Baghdad Rule of Law complex, see MNF-I Staff Judge Advocate's Office, "Report to the Ministerial Committee for Rule of Law and Detention on The Rule of Law Complex in Rusafa: June to December 2007," January 2008.

129 SIGIR interview with Colonel Mark Martins, former MNF-I Staff Judge Advocate, July 24, 2008.

130 The State Department notes that these 5,000 guards are contracted to the Iraqi Facilities Protection Service, and that because their effectiveness is suspect an effort is underway to form either a federalized Judicial Protection Service under the employ of the Iraqi judiciary or have guards provided by the Ministry of the Interior. State Department, comments to SIGIR, October 28, 2008.

131 SIGIR, *Quarterly Report to the United States Congress,* July 2008, 86-88.

132 Prime Minister Gordon Brown, official correspondence to Prime Minister Nouri al-Maliki, official correspondence, July 29, 2007.

133 Suleiman al-Khalidi, "Iraq Needs $100-150 Bln for Reconstruction: Finance Minister," *Reuters,* August 20, 2007.

134 Alissa J. Rubin, "Sunni Sheik Who Backed U.S. in Iraq is Killed," *New York Times,* September 14, 2007.

135 DoD, *Measuring Stability and Security in Iraq,* September 2007, 21.

136 DoD, *Measuring Stability and Security in Iraq,* June 2007, 21.

137 P.L. 110-28, U.S. Troop Readiness, Veterans' Care, Katrina Recovery, and Iraq Accountability Appropriations Act, 2007, May 25, 2007.

138 NSC, "Initial Benchmark Assessment Report," July 12, 2007.

139 GAO Report 07-1195, "Securing, Stabilizing, and Rebuilding Iraq: Iraqi Government Has Not Met Most Legislative, Security, and Economic Benchmarks," September 2007; David M. Walker, Comptroller General, Testimony before the Senate Committee on Foreign Relations, September 4, 2007; and White House Press Release, "Benchmark Assessment Report," September 14, 2007.

140 General David Petraeus, MNF-I Commander, Testimony before the House Committee on Foreign Affairs and the Committee on Armed Services, September 10, 2007; and Ambassador Ryan C. Crocker, U.S. Ambassador to the Republic of Iraq, Testimony before the House Committee on Foreign Affairs and the Committee on Armed Services, September 10, 2007.

141 International Compact with Iraq, "About the Compact," updated June 8, 2008, http://www.iraqcompact.org/en/about.asp.

142 Daniel Kaufman, Aart Kraay, and Massimo Mastruzzi, "Governance Matters IV: Governance Indicators 1996-2006," World Bank Policy Research Working Paper no. 4280, July 2007; and SIGIR, *Quarterly Report to the United States Congress,* April 2008, 34.

143 BBC News, December 18, 2008, "Iraq economy 'on track' says IMF."

144 DoD, *Measuring Stability and Security in Iraq,* June 2008.

145 Jay Price, "Calmer Iraq a Big Boost to RTI's work," *News and Observer,* July 16, 2008.

146 SIGIR interview with Jeremiah S. Pam, former Treasury Attaché, September 9, 2008.

147 Ambassador Ryan C. Crocker, U.S. Ambassador to the Republic of Iraq, Testimony before the Senate Armed Services Committee, April 8, 2008.

148 SIGIR, *Quarterly Report to the United States Congress,* April 2008, 24.

149 SIGIR, *Quarterly Report to the United States Congress,* January 2008, 3.

150 SIGIR, *Quarterly Report to the United States Congress,* October 2008, 6.

151 SIGIR, *Quarterly Report to the United States Congress,* April 2008, 32.

152 SIGIR conversations with Terrence K. Kelly, former JSPA director, September 2008.

153 News organizations, brigades and some USAID programs have each at different times produced data on a variety of measures. See, for instance: ABC News, USA Today, BBC and ARD, "Opinion Poll: Conducted Feb 25-March 5, 2007," March 19, 2007, http://www.usatoday.com/news/graphics/iraqpoll_pdf/iraq_poll.pdf; and World Public Opinion, "What the Iraqi Public Wants," conducted by the Program on International Policy Attitudes, January 31, 2006, http://www.worldpublicopinion.org/pipa/pdf/jan06/Iraq_Jan06_rpt.pdf. Fuel delivery includes benzene, diesel, liquefied petroleum gas, and kerosene.

154 DoD, *Measuring Stability and Security in Iraq*, reports for 2006 and 2007.

155 Secretary Rice is quoted in Michael R. Gordon, "The 2000 Campaign: The Military; Bush Would Stop U.S. Peacekeeping in Balkan Fights," *New York Times*, October 21, 2000.

156 Yochi J. Dreazen, "New Rebuilding Plan in Iraq Stirs Debate about Tactics," *Wall Street Journal*, April 19, 2007.

157 SIGIR interview with Iraqi team leader employed by a USAID program, August 2007.

Essential Services Overview – After the Surge
158 SIGIR, *Quarterly Report to the United States Congress*, July 2008, 11, 14-20, 58-60, 64; DoD, *Measuring Stability and Security in Iraq*, June 2008, 35; SIGIR, *Quarterly Report to the United States Congress*, October 2008, 68; World Bank Operations in Iraq, "Status of Projects in Portfolio," February 29, 2008; Iraq Coalition Casualty Count, "U.S. Deaths By Month," updated September 2008; and Iraq Body Count, "Documented civilian deaths from violence," updated August 24, 2008; P.L. 110-28, U.S. Troop Readiness, Veterans' Care, Katrina Recovery, and Iraq Accountability Appropriations Act for Fiscal Year 2007, May 25, 2007; P.L. 110-92, P.L. 110-116, P.L. 110-137, P.L. 110-149, 2007 Foreign Assistance Continuing Resolutions, December 21, 2007; P.L. 110-161, Consolidated Appropriations Act for Fiscal Year 2008, December 26, 2007; and P.L. 110-252, Supplemental Appropriations Act for Fiscal Year 2008, June 30, 2008.

159 SIGIR, *Quarterly Report to the United States Congress*, July 2008, 64; and International Compact with Iraq, "A New Beginning: Annual Review," May 2007-April 2008, 50.

160 SIGIR, *Quarterly Report to the United States Congress*, July 2008, 60-62.

Chapter 27

1 SIGIR interview with James Kunder, USAID Acting Deputy Administrator, February 15, 2008.

2 SIGIR interview with General (Ret.) Colin Powell, former Secretary of State, February 4, 2008.

3 Donald Rumsfeld, former Secretary of Defense, letter to Stuart Bowen, Special Inspector General for Iraq Reconstruction, April 4, 2008.

4 Condoleezza Rice, Secretary of State, Statement before the House Foreign Affairs Committee, February 13, 2008.

5 NBC interview with Condoleezza Rice, Secretary of State, December 21, 2008.

6 SIGIR interview with Lt. General (Ret.) Ricardo Sanchez, former CJTF-7 Commander, October 26, 2007.

7 SIGIR Audit 09-005, "Agencies Need Improved Financial Data Reporting for Private Security Contractors," October 30, 2008, i, 3, 6.

8 For a cumulative analysis of SIGIR inspections and audits, see SIGIR PA 08-139, "Summary of Project Assessments Through April 2008," July 24, 2008; and SIGIR Audit 08-020, "Key Recurring Management Issues Identified in Audits of Iraq Reconstruction Efforts," July 27, 2008.

9 SIGIR Audit 07-008, "Fact Sheet on the Roles and Responsibilities of U.S. Government Organizations Conducting IRRF-Funded Reconstruction Activities," July 26, 2007, 2.

10 For a detailed analysis of the history of Army contracting, see Jacques S. Gansler, Chairman, "Urgent Reform Required: Army Expeditionary Contracting," Commission on Army Acquisition and Program Management in Expeditionary Operations, October 31, 2007, 17, 29.

11 The number of government employees has fallen from 4,058 in 1980 to 2,200 in 2008. Brian J. Atwood, M. Peter McPherson, and Andrew Natsios, "Arrested Development: Making Foreign Aid a More Effective Tool," *Foreign Affairs* 6 (October-November 2008).

12 Secretary of Defense Robert Gates, "Remarks at Landon Lecture, Kansas State University," November 26, 2007.

Afterword

1 SIGIR, *Quarterly Report to the United States Congress*, October 2008, 9.

2 SIGIR, "Iraq Reconstruction: Lessons in Human Capital Management," January 2006; SIGIR, "Iraq Reconstruction: Lessons in Contracting and Procurement," July 2006; and SIGIR, "Iraq Reconstruction: Lessons in Program and Project Management," March 2007.

3 S. 3001, "Duncan Hunter National Defense Authorization Act for 2009," Title XVI: Reconstruction and Stabilization Civilian Management.

4 S. 3001, "Duncan Hunter National Defense Authorization Act for 2009," Sec. 1605.

5 S. 3001, "Duncan Hunter National Defense Authorization Act for 2009," Sec. 1605.

6 National Security Presidential Directive 44, "Management of Interagency Efforts Concerning Reconstruction and Stabilization," December 7, 2005. For an overview of State Department actions in response to NSPD 44, see DoS, Office of the Spokesman, "President Issues Directive to Improve the United States' Capacity to Manage Reconstruction and Stabilization Efforts," December 14, 2005.

7 Office of Management and Budget, "Appendix to the Budget of the United States Government for Fiscal Year 2009," 771-772. In February 2008, the Administration requested almost $649 million for the Civilian Stabilization Initiative (CSI) to develop "a coordinated capacity across the 15 United States Government civilian agencies and the Department of Defense for a 'Whole of Government' response to emergent Reconstruction and Stabilization crises." DoS, *Congressional Budget Justification Fiscal Year 2009*, 531-533. The Congress later appropriated around $75 million to support the CSI. Nina M. Serafino, Congressional Research Service Report RL32862, "Peacekeeping/Stabilization and Conflict Transitions: Background and Congressional Action on the Civilian Response/Reserve Corps and other Civilian Stabilization and Reconstruction Capabilities," updated September 18, 2008, 2.

8 For a review of the government's reform efforts to date, see GAO Report 08-39, "Stabilization and Reconstruction: Actions Are Needed to Develop a Planning and Coordination Framework and Establish the Civilian Reserve Corps," November 2007.

9 Project on National Security Reform, "Ensuring Security in an Unpredictable World: The Urgent Need for National Security Reform," Preliminary Findings, July 2008, 60-61; and Derek Chollet, Mark Irvine, Bradley Larson, "A Steep Hill: Congress and U.S. Efforts to Strengthen Fragile States," CSIS, March 2008, 27-29.

10 DoD Directive 3000.05, "Military Support for Stability, Security, Transition, and Reconstruction (SSTR) Operations," November 28, 2005, 2.

11 Michael A. Alexander, Army War College Report A270974, "The U.S. Army Corps of Engineers Support of Combatant Commands," March 15, 2008, 5.

12 FM 3-07, "Stability Operations," Department of the Army, October 2008.

13 Jacques S. Gansler, Chairman, "Urgent Reform Required: Army Expeditionary Contracting," Commission on Army Acquisition and Program Management in Expeditionary Operations, October 31, 2007, 2-4; and Robert Gates, "Report to Congress on the Implementation of DoD Directive 3000.05 *Military Support for Stability, Security, Transition and Reconstruction (SSTR) Operations*," April 1, 2007.

14 SIGIR interview with General David Petraeus, Commander of MNF-I, March 2, 2008.

15 Project on National Security Reform, "Ensuring Security in an Unpredictable World: The Urgent Need for National Security Reform," Preliminary Findings, July 2008, 30, 32.

16 Robert Gates, "Remarks before the U.S. Global Leadership Campaign," July 15, 2008.

Annex A

1 The Office of the Special Inspector General for Iraq Reconstruction was created by Congress in 2003 as the Office of the Inspector General of the Coalition Provisional Authority. The CPA-IG was created by the Emergency Supplemental Appropriations Act for Defense and for the Reconstruction of Iraq and Afghanistan (P.L. 108-106, Section 3001), enacted November 6, 2003, in order to provide for independent and objective conduct and supervision of audits and investigations relating to the programs and operations of the Coalition Provisional Authority. The Ronald W. Reagan National Defense Authorization Act for Fiscal Year 2005 (P.L. 108-375), enacted October 28, 2004, redesignated the CPA-IG as SIGIR.

2 P.L. 108-106, Emergency Supplemental Appropriations Act for Defense and for the Reconstruction of Iraq and Afghanistan for Fiscal Year 2004, Section 3001(a)2(A), November 6, 2003.

3 For previous lessons learned reports, see SIGIR, "Initiatives: Lessons Learned," http://www.sigir.mil/initiatives/lessonslearned.aspx.

Annex B

1 SIGIR, *Quarterly Report to the United States Congress*, October 2008, 16; and GAO Testimony 08-568T, "Stabilizing and Rebuilding Iraq: Actions Needed to Address Inadequate Accountability over U.S. Efforts and Investments," March 11, 2008, 1.

2 The Department of Treasury Office of Inspector General also issued one report reviewing the agency's activities in Iraq. See Treasury OIG Audit 06-029, "International Assistance Programs: Review of Treasury Activities for Iraq Reconstruction," March 23, 2006.

3 Commission on Wartime Contracting, "Background Information and Chronology," http://webb.senate.gov/pdf/wtcontractbg.pdf.

4 Duke of Wellington, letter to the Foreign Office, 1812 as cited in: Clive Grace, "The Rapidly Changing World of Audit and Inspection," *Public Management and Policy Association*, October 11, 2004.

5 SIGIR interview with Joseph Farinella, Acting Assistant Inspector General for USAID, October 31, 2005.

6 P.L. 108-106, Emergency Supplemental Appropriations Act for Defense and for the Reconstruction of Iraq and Afghanistan for Fiscal Year 2004, November 6, 2003.

7 USAID OIG, "Iraq Information: Reports to Management," http://www.usaid.gov/oig/iraq_information_rptsmemos.html; and SIGIR, *Quarterly Report to the United States Congress*, October 2008, Appendix N.

8 GAO, "Topic Collection: Iraq and Afghanistan," http://www.gao.gov/docsearch/featured/oif.html; and SIGIR, *Quarterly Report to the United States Congress*, October 2008, Appendix N.

9 DoS OIG, "Office of Inspector General: Iraq & Afghanistan," http://oig.state.gov/c26058.htm. For a list of completed audits, reports, and testimonies of various oversight agencies see SIGIR, *Quarterly Report to the United States Congress*, October 2008, Appendix N.

10 DoD OIG Report D-208-086, "Challenges Impacting Operations Iraqi Freedom and Enduring Freedom Reported by Major Oversight Organizations Beginning FY 2003 through FY 2007," July 18, 2008, i.

11 SIGIR, *Quarterly Report to the United States Congress*, October 2008, Appendix N.

12 DoD OIG Report D-2008-086, "Challenges Impacting Operations Iraqi Freedom and Enduring Freedom Reported by Major Oversight Organizations Beginning FY 2003 through FY 2007," July 18, 2008, 1-2, 5.

13 For a list of completed USAAA audits, see SIGIR, *Quarterly Report to the United States Congress*, October 2008, Appendix N.

14 SIGIR, *Quarterly Reports to the United States Congress*, October 2005, 104; April 2006, 216; July 2006, Appendix L; January 2007, Appendix K; and April 2007, Appendix L.

15 SIGIR, *Quarterly Reports to the United States Congress*, July 2007, Appendix L; and October 2008, Appendix M.

16 DCAA, "DCAA History," http://www.dcaa.mil/.

17 DoD OIG Report D-2004-057, "Acquisition: Contracts Awarded for the Coalition Provisional Authority by the Defense Contracting Command-Washington," March 18, 2004, iii.

18 DCAA Audit 3311-2004K17900055, "Report on Audit of Proposal for Restore Iraqi Oil Task Order No. 5," October 8, 2004.

19 James Glantz, "Army to Pay Halliburton Unit Most Costs Disputed by Audit," New York Times, February 27, 2006.

20 P.L. 108-106, "Emergency Supplemental Appropriations Act for Defense and for the Reconstruction of Iraq and Afghanistan for Fiscal Year 2004," Title III, Section 3001, November 6, 2003.

21 SIGIR Audit 05-004, "Oversight of Funds Provided to Iraqi Ministries through the National Budget Process," January 30, 2005, 9-11.

22 Congressional Record–Senate, "Emergency Supplemental Appropriations for Iraq and Afghanistan Security and Reconstruction , 2004-Continued," Amendments 1846 and 1847, October 15, 2003, S12585-S12589; and P.L. 108-106, "Emergency Supplemental Appropriations Act for Defense and for the Reconstruction of Iraq and Afghanistan for Fiscal Year 2004," Title III, Section 3001, November 6, 2003.

23 George W. Bush, "Statement on Signing the Emergency Supplemental Appropriations Act for Defense and for the Reconstruction of Iraq and Afghanistan, 2004," Weekly Compilation of Presidential Documents 39 (November 6, 2003), 1549.

24 P.L. 108-106, "Emergency Supplemental Appropriations Act for Defense and for the Reconstruction of Iraq and Afghanistan for Fiscal Year 2004," Title III, Section 3001, November 6, 2003. The legislation stated that: "The Office of Inspector General shall terminate six months after the authorities and duties of the Coalition Provisional Authority cease to exist."

25 P.L. 108-375, "Ronald W. Reagan National Defense Authorization for the Fiscal Year 2005, October 28, 2004.

26 SIGIR, "Audits," http://www.sigir.mil/audits/Default.aspx.

27 SIGIR, "Inspections," http://www.sigir.mil/inspection/Default.aspx.

28 SIGIR Audit 08-020, "Key Recurring Management Issues Identified in Audits of Iraq Reconstruction Efforts," July 27, 2008, ii.

29 SIGIR, Quarterly Report to the United States Congress, "SIGIR Summary of Performance," January 2009.

30 SIGIR, "Initiatives: Lessons Learned," http://www.sigir.mil/initiatives/LessonsLearned.aspx.

31 110th Congress, 1st Session, S.680, "An Act: To ensure proper oversight and accountability in Federal contracting, and for other purposes," passed the Senate November 7, 2007.

32 SIGIR, "Reports: Quarterly Reports to Congress," http://www.sigir.mil/reports/quarterlyreports/default.aspx.